Carol Weiss King

Carol King, ca. 1951. (Photographer unknown.)

Carol Weiss King
Human Rights Lawyer, 1895–1952

Ann Fagan Ginger
With a Foreword by Louis H. Pollak

UNIVERSITY PRESS OF COLORADO

Copyright © 1993 by the University Press of Colorado
P.O. Box 849
Niwot, Colorado 80544

The University Press of Colorado is a cooperative publishing enter-
prise supported, in part, by Adams State College, Colorado State
University, Fort Lewis College, Mesa State College, Metropolitan
State College of Denver, University of Colorado, University of
Northern Colorado, University of Southern Colorado, and Western
State College.

Library of Congress Cataloging-in-Publication Data

Ginger, Ann Fagan.
    Carol Weiss King, human rights lawyer, 1895–1952 / Ann
Fagan Ginger; with a foreword by Louis H. Pollak.
        p.   cm.
    Includes bibliographical references and index.
    ISBN 0-87081-285-8 (alk. paper)
    1. King, Carol Weiss, 1895–1952. 2. Lawyers — United States
— Biography. 3. Civil rights — United States — History. I. Title.
KF373.K48G56   1993
342.73'085'092 — dc20
[B]
[347.30285092]
[B]   92-40157
                                                         CIP

The paper used in this publication meets the minimum requirements
of the American National Standard for Information Sciences—Perma-
nence of Paper for Printed Library Materials. ANSI Z39.48–1984
∞

10 9 8 7 6 5 4 3 2 1

Louis H. Pollak was a member of Yale Law school faculty from 1955
to 1974 and of the University of Pennsylvania Law School faculty
from 1974 to 1978; in 1978 he became a United States District Judge.

To the people who try to save the world
by changing it
and to their families,
especially their children

To the lawyers
who defend their rights
and to the secretaries, organizers, and fund-raisers
who work for their cause

To the jurors, judges, and lawmakers
who vote for them,
and to the laws they hold fast
and strengthen by their struggle

Other Books by Ann Fagan Ginger

Human Rights & Peace Law Docket: 1945–1991 (1992)

Peace Law Almanac (1991)

The National Lawyers Guild: From Roosevelt through Reagan (with Eugene M. Tobin) (1988)

The Cold War Against Labor (2 vols) (with David Christiano) (1987)

The International Juridical Association Bulletin 1932–1942 (3 vols, reprint edition, editor) (1982)

Jury Selection in Civil & Criminal Trials (2 vols) (1984, 1985)

Human Rights Docket US 1979 (1979)

The Law, the Supreme Court and the People's Rights (1974, 1977)

The Relevant Lawyers (1972)

Civil Liberties Docket 1968–69 (1970)

Civil Liberties Docket 1967–68 (1968)

The New Draft Law: A Manual for Lawyers and Counselors (1965, 1969)

Civil Rights & Liberties Handbook: Pleadings & Practice (2 vols) (1963)

Contents

Foreword   ix

Preface   xiii

Introductory Quote   1

PART I: THE ROARING TWENTIES, 1920–1929
Learning to Practice Law   3

1. Attorney General Palmer's Raids   6

2. Discovering How to Fight Back   23

3. Beginning to Practice Law   36

4. From Hell to Horatio   46

5. Grasping a Victory Out of Defeat   59

6. Shorr, Brodsky & King — and Jonathan   71

7. Watching Darrow Work a Jury   80

PART II: THE DEPRESSION THIRTIES, 1930–1938
Practicing in the Left of Times   97

8. Suddenly Alone, With Jonathan   100

9. After the Crash   104

10. Dnieprostroy, Berlin, and Harlan County   114

11. Defending the Right to Revolution   128

12. Getting on With the *Bulletin* and With Life   146

13. Saving the "Scottsboro Boys"   170

14. A New Deal for Aliens?   182

15. Representing Clients in Warsaw and Dixie   197

16. Building a Guild of Lawyers   212

17. Uniting on Many Fronts 233

PART III: THE WORLD WAR FORTIES, 1939–1945
Winning Cases in the Supreme Court 253
18. Moving Onto Page One 256
19. Harry Bridges: Round One 267
20. Proving a Government/Business Conspiracy 288
21. Fighting Fascism and the FBI 304
22. Harry Bridges: Round Two 325
23. The Cumulative Effect of Five Liars 342
24. Getting a Republican to Represent a Communist 363
25. Folks Have to Be Themselves 381
26. Winning in the Highest Court 398
27. Winning in the Highest Court, Doubled 412

PART IV: THE COLD WAR FORTIES AND FIFTIES, 1946–1952
Holding the Line 423
28. The Attorney General Threatens Revenge 427
29. Making a Noise Like a Lawyer 440
30. "The Hell With You! Love, Carol" 458
31. A New Kind of Woman Fights the Cold War 465
32. An Incredible Case 481
33. Once in a Lifetime! 494
34. A Big Fraud in a Little Palmer Raid 507
35. "The Communist's Dearest Friend" 516
36. Finally, the Supreme Court 522

Afterword 535
General Sources/Specific References 545
Index 577

Foreword

Ann Fagan Ginger, scholar and practitioner of the law of civil liberties, has written an important book. The book is important because it recounts, in rich and perceptive detail, the life story of an American whose remarkable — indeed, unique — achievements have never before been chronicled: Carol Weiss King.

Carol King practiced law in her native Manhattan from 1920, when she graduated from New York University Law School, until her death in 1952. For three decades, Carol King was a formidable lawyer for the underdog. She devoted her seemingly inexhaustible professional energies chiefly to the representation of a very select clientele who, but for her, might well have gone undefended — the "poor, [the] huddled masses yearning to breathe free" to whom the United States has extended ambivalent welcome. With a generous heart, and little reason to expect an adequate fee, Carol King deployed her skills on behalf of hundreds upon hundreds of the truly dispossessed — aliens, generally of left-wing political persuasion, whose principal resource was their remarkable lawyer. Over the years, Carol King achieved an unmatched mastery of immigration law.

Not all of Carol King's clients were humble and unknown. Harry Bridges, the militant longshoreman who in the 1930s and 1940s ruled the docks of the West Coast, was one of the most flamboyant and effective labor leaders of his time. Charging Bridges with being a Communist, the government waged a seemingly endless campaign to deport him to his native Australia. But the government was out-generaled at every turn by Carol King. Another client as celebrated as Bridges — but, unlike Bridges, a native-born American — was Earl Browder, the head of the Communist Party. Despite Carol King's best efforts, Browder went to prison (until President Roosevelt commuted his sentence).

Others achieved prominence as a result of the legal battles Carol King waged on their behalf. One was Angelo Herndon, a Black Communist

organizer whom the Georgia courts sentenced to eighteen years in prison
for inciting insurrection, a charge the Supreme Court found to be barred
by the First Amendment. Another was William Schneiderman, a naturalized citizen whose citizenship the government sought to revoke because
he was a Communist; in one of the tactical masterstrokes of her career,
Carol King persuaded Wendell Willkie to argue Schneiderman's case in
the Supreme Court, and the government was checkmated.

Enlisting the aid of Wendell Willkie brought victory to Schneiderman;
and to Carol King it brought not just a new professional colleague but
also a politician-turned-world leader — and a new friend. But enlisting
Willkie's aid was also symbolic of an important incompleteness in Carol
King's professional armament; she was a woman lawyer in an era when
there were very few women members of the profession. This enormously
capable lawyer — bullied by male adversaries and condescended to by
male allies because she was a woman — took it as a given that she was
not a proficient courtroom advocate, and so it was common practice for
her, especially in the Supreme Court, to retain a man to argue the brief
that she had predominantly written.

Carol King was an iconoclast. She viewed the United States's political
and social structures form the left-wing perspective she shared with many
of her clients. But she was not a member of the Communist Party. She
was far too independent-minded to submit to stifling Party discipline.
Representing Communists was one thing; subscribing to the tedious
shibboleths of the Party quite another.

The philosophic structure to which Carol King was committed was
the law. She derided the law's imperfections but she went to court to
correct them. When Gerhart Eisler — the East German Communist whose
contempt-of-Congress conviction Carol King brought to the Supreme
Court — jumped bail and fled the United States before the Supreme Court
decided his appeal, lawyer King was profoundly shaken by the fact that
her client had run out on the judicial process.

꙳

Writing this Foreword is professionally gratifying because it affords
me an opportunity to salute a penetrating study of a hitherto unsung

lawyer who accomplished much during a difficult era in our nation's history. Writing this Foreword is personally gratifying because it brings into close focus a cherished friend of my younger days. Carol King was a close friend of my parents, and she worked on some major cases with my father, Walter H. Pollak, a leading civil liberties lawyer. So from my infancy I knew Carol King: her boisterous laughter, her strongly held opinions, her kindness — all of these were part of my childhood. And as a law student and in my first years as a lawyer, I argued with her and learned from her.

Carol King died in 1952. For those who cared about law and liberty, the early fifties was not a good time. Joe McCarthy was reaching for center stage. The lamp of liberty seemed to be flickering. Starting with the Army-McCarthy hearings, McCarthy's popularity began to wane. And in 1954 the Supreme Court — a court in which Carol King had won some of her greatest victories — delivered the most resounding blow for liberty since the Civil War: the decision in *Brown v. Board of Education*.

In the years that followed, the Court began to recognize that in a free society, gender equality has as strong a claim as racial equality — an understanding that culminated in 1973 in *Roe v. Wade*. In 1992, in *Planned Parenthood of Southeastern Pennsylvania v. Casey*, *Roe v. Wade* was reaffirmed. The opinion of the Court — an opinion written jointly by Justices O'Connor, Kennedy, and Souter, and in which, as to this issue, Justices Blackmun and Stevens joined — stated the following:

> Like the character of an individual, the legitimacy of the Court must be earned over time. So, indeed, must be the character of a Nation of people who aspire to live according to the rule of law. Their belief in themselves as such a people is not readily separable from their understanding of the Court invested with the authority to decide their constitutional cases and speak before all others for their constitutional ideals. If the Court's legitimacy should be undermined, then, so would the country be in its very ability to see itself through its constitutional ideals. The Court's concern with legitimacy is not for the sake of the Court but for the sake of the Nation to which it is responsible.
>
> The Court's duty in the present case is clear. In 1973, it confronted the already-divisive issue of governmental power to limit personal choice to undergo abortion, for which it provided a new resolution based on the due process guaranteed by the Fourteenth Amendment. Whether or not a new social consensus is developing on that issue, its divisiveness is no less today than in 1973, and pressure to overrule the decision, like pressure to retain it, has grown only more intense. A decision to overrule *Roe's* essential holding under the existing circumstances would address error, if error there

was, at the cost of both profound and unnecessary damage to the Court's legitimacy, and the Nation's commitment to the rule of law. It is therefore imperative to adhere to the essence of *Roe*'s original decision, and we do so today.

I think that Carol King, an eminent member of the bar of the Supreme Court, would have agreed.

LOUIS H. POLLAK
Philadelphia, Pennsylvania

Roe v. Wade, 410 U.S. 113 (1973)
Planned Parenthood of Southeastern Pennsylvania v. Casey, 112 S. Ct. 2791 (1992)
Brown v. Board of Education, 347 U.S. 483 (1954)

Preface

Carol Weiss King was a pioneer as a lawyer and as a woman. She was a hidden human rights hero, working behind the scenes with a remarkable group of activists and lawyers to make real the promises of freedom of speech and the First Amendment from World War I to the cold war.

King was full of contradictions, collaborations, and exuberant insights that led her to significant victories. She persuaded the head of the Republican Party, Wendell Willkie, to represent a leader of the Communist Party before the Supreme Court. They won in 1943. She convinced the dean of the Harvard Law School that some big business and government officials were conspiring to deport a radical union leader in San Francisco in 1939. She located a Georgia judge whose guilty conscience might lead him to do justice to a Black youth in a civil liberties case in 1935. She helped stop the Immigration Service from holding any deportation hearings in 1950 because they were breaking the law in every case. She even shamed the FBI into taking its tail off one of her clients whom they labeled "a dangerous international Communist" after the cold war began. And on Saturdays she visited the latest art exhibits with her colleagues and friends.

When Carol King died in January 1952, the *New York Times* ran a full-column obituary describing the landmark human rights cases she had helped win — *Scottsboro, Herndon, Bridges, Schneiderman,* and, in a way, *Eisler.* Now that the cold war is officially over, these victories will give her the place she earned in any guide to history, law, labor, women's, and ethnic studies.

Carol King turned her back on the Wall Street law firm model. She moved beyond Clarence Darrow's individual defense of the damned to build a collective of colleagues and clients who based their work on inspired mass action and the creative use of democratic legal principles. Her work transformed King into a new kind of woman, standing somewhere between Mrs. Eleanor Roosevelt and Comrade Elizabeth Gurley Flynn.

Attorney Carol King established a room of her own in 1921 in a suite with other lawyers. She joined the small network of Leftists and Liberals who came together in the roaring Twenties to stop persecution by the Attorney General and the young FBI. The network grew into a movement that marched in the Great Depression to achieve insurance against unemployment and a New Deal; they sat down at their machines so they could sit down at the bargaining table with Big Business; they got some political prisoners released, won several major cases, and, in the process, got the Supreme Court to enunciate a few enduring rules of law. In the forties they fought World War II to defeat fascism abroad and to expand democracy at home. Many of them kept talking in the Silent Fifties to slow down the cold war assault on the Constitution, human rights, and peace. Their commitment and audacity magnified their victories and in fact spawned generations of movement activists and lawyers who have been kept largely ignorant of their rich heritage.

Carol King's life is a good place to begin to redress this grievance, to uncover what the Left was doing in the thirties when they were not fighting the good fight in Spain or winning the 1934 general strike in San Francisco, events recorded in revisionist history. It's time to let these folks describe how they developed their politics and their craft, to hear the Democrats declaim their New Deal, the Communists proclaim Marxism, the old-fashioned Republicans quote Abraham Lincoln, and the women sound militant while the FBI taps and reports on them all, turning only a handful into turncoats. This firsthand material will make it possible to see how the faith of the thirties was transformed into folk songs and slogans of the sixties civil rights movement, requiring reassessment of the assumption that the Old Left was defeated and destroyed, leaving barely a trace, and that the New Left sprang up from the void by spontaneous combustion.

The dawning of the twenty-first century is a good time to present the first major biography of a woman lawyer and a lawyer woman. King's story is part of the outsider's jurisprudence now being written by feminists and people of color, using sources often ignored, as she used unreported "little" cases to help win the big ones.

Carol King came from an upper-middle-class, intellectual, New York Jewish family. Her father, Samuel Weiss, once represented Standard Oil; her brother Louis S. Weiss founded the Paul, Weiss law firm. She always

acknowledged these roots and relatives and never let the resulting contradictions cramp her style. She fell in love, married early, bore a son, and
was left a widow at thirty-five. She built a busy life in the law and the
arts, full of friends and relations whom she enjoyed shocking, then asking
for help on her causes. Her daring at some points was matched by
unnecessary caution at others; occasionally her individualism overcame
her colleaguial style. Her life was the stuff of guffaws and legends. She
tried to have it all: professional success, love, motherhood, friendships,
privacy, and fun. The FBI and the Immigration Service worked to thwart
the efforts of "the King woman" to achieve several of her goals, reporting
on her as if she were a conjure woman, almost a witch.

King practiced law as a large family business, treating every friend
and opponent as an individual who might be persuaded to do right by
logic, or might be stopped from doing wrong by an appeal to someone
with more power, all the way up to President Franklin D. Roosevelt. King
rejected sterile, "neutral" legal principles and would be pegged today as
one of the critical legal theorists. She would have scoffed at their academic
stance while she enticed them to work on her next hard case. If I have
caught her accurately in these pages, she will both exasperate and inspire
you, as she did many of her friends and opponents.

This large tale must be spread like a mural on a large public space.
King and colleagues took up the challenge to save war protestors in New
York, Sacco and Vanzetti in Boston, and Dimitroff in Leipzig; the attorneys represented prisoners in Warsaw, Poland, and Atlanta, Georgia; they
participated in hearings on Ellis Island and Capitol Hill, in the chambers
of the Supreme Court and the United Nations General Assembly. Their
story could fill a twelve-part television series with spies and stowaways,
murders and suicides. It includes some stunning victories and many
standoffs in a mix as fascinating as any overplotted opera.

King worked her way into the center of this group of lawyers and
activists who learned to stick together to win through fraying egos,
unpaid legal fees, and changing political lines. They challenged the system
to live up to our most common boasts — that the Bill of Rights housed
in a free market economy protects the rights of U.S. dissidents; that we
are a peaceful nation; that people of color can achieve equality; that we
always welcome immigrants from all countries into our melting pot; that
we permit freedom of association for labor unions, nationality groups,
and minority parties; that the New Deal was only an emergency measure.
They probed the degree of reality behind the image of great legal battles

being played on a level field; of our judicial system operating in the open according to stated rules without interference from a secret police; of local police officers obeying Supreme Court decisions; and of a woman gaining equal treatment in the worlds of government and business.

These lawyers and clients learned how to slow down the machine intended to destroy them. They found ways to cut the financial and emotional cost of long litigation battles, ways to insert short sentences into pending congressional bills that would benefit specific groups in the movement. They learned to count as victories every sentence (and footnote) in a majority Supreme Court opinion that could be used by their side later, and how to turn every telling phrase in a dissenting opinion into a majority opinion in the course of decades.

King learned early that she could not practice law successfully like a man — that is, in the trial courts — so she recruited men trial lawyers and fed them her ideas. The *Saturday Evening Post* in 1951 described her as playing both sides: the International Labor Defense "sought to rip down one legal structure," the International Juridical Association "tried to build another, more advantageous one," although it was "rare" to have "the reins of both operations largely in the hands of one person."

One could write a study of this one person as an expert on immigration law, but her acknowledged greatness in this field was built on the significant role she played in major constitutional law cases in support of the rights of workers, labor unions, Negroes, Jehovah's Witnesses, and, incidentally, counterfeiters. Her generalist experiences and interests made her the great specialist.

I decided to try to write a life, following chronological order when possible, because King, like other solo practitioners, was very much affected by the flow of events and was never able to concentrate on one case or issue at a time, except for the *Bridges* case. To understand her actions and reactions, it is necessary to know what was happening in the world in general and in the local/political world in which she lived, where timing was often decisive.

Yet a strict chronology would be confusing because King was constantly involved in more than one important cause at a time, while a series of neat narratives of King's cases would belie the daily patchwork of her life. She relied on qualities common to many women, permitting us to mind several children of different ages, a spouse, a job, and an organization at the same time. In her case this meant relating to one real-life son while also "playing mother," as she sometimes put it, to numerous younger lawyers, clients, cases, and publications.

Her strength as a legal mother was also her weakness. After the death of her husband, her public persona was bluff, open, hard-hitting. She made a poor media figure in a nation that does not know how to respond to strong-minded women. And she sandwiched her personal affairs in between her cases in an awkward manner, which is how I saw her live her life — puffing cigarettes while working on the latest brief between phone calls from her relatives and friends, especially her housekeeper, her clients, attorneys, and reporters around the country, never knowing how many of these calls the FBI was tapping.

The best way to present the life and times of Carol Weiss King turned out to be as a mystery story, slowly uncovering the role King actually played while carefully covering her tracks to avoid discovery as the legal strategist in the key constitutional litigation. Her gender, her politics, her profession, her heritage, and her era determined her style. To succeed she had to use many tactics different from a man's in order to accomplish the same result, without seeming to be behaving differently.

Sources and Citations

I started work on this book in 1953 by going through Carol King's office files and some personal correspondence, making copies of some material and taking shorthand notes on the rest. To get the feel of the periods as King lived through them, and some personal history, I relied heavily on the notes she made in 1948 for the banquet in her honor and on the publications she mothered and edited continuously from 1924–1947. I selected as illustrations contemporaneous cartoons that seemed to capture the mood of Carol King and her clients, although these are not the paintings art collector Carol King would have selected. (Their study would have added another facet to the personal side of King not covered here.) I have included as illustrations some FBI reports that captured their view of "the King woman" and her colleagues.

I met Carol King in 1944 and got to know many of her colleagues, clients, and organizations from then on. I have drawn on memories and on several similar experiences — marrying before entering law school, arguing before the Supreme Court, being a single mother, and having a close relative stricken by multiple sclerosis. I talked and corresponded about Carol King and her times with seventy lawyers, clients, judges, secretaries, relatives, and friends in 1953–1954 when the first, short draft of this book was written; between 1979 and 1991 I corresponded with twenty-five other people. Soon after her death, Carol King's niece, Peggy Stern Kahn, and her brother-in-law, Howard King, each wrote several pages about the personal life of Carol King and Gordon King that I have used, along with personal anecdotes of Clara Binswanger, Justine Wise Polier, Sol Cohn, and Solon DeLeon from the early days. In the late 1980s Peggy Kahn and Louis H. Pollak supplied more information on her personal life. Almost everyone who knew her had a Carol King story; I have included as many as I could, and the sources are usually identified in the text. I have sought to check the accuracy of personal, political, and legal descriptions with a variety of people listed in the Acknowledgments, General Sources, and Index (with names in bold type).

The FBI admits that it opened a surveillance file on Carol King in 1941 and subjected her to continuous investigation until she died. I used 1,500 pages in the FBI's file on King and the 1951 *Saturday Evening Post* article on her.

All of the materials I collected, as well as secondary material, are now part of the Carol Weiss King Collection at Meiklejohn Civil Liberties Institute in Berkeley, which also houses related major archives of the National Lawyers Guild, the *Harry Bridges* cases, the International Labor Defense, the American Committee for Protection of Foreign Born, and Labor Surveillance Papers.

The General Sources/Specific References provides official and unofficial citations to every case discussed in the text, along with citations to descriptions of some of the cases, often written by King, in periodicals she edited. Thanks to the Freedom of Information Act in the United States and glasnost in the Soviet Union, documents are becoming available on the roles of the FBI, CIA, KGB, Trilateral Commission, Council on Foreign Relations, and other leading organizations and individuals, which should permit more definitive historical assessment of those aspects of the period that touched Carol King's life and work at the national and international levels.

Acknowledgments

I want to thank everyone who supplied information for this book, including Robert Cherny and the staffs at New York University Tisch School of the Arts and Tamiment Library, who shared documents, and each person I interviewed or who corresonded with me. I want to thank especially those on the original committee supporting the research in 1953 and those who read all or part of the manuscript, including the late Ray Ginger and the late Thomas I. Emerson, the late Clara Binswanger and the late Abner Green, and Doris Brin Walker, Norman Leonard, Louis H. Pollak, Peggy Stern Kahn, Alain Henon, William Preston, Jr., Sam Rosenwein, Marilyn Berger, Ira Gollobin, Aubrey Grossman, Ben Margolis, Zipporah Collins, Mary Ratcliff, Ann Mari Buitrago, Pearl Bates, and Neil Lester. I also want to thank innumerable librarians across the country, especially the staff at Meiklejohn Institute, and those who typed and input the many drafts, including Linda Richter, Phoebe Watts, Nancy Ammons, Miriam Berg, Melanie Heath, Frank Cialone, Christopher Weills, Sarah Shapiro, Isobel White, Elizabeth Maker, and Linton Hale; Myriam Godfrey and Rick Davis, who helped with computer problems; and James Fagan Ginger, who did most of the work on the Index.

My telling of the story of Carol Weiss King, her colleagues, and her clients has been unconsciously colored by similarities and differences in our heritage and experiences. I grew up during the Depression in a Socialist/Irish/Russian/Jewish/Quaker family in the Midwest. My father was a newspaperman, my mother a teacher and activist. I worked my way through the University of Michigan from 1941–1947, as the FBI started its file on me. During law school I was a member of a Marxist study group of inspired historians and doctors. After graduation I was one of the last to join what came to be known as the Old Left, as the cold war kept me from finding a job or winning cases for my political clients. I turned to Carol King for advice and encouragement, accepting many of her approaches and rejecting others that did not fit my status or style.

To capture more of the flavor of the times, I have often used the language then in vogue. Almost everyone who knew her, friend and foe alike, called her "Carol" or "Mrs. King," never "King." The FBI called her "the King woman" and court opinions often listed her as "Mr. Carol King." People of color were usually called "Negroes" with a careful capital "N" to show respect and equality; the words "Black" and "African-American" were rarely used. The defendants in the famous case were called "the Scottsboro Boys" to emphasize their youth. Workers were often called "members of the working class" by popular writers as well as by "Communists," and everyone called all secretaries "girls." There are very few "he" or "she" references because there were almost no shes in the lists of powerful people with whom King dealt.

Quoted material is indented or marked by double quotes. Material that is slightly abridged or paraphrased is marked by single quotes. Capitalization, hyphenization, and citations are all compromises between legal style and other research styles that may not completely satisfy everyone.

I am grateful for the humor and forbearance with which my family has put up with this book for many decades as Jim, Tom, Jim, and Nina, Viola, Paul and Mary, and Jean and Ed listened to one more Carol King story.

And I deeply appreciate the zest and skill Luther Wilson, Jody Berman, and Pete Hammond put into the production of this book by the University Press of Colorado.

ANN FAGAN GINGER
Berkeley 1992

Carol Weiss King

As Americans we learn from our earliest days about the Bill of Rights in the United States Constitution. . . . [W]e are told much less, or nothing at all, about how these rights have been maintained and about how the people have had to fight continuously to protect and extend their rights of free speech, free press, free association and due process of law.

In that struggle the protection of the rights of minority groups has played a large part. One of those minority groups has been the foreign-born. The protection of the foreign-born is an important chapter in the history of the preservation of the Bill of Rights.

Carol King, General Counsel
American Committee for Protection of Foreign Born
1949

PART I:
The Roaring Twenties, 1920–1929
Learning to Practice Law

The Attorney General rounded up 10,000 immigrants.
The Immigration Bureau deported Emma Goldman.
Massachusetts threatened to execute Sacco and Vanzetti.
The United States sent an expeditionary force against Soviet Russia.

The Constitution said:
"Congress shall make no law . . .
abridging the freedom of speech, or of the press;
or the right of the people peaceably to assemble,
and to petition the government for a redress of grievances."
— First Amendment

In New York City on the night of November 7, 1919, a battery of local police and federal agents under the direction of the United States Department of Justice descended on the Russian People's House at 113 East Fifteenth Street. The law enforcement officers found several hundred refugees from the czar attending meetings and English classes at their cultural center.

As the officers marched ahead, people began asking them the meaning of their intrusion.

'Shut up there, if you know what's good for you!' the people were told.

The law enforcement men went through the building, beating up people with blackjacks and stair rails, breaking up and destroying most of the furniture, desks, and typewriters. They burst into classes and herded the students to the stairs, beating them as they went, shoving them from the landing onto the stairway so that many fell, rolled down the stairs, and were trampled on by those shoved after them.

The agents arrested hundreds of prisoners and took them to the office of the Department of Justice at 13 Park Row and put them through a third-degree inquisition.

The Justice Department's Bureau of Investigation made similar raids that night in Philadelphia, Newark, Detroit, and fourteen other cities. The *New York Times* reported the next day that thirty-three men, "most of them with bandaged heads, black eyes or other marks of rough handling," were taken to Ellis Island for deportation. The government freed 150 others, although "most of them also had blackened eyes and lacerated scalps as souvenirs of the new attitude of aggressiveness . . . assumed by the Federal agents against Reds and suspected Reds."

Within a few days, the *Times* reported that Justice Department agents did not have warrants for the arrest of most of the people they had picked up. Eighty percent had to be released because they were citizens or aliens legally present in the United States and clearly innocent of any wrongdoing. Justice turned the rest over to the Immigration Bureau of the Labor Department for deportation.

Aliens were not the only targets of the raid. According to the *Times,* another goal was "to break up sources of propaganda. . . . It was reasonably certain that the whole editorial staffs of most of the Communist party newspapers had been taken," citizens and aliens alike.

The Immigration Bureau promptly held deportation hearings on the well-known anarchists Emma Goldman and Alexander Berkman and other aliens the agency had arrested. All were ordered to leave the country. On December 21, 1919, the *SS Buford* dutifully headed out of New York harbor with its cargo of four "organized anarchists"; forty-seven of whom had been "heard to say they did not believe in government," and 198 of whom were simply members of the Union of Russian Workers. They sailed past the Statue of Liberty, out the golden door they had entered so hopefully some years before, half of them leaving wives and children behind.

Two months later, on the night of January 2, 1920, Attorney General A. Mitchell Palmer and J. Edgar Hoover, head of the new General Intelligence Division of the Justice Department's Bureau of Investigation, led a second round of raids. This time they attacked in seventy cities, breaking into halls where foreign-born workers were gathered, and into private homes. In a single night they arrested between 6,000 and 10,000

people in New England, Buffalo, New York City, Philadelphia, Pittsburgh, Cleveland, Toledo, East St. Louis, Chicago, and Detroit. They
arrested many citizens; the best known, perhaps, was Louise Bryant, wife
of citizen John Reed, who was on assignment in Moscow.

1.
Attorney General Palmer's Raids

Early in 1921 Carol Weiss King applied for a job with Hale, Nelles & Shorr, a law firm frequently mentioned for its role in combating the outrageous Palmer Raids. Mrs. King hoped their progressive views were not limited to aliens and socialists and that they would be willing to hire a woman. She walked into their small office at 80 East Eleventh Street wearing no corset on her full figure and no blinders on her broad mind.

She probably did not bring gloves to the interview, although that was the custom. She probably did bring the brief she had written as a law clerk although having her name on the cover was not the custom.

She certainly brought with her some ideas about law practice from her first temporary job at Lowenthal & Szold. She had been hired easily by Max Lowenthal, just as she would have been if she had been a man. Lowenthal knew her father's reputation as a first-rate corporation lawyer, may have seen her grades, and liked her style. He represented the Amalgamated Clothing Workers as well as more traditional business clients who could afford his fees. Lowenthal & Szold were not handling any Palmer Raid cases, but they assigned Mrs. King to work on a brief for the union during the great strikes and lockout of 1920. They took the unusual step of printing her name on the cover even though she had not yet been admitted to practice.

King had gone to law school because she did not enjoy fighting for causes and people she believed in from the wrong side of the tracks of power. She had become a lawyer so she could fight in the forums used by corporation lawyers, the courtroom, and the Congress. She never considered applying for her first job with one of the corporate law firms where her father's name might help. She did not want to go into practice with her two brothers, who were only liberals. A self-assured young Carol Weiss King was ready to begin her practice of the law on her own terms.

She described her job interview with gusto twenty-five years later. Walter Nelles had begun by introducing himself and his two partners, Swinburne Hale and Isaac Shorr. Nelles was relatively short and slight with a black mustache and glasses. His manner was scholarly and reserved until he launched into his experiences as a conscientious objector during the recent World War. He had started handling "CO" cases for the new National Civil Liberties Bureau in 1918. Suddenly, agents of the Justice Department raided his New York law office, apparently in retaliation; his pacifist response stood him in good stead. In 1920 the bureau became the American Civil Liberties Union, and Nelles continued his volunteer work. He revealed himself to be a deep and radical thinker.

Captain Hale had played quite a different role during the War. Coming from an old American family, he had taken a leave from the office he shared with Nelles to serve in the Military Intelligence Division of the United States General Staff. He was a wealthy man in his forties who was busy enjoying life. He came into the office irregularly to work on cases that attracted his interest.

When the conversation shifted to Isaac Shorr, King faced an impressive figure puffing pipe smoke and speaking with a noticeable Jewish accent. Shorr seemed completely absorbed in his clients' individual problems. She liked him immediately and felt she could rely on his strength and sensitivity, which had been molded in a Russian ghetto and honed in the New York cigar factory where he worked while attending law school.

Carol King found herself in animated conversation with each of the three partners, gladly shaking off the stance required of a law student drinking in the common law from learned professors. After a brief huddle with Hale and Shorr, Nelles turned to King. 'We're not making a living for ourselves,' he confessed, 'so we couldn't possibly afford to hire you. But we do have a suggestion. Why not rent a room in our suite and open up your own office?'

King had come looking for a traditional job and had not considered going into business for herself. Still, it was a tempting offer. The men, beleaguered but unbowed, exuded a sense of certainty in these difficult times. Clearly they were fighting for principle as well as trying to earn a living. They were very different from each other, and she liked that fact because she also was an individual. She liked the spirit of rebellion against injustice that resonated in their office, and the shelves of books that lined the walls.

Without either side characterizing the proposal, Nelles was offering Carol Weiss King a premature room of her own; her father's will had provided her the necessary "500 pounds a year" to make her independence possible, as Virginia Woolf would advocate a few years later. Her acceptance of the proposal at age twenty-five would launch a career that maintained a room of her own to the end of her life. Eventually the room would generate the necessary income to sustain her.

Nelles's offer sounded like a real opportunity. She would be practicing law in a suite with distinguished lawyers who appeared ready to be the mentors and role models that every young professional needs. She certainly could not hope to find an older woman lawyer to train her.

Of course, if she opened her own office, she and her husband would have to continue spending carefully. Still, Gordon would probably approve of the offer since he, too, had embarked on an unconventional path in his career, and the Nelles office handled the kind of case he had gotten involved in during his one brush with the law.

The case arose one Sunday in 1914 in an unlikely setting: the Calvary Baptist Church on Fifty-seventh Street. Gordon was teaching Sunday School there, as his father had done before him. During the service, a minister from another church stood up, looked at John D. Rockefeller sitting in his pew, and hotly charged him with the responsibility for killing thirty-three strikers and their families in Ludlow, Colorado during the previous week. Reverend Bouck White said Rockefeller owned the major share in the struck Colorado Fuel and Iron Company. Suddenly special police appeared in the aisles, eager to jump on Reverend White and his supporters. This they did, with considerable help from city police and even from the church ushers dressed in their cutaways and striped pants.

Gordon King was shocked and decided he had to do something about this outrage. He became a witness on behalf of the Socialist minister and the other ten protesters. His testimony made no difference. The defendants were all convicted and spent six months on Blackwell's Island, which fed Gordon's skepticism about the law.

Like his college friend Bernard DeVoto, Gordon's own career commitment was to writing. When he graduated from Harvard, Gordon decided not to get a regular job but to devote himself to this pursuit. If Carol did not find a salaried position, she and Gordon would have to continue to

Drawn by John Sloan.

IN THIS ISSUE
CLASS WAR IN COLORADO—Max Eastman
WHAT ABOUT MEXICO?—John Reed

Ludlow, Colorado. During the bitter strike of mine workers, the Rockefeller company evicted strikers from their homes; militia set fire to the strikers' tents, shooting people as they fled into the snow. Thirty-three children, women, and men died of burns and bullets in the Ludlow Massacre. By John Sloan, front cover, *The Masses,* June 1914, reprinted in Rebecca Zurier, *Art for* The Masses *(1911–1917): A Radical Magazine and its Graphics.* New Haven: Yale University Art Gallery 1985 (exhibit guide), p. 66.

live on her inheritance until his writing and her practice started to pay off.

Fortunately, their housing was assured. When Gordon was discharged from the infantry after the Armistice in 1918, Carol's mother had given them a new home in the Chelsea district. It was a charming place with built-in bookcases from floor to ceiling and a fireplace. Mrs. Weiss had also made it possible for Mrs. Barkley to move in as their housekeeper while Carol was finishing up her law degree. Thanks to the Weiss inheritance, Carol could keep both the house and Mrs. Barkley to take care of it, even if she took this non-job. Under these auspicious circumstances, Carol accepted the firm's proposal.

Soon a new name was painted on the door beneath the others:

HALE, NELLES & SHORR
JOSEPH R. BRODSKY
CAROL KING

She moved in enough furniture to look presentable and put her diploma up on the wall.

If her experience was typical, nothing happened. No one walked into her office with a specific case, to say nothing of a tangible fee. In fact, she probably had to admit that she had no precise idea of what to do when her first client actually appeared. She had attended New York University Law School, a good law school, from 1917 to 1920, so of course she had not received any practical, clinical training. She hadn't learned how to interview a client or prepare a complaint. In fact, she knew a lot less about law practice than Fay Seagartle, the secretary to the firm.

Carol King, Esq., had time to notice her surroundings and absorb the smells common to office buildings — the mixture of age, waxed marble floors, steam heat, and humanity rushing through from 9:00 to 5:00. She decided to do her own typing and, toward the end of the day, brew her own tea. On one of her first days in the office, she had trouble with the little alcohol stove, which led to her dramatic meeting with the other lawyer in the suite, and a story she loved to tell. In trying to light the stove, she spilled the fluid. "With a burst of flame, the whole room threatened to disappear forever. As I madly tried to extinguish the fire, a large man, too voluminous in size and character to compress into a few sentences, stuck his head in my door. Showing no concern at the blaze, he blandly inquired, 'Do you do this every afternoon at 4:00 P.M. sharp?' "

This was Joseph R. Brodsky, as jovial as Saint Nick and a good street fighter. He had been a classmate of Shorr's at NYU Law School and, like him, an immigrant. Now he rented space from the firm. He got what he called his "class instinct" from his upbringing in a four-room, cold-water flat on the East Side of Manhattan. His father tried to support his wife and eight children as a shirtmaker but was often out of work. His mother kept three boarders and sewed buttons onto trousers at night. Many days the family went hungry. Many nights the father went to meetings of Branch 1 of the Workmen's Circle, where he fought Morris Hillquit and other "opportunists" in the Socialist Party.

Joe Brodsky worked on many cases with the Nelles firm, and the four men had a reputation for fighting well together, despite deep differences in their backgrounds and politics. Hale was a wealthy liberal with many ties to the establishment and some continuing commitment to the practice of law. Nelles was a pacifist and former teacher with a sardonic side. Shorr was a ponderous philosophical anarchist; Brodsky a young, flamboyant Marxist advocate. They were half Jewish, half Gentile; half old-American stock, half immigrants. All were committed to finding the law that would help their clients win against enormous odds.

Carol King was also a rebel but she was younger and her background was different. She was of the other gender and had developed her radical stance as she rejected some of her parents' standards and transformed others.

Her father, Samuel Weiss, had been brought up on a farm in Wilkes-Barre, Pennsylvania, by immigrant parents. Their neighbors had been so impressed by his intelligence that they donated money for him to go to Yale University, which led him into the law. He assessed the new monopoly structure of U.S. business and set out to succeed in 1871 by building Frank & Weiss into a small law firm representing the new trusts. He marked his success by the stature of his clients, starting with Seeman Brothers, a wholesale grocery business that sold White Rose Tea. While representing Seeman Brothers, he met his client's young daughter, Carrie Stix, and married her. After Teddy Roosevelt and the Supreme Court began trust-busting, Standard Oil needed new incorporation papers to show that the company had divested itself of some of its subsidiaries. They retained Weiss to do the drafting.

It had been fun growing up a Weiss, by all accounts, with plenty of money and intellectual interests. But this was the Victorian era. Fathers were expected to be domineering and daughters were supposed to be ladies. Samuel Weiss certainly played his expected role; his much younger wife played her subordinate role without surrendering her own spirit. But his fourth child refused to play her part.

Mr. Weiss was firmly committed to the concept of citizen participation in government and to strict discipline in the home. His concept of virtue and the good life led him to read aloud in Latin and Greek to his four children. He was a liberal intellectual Jewish father and, with his wife, provided a spacious and carefree environment for their family. During the winter they lived in a fine colonial homestead they built in Fort Washington, New York, and in the summer they lived at a spacious, rustic campsite in Maine named Lorac Lodge after Carol, spelled backward.

Carol's parents cared deeply about education and thought carefully about where their children should be educated. They followed others of their class in deciding on private schools, which they could easily afford, and sent Carol to progressive Horace Mann School. This was the era of women demanding votes and birth control, Eugene V. Debs running for president on the Socialist ticket, and the Industrial Workers of the World organizing IWW unions and waging free speech fights out West. When Carol was fifteen, her father died. She turned to her two older brothers and sister for family support.

She was a rebellious spirit and entered Barnard College in style in 1912. Knowing that freshmen were not permitted to go up the front stairs, she rushed for the stairs as soon as she got on campus. As she liked to tell the story, she was soon spotted and pursued by an entire and enraged sophomore class. Nonetheless, she gained the top step before her pursuers caught up with her and pushed her down the whole flight. Luckily all she broke in her descent was a front tooth. Carol Weiss was proud of her athletic ability and after this memorable solo entry into campus life, she went out for team sports. She really liked the competition in hockey and basketball, and wrote many letters to her brother Louis about the exploits of her team. She made many friends. One was a progressive coed, Honi Pollitzer, who soon met Louis and in due course married him.

Carol was a good student at Barnard and worked on the *Barnard Bulletin* with an aspiring writer, Babette Deutsch. As editor-in-chief, Miss Weiss put out an issue dealing with women's suffrage; she was called down for it and almost expelled. She was also observed crossing Broadway without a hat. The dean reprimanded her for this violation of accepted conduct.

When Carol signed up for a history course with Juliet Stuart Poyntz, she met an inspired professor who pulled her into concern for the problems of working people, especially working women, a group of people she had never really gotten to know. Her conscience and curiosity soon led her to the office of Local 25 of the International Ladies Garment Workers Union, where she began working as a volunteer among the many immigrant men and women workers.

As Professor Poyntz and the union were developing her social conscience, a shocking case of anti-Semitism hit the front page. A young New Yorker, Leo Frank, had moved to Atlanta to work for his uncle's company. When a young woman employee was killed in 1913, he was charged with murder. He professed his innocence. The courtroom during his trial reeked of anti-Semitism. The jury quickly convicted him. He was sentenced to death. The United States Supreme Court affirmed the conviction, with Justices Oliver Wendell Holmes and Charles Evans Hughes dissenting. When the governor commuted Frank's sentence to life imprisonment, twenty-five Atlanta citizens were able to break into the prison, carry him off, and hang him. This shocking conclusion led many Jews to move out of Georgia, as racists revived the Invisible Empire, Knights of the Ku Klux Klan. New York liberals, in turn, founded the Anti-Defamation League of B'nai B'rith. Carol never forgot the incident and used it twenty years later to help win a case.

In her senior year Carol was eligible for the honorary society but didn't make Phi Beta Kappa. She assumed her nonconformist views were the reason. They were certainly well known. The quotation under her picture in the 1916 Barnard yearbook was "Give me your gloves; I will wear them for your sake."

Miss Weiss took her Bachelor of Arts degree in her bare hands to apply for a job with the American Association for Labor Legislation, which was working for occupational health and safety and worker's compensation for injuries on the job. The association even advocated the radical idea of paying workers when they got laid off through no fault of their own. Germany had instituted this reform in the 1880s as part of the first capitalist social insurance program, including compensation for illness, accident, disability, old age, and unemployment.

Carol got the job and made two close friends at work, Doris Maddow, an artist she had known at Barnard, and Solon DeLeon. Doris remembered that Carol often seemed to be struggling against her father's influence and ideology. Solon's father was also a strong personality.

Pittsburgh. The steelworkers strike of 1916 began in the Mesabi Range; this
scene in crayon and india ink is from Pittsburgh, Pennsylvania. By Robert
Minor in *The Masses,* August 1916, reprinted in Rebecca Zurier, *Art for* The
Masses *(1911–1917): A Radical Magazine and its Graphics.* New Haven:
Yale University Art Gallery 1985 (exhibit guide), p. 117.

Daniel DeLeon was the first Marxist scholar in the United States and
founder of the Socialist Labor Party. He convinced his son that dialectical
materialism is a sound philosophy, in the process leading Solon to reject
unthinking filial devotion. Solon recalled discussions with Carol about
their domineering fathers on many daily walks from Eighty-sixth Street
and Fifth Avenue, where they both lived, down to Twenty-third and
Lexington, where they worked.

   After work Miss Weiss went swimming, played tennis, and hiked with
her friends and relations. She was twenty-two, busy, but not content. Her
hard work for John B. Andrews and the Association for Labor Legislation
was defeated repeatedly by corporation lawyers. She was determined to
best them at their own game. She acknowledged that her father's career
had influenced her decision. If he could utilize the law to protect the rich,
she reasoned that she could use it to safeguard the rights of the poor. As

he had looked after the interests of Standard Oil, she would represent the interests of the workers.

That would require going to law school, but she had no reason to think that task would be too difficult. How could her family of lawyers disapprove? Her brother Billy was already a lawyer, Louis was in law school, and Nina was married to a lawyer. There was a little problem of where she could study: many schools had a quota on Jewish students and none of the "best" schools would accept her. Harvard, Yale, Columbia, and the others didn't admit women. No matter. NYU did.

In 1916, with war raging in Europe, Woodrow Wilson had gotten himself re-elected president under the slogan HE KEPT US OUT OF WAR. Safely ensconced in the White House, Wilson embarked on the path that sent U.S. troops "over there." When everyone did not fall into line immediately, Congress quickly responded with the Espionage Act of 1917.

While waiting to enter law school, Carol Weiss attended a party at the home of a college friend, Mary Powell, who introduced a cousin, Gordon King. He and Carol started talking easily, and she told Solon later that somehow they never stopped. When neither felt like dancing, they talked their way from philosophy on to art and finally to Gordon's first love, books and the art of writing them. Carol was charmed by his analytical way of thinking and was as unaffected by his traditional Baptist background as he was by her not wearing traditional gloves. Gordon was tall, fair-haired, slim, with regular aquiline features and a slight, appeall-ing stutter. He always dressed fashionably while, from the first, he accepted her lack of fashion.

She fell deeply in love with Gordon, and he with her. Within a few months, they decided to marry. No one in the family could chide Carol for "not following tradition" or for taking a "wrong career turn" since there were so few women lawyers that her proper path was uncharted.

She spent her three years at NYU uneventfully, a gregarious young married woman in a sea of men, among whom she found no kindred spirits. There was no course on civil liberties or labor law, and she found workers' cases by looking under "Master/Servant" in the digests. Her professors virtually ignored the headline stories that she, Gordon, and their friends chewed over on weekends as the world suffered through war and revolution. There were reports of Wobblies and Socialists getting arrested for opposing U.S. participation in the "imperialist war" and of people getting killed in race riots at home. The Attorney General had a thousand people arrested and tried under the Espionage and Sedition Acts of 1917 and 1918, accompanied by appropriate scare stories in the press. Ultimately he reported 877 defendants convicted, including Eugene Debs, who was sentenced to prison for ten years for telling young men not to go to war, and Congressman Victor L. Berger (Socialist-Wis.), whose conviction was overturned after Congress refused to swear him in. (The Left press duly pointed out that the government never proved one act of injury to the U.S. military services by any of the 877 convicted defendants.)

Then Congress amended the deportation law so that "dangerous aliens" could be sent out of the country regardless of the length of time they had lived in the United States. And they said aliens could be excluded or deported if they "belonged to or were affiliated" with an organization that taught anarchy or "violent overthrow." The government would not have to prove that an alien personally believed in or advocated "violent overthrow;" it merely needed to prove membership in the organization and that the organization advocated violent overthrow.

The professors at NYU did not protest the postmaster general's warning that he would bar *The Masses* from the mails under the Espionage Act. This "monthly revolutionary journal," with a circulation of over 20,000, carried Jack Reed's stories from Petrograd about Lenin and the establishment of the first workers' state. The professors did not discuss Judge Learned Hand's preliminary injunction against the New York postmaster or protest when the Second Circuit Court of Appeals reversed his order.

The papers reported the government's arrest of a socialist professor and author, Scott Nearing, and his publisher, the American Socialist Society, charging them with feloniously obstructing army recruitment. The firm of Hales, Nelles & Shorr tried the case to a jury of twelve and put up a strong defense. The jurors were troubled by the First Amendment argument and decided to acquit the author. Then, following a logic of their own, they found the publisher guilty.

The Armistice was declared November 11, 1918, as the world mourned the more than thirty million soldiers and civilians killed,

Having Their Fling. One of several cartoons for which the artist was indicted during World War I; the picture is done in crayon and graphite on board. By Art Young in *The Masses,* September 1917, reprinted in Rebecca Zurier, *Art for* The Masses *(1911–1917): A Radical Magazine and its Graphics.* New Haven: Yale University Art Gallery 1985 (exhibit guide), p. 44.

wounded, and imprisoned. Socialist Elizabeth Gurley Flynn wrote that 1,500 opponents of the war were in jail in the United States: Socialists, IWWs, other radicals, and conscientious objectors.

The Immigration Bureau in the Department of Labor slowly began enforcing the new deportation act. The Secretary of Labor was solely responsible for enforcement; the Justice Department had no jurisdiction over immigration or aliens. Labor Secretary Wilson and Attorney General Gregory declared that "guilt is always personal," so "no person should be prosecuted or interned solely by reason of his membership" in an organization holding proscribed views. But as President Wilson lost his grip in the fall of 1919, Gregory stepped down and Labor Secretary Wilson became ill. The ambitious A. Mitchell Palmer became Attorney General, filling the vacuum as the United States lurched toward peace.

The international armistice did not bring peace at home. The war boom and booming profits burst into postwar strikes, lockouts, and unemployment in the cities; it turned into panic on the farms. In January 1919 the press began reporting on the "Red Peril" and a plan to deport aliens to meet it. Early in February, Seattle bubbled up into a general strike. It was short and completely peaceful, but it terrified local and national leaders. On Lincoln's birthday the government ordered fifty-four members of the militant IWW deported. On May 1, 1919, Palmer reported that twenty-nine packages of bombs were found in the mails addressed to prominent citizens; he said they were sent by Reds, labor agitators, and aliens. One exploded and wounded a maid. Jack Reed, of the Left Wing of the Socialist Party, suggested that the bombs were part of an attempted frame-up; they were discovered for insufficient postage before they were delivered because they had been planted by anti-labor forces.

At the same time, in this frightening period of layoffs due to the end of the war, whites attacked Blacks in a Chicago race riot in late July that lasted five days, leaving thirty-eight dead, fifty-three wounded, and hundreds homeless. Attorney General Palmer admitted in the July 31 *New York Times* that the Washington and Chicago race riots were "due solely to local conditions," not to outside agitators or Reds. Bombs continued to demolish homes in Black communities throughout 1919 and 1920; their perpetrators were never found or prosecuted.

Toward the end of this long, hot summer, workers throughout the United States embarked on a long march. On September 1, the railroad workers went out in a national strike. On September 22, 340,000 steelworkers went out on strike under the leadership of William Z. Foster. On November 1, 400,000 coal miners struck, joining the railroad and steelworkers who were still out.

The new Attorney General repeatedly said there was danger of a Red revolution in the United States on the second anniversary of the November

1919 Red revolution in Russia. To many, the signs seemed clear. In September during the Socialist Party convention in Chicago, 60,000 members split away to join the new Communist Party and the new Communist Workers Party. By this time, 250,000 workers in Chicago were on strike, locked out, or threatening to strike.

Unemployment and anger at working conditions were also widespread in Europe. In the wake of the successful Russian revolution, the Allied leaders formed the International Labor Organization to keep workers from organizing to overthrow capitalism. In the constitution of the ILO, the leaders pledged efforts to reform hours of work, prevent unemployment, raise wages, and protect workers from disease and injury.

In this tense climate, Attorney General Palmer ordered raids on the Union of Russian Workers in New York City and on the offices of the Communist (Workers) Party. Within five days, the press chronicled several historic events:

Nov. 7, 1919:
SECOND ANNIVERSARY OF BOLSHEVIST REVOLUTION

Nov. 8, 1919:
ALL RADICAL LEADERS TO BE DEPORTED — BOMB SQUAD ARRESTS 150
IN RED ROUND UP AIMED AT PLOT FOR REVOLUTION IN U.S.

Nov. 11, 1919:
CENTRALIA, WASHINGTON, LYNCHING OF WESLEY EVERETT, I.W.W.,
AFTER "PATRIOTIC PARADE" ATTACKED I.W.W. HALL

The U.S. Senate soon voted against joining the new League of Nations, reflecting a desire to turn away from involvement with the people of the rest of the world — foreigners.

Early in 1920 Attorney General Palmer rushed into action with his sights on the White House. The *Times* headlines told the story:

Jan. 4, 1920:
REDS PLOTTED COUNTRY-WIDE STRIKE —
ARRESTS EXCEED 5,000; 2,635 HELD
THREE TRANSPORTS READY FOR THEM

Jan. 5, 1920:
REVOLUTION IS SMASHED

Palmer took credit for the arrests of thousand of people in his second raid, then left the Labor Department immigration inspectors with the "technical task" of trying to discover which of the approximately 6,000 warrants that had been issued applied to the particular individuals who had been swept into the dragnet.

The editors of the *New York Times* applauded the raids and the "resolute will" of the Department of Justice "in hunting down these enemies of the United States." The *Times* assured its readers, "This raid is only the beginning. It is to be followed by others. Without notice and without interruption the department will pursue and seize the conspirators against our Government." The *Times* also liked round numbers, reporting that "some 60,000 Bolshevists' names are recorded in the department." The *Times* said, "Some of [the Reds] are making mischief, or trying to," in unions, in hope of "agitation among the Negroes, regarded as victims of 'economic bondage' and material for proletarian propaganda. These communists are a pernicious gang. In many languages they are denouncing the blockade of Russia."

On January 7, the coal miners admitted they had lost their strike. The next day the steel workers admitted defeat. On January 10, 1920, the League of Nations was born in Geneva, a historic event in which the United States did not participate. Then the Allied leaders met in Paris to decide what to do about the failure of their blockade of Soviet Russia. Taking account of the hunger and war-weariness of their own people, they decided to turn toward peace, and perhaps even to accept tempting offers of commerce from the Soviets.

Jan. 17, 1920:
NO WAR WITH RUSSIA, ALLIES TO TRADE WITH HER;
BLOCKADE SUDDENLY LIFTED BY PARIS COUNCIL

꙳

After graduation from the law school's narrow confines in 1920, Carol King needed a clerkship to fulfill a requirement for admission to the bar of New York. She quickly found a temporary position with Max Lowenthal and enjoyed her relationship with the senior partner, who remained her mentor and friend throughout her career.

Now in 1921 Carol King had found a permanent slot for herself in the Nelles office and had begun to figure out how to fit in. The atmosphere was totally different from Lowenthal & Szold. Lowenthal obviously held some of the beliefs of Hale, Nelles, Shorr and Brodsky, but he evidently preferred, or felt compelled, to divide his time between business clients and a few labor unions, whereas Nelles and Shorr poured all their energies into one basket and Brodsky did the same. When one got a hard case, they all discussed the facts and issues. They wrote briefs and argued cases for each other depending on who was best equipped. There was no clear pecking order from senior partners to junior partners to law clerks and secretaries. Two senior partners worked on the premises; the third was frequently away. Office procedures depended on the habits of the particular lawyer. They had yet to afford a clerk.

It was obvious that Fay Seagartle ran the office and kept it functioning smoothly. Fay was an energetic and attractive young woman whom Walter had hired straight out of business school so he could shape her into the kind of legal secretary he knew they needed. Now she took dictation, filed correspondence, kept a calendar of deadlines for papers to be filed in court, and got them filed properly. She typed statements to paying clients, paid the bills, and warned the lawyers when their bank balances were about to be overdrawn. She was as committed to the clients as the lawyers were.

Carol had expected to be drawn to Joe's labor clients. They had been arrested for picketing, passing out leaflets, or making soapbox speeches on the streets of New York. Some, like Joe, were members of the new Communist Party. They wanted a lawyer who could pick a good jury and then convince twelve citizens that the defendants had not done what they were charged with or that they had been justified in their actions. Joe's other clients hobbled in on crutches or swathed in bandages, seeking compensation for injuries they had suffered on the job.

For some reason, their cases did not seem to hold the legal challenge she was seeking, and some of the clients seemed well able to take care of themselves. The people who aroused Carol's sympathies were the clients with immigration problems arising from the Palmer Raids. A lawyer was supposed to help a victim, but there were no hornbooks on how to deal with massive repression by the government. There weren't even any books summarizing the basic rules of immigration law. There were few law review articles on the subject, and no known experts because the Supreme Court had decided only a few deportation cases and none of them recently. This was a virgin field for a young, ambitious lawyer with a creative turn of mind and a need to be needed.

Hale, Nelles, Shorr, and Brodsky had responded to each shift in government policy by trying to take the offensive in their deportation and criminal cases. They were a small office with no basis for thinking they could win a challenge to the Attorney General in the Supreme Court. There was every reason to believe that adding attorney Carol King to their roster would make life and the law more interesting, but no reason to believe it would change their situation.

2.
Discovering How to Fight Back

Carol King needed to find out what tools and tactics had been most effective in the campaign against the attorney general of the United States. No one was assigned to supervise her introduction into the practice of law, but the office files were full of memos and correspondence showing that the lawyers fought each case to the hilt based on the particular facts and defendants. At some point they had also decided a case-by-case approach would not suffice. They would have to attack the underlying legal issues raised by the raids, based on the rights of the people enunciated in the U.S. Constitution.

The Bill of Rights was at the core of the defense. The First Amendment guarantee of freedom of expression was perfectly clear:

> Congress shall make no law . . . abridging the freedom of speech, or of the press; or the right of the people peaceably to assemble, and to petition the government for a redress of grievances.

It contained no hint of an exception for aliens or for a period of war preparation, and Justice Oliver Wendell Holmes, Jr., had just issued an opinion to that effect. One year after the Armistice, Holmes had decided that a Russian immigrant named Jacob Abrams and three friends had not violated federal law when they attacked U.S. government policies in print. They had published leaflets protesting President Wilson's joining forces with the British and other wartime allies and sending U.S. troops to try to overthrow the new "Workers' Republic of Russia" after the end of the war.

For the first time, a United States Supreme Court opinion maintained that the right to criticize the policies of the federal government is a safety valve protected by the First Amendment; at the same time it may help pressure the existing system to make necessary changes. The vote was 2 to 7, and Holmes's dissenting opinion was not considered significant. The *New York Times* ran the story on the case as the second item on an inner page of the third section of the Sunday paper as Abrams began serving his twenty-year term.

But to the lawyers on East Eleventh Street Holmes's opinion was a candle they meant to fan into a beacon. They would try to convince lower court judges to accept this minority view, and "*See* Holmes, J., *dissent* in *Abrams v. United States*, 250 U.S. 616 at 624 (1919)" became a standard citation in their briefs.

Oliver Wendell Holmes, Jr., the Boston Brahmin, had been profoundly affected by his service in the Civil War as a young man. Coming from education and privilege to fight a war to save the United States from dismemberment, he had learned that change is necessary, even a basic change like the abolition of the system of chattel slavery, even confiscation of private property when that property consists of human beings. None-theless, Holmes had written the majority opinion in 1919 holding that First Amendment protection did not apply in wartime when there was a "clear and present danger" to the government, as in the *Schenck* case. He had written the opinion that sent Eugene V. Debs to prison for a long term solely for making a long speech about socialism in which Holmes also found a "manifest intent" to encourage the obstruction of the recruiting service for U.S. participation in the imperialist war.

This opinion had not sat well with Judge Learned Hand, who had observed "the merry sport of Red-baiting" and was dismayed at "the pack" showing "symptoms of apparent panic." Hand wrote a careful, respectful letter from his lower court bench raising basic questions with Justice Holmes about the First Amendment. Hand preferred his test in *The Masses* case to Holmes's "clear and present danger" test. Hand's test was strict, "hard, [and] objective": speech was protected unless it was solely speech of direct incitement to illegal action. Hand's letter led Holmes to deeper thought and to change his mind, or to see a distinction in the facts in the *Abrams* case. He held that the Court should not punish the peaceful exercise of First Amendment liberties by Abrams. This decision would be the safest course for the republic:

> But when men have realized that time has upset many fighting faiths, they may come to believe even more than they believe the very foundations of their own conduct that the ultimate good desired is better reached by free trade in ideas — that the best test of truth is the power of the thought to

get itself accepted in the competition of the market, and that truth is the only ground upon which their wishes safely can be carried out.

That, at any rate, is the theory of our Constitution.

It is an experiment, as all life is an experiment. Every year if not every day we have to wager our salvation upon some prophecy based upon imperfect knowledge. While that experiment is part of our system I think that we should be eternally vigilant against attempts to check the expression of opinions that we loathe and believe to be fraught with death, unless they so imminently threaten immediate interference with the lawful and pressing purpose of the law that an immediate check is required to save the country.

Only Justice Louis D. Brandeis concurred in this memorable opinion.

The lawyers in the Nelles office also knew the Fourth Amendment was on their side:

The right of the people to be secure in their persons, houses, papers, and effects, against unreasonable searches and seizures, shall not be violated, and no Warrants shall issue, but upon probable cause.

"The people" had a right to be secure, not only "the native-born."

The Fifth Amendment guaranteed:

No person shall . . . be deprived of life, liberty, or property, without due process of law. . . .

The Sixth Amendment guaranteed every accused person:

the right . . . to have the Assistance of Counsel for his defence.

And the Eighth Amendment said:

Excessive bail shall not be required, . . . nor cruel and unusual punishment inflicted.

The lawyers maintained that the Attorney General of the United States had clearly violated the Bill of Rights; they set out to free the prisoners he had taken and to enforce the first ten amendments. They were joined in their efforts on January 12, 1920, by the U.S. Attorney for eastern Pennsylvania who resigned with a blast at the Attorney General for denying alien Americans the most basic due process. Francis Fisher Kane had to speak out because he felt U.S. Attorneys were involved, even though "the crusade" was operated not by them, but by "professional detectives." Kane's attack supported efforts by Isaac Shorr and Walter Nelles to seek release of each individual client held on Ellis Island. They lost. Federal judges refused to release any aliens on bail.

Watching their opponent take to the press, Swinburne Hale followed suit. As senior partner of the firm, Captain Hale appealed to the court of public opinion, as Clarence Darrow always did. He made fun of "The Force and Violence Joker" in an article for the *New Republic,* blasting the "criminal anarchy" charges against New York radical Ben Gitlow. Then he appeared before the House Rules Committee as an expert, speaking with authority based on his position in Military Intelligence during the recent war. The American Federation of Labor found its voice and also testified against Palmer's sedition bill before the committee, fearing attacks on the basic right to strike. The new American Civil Liberties Union and the progressive National Popular Government League testified, followed by the American Newspaper Association, which feared censorship of news and editorials.

By the end of January, Hale could report victory on his front: the Rules Committee chairman referred Palmer's bill back to the Judiciary Committee for reconsideration.

In March, Isaac Shorr journeyed to Hartford, Connecticut, to represent forty-seven men picked up in Bridgeport in the first raid. Friends of the men told Shorr they had been arrested without warrants, held for two days in the Bridgeport police station, then transferred to the Hartford jail. Friends who went to visit them were also arrested, until ninety-seven people were incarcerated. Shorr wrote a careful letter to Attorney General Palmer inquiring whether the acts of the department's agents in the November 1919 raid had been committed by authority of the department. If not, he requested an investigation to fix the responsibility for this lawlessness.

The Attorney General did not answer the letter.

When Isaac finally met his clients, they had been held for five months with no information about the charges against them or the bail required for their release. Most of them were not political, he learned; they were foreign-born workers who could not speak English. He found them isolated in their cells, denied all reading matter, prohibited from exercising, given what a later report termed "foul and insufficient food." For trivial offenses, prison officials sent them to punishment rooms built over the boiler: hot, unventilated cells without lights. Bailiffs sent in one glass of water and one slice of bread every twelve hours. The prisoners asked for permission to contact a lawyer. This request was denied from their arrests in November 1919 until March 1920.

Isaac was determined to get the prisoners out of the Hartford jail immediately, but he knew no federal judge would issue a writ. When it was announced that Assistant Secretary of Labor Louis F. Post had become acting secretary of labor, success suddenly seemed possible. Post was an older man known as a progressive and a believer in an early tax reform, the "single tax." Post quickly wrested control over deportation matters from Palmer and the Justice Department, reasserting the Labor Department's exclusive jurisdiction. Palmer did not like Post's actions, but the law was clearly on Post's side.

Isaac wasted no time in writing to Post about the conditions at Hartford. Post reacted instantly, transferring Shorr's clients to Deer Island, Boston, where many other victims of the raids were still being held. Conditions there were chaotic, and according to a later ruling by a federal judge, "inhumane," but they did not compare with the horrors of Hartford. Post kept a careful record of these detentions and other facts and decisions, publishing them in 1923 in his book *The Deportations Delirium: A personal narrative of an historic official experience*. Release on bail continued to be impossible.

In April the New York State Assembly refused to seat four members re-elected from New York City on the Socialist Party ticket and a fifth new Socialist assemblyman. Only five assemblymen dissented from this decision, and the *New York Times* supported the expulsion on April 2. In Washington, Attorney General Palmer urged Congress to pass a strong *peacetime* sedition law. He said he had to move against 60,000 *citizens* considered "suspect" by J. Edgar Hoover's newly established General Intelligence Division of the Bureau of Investigation. Palmer's bill would prescribe the death penalty for certain "seditious offenders," give him sweeping police powers, and virtually outlaw all meaningful dissent from government policy.

This legislative assault led Hale to action in yet another part of the forest. He helped initiate a committee of eminent lawyers who could expose those facts about the Palmer Raids that had never appeared in the press. Their report would undercut Palmer's campaign. Hale started with the Harvard liberals, law school dean Roscoe Pound and professors Felix Frankfurter and Zechariah Chafee. Chafee had just gotten started on civil liberties issues after reading Hand's decision on *The Masses* and talking with Harvard tutor Harold Laski.

All this work by Shorr and Hale was a far cry from what Carol King had been taught to consider "practicing law." So was the work of Walter Nelles, who had started to publish the *Law and Freedom Bulletin* for the ACLU. In each issue of the mimeographed *Bulletin,* Nelles reported the latest decisions of the Supreme Court and lower state and federal courts on immigration, labor law, free speech, and similar questions. He began to chronicle the development of constitutional law just as the field of civil liberties came to life in 1919 in reaction to the repression of political dissent during the Great War. After the Palmer Raids, he spent considerable time on this publication, so that the little band of willful lawyers representing dissenters around the country could take immediate advantage of the latest cases.

Carol King's impression of Walter Nelles changed as she got to know him. His reserve and shyness turned to warmth with personal friends. He had been a teacher before going back for his law degree and was a real intellectual, completely absorbed in where ideas come from and how they manifest themselves. In the *Bulletin* Nelles could take a crack at analyzing Justice Holmes's new opinions on the meaning of the First Amendment and Judge Hand's different approach in *The Masses* case. Nelles could suggest how other lawyers could use these opinions in representing labor and alien clients. He was also beginning a collection of cases that might lead eventually to statistical studies of the operation of the legal system.

Carol began to regale the lawyers in her family with stories from the office about the ineptitude of Attorney General Palmer and other government officials. She loved to boast about the significance of the cases her colleagues were handling. The best example was Walter Nelles's involvement in the incident that set the stage for the Sacco-Vanzetti case that was beginning to hit page one of the newspapers.

In early March 1920, agents of the Justice Department picked up two printers in New York on warrants of arrest for deportation to Italy, without notifying the Labor Department. They did not turn Andrea Salsedo and Robert Elia over to the immigration authorities as the warrants required and did not give them a hearing of any kind. When friends inquired as to the whereabouts of the men, they got the runaround.

On May 3, the newspapers reported that the body of Salsedo was found on the pavement at four o'clock in the morning, fourteen stories below the offices of the Department of Justice at 13 Park Row. Reporters learned that Salsedo and Elia had been held there, incommunicado, for more than seven weeks.

At first the Justice Department announced that Salsedo and Elia were vital witnesses in connection with the unsolved Washington bombings of 1919, that they had remained in custody voluntarily, that the department could not release them, and that Salsedo had jumped to his death. Within a few days, however, Justice found it could turn Elia over to Immigration, and it was desperately anxious to have him deported.

Walter defended Elia in the deportation hearing at Ellis Island. The minute the hearing was over, Nelles filed suit for Mrs. Salsedo, seeking damages from the attorney general and other officials on account of her husband's death. Judge Martin T. Manton dismissed the suit and denounced Nelles's allegations as untrue "and directed the United States Attorney to institute an inquiry as to whether Mr. Nelles was guilty of perjury or unprofessional conduct." Nothing came of this threat or of Nelles's effort to disprove the charges.

Two days after Salsedo's death, the police in Boston arrested two Italian workers, Bartolomeo Vanzetti and Nicola Sacco, and charged them with a payroll robbery and the murder of a guard. A committee was quickly formed for their defense by supporters, who said Sacco and Vanzetti were among the millions who came to this country with a vision sold by agents of U.S. firms promising streets paved with gold and votes for every man, including poor men. Having fled tyranny in Italy, they had fled to Mexico rather than go into the U.S. army in a world war that would only help Big Business and kill their working-class brothers.

At their trial in 1921, the prosecution described the suspicious actions of Sacco and Vanzetti when arrested and said their efforts to destroy their radical literature pointed to their guilt.

The defense replied that Vanzetti went to New York to learn the whereabouts of Salsedo and Elia, without success. On his return to Boston he gave a speech that Sacco heard. Vanzetti said another roundup of alien radicals was imminent, and they should dispose of all their radical literature.

The Left attacked the trial of the good shoemaker and the poor fish peddler, describing in detail the Back Bay prejudice against workers in general and aliens in particular. They made the two men known the world around as victims of American injustice. The jury convicted them of murder and they were sentenced to death.

২৯

Finally in the spring of 1920 in Boston, federal judge George Anderson began hearing *Colyer v. Skeffington,* the lawsuit seeking release of 800 to 1,200 aliens arrested on January 3 and still held on Deer Island. The judge had been head of the anti-espionage efforts of the Department of Justice in New England during the War; his loyalty was unassailable. He welcomed the assistance offered him by Harvard law professors Felix Frankfurter and Zechariah Chafee, appearing not as attorneys for specific clients but as friends of the court (amici curiae). Chafee's new book, *Free Speech in the United States,* was the first on the subject and an instant classic.

Chafee and Frankfurter soon joined one of the sharpest attacks ever made on law enforcement: "Report Upon the Illegal Practices of the United States Department of Justice," published in May 1920 by the National Popular Government League. Prepared by Hale's committee of prestigious lawyers, the signatories also included Pound from Harvard; Professor Ernst Freund of the University of Chicago Law School; Frank P. Walsh, Joint Chairman of the National War Labor Board; and other Republicans, Presbyterians, and former judges. In seven short pages this report made its case against the government and then added fifty-seven pages of supporting documents.

The report called to the attention of the public many "utterly illegal acts" committed by agents of the Justice Department in making 5,500 arrests of citizens and noncitizens. They had imposed cruel and unusual punishments, made arrests without warrants, conducted unreasonable searches and seizures, and compelled persons to be witnesses against themselves. They had planted undercover agents in radical organizations who had "occupied themselves with informing upon or instigating acts which might be declared criminal, and at the express direction of Washington" had brought about meetings of radicals in order to make possible wholesale arrests at such meetings. They had made the arrests for the purpose of indefinite detention, and manacled many of their victims, marching them through the streets so they could be photographed in this condition. They had terrorized many citizens as well as aliens, arresting people in their homes in the middle of the night.

The report specifically found that the Attorney General had not limited himself to bringing people before grand juries to investigate whether they had violated the law; he had gone into "the field of propaganda against radicals," and in so doing had been guilty of "a deliberate misuse of his office and a deliberate squandering of funds entrusted to him by Congress."

The report declared, "Since these illegal acts have been committed by the highest level powers in the United States, there is no final appeal from them except to the conscience and condemnation of the American people."

The newly organized ACLU co-sponsored the report and circulated copies among key government and business figures in Washington and New York. It swelled the chorus of opposition to the raids, which by now included some strange bedfellows. Bethlehem Steel magnate Charles M. Schwab denounced the mass deportation of cheap foreign labor, while Senator William E. Borah (Rep.-Idaho) deplored the scuttling of individual rights and freedoms, as he had earlier opposed U.S. entry into the war. Carol King came to refer repeatedly to the careful findings in this report to support the need for judges to order the Immigration Bureau to afford due process to her clients.

Early in 1920, in his role as Assistant Secretary of Labor, Louis F. Post was busy reviewing 1,600 deportation cases arising from the raids. Over the objections of J. Edgar Hoover of the FBI, Post guaranteed release of deportees on reasonable bail, the right to counsel during deportation hearings (if the aliens could pay for it), and a speedy review of all pending cases. In making the final administrative decisions, Post announced that he felt bound by certain minimum standards of due process of law and would not order the deportation of an alien just because he had belonged to a proscribed organization. He would not order deportations on the basis of evidence that the government had procured illegally, or return aliens to any country where they might be arrested or tortured for their political views. And if deportees had dependent children who were citizens of the United States, he would give *them* the benefit of the doubt, not the government.

The House Committee on Rules called on Post to explain his decisions in mid-April 1920, threatening impeachment. Post was an elderly and determined man, and the ACLU and the National Popular Government League saw to it that he was provided with free legal counsel.

Post patiently reviewed the procedures required in deportation cases. He walked with the nation's heroes as he made a strong defense of his actions: "I can remember my grandfather telling me . . . how Thomas Jefferson was denounced as a 'red republican,' so . . . in that period the red color prevailed as the best way of denouncing an opponent with whom one did not agree and whom one could not answer by argument. . . . A little later . . . the color scheme was changed from red to black and Abraham Lincoln . . . [was] in my time a 'black republican'; . . . and all you had to do . . . to avoid answering an unanswerable proposition was to say 'You are a black Republican.' "

Before he left the stand, Post had convinced his congressional questioners that his decisions were justified; an opposition congressman apologized to him.

Suddenly the committee called A. Mitchell Palmer to account for *his* extralegal deportation activities. On the stand the Attorney General peppered his statements with sneers at the "twelve gentlemen said to be lawyers" who had submitted the "Report Upon the Illegal Practices of the United States Department of Justice." He said, "I apologize for nothing that the Department of Justice has done in this matter. I glory in it. If . . . some of my agents out in the field . . . were a little rough and unkind . . . with these alien agitators whom they observed seeking to destroy their homes, their religion and their country, I think it might well be overlooked in the general good to the country which has come from it."

In June 1920 Palmer went to the Democratic Party convention to seek the presidential nomination. After many rounds of voting, he conceded defeat. He had become "somewhat of an extremist on the radical question," a man who lacked electability. And when Republican Charles Evans Hughes gave the graduation speech at Harvard Law School, he supported the Bill of Rights and denounced the deportation outrages, as he had earlier opposed the expulsion of the Socialists from the New York Assembly because "guilt is personal and cannot be attributed to the holding of opinion or to mere intent in the absence of overt acts; . . ."

The New York State prosecutors responded in their own way to the hysteria that spawned the Palmer Raids. They convened a grand jury to look for anarchists who had violated the New York criminal anarchy law. They found instead members of the Left Wing of the Socialist Party, the Federated Union of Russian Workers in the United States and Canada, the new Communist Party, and the Finnish Branch of the Industrial Workers of the World (IWW). Several of these people became clients of Brodsky and Shorr. Of these sixteen defendants, seven were convicted and sent to Sing Sing Prison for long terms, five were deported, one fled the country, two renounced the Communist Party and received suspended sentences, and five men could not be apprehended.

The grand jury was not satisfied. In its report, which Nelles quoted in the *Law and Freedom Bulletin,* it recommended that the state anarchy statute be broadened. Then it made a 180-degree turn, finding that "repression of free speech tends directly to the embittered exaggeration of impulses which, if allowed a reasonable liberty of expression, would very largely satisfy or dissipate themselves. . . . It is not a skillful means to the proper development of character, and should not be carried to extremes." The jury was troubled by imprisoning 400,000 people each year in the United States, which "suggests reason for disgust, censure of our institutions, and explanations, if not supporting argument, of radical counter-action in political doctrine."

The lawyers in the Nelles office appealed to the second half of this contradiction in every case, and it determined the decision that finally held the Palmer Raids unconstitutional. It was not a Supreme Court case but the decision of Judge Anderson of Boston, who had listened to fifteen days of testimony covering 1,600 pages of transcript from people arrested in the raids in Boston and incarcerated thereafter. He had ordered agents of the Justice Department to testify about their actions and to produce in court intradepartmental memoranda and telegrams. He put this material into his sixty-four-page opinion in *Colyer v. Skeffington,* issued in June and laying a strong basis in fact for his ultimate conclusion: the law enforcement officers involved in the raids had been a "mob."

Judge Anderson found that almost one thousand aliens had been denied due process of law in the cradle of liberty and ordered them released for this reason. He found that the immigration officials, rather than being impartial, had felt strong pressure to order deportation in as many cases as possible. He held that aliens could not be deported merely for being members of the Communist Party if they did not understand its policies because they did not know the English language in which it stated its platform. And he held that aliens could not be deported even if they did understand Party policies.

The Department of Justice did not contest Judge Anderson's general findings. It limited itself to an appeal to reverse his decision permitting four aliens from England to remain in the United States since they were admitted Communist Party members and could read and understand the Party doctrine. The Court of Appeals in time agreed that "conscious" Communist Party membership was a ground for deportation.

Secretary of Labor William B. Wilson, like the Court of Appeals, ruled that certain organizations such as the Communist Party advocated the violent overthrow of the government, so that mere membership was a basis for deportation under the 1918 Sedition Act. Following this rule, Post ultimately canceled more than 3,000 deportation arrest warrants. He signed 500 deportation orders, concluding that "there could hardly have been, out of the thousands of aliens charged with deportable offenses, more than a canoe load of deportees."

By the November election, the hysteria had partially spent itself. In the secrecy of the voting booth, one million citizens marked an X for President for a man serving time in prison for violating the Sedition Act by opposing U.S. entry into the recent War — third-party candidate, Eugene V. Debs of the Socialist Party. The majority voted out the Democrats and voted in Republican Warren G. Harding, who felt he could release Debs from prison in the Christmas season of 1921.

Carol King had followed some of these events in the newspapers, had participated in others herself. Now she studied the smashing series of legal victories that had never reached the Supreme Court at all. This approach was all new to someone who had just spent three years in school reading Supreme Court opinions. As a matter of fact, the Boston case before Judge Anderson had never gone to trial but had only been a hearing on a habeas corpus petition. The whole fight would never appear in law school casebooks because only the Boston case led to a written opinion, and it was by a lower court on a habeas petition. In many of the other habeas cases, the judges did not even file written opinions.

Still, the people and their lawyers stopped 3,000 deportations. They killed the attorney general's ambition to be President and a repressive new peacetime sedition bill he sponsored (although they might expect the bill to be resuscitated in the next era of anti-Red hysteria.) They did all this without arguing a single case in the Supreme Court, appealing to the President, or getting a new bill through Congress.

Joe Brodsky would say they accomplished this by carrying on a struggle in every available forum — in mass organizations, the press, the local bar association, the lowest federal courts, the highest administrative review agency, and in a congressional committee — always conscious of the contradictions in the ruling class between the desire for trade with the new Soviet Union, and the drive to another war with the Russian Reds requiring attacks on native Reds.

A broad range of organizations and individuals led the fight against the Palmer Raids — union members, rank-and-file aliens and citizens, one group of businessmen, and one group of lawyers with and without individual clients. They were so successful that many specific charges of misconduct by Palmer, Hoover, and their agents were spelled out in 1921 in hearings before the U.S. Senate Judiciary Committee on Charges of Illegal Practices of the Department of Justice. The ACLU observed that the Justice Department never did discover who sent the bombs in 1919 and 1920, almost all of which had been stopped by the postal service in an unparalleled example of efficiency. Finding the culprits had been the only constitutionally authorized duty of the Justice Department in the whole anti-alien drive, the ACLU concluded in its 1924 pamphlet, *The Nation-wide Spy System.*

Starting her career in the midst of the Palmer Raid cases, Carol King found a model for constitutional litigation that was without parallel. After this introduction to the practice of front-page constitutional law, she could start handling her share of the cases that came to the office.

3.
Beginning to Practice Law

Carol King was starting her practice in 1921 at the desperate moment when the leaders of government and industry were on a strikebreaking, Red-baiting spree accompanied by race riots and attacks on aliens, and when labor law was still reported under "Master/Servant" in the law books. It was the exciting moment when civil liberties law was being born. Oliver Wendell Holmes had just become the first Supreme Court Justice to rule on the meaning of the First Amendment. Holmes was also the first to decide that this amendment protects individual liberties against arrests by the federal government under some circumstances (although his was the minority view and was for limited protection). The American Civil Liberties Union had just begun to defend the right to organize unions and object to war. The National Association for the Advancement of Colored People was becoming a force against segregation and lynchings. Women's groups were celebrating their right to vote. The Anti-Defamation League was fighting anti-Semitism. The new Communist Party was supporting Marxism and the new Soviet Union, and Clarence Darrow had started losing cases again, this time for members of the new Communist Party.

Dozens of people remained in custody at Ellis Island as Carol King sat in her new office waiting for work. At the same time, Hale, Nelles & Shorr, and Brodsky had scores of cases; many involved complex sets of facts hidden in documents issued over many years in many languages by several governments. Their new law clerk, Sol Cohn, remembers how different each lawyer was in his style of work. The senior partner, Swinburne Hale, would pop in looking like a man who had just sailed the seven seas on his yacht with his wife, which is exactly who he was and what he had been doing now that his presence on Capitol Hill was not urgently needed. He would make appearances at night court for an indigent criminal defendant but wouldn't take on a major issue because he wouldn't be around long enough to see it through.

Isaac Shorr worked slowly. He talked as a person in ceaseless battle with other lawyers, teaching respect for his clients regardless of who they were or the condition of their clothing. He related to each client as an individual with a legal problem. He would sit down with his pipe and try to analyze what the equities and justice in this case really were, concentrating for hours at a time, scrawling arguments on pieces of paper and throwing them away one by one as he figured out how his opponent would counter each point.

Sol would come in and say, "It's time for coffee," and walk Shorr to a distant coffee shop to give him some respite from his labors. Isaac would start talking about the problem as they walked, logic his only tool. 'Maybe it would be possible to do this or that? . . . No, that wouldn't work for such and such a reason.' By this slow and tortuous method, he singled out the issues he was prepared to take to the state and federal supreme courts. But he needed help.

So did Joe, who was busy not only on his law cases but also with organizational work — in defense of Sacco and Vanzetti, his New York comrade Ben Gitlow, and other victims of the Red scare. He nonetheless had time to describe the theory behind his approach. He would explain that 'the economic system is the base, and the legal system is part of the superstructure of society.' He saw a political democracy housed in the capitalist economic system in the United States. This condition created built-in contradictions that he could use to the advantage of his clients if he worked hard enough to ferret them out in each case.

Joe had read *The Communist Manifesto* and Engels's *Origin of the Family, Private Property and the State*. His clients were uniformly from the working class, and they faced members of the ruling class in court — police officers in criminal cases, employers or landlords in civil cases. Both sides knew that political and legal forms are conditioned by material, economic factors. So Joe said his job as a lawyer was to study the specific features of a case and then to find provisions in the Constitution and laws protecting the rights of his clients. Since the Constitution was written by men who had helped make a revolution against the British king and ruling class, it contained clauses he could use to protect his working-class clients, and he should be able to find them. And he should be able to find some statutes passed by Congress during periods when the people had elected progressive-minded people to office.

He realized that almost all judges come from the ruling class, but he maintained that this situation did not end the matter. Some had been taught, or had learned from history, that social stability requires the rich to mitigate the worst injustices to the poor. Joe appealed to this precept. He called this a contradiction between democratic, egalitarian aspects of the legal structure in the United States and the class stratification of the capitalist economic system. Of course, as a Marxist, he had no illusions about having "justice" meted out "impartially" by "neutral" men on the bench, as he had no illusion about getting "justice" from the Department of Justice. But that would not excuse laziness in a working-class lawyer because hard work at every stage in a case should pay off.

The fact that Joe could tell an amusing anecdote to make a point in the middle of this heavy theorizing made such pronouncements memorable, whether or not one accepted them. He, Nelles, and Shorr often spoke at the Rand School of Social Science run by the Socialist Party, where columnist Heywood Broun taught a class. The lawyers were romantic figures to young workers like Sender Garlin because they were handling cases of alien workers and other persecuted people, undaunted by the power of their opponents. Walter Nelles had quite a different philosophy and style from Brodsky. Busy as he was, he took the time to introduce Carol to the Civic Club on West Twelfth Street, and to Louis Waldman.

Waldman was an old-line Socialist Party lawyer who recorded his impressions of both lawyers for an article in the *Saturday Evening Post* in 1951. Waldman characterized Walter Nelles as far from a radical, although he did "burn with a crusader's zeal to protect civil liberties against all encroachments," and seemed to find his most congenial companionship among the socialists who frequented the Civic Club. Waldman's reaction to Carol Weiss King was sharp and negative. He knew that her father had been a successful commercial lawyer and that her brother Louis was following in his footsteps with his new firm of Weiss & Wharton. As for Carol, he had to mention that she was "a bright girl who would never be a beauty."

When he met Carol's husband, Waldman noted that "seldom had more opposite opposites mated" — Gordon liked to lunch at the Harvard Club while Carol paraded on picket lines; he wrote experimental plays while she represented aliens arrested for deportation; he meticulously put on a black tie and dinner jacket every evening while she never seemed to give a thought to what she wore. Waldman thought Carol visited the Civic Club while "slumming in search of a career."

Carol King had learned to notice people's reactions to her, but there is no record that she knew how she affected people like Waldman when she invaded what they subconsciously perceived to be their domain. She was terribly preoccupied with finding her niche in the office where she worked while at the same time trying to fit in with her husband's needs and schedule.

Gordon was cooped up every day in their apartment writing, and welcomed the chance for a change of pace. Occasionally they would interrupt their work to meet in the park for a quick chat. One day they had repaired to a favorite park bench where they sat, totally absorbed in each other, when a policeman came up and chastised them for being so affectionate in public. Gordon protested that they were a married couple. The officer appeared skeptical. Gordon offered to produce their marriage certificate. The officer said that didn't make any difference to him. 'You better learn to curb your passions in public if you want to stay out of jail!' he warned. Gordon said they would do so and the officer let them go. (His wife told the story with joy fifteen years later to a young Columbia Law School couple, Norman and Marjorie Leonard.)

Their easy brush with the law befitted their status as a young white American professional couple violating social taboos. Most of the clients who came to East Eleventh Street did not fall into these categories, and they had become so numerous that the other lawyers began asking Carol to make appearances for them, particularly in deportation and exclusion cases. This led Carol to the forlorn federal enclave known as Ellis Island. None of the lawyers had time to show her the ropes there. They assumed she could figure things out for herself, as they had done when they started practicing. Attorney Carol King, therefore, set off for Ellis Island prepared to rely on her instincts if she found herself in a tight spot.

First she would go down to the waterfront launch station for a pass. Waiting for officialdom to sanction her movements, she got a taste of how her incarcerated clients felt. The launch ran through New York Harbor past the Statue of Liberty until it reached the Ellis Island pier. To the left was the Coast Guard station; straight ahead, Immigration. There were bars on the windows and nobody could leave without authorization from the Immigration Bureau or a federal court; still, the island was not labeled a jail.

Lawyers found the counsel room forbidding. They and their clients gained admission through locked doors. The room had no windows at eye level. The walls were institution green, the tables long, the chairs dark.

The attorneys usually had no news for their clients, intensifying their alienation: they were nobodies; they could make no plans for the future. Who knew how long they would have to stay on the island? Some of their babies would be born there; their children would be taught to sing "The Star-Spangled Banner" before they understood English or knew whether they would ever set foot in the United States.

Attorney King soon discovered that her success as an immigration lawyer depended in part on her prowess as an athlete. In 1921 all deportation hearings were held on the island. The Immigration Bureau would send out letters scheduling hearings in a hundred cases for the same time on a certain day. The first attorney to hand in a card to the hearing officer was the first to be served; latecomers might sit around waiting all day and then have their hearings postponed. Looking back on these days, Carol recalled catching the first launch for Ellis Island on the appointed day and sprinting from the landing to the hearing room. She might not look dignified, but at least she got her cases heard.

Wherever she went as a lawyer, Carol King was breaking new ground. Three million women had been pulled into work in various industries during the War, but most people had never seen a woman lawyer before. When Mrs. King met bailiffs, immigration officials, other lawyers, law clerks, legal secretaries, judges, court clerks, and clients, it was usually a first for all of them. Apparently she figured out that this made it feasible for her to act like herself. Since no one knew what a woman lawyer looked like, she could set the fashion. Everyone expected to be uneasy with this new phenomenon — The Woman Lawyer — so Carol King, Esquire, had to teach herself to get through that awkward moment when she was being sized up by each new person she met professionally.

Basically friendly and gregarious, she began handing out her card to elevator operators and people she talked to on subways. From her background she knew, without being shown, how to treat administrative underlings and upperlings. Since her clients lived for long periods on Ellis Island, their living conditions were important. If she could not get them out on bail, at least she might be able to humanize some of the treatment they received in custody. She got into the habit of making small talk with the bureaucrats and civil servants she met and, when she could, became friendly with them. Later, if she needed to ask them to call a doctor for a client who became ill on Ellis Island, or for some other personal consideration, there was a greater chance the civil servant would find an exception to a rule and respond like a human being.

Carol King seldom won a case. No one representing aliens was winning cases in this difficult period. Yet the resistance to the Palmer Raids had made a difference, although it had not touched the underlying problem in the handling of deportation cases. The Supreme Court was the problem: it refused to rule that deportation is punishment. This meant a person could be arrested without being charged with any crime and could be sent to jail awaiting deportation. From that point on, a person charged with murder had more constitutional rights than a worker from another country labeled an alien. Clerks in the Labor Department, protected by civil service, could make life-and-death decisions about an alien whose views they opposed, without being subject to review or censure in the courts. Even native-born radicals were being arrested for "criminal syndicalism" when they simply participated in peaceful strikes.

In this political climate, lawyers found little hope of due process for aliens. Deportees were not told they had a right to counsel after they were arrested for deportation. They were asked to make damaging statements. They were not permitted the assistance of lawyers until the deportation hearings began. By then it was usually too late for them to prepare a successful defense. And they could be forced to be witnesses against themselves at the hearings, which were closed to the public and even to the press.

On top of all this, one person, an inspector of the Labor Department, usually acted as investigator, prosecutor, and judge at the hearing. He collected the evidence against the alien before the hearing, presented it at the hearing, then decided whether the evidence was sufficient to justify deportation. Combining those functions could never result in a fair decision because the hearing officer had a stake in upholding the work he had done on the case as an investigator and prosecutor.

After the hearing, the attorneys for both sides needed a transcript in order to write a meaningful appeal; only the government lawyer got access to this document. The Labor Department did not publish any of its opinions in deportation cases but made them available to counsel in the department, not to counsel for the aliens.

When Carol saw that this was the state of the law, she began wearing a path from the Ellis Island launch to the U.S. District Court in New York. As she explained repeatedly, one couldn't just let one's clients sit on the island indefinitely while their rights were being denied! They ought to be released while their deportation cases were going through the long administrative procedures required by immigration rules. Her weapon to secure their release was the writ of habeas corpus, "the great writ" wrung from King John in 1215 by English lords, enshrined in Magna Carta and in the Constitution of the United States. The minute she filed her habeas petition, a federal court judge had to order the prisoner brought into court so the judge could look at the person and decide whether the petition should be granted and the person freed.

Each decision meant the difference between life in the United States and deportation to some other country where one might face death or prison. This knowledge led committed immigration lawyers to feel in their bones that a case was more than a case in the law school sense. To the people in Carol's office, a case was both an important person and a significant legal principle. It was not a fee and an inanimate file to be dropped at quitting time and forgotten till tomorrow morning. Clients were more like relatives with quirks and mannerisms that must be tolerated over long periods of time while the courts were deciding their fate. The issues in their cases became old friends whose many facets became familiar long before the courts permanently settled them.

One of the first cases Carol handled fell into this category; it lasted for several years and creating an amusing, and expensive, problem for the U.S. Attorney. She loved to tell the story step by step, emphasizing the thrust and parry that mark litigation duels, with no automatic victories even on obvious facts.

A man named Okolitenko was ordered deported to his native land, Russia, so the Immigration Bureau went to the Russian Embassy in Washington for the necessary papers for his readmission to that country. The embassy was still staffed by Russian officials of the Kerensky regime who had stayed on after Kerensky was ousted by Lenin in the October 1917 revolution. They issued the papers for Okolitenko.

Carol promptly filed a petition for a writ of habeas corpus for the release of Okolitenko, explaining that the "Russian" government did not exist any longer; it had been permanently replaced by the "Soviet" government. Kerensky had no standing; neither did his Washington attaché or his visa. John Reed and other Reds from the United States had explained the Palmer Raids to their comrades in the new Soviet government, who adopted a policy to thwart the deportation delirium, at least as it concerned Russians. As a result, the "Soviet" government refused to admit entry of people who had left old "Russia," had lived in the United States, and were now being deported from the United States because of their political beliefs or activities in the United States.

The U.S. Attorney denied all of Mrs. King's allegations about the lack of authority of Kerensky's agent, the demise of the Russian government, and the Soviet policy on political deportees. The judge took his word over hers, and dismissed her petition.

Okolitenko was sent back to "Russia." When he arrived there, the new "Soviet" government denied him admission, as his lawyer had predicted. They returned him to the United States.

When Okolitenko called Carol from Ellis Island on his return, she copied her old habeas corpus petition, added a paragraph or two about his round-trip journey, and sought his release, as before.

The U.S. Attorney denied the facts in her pleadings, as before. The judge believed him and not her, as before. Okolitenko was again sent to Russia, where he was promptly denied entry by the Soviet Union and returned to the United States.

When he called her from Ellis Island for the third time, Carol explained to the Immigration Bureau that these boat rides could continue indefinitely, and they were costing the government a lot of money.

They agreed. After four trips across the Atlantic, they released Okolitenko from custody in the United States. Carol could boast that she had bested the Bureau, although she had set no precedent because no appellate court had written an opinion granting her a writ.

This victory did not change the policy of the U.S. State Department, which continued to recognize one Bakmatieff as the representative of the Russian government long after the fall of Kerensky. The United States refused to recognize the Soviet representative, Ludwig C.A.K. Martens, a Russian engineer who had lived in the United States since 1916, although Martens presented his credentials to the State Department early in 1919, properly signed by Soviet Foreign Minister Chicherin. Martens then opened an office in New York and made thirty million dollars' worth of tentative contracts with U.S. corporations on behalf of his government before the U.S. government stepped in. They arrested him for deportation for membership in an organization that advocated the violent overthrow of the U.S. government.

In the end, however, caution prevailed. Carol must have been amused to discover in January 1921 that Martens was permitted "voluntary departure" instead of deportation, which meant he could be readmitted if the United States ever got around to recognizing the existence of the Soviet government.

❧

Cranking out petitions, motions, and writs, Carol King began to fit into the office setup established by Hale, Nelles, Shorr, and Brodsky. She had to learn how to get pleadings and briefs out "instanter," although she had never seen a woman dictate anything and neither Fay Seagartle nor the other legal secretaries had ever worked for a woman before. Fay recalls the general informality in the office and the dedication everyone felt for the work at hand. You could not worry about working for a woman when a client might be arrested and deported before morning. Besides, women had just gotten the vote. There were certain to be more women lawyers and women in every field.

Carol began to participate in almost every aspect of office life — except writing the checks to pay the salaries of the secretaries and the clerk and the other bills that made up the office overhead. Her own bills were few and small — the rent of her room, stationery, stamps, and the law books she was beginning to accumulate. Her fees were small because most of her clients had low incomes. Her commitment to her clients had become enormous. She began to call them "my little aliens." They were rank-and-file, anonymous workers facing the awesome power of the federal government. It was her responsibility to protect them. Their cases were, in a sense, her property. They would not set any precedents, but some of them could be won.

Sol Cohn described what happened when a typical client walked into Carol's office with a legal problem. They came, men and women, often with their children, so upset they could barely explain what their problem was. She talked a little to calm them down, then asked a few questions. Her questions reminded them of the really important facts they wanted to tell her. After she had the whole story, or at least the basic outline, Mrs. King told them frankly what she thought she could do for them under the circumstances. She also told them what she could not do, in English, not in legaleze.

When they left her office, they felt relieved. Most of their problem was now sitting on her cluttered desk. Only later, on the way home, they remembered that Mrs. King had not asked them for money or told them what her fee would be. This did not seem too strange, however, because they had never visited a lawyer before, and they already considered her a friend.

As for Carol King, she was more than ready to move from Ellis Island hearings and habeas petitions to her first jury case.

King was one of the small group of women who began their careers at the successful conclusion of the long struggle for suffrage, forming a tiny, invisible sorority of government officials with an occasional engineer, lawyer, doctor, scientist, editor, or social worker.

Many of these women benefited from the prosperity the 1920s offered to some professionals and intellectuals in Manhattan. It led them to espouse a freer style of life for women as well as men, as the flapper image took hold within the United States and the expatriate image emerged in Paris. While Dorothy Parker and Edna Ferber were writing alone and being discovered by the Alexander Woollcott/Heywood Broun crowd and while Mrs. Eleanor Roosevelt was beginning to organize the Women's Division of the Democratic Party, Carol King was becoming a behind-the-scenes member of a legal collective that was closer to people in trouble, even in these roaring twenties.

As a bright, self-confident, New York woman lawyer, King knew something about the tactics that had finally led men to vote for woman's suffrage. She could use these methods to achieve the equality she expected. The elbow of time had jostled her into position to succeed as a lawyer, as it would have barred her path just five years before. But when she espoused the cause of the downtrodden, of unorganized workers, and particularly of aliens, she could never know whether a defeat in court was due to bias against her sex, prejudice against her clients, or to her own inadequacy. She simply had to proceed regardless and still find time for her rich personal life and relationships.

4.
From Hell to Horatio

As Carol began to spend part of her office hours watching for her first jury case, her husband continued to work at home on books set somewhere between twentieth-century America and ancient Greece, often writing about relationships between men and women. In 1921 Gordon completed *Too Professional: A Comedy of Manners in Four Acts* and in 1923 copyrighted *The Ostriches: A Political Fantasy after "The Frogs" of Aristophanes.* When he needed inspiration, he tried various remedies, often inviting friends over for some good conversation, sometimes going out on the town with them in search of the proverbial wine, women, and song. He did not always invite his wife to go along.

Carol's feelings were those of any wife's under similar circumstances, although having been out all day doing intense work among groups of people, she may have preferred to stay at home on some evenings. At the same time, some of their acquaintances were beginning to experiment with what they called "open marriages," along with popular columnist Heywood Broun and his wife, Ruth Hale. And Carol had been raised a Weiss, which meant that she should recognize each individual's rights as an independent person.

It wasn't as if Carol and Gordon had not known they would have differences. Some had appeared right after they met in the spring of 1917. Gordon had not shared her enthusiasm for socialism or her opposition to the War. He felt a responsibility to share in the duties of citizenship as he shared in the exercise of its freedoms, and that included service in the military, as far as he was concerned.

Their differences hadn't interfered with their joy in each other, since Carol was accustomed to disagreeing politically with the people she loved. After all, her brother Louis had worked in the legal division of the wartime government in the U.S. Housing Corporation of the Department of Labor during a war she did not support.

Gordon and Carol explored many other differences as they became intimate. His family background had been less affluent to start with, never secure, and finally impoverished. The Kings were plain people with roots in Massachusetts at the time of the Revolutionary War. Gordon's father, Louis Cass King, was a businessman who read a great deal and loved to talk ideas. He was fairly successful after he came to New York City in 1880, excited by the gamble of buying and selling coffee and other commodities. His son Howard remembered his father's delight in showing his four children the sailing ships carrying goods he traded that were being unloaded in the harbor. In 1898, when a commercial dispute arose between Great Britain and Venezuela, he lost heavily and was forced into bankruptcy. He died of pneumonia in 1900.

Kittie Bruen King was thirty-nine when she had to face the task of bringing up four children alone, the oldest thirteen and the youngest, Gordon, age six. Her immediate family was usually impoverished due to the drinking habits of her father, a shipbuilding carpenter in the Brooklyn Navy Yard. She had planned to earn her living by drawing or calligraphy and took courses for that purpose at Cooper Union. When she became a widow, she had some life insurance money available, and moved the family to a series of apartment houses on the Upper West Side from 112th Street to Moshulu Parkway. Gordon came to hate that spartan life and was often lonely. He was considerably younger than his brothers and sister, and his mother was much too burdened down to be a good companion. He wrote later about a character who was alone too much when young: "It made me grow up all awry. I have a horror of being alone."

He became something of a rebel and did not feel obligated to follow what he considered the dull and rigid mores of the family. He was eager to have friends who wanted to discuss the ideas that were on his mind. As a freshman at City College, he became serious about church membership and his religious beliefs, noting with displeasure an aging leader in the Calvary congregation whom he found to be "a colossal bluff."

After two years at CCNY, Gordon rebelled against the closely prescribed course of study. He asked his mother to let him go to Harvard so he could concentrate on English literature, Jean Jacques Rousseau, and writing. Nearing the end of her battle to put all four children through college, Mrs. King was able to agree. At Harvard, Gordon made a few

really intimate friends with whom he talked late into the night, supported
by quarts of black coffee.

That first summer after he met Carol, he came over often to see her
and soon met her warm, talkative, Jewish family. He was working on his
first play, *The Girl Pygmalion: A Comedy in Three Acts,* as Carol was
getting ready to enter law school.

Neither was bound by convention, and Solon DeLeon recalled Carol's
reporting one day in August that she had just sent Gordon a telegram:
HURRAY FOR THE RUSSIAN REVOLUTION STOP I WILL MARRY YOU.

In light of their passion, and in the face of their differences and the
fact of the War, they decided to marry quickly. A few days after their
wedding on September 14, 1917, the army called Gordon to serve and
sent him to Fort Niagara while Carol stayed in New York to attend her
first semester at New York University. After a few months Gordon was
assigned to the infantry on Governors Island, and Carol rushed to move
in with him. She woke up on a military base, then started her curious
daily commute between the disparate disciplines of Mars and Moses.

Once the War was over, Mr. and Mrs. Gordon King moved into the
house on West Twenty-second Street made possible by her mother's
thoughtfulness. When Mrs. Weiss saw them settled in, she offered to help
them buy the building, and then suggested that Mr. and Mrs. Matthew
Barkley move into the basement flat so that Mrs. Barkley could keep the
building in order, a job she had been doing for the Weisses for many years.
The couple agreed to both proposals, and soon made their apartment into
a perfect place for a party, creating an atmosphere completely divorced
from Gordon's spartan childhood and the mansion on the Hudson where
Carol had grown up. They selected the furnishings with care: antique
chairs and sofas, batik over the marble mantel, and avant-garde paintings
by Bertram Hartmann and William Zorach on the walls.

Gordon selected his friends with equal care — John van Druten, the
young dramatist, and his friend from Harvard, Bernard de Voto, who
considered Gordon one of the best talkers who ever lived, with a singu-
larly deep and winning nature among his friends. Another young writer,
F. Scott Fitzgerald, came to one of their frequent gatherings, where people
often revealed their characters, then acted out their roles almost as if they
were on stage, going further than they expected to.

Doris Maddow and other friends from college remarked that Gordon
was an active participant in these formal parties, discussing the matters
that intrigued him, questions of literary style and the ethical problems

that men have written about since the days of Athens. He was the center of conversation and attention; Carol seemed to be more of an appreciative onlooker. Some of her friends began using crimson lipstick, bobbing their hair, and buying short, flapper skirts, but after several experiments with her own appearance, she put what she liked on her short, stocky figure, without a brassiere, and adopted the stance that she preferred to be "inconspicuously badly dressed."

Her liberated spirit on the question of attire fitted into the literary/art-loving crowd with whom she and Gordon spent most of their free time. Their apartment gave them plenty of room for roaming about. And as landlords, their own rent never went up, and they could set high standards for the painting and repair of the building.

Mrs. Barkley turned into permanent live-in help. Having worked for the senior Weisses during Carol's youth, she knew how to keep the apartment in pretty much the style Carol expected, which gave Carol complete confidence in the appearance of her new home and freed her from household chores she did not have time for and knew relatively little about. Mrs. B. even kept the newspapers picked up, learning early never to touch the papers on which Carol and Gordon were working. Peggy Stern remembers Mrs. Barkley's natural tact, good humor, and forbearance, which made her unflappable in the midst of the legal, literary, and domestic crises that occurred upstairs. Downstairs she maintained her own life with her neighbors in Chelsea and her night watchman husband, but since he slept during the day, she spent a lot of time at the Kings and clearly enjoyed her role in their lives and the knowledge that she was indispensable.

Her presence meant that Carol never had to take time out to advertise for, interview, and train a series of housekeepers, which was the fate of many of her friends. They were all alert, well-educated women who exercised their critical faculties at theater parties and literary affairs, and sometimes on assignments as volunteers, but whose major roles were as wives and mothers. Carol's close friend, Marion Pollak, for one, felt somewhat ambivalent about being a full-time homemaker.

Carol was different from almost all the women of her era. For her, Monday was the day the U.S. Supreme Court handed down its decisions, not the day to deal with the family washing, and some evenings were for planning the legal work to do at the office the next morning.

In 1923 Carol took a short breather from practicing law when Hunter College asked her to give a course in parliamentary law. The college apparently thought this was a branch of the law and in the fall semester called on Mrs. King, the expert woman lawyer, to teach a course on proper procedures to follow in organizational meetings.

By deciding to become a constitutional lawyer, an appellate lawyer, an immigration lawyer, and Carol King was deciding to spend most of her working time with other lawyers whose gender was male, whose style was aggressive, and whose gratifications came from thinking, writing, arguing, and winning.

By deciding to be successful in this work, Carol King was deciding, consciously and unconsciously, to copy the styles of the other lawyers in some ways. In other ways, to achieve the same result she began to act quite different.

Every woman lawyer to date has probably faced a moment when she can not do what a man lawyer would do, or she cannot do it in exactly the same way a man lawyer would do it. The choices, then, are to imitate the male pattern as closely as possible and hope the difference will not be noticed; to get out of law practice; to step back and become a glorified legal secretary or assistant to a successful male lawyer; or to invent a new way to win that is different from the way a man lawyer would win but that cannot be attacked as unprofessional.

Carol Weiss King did smoke and drink and swear, as did most of her male colleagues, or as she supposed most of them did. Some men said she always sounded somewhat affected when she swore. She did not have affairs with other men, and some of her letters suggest that she was both naive and off-putting with men who might have gotten interested in her.

Now she was anxious to try a case to a jury, as her (male) colleagues often did. The jury would obviously consist of twelve men, as women had just gotten the vote and few, if any, had made it onto jury panels. She could not know how she would fare before a jury of twelve women and could not expect to face such a jury in her lifetime. Since she liked to meet people and make new friends, and had countless close women friends — women of all ages, religions, and economic classes — it seems likely that she would have made friends with at least some of the women jurors and that they would have voted for her client if she made a decent case, as men jurors voted for Darrow's clients because they liked Darrow, even when they rejected the politics and actions of his clients.

The question King faced at this point was whether she could learn to succeed in trying cases before a jury of twelve men with, perhaps, an occasional woman thrown in. One problem was that she did not think like a man lawyer. She thought like a lawyer and she thought like a woman. Honest male lawyers, and presumably jurors, could not deny her legal ability while most of them could not comprehend or accept her different intuitions or ways of working.

In this period, one of Carol King's clients finally came to her with a traditional civil case to be tried in a regular court, rather than an immigration case to be tried in an administrative hearing. This gave Carol the chance to file suit and begin preparing for her first jury trial.

She was scarcely walking onto a level playing field. Mrs. Mary Goldburt Siegel, another NYU Law School graduate, recalled her first courtroom experience at about this time. When her first case was called, Mrs. Siegel walked over to the appropriate table in the New York City courtroom to sit down. A bailiff rushed over to direct her to sit on the spectator's bench, where he was sure she belonged. A few minutes later, the presiding judge asked to speak to the lawyers. "As I walked toward him, I was reproached by the judge, who virtually sneered when he repeated that he wanted to confer with the legal representatives, not an office stenographer."

Mrs. Siegel and Mrs. King may not have known each other, and Carol may not have had any way of knowing how other women lawyers were faring in the trial courts. She never forgot her own feelings during this period and described them years later to Joan Isserman, the wife of a colleague. King did not mention the pervasive sexism, but talked as if her problems were caused by her own style.

She had been excited about trying her first case before a real judge and a jury, with a chance for a quick victory based on her presentation of the facts. For once, she would not be hampered by the lack of due process inherent in immigration cases governed by administrative law. She told Mrs. Isserman that she had put everything she had into this case, relying on her own hunches. She had been doing this since her teens, when there had been talk in the closely knit clan that she was too heavy and should pay more attention to her appearance. She should stop limiting her wardrobe to middy blouses and bloomers, and it was time for her to wear a proper brassiere. Carol had rejected their advice and decided to find her own style. This approach had gotten her through law school, and she had done remarkably well, up to now.

She followed her own style in her first courtroom trial, calling her witnesses, cross-examining the witnesses for the other side, arguing to the jury.

She lost the case.

At the age of twenty-eight, she had never really experienced personal failure before. She was very bright and quick; she had always worked hard, and she had figured out creative ways to win at least something for her clients. Now she did not know how to take this defeat. She not only lost confidence in herself but also felt guilty for having lost the case for her client. For some reason, she was not effective in the courtroom, and she was convinced she never would be. What made it even worse was that she was one of the very few women appearing in court, which meant that she would always be scrutinized by the judge and everyone else in the courtroom in a very critical way; anything she did wrong would be noted and commented upon.

She didn't even bother to ask the older men in the office whether they had ever experienced this kind of failure. She was sure they had not (although in fact they had). Carol was convinced that her career as a lawyer was over: the people she had begun to call her "little aliens" would have to manage without their selfless champion.

She went home after her defeat and stayed there for a week, totally isolated. Gordon could not help her; he was an author who worked alone with words, not a lawyer in the public eye. And he was a man who had suffered personal defeats whenever an editor rejected one of his articles or books. Her sister, her mother, her sisters-in-law had no experience that could shed light on her troubles. Neither did her friend Marion Pollak, or her housekeeper, Mrs. Barkley. She would have to fight this through alone. She did not record her travail, although her niece Peggy Stern knew of it. Her dream had become a nightmare.

Finally the Weiss in her apparently asserted itself, and she began to ask a practical question: what could she be, if not a trial lawyer? She liked working and there was no question she was good at it. So why couldn't she become expert in noncourtroom law? Before a trial, there was always a tremendous amount of preparation. During a trial, there was night work in the library and early morning work in the office before court, getting witnesses ready to appear. After a trial, if the verdict went against her side, she could pick up the pieces left by the trial lawyer and prepare the appeal. Few men would compete with her for this hard labor at low fees outside the limelight. She could even find the right trial lawyer for a particular case, using her wide acquaintanceship and her knowledge of the issues — and the judges.

In fact, her brother Louis was following a similar course in his own career. As a practicing commercial and domestic relations lawyer, Louis S. Weiss was making a name for himself by specializing in negotiating settlements for clients who warmed to his sympathetic attention to their problems and wanted to avoid the publicity of trials. These qualities made him a rising member of the bar and helped him found one of the first integrated law firms in the City, that is, including both Jewish and Gentile lawyers.

Carol Weiss King practiced in a different arena. Among labor and criminal defense lawyers on the Left, a good lawyer was a good trial lawyer; a great lawyer was a master before a jury. Lawyers were not expected to be able to negotiate settlements in most of their cases because their opponents were "the class enemy," that is, prosecutors, immigration officials, employers, landlords, and their ilk. If a Left lawyer could negotiate successfully with such an adversary, there must be a joker in the deck.

৯৫

Carol returned to the office after her interlude in hell. She never again tried to practice law like a man and soon got involved in the next case on her new terms. She did not insist on getting paid — in fame or in fees. She insisted on doing research, coming up with ideas, trying them out on other lawyers, and getting them presented properly in court by the person most likely to convince the judge.

King became totally immersed in the practice of immigration law. Ultimately this absorption overcame the anguish of her defeat and led her to study and speak on the history of the treatment of immigrants to the United States.

King wrote later that Americans have always been conflicted about aliens. Even before the War of Independence, the colonists tried to exclude certain types of immigrants — Roman Catholics and Quakers. They complained about England's interference with immigration to the colonies in the Declaration of Independence, but the minute they won independence, they went after "aliens."

Then the Federalists (Carol called them "the moneyed interest of their day") passed the Alien and Sedition Acts in 1798 to cut the votes for the Jeffersonians, who had won the support of the foreign-born. These acts authorized the President to deport any alien he thought dangerous, and they also contained criminal provisions. The acts "aroused a storm of protest" that helped elect Jefferson. He said the law was unconstitutional but it was never tested in court.

Fifty years later, in the mid-1800s, the Irish fled both the brutality of the British and their induced potato famine. The massive Irish immigration led to counter-demonstrations and the organization of the Know-Nothing Party and the American Protective Association, finally succeeded by the Ku Klux Klan.

The Civil War put an end to Negro slavery and to the Know-Nothing movement. Soon Congress passed laws encouraging immigration. The United States advertised that it was "the asylum of the oppressed of all nations" and signed the U.S.–China treaty. Chinese began arriving to do the rough labor and agricultural work that built up the Pacific Coast during the gold rush. But in 1875 Congress finally passed a law prohibiting the entry of alien prostitutes and criminals. Employers raised a false cry of "yellow peril" and "even the trade unions joined the outcry," Carol wrote. In 1882 Congress began passing a series of laws to exclude from this country not only Chinese but other "Oriental laborers." From the beginning, "non-white peoples" were denied naturalization; they were often arrested and jailed without a criminal trial on charges of illegal entry. It was 1896 before the Supreme Court declared this practice unconstitutional in the *Wong Wing* case.

Summarizing the "persecution of aliens" twenty-five years later, Carol wrote that "before the turn of the century, enforcement of exclusion and deportation was arbitrary . . . without any safeguards in the procedure used. Gradually, however, the courts recognized that aliens, no less than citizens, were entitled to the full protection of due process of law guaranteed in the Fifth Amendment." More than sixteen million people arrived on the shores of the United States between 1899 and 1921 according to the report of the commissioner general of immigration for 1921. This was many times the total populations of several of the nations the immigrants had left.

In 1901 a foreign-born anarchist assassinated President McKinley. His act opened "a new chapter in the country's deportation laws." Instead of using existing laws, "the government obtained immediate passage of a law against the entry of Anarchists — whether violent or peaceful." The lawyer/poet Edgar Lee Masters argued for such an alien in the Supreme Court. In 1907 the Justices decided against them: an immigrant anarchist not yet in the country could not rely on the First Amendment to protect his right to come in.

But for a time no one moved against the noncitizens already in the country, and radical aliens began to relax. Some began to exercise the freedom of speech and press they had heard so much about before they left the tyranny in their homelands.

Then, during the recent war, "to make the world safe for democracy," Congress passed the Espionage and Sedition Acts and free speech for aliens came to an abrupt end. Now Carol and her colleagues were trying to figure out the next steps in defense of their clients in deportation cases.

Thinking is hard work, and trying to think new thoughts requires that creative leap from the known to the unknown or suspected. Carol apparently decided it was time to follow the advice of older lawyers in the office who sharply separated their professional and personal lives and relaxed at home.

At night after work Carol could turn to a special diversion when her husband finished his new novel, *Horatio's Story*. The plot involved the love of a father and son for the same woman, a distant poor relation seven years younger than the one and seventeen years older than the other. And Gordon created an Englishman who defended the bohemian existence Gordon had elected to lead, explaining:

> When you get right down to it, the bohemians are the only people who have a decent life socially. They make themselves ridiculous, of course; but among themselves they seem to be having a jolly good time, whereas we respectable people never seem to be quite able to play the formal conventional game that we put before us. Either we get hurt, or we break the rules deliberately, or the rules break us. If one is to be formal one should be a member of the French aristocracy before the revolution. Otherwise the only thing I can see is to be out-and-out-bohemian.

Gordon made his female character beautiful in face and form, and dressed her well, although Carol could have detected some of her own mind and determination in Rhoda Lispenyard. Gordon posed two questions for Rhoda: whether she had enough drive to succeed in her chosen field, and whether her marriage to a professor could survive such success.

Gordon described a confrontation between his fictitious husband and wife based on a problem that arises when a couple both work at home: " 'I don't like being in the same room with you unless you feel like giving me your first attention.' It sounded stupid as she said it, but there was no help for it. One has to say stupid things frankly now and then if one is to express oneself. If he got her meaning it did not really matter how it sounded."

Gordon tried to write his novel from the perspective of a modern woman. He portrayed the frustration a woman like Carol must feel, based not only on the behavior of Rhoda's husband's colleagues at the university but particularly on the behavior of their wives. Rhoda's English friend explained that this behavior of the wives was the most natural thing in the world: "Use your sense of humor. . . . You can't possibly hope to get on in a set of idle, vain, and useless women. You can't expect them to like you . . . they're jealous of you. And the men feel they have to take the part of their women."

If Gordon expressed some of his feelings about himself and his own work in his novel, he did so through the wife, rather than the husband: "Rhoda, too, had wanted to take the world by storm. But if she had not succeeded in taking many fortresses, she had a few valid excuses. In the first place, Rhoda wanted to be a complete personality; . . . her career often met disaster largely because she never thought of it except as a means to preserve her self-respect. She worked because she believed that a woman ought to work."

One of Rhoda's younger male friends understood one problem of a working wife and advised Rhoda to have small intimate gatherings after work so she could excuse herself and take it easy. She shouldn't try to put on large parties: "It's all right for women who are home all day to plan and fix and fret; but when you come home at night you need relaxation."

Gordon went on to have his English character describe the relative merits of men and women in the United States.

It's a land of interesting women and dull men. In any level of society the women have more character than the men. And a large part of the social difficulty is that the men feel it and react to it dishonestly. While they pretend an equality of sex as no other race pretends it, they treat women as inferiors in fact, which is of course the bane of any social set. The American likes to honour women with many words; he likes equality in law and politics and business. But in society he doesn't treat a woman as an equal; . . . it would make him conscious of his inferiority.

Gordon's character found Mrs. Child superior in every way to Mr. Child: "[S]he's rounded, luxurious, full of emotion, and not ashamed of her better nature. Now her husband is a very promising young university don, but he goes about being a success in the world." Later Gordon described Rhoda in terms Carol might well have inspired: "In most things she was generous by nature. The sacred integrity of her personality she guarded against every intrusion; but, when she was asked to give, she could keep nothing back."

Gordon proceeded to probe the development of a modern woman and how this affected her marriage. At one point, after a long discussion, Rhoda and her husband were overcome by emotion and, in the heat of their feelings, came together again. But as they talked on, they seemed to recede to their former hostile positions. "That they loved each other profoundly" Rhoda still believed

> it was in mind and character that they were drifting apart. A candid realization of the situation was perhaps all that was necessary, though such a realization was in itself suggestive of future difficulty. Then and there she gave up the all-or-nothing theory of marriage. She would go on on a natural basis. Certainly it was worth trying; . . . It meant that there was nothing static in their marriage; that it was something to fight for, to preserve.

At the end of the scene, Rhoda said to her husband, "I want you to know many women, O. F., in order that you can come to understand one a little better." Later Rhoda Lispenyard-Child broke up her marriage over her husband's insensitivity and floundered into a relationship with the Englishman. In the end she sought and obtained a suicide assignment on a foreign mission, dying abroad covering a story, which John Reed had just done in real life, leaving her problems unresolved, perhaps incapable of resolution at that point.

Gordon dedicated his book to "C.W.K.," not simply to "My wife" or "C. K." It was published by Boni and Liveright in 1923.

But Gordon wasn't satisfied with his writing. Some of the effects he had hoped to achieve in the book had not come off. The *New York Times* reviewer said, "It is a book of talk, level and truthful, but it misses the electrical spark that holds a reader's interest." The *Springfield Republican* gave the book high praise: "[a] fine piece of prose writing and an unusual study of character." Others praised King's "unusual promise," but Gordon King kept dwelling on his failures.

He got restless and depressed. He couldn't seem to get to work properly on his next book. He finally decided he needed a change of scene. A great many American writers were making the trek to Paris in this postwar era, searching for something in themselves they could not seem to find in this country. Gordon was not part of the Algonquin crowd that ended up in *The New Yorker* and Hollywood, although he was a confessed conversationalist who could easily talk instead of doing the writing he felt was his real meat. Gordon did not want to become an expatriate, but he discussed with Carol the possibility of going off to the provinces of France for a few months, alone. At Perpignan he would bury himself in study and writing, living frugally and without interruptions from his family and friends for a few months.

He hated his life and was trying to make it over, Carol wrote later. She accepted this jaunt, as she did the other vagaries arising from his needs as a writer, because he remained the love of her life.

Carol was intrigued by Gordon, and had been taught in her own family to accept and even relish individuality, and to be fair. If she wanted him to continue to accept her work habits, she would have to accept his. She should also admit that she was beginning to feel somewhat established in her career as a lawyer among lawyers, despite all the odds. Such acceptance had so far eluded her husband in the much lonelier field of writing.

During Gordon's absences, Carol spent more time than ever at the office. Even when he was at home, Carol had learned to keep her life with Gordon in a separate compartment. When she was hurt by something that happened between them, she put it into that compartment and then moved back into other parts of her life — or at least, that is how it seemed to her niece Peggy Stern, recalling these years. Now Carol found it easy to immerse herself in her work because several cases from the office were on their way to the Supreme Court, giving her a chance to participate in opening up new vistas in constitutional law.

5.
Grasping a Victory Out of Defeat

The issues the lawyers faced in 1923 were not the broad philosophical questions Gordon King liked to play with, but they were equally thorny. No matter how much time and thought Carol expended on them, she could not make much progress. The difficulty arose out of the very success of the Left defense/offense against Attorney General Palmer.

The immigration cases arising from the Palmer Raids had usually involved flagrant denials of due process and fairness. After 1921 the issues became more subtle because the Immigration Bureau had stopped its outrageous actions and "returned to normalcy." It again followed legally sanctioned procedures in handling deportation cases. Even Assistant Secretary of Labor Louis F. Post could not cancel a deportation order when it was valid under a statute at a time when the Supreme Court would not consider the constitutionality of such a statute, and Congress was in no mood to soften the deportation laws against aliens as unemployment was rising among citizens.

The lawyers in the Nelles office, therefore, took the traditional route leading to the nine Justices on the United States Supreme Court to reverse unfairness in individual cases. The Justices had affirmed the convictions of numerous citizen-opponents of the Great War, with Justices Holmes and Brandeis sometimes dissenting. Nonetheless, that war was long past. The lawyers in the Nelles office thought the Justices might overturn some deportation orders against alien opponents of the War. The Court had never ruled on the deportation arrests in the Palmer Raids, so there were no recent bad precedents to overturn. The lawyers hoped the Justices would agree to hear their cases and then decide in their favor. Justice Brandeis might take the lead, given his liberal approach to social questions.

Louis D. Brandeis was the first Jewish Justice on the United States Supreme Court, appointed despite the bitter opposition of the traditional leaders of the bar before the War. His wife was an immigrant and his friendships were international. He had voted against the repression of speech and press, against unreasonable searches and seizures by police officers, for the First and Fourth Amendments. He was not afraid of socialists, although he did not agree with them. If Justice Holmes would join him on civil liberties grounds, the lawyers hoped three other votes could be found somehow to make the winning five out of nine.

Nelles and the other lawyers agreed that their best chance of winning would be to show that their clients had not been treated fairly, that their right to due process of law had been violated by the government. Judges were more likely to agree on this point than to uphold a First Amendment right of aliens to have their own ideas and to express them publicly. Following this strategy, in late 1923 Carol helped Isaac Shorr and Walter Nelles prepare appeals in four key cases they had lost in the lower courts. Michael Bilokumsky, Catoni Tisi, Nicolai Mensevich, and Herbert Mahler had all lived in the United States a dozen years or more. They had opposed U.S. participation in the War and were serving sentences solely for possessing literature the government said advocated the violent overthrow of the U.S. government. They were not charged with any violent act or even with membership in a proscribed organization. They would be the first political deportation cases to come to the Supreme Court under the 1918 act.

In the *Bilokumsky* case, Nelles argued that the Immigration Bureau admitted it had violated its own rules by failing to warn Bilokumsky he was entitled to a lawyer and did not have to answer questions. Nelles emphasized that the only evidence that Bilokumsky was an alien had been obtained by unlawful search and seizure. In the *Mensevich* case, Nelles argued that his client could not be deported to Poland because the boundary line making him "Polish" had been changed after he left what was then Russia. In *Tisi,* Nelles argued that his client could not be deported for possessing leaflets written in English since he could not read English and could not have known their content. In *Mahler,* Nelles argued that his client could not be deported for an act committed before the law made that act deportable.

Nelles lost all four cases, with Justice Brandeis writing three of the opinions upholding deportation. Brandeis held, for the Court, that deportation is not punishment. Therefore, the alien Bilokumsky could not refuse to admit that he was an alien on the ground of possible self-incrimination; silence can be proof. Brandeis held, for the Court, that the Russian Mensevich could be deported to Poland. Brandeis held, for the Court, that Tisi could be deported for possessing leaflets he could not read. The Immigration Bureau itself later recognized the lack of evidence against Tisi and canceled the warrant of deportation against him. But Brandeis set the illiberal precedents in cases never mentioned by his biographers.

In the *Mahler* case, Chief Justice Taft, the conservative, wrote the opinion. He ruled that the prohibition against ex post facto laws did not apply to deportation, so Mahler and his four co-appellants could be deported for an act he had committed before the law was passed, making it a deportable offense. But Taft gave Nelles a technical victory. The government had made an error in the proceedings, so the Supreme Court reversed the judgment of the district court, with the direction that the petitioners should not be released until the Secretary of Labor had had time to correct this error.

The lawyers found this another infuriating decision. When a person is charged with committing a crime, the prosecutor has one chance to try to convict; if he fails to try the case properly, he gets no second chance. Certainly the Immigration Bureau should not have a second chance to prove a deportation case against an alien who had done nothing criminal in the first place!

Since they couldn't stop deportations in the federal courts on habeas corpus petitions, Carol and Isaac looked for another avenue of redress. They decided to appeal to the chief executive. They asked Republican President Calvin Coolidge to grant a "full and unconditional pardon" to their client Joseph Oates, one of the five appellants in the *Mahler* case. A presidential pardon would make it possible to petition the secretary of labor to hold that Oates was not an "undesirable alien" and therefore could not be deported. In January 1925 the President granted the unconditional pardon on a finding by Attorney General Harlan Stone that Oates had "conducted himself as a law-abiding citizen" since his release from prison in May 1922.

The Immigration Bureau had a different agenda, arresting Oates for deportation despite the pardon. The lawyers immediately filed a habeas petition protesting the arrest as unlawful, and the district court agreed. But the circuit court held that a person could be pardoned only for *criminal* offenses; the president had no power to pardon anyone to prevent the *civil* penalty of deportation. The Immigration Bureau *had* made an error — it had not issued a finding that the men were "undesirable aliens." But the court gave the bureau time to correct this failure. Judge Learned Hand dissented from this decision in *Brazier v. Commissioner.*

After this series of defeats, the older lawyers in the Nelles office saw little hope of winning any deportation cases in the Supreme Court. The precedents set in their cases were all bad. The newest lawyer began to build her practice in immigration law at the administrative level.

The other lawyers turned to a criminal case that was to become a major U.S. Supreme Court decision. It arose out of the Palmer Raid hysteria in 1919–1920 when a New York grand jury indicted John Reed, Jim Larkin, Ben Gitlow, and three other American and Irish radicals for criminal anarchism.

When charges of "criminal anarchy" or "criminal syndicalism" were made, Brodsky, Nelles, Shorr, and King knew that logic was useless, whether they were talking to laymen on juries or to most judges. The phrases had become code words to attack the current form of witchcraft, that is, "advocating basic social change." Like "obscenity" and "disloyalty," "criminal syndicalism" could be detected by any true patriot even when it was occurring one hundred yards away on a picket line. Criminal syndicalism meant opposing United States entry into the recent war, trying to organize unions, and calling work stoppages. It meant demanding free speech and then using it to attack child labor and lynchings, or to support birth control or the Bolshevik overthrow of the Russian czar.

The new defendants had published and distributed a *Manifesto* of the Left Wing of the Socialist Party, written in the glow of the first successful Bolshevik revolution against the czar. *The Manifesto* proclaimed: "The old order is in decay. Civilization is in collapse. The proletarian revolution and the communist reconstruction of society — *the struggle for them* — is now indispensable."

Reed was in Moscow living the "ten days that shook the world" and was never arrested, but the New York court conducted four jury trials of Gitlow, Larkin, Charles Ruthenberg, and the others. Sol Cohn recalled Joe Brodsky's description of the trials. For the first trial the defense retained "the great mouthpiece," Bill Fallon, considered the best trial lawyer in New York. He put on a remarkable defense, but he could not convince the jury to acquit. So for the second trial the defense decided they had better retain Clarence Darrow, considered the best trial lawyer in the country. He presented a remarkable closing argument, but he could not convince the jury to acquit. In this situation, for the third trial the defense turned to Joe Brodsky. If they couldn't win with Fallon or Darrow, they'd give Brodsky a chance. He had built quite a reputation by this time. Everyone said he put on a magnificent performance, but he could not convince the jury to acquit. Finally, for the fourth trial the defense told the lawyer/defendant Isaac Ferguson to represent himself. He was a careful, competent lawyer, but he could not convince the jury to acquit. Brodsky let out a booming laugh as he concluded that each of the cases had to be appealed.

To handle the first appeal, Gitlow turned to Brodsky, his comrade and attorney for the Communist Party. Brodsky naturally turned to the other lawyers in his office. Nelles had been corresponding with Judge Learned Hand on his First Amendment decision in *The Masses* case, which had stated a stronger rule than Holmes had stated in *Abrams*. But Hand would not hear the *Gitlow* appeal. Walter, Joe, and Carol concluded they needed "leaders of the bar" to make their First Amendment argument upstairs. Swinburne Hale and Walter Nelles would work with Murray C. Bernays, a well-known New York trial lawyer, on the appellate brief. Charles Recht, a leader of the New York appellate bar, made the oral argument.

The Appellate Division was not impressed with this array of talent and affirmed the first conviction.

On their second appeal, to the New York Court of Appeals, the lawyers lost again, but at least they got two dissenting votes from Judges Cuthbert Pound and Benjamin Cardozo. Pound explained what had always seemed obvious to the defense: that "anarchy" and "communism" are different. The 1902 statute was aimed at assassins who were anarchists and rejected all government, Gitlow was not an assassin or an anarchist; therefore, his conviction for anarchy must be reversed.

The lawyers all wanted to save Communist Gitlow from prison: Isaac Shorr, pacifist/philosophical anarchist "office" lawyer; Carol King, behind-the-scenes civil liberties lawyer; Walter Nelles, constitutional scholar; and Joe Brodsky, Communist trial lawyer. They also wanted to get a ruling that the criminal *anarchy* law was unconstitutional, which should then lead to a decision that the criminal *syndicalism* laws were also unconstitutional.

Carol suggested they call in an outside appellate lawyer, Walter H. Pollak, to take the case to the U.S. Supreme Court. This "minor" contribution — on personnel rather than issues — proved to be significant.

Pollak had become a partner of her brother-in-law, Carl Stern, and came from the encyclopedic eastern European Jewish tradition. Pollak's grandfather had fled the 1848–1849 Hungarian revolution; his immigrant father had been an editor of *The Nation*. Pollak was the sort of lawyer Carol liked, a witty conversationalist, and he had a strong and charming wife, Marion, who had become a close personal friend of Carol's. Walter, who had graduated cum laude from Harvard Law School, left Sullivan & Cromwell because it was becoming too large (with twenty lawyers). In 1912 he moved to Simpson, Warren & Cardozo, where Benjamin Cardozo implanted in Pollak habits of meticulous and imaginative lawyering. Pollak began a friendship with Cardozo that endured when Cardozo became a judge in 1913 and the heir apparent to Justice Holmes.

As Walter Pollak moved into the *Gitlow* case, Carol moved back into her own world of immigration law. In 1924 Congress passed an immigration act raising terrible new problems for aliens. The clear purpose of the 1924 act seemed to be to destroy the families of aliens who had come to the United States before 1914, leaving their wives and children in eastern Europe until they found steady jobs and could save enough to pay their families' passage. The War had smashed all their plans, enforcing long separations. After the Armistice, the men in this country immediately tried to bring their families over. They were told it would be much more difficult to be reunited in this country under the new quota and literacy laws passed by Congress in the xenophobic year of 1921. For the first time, Congress had limited immigration in any year to three percent of the nationals of each country resident in the United States in 1910, and three percent of eastern European immigrants was a low number.

Congress passed the 1924 act at the tail end of the anti-alien hysteria of the Palmer Raids, reflecting the worried 1920s and the rightward move in the 1924 election. Calvin Coolidge won the presidency over the undistinguished Democrat. Robert M. La Follette, running as a Progressive Party independent, received the biggest-ever third party vote — almost five million. In 1924 Congress further restricted immigration from eastern and southern Europe, cutting the annual quotas from three to *two* percent of the nationals of a country resident here in *1890* and virtually ending immigration from Asia. Having enticed workers from other countries to fill our mines and factories, Congress was fighting now to make the United States a country of western and northern Europeans.

The 1924 act also placed on the noncitizen in any deportation proceeding the burden of proving the time, place, and manner of entry into the United States. This statute wiped out the ruling of Louis Post in 1920 and turned the *Bilokumsky* decision by the Supreme Court into a statute. Congress shifted the responsibility of screening would-be immigrants abroad from the shipping companies to the State Department, while leaving enforcement of the exclusion laws at the border to the Labor Department. All of these changes meant more work for immigration lawyers and less chance of winning their cases.

At this point, Attorney General Harlan F. Stone took a step in the opposite direction. He found that the staff of the Federal Bureau of Investigation had swollen under William J. Burns. He reduced the staff and abolished the General Intelligence Division headed by J. Edgar Hoover from 1919 to 1924, although he retained Hoover.

༄

While Carol was figuring out her next move in immigration law, the two Walters, Isaac, and Joe had devised a novel issue to raise in the *Gitlow* case in the Supreme Court, which Walter Pollak worked out in his brief. It was based on a deep appreciation of U.S. history and the recognition that the Civil War and the Thirteenth, Fourteenth, and Fifteenth Amendments had done more than abolish the system of chattel slavery, more than require equal protection for exslaves and all people of color.

The lawyers maintained that the Fourteenth Amendment guarantee that *no state* shall "deprive any person of life, liberty, or property without due process of law" was a guarantee by the *federal government*. In other words, they argued that the *federal* government must now protect people from violations of their political rights *by the states,* as the First Amendment had always protected people from violations by the *federal* government. In shorthand, they were saying that "states' rights" to limit the political liberty of their residents had also been buried at Appomattox. The new Fourteenth Amendment "incorporated the First Amendment" and made it applicable to the states. In 1924 the lawyers sent this new concept to the Supreme Court.

At the same time, Walter Nelles convinced Carol King to help him put out the ACLU *Law and Freedom Bulletin.* This was the first continuing effort to collect state and federal cases in the United States raising issues of constitutional law. Socialist Party lawyers had collected anti-war cases during the recent War and published a small manual on how to handle them, but there was no follow-up. Now Nelles was determined to record the "little" cases won or lost at trial that are never reported in traditional law books, which only report written opinions by appellate courts (and federal district courts). Nelles maintained that the few victories for civil liberties and labor were most likely to come out of trial court juries and judges, and that trial lawyers needed to know how these victories were achieved so they could follow the same approach. He would also comment on the Supreme Court opinions that set precedents. This collection would make it possible to count cases and to analyze how constitutional rights were being protected *in practice* at the local level. To this end, Carol reported that three California decisions and one from Idaho somewhat limited prosecutions for criminal syndicalism in those jurisdictions.

Having taken on a long-range commitment to her first publication, she discovered that she was about to take on another long-range commitment — to her first baby. She was in robust health and could share the morning sickness and awkwardness of pregnancy with some of the secretaries at the office, if not with the other lawyers.

She had the energy to work on a second publication, an ACLU pamphlet called *State Laws Against Free Speech*. In it Carol was happy to report that appellate courts in New Mexico, Montana, and New Jersey had declared restrictive laws unconstitutional and only ninety-five political prisoners were currently serving sentences under such laws, including eighty-eight in California who were all members of the IWW. King and Nelles soon delighted in Chief Justice Taft's opinion in the *Hammerschmidt* case, reversing the convictions of thirteen Cincinnati Socialists who had opposed the draft in the recent War. The Court held that the government had overreached itself by charging them with "conspiracy to defraud the United States" during the War. All these individuals had done was to distribute anti-conscription literature — and this was done before Congress had passed a statute on the subject. The lawyers hoped this decision was an omen for the *Gitlow* decision.

Finally, in June 1925, the Supreme Court handed down its decision in *Gitlow v. New York*. Six Justices voted to affirm Gitlow's conviction, including Chief Justice Taft. The majority explicitly upheld the constitutionality of the state criminal anarchy statute against all the weaknesses listed by the defense. The statute was not "an arbitrary or unreasonable exercise of the police power of the state, unwarrantably infringing the freedom of speech or press." The statute did cover the Communist Gitlow, who was no anarchist (rejecting the dissent of Pound and Cardozo below). The statute could be used against "every utterance — not too trivial to be beneath the notice of the law."

But wait. The majority *did* take up the novel point raised by Walter Pollak. They explicitly held:

> For present purposes we may and do assume that freedom of speech and of the press — which are protected by the First Amendment from abridgment by Congress — are among the fundamental personal rights and 'liberties' protected by the due process clause of the Fourteenth Amendment from impairment by the States.

So the lawyers had won — if not for their client, at least on their principle. Hereafter, anyone arrested by a local cop or high sheriff and tried in a state court could claim rights under the First Amendment. For the first time, the United States Constitution and Bill of Rights would govern the behavior of *state and local* police officers.

Nelles wrote later that "if the sweep of the Fourteenth Amendment is to be broad, logic requires that it be broad consistently." The propertied interests could not forever have the Supreme Court uphold the rights of corporations under the Fourteenth Amendment against attacks by the states without eventually having to uphold the rights of speakers and activists under the Fourteenth Amendment against attacks by the states.

And there was more to *Gitlow*. Justice Holmes, joined by Justice Brandeis, had filed a dissenting opinion written in the magnificent language he had begun to use in *Abrams:*

> It is said that this *Manifesto* was more than a theory, that it was an incitement.
>
> Every idea is an incitement. It offers itself for belief, and if believed it is acted on unless some other belief outweighs it or some failure of energy stifles the movement at its birth. The only difference between the expression of an opinion and an incitement in the narrower sense is the speaker's enthusiasm for the result. Eloquence may set fire to reason. But whatever may be thought of the redundant discourse before us it had no chance of starting a present conflagration.
>
> If in the long run the beliefs expressed in proletarian dictatorship are destined to be accepted by the dominant forces of the community, the only meaning of free speech is that they shall be given their chance and have their way.

In the next *Law and Freedom Bulletin,* Carol admitted defeat on the unconstitutionality of state criminal anarchy and syndicalism statutes, but concluded:

> Although the court held that the due process clause did not protect Gitlow's publication of the *Left Wing Manifesto,* the court sustained the contention, never successfully argued before, that the due process clause of the 14th Amendment limits the right of a state to abridge free speech.

Most local judges were still hard of hearing when defense counsel talked about the First Amendment rights of their clients, so appellate lawyers knew they would be citing *Gitlow* in every appeal to the United States Supreme Court for years to come.

By late 1925 Hale, Nelles, Shorr, Brodsky, and King were able to relax a little. In addition to Sol Cohn, they had another young law clerk, Vito Marcantonio, to help on the work and to translate for any Italian clients who k .ew no English. They were a close-knit, efficient, experienced team of lawyers specializing in immigration, labor, criminal, and constitutional law, with plenty of clients and enough income to survive.

Suddenly Swinburne Hale was killed in an accident, and the surviving lawyers' sense of security died with him.

Walter Nelles was able to analyze the situation dispassionately after the clients had gone home with their bread-and-butter problems. He enjoyed doing research on broad legal questions, but in the current climate in the Supreme Court, he could not write winning briefs. Having turned over to Carol the *Law and Freedom Bulletin,* he decided to stop practicing law and accept the chance to teach and do research at Yale Law School.

Isaac Shorr never considered leaving his practice. This plodder, who was never without his pipe or his clients' problems, was a Tolstoyan believer in the dignity of each individual with a vast love for humankind. He wanted to make new office arrangements that would permit him to continue what he was doing with as little disruption as possible.

Joe Brodsky would go on with his legal work, of course, in labor and criminal cases, and with his political work in the Communist Party. He had joined the new International Labor Defense when it was founded in the summer of 1925 in Chicago to strengthen the work in political cases, starting with a campaign to save the lives of Sacco and Vanzetti from the Massachusetts hangman. Brodsky could work best out of a New York law office staffed by bright, dedicated lawyers and secretaries handling cases in the trial courts before juries, and in the court of public opinion whenever possible.

Carol Weiss King also intended to go on practicing law. She and Gordon, with the help of Mrs. Barkley, would manage things when the baby arrived in a few months. Since she did not have a job and was no one's law partner, she could have closed down her cases relatively easily and taken off for a few months, or years, to stay home with the baby. She and Gordon could afford it, thanks to her family inheritance. But she had just built her practice, and she wanted to get back to work full time very soon after she returned from the hospital. She figured she could do this with the help of Mrs. B. and Gordon at home. The fact that women "did not do" what she was contemplating did not deter her.

In a sense, the Kings' arrangements had always been unconventional without calling attention to that fact. At the office Carol acted just like a man — she played her full role for forty hours a week and put in all the overtime necessary in a crisis without letting on that she was also responsible for running her household at home. Any time she spent talking to Mrs. B. on the phone to plan dinner and marketing she more than made up for by her efficiency and speed in doing research and by her willingness to come back to the office at night to finish a job. At home on nights and weekends, she appeared to be a relaxed hostess with leisure time to see to the arrangement of bouquets of flowers and other nice touches. Carol relied on her good health and great energy to see her through her pregnancy, the birth of the baby, and her new maternal tasks. To make things more comfortable after the baby arrived, she and Gordon had just enlarged their quarters, turning the low attic space above their apartment into a spacious studio room with French windows opening onto a small outdoor roof terrace.

Isaac, Joe, and Carol decided to keep the office open. It was the logical thing to do. The fact that there were few, if any, other partnerships across the gender line was not a cause for comment or publicity; Carol was totally accepted as "one of the lawyers." They had clients to represent and a tradition to maintain. Since 1920 Hale, Nelles & Shorr and Brodsky and King had handled literally hundreds of deportation cases. They had won some victories in representing unions and individual workers. They had helped put a stop to the raids and mass arrests of 1919 and 1920.

The fervor with which they had contested each case had forced the Immigration Bureau to reconsider its worst decisions and caused judges to issue occasional writs. But the courts had repeatedly upheld deportation orders based on procedures that would not satisfy a criminal court. The lawyers had made no progress on this issue.

They had helped expand the protection of the First Amendment against violations by state officials in the *Gitlow* case, although for Ben Gitlow himself the decision had been a disaster. The client who had walked into the case as a revolutionary walked out of prison an embittered man after serving three years of his ten-year term. In this time of peace and prosperity, Governor Al Smith pardoned Gitlow and other defendants soon after the opinion in *Gitlow* and stopped further prosecutions because "political progress results from the clash of conflicting opinions. The public assertion of an erroneous doctrine is perhaps the surest way to disclose the error and make it evident to the electorate."

Carol King looked forward to practicing law in this new climate. She would be expected to play a major role in the new, smaller law firm of Shorr, Brodsky & King. She couldn't know exactly what would happen when her baby was born, but she was ready to take up the challenge.

6.
Shorr, Brodsky & King — and Jonathan

Carol King spent the early hours of New Year's Eve 1925 contemplating the imminent birth of Shorr, Brodsky & King out of Hale, Nelles & Shorr, and Brodsky, and King. As the evening wore on, her enjoyment was interrupted by intermittent messages that finally could not be ignored. At a certain point, she and Gordon agreed they had better head for the hospital with the bag Mrs. Barkley had packed for the occasion.

Two hours before midnight, Carol gave birth to a boy. They had already decided on the name Jonathan. Carol told her friend Solon DeLeon that the first glimpse of her son was "the most beautiful sight I've ever seen."

But when the baby cried for food or needed to be changed, she found she had no natural knack for the work. She had spent little time around babies and loved the feeling of motherhood long before she felt she knew what she was doing. She decided not to have Mrs. Barkley bottle-feed her baby or to hire a wet-nurse, but to do what everybody else was doing, more or less. Since she liked to walk, she would nurse the baby at breakfast, walk to the office, work three hours, walk home to nurse the baby and eat the lunch Mrs. Barkley had prepared, walk back to the office, work another three hours, and walk home in time for the next feeding and her own dinner.

This schedule apparently made her feel she was being as good a mother as her friends were (who occasionally left their offspring with relatives or nursemaids while they shopped or visited art galleries), and as good a lawyer as her partners were (who occasionally took extended lunch hours with their clients). She evidently decided that the main thing was to behave as if nothing unusual was going on, which meant being prepared for a client and a baby as circumstances required. Fortunately, she had the ability to keep several pots boiling at the same time, shifting her attention quickly to the one pot most in danger of burning or boiling over.

She must have discovered very soon that her son was not an automaton, and neither were her clients. One or the other must have needed her a little earlier or later than usual. Frequently pulled in two directions, Carol relied heavily on the people at the office and on Mrs. Barkley at home. Everyone at the office had been her friend for years, as well as her partner or secretary, and they all filled in for her as needed. The office had never been simply a 9:00 to 5:00 operation because too many clients got arrested at night or on weekends. Now Joe and Isaac simply extended themselves, knowing Carol had done the same for them. Sol Cohn and Fay Seagartle were always helpful. So were the other secretaries, many of whom were the daughters of clients or union leaders. As a result, Carol never left the office fearing she had abandoned a client in need.

Mrs. B. had helped rear Carol a generation earlier, and she was soon helping rear Jonathan. Gordon pitched in enthusiastically with this new and wonderful addition to their family life. As if by magic, Carol never came home to a living room strewn with yesterday's newspapers, a sink full of dirty dishes, a bathroom smelling of unwashed diapers, and a screaming baby. Mrs. Barkley managed her end so efficiently that the baby was neat and clean and dinner was partially prepared when Mrs. King shifted from lawyer to housewife and mother. In constant touch by phone, Carol knew what food was in the pantry, what leftovers were in the icebox, and whom Gordon had asked over for dinner.

Shorr, Brodsky & King handled cases for three discernible kinds of political clients: anarchists and members of the League for the Rights of Man who came to see Shorr; Communists who came to see Brodsky; and ACLU members and writer friends who came to see King. Of course, the bulk of their clients were like the clients of other lawyers — basically nonpolitical but sometimes drawn into politics by a strike or a cause. The firm also handled many commercial cases in which Carol participated with as much interest as in the civil liberties cases.

Joe Brodsky was the kind of lawyer other lawyers listened to when he argued a motion in court. Usually lawyers sit waiting for their own cases to be called, riffling through their papers and jotting down notes about what to say on an important point. But when Joe Brodsky got up to argue, the lawyers put down their briefs to listen. He was a street lawyer with a booming voice. His tool was persuasion, making socialist speeches on soapboxes on New York's East Side in the 1910s. Whenever he came back from a trip to Albany, New York, or some other foreign country, he brought back a story that added to the legend of Shorr, Brodsky & King.

One day Brodsky came back from Albany with the perfect story. While arguing a criminal case before the local judge, he had tried to explain, "Your honor, my client has chutzpah."

The judge: "I don't know what you mean. Define the word."

Reaching back into his own Jewish heritage, while acutely aware of the judge's small-town Gentile roots, Brodsky said, "Your Honor, when a man kills his mother and father and seeks leniency from the court because he is an orphan, that's chutzpah!"

Joseph R. Brodsky was proving to be long on chutzpah himself. An early Left Socialist and a charter member of the Communist Party, he welcomed the organization of the International Labor Defense in 1925, and thereafter made himself available when ILD members needed legal advice or representation. This meant that he called in his partners to help in ILD cases as well.

Isaac Shorr's quiet manner and indefatigable spirit also provided support for Carol's professional work. Isaac never regarded the law as a code rigidly bound by precedent. Instead, he approached each case in terms of certain human equities that seemed to him clear and irrefutable. Equity was not determined by what courts had decided in previous cases, he taught Sol Cohn, who had graduated from law clerk to lawyer; law was determined by the facts in the individual case. If the courts had not yet recognized the equities present in his client's case, this only meant that the courts were wrong and needed to stretch the law a little.

Brodsky was also deeply interested in political questions, Shorr less so, and Carol not much. She respected the importance of questions of political theory and wanted them properly handled, but she did not agree with her Communist friends that you should "hammer out the Party line" in endless discussions at Party meetings. Or at least, she did not choose to spend her precious free time in this way. She wrote later, in reviewing a biography of Debs, that she was convinced that people draw different conclusions from the same facts because of their pre-existing experiences and prejudices. This view led her to practice politics by ear, reserving her note-reading for the law.

(c)

On May 12-15, 1927 the Police of the City of London
conducted a raid upon the joint headquarters of the Russian Trade
Delegation and Arcos located at 49 Moorgate, London.
was employed by the Russian Trade Delegation in London
and on his person were found certain documents by London Police.
One item in the documents found   possession
bore the inscription:

> "For money, per Bank: (No. 8) Joseph R. Brodsky
>   799 Broadway,
>   New York. "

Also found   possession was a notation:

> "Joseph R. Brodsky,
> Room 703 41 Union Square,
> New-York."

Another document found   possession bore the following:

> "Adresse fur Geldsendungen: ——
> 1. Joseph Brodsky room 703 41 Union Square New-York
> /fur die Partei und andere Organisationen/"

FBI File: Joseph Brodsky (1927). One of the early entries in the FBI file on
attorney Joseph Brodsky. Facsimile reproduction of photocopy supplied on
FOIA request.

She was devoted to the clients who came to her office with specific
problems. They did not want to discuss the state of the world — at least,
not with her. After she got their brothers or friends out of jail, they would
love to go to a meeting and expound on the best way to rebuild society
so there would be fewer jails — and perhaps fewer lawyers. Or they would
discuss with Joe how to organize a union or a Communist Party club, and
how to pass out leaflets without getting themselves arrested or having
their timid fellow workers fall into the clutches of the law.

Isaac would get a case involving a will or a small piece of property
and sit down with Carol to discuss how to handle the legal issues.

Then Joe would rush in. 'We just got ruled off the ballot in Podunk
County!' he would report. 'What should I do?'

After listening briefly to the facts in both cases, Carol would spurt
into action. She liked thinking fast, and she would go to the office library

and find a case or two to support her proposed line of action and be ready to make the first move on each case within fifteen minutes. Sol Cohn said he had never seen anybody like her — she was like a fire horse whenever she got a new problem. Other times, she would go to the bar association library and stay there night and day until she found every case on a subject. Gordon didn't seem to mind. Mrs. Barkley was handy, and after Jonathan started sleeping through the night, Carol again had energy to burn.

The three partners shared office expenses and reputation and staff, working together frequently on cases. But they did not put all their fees into the pot and divide it three ways. They remained three quite distinct individuals taking advantage of the position of lawyers in society and taking their differences for granted. They kept their office small and geared it to the individual clients, habits, and foibles of each partner, which could be respected or ignored in return for acceptance of the other's ways. They worried about each other's slow months and rejoiced when any of the partners got a good settlement or a high fee. But they never gave up their individualism in favor of central planning.

The three lawyers followed the custom in law offices of acting as witnesses on wills and other legal documents drawn by one of the other two. Such documents needed the signature of someone likely to be available if required later to authenticate the document. This custom led to an early item in the Immigration Bureau's file on Carol, which was repeated in her FBI file: she subscribed to the certificate of incorporation Joe drew up for the *Daily Worker*, which the FBI termed "Central Organ, Communist Party of U.S.A."

The lawyers assigned to Fay Seagartle the tasks of billing clients and getting the lease signed on time, giving her neither the title nor the pay commensurate with running the office. She did not complain because "good legal secretaries" traditionally carried out these responsibilities, and she knew her own worth and the significance of the cases the office was handling.

Early in 1926 Shorr, Brodsky & King were trying to get the U.S. Supreme Court to rule on several of their cases. By June the Court had ruled against them on all but one, which it refused to review. Carol left for a holiday in England with Gordon and Jonathan. She returned in time to help Shorr prepare the briefs for Emanuel Vajtauer, the editor of a Bohemian newspaper. First the postal authorities had revoked his mailing permit because of his opposition to the war. Then he was arrested for deportation. The lawyers asked Walter Pollak to argue his appeal. Having just won the *Gitlow* case, Pollak had decided to take the time from his own office to argue the appeals Shorr, Brodsky & King offered him. They had broader constitutional implications than the run-of-the-mill commercial cases he handled. And he couldn't help noticing that their Gitlow case was becoming one of the most cited cases of the era.

But they lost *Vajtauer v. Commissioner* in an opinion by the new Justice Stone, who had recently clipped J. Edgar Hoover's wings while serving as Attorney General. The new Justice ruled that, in a deportation case, "a want of due process is not established by showing merely that the decision is erroneous . . . or that incompetent evidence was received and considered." *Some* evidence against the immigrant in a habeas corpus case will justify deportation. And once an alien is sworn, he can be compelled to testify, even if it requires him to incriminate himself.

With no room to maneuver and no way to win, Carol, like her partners, had to find outlets for her frustrations at the snail's pace of the law to face injustice.

One of her pleasures was getting out the *Law and Freedom Bulletin*. It was also work, month after month, and that was a problem when she was already busy as wife, mother, and working lawyer. But at least the preparation of the *Bulletin* had a beginning, a middle, and an end, unlike a case that might drag on for years, or might end suddenly when the client gave up and left the country, or died. Few of her cases resulted in written opinions — and most of those were defeats. So she had little tangible reward for her efforts. But her work on the *Bulletin* ended up on a piece of paper that might endure, especially as libraries started to subscribe to the publication.

Besides, the *Bulletin* permitted the kind of analysis of cases and statutes she enjoyed, providing a medium through the editorial "we" for letting off steam (politely and legally) against outrageous actions by judges. It put her in touch with lawyers all over the country, which built a feeling of strength or at least of having colleagues to turn to in case of need. And occasionally it was clear that an article in the *Bulletin* gave someone an idea whose time had come, leading to victory in a case that otherwise would have been lost.

When she came home from work, Carol had Gordon to talk to about nonlegal affairs, especially the questions asked by their growing offspring, who was full of wonder about the world around him. Jonathan was now two and talking, which made him another person entirely to his conversational parents. When he woke up at night, terrified, his mother could explain that he had only heard a train whistle, and Jonathan could understand.

Gordon was still searching for his niche as a writer, still seeking critical acclaim. He began looking for books to read to Jonathan but was disappointed in his quest. He took his job as parent seriously. In his 1923 novel one of his characters discusses a father's chance to undertake his son's education as one of the most important tasks in life: "I had felt — it was my secret vanity — that no school was good enough for him, and I therefore spent a very large part of my time trying to be a model schoolmaster." Now Gordon began to write books for juveniles, editing Herodotus for children and writing a children's history of Rome. He was trying to develop a new approach to children's literature. Talking to Jonathan and to his nieces and nephews, he assumed a child was capable of understanding a complex situation if the writer presented it clearly enough.

After Jonathan went to bed, Arto Funduklian often stopped in, as did other tenants Carol and Gordon had selected for congeniality and intellectual stimulation as much as for ability to pay the rent. Funduklian was a favorite, a studious and retiring Armenian who had used his education at Oxford to become literary critic for the *Manchester Guardian*. On emigrating to the United States, this well-read and extremely sensitive man became advertising manager for a carpet firm. He enjoyed his apartment on Twenty-second Street and the opportunities it provided for long talks on all kinds of matters with Gordon King.

Carol was usually too busy for socializing, and that condition intensified when she agreed to write a law review article with the new Yale law professor Walter Nelles. Of course there was no money in it, but as Walter described the project, it looked like fun and a chance to work on one of those germinal law review articles that would be cited for the rest of their lives. It was to be the definitive discussion of freedom of the press and the problem of judges who charge people with contempt for attacking them in print. It would discuss every case decided by state and federal courts on the subject, even though, Nelles wrote, "Messrs. Frankfurter and Landis" felt that state cases "contribute only to confusion" and are far from harmonious. Nelles believed, rather, that to "resort to the whole mass of legislation and decision on the subject throughout the United States, far from proving 'treacherous,' may pave the way for a solution which may deserve to be called 'scientific.' "

Walter would write the main text if Carol would just find all the state and federal cases and statutes and do the footnotes. His thesis was that judges in the twentieth century were violating a clear 1831 statute limiting contempt power by judges.

So Carol began her search for all the "little" cases to illustrate the point, somewhat as Louis Brandeis had collected all the little bits of data from many fields in pioneering "Brandeis briefs" in the new era of applying the scientific method to the natural, and now the political, sciences. Walter began his writing by contrasting the ideal of the law as "some ultimate basis, beyond reach of the individual human will, that stands fast in the whirl of change of which life is made up" with the true picture: "a pastoral" in which "docile human sheep lick the hands of omnipotent shepherds." He rejected Dean Roscoe Pound's theory of law "as a process of reconciling the conflicting claims and demands of civilized society." Nelles said the theory did not hold in contempt of court cases; they deal with "power — personal power for men who happen to be judges — power to maintain at any social cost the prestige of the class or clan."

Carol applauded these views (and, according to the custom of the time, made no complaint against the use of "men" to include women, since in fact, there were then few women indeed "who happen[ed] to be judges"). Her appendix was a work of art — nine pages of small type in three columns summarizing the character of publications held punishable as contempt in forty-eight states, together with a short statement of the "theory of power" in each case.

Walter concluded that "it may well be doubted whether any consistently able and impartial court has ever imposed a summary punishment for aspersion of itself" and said simply, "Bad courts should not be respected. Good courts, even, should not be respected in their aberrations. Public discussion outside of court rooms, at such time as it is most likely to command attention, is the nearest we have to a practical means of working for consistent judicial respectability." The article was published in two issues of the *Columbia Law Review,* April and May 1928, covering sixty-seven printed pages including 271 footnotes, without mentioning that one author was a woman, the only one in that or many other volumes of the *Columbia Law Review.* The article was widely read at the time and frequently quoted. Wherever Carol King went thereafter, she met lawyers and judges who had read it, and many who had used it in contempt cases.

After finishing work on the article, Carol had time to really enjoy young Jonathan. She and Gordon could teach him a small lesson in some esoteric subject like where his shadow came from, or butterflies, or the sun.

At the office she continued to think more about the clients' problems and their broader implications than about the fees they paid her. But she was learning the economics of law practice and always welcomed a client who needed to have a will drafted or an estate administered because the fees were easy to set and collect. She was both gregarious and iconoclastic. Somehow this combination made her good at getting business.

Her brother Louis had turned out to be great at getting business and was slowly carrying out his plan to build a major New York law firm. At the same time, multiple sclerosis was slowing down their older brother, Billy. The Weiss/Wharton firm joined the Weiss family firm to become Cohen, Cole, Weiss & Wharton, and Louis continued to bring in clients through his charm and craftsmanship, clients who could afford to pay the fees appropriate to a Wall Street firm handling commercial and domestic relations cases.

Carol was moving in almost the opposite direction financially. Although she had plenty of clients, she still needed small payments from the Weiss inheritance Louis continued to administer. She and Gordon lived on these payments, rentals from the other apartments in their building, the small return from her practice, and small royalties from Gordon's writings. With their housing assured, money was not overly important to either of the Kings, although Howard King noted that his brother Gordon seemed depressed by his lack of any conspicuous monetary success. Howard thought this situation caused Gordon to imagine that other people thought of him as one who never had to earn a living.

In fact, Gordon became rather cool toward his brothers and sister at this time because he thought they did not approve of him. He was engrossed in his writing, his endless curiosity regarding people and ideas, and his role as a father, as his wife returned to work before a jury.

7.
Watching Darrow Work a Jury

In 1927 Isaac Shorr asked Carol King to help him defend murder charges against three Italian-American anti-fascists in New York. She agreed to work on these cases immediately, knowing that political disputes overseas nestled in the luggage of many immigrants to this country.

When Benito Mussolini came to power in the 1920s, fights broke out in Italy and in Little Italys all over the United States. Calling himself a socialist and appealing to Italian nationalism, Mussolini became a fascist dictator in the deep economic depression after World War I. By 1927 he was sporting a black shirt and harsh military bearing, creating an image of a man who made his nation's trains run on time. These cases led Carol to work with Clarence Darrow, a man of quite different style and dress.

The basic facts in the first case were reported in the press. About 8:00 A.M. on Memorial Day 1927, a group of black-shirted Fascisti gathered at a station on the elevated commuter line in the Bronx en route to Manhattan to march in the Memorial Day parade, ignoring numerous warnings in Italian-American radical journals. Suddenly two men wearing flaming red neckties emerged from the door of a restaurant. One of them ran to Joseph Carisi and stabbed him six times in the neck. The second ran toward Nicholas Amorroso, whom he stabbed once and then shot through the heart. Carisi and Amorroso died. Both assailants escaped.

The Italian fascist community in New York claimed the two as Fascist martyrs, conducting their funeral with full military honors. Black-shirted fascists stood guard over the double bier, and the Italian ambassador came from Washington for the occasion before the bodies were shipped to Naples. Mussolini and the Italian Chamber of Deputies stood in silence while a deputy exhorted all fascists to avenge the murders by actively promoting fascist ideals.

On July 12, the New York police went to the homes of Donato Carillo and Calogero Greco, arrested the men, searched their homes, then rushed on to the offices of the daily newspaper *Il Nuovo Mondo* and arrested five men, including a brother of Carlo Tresca, internationally known labor radical and anti-fascist leader. The police said they were convinced that the newspaper warnings were causally related to the murders. They held Greco, Carillo, and three others as material witnesses to the murders under bond of $50,000 each.

Carlo Tresca, casting about for a lawyer, recalled Isaac Shorr's militant representation of Elia and the widow of Salsedo during the Palmer Raids of 1920. He probably heard about Carol King from his close friend and comrade, Elizabeth Gurley Flynn, who knew Carol from their work in the ACLU. Tresca retained Shorr and King to handle the new cases.

The lawyers promptly began efforts to secure the release of the prisoners, arguing that they were workers and family men who would not flee to avoid trial. Carillo lived with his wife and two young children, Greco with his sixty-one-year-old mother. Both men were members of the Amalgamated Clothing Workers Union and committed anti-fascists.

On July 26, the grand jury indicted Greco and Carillo on two charges of murder. All summer the prosecution made no move while the two men sat in jail, but the defense was busy, working through the International Labor Defense.

The ILD was organized in 1925 to move beyond the sporadic and temporary defense groups and "prison comfort clubs" established for some "class-war defendants and political prisoners." These clubs had functioned for labor organizer J. B. McNamara, imprisoned in 1910 after the dynamiting of the *Los Angeles Times* building; for Tom Mooney and Warren Billings, labor organizers imprisoned in 1916 in San Francisco after an anti-war protest; for the IWW prisoners jailed in Centralia, Washington, in 1919. A Labor Defense Council had been established to build support for leaders of the Communist Party who were arrested after their 1922 national convention was broken up in Bridgman, Michigan. In May 1925 this council had issued a call to all defense groups and concerned people inviting them to a convention on June 28, 1925, in Chicago where seventy-eight delegates from trade unions and fraternal organizations and twenty-three delegates from locals of the

Labor Defense Council decided to found the ILD. Joe Brodsky got involved in the ILD at its inception and kept his law partners informed of its work.

The ILD national committee included a Who's Who of the Left: muckraking novelist Upton Sinclair, Socialist Eugene V. Debs, economist Scott Nearing, Communist William Z. Foster, suffragette Alice Stone Blackwell, defendant Benjamin Gitlow, Wobbly Ralph Chaplin, radicals James P. Cannon and Max Bedacht, Bishop William M. Brown, and many others. The ILD's constitution stated its aim:

> to fraternally unite all forces willing to cooperate in the work of labor defense into a broad national organization based upon individual and collective membership that will stand as an ever-willing and ever-ready champion for the defense and support of all workers and exploited farmers, regardless of their political or industrial affiliations, race, color, or nationality, who are persecuted on account of their activities for the class interests of the workers and exploited farmers.

The ILD grew rapidly. By the end of 1925 it boasted 120 locals and branches throughout the country with thousands of individual members, including many noncitizens, contributing monthly relief checks for the 106 "class-war prisoners" they knew about and to their dependent families. The ILD soon affiliated itself with International Red Aid, which had grown out of the Society for the Aid of Revolutionary Fighters (M.O.P.R.), founded in 1923 by workers in the Soviet Union who, remembering their days as political prisoners in Siberia, stressed the need for international solidarity with political defendants and prisoners. The German Left soon founded the Rote Hilfe and joined International Red Aid. The ILD constantly exhorted its members to send letters of condemnation to the governments of Germany and Japan, to send money and letters of support to Mathias Rakosi and his comrades facing death by Horthy's hangmen in fascist Hungary, and to send money and support to other prisoners of conscience abroad.

Now the ILD highlighted the *Greco-Carillo* case. Its international implications were obvious, as the conflicts between fascists and anti-fascists in New York were mounting. But it was the execution of Sacco and Vanzetti after seven years of suspense, agitation, and vigorous partisanship that made it possible for the Greco-Carillo defense to raise funds quickly through a large committee chaired by Robert Morss Lovett of the *New Republic,* working with the ILD. Everyone felt they had no time to

Looking at the Month with Hay Bales. A regular magazine feature depicting the events considered most newsworthy for members of the International Labor Defense and other readers of its monthly magazine. By Hay Bales (real name unknown) in *The Labor Defender*, July 1928.

lose in developing mass support for the second pair of radical Italian-American workingmen to come into the clutches of the law.

They did build popular support, working together as activists and attorneys, through meetings and the ILD's monthly *Labor Defender*. But still Greco and Carillo were neither bailed nor tried. On November 7, Judge Albert Cohn overruled motions to dismiss the indictments and set the trial tentatively for December 5, 1927.

There was only one issue in this case, an issue of fact: were Greco and Carillo the assailants? This was a new kind of problem for Carol. In her deportation cases, everyone knew who the alien was; usually the person had admitted the basic facts of alienage and of political activity before realizing the need for a lawyer. As a result, the only issues were legal ones: had the alien been denied due process and was the applicable deportation statute constitutional? In this case Carol had to concentrate on the facts, not the law. She started interviewing potential defense witnesses and found many ready to furnish alibis for the defendants. Unfortunately, their stories often conflicted with each other, as well as being extremely implausible. They would not convince a jury.

Carol was back in the forum that had marked her first major defeat — a trial court. She knew that a jury can hold the key to victory in a political trial, although juries convicted Left-wing defendants quite regularly during and after the War. Still, jurors don't have to 'obey the law' as they are instructed by the judge. They can make their own law in a particular case if the defense lawyer can convince them to do so before the judge holds the lawyer in contempt for suggesting such a thing. Jury trials are a kind of wild deuce in our legal system, Joe Brodsky implied, a democratic institution fought for and won by the people. They are not part of the predictable U.S. legal structure because the decision-makers are not lawyers from the ruling class who have made it onto the bench. Jury commissioners can be as careful as possible in trying to restrict jury duty to those in the bluestocking districts, but one or two workers are likely to make it onto a jury panel — and in New York, an anti-fascist or two.

It would take an expert trial lawyer to find and keep workers and anti-fascists on the jury in this case, and then to try the case to them. But Joe was too busy, and Shorr and King knew they could not fill his trial shoes even if the ILD raised the kind of mass pressure that would forestall another Sacco-Vanzetti defeat. Carol therefore convinced the ILD to retain Arthur Garfield Hays, a well-known trial lawyer with whom she had worked on numerous issues in the American Civil Liberties Union.

In mid-November Hays's friend Clarence Darrow was in New York to lecture on his successful defense of Loeb and Leopold in Chicago and of Dr. Ossian Sweet and his family in Detroit. Sweet was an African-American physician who had moved his family into a white neighborhood. When a mob surrounded his home, a shot was fired and a white man in the mob was killed. Sweet was charged with murder. Darrow talked to his audience about racial prejudice and how it had been overcome in two trials in the Sweet cases. Afterward, Hays and Greco's distraught brother went to Darrow's hotel room to plead with Darrow to take on the case. Greco's tears convinced Darrow, and Carol could (privately) take credit for making a major contribution to a case by pulling in a broad figure who pulled in someone even broader and much more likely to win.

By now Darrow had regained confidence in his skill before a New York jury. It had been a long time since he lost the *Gitlow* case. He confidently announced to the press, "It should be an easy task to convince a jury that these men are innocent."

Once Darrow took hold of the case, it became *his* case, and Carol had none of the feeling of participation that accompanied work on cases handled by the other lawyers in her office. But it paid off. According to Sender Garlin, who was covering the case for the *Daily Worker,* when Clarence Darrow appeared in the Bronx County Court on December 9, Judge Albert Cohn practically genuflected toward the great criminal lawyer. And when Darrow slowly raised himself up to his full height and moved that the defendants be tried only on the indictment accusing them of the murder of Carisi, the judge quickly granted the motion. Shorr and King knew that they might not have gotten the same decision, which increased the chances of the defendants going free by at least 50 percent.

Darrow was famous for taking two months to select a jury in a murder trial, slowly teaching prospective jurors, and the communities from which they came, that there was a strong core of prejudice in each of them and that this prejudice must be faced and consciously overcome before a defendant could get a fair trial. But Darrow did not dig into the subconscious prejudices of the New Yorkers called for jury duty in this case, and the twelve men were chosen in one day.

His inaction was cause to worry.

Then, the State began to put on its witnesses. Darrow did not seem to be paying close attention either to the broken and imperfect English of the witnesses or to the translations from Italian into English by the court translator, Vito Marcantonio, a former clerk at Hale, Nelles & Shorr.

Most of the time Darrow slouched in his chair and looked absent-minded, although every eye was nonetheless on him, including the jurors' — even when he seemed to be doing nothing, even when the prosecutor was standing at the bar. And when Darrow rose to make an objection to a question, his slow motion and his drawl riveted every eye to his. But when it came his turn to cross-examine a witness, Darrow seemed lethargic. Spectators wondered whether this was the way a great criminal lawyer should act. Had he grown senile?

His old friend Lincoln Steffens had the answers. "[A]t three o'clock [Darrow is] a hero for courage, nerve and calm judgment, but at 3:15 he may be a coward for fear, collapse, and panicky mentality. . . . [H]is power and his weakness is in his highly sensitive, emotional nature which sets his seeing mind in motion in that loafing body."

When the prosecutor asked a key witness to make a positive identification of the defendants, the witness paused. The prosecutor pushed him. Finally the witness answered, "If you want me to say it's him I'll say it's him and I'll go away, but I am not sure. Why should I send an innocent man to jail for nothing when I'm not sure?"

"Are you changing your testimony because you're afraid?" the prosecutor demanded. "I am not afraid of no one," the witness replied. "I am going to die just the same. I am a Catholic."

Luigi Alfano, another prosecution witness, testified that he was shown photographs of numerous anti-fascists while he was in the company of several detectives and Alexander Rocco, organizer and secretary of the Bronx branch of the Fascist League of North America, who had a reputation for vicious behavior toward opponents.

When Rocco himself took the stand, he created further problems for the government because immediately after the killings, he had stated that the man who did the stabbing was "almost six feet in height. . . . The fellow that done the shooting was about five feet ten inches high, had a long face. And the left part of his face was yellow."

The defendants in the box were short: Greco five feet, five and a half inches tall and Carillo an inch taller. The other descriptions did not fit either man.

Next, a patrolman testified that Rocco had not been observed at the scene of the crimes until thirty minutes after the events.

When the prosecution rested, Darrow started putting on the defense. He called Mrs. Greco as a witness. She testified that on Memorial Day she had breakfast with her son. That was all. She was "a fine type," Darrow wrote later, "like one who had stepped out of an old Italian landscape by some master." When she had given her brief testimony, she turned to the judge and asked with motherly affection and womanly dignity, "Please, may I embrace my son?"

Greco had shown no emotion until then; suddenly he broke into tears, and Darrow wrote, "There were few eyes in that courtroom that were not equally affected."

The trial lasted two weeks and convinced the reporter Garlin that Darrow was an awesome guy. When it was time for Darrow to make the final argument for his clients, he rose slowly to his feet and began talking to the jury as he would to any group of friends: "Everybody knows the difficulty of identification, of remembering even the people you know — much less a man who you had never seen before."

Slowly discussing the facts, he paused at 1:00 P.M. to ask if the jurors wanted to go to lunch. They did not.

He asked the same question at 2:00 P.M. Nobody was hungry. By 3:00 P.M. it was too late to eat. Nobody had lunch that day.

Now Darrow was thundering to the jury, "If you can convict on this evidence, silly, foolish, impossible stuff that it is, then life is cheaper here than in Italy." Thrusting his left hand deep into his coat pocket, gesturing with his right, he concluded quietly, "I ask you, gentlemen, to take this case as you find it — these children of Italy who came here to better their condition, who have lived honest lives, who have worked for their families, worked at plain, manual toil, who bore the bullets of the enemy in defense of America and in defense of Italy, who loved freedom and hated despotism, and, therefore, hate Mussolini . . . I ask you for their sake, gentlemen, for a verdict of 'not guilty.' "

The jurors went into the jury room on Christmas Eve with Darrow's words ringing in their ears. They stayed out seven hours and fifty-six minutes. Their verdict: not guilty.

The district attorney moved to have the other indictments against the two men dismissed, and Judge Cohn granted the motion. This was his great moment, undoubtedly recounted later to his son, Roy (who became a young lawyer for Senator Joseph McCarthy during the cold war).

Greco and Carillo rushed home to spend the holidays with their families, rejoicing after almost six months in jail.

When Carol spoke briefly at the testimonial dinner for Darrow on December 28, she was prepared to honor him as a great criminal lawyer. He knew the secret: how to help people acting as jurors look at the defendant as a human being charged with a crime of which he may be innocent.

In its write-up of the victory, the ILD's *Labor Defender* did not mention the work of any of the lawyers, simply running their pictures along with a story highlighting the ILD's mass campaign and the phony identification testimony.

Soon Carol and Isaac represented another Italian American, arrested on August 22, 1927, during a protest meeting held in Cheswick, Pennsylvania, against the execution of Sacco and Vanzetti. Three thousand workers, mostly striking miners, attended the demonstration along with their wives and children. Many state troopers, some on horseback, surrounded the crowd. Finally the troopers hurled tear gas bombs; some of their horses trampled workers under their hoofs.

The workers fought back fiercely. In the ensuing melee, trooper John J. Downey was shot and killed while standing 300 yards from the scene of the meeting.

Nineteen months later, Pennsylvania charged Salvatore Accorsi with the murder. The New York police arrested Accorsi, age thirty-eight, and the father of three young children, on June 13, 1929, on a warrant charging him with another crime under New York law. Soon a Pennsylvania officer arrived in New York to take Accorsi back to Pittsburgh to stand trial for murder.

The defense retained Shorr to oppose extradition. He appeared with King before New York governor Franklin D. Roosevelt in Albany. Shorr convinced Governor Roosevelt to refuse to sign the warrant. But when a third Pennsylvania policeman signed an affidavit the next day, swearing he had seen Accorsi shoot Downey and that he had identified Accorsi on June 17, 1929, in the New York jail, Roosevelt signed the warrant.

Shorr and King immediately asked a New York judge for a writ of habeas corpus. When he dismissed their petition two weeks later, Shorr filed a notice of appeal.

In the end he lost, and Accorsi was sent back to Pittsburgh for trial. The jury voted to acquit him. Shorr and King were convinced that his defense would have been infinitely more difficult if he had been returned

Sacco-Vanzetti Demonstration in Berlin (1927). Illustration for an article by attorney Leo Gallagher on "Our Anti-Fascist Campaign." In *The Labor Defender,* June 1934. (Photographer unknown.)

to Pennsylvania promptly in June. Legal delay had served the ends of justice.

The lawyers' next anti-fascist client was Mario Giletti, ordered deported to Italy for assaulting two fascists. Isaac and Carol asked the Second Circuit Court of Appeals to permit Giletti to take "voluntary departure" to another country, because if he were returned to Italy, he would be subjected to violence and perhaps to imprisonment for political reasons. Giletti was another ILD defendant, and the organization quickly appealed to International Red Aid for evidence of violations of human rights by the fascist government of Italy. The IRA came through in time for the hearing.

Judge Learned Hand wrote the opinion deciding against Giletti. "All we can do," he confessed, ". . . is to suggest that if it prove possible, it would seem most desirable that he be allowed to go elsewhere. . . . His offenses [in Italy] are apparently political, for which he could not be extradited. . . . It has been our traditional policy from the outset not to assist in the prosecution of political offenses," and when possible, U.S. laws should not be enforced in such a way as to cause a person to be charged with political crimes in another country.

This decision from the great liberal, Learned Hand, who had nudged another great liberal, Oliver Wendell Holmes, to think again about the First Amendment! Hand seemed determined to teach King the bitter difference between practicing immigration law — administrative law — before an administrator, and practicing "real" law — common law — before a jury. In *Greco-Carillo,* an outstanding jury lawyer had shown King the majesty of the criminal justice system when it is worked properly. And in *Accorsi,* good lawyers had also worked the timing of the system to bring about justice in a jury trial. But in a deportation hearing there was no point in putting the deportee's mother on the stand. There was no jury, not even an impartial judge, to impress. There was instead a hearing officer following nebulous administrative law being made in Washington, D.C., and a judge who accepted the facts as found by the hearing officer.

At this point, Isaac, Carol, Joe, and the ILD could not muster the power to overrule them either through logic or mass pressure. They might better turn outside their work for some feeling of success.

∂❧

Carol turned to her son, Jonathan, especially after he learned to talk and could share with her his wonder at the world. He was a miniature version of his father, but very much himself. His sharp blue eyes seemed to take everything in, and even when he first started talking his speech was clear and articulate. Independent and self-sufficient, he was a boy on good terms with his parents but, very early, intent on living his own life.

This approach suited Carol, who was a pioneer in seeking the proper balance for a career woman-mother raising a son. No one knew the exact proportions of selflessness and self-interest in the perfect parent, as no one knew the precise age at which selflessness is no longer appropriate. Probably no one thought Carol did her job as a parent perfectly. But Carol, Gordon, and Mrs. Barkley somehow achieved an extended family relationship that assured Carol that Johnny was never without loving adult companionship.

Carol and Gordon believed in taking people seriously and listening to what they had to say, regardless of their age or situation. Gordon followed this approach with all the children coming up in the clan, as he began writing books for the daughters of Carol's sister, Nina, and her husband, Carl Stern.

By the time Peggy Stern was nine, she already knew that her aunt was busy, which made it even more impressive when Carol took the time to notice her. Peggy heard Carol say, "She hasn't a Weiss mind; she thinks like her father." Imagine any adult noticing what kind of mind she had!

Then Aunt Carol took her niece out for an evening, and teenage Peggy was entranced. "First she quite properly took me to a play, as aunts are wont to do. But afterwards she rounded off the evening at Johnnie's, complete with password, an entourage and so charming I still remember the details." It illustrated one of Carol's basic tenets: that you treat a child as a personality. "None of this was ever done solemnly, according to some principle of child psychology, but because it was part of Carol's most militant conviction that the individual and his rights are the most important consideration there is."

Carol King, the attorney, was trying to make this point in each of her cases, and she made it in a speech she gave to a comfortable middle-class audience. She told these citizens that by 1896, the balance of immigration had shifted from western Europeans to eastern Europeans — Italians, Greeks, Russians (including Poles), Austrians, and Hungarians. In 1907, the peak immigration year, 1,285,000 immigrants arrived, 81 percent of them came from southern and eastern Europe. She ticked off the charges against these new immigrants, answering each in turn. *They do not become citizens:* "But for this our own laws are at least in part responsible," she said, because the 1906 act requires applicants to speak English and to have their certificates of landing, which some never had. *They are "the criminal type":* But "Congestion in cities and not nationality may as easily account for these statistics," and the 50,000 immigrant criminals "scarcely account for most crimes in this country." She reminded her audience that "We are all immigrants and the children of immigrants. Why then should we suddenly in our superiority turn away from the immigrant and hold ourselves better?"

Even before a conservative audience, she could not resist discussing the role of birth control in the older immigrant group, the so-called American stock. She said that a judge turned to her in chambers after signing an order sustaining a deportation and asked, "Well, if you were the government, how would you solve this immigration question?"

She knew he had been instrumental in excluding and deporting more aliens than any other judge in New York. Nonetheless, she told him, "I would have immigration unrestricted and pay more attention to the birthrate." The judge was unconvinced but went so far as to say she might be right at that.

She insisted that we should "allow the families of resident aliens to join them here," and permit "peaceful and unoffending aliens" who have lived here sometimes twenty years to become citizens "regardless of the manner of their coming." Immigrants should "not meet prejudice everywhere, in our schools, our courts, our economic and social life."

Carol soon faced some prejudice in her own social life when the ACLU sent her as an observer to the strike of the dressmakers' union against an exclusive dress shop near Fifth Avenue and Fifty-eighth Street. Pickets were handing out handbills perfectly peacefully, and the police were arresting them very promptly.

Carol Weiss King was in a ticklish position. In fact, she had been raised in the upper-middle class, and she had both a college degree and a law degree. At this point, many of the people she respected most were workers who came from the working class and had no hope of a college education. What they were doing — striking a fancy dress shop — seemed the thing to be doing. In this setting, King and others of her class and gender were defensive about their class position and their educations. Anna Rochester and Grace Hutchins were two such "lovely ladies," according to Sender Garlin, making significant contributions through research and writing as they moved from their DAR status to embrace the working class and its struggles.

In this mood, when one of the strikers handed Attorney King some leaflets, she accepted them as the police started arresting everyone in sight. Attorney King suddenly found herself in jail.

While she wasn't the first lawyer to be arrested along with her future clients, it certainly was not a common occurrence and might not have happened to a male lawyer, or to a woman lawyer dressed very formally who was not holding any leaflets.

Defendant King made her one permissible telephone call to her husband. Gordon King arrived very soon to reclaim his wife. Attired in evening clothes and a wrathful disposition, he let it be known that the police officers had arrested a lawyer by mistake. Private citizen Gordon King did not like this reminder of the arrest of the Reverend Bouck White some years before at his church.

LOOKING at the MONTH with HAY BALES

Looking at the Month with Hay Bales. By Hay Bales (real name unknown)
in *The Labor Defender*, December 1928.

Carol crowed later, "Not only was I released, but so were all the pickets, and the law became established in New York that leaflets could be distributed in connection with a strike."

That wasn't enough for Carol. She promptly sued the police officer who had arrested her, seeking $3,000 damages for false arrest. Although she pushed her case along as fast as she could, it seemed to get stuck for months at a time. It would probably take years to come to trial.

In the meantime, Gordon was immersed in his new book, *The Rise of Rome,* a children's version of Herodotus that would make one of the world's best storytellers accessible to the young. He dedicated it to his niece Anne Stern, because at ten, she was the age and kind of child for whom he was writing. Anne was suddenly the center of attention among the cousins when the book appeared.

Carol often found Gordon far away in space and time when she came home from the office. He was determined to write in a clear and exciting style for young readers and to find illustrations that would appeal to them. He found one image in the National Museum in Naples of a young Roman student with pencil and tablets in a fresco from Pompeii, dated about 70 A.D. As an unusual touch, the student was a girl.

As Mussolini built his fascist power in Rome, Gordon conjured up a Julius Caesar who "was powerful enough to be dangerous" and "well out of the way in Gaul." Toward the end of his book, Gordon turned again to a strong, ill-fated woman character, as he had in *Horatio's Story,* providing a warm and respectful description of Cleopatra, the most important woman of the era: "It was a pleasure merely to hear the sound of her voice, with which, like an instrument of many strings, she could pass from one language to another."

Gordon was completing *The Rise of Rome* early in 1929 as the stock market was also rising. In 1925 the Dow-Jones average stood at 99.18. By September 9, 1929, it registered 381.17 and Irving Fisher, a well-known economist, predicted that stock prices had reached "a permanently high plateau," although the International Labour Organization estimated that at this point there were 2,286,000 unemployed in the United States.

Carol King was overjoyed when the ACLU leadership told her they were able to establish a fund of $100,000 to provide bail where necessary in civil liberties cases. They decided to exclude deportation cases because in the past bail in these cases had often been tied up for several years, or had been lost entirely when the alien did not appear at deportation proceedings.

Carol protested loudly that the problems could be solved by better administration of the fund, not by arbitrary denial of bail to aliens. She described a case in which "if the United States Attorney had not been very kind, and perhaps a little stupid, the deportee would have had to put up bail pending the appeal, even though he had won in the lower court." But she could not convince the ACLU to reverse its policy.

Isaac and Carol handled an occasional real estate case at this point, and many workers' compensation cases in New York, which had passed one of the first workers' compensation acts in the country. Carol represented a nurse who contracted tuberculosis from working in a hospital. She built a very careful record in her case, but lost nonetheless. Later, cases on this point were won on the basis of the record she had made.

⅔

Then the stock market crashed in October 1929. By November it was down 182 points. Almost everything began to change. A few rich men jumped from their corporate suites, for shame or for insurance premiums for their families. Millions of men feared loss of their jobs and small businesses and fell into individual despair and retreat. But the people who were rammed in together, in tenements by night, on subways and narrow streets by day, began to discover that almost everyone else was in the same boat. Men who stood for hours in soup lines began to talk together. Some lost their shame and began to gather to discuss what to do. In late 1929 the Communist Party's Central Committee listed its demands:

> unemployment insurance administered by workers; abolition of private employment agencies and establishment of free agencies administered by workers; a 7-hour day and a 5-day work week; no underground work for women; no child labor; no evictions; public funds for emergency relief; union pay on public works projects; recognition of Soviet Russia.

U.S. Communist leader William Z. Foster, who had led the postwar strikes across the country, went to a meeting in Moscow of the Communist International. The CI called for worldwide demonstrations against worldwide unemployment in February 1930.

Carol and Gordon King were not affected immediately or directly by the Depression in their private lives. They were actually beginning to feel somewhat established. They had lived in the same house throughout their married life, assisted by Mrs. Barkley. At thirty-five, Carol King was a seasoned lawyer who had started practicing at the lowest point in immigration law in U.S. history. She and her colleagues had stopped the worst abuses of the Department of Justice and the FBI and had helped many individual clients. They had, however, won no new rules of immigration law in the Supreme Court. At thirty-six, Gordon King was finding himself as a writer, although he still had more works in manuscript than in print. Their son Jonathan was approaching school age. Their personal future looked more or less secure in a rapidly changing world.

PART II:
The Depression Thirties, 1930–1938
Practicing in the Left of Times

One-third of the nation was ill-fed and ill-housed.
Millions of workers went on strike and built unions.
Alabama tried to execute "the Scottsboro Boys."
Hitler threatened to take over Europe.

The Constitution said:
"nor shall any State . . .
deny to any person within its jurisdiction
the equal protection of the laws."

— Fourteenth Amendment

The Communists of the world proclaimed March 6, 1930, International Unemployment Day. The Communist International had to shift the date from February to March when national movements, like the one in the United States, said they could not get the word out any sooner.

The word did get out. On one side, it was disseminated through the *Daily Worker* with its 10,000 readers, through two Finnish-language dailies, one daily in Russian, one in Yiddish, and twelve weekly language newspapers. That made a total of 250,000 readers who could be counted on to use every form of publicity, including holding smaller rallies to build for the big one and furtively pasting posters on the walls of big buildings in the dead of night. On the other side, scare stories in the major newspapers warned of the threat of a red revolution in this country because of mass unemployment.

Senator Robert Wagner (Dem.-N.Y.) decided to schedule hearings on March 6 in Washington, D.C., on three bills that "for the first time [put] the federal government in the business of alleviating unemployment." In Albany, Governor Franklin Roosevelt scheduled a press conference to announce his support for unemployment insurance and said that state-owned armories could be used thereafter to shelter the homeless. The governor also announced the first statewide emergency relief apparatus.

> *New York Times,* March 6, 1930:
> ALL POLICE ON DUTY TO AVERT VIOLENCE AT RED RALLY TODAY
> Fire Department Also Held in Readiness To Quell Rioting Anywhere in the City
>
> WHALEN TO COMMAND BIG FORCE EQUIPPED WITH TEAR
> AND GAS BOMBS AT UNION SQUARE

At noon the demonstration officially began with a speech by Communist William Z. Foster. He told the crowd about his meeting with Police Commissioner Whalen:

> Our committee demanded a parade permit. We pointed out that the Queen of Rumania, sundry military butchers and many capitalist organizations had been allowed to parade freely. But now the class that built Broadway was being denied the right to walk along it.
>   Are we going to take 'No' for an answer?
>   'No!' roared the crowd.

Soon after Foster finished his speech, the police attacked. The *New York World* reporter gave the following account:

> [Demonstrators and bystanders] were slugged and kicked, blackjacked and knocked down by mounted police in the frantic fifteen minutes that followed the policemen's charge on the straggling parade of placard carriers. That attack altered the scene with incredible swiftness from one of good-natured mass apathy and order to the most panic-stricken confusion. . . . Mounted police were setting their horses at the trot into mobs so tightly packed that there was no escape.
>   [There were] women struck in the face with blackjacks, boys beaten by gangs of seven and eight policemen, and an old man backed into a doorway and knocked down time after time, . . .
>   Their faces contorted and raving and cursing, [the police] plunged into the crowd . . . which did its terror-stricken best to flee.

Altogether 130 were injured and 37 arrested, including Foster. They were held without bail.

The next day the *Times* estimated the crowd in New York at 35,000. The *Daily Worker* said 100,000. Within a few days, the *DW* listed the crowds in other cities, along with the numbers injured and the number arrested. In Detroit, hard hit by plant closures, another 100,000 demonstrated. When the police launched an attack, the fighting lasted two hours. Twenty-five were injured, 45 arrested. In Chicago 50,000 demonstrated; another 50,000 in Boston, plus 50,000 in Philadelphia, 25,000 in Cleveland, 20,000 in Youngstown and Pittsburgh. In Los Angeles, 20 were injured, 60 arrested; in Seattle 10 were injured, 12 arrested; in Washington, D.C., 6 were injured, 11 arrested.

Altogether an estimated 500,000 people demonstrated on March 6 in the United States. "The magnitude of this response not only shocked the authorities in New York but also surprised the organizers," according to Franklin Folsom, participant and chronicler in *Impatient Armies of the Poor.*

Foster and the other CP leaders were charged with unlawful assembly. They were denied jury trials.

8.
Suddenly Alone, With Jonathan

The offices of Shorr, Brodsky, & King were soon filled with people needing lawyers to defend their relatives against criminal charges and deportation after the demonstrations of March 6, 1930. Brodsky represented Foster and the other Communist Party leaders before a judge. He conducted such a blistering cross-examination of police witnesses that it became a model in future trials. The judge convicted all the defendants, sentenced each to three years, and sent them to different city prisons, where Foster reported that the meat was full of maggots and the other food inadequate.

After six months, when the headlines had died down and the demand for unemployment insurance had lost its horns, Foster was released on parole as Carol King continued to represent the demonstrators arrested for deportation.

In the summer of 1930, Carol and Gordon sent their son, Jonathan, off on vacation to the Weiss's summer place in Maine with cousins, aunts, and uncles, as they did every year. It gave him some priceless time in the country and his parents some priceless time to enjoy each other without a youngster tagging along.

In early July Gordon became ill, and Carol rushed him to the hospital. It was pneumonia. Nine days later he died.

It was unbelievable. Tragic.

Numb with shock and grief, Carol and the family went through the motions required at such a time. Jonathan had to be told in Maine. One of his uncles took him out in a rowboat and explained to him what had happened.

The *New York Times* obituary soon supplied one bit of reality, one proof that Gordon was really gone, that he would never be able to complete the works he had planned. The brief article noted that "critics have watched Mr. King's work with interest. In his books for children he developed a new approach to young readers, treating them as capable of absorbing serious facts which are presented clearly."

Mrs. Gordon King got through the funeral of her husband somehow, even comforting some of her husband's friends she met for the first time at the ceremony.

Afterward, Carol Weiss King had to mourn in her own way, mourn the contentious, difficult times as well as the glistening moments. And even in her mourning, she had to be aware of Johnny and his four-year-old needs.

Gordon's presence still filled every room with the richness of their conversations and debates. Every corner spoke of the intimacy she had lost forever, leaving no space in which to be transformed from wife to widow. There was no place to find respite after the abrupt end of an intense life with a creative, frustrated personality. There was no way to go through Gordon's things. Not now. She had them packed away quickly, unsorted. In the passion of her loss she asked Mrs. Barkley to destroy all the photographs she had of her husband. (Mrs. Barkley said she saved one, nonetheless.)

As soon as she mustered the energy, Carol decided that she and Johnny would have to leave their old home so that she could make a new life. Yet the building on Twenty-second Street was part of her, too. So was Mrs. Barkley, who had become more indispensable than ever. So were her friends and congenial tenants, Doris Maddow and Arto Funduklian. Carol found a graceful solution, moving all of her things and Jonathan's into Arto's apartment while he moved elsewhere in the building.

And she made other changes, proving that, like Gordon's young readers, she was capable of absorbing serious facts when they were presented clearly. The facts were that she was an adult with a dependent child, a widow in a man's profession. Since fate had made her solely responsible for herself and Jonathan, she decided to go further. She would stop asking her older brother for money from the family trust and live on what she earned, using the room of her own she had established but forswearing the 500 pounds a year Virginia Woolf required for woman's independence.

This decision did not mean she was joining the working class. She would continue to live in the house provided by her mother, and for the rest of her life she would know in the back of her mind that she had the cushion of her inheritance if she really needed it. But she would not have the cash in the bank to allow her to act well-to-do. If she wanted to splurge on a painting, she would have to plan how to get the cash to pay for it. She would have to set proper fees for her clients, bill them for expenses, and make sure they paid.

Carol King, new widow, enrolled Jonathan in The Little Red Schoolhouse, just as her parents had sent her to a private school. Johnny was a schoolboy now, spending his days with kids his own age, not with a father who worked at home with Mrs. Barkley nearby.

Those matters settled, Carol hurled herself into her law practice with almost frenzied vigor. She could lose herself at the office working to defeat violations of the rights of her clients, and continue to puzzle out the best approach on her walk home to Twenty-second Street. Once she opened the door to her new apartment, reality hit her in the face again. Gordon was dead — without warning, without logic. So fast.

By now she could get up every morning and see Johnny off to school. She could plan the meals with Mrs. B. for the next few days. She could work with Joe, Isaac, Sol, and Fay at the office and see her clients. She could talk to friends and family.

But she had no adult to talk to at dinner, or even to chide for being absent or inattentive. No man to share the sex and pillow talk that make a sleepless night worthwhile. No one to share breakfast and enjoy the chatter of their son. And no likelihood that she ever would again.

As soon as she could, she began to fill the empty spaces with phone calls and weekend breakfasts. She kept friendships with some of the people she had met through Gordon. She often went over to the Pollaks by herself for a chat with Walter or Marion, whose children had grown old enough for Marion to do volunteer work outside her home, pulling her closer to Carol's life-style. But the void in Carol's life was deep. She built many bridges over it and apparently learned never to look down.

After a while she could go to an art show again and think about buying a new painting by an artist she had discovered. She gained an artistic ally on the Stix side of the family when Margarite Stix became a sculptor and opened a gallery.

So Carol did what she could. What she could not do was to sit down and put out the *Law and Freedom Bulletin*. The next issue was, of course, impossible. And the next. She had been able to put out the *Bulletin* without a break after Jonathan was born. That was an affirmation. Gordon's death was devastating.

9.
After the Crash

The 1929 stock market crash hit New Yorkers hard. It marked the end of the carefree and reckless twenties. Citizen radicals began asserting themselves on picket lines and at innumerable demonstrations. So did noncitizens. They told their lawyers their stories so they could plan their defense against criminal charges and deportation.

Many immigrants were Reds when they arrived in the United States; many were youngsters who became Reds while growing up here; others learned Marxism on the breadlines. They were determined to participate in demonstrations and union organizing drives regardless of their status as aliens. Some had been silenced by the Palmer Raids long ago. Now immigrant Ben Gold led the fur workers, James Matles the electrical workers, Ferdinand Smith the sailors. Peter Harisiades became a Communist Party leader while an alien; William Schneiderman became a Communist and then a citizen.

Lawyers for aliens faced the same problem repeatedly: how to keep their clients from spending endless time in jail on deportation warrants. Ultimately the lawyers could save most of their clients from deportation on some ground or other. The Russian clients could not be deported because the USSR had continued its post–Palmer Raid policy of not accepting political deportees from the United States. There was no evidence against other clients, or the law provided some technical relief. But the lawyers thought there must be some way to prevent long periods of detention while their cases were pending.

Carol King and Isaac Shorr decided to make a test case out of the detention of Loucas A. Loucas. The New York police picked him up for allegedly painting radical signs on the sidewalk, but the magistrate set him free. Then the Immigration Bureau arrested him for deportation on the ground that he did not have an unexpired immigration visa when he entered the country. Loucas retained Mrs. King. She insisted that Loucas had a valid visa, but the Bureau refused to discharge him.

Carol went straight to court for a writ of habeas corpus, even though the deportation proceedings were still pending before the commissioner. She knew that a habeas petition can be filed to challenge an illegal arrest: this was an illegal arrest; therefore, a habeas petition was appropriate. She could not find any precedents for going to a judge *while* an immigration officer was considering deportation. But lack of precedent did not deter her for more than a moment.

Judge Woolsey agreed with her, and sustained the writ.

Carol had barely told her client and her colleagues about the success of her latest counterattack when the judge, in an almost unprecedented move, reversed his decision. He declared that court *rules* required the alien to "exhaust his administrative remedies" before coming to court, even though there were no court decisions or statutes requiring this procedure.

Carol was furious. She hurried to the U.S. Court of Appeals for relief, got the record and her brief printed, and was preparing for argument when the Labor Department canceled the warrant of arrest. "This was all the more extraordinary," Carol explained, because the department insisted, "It is without power to do anything in a case once the court has taken jurisdiction." She charged, in print, that "the arrest was clearly vindictive": because the magistrate had not punished the alien, the Labor Department was determined to do so. Then the department canceled the warrant to prevent an appellate federal court "from looking into the methods resorted to." The Labor Department did not deny this charge. So Carol won the case for her client, not only getting him released but actually getting his arrest warrant canceled.

But she got no court opinion to cite as precedent in later cases. Thanks to the *Law and Freedom Bulletin,* the few lawyers who subscribed could cite this unreported case if she wrote it up giving the details, the Immigration Bureau docket number, and the date of the decision to substantiate the outcome.

The next case Carol got into was also typical of the times. Spiro Pieratos was arrested in February 1931 for disorderly conduct in connection with a strike. Instead of being taken to court, he was turned over to an immigration inspector. Under questioning, he admitted his membership in the Food Workers Industrial Union. The inspector immediately had a deportation warrant issued on the ground that Pieratos belonged

International Labor Defense. Full-page ad for the International Labor Defense by a young artist. By William Gropper in *The Labor Defender*, October 1930.

to an organization advocating the violent overthrow of the government, and had him arrested.

When he was released, Pieratos came to the Shorr office, where Carol interviewed him with the help of a translator because he could not speak English.

At his deportation hearing the Bureau introduced exhibits to show that the Food Workers Industrial Union was affiliated with the Trade Union Unity League, which was affiliated with the Red International of Labor Unions, which was affiliated with the Communist International, which had headquarters in Moscow, capital of Soviet Russia! The program of the Communist International was then offered in evidence as the final devastating proof that Pieratos should be deported. The Bureau called as witnesses against the deportee the police officers who had made the original arrest and a clerk employed at Ellis Island. The clerk said he was in an adjoining room when an immigration inspector had asked Pieratos, "Are you an anarchist?" He testified that Pieratos had replied, "No, I am a communist."

Pieratos took the stand to deny under oath that he was a communist. He testified he had misunderstood the inspector and the interpreter and that later in that preliminary hearing he had testified he was neither an anarchist nor a communist. He testified that he did not know that the Food Workers Industrial Union was affiliated with the Trade Union Unity League, of which he had never heard. He didn't like the FWIU anyway because it had never gotten him a good job. (This was the kind of offhand jab at the Bureau's neat stereotype of "a typical radical alien" that Carol savored and repeated at home.) The hearing officer nonetheless sustained the charge against Pieratos and ordered him deported.

Soon the New York City police commissioner was urging summary deportation of all noncitizens involved in violent strikes, declaring that every noncitizen should be required to prove his or her right to remain in the United States. The commissioner could cite no law to support this proposal.

❧

Carol stuck to her task at the office and learned to endure the loneliness at home. She received help from an unexpected quarter in her work.

An official government report was issued by the National Commission on Law Observance and Enforcement, which had been appointed by President Herbert Hoover. This businessman Republican president ultimately had to deal with the massive charges of misconduct by law enforcement agents during the 1920 Palmer Raids and the 1923 Teapot Dome scandal in the fat Harding White House. In 1931 the Wickersham Commission finally issued its "Report on the Enforcement of the Deportation Laws of the United States" by Reuben Oppenheimer. After reviewing 500 case records, the report came to devastating conclusions: the enforcement of the deportation laws was "often characterized by methods unconstitutional, tyrannic, and oppressive" and led to results "that violate the plainest dictates of humanity."

The report made several recommendations: the findings of the Immigration Bureau should be published; the system under which the same agency, often the same man, acted as investigator, prosecutor, and judge, should be stopped; the government should establish an independent "board of alien appeals" to issue warrants of arrest, conduct hearings, and decide when warrants should be issued; the Secretary of Labor should have greater discretion to afford relief to deserving aliens.

The report was distributed widely among government officials and libraries, and Carol quoted it frequently. Like her own work, it was based on all the "little" alien cases that were not even reported. Carol was critical of the report's proposal for a Board of Alien Appeals in the Labor Department because "the Department is so shot through with antagonism to the alien that even a new, relatively independent and highly paid board to review appeals does not seem likely to remain free of the taint." She flatly rejected a congressional bill that would authorize direct appeal from the proposed board to the U.S. Circuit Courts of Appeals (C.C.A) because "the District Court is . . . the only place now where an alien gets even the suggestion of a fair deal. The C.C.A. is much too busy to bother with mere aliens. . . ."

By the spring of 1931, Carol did not have much time for simply criticizing government policies. The office was constantly full of new and old clients needing help on new and old kinds of problems — immediately, matching the change in the legal/political air.

She and her colleagues and clients had spent most of the 1920s cleaning up the defeats suffered during the hysteria of the late 1910s. They had not been able to stop new restrictive laws against labor and the foreign born. They had lost almost all their deportation cases in the

Supreme Court, although they had won the First Amendment point in *Gitlow* and the friendship and respect of a great many clients and lawyers across the country.

Now in the spring of 1931, all these events were history. There was a hungry, angry tension at each strike and demonstration seeking jobs and welfare, with many people chanting newfound Marxist slogans. The people were quick with their demands; the cops were quick with their nightsticks. Active people were meeting under many banners. The Group Theatre was formed by radical actors; the ACLU grew; so did the NAACP and the Communist Party.

With Joe Brodsky's inspired assistance, the International Workers Order came into being out of the 5,000-member Jewish Workmen's Circle. After a national conference in March 1930, the IWO was incorporated under the insurance law of New York State to provide insurance benefits and to advance "the mutual protection, health, cultural, educational and recreational interests and well-being of its members." The IWO embarked on a spirited campaign to build societies among the major nationality groups in the United States. Within a year Joe could boast of functioning IWO lodges of Polish-American miners in Pennsylvania, Italian-American garment workers in New York City, Ukrainian-American steel workers in Michigan and Ohio. Many of these people looked to Shorr, Brodsky & King when they needed a lawyer.

The International Labor Defense moved into high gear, setting up a bail fund that was available in deportation cases, unlike the ACLU fund; it could also be used in criminal cases against victims of the Depression repression. The certified public accountant for the ILD reported that on August 1, 1930, $142,500 in securities had been deposited as bail, along with $36,275 in cash and $8,000 in collateral, but this sum was offset by loans payable for bail amounting to $204,134 for a net liability of $17,350 — all enormous sums in 1930.

Joe was repeatedly called out of the office by the ILD — to a strike situation in New Jersey or a vigilante situation in the South. He provided a sense of strength and righteousness to clients and to lawyers new to civil liberties law. Many ACLU lawyers worked with the ILD, savoring its more militant flavor and talk about 'defending the working class.' Many Communist Party members and supporters became active — giving assistance to the ILD and often receiving assistance as defendants. They came and went to Joe's office as events pulled Carol past her widow's weeds into a position of prominence in her field.

THE MONTH IN CARTOONS   *By Bill Gropper*

THE LABOR DEFENDER—October, 1930. Vol. V. No. 10. Published monthly by the International Labor Defense, 80 E. 11th St., Room 430, New York City. J. Louis Engdahl, Editor; Sender Garlin, Associate Editor. Subscription $1.00 year. Entered as second class matter November 5, 1927, at the Post Office, at New York, N. Y., under the Act of March 3, 1879. National Officers: J. Louis Engdahl, General Secretary; Sam Darcy, Assistant Secretary; A. Jakira, Organizational Secretary.

The Month in Cartoons. Quick, short slogans and images to attack clear-cut issues for International Labor Defense members and activists. By William Gropper in *The Labor Defender,* October 1930.

As her career quickened, her older brother's ended. Billy Weiss reluctantly moved out of his office at Cohen, Cole, Weiss & Wharton, where he had specialized in real estate law. He had been afflicted with multiple sclerosis for many years, and now each trip downtown was a painful exercise. At forty-three, he could look back on a successful career as a traditional office lawyer, but he could no longer keep it up. Manhattan had no graciousness of style to offer the physically disabled.

ᣅᣞ

And the South had no simple justice for Negro youths, as Carol began to learn. The press reported in March 1931 that nine young Negroes (ages fourteen to twenty) were arrested at Scottsboro, Alabama, on a charge of forcibly raping two young white women in a freight train — a capital offense. Rootless, unemployed white and Black young men and a few young women had been riding in an empty freight car when the acts allegedly occurred. Stephen Roddy, a white Chattanooga attorney, would represent all the Black defendants at trial. The new southern organizer for the ILD quickly departed from Chattanooga for Scottsboro to attend the preliminary hearing. He phoned in a report to the ILD office in New York. By this time, James S. Allen and another reporter for the *Southern Worker* had located the families of the defendants living in Chattanooga.

Within two weeks the state of Alabama conducted three trials; all-white juries were selected, heard the evidence, and immediately voted to convict all of the defendants and to sentence them to death in a courtroom atmosphere "tense, hostile and excited." The jury could not agree on the ninth young defendant — at fourteen should he get life, or death?

In April the ILD sent its first telegram on the case to the governor of Alabama protesting the attempted legal lynching of the defendants, demanding immediate change of venue (place of trial), new trials, and dismissal of the "court-appointed lawyers openly advocating quick execution." The ILD warned the governor of the imminent danger of lynching and concluded, as to the lives of the defendants: "WE HOLD YOU RESPONSIBLE."

Anna Damon, head of the ILD, asked Joe to go to Scottsboro immediately. He agreed. There he met with the parents of the defendants. They decided to retain this New York Jewish lawyer and the Left-wing ILD to try to get their sons' convictions overturned. Joe returned to New York with the trial record and set about organizing lawyers to prepare

35 MINERS FACE THE ELECTRIC CHAIR

in Harlan, Kentucky
Because they refused to let their families die of starvation.
SHALL THEY BE MURDERED?

NINE. SCOTTSBORO NEGRO BOYS FRAMED-UP
Doomed to Die in the Chair   **SHALL THEY BE MURDERED?**

1,000 Imprisoned in the Penna.-Ohio-W. Va. Coal Strike!
The Imperial Valley Prisoners Are Still Behind Bars!
Mooney and Billings Buried Alive   *Deportations Mounting Sky High*

Camp Hill share-croppers

BOSS TERROR INCREASING
DAILY
CHICAGO—THREE KILLED
CAMP HILL—ONE KILLED—FOUR MISSING
BIRMINGHAM—
Negro and White Workers Are Fighting Back! They Must Halt This Reign of Boss Terror!

Build the INTERNATIONAL LABOR DEFENSE—Your Shield!
Rush Funds
NATIONAL OFFICE — INTERNATIONAL LABOR DEFENSE
80 EAST 11th STREET   *Room 430*   **NEW YORK CITY**

35 Miners Face the Chair. A one-page summary of civil rights cases, North and South. In *The Labor Defender,* September 1931. (Artist unknown.)

the appeals to the Alabama Supreme Court. Joe asked Elias Schwarzbart, a new associate in the office, to work with him, and he agreed. They enlisted Carol to help on the brief for "the Scottsboro boys," as they were called. She started studying the meager trial record to find out exactly what had occurred in that Alabama courtroom and what specific rules of law had been violated. She was soon immersed in the case.

From then on, Carol kept working on this case, trial after trial, appeal after appeal, defeat after partial victory after delay. Whenever she was asked to get "a little memo" on "a small procedural point" in the mail by tomorrow morning, she agreed and did. All the while she was concentrating on the problems of her foreign-born clients.

Then lawyers for the United Mine Workers and the IWW General Defense Committee called her attention to a large shoot-out in Evarts, Kentucky, between union miners and mine guards. In May 1931 the state indicted forty-one people for murder and criminal syndicalism. The reports of events in Bell County showed a denial of constitutional rights that was horrifying. One wondered how this new outrage could possibly be handled, since the lawyers for the miners were going to need massive assistance in order to get any kind of justice for their clients.

But the main pull was *Scottsboro*, turning the attention of Carol King, her colleagues, and political friends from workers and aliens in the North and West to Negroes in the South. Alabama suddenly became real to them. They had to move on from the issues of free speech and fairness they had worked with in the twenties. The First Amendment was not the issue in this case, nor were the rights of aliens. The issue was not the Fifth Amendment guarantee of due process by the federal government, nor the rights of workers. The issue was civil rights, the Reconstruction Amendments' guarantee that the federal government would require the states to provide due process in dealing with Black people — that is, equal protection of the law, as spelled out in the Fourteenth Amendment:

> No State shall make or enforce any law which shall abridge the privileges or immunities of citizens of the United States; nor shall any State deprive any person of life, liberty, or property, without due process of law; nor deny to any person within its jurisdiction the equal protection of the laws.

The people in the *Scottsboro* case somehow transmitted to Carol King the energy to take on the civil rights issues in the case. She finally worked herself around to the point where she could also put out an issue of the ACLU *Law and Freedom Bulletin*. June 1931 was the first issue published since Gordon's death a year before. It was shorter than some issues had been. But at least she got it out.

10.
Dnieprostroy, Berlin, and Harlan County

In the summer of 1931 Doris Maddow, Carol's old friend from the American Association for Labor Legislation, suggested a trip to Europe. Doris had lived in the King's studio apartment for many years, and Carol had bought several of her paintings. The two talked it over. World Tourists was advertising "12 thrilling days in the U.S.S.R.," including Leningrad, Moscow, Kharkov, Kiev, and Dnieprostroy, for $250. It sounded like a real bargain, and an adventure! Fourteen years after Lenin's October Revolution, the United States still had not recognized the existence of the Communist government, and relatively few people from the United States had made the trip to Moscow, although Joe Brodsky had led a six-week tour in July 1928, returning with an enthusiastic report.

Carol wanted to go, but worried about what would happen to Johnny, age five and a half, if she left for a month or so. Mrs. Barkley said they would manage perfectly well — of course Carol should go for a holiday.

Doris and Carol decided to visit the Soviet Union first. When they arrived, they saw examples of rapid expansion on every side, in sharp contrast to the Depression decay surrounding them in New York City. The Soviets boasted that they had not had any serious unemployment in several years; now they were putting to work the very last unemployed men and women under their first five-year plan. This was a totally new concept in the history of the world — a massive central plan encompassing every industry and agricultural enterprise in their country and all of their 155 million people.

The tourists were duly impressed as they met and talked to some of the U.S. specialists who had answered the Soviet call for help, and they talked, through translators, to some of the Russians working at various trades. The Soviet papers were full of stories about teams of workers determined to beat the production quotas set in the plan for their enterprises.

Anna Louise Strong, West Coast journalist stationed in Moscow, reported that the Soviet Union was in a war — a war to move this semi-feudal nation into the twentieth century, to industrialize the cities, and to electrify the rural areas. Strong found Communist Party members everywhere acting as shock troops in this peaceful assault on ignorance, backwardness, hand tools, superstition, and fear. Anyone who knew anything about production was quickly put in a position to teach it to others. The air was full of activity and excitement. To some of the Soviet people, nothing seemed impossible.

Carol and Doris also noticed examples of what they considered comic disorganization. The water did not always run in the beautiful marble bathtubs, and the food was not very good in some of the hotels. The hotel at the site of the new Dnieprostroy Dam was an exception. This massive structure, of which the Soviets were so proud, was the largest dam in the world. As workers had spaded the earth for its construction, others had begun building the city that would surround it. Thousands of Soviet workers had come to work on the site before there was sufficient housing or other facilities for them.

By the time King and Maddow visited the dam, the housing situation had improved considerably. They had to share their room with only five other people, each from a different Soviet region and speaking a different language.

Changing for dinner, Carol and Doris wondered what to expect in the way of food. When they entered the hotel dining room, they were escorted to a luxurious table. Before they could order, the waiters began serving an excellent dinner, starting with steak and ending with ices. The women enjoyed themselves thoroughly. As they were leaving, they discovered that they had been mistaken for a pair of German trade unionists who had placed an advance order.

In Moscow Carol met Henry Shapiro, one of the small group of Americans living in the Soviet Union, and they struck up an immediate friendship. Over a drink he described his move to the Soviet Union after graduation from Harvard Law School. He wanted to become the first person from the United States to practice law in the first socialist society, as others had emigrated to be among the first in their fields. This idea proved utopian for Shapiro the lawyer, and he turned instead to journalism, retaining his interest in law. Now he was delighted to discuss with a

You Are Now a Free Woman/Help To Build Socialism. Poster in warm browns and black with rust-red ink calling Soviet women to work. By A. Strakhov in *Proletariy* (Kharkov, 1926), reprinted in Nina Barburina, *The Soviet Political Poster 1917/1980.* London: Penguin Books, 1985, p. 49.

lively and knowledgeable U.S. lawyer the activities of the ILD in the United States and of its Soviet counterpart, MOPR.

Shapiro probably talked about the recent plenum of the Executive Committee of International Red Aid (IRA) in Moscow, attended by representatives of nearly nine million members worldwide. The IRA had made its report to its members in the same way that boards of directors report to their stockholders; only the items differed. The IRA said that in January 1931, 170,759 workers were in prison, the greatest number, 60,000, in Great Britain's India, while the nationalist government in China and its allies were holding 50,000 workers and peasants. Poland led the list in Europe with 7,000 victims. These figures did not include hundreds of thousands arrested and sentenced to serve short prison terms or tens of thousands put to death, especially in China and India. At the same time, the IRA boasted sixty publications in twenty-five languages outside the Soviet Union, with circulations totaling 6,421,000 copies. The Chinese section had the only daily paper, with a circulation of 2,400,000.

Shapiro urged King to help organize a new association of lawyers in the United States to fight repression on many fronts: the IRA sections in thirty-four countries had been forced into illegality, and five more were facing illegality. Only twenty-five sections were legal at this juncture.

Carol was on holiday, but she listened to Henry's pitch and wrote down names of lawyers to contact in Berlin, as he wrote down her name to pass on to other American lawyers who might visit Moscow.

When she and Doris went on to Germany and France, they found the mood a sharp contrast to Dnieprostroy and Moscow. In Germany they found some good restaurants, and the plumbing in the hotels worked. The politics did not. Everywhere the travelers saw signs of the struggle for power between Left and Right, between Communists and Nazis, between Social Democrats and Nazis.

In Berlin Carol looked up Dr. Alfred Apfel, international secretary of the new organization Henry Shapiro had mentioned, the International Juridical Association. Apfel explained that the IJA had built branches in Germany, France, and Austria that would concentrate on denials of civil liberties in their countries and on problems of labor unions. As the Great Depression spread through country after country, there was a dramatic increase in the attacks on traditional liberties. In Germany the Nazis attacked unions in particular and democratic rights in general. Communists and some Social Democrats responded with demands for further extension of civil liberties in the face of the rising terror of the National Socialists and their leader, Adolf Hitler.

Dr. Apfel asked Mrs. King what she could do about these issues in the United States. Mrs. King promised to think about it when she got home. She actually started thinking on the return ocean voyage. She was, of course, accustomed to hard work for unions and civil liberties in the United States. But she was not accustomed to working internationally, or to starting organizations or running them — at least not up front. She was good at figuring out tactics and working behind the scenes.

⁊⁊

After docking in New York, Carol rushed home to Jonathan. Perhaps she had to be away before she could realize how fast he was growing up. Later, opening her mail, she found a letter from Gordon's brother Howard telling her that his sister, Edith, had died. Carol replied:

> I have tried ever since I received your letter to
> find some words in answer. The reason for telling
> me so slowly I realized. I think we must have all
> felt the same thing, the strange fatality of
> Gordon's death followed so closely by Edith's.
>   Perhaps it was my very understanding of Gordon
> that made me love and understand Edith. He hated
> his life and made it over more nearly to the
> heart's desire. She was always fighting the
> artificial standards she despised but never quite
> built anew. . . . They wanted to live decently. . .
> . There was something the same in the stuff of
> which they were made. The best of them was young
> and full of struggle and protest.

Her trip had done her good; she was able to close on a positive note:

> The experiences of the summer were tremendous. I am
> still stunned. It is like going to another world
> and then coming back. I shall tell you a little of
> it soon but there is nothing I saw that has not
> already been written about. But to see it makes all
> the difference in the world.

It took Carol King a while to settle into her daily routine at home and at work after her return. Her perspective had been forcibly enlarged, and her energy level seemed to increase to meet the new demands. In particular, the German lawyers wanted her to play a role in the United States as part of an international effort to stop the Nazi Party in Germany. They argued that she was not just an independent, conscientious, liberal U.S. lawyer; she was part of a worldwide movement among lawyers — to support new efforts of the working class and to stem the rise of fascism. She must become an organizer of other lawyers, not just a recorder of their work as she had done in the *Bulletin*. Her clients would expect her to continue working on their U.S. cases. But with proper organization, she and other U.S. lawyers could also start to attend international meetings, send observers to crucial trials in other countries, and assist international political activists needing legal counsel in the United States.

Carol began talking about the IJA to her partners. Joe was enthusiastic — but he was obviously completely tied up with the CP, the IWO, the ILD, and with each new crisis in the *Scottsboro* cases that would certainly continue for years. Isaac was interested — but he was also busy with cases, some of which had to produce fees to pay the office overhead. Eli Schwarzbart was busy on *Scottsboro* with Joe. Sol Cohn was enthusiastic, and *he* was prepared to devote some time to the new IJA — American Section.

Carol proposed that their section work on civil liberties and labor law problems. It would not compete with the existing defense groups — the ACLU, the ILD, and the NAACP; on the contrary, it would assist them in their legal defense work. Building on the European models, she planned a legal research group that would hold forums on current legal problems, draft new social legislation, write briefs in pending cases, and publish a monthly legal bulletin on labor and civil rights law.

The IJA would give equal urgency to working on cases and working on statutes. It would draw into its work the more intellectual, library-loving lawyers, people with full-time jobs who could work on ILD cases only at night writing briefs. The bait would be the chance to save a life, write a law, make a headline, or, just possibly, win a precedent from the Supreme Court.

Carol rented an office for the IJA in the St. Denis Building at Eleventh and Broadway and had some stationery printed, giving the name of the organization and her name as secretary. Within a few months she had forty-nine names from twenty states to put on the letterhead, including not only the customary East Coast liberal names but writer Sherwood Anderson from Virginia, and two each from Tennessee and Louisiana, one each from Canada and Puerto Rico. As the Depression spread across the continent, so did the response. Money was less forthcoming, however, and Carol soon had to move the IJA into her office at 100 Fifth Avenue. By now the executive committee also included a pretty good spectrum: Osmond K. Fraenkel, representing the ACLU; Joe Brodsky, representing the ILD; and Roy Wilkins, representing the NAACP; well-known professor Paul F. Brissenden and law professors Jerome Frank and Karl Llewelyn; writers Charles Erskine Scott Wood and Floyd Dell; and one woman in addition to the executive secretary — labor lawyer Yetta Land of Cleveland.

❧

In the winter of 1931 Joe Brodsky became involved in another case as counsel for the International Labor Defense. This paunchy, jovial man had no fat on his legal mind when he went to the Eastern Shore of Maryland to defend Orphan Jones (Euel Lee), who had been arrested in October, held for sixteen hours, mistreated by his jailers, and charged with murdering a farmer, his wife, and their two daughters.

Four times in the next two months white mobs marched through the county to the jails where they thought this Black defendant was being held. They threatened his ILD attorney as well. Twice Brodsky and the Maryland counsel succeeded in getting the trial moved because of the anti-Negro prejudice of the Eastern Shore. But the move was no solution, because the defendant's second trial took place in Baltimore where no Black had been selected for jury duty in twenty-six years (if ever). The Maryland Court of Appeals granted a new trial on this ground.

Six Negroes were on the panel of two hundred at the new trial — and their presence was a victory. The prosecution dismissed all of them with peremptory challenges (requiring no justification) — a defeat. The second all-white jury convicted Jones. The Maryland Court of Appeals said this was not "exclusion of Negroes from the jury," and the execution day was set.

Carol filed her papers to convince the United States Supreme Court to hear this case, although they had not heard an appeal involving exclusion of Negroes from juries for more than twenty years. It takes four Justices to vote to hear a case. They did not come forward in *Jones,* as they had not come forward in *Sacco-Vanzetti,* cases challenging Northern justice for both Italian- and African-Americans. The "old" liberal Justice

Brandeis and the "new" liberal Justice Cardozo did not file dissents from the denial of certiorari. Orphan Jones was executed in 1933.

King, Brodsky, and the people in the IJA and the ILD were determined to bring about a different outcome in the *Scottsboro* cases.

The whole Communist movement was facing up to the problem of racism in the United States, going far beyond the Socialist Party attitude under Debs. As the *Scottsboro* cases went forward in court, the Communist Party decided to try an experiment in order to fight racist attitudes among its own members. On February 27, 1931, the New York Party announced that it would hold a public trial of one of its members, August Yokinen, on the charge of white chauvinism. They said he had discriminated against Negroes in his position as janitor of the Finnish Workers Home. The mock trial was held before 2,000 people at the Harlem Casino, with seven white and seven Black jurors selected to hear counsel for each side describe the position of the Party and of Finnish immigrant Communist Yokinen. The mock jury voted to expel Yokinen from the Communist Party, with the condition that he might be readmitted after he demonstrated his solidarity with Negro workers and proved his worthiness by performing certain tasks in relation to the struggle for Negro rights.

This early effort to fight racism in a U.S. political party had disastrous consequences for the individual. Yokinen had been an inconspicuous member, but when the trial was reported in *The Afro-American* and the *New York Times*, the U.S. government stepped in to punish him by arresting him for deportation. He was not a Communist Party member when his hearing was held, as Carol pointed out in her write-up of the case in the *Bulletin*, although he was attempting to regain membership by performing the prescribed tasks. The government ordered him deported as a past member of the Party. The court of appeals affirmed and the Supreme Court denied certiorari. In January 1933 Yokinen sailed to the Soviet Union in order to avoid deportation to Mannerheim's reactionary Finland.

❧

The *Scottsboro* defendants, meanwhile, faced death because of racism, according to their defenders. King's role in this case was to suggest where to find lawyers to do the public — and library — work needed to save their lives. After the U.S. Supreme Court agreed to hear the appeal,

Carol suggested to Joe and the defense committee that Walter Pollak be asked to argue the case there, as he had done in *Gitlow*. Pollak accepted Brodsky's request. He would cite the strong dissent by Chief Judge Anderson of the Alabama Supreme Court that none of the defendants had been accorded a fair trial. Charles Evans Hughes would preside over the Supreme Court as Chief Justice.

The ILD *Labor Defender* said Hughes "has such an outrageous record as a corporation lawyer for big capitalists that even the liberals raised a yell when he was appointed." He had represented Standard Oil, the meat packers, "the power and radio trust," and as secretary of state "he was responsible for sending U.S. marines to suppress the workers in Nicaragua and Haiti; . . ." His rejection of Attorney General Palmer's attacks on immigrants twelve years before was not mentioned.

The *Labor Defender* also excoriated Justice Cardozo, "hailed as a liberal" because "his decisions have always been in the interests of the propertied class." As a New York state judge in 1921, Cardozo had ruled that a Communist prisoner in jail could not be a candidate "although the law . . . clearly permitted it." And he had upheld the conviction and one-year sentence of Carol's client, YCL member David Gordon, for his poem "America," published in the *Daily Worker* in 1927. His vote to reverse the conviction of Ben Gitlow was not mentioned.

The ILD therefore, quoted Vanzetti: " 'Mobilize a million men' . . . standing up, moving forward, fists raised, . . . calling to you to join them . . . in a surging chorus, 'FREE THE SCOTTSBORO BOYS.' "

The defense raised two basic constitutional issues in the U.S. Supreme Court: the defendants had been denied their right to counsel, and they had been tried by juries from which Negroes had been systematically excluded. The lawyers could not tell whether their arguments had convinced the Justices.

ॐ

Busyness had become Carol's hedge against loneliness. Now she began to learn how to enjoy herself by herself, and with new friends. She particularly liked going to art galleries and getting to know young artists who needed the encouragement of selling an occasional painting. Her niece Peggy Stern remembers that "the inarticulate somehow assuaged their longing in Carol's company. This longing beyond what one could fulfill interested Carol more than the artist who was able to give his vision full expression."

On one of her visits to the Julien Levy Gallery, Carol saw a short art film, *A Bronx Morning,* which she really liked, and soon met the young photographer whose first work it was. Jay Leyda came from Ohio and said he had worked on a punch press in Dayton before daring the move to New York to launch his career by working as a darkroom assistant to Ralph Steiner in 1929. By 1931 he was recommended to give Margaret Bourke-White lessons on how to use a sixteen-millimeter camera.

Carol soon introduced Leyda to her friends. Doris Maddow's brother was a filmmaker and they became close friends.

Jay, age twenty-two, was clearly intrigued by thirty-seven-year-old Carol. They had much in common: their excitement and commitment to the growing Left movement, their love of art and work. Jay soon moved into a vacant room in Carol's apartment and started to make friends with Jonathan and Carol's other personal friends.

Carol's main source of new friends was her professional work. One evening a newcomer, attorney Isadore (Shad) Polier, came to an IJA meeting and soon became a public and personal friend. Polier was a leader — energetic, dynamic, and ruthlessly honest. He was a very warm person but considered somewhat intolerant of people whom he thought were not bright or who did not agree with him. On this occasion, without hesitation, he criticized something Carol had published on behalf of the IJA.

"If you can do it better, you take it over," Carol said without rancor. So Polier became IJA director and King IJA secretary.

Soon Carol invited a group of bright young lawyers to her apartment for a drink — and a chance to become founding editors of the *International Juridical Association Bulletin.* They had all been touched by the "cruelty, injustice and irrationality of capitalism and its brutal suppression of peaceful mass demands for change," John Abt wrote later. They had rejected the ivory tower for active participation in the midst of the madding crowd. Having been near the seats of power at Harvard and Wall Street, they had confidence in the power of their intellect to help bring about basic social change.

The group soon included Tom Emerson, Alger Hiss, Nat Witt, Lee Pressman, and Abe Fortas. Hiss and Pressman had worked together on the *Harvard Law Review* and studied under Professors Felix Frankfurter and Thomas Reed Powell. Witt came from an immigrant family on the Lower East Side and drove a cab for two years to earn the money to go to Harvard. After graduation Frankfurter sent Witt down to work for William Donovan's firm doing corporate reorganizations so he could get a taste of Big Business law. By night Witt gave some time to the IJA toward his long-term goal of becoming a labor/civil liberties lawyer. Emerson had graduated from Yale, and Fortas had stayed on at Yale to teach. The group named Joe Kovner as editor in charge of the *Bulletin*. Kovner was very bright, able, and decent, a compassionate person amid the sharks of the New York legal world. He and the other editors argued out the jurisdiction and style of their new periodical with care.

Since existing law journals dealt only with "property rights," the *IJA Bulletin* announced that it would provide a "compilation of cases involving human rights." Current economic and social problems, "with which all intelligent persons are today concerned," would be treated in the *Bulletin* "as they are not in any other legal publication." There would be no ponderous articles by respectable law professors, but Carol insisted that every factual statement be documented and every case cited accurately so that lawyers could rely on the material and use it in their briefs.

As the evening meetings multiplied, they were invariably held at Carol's apartment. (She asked Jay if he would mind the commotion; it really was the best place to meet.) The work sessions finally produced the first issue of the *Bulletin,* dated "May Day 1932." In eight pages it discussed the status of the *Scottsboro* case; the coal miners' struggles in Harlan and Bell Counties, Kentucky; the new Norris-LaGuardia Anti-Injunction Act; and criminal syndicalism cases in Ohio and Oregon. The "Recent Items" section included notes on a lynching in Maryland, white primaries in the South, and several new deportation cases. Carol included a note on the death of one of the lawyers in the informal national network the movement had been building for years: Elmer S. Smith, valiant attorney for the IWWs of Washington State, disbarred and impoverished after his clients had been routed at Centralia and Everest in 1921 — "truly a labor lawyer."

Later in May the ACLU decided to send a delegation to investigate conditions in Bell County, Kentucky, where bloody battles were reported between coal miners and scabs. The group was headed by attorneys Arthur Garfield Hays and Dudley Field Malone and included professors from Johns Hopkins and the Union Theological Seminary; leaders from

Washington, D.C., Knoxville, and Memphis; and Carol King of the IJA. The delegation asked the federal judge at London, Kentucky, for an injunction permitting them to enter Bell County, based on threats of violence from the local prosecutor. In two days the judge moved from sympathy to denial of the petition, saying finally that Bell and Harlan counties had a right to be protected "from free speech," and warning the delegation not to stir up trouble.

The group nonetheless left by auto for Bell County. On May 13 county officials stopped them at the county line, saying that a mob was in control of Pineville, the county seat, and the officials were determined to protect the ACLU party by refusing them entry into Bell County. Hays and Malone went back to the federal court at London to file a suit for damages against the county officials. On their return to New York City, Hays and the others were called to Washington by a friendly subcommittee of the Senate Committee on Manufactures investigating the Kentucky coal area. King continued to concentrate on the IJA.

The growing intimacy between Carol and Jay did not come as easily as did their lying together before the fire. She wrote later that she just couldn't believe "that some one young and great and direct as you are can want to be permanently tied to what is left of my life. It isn't only a question of age — it's the amount of living I did without you. I am always torn between a desire to throw it all at you and a feeling that if we are to live our lives together it should begin where we began." And she wanted conflicting things from Jay. "I want accomplishment and the drive and ability which makes it possible but I can't do without the continual give and take of daily intercourse which interferes so with getting things done." While she loved him first for his film, "A Bronx Morning," "you have hurt me most when the movies have completely wiped me from your consciousness. I want a genius and a devoted husband. They don't go together and neither is enough. On the other hand I want to be free to have meetings of the I.J.A. or work at night when I want and have no demands made on me but other nights I want to be needed and talked to and made love to."

Soon Jay convinced Carol and Doris Maddow to pose for a portfolio of portraits that was hung in the new Museum of Modern Art. Leyda caught Carol Weiss King in a mood never even approached by any other

Carol King. Gelatin-silver print. By Jay Leyda in *A Portfolio of Photographs New York 1931–1933*. In the collection of the Museum of Modern Art, New York, published with permission.

photographer — relaxed, open, vulnerable. Art critics later described Leyda's work as "fundamentally constructive": that is, "the spectator or reader must work in order to *produce* meaning. A synthesis must take place in one's imagination, and nothing is meant to be passively consumed."

Jay was increasingly fascinated by filmmaking and shared with the two recent Soviet tourists his plan to apply for Sergei Eisenstein's classes at the Moscow Film School, which would require a three-year stay in the Soviet Union.

Carol enthusiastically supported this decision. She wrote that she was "terribly eager for you to get a hell of a lot out of this experience." Although, or perhaps because, she had "spent such a lot of my life carrying other people along I terribly want you to swing your own life. And you can't do that if you're frustrated."

It had only been one year since Carol's trip to the Soviet Union as an exhausted widow. Incredible how much everything had changed! She had been part of the Roaring Twenties, working hard at the office, having fun at home, talking, drinking, partying with her writer husband and other young, talented people. Now she was part of the thirties, working hard at the office, going to meetings at night — often in her own apartment — talking, drinking, planning with her artist friend and other young, talented people. Jay Leyda had made her personal life "full and vivid again," she wrote, helping her face the deep problems and probe the possibilities for action in the Great Depression.

11.
Defending the Right to Revolution

During her days at the office, Carol King was now surrounded by the most militant men and women in trouble with some part of the government for their activities. The language of her colleagues and clients affected her own. She was surrounded by members of the working class, by their own definition and statements of faith. She was moving toward becoming part of their movement, which led her to warn her liberal friend I. F. Stone, "Don't sell out the working class, Izzy," a remark he long remembered. She spent some of her free time with her brothers, sister, and their families, who were surrounded by people in business and the professions trying to work their way up from the Crash. She had the urge to shock them out of their sense of relative well-being as she shifted from attorney for the movement to recruiter for the movement, trying to draw into the work every bright and principled person she could, through suasion or scorn.

She liked being busy in this gray season of hunger, broken occasionally by a red banner waving in the wind. But as the Depression deepened, she and her colleagues began to feel swamped. Across the country millions of workers were laid off, evicted from their homes, forced onto the streets. They were broke and homeless, eating out of garbage pails, sleeping on the roofs of trains, hurtling from one hobo jungle to another.

People slowly began talking to each other. They said they had been taught that, in the United States, if you work hard enough, you get ahead. People who lose their jobs are lazy, Blacks, aliens, women, slackers, Communists — "the others." The President kept telling them the worst of the hard times was already over. But when white native-born men with long seniority got pink slips in massive layoffs, first they asked, 'Why me?' Finally they asked, 'Why?'

In New York people began calling small demonstrations against evictions for nonpayment of rent. Soon coalitions were mounting mammoth demonstrations for relief and unemployment compensation. Oldtimers got arrested and beaten; they called on Joe Brodsky to represent them. People new to the movement heard about the International Labor Defense; they rushed to the office for help.

Some of Joe's clients thought the stock market crash signaled the possibility of a revolution. It would lead to the overthrow of the capitalist system, the chance to usher in a socialist society in the United States. The more demonstrations they attended, the more times they moved furniture back into apartments of evicted tenants, the more Communists they listened to, the more convinced they became. And the redder they got, the more they got arrested.

The ILD lawyers had to send out a call for volunteers. Over a hundred lawyers responded in New York City. After a short briefing, they hurried to courts all over the city to defend their new clients. First, they argued to judges on pretrial motions; then, if the charges were not dismissed, they argued to juries. A group of dedicated young Left and Communist lawyers did the briefing — Joe Tauber, David Freedman, Ed Kuntz, Abraham Unger, and David Scribner, among others. They had stepped up their commitment from part-time to virtually full-time without pay. People had no money to pay the rent; they couldn't possibly pay legal fees. The lawyers established a formal ILD legal staff. But still they could not keep up with the daily arrests in the city.

The same problem existed in industrial areas all across the country. The young lawyers sought out Brodsky, streaming into the office at 100 Fifth Avenue for advice and encouragement. Often Joe couldn't see them because he was out organizing the defense of the Scottsboro defendants, with all the crises and deadlines that imposed.

King was doing research for *Scottsboro*. She was also trying to help new lawyers by writing her "Recent Items" column in the *IJA Bulletin*, describing the latest ideas lawyers were using in representing alien workers and strikers of all nationalities. Carol saw no need to spell out the strategy underlying the lawyers' moves. She evidently assumed that a reader should be able to figure out the strategy from the case digests she provided and quickly get on with the courtroom work.

This approach was not enough for the ILD. They were trying to carry out their principles: championing "the defense and support of all workers and exploited farmers" regardless of their political affiliation, race, color, or nationality, when they were persecuted for fighting for their "class interests." The ILD was trying to be the "Red Cross of the labor movement," as Big Bill Haywood described it from his exile in the Soviet Union.

But the organization had run out of experienced lawyers, and an untrained ILD lawyer was sometimes worse than no lawyer at all, the veterans found. A novice lawyer might discourage a militant client from simply demanding his or her rights and getting friends to pack the courtroom while the lawyer told the jury what was really happening in the streets and in the shops. Or an inexperienced lawyer might tell the defendant's family not to waste what little money they had on a bail bondsman to get the prisoners out of jail quickly, because putting up bail would leave nothing to pay for investigators and lawyers to make a strong defense. Older lawyers worried about radical clients being attacked by vigilante-type prisoners if they were not bailed out of jail.

King and the other seasoned lawyers knew they needed many things to win: clients with guts and wit; time and forces to build a mass campaign; diligent effort to uncover the facts to prove the client's innocence; hardworking, devoted, bright lawyers who were not afraid to try something new; and a jury with a few workers on it. And of course they learned that victory often consisted not in acquittal, but in delaying a decision until a strike was won or an agreement was reached to drop criminal charges when the underlying dispute was resolved.

The debates around legal defense waxed hotter as the alternatives disappeared. Finally some fiery clients reminded some fiery lawyers about cases won by ILD members without any lawyers! Remember the 1930 delegation of unemployed workers to see Mayor Jimmy Walker? Three men were arrested. They walked out of court as free men "because of their brave self-defense and . . . mass pressure both in and outside the courtroom," according to the *Labor Defender*.

William L. Patterson, an African-American lawyer and ILD leader, went further in his column in the *Labor Defender*: "It is the worker defendant who uses the court as his forum" to raise social and economic questions "so vital to an exposure of the court as a weapon of class rule. It is not the lawyer who politicizes the defense struggles. . . . The courtrooms of the working class are the streets." There workers "pass their verdict of innocence on a class war victim." When they have done this in sufficient numbers, that verdict "will be reflected by judge and jury in capitalist courts."

Class Struggle in the Court Room.

Class Struggle in the Court Room. "Mass support for workers on trial. Very often a court room packed to the doors with workers has been the decisive feature that won the workers' case." By Bard in ILD pamphlet (n.d. ca. 1933).

But Patterson the activist did not deprecate the role of Patterson the lawyer. "Mass pressure" to bring about the release of "class war prisoners" must be supplemented by legal defense, which "must be of the most expert character. Every legal technicality must be used." The better the lawyer retained by the ILD, "the more easily and effectively can the worker be shown that the guarantees of justice extended him by the ruling class are meaningless." (Patterson did not mention what many lawyers felt: that the better the lawyer, the greater the chance of winning, which would prove the opposite to workers — that the guarantees of justice are *not* always meaningless in the U.S. constitutional system, even though it is housed in the capitalist economic system.) Marxists accepted this as another contradiction in society.

Patterson took pains to correct the rumor that "the I.L.D., when it retains lawyers, swears them to silence 'on all points where they disagree with it.' " Patterson wrote, "This is not so. The I.L.D. imposes no such obligation, nor is it so simpleminded as to regard this as possible."

The ILD finally decided to publish a pamphlet guide for defendants and their supporters, based on the lessons the organization had learned in its victories and defeats since its formation in 1925. It would carry out the decisions of 247 delegates to the ILD's fifth national convention in 1932, which had considered the rise of fascism in Europe and had "lashed mercilessly the stubborn sectarian methods that isolated us organizationally from the broad masses."

Patterson, recently returned from years in the Soviet Union, was busy trying to prevent a recurrence of the injustice he had fought against so hard in the case of Sacco and Vanzetti before his mission to Moscow. This case had taught the ILD the necessity of a united front with members of the ACLU and NAACP, although the ILD differed sharply with what it considered the cautious, legalistic stance often urged by those organizations in the handling of tough cases. "Pat" wanted the ILD to broaden out while maintaining a militant posture in handling its cases. He was primarily concerned with criminal cases.

For the cover of the ILD pamphlet published in June 1932, young artist Bill Gropper drew a strong, determined young man in work clothes pulling up a fat judge's robe to reveal three weapons strapped to his judicial belt: a contempt of court axe, a jail-term blackjack, and an injunction knife. *UNDER ARREST! Workers' Self-Defense in the Courts* was pamphlet number five, to be sold for five cents by ILD branches and individual members.

One of the nontechnical defenses on which the ILD relied was the First Amendment. Many leaders of the ILD, along with William Z. Foster of the Communist Party, had participated in the free-speech fights by the IWW in the western states in the first two decades of the century. They wrote in their pamphlet: "The capitalist laws theoretically grant the right of freedom of speech and press. These rights should be used as a weapon of the worker on trial for these crimes. The workers should expose the contradictions and demand that this right to express themselves be given to the workers, as well as to the boss class."

Carol saw to it that this advice was not repeated when discussing aliens and deportation. There was no way to turn an Ellis Island hearing into a forum for discussion of the underlying ills of the capitalist system. The pamphlet said clearly: "Deportation hearings are held in private. The only people present in the room are the commissioner, the stenographer, the alien, and the alien's lawyers. The testimony is secret and is not given to the newspapers. Do NOT try to propagandize the government officials at such a hearing. You will only be talking yourself into a swift deportation."

The pamphlet repeated Carol's constant plea to clients and future clients: "The government seldom has much information about a worker when a deportation proceeding starts, but usually obtains enough information when the worker talks freely with an inspector. In many instances the alien worker has lost his case by loose talking before his hearing."

At the same time, the ILD was determined to present the full picture to its readers, alien and citizen alike:

Is There a Right of Revolution in America?
  District attorneys will often attempt to prove that a defendant in a working class prosecution advocates "R-r-r-revolution." The way he rolls the word off would make you think that this is the worst crime there is. Point out, if you are compelled to answer this question, that revolution is a word which should have a particularly favorable meaning to an American. The right of revolution has never been taken away, and never can be. . . .

The pamphlet was written for defendants with an oratorical bent — Irish, Jewish, Italian, and Negro workers who had memorized poetry in school or church and knew how to deliver it in style. They could use the quotations starting with the Declaration of Independence, when talking to a jury:

UNDER ARREST!

Workers' Self-Defense
in the Courts

Issued *by the* INTERNATIONAL LABOR DEFENSE

PAMPHLET No. 5   FIVE Cents

Under Arrest! Workers' Self-Defense in the Courts. By William Gropper in
The Labor Defender, April 1932, and in the ILD pamphlet of the same title.

> Governments are instituted among men, deriving their just powers from
> the consent of the governed; . . . whenever any form of government
> becomes destructive of these ends, it is the right of the people to alter or
> abolish it, and to institute a new government. . . .

Then the pamphlet quoted President Thomas Jefferson: "I hold a little rebellion now and then is a good thing, and as necessary in the political world as storms in the physical"; President Abraham Lincoln: "Whenever [the people] grow weary of the existing Government, they can exercise their constitutional right of amending it or their revolutionary right to dismember or overthrow it"; and President Woodrov Wilson: "We have forgotten the very principles of our origin if we have forgotten how to . . . pull down and build up, even to the extent of revolutionary practice."

The whole thrust of the pamphlet was away from the great individual trial lawyer with charisma — the Clarence Darrow image — toward group and mass defense. Darrow had learned that sometimes he could convince ordinary Americans sitting as jurors that the rights of his clients had been violated and that the defendants did not belong in prison — or in the gas chamber — even though their views differed from the jurors. But Darrow had also learned — in cases involving Communists and other radicals — that he could not convince ordinary Americans that his clients were correct in their assessment of the state of the country or in their demands for social change. So he tried to focus attention on *his* perception of what was unfair about the way society treated his clients and their fellows. He did not permit the focus to shift to his clients or to *their* perception of racial prejudice (in the *Sweet* case in Detroit) or to *their* horror of fascism (in the *Greco-Carillo* case in New York). When Gitlow insisted on shifting the focus to himself in his case, he lost.

The ILD went in the opposite direction. But it also recognized that a case like *Scottsboro* continually raised issues going far beyond the advice in its pamphlet, and the organization counted on individual ILD lawyers to go beyond the advice in the pamphlet to win the cases they handled. Joe Brodsky had his remarkable oratorical skills, developed on many a soapbox when he was making socialist speeches on the Lower East Side as a kid. He also had his jovial-fisherman side to show a judge or jury in a farm community as the first step toward walking his client out the courthouse door after trial.

Carol King had a different tool. In a profession in which contacts are power, she had a large portfolio. She was a Weiss, daughter of corporation counsel Samuel Weiss, and she carried herself accordingly. She had argued before many judges since her admission to practice right after the Palmer Raids. Her brother was Louis Weiss of the rising firm of Cohen, Cole, Weiss & Wharton. Her brother-in-law was respected lawyer Carl Stern, and her friend Walter H. Pollak also practiced law close to Wall Street. A reference to one of them was no open sesame, but she felt it evened the contest somewhat.

She also tried to have a friendly chat with a judge before court opened, as the other side customarily did, or at least with the judge's clerk, who was often bright and sometimes liberal. Occasionally she could use the old school ties she still had — with NYU Law School classmates, or with members of Max Lowenthal's firm. Her political friends noticed that in making these contacts, Carol showed a clear perception of what they called 'the nature of the ruling class' in general and of the judiciary in particular. They realized that her parentage and a broad range of relatives, friends, and acquaintances had given her miscellaneous background facts about a judge that helped her gauge what (and who) might appeal to him when he sat in judgment on a Communist, Negro militant, unemployed worker, or alien.

She was also developing a feel for the issue in a case that would appeal to a decent judge — the particular narrow legal issue that might permit a ruling for her client even in the charged political climate that gave rise to the case.

❧

Early in the summer of 1932, the *IJA Bulletin* began reporting on another potentially "big" case. Angelo Herndon led a demonstration of 1,000 whites and Negroes to the courthouse in Atlanta, Georgia, to demand relief. This immense, unprecedented, integrated outpouring of Southerners was entirely orderly, according to all accounts. Herndon was a nineteen-year-old Negro coal miner who had gone to organize the unemployed in Atlanta for the Communist Party. He was overjoyed when the city government voted relief funds the day after the demonstration. A few days later, Herndon went to the post office to get his mail. The police arrested him. They also searched his room without a warrant and held him for two weeks without charges.

Someone notified Anna Damon, leader of the ILD, of Herndon's arrest. She called Joe Brodsky, who contacted Herndon's local lawyer and offered to help him in any way. This offer was gratefully accepted. The local grand jury quickly indicted Herndon under a statute forbidding "any attempt, by persuasion or otherwise, to induce others to join in any combined resistance to the lawful authority of the State." The penalty for violation was death unless the jury recommended mercy, in which event the penalty was five to twenty years in prison. Georgia had enacted this law in 1866 as its contribution to the Black Codes, passed to retard the Reconstruction era after the South lost the Civil War. Only one previous indictment had been returned under this act.

The ILD (via Joe Brodsky) promptly requested the IJA (in the person of Carol King) to help with the legal research on the Herndon case. Carol took on this new commitment, relying on Anna Damon for strength and inspiration. Damon was a woman with keen, gray eyes and strong, outstretched hands, known for her calm and courageous manner that slowly brought many kinds of people into the defense of the "Scottsboro Boys" and Angelo Herndon, and brought them back again and again after year-long waits for trials and appeals.

The campaign for Herndon began as the 1932 national presidential campaign got under way. Herbert Hoover was seeking the traditional second term. To run against him, the Democrats nominated Governor Roosevelt of New York, a man who looked and acted like the aristocrat he was, but who talked with feeling about "the common man." The Democratic Party wrote a platform that promised to tackle the real problems created by the Depression. They promised "to provide unemployment relief" and "the spread of employment by a substantial reduction in the hours of labor." They promised "unemployment and old age insurance under state laws." These demands had given activists cracked heads at the hands of New York City cops only two years before, and defending their supporters had helped build Joe Brodsky's reputation as a fiery lawyer.

Carol King, Joe Brodsky, and many of their friends opposed Roosevelt, supporting instead the Communist Party candidates William Z. Foster and his Negro running mate, James Ford. They had no faith in the gentleman from Hyde Park and the combination of northern Tammany Hall politicians and southern Democrats he was putting together to defeat the reactionary and obviously ineffectual Hoover.

At this point the ILD was also busy warning of the new threat of war from U.S. acceptance of the Japanese invasion of China. Theodore Dreiser wrote in the *Labor Defender* about "American money-masters" wanting Japan to "hold as much of China as will safeguard her checking of Russia" until both nations are destroyed. Then "if Japan does not then share the great loot of Asia with us, we will turn and attack her" to remain the "imperial war lords of the world."

As Dreiser was writing, the Republican Department of Labor was ordering three political dissenters deported: one to China, Communist Tao Hsuah Li; another to Italy, anti-fascist Guido Serio; the third to Venezuela, Eduardo Machado. Then the government refused to let the three seek "voluntary departure" to countries that would not jail or kill them on their return. On the very eve of the appellate court argument, the department finally yielded the right of the three to go to safe countries.

Carol King had proposed reforming this law in the *Law and Freedom Bulletin* in 1925. Now in 1932 the IJA legislation committee made this argument: there is no reason why the government should care where an alien goes so long as he does not go to foreign contiguous territory from which he could more easily sneak back in the United States. But political aliens "are vitally interested in their destination." In June 1932 Congressman Fiorello La Guardia (Rep.-N.Y.) introduced the IJA bill.

Instead, the House passed the Dies Deportation Bill that would make membership in the Communist Party a ground for deportation or exclusion from citizenship. Congressman Martin Dies (Dem.-Tex.) proposed the new bill to reverse the decision of the Ninth Circuit Court of Appeals in the *Fred Fierstein* case, which held that the government must establish the proscribed character of the organization in each proceeding. Carol urged defeat of the bill because under it, "White Russians are thus free to come to this country and conspire against the Union of Soviet Socialist Republics, but anti-Fascisti who plot the overthrow of Mussolini are immediately deportable to Italy." The bill did not pass in 1932, and Fierstein continued struggling to remain in the United States (which he did successfully for the next fifty years).

During the election campaign, the "little clerks in the Labor Department" whom Carol scorned got a chance to exert their power over another dozen aliens in August 1932. Carol reported in the *IJA Bulletin* on the outcome of an open-air meeting of the Unemployed Council in White Plains, New York. No ordinance required a permit, and the meeting was orderly. Nonetheless, the police arrested a citizen on the charge of unlawful assembly for speaking without a permit. A crowd of workers attended her trial. When her case was called, the city judge ordered the courtroom cleared. As the spectators filed out, the police surrounded them and took forty-two to police headquarters, where agents of the Immigration Bureau questioned them. Twelve were not able to produce citizenship papers or other evidence of their right to remain in the United States. They were promptly sent to Ellis Island to face deportation. What had started out as a show of support for a fellow worker on trial in a city court had become a terrifying stay in prison that could lead to expulsion from the United States. Each case would have to be fought before and after the election.

Just before the election, the Republican Labor Department refused re-entry to resident aliens because "they are liable to become public charges." These people were married to U.S. citizens and were trying to return from quick trips to see relatives in their native lands. And in November 1932 the department ordered a mass round-up of Mexican workers in Detroit, leading to the deportation of 400 people.

Carol responded to all these government attacks with a recruiting letter for the IJA: "Present America offers the example of a country discarding traditions of liberty and freedom, and substituting legislative, administrative and judicial tyranny," citing deportations, persecution of political dissenters, ouster of radical teachers and professors, and injunctions against organized labor. "It is the purpose of the IJA to combat these tendencies." The letter concluded with a plea for "not only your financial but your moral support."

This letter was delivered just as Roosevelt trounced Hoover at the polls. Many joined the IJA in the first flush of this victory.

❧

October 11, 1932:
GUARDED HIGH COURT HEARS NEGRO PLEAS
Reds Protest in Paris

New York Times, November 8, 1932:
NEW TRIAL ORDERED BY SUPREME COURT IN SCOTTSBORO CASE
Police Wield Clubs Freely on Radicals Attempting to Picket Court Chamber
Many Hurt, 14 Arrested

In November 1932 Justice Sutherland issued the opinion of the Supreme Court in the *Scottsboro* case. The opinion marked a significant

Scottsboro Case Discussed in Soviet Russia. "World-wide protest on
Scottsboro: In Soviet Russia, colonial peoples liberated from Czardom carrying Scottsboro appeals and pamphlets to a protest meeting, demanding Wall
St. government free the boys." In *The Labor Defender,* July 1932. (Photographer unknown.)

change in the law. By a vote of 7 to 2, the Court accepted Pollak's
argument and reversed all of the convictions because the defendants had
not had a proper opportunity to prepare for trial and had not been
represented by effective counsel. As in the *Gitlow* case, the Supreme Court
held that it had to consider whether the action of the *state* had violated
the *federal* Constitution, and found it had. Finally the Court set forth the
rule:

> In a capital case, where the defendant is unable to employ counsel, and is
> incapable adequately of making his own defense because of ignorance,
> feeble-mindedness, illiteracy, or the like, it is the duty of the court, whether
> requested or not, to assign counsel for him as a necessary requisite of due
> process of law. . . . To hold otherwise would be to ignore the fundamental
> postulate . . . "that there are certain immutable principles of justice which
> inhere in the very idea of free government which no member of the Union
> may disregard."

Defense counsel and the ILD were jubilant. They had stopped the executions of the Scottsboro defendants. They did so by raising the big questions of "right to counsel" and "due process of law in all criminal cases," not by asking the Court simply to help out "these poor defendants." They felt their mass campaign had been successful in convincing the liberals Brandeis and Cardozo and corporation lawyer Hughes to vote differently than they had in the past, taking with them four conservative Justices.

The *Scottsboro* opinion began to have an effect almost immediately. The *IJA Bulletin* reported that the Oklahoma Court of Criminal Appeals reversed the conviction for rape of a white woman by a Negro man because his right to effective assistance of counsel had been denied. Eventually the opinion would be applied in cases of indigent *white* defendants.

Early in December 1932 Carol King was called to another front. Two thousand hunger marchers from all over the country were nearing Washington, D.C., by foot, jalopy, bus, and truck. They came under the banner of the Unemployed Councils of America to demand jobs, food, and housing from Congress and the lame duck President. The Washington police announced they would keep the marchers from reaching their goal, the Capitol. President Hoover acquiesced by his silence.

Carol King, as IJA secretary, quickly joined a delegation of New York women trying to see Hoover to convince him to change his policy. Hoover refused to see them.

```
CONFIDENTIAL
[Forwarded to the (FBI) Bureau on 12/3/32
Re: Hunger Marchers 61-6699-313 (80)]
   FRANCIS RALSTON WELSH (NOT IDENTIFIED) IN A LET-
TER TO PRESIDENT HERBERT HOOVER, DATED DECEMBER 1,
1932, WROTE AS FOLLOWS:
      "I SEE THAT VARIOUS LADIES HAVE MADE AN APPEAL
      TO YOU FOR THE COMMUNIST HUNGER MARCHERS. THESE
      ARE LARGELY PART OF THE AMERICAN CIVIL
      LIBERTIES UNION-COMMUNIST-AIDING CROWD WHICH
      PUT AID FOR COMMUNISM BEFORE PATRIOTISM."
AMONG THE WOMEN DESCRIBED WAS MRS. CAROL WEISS
KING. REGARDING HER WELSH WROTE:
      MRS. CAROL WEISS KING WAS ATTORNEY FOR DAVID
      GORDON, AUTHOR OF THE FILTHY AND OBSCENE POEM,
      AMERICA, WHICH WAS PUBLISHED IN THE COMMUNIST
      ORGAN THE DAILY WORKER. SHE WAS OF THE
```

COMMUNIST INTERNATIONAL LABOR DEFENSE. SHE
DEFENDED DISLOYAL STUDENTS ARRESTED AT A
MEETING ON THE COLLEGE OF THE CITY OF NEW YORK
CAMPUS. SHE WAS ATTORNEY FOR THE AMERICAN CIVIL
LIBERTIES UNION AND WAS ARRESTED DISTRIBUTING
PAMPHLETS AT AN INTERNATIONAL LADIES GARMENT
WORKERS' UNION STRIKE. SHE WAS ATTORNEY FOR
ELSA HEWITT, RADICAL LABOR TEACHER. SHE WAS
COUNSEL FOR TAO HSUAN LI, CHINESE COMMUNIST
SENTENCED TO BE DEPORTED. SHE WAS ON THE
NATIONAL COMMITTEE TO AID STRIKING MINERS
FIGHTING STARVATION, WHICH WAS COMMUNISTIC AID
TO A COMMUNIST STRIKE. SHE WAS PART OF THE
AMERICAN CIVIL LIBERTIES UNION EXPEDITION TO
KENTUCKY WHICH WENT THERE TO MAKE TROUBLE IN
THE INTEREST OF COMMUNISM.

On December 5, 1932, Carol King sent telegrams on behalf of the IJA to President Hoover and the commissioners of the District of Columbia requesting them to exert their "influence to secure for hunger marchers their right to passage through Washington . . . [since] legal authorities establish the undoubted right of persons to move about freely in this country." King clearly expressed the view of law-abiding, concerned citizens: "When conditions are as tragic as they are today the least the government can do is to give some of the victims an opportunity to present their grievances."

Carol received no reply as two thousand people gathered in the nation's capital. They had no cots or beds, although "Quakers, workers, humanitarians and radicals" had offered accommodations that the police would not permit them to use, according to the story in the *New Republic*. Someone produced a mandolin and a group of the marchers started singing as others lay down on the cold asphalt to try to sleep. The next day 1,200 policemen; 700 deputized firemen equipped with tear gas, sawed-off rifles, and submachine guns; and the militia prepared to meet the hunger marchers while Carol and others approached members of Congress to guarantee the marchers' right to assemble and parade peacefully.

On the second day the newspapers ran stories that each hunger marcher was receiving five dollars a day from Moscow. A headline ran: "RUMOR, DYNAMITE IN COMMUNISTS' TRUCKS"; below, in small type: "Rumor Unfounded." By this time Senator Edward P. Costigan (Dem.-Colo.) had visited the hunger marchers' camp. So had Congressmen La Guardia

(Rep.-N.Y.), Edward Irwin (Rep.-Ill.), and Thomas R. Amlie (Rep./Prog.-N.D.). They were all indignant at the treatment of the marchers, as Edward Dahlberg reported in *The Nation*.

Finally, at five o'clock on Monday afternoon, the marchers lined up for a parade with their banners as the Red Front Band struck up a tune and the line moved forward. "Come on, you yellow bastards," one of the policemen shouted. The line of marchers came on step by step, till they almost touched the rope that marked the limits of their prison. The police stirred; the movie men got out their gas masks. Suddenly the leader of the marchers ordered the column to swing left and left again, and the disciplined marchers retraced their steps to avoid a riot.

The next morning, the work on the Hill paid off: the marchers won a parade permit. They walked with police lining both sides of the street. The spectators were largely silent. Once or twice someone tried to cheer from the sidelines but stopped when a policeman jostled him. As the marchers climbed the Hill, a delegation finally took their petition for a redress of grievances rooted in the Great Depression and handed it to congressional leaders. The marchers demanded $50 in cash for every unemployed worker for the winter, plus $10 for each of their children; immediate unemployment insurance paid for by the government and the employers; an end to tax rebates for the wealthy and their corporations; a halt to military expenditures; and a tax levy on the capital of large corporations.

Democrat John Nance Garner, incoming Vice President, seemed as hostile to their demands as Republican Vice President Curtis, who was on his way out.

That day the *Times* carried a story from Berlin on another nagging problem exacerbated by the economic crisis in the capitalist world. Professor Albert Einstein had been summoned to the United States consulate in Berlin to discuss his application for a visa because the U.S. Woman Patriot Corporation had told the State Department that Einstein was a Communist and should be barred from the United States. After forty minutes of questioning about his political views and his eligibility to enter the United States, Professor Einstein "got mad and got the visa," according to the World Almanac report. No one at the time envisioned the mushroom cloud that would be one ultimate contradictory outcome of this decision concerning the admissibility of one German Jewish alien intellectual into the United States during the Great Depression.

We Will Not Forget! One of the early U.S. depictions of the Hitler terror.
By Hof in *The Labor Defender,* July 1933.

Carol and Jay planned joyfully for Jonathan's Christmas stocking, and for each other's. This Christian custom was probably one Carol had enjoyed with Gordon and Jonathan but one she couldn't very well ask her Weiss relatives to share.

In January 1933 *King v. New York City Police Department* finally came to trial. King testified that she was a lawyer and that she had gone to the scene of the dressmakers' strike in 1928 for her client, the American Civil Liberties Union. She had been watching the efforts of the pickets to distribute handbills, but she had not been passing them out herself and her arrest was totally without cause. (Her testimony must have brought back, with a start, the striking image of Gordon King striding into the police station in evening clothes to demand her release.) Several witnesses corroborated her account.

The defendant policeman testified that Mrs. King had not simply been observing; she had been passing out the leaflets, which the police had been instructed to prevent. Another policeman supported his story.

The jury believed the policemen and not the lady lawyer. Carol King had no victory to report in the *IJA Bulletin* as the Hoover administration was ushered out and the pace of her life quickened.

12.
Getting on With the *Bulletin,* and With Life

Whatever else she might be doing, Carol King got each monthly issue of the *IJA Bulletin* to the printer more or less on time, but not without fights with the other editors who were polishing their articles. ('Just a few more days — Oh, all right, Carol! You'll have it Monday morning!')

The *Bulletin* described new efforts to prove the innocence of Tom Mooney, San Francisco labor hero, in prison since 1916 for allegedly planting a bomb during a Preparedness Day Parade supporting United States entry into the World War. The *Bulletin* discussed the unconstitutionality of a New York City ordinance prohibiting street-speaking without a license. It attacked the collector of customs for censoring foreign publications entering the United States. And each issue reported the unfolding story of the *Scottsboro* case.

Joe Kovner was the editor of the *Bulletin,* and he soon recruited another editor. Young Wall Street lawyer Nathan Greene had recently graduated from Harvard Law School, where he had collaborated with Professor Felix Frankfurter on *The Labor Injunction* (1930), an instant classic. Now he spent his evenings writing one piece after another for the *Bulletin.* Days he worked for Lehman & Greenman, the firm run by Governor Herbert Lehman's brother, representing the *New York Times* and other prestigious corporate clients. Nuddy Greene was small and slender in stature, with a dark complexion. Under Carol's unobtrusive management of IJA meetings, his remarkable abilities as thinker, author, and editor soon became apparent. Everyone's pieces on the *Bulletin* were edited and re-edited, except Nuddy Greene's; by common consent, by the time he submitted them, they required no further work.

Greene had become absolutely convinced, from his work on the injunction book, that workers and unions are essential to democracy. Soon he met Communist fur workers Ben Gold, Irving Potash, and others who were trying to get rid of the racketeers in their union. He helped them prepare their testimony before the Seabury Commission on this subject, as Leftists were also trying to clean up the hotel and restaurant workers unions. These problems found their way into discussions in the *Bulletin.*

Each month the editors tried to select an economic or political issue emerging out of the myriad of events demanding their attention. Several represented labor unions or New Deal agencies; others were active in a CP neighborhood club or unemployed council engaged in some crucial campaign. They wanted to display their new radical ideas and to cover up or atone for their "middle-class backgrounds" in this era of strong "working class consciousness." They felt they were at the center of "the movement" and were determined to have their subject covered properly in their publication. Other lawyers had ordinary jobs in the daytime but the willingness, the need, to participate in the struggle in their spare time — and they could write. Most were young Jewish intellectual men from Harvard, Yale, or Columbia, with an occasional Gentile, woman, or Midwesterner joining the magic circle.

The *Bulletin* editors argued and wrote about the social origins and functions of the law. When the police in Bayonne, New Jersey, severely beat John Kasper, a Communist Party member who asked for a parade permit for the Unemployed Council, Kasper filed a federal suit for damages. The jury decided for the police defendants. The editors quoted Judge Clark in the *Bulletin,* saying that "a man has a right to say he is a Communist, and a Communist is entitled to his rights just the same as a Republican or Democrat." But the outcome of the trial "tends to disprove this," the editors wrote. Even against the police, a Republican or a Democrat would probably have fared better. However, the editors concluded, "it remains true that no communist has been beaten by the police of Bayonne in 1932," so the bringing of this suit "was not altogether futile."

On the criminal law side, in June 1933 the editors reported a two-year sentence for a demonstrator at the New York City Home Relief Bureau protesting the bureau's recent policy of paying no rent for families on the relief lists. The magistrate's action was upheld on the first appeal despite "clear" disregard of notice and hearing requirements. The editors worried that this practice, if upheld, "opens the way for imposing harsh sentences upon strikers and other persons active in social struggles. It is another illustration of the readiness of courts to fashion innocuous and inapplicable legislation into weapons against workers."

The editorial group of fifteen or twenty met in the evening at King's apartment on Twenty-second Street, where she sometimes greeted them in lounging pajamas. Carol described one of these affairs in a letter to a friend:

> The meeting was a rather jovial occasion at which
> in my opinion nothing was accomplished except the
> disappearance at supper of the balance of my birth-
> day cake and the disappearance, after the technical
> adjournment of the business meeting, of one bottle
> of Johnny Walker, Black Label,

which, she explained, came into her possession as a dividend from her stock in the distilling firm. And to another friend:

> I'm thinking of opening a bureau, sort of Dorothy
> Dix advice to young and troubled males. Felt as if
> my knowledge of human nature was going overtime
> when I rightly sized up [X] as a man who had gone
> to bed with a woman but never lived with one. Altho
> I talk so flipply I was tremendously interested in
> what both [X] and [Y] had to say and tried my
> damnedest to be helpful.

The "IJA boys" agreed that Carol was always stimulating, and she had a broad perspective. She would discuss the making of salad dressing with the same enthusiasm as the drafting of a petition for a writ of habeas corpus. She was a complete person and drew innumerable lawyers to her and the IJA. Sol Cohn remembers that the conversations at these meetings were always twisted and scattered, usually including references to some-one's having a new baby or mother-in-law. Carol sometimes went to sleep while the verbal battles raged around her head. But the discussions always seemed to end with general agreement as to the most pressing topics for analysis in the next issue. Even more surprising, the analyses were actually prepared and appeared in print — the next month.

And somehow, before she fell asleep, Carol had offered an apartment at West Twenty-second Street to someone like Jerome Hellerstein, who had hinted to someone that he might be getting married soon. (He and his wife moved in and stayed for two years.)

Nathan Greene knew how Carol worked by this time: "She made you feel that unless you took the case or wrote the brief, the guy would be deported and maybe killed in his home country. Once you grudgingly committed yourself, you got interested in the legal problems themselves and they kept you going and doing the best you could. I'm a lazy guy myself, but I really worked on cases Carol got me into."

Her gift for flattery was coupled with a startling command of invective that she picked up from her clients, especially the seamen. She always swore with good nature about her opponents, but toward her colleagues and intimate friends she could be genuinely abusive. None of this invective was spontaneous. Her associates came to recognize that both methods were calculated to achieve a specific result from a specific person based on her keen sensitivity to the moods and feelings of others.

Occasionally the sheer pressure of work dictated her conduct, which somehow had the same affirmative result as her invective. That's how she had recruited Hellerstein in 1933, he recalled. He had written the case notes on labor law for the *Harvard Law Review* as a student, and when he started practicing in New York he missed the excitement of writing for publication. When he heard about the *IJA Bulletin* and its work on labor law, he naturally went to see Carol King. He never forgot the picture: a woman sitting at a desk piled high with law books, hair sticking out from her head, busy on the Scottsboro case. The cigarette in her mouth was scattering ashes down the front of her blouse. The only tidy things he noticed in the room were the excellent modern paintings on the walls.

Mrs. King scarcely bothered to look up when he introduced himself. She just said, "I'm very busy now. Here, write your name on this sheet of paper. I'll get in touch with you later." He thought she would probably lose the paper, but she called him finally, and within a few months Hellerstein was chairman of the legal research committee of the IJA. This committee provided its services to attorneys all over the country who faced novel legal problems in the deepening depression.

As Carol worked on political questions and the proper legal response, Jay was working on the same questions and the best artistic response. Both were deeply internationalists, one just back from a brief stay in the Soviet Union, the other determined to spend three years there as soon as he could. And both were deeply concerned about events in Europe, especially in Germany, which cast a constant shadow over their work in the United States. At the time of the November 1932 presidential elections in this country, Germany was in the midst of a strike wave supported by the German Communist Party and others against wage cuts and the rise of fascism. The Nazi Party opposed the strike. In January 1933 President

Von Hindenburg appointed Adolf Hitler chancellor of Germany. On February 27, before elections to the Reichstag (parliament), the Reichstag building was destroyed by fire. The government arrested Georgi Dimitroff and three other Bulgarian Communists for arson. The defendants pleaded not guilty; the German Communist Party denounced the frame-up and polled nearly 5,000,000 votes on March 5. But the successful Nazi Party soon forced the CP underground.

A few days later, Carol was informed of the arrest of Dr. Alfred Apfel, secretary of the International Juridical Association, whom she had met in Germany two years before. She sent a telegram to the German ambassador to the United States protesting the arrest. She admitted civil liberties violations in this country, "BUT AS YET NONE OF OUR ATTORNEYS HAVE BEEN ARRESTED BECAUSE OF THE DEFENSE OF MINORITY GROUPS." The German ambassador did not answer the wire.

Later that month, Carol received word that Dr. Apfel had made an unsuccessful attempt at suicide. Still later it was reported that he had died in jail, apparently as the result of torture.

In June the ILD received a telegram from an attorney in Germany stating that German lawyers were told they would be arrested if they defended Dimitroff and his co-defendants. The German lawyer asked the ILD to find a U.S. attorney who would come to defend the three, even though the German government would not provide a copy of the official charges or grant counsel permission to confer with the defendants.

The ILD asked the IJA for help. Carol King issued a press release protesting this challenge to the right to counsel and the right of German attorneys to represent whomever they saw fit, and then set about finding a lawyer to undertake this assignment. She selected Leo Gallagher, recently fired from Southwestern University Law School by a dean who said he had no room "for attorneys who defend the rights of political minorities." Gallagher had just won nominal damages against Los Angeles police officers for sending him to a hospital after they broke up a meeting and banquet of the Workers' United Front Election Campaign Committee. This experience, and his fighting Irish heritage, seemed to qualify him to undertake to represent a client under the most difficult circumstances. Gallagher was to keep the IJA informed of developments.

Carol and Jay talked often about the future, their future, and his future. He proposed marriage; Carol said no, but "If I ever love anyone again I think it will be you."

Time rushed by. It was late summer. Finally it was the day for Jay to leave for Moscow, with a short stop in England en route, where he would stay with some friends of Carol's. Carol started writing to Jay almost as soon as he got on the ocean liner. She wrote about her work and Jonathan, and more about her work.

> We had a swell time in the Pa. Station Sunday looking at all the exhibits and finally going down to the trains. The engineer of the Broadway Limited took Jonathan aboard the engine. He nearly burst.
> Saved this for you tho Jonathan isn't a daughter. [Enclosing a piece from the New York Times Book Review, "Should a Woman Let Herself Fall in Love with a Younger Man?" by popular novelist Kathleen Norris, who began her piece: "Lee Fargo had forgotten what it meant to be a woman, lovely, desired and desiring, till a man ten years younger, reminded her. Then came the question, does age make a difference in love?"]

A few days later Carol alluded very indirectly to her continuing concern that Jonathan was slow to learn to read and that one "expert" had cautioned about his ability to learn.

> Sunday, Sept. 24 [1933]
> I happened in connection with a tale I was telling to ask J. K. if he was glad he was born or sorry. "Sometimes one, sometimes the other," the young man replied. "I'm sorry when I'm mad at myself and unhappy." "And when you're happy?" the old lady inquired. "Then I don't think of it." That's my notion of articulate.

Finally Carol wrote a real letter to Jay.

> Sunday evening
> I feel very good tonight, Jay, to use a phrase of your own, and perhaps for that reason I have more courage about writing to you. . . .
> It's as if a great weight had lifted — For months now I've been feeling responsible for us and what

*came of it. Now suddenly I feel easy and ready for
whatever does come.*

*One of the worst things about my being older is
that I feel as if I ought to take all the
responsibility and I hate that. It was one of the
reasons I really felt comfortable and content after
you went away. It was like a vacation.*

*If you come back I'm not going to quarrel with
you any more about whom the home is run around but
I am going to be a lot more on my own. I want to be
alone more and go out alone more. And when we're
together I want to be more together. I want
everything to be more so. And I hope to hell we
aren't worried about money or careers or what not.
I want to have a good time. I love life, and I want
you to a lot more. I feel like a kid mostly wanting
someone to play with, and instead of that we get
all wound up inside and are sensitive and solemn.
Why don't you like to do nothing more?*

*And probably the next three years in the Soviet
Union will make you more your way. . . . If you
come back without drinking the cup dry as it were I
shall be terribly disappointed. Little things are
going to be frightfully discouraging but you
mustn't let go the main thing. One of your biggest
difficulties with life is just going to pieces over
the obstacles that interfere instead of somehow
climbing under, over, or around them. . . . Almost
everyone I know or ever cared about was a
frustrated personality, and if you manage to
conquer your problem it will give me a great sense
of release. . . . You must win out — learn what you
need to learn, get a chance to use every bit of
yourself. Then if we both feel as I do tonight
you'll come home and we'll get married, have a kid
and everybody live happy ever after.*

Meanwhile my salutations from afar.

Me

Soon Carol wrote in a different vein.

Oct. 17 [1933]

. . . I waited [for a letter and] *I had somehow
come to feel that you were slipping away — Then you
come back with a jolt. I don't quite know what to
do with the idea of you because for you in the
flesh right now I wouldn't have time or energy. And*

*so I am all mixed up. It is so pleasant to adjust
to no one and yet way deep down I know that I can't
live forever preoccupied with the I.J.A. and the
office. But just now there isn't enough of me left
for anything else. I vaguely wonder sometimes if I
shall ever go to bed with anything but an idea
again.*

*. . . Jonathan is gradually learning to read tho
his resistance to formal education remains
powerful. His hair is cut off short and he has even
greater self assurance.*

In a later letter, Carol acted as scribe for her son, sending his news —
that they had been to the rodeo — and "Hope I meet you some day again."
For herself, she wrote

*Sat. & Sun. Oct 21-22, [1933]
. . . My own life has always been just a little too
complicated for comfort. I want it to be easier and
more peaceful at home so that I'll have more fight
left in the rest of it. . . . I want big things to
stay important and the others to sink into
insignificance. . . . Of course no one lives his
life ideally but the horrid thing is to lose even
the dream in the everyday complications. And one of
my great hopes has always been to make every day
satisfactory, not without its own beauties and
pleasures. In other words I still have absurd
illusions and I can't reconcile myself to giving
them up. Which is of course one of the reasons you
like me.*

*Your letters have brought you insistently back
into my life. It is pleasant to feel that some one,
even if it's half across the globe, gives a dam
about you. I had come to be reconciled to being
utterly alone but it's warmer not to be even if
more disturbing in some ways.*

She explained, "Except for the I.J.A. the office is still dead and no
prospects of decent business ahead. The 'new deal' hasn't hit S.B. & K."
Isaac had four months of not even making expenses. "It makes him jumpy
with no prospects ahead." Her solution? Borrowing $2,000 from a friend,
"a crazy idea but I couldn't see any other solution. . . . It was one of my
best ventures in high finance."

She concluded, "Your letters haven't been exactly suitable for loud reading," which was awkward because many friends had asked to hear them. "Isn't it swell about recognition [of the Soviet Union by the United States]! It's 6:30 a.m. & still I love you."

Carol King's letters bring to life the daily activities, worries, and busyness of radical lawyers in the United States during the Depression.

Friday afternoon
Oct. 27, [1933]
Dear Jay,
   The formality is due to the fact that I am
sitting in [my brother] Louis's law office, in a
spotless walnut desk chair with my foot on his
spotless walnut desk. I have been helping him on a
small job, and he being a busy and important lawyer
has left the place to me while papers are being
typed and until witnesses come back to sign them.
It is incredibly different from our place, so much
more formidable and all sorts of people to carry
chairs, answer bills, etc.
   . . . Life has been hectic in the extreme.
Stupidly enough Doris & I let the Am. Com. for the
Defence of the Victims of German Fascism use the
apt for a party Sat night — God what confusion.
Doris wasn't able to move back till today. Jonathan
and I spent the week-end with Sophie — the only
pleasant spot in the immediate past. Sunday
afternoon — after sunning myself in the Park all
morning & clearing the channel of one of the
streams so J. K.'s boats could take the rapids well
— worked at the Library (on the status of
deportable Russian aliens after recognition).
   . . . [Our] office has been in a whirl of non-
paying work. . . . I have become completely
discouraged about S.B. & K. ever working its way
out of the depression or my making ends meet by
borrowing and skimping. So today I told Joe I was
quitting and looking for a job as a clerk in some
other office. It remains to be seen if I shall find
one. But it was heart-breaking business. I don't
mind so much about Joe who is a pretty tough
specimen and somehow bobs up serene whatever comes
but I really feel terrible about Isaac. Eli is also
quitting because he has got to have more money. I
feel as if all my life was tumbling down around my
ears. S.B. & K. was such an important thing to me —

it had continued where everything else was gone.
But I can't let things drift any longer for I don't
see an end to the present situation. Even [J's]
$2,000 [loan] was immediately swallowed up by our
debts and as you know I owe . . . more beside that.
I have got to have a steady income and there's
really no reason why I should make such a fuss
about earning it — that is if I can possibly get a
job.
    Curiously enough this all came over me when and
perhaps because at the moment I am solvent. That
gave me a little perspective and I realized quite
suddenly that the present situation can't go on —
Probably just after I've reorganized some rich
relative will die and leave me a million dollars
making this all unnecessary. But I am determined to
see it through.

By November Carol wrote to Jay that Isaac "assures me, without my
having made the least attempt, that I can't possibly get a job." Then a
friend "unsettled me completely by offering to take care of the situation
financially practically indefinitely. I somehow feel I can't take her up, that
there is a moral obligation to carry my own load."

Sunday, Nov 12, [1933]
I have reached the please stage, Jay. Have you
stopped writing because I did, and now am I to
stop, and then you again. . . .
    Took the first step today with reference to a
job, or rather the second. The first step was
getting some presentable clothes. You really
wouldn't know me with three new dresses in a week —
and gloves. Attired in a red silk dress, a felt hat
to match and the gloves, I was marched by Max
Lowenthal to see the "right man." I'd rather not go
into details until there is something definite to
tell — Suffice it to say that you will probably be
no end disgusted with me for "selling out."
Whatever I do I hope I won't befuddle myself into
believing in a lot of nonsense.
    There are so many things I want to talk to you
about and you seem suddenly to have disappeared.
What I want most is a friendly shoulder to cry on.
After that I think I'd feel a lot better. But what
good is a shoulder in Moscow, and especially when
it doesn't even drive a pen.

> . . . *It's good to have the decision about the*
> *office behind me. I feel already as if I was free*
> *from the worry of it. I have opened negotiations*
> *for the sale of the library. . . . I am lazy and*
> *now I'm letting myself be, because it was all too*
> *complicated.*

Carol started her Christmas letter to Jay describing how the day went without him.

> *Dec. 26* [1933]
> *Christmas is over, Jay, and I missed you incredibly*
> *in connection with it. It wasn't as much fun*
> *filling Jonathan's stocking and Adelaide and Peggy*
> *didn't make up for you. But Jonathan has the idea*
> *much more and went in heavily for getting me gifts,*
> *filling my stocking, etc. All in all tho a pleasant*
> *time was had by all.*

This letter then turned into a remarkable parallel to a passage Gordon King had written a decade earlier in his novel *Horatio's Story*, about a husband/wife two-career relationship.

> *You know I think you took an unfair advantage by*
> *going away. I can endow my fictitious picture of*
> *you with all the virtues. My imaginings are always*
> *realer to me than reality, and now that you have*
> *indicated a definite intention of returning to my*
> *heart and hearth I allow myself the luxury of*
> *dreaming all kinds of impossible dreams about you.*
> *The real you is bound to be a disappointment. You*
> *will continue to come home late to supper so that*
> *when I am played out with work and one supper for*
> *Jonathan there will have to be another for you.*
> *Then when I want to sleep you will want to work in*
> *my room. But most of all when I want to talk, to*
> *pour out all that is in me, you will be preoccupied*
> *with study or work of some sort.*
>   *Why can I never reconcile myself to reality but*
> *always dream glowingly? I meant to give you a quote*
> *from Lincoln Steffens Autobiography in my last*
> [reading about himself in his wife's diary after
> her death:] *"The fact that I was the husband did*
> *not hinder me from seeing what an ass a 'good*
> *husband' is in the eyes of an intelligent wife who*
> *is thinking of him, who is thinking always of graft*

or business or — something else; who is always at
hand but never at home."
    I think most women feel that. They want to build
a relationship which takes time and patience beside
a depth of emotion. Most men have the emotion but
are preoccupied with their profession or something
of the sort. I was really scared when you suggested
that I was to prevent your wasting spare time. From
my point of view you waste far too little time.
Real mellowness of experience and of relationship
can come only with infinite waste of time,
sometimes described as leisure. And it is so
difficult for two busy people to have that at the
same moment of the same day. Curiously enough Solon
De Leon posed the same problem to me on Sunday. He
is immensely busy, and feels his wife's loneliness,
her disappointment that he should always work when
she wants his company and his time. What, he asked,
is the solution? I said intensity of emotion and
experience but he wondered if he had the capacity
for that. . . .
    I want everything all at once, which I know to be
outrageous but knowing that doesn't make me feel a
bit different. I want the freedom of your being in
the Soviet Union and the closeness of your hands
upon my skin. I even want to write on endlessly and
yet go to sleep because I am so tired. And I'm
going to sleep. I've said too much. I always want
to tell you just everything — and then not to have
said it at all. . . . Good night, my man-boy from
whom I demand all love, all work, all understanding.

    I don't dare to read what I wrote some days ago
lest I tear it up.

During her days at the office, Carol was called on for help more often
than ever. Abe Isserman was an early and frequent recipient of help from
his "IJA friends in New York." A young worker from Belgium, he came
to this country and skipped college in his haste to become a lawyer. Now
he was active in the civil liberties and labor union struggles in Jersey City;
in the textile, garment, shipbuilding, and electrical industries, and in a
long, drawn-out farm workers strike at the Seabrook Farms in Bridgeton,
New Jersey. When a flurry of arrests erupted, Isserman simply could not

do justice to clients in both areas at the same time. He called Mrs. King for help.

She immediately got on the phone to a number of New York lawyers who knew something about the emerging labor law or were willing to find out about it, and she called Columbia law student Howard Meyer. They all had a deep sense of the terrific suffering that was all around them, and a wonderful optimism: "If we work hard enough, we can change things!" They lived two lives: "One worked during the day at one's job, and then one pitched into the things that seemed most important at night. There was no such thing as hours," Justine Wise Polier remembers. "Carol was one of the people who represented that approach all through her life; but there were others as well, like Nathan Greene."

This time Carol convinced several lawyers to do "the paper work" Isserman needed so he could operate "in the field." From their Manhattan law libraries they cranked out complaints and briefs raising the hottest issues being argued anywhere in the country. They forwarded these to Isserman with advice on the best strategy to follow, delighted to have their research put to immediate use in trial. With this kind of backup, Abe Isserman could walk into a New Jersey court with perfect confidence and a good chance to win — if not there, then on appeal.

As Carol went job hunting, she wrote Jay about one side effect if she were successful:

> Of course that will mean no more I.J.A., or at any
> rate very little more to do with it. No boss will
> be willing to have me spend much time on anything
> but his work. And to a degree I'm glad of that.
> I've been fearfully driven of late, no time for
> anything but work and up too late that I'm tired
> all the time. I want evenings to myself and for
> reading. The organization has profited; made
> contacts, had a better [B]ulletin and built up a
> bank balance of more than $100 dollars, but I've
> gotten the short end of it somehow. I refuse to be
> worked to death all the time and to not even have
> made expenses by the end of the month.

At the same time, the IJA had to assure its own survival, as Sol discovered after Carol recruited him to serve as treasurer. In 1933 the IJA spent $600 on all its activities. Shorr, Brodsky & King (sometimes) received $10 a month for providing an office; the Jewish Social Service

Agency provided a full-time stenographer free. And the *Bulletin* conducted a never-ending subscription drive at one dollar a year for twelve
issues. The ACLU paid $100 a year for copies to distribute to its
cooperating attorneys, and the lawyers put on three social events that
raised $150. The editors listened gleefully as they read the names of new
subscribers, including some of their old law professors and judges for
whom they had clerked. There were no complimentary subscriptions to
the *Bulletin*, so when judges renewed their subscriptions year after year,
the editors could tell that they probably read the *Bulletin*.

One of the most important functions of the *Bulletin*, in King's eyes,
was the noting of all the "little" cases filed all over the country that
received no national attention. This was in addition to describing the
technical side of the big *Scottsboro* cases. She was figuring out the main
categories: labor injunctions, criminal syndicalism, academic freedom,
civil liberties, political criminal cases, rights of Negroes, rights of aliens,
and, of course, miscellaneous. The items did not come in automatically.
She clipped short articles from the *New York Times, New York Herald-
Tribune, New York Call,* the *Daily Worker,* the ACLU News, the ILD
News, the IWW News, press releases from the Socialist Party lawyers'
group, the Non-Partisan Labor Defense, the Labor Defense League, and
the National Committee for the Defense of Political Prisoners. The news
was often of judges setting bail of $3,500 for each penniless, peaceful
protestor, as in New York City, and of police officers brutally beating
peaceful hunger marchers, as in Albany. When there was no news from
certain parts of the country for a while, King would write to the lawyers
and other subscribers there, demanding information.

Carol never explained why she insisted on spending her time, month
after month, collecting "little" cases from all over the country. She always
said she was not interested in the ideologies of the people in these "little"
cases, although she was clearly intrigued by the individuals and their
idiosyncracies and passionately interested in their right to struggle for
their ideas. It had become a habit to record the facts and describe the law
accurately, first on the *Law and Freedom Bulletin,* then in collaboration
with Nelles on the contempt of court article. In fact, although she would
deny it, she was also interested in the law itself and in its development.
So she preferred the anonymous, thankless task of writing the "Recent
Items" column to the more traditional one (for men) of analyzing
appellate court opinions in two or three "big" cases in a major essay in
the *Bulletin,* or even in a traditional law review article.

```
       On November 23, 1933, in a letter addressed to Milton
Katz, Esq., Sunward, Alexandria, Virginia, an individual dictating
with the initials, I.P. stated that the International Juridical
Association in a year and a half of its existance had grown to in-
clude a number of Mrs. Katz' colleagues in Washington, including
"Jim Landis, Alger Hiss, Nat Witt, Lee Pressman, Jerome Frank,
Margaret Bennett and Moe Huberman. In fact the recovery has hit us
hard, taking Witt and Pressman who were editors of the Bulletin, Hiss
who was chairman of our research committee and Frank who was a member
of our executive committee. I can recall at least two other people
in Washington, J. Tommy Austern and Louis Jaffe. In the depleted
Harvard School, we still have Frankfurter and Feller as well as a
half dozen second and third year students." (Source unknown
                                              100-25836-41 P 5)
```

FBI File: Carol King (4-14-51). Contents of a letter from Isadore (Shad) Polier to a Virginia lawyer boasting about the lawyers working with the IJA.

The results of her work are clear. For the first time in U.S. legal history there is a record of the ebb and flow of new ideas, New Deal and revolutionary ideas, how lawyers developed them into new legal issues, and how they played in the trial courts, in local and state legislatures, in administrative agencies, and not only how they were decided later on appeal.

The *Bulletin* office kept a current index to its articles and notes in order to supply clients and lawyers with copies of briefs or articles they had mentioned. The IJAers took great pride in this service, which was provided free.

Soon the editors started writing longer analytic discussions of broader topics: the unfolding New Deal legislation; the National Industrial Recovery Act with its section 7a protecting the right to organize unions; state labor legislation; cases on the rights of Negroes; illegal activities of the police in strikes; and the status of labor and civil liberties in Germany.

The young editors and contributors talked about signing articles, following the practice of the law reviews on which they had worked at Harvard, Columbia, or Yale. But they rejected the suggestion because the articles really were cooperative efforts of an unprecedented character for lawyers who shared a common purpose, like their counterparts in the Group Theatre who rejected the star system at this time and had a common Left ideology.

Shad (Isadore) Polier sent out a mimeographed promotional letter on November 25, 1933. He boasted about a "growing recognition of the authoritative position in the labor field of the *Bulletin*" indicated by republication in extended form in the *Yale Law Journal* of one article, by citation of the *Bulletin* in several law reviews, and by requests from law review editors and attorneys for information on labor cases. In December

1933 the *Bulletin* proudly announced formation of a Chicago branch of the IJA and its first forum on the use of habeas corpus.

Lawyers, judges, and law professors from all over the country wrote letters indicating that they were waiting to see what the IJA had to say about the latest legislation and Supreme Court opinions on labor and civil rights; what did the editors think would develop from this new law?

Carol kept working on the *IJA Bulletin,* on nonpaying cases, and on trying to get a paying job as the winter passed. Suddenly it was spring and she wrote to Jay:

```
Friday evening, April 6 [1934]
. . . I feel as if I kept writing and writing but
never saying what I really felt. I don't even know
how I feel except that I am lonely and want to feel
warm and close. But I am getting so used to not
feeling that I wonder if I'll ever be able to break
down the barriers I have unconsciously been
erecting. This winter has been utterly selfish,
everything has been run around me — my needs have
been met — You want and need different things and
I'm getting out of the habit of making adjustments.
If you are coming back don't stay gone too long or
you will find me much more difficult and set. Maybe
you'll like it better if we each go our own way. I
know that I want to love you utterly and completely
and that mostly I have respected and liked you, and
felt that we understood one another. But lately you
have been slipping away, so that I can't find you,
the you I have lain before the fire with. . . . I am
suddenly afraid of you, of us, of love itself. . . .
```

In early May, Carol wrote to Jay that she had been hired by a "down town lawyer" who was fussing "about nobody having the right to defame Jews" as the Silver Shirts (new fascists) had been doing in their publication that had recently gone into bankruptcy. This decision led Carol "to plunge [into] Jefferson's complete works," and more. "My room is piled high with books — desk, table, book case and children's books, novels, politics, etc. I wonder if I'm actually going to take to reading again."

She wrote on:

I want to laugh with you and cry with you and lie
with you and always I feel that I shouldn't as if
it were wrong, just as I feel now that writing to
you this way is wrong. My conscience, that curious
relic of Christianity in my pagan life, brings me
up short and forces me to play a part.

And so just tonight let me send all my love, but
don't expect it tomorrow morning when I may put the
breaks [sic] on again.

The mail from Moscow was slow. Finally Carol received the letter she
had been expecting. She answered it the same day.

May 19 [1934]
Your letter this morning was a relief, Jay. I felt
very much like the time when I came back from
Harlan, Kentucky with the mumps and fought the
thing and fought the thing until it was finally and
definitely proclaimed mumps. It was delightfully
comforting then to take to my bed as it is now to
know just where I'm at. I know it annoys you but my
knowledge of human nature told me from the very
beginning that this was bound to happen. Thank God
you never persuaded me to marry you so that there
were all sorts of legal and other complications as
well. My snap judgment is that the only steps I
shall take now is to stop your telephone listing
and take your name off the door. As your attorney
in New York I shall be glad to take care of loose
ends that need attention and can't be managed at
long distance.

It will take me a while to reorganize life but as
a sensible human being I can't help but see that
this is the best solution all round. You and I
really never were a well adjusted permanent
arrangement. . . . What we had — and it was a lot —
nobody can take from us. It's just good that we
didn't mess up each other's lives getting it.

. . . I think you should write Jonathan, not nec-
essarily about this but in general. Eventually,
when it is less fresh, I shall tell him as I think
he is entitled to the truth, nor do I find that I
can blame you in the least for what you did. Your
only mistake was in not knowing yourself well
enough.

I am up to my ears on the Scottsboro case and
shouldn't even have taken this much time off. I

```
will write you the news some other time. Here's
luck —
                                            Carol.
```

⁊⧳

Carol King, of the now defunct firm of Shorr, Brodsky & King, did not take a job with another lawyer or firm. She managed, somehow, to become a sole practitioner, staying in the same office and sharing what was left of the library with Isaac and Joe.

And she managed to invite new people over for dinner during the week, for a long lunch on Saturday, for Sunday brunch now that she was alone a second time and Gordon's death was further behind her. She had a lively interest in the affairs of people she liked, and she liked almost everyone she met. When she risked a large party, people who considered themselves her close friends met large numbers of other people who also considered themselves her intimates: artists, businessmen, neighbors, lawyers, and politicians. In introducing friends from two worlds, Carol had a knack for mentioning some personal quality the two might have in common, or some issue on which they could have a good fight.

There were certainly plenty of issues to fight about in the spring of 1934, as the long Depression hit more and more people at deeper and deeper levels. Carol wrote to a friend that she was bothered about what would become of Jonathan "this summer as Maine has been given up for financial and other reasons. Poor kid, I haven't told him yet because I don't know how to, he's looking forward to it so."

As the middle class gave up its summer places, the upper class openly attacked workers fighting for their rights, their jobs, and their lives. On July 5, 1934, the shipping companies in San Francisco convinced the authorities to break the long longshoremen's strike. By night 400 men were wounded and two were left to die. On Monday, July 9, 40,000 people walked in the funeral procession on Market Street. A general strike was called for July 16; it was successful, and the longshoremen ultimately won their basic demands.

⁊⧳

```
[undated July 1934]
I have vaguely waited, Jay, to hear further from
you, but apparently you have nothing further to say.
```

To Bury Their Murdered Dead. Funeral procession down Market Street in San Francisco for two workers killed by the National Guard during the San Francisco longshore strike, leading to the general strike in 1934. By Bits Hayden in *The Big Strike* by Mike Quin. Olema, California: Olema Publishing Co. 1949, front matter.

I have a few things which I want to say, but unless
you want to answer, this will be all.

In the first place I wanted to send you the two
enclosed clippings which I thought you would like
to see. . . .

By the way I came home last Sunday evening at
eight or a little after with Jonathan. Jim
Hendrickson was sitting in the fading light looking
over your art books or whatever you want to call
them. Later Jonathan said, "I thought it was Jay."
Curiously enough for an instant I had the same
illusion. Jim . . . is to be in New York next
winter so I am being very cautious. I had to tell
him to leave at midnight as I had a big day Monday.

I hope you are properly proud of the fact that
the rest of this yellow pad is being used for the
Herndon case. We are swamped with work —
Scottsboro, Herndon, the repression of all labor
activity in New Jersey, etc. etc. The night of July
4 Leo Herwitz phoned me that the police insisted on
arresting pickets of the Film & Photo [League] in
front of Proctors on 23rd Street who were
distributing leaflets calling attention to the fact
of its being a pro war movie. I came over and
finally talked the cops out of it.

Just one thing more. I want you to know, Jay,
that I believe in you. I hope the film in Siberia
is going well and that somehow you're getting
started really making the kind of movies you care
about. . . . I still expect great things of you as
a movie man and wonder when I'll see your work on
the screen over here. That sounds completely trite
and like your Dayton family but I mean it. Jay
Leyda is an artist. He must give the world
something.

Carol referred to Jay's new girl, Sylvia/Si-Lan Chen, a Chinese dancer
whom he had met through her sister, another camera student at the Film
School.

Don't let any confusions in your personal life
interfere with this your main purpose. But perhaps
everything is smoother now, although it must be
difficult having Sylvia half across Russia and
yourself being a person with your roots in the
United States and not in the Soviet Union. But
remember you must come thru. . . . Also, and as

*long as I am saying "good-bye" I want to say again
that I'm not sorry for our life together, that what
we got will always seem to me important and worth
while and that you go with my blessing.*

*Everything good come to you both. If you feel
like it tell Sylvia from me that she has my very
best wishes and somehow my warm affection because
she is Jay's girl. . . .*

                                                        Carol

Carol wrote one more letter (which Jay and his wife saved for fifty
years until, at his death, all her letters to them became part of the Jay
Leyda Collection at Tamiment Institute).

Sept. 3 [1934]
Dear Sylvia,

*I was very glad indeed to get your letter but it
was not until now during a week-end in the country
with the Lowenthals . . . that I have really had a
chance to answer it.*

*First of all I want to say that I don't hold you
in any way responsible for what happened between
Jay and me which I regard as inevitable, not only
from his point of view but from mine. I was fond of
Jay and respected him but I don't believe I ever
loved him as you do. I am left lonely now, but that
is rather through the death of my husband than
Jay's desertion. My great love affair was not with
Jay, which was one thing that made for
difficulties. He made life full and vivid again but
my big romance was not connected with him. I say
this to you rather than to him. . . .*

*[A paragraph of suggestions on how/where Sylvia
could work in the United States in answer to her
query, concluding:] If you ever feel like writing
again I shall be glad to hear from you. Jay has
apparently decided to put a complete stop to our
correspondence, and perhaps he is right. When an
intense situation is finished the friendly warmth
that succeeds it may be a bit pale and
insubstantial — not quite worth bothering about. I
too hope that you and I may meet. With all our
differences we must have much in common. May I in
all sincerity offer you my friendship?*

                                                    Carol King

꿎

Carol King continued recruiting lawyers to do writing and research for the IJA. The IJA Research Committee reported that its thirty lawyers did a prodigious amount of work on many topics in 1934 for groups in nine states from Alabama to Michigan and Nebraska to New Mexico. Columbia law students collected material and IJAers wrote the text for a "readable manual" on civil rights for the ACLU. Columbia law professor Herbert Wechsler prepared a memo showing that the conduct of Governor James Rolph of California and his statement concerning lynchings had encouraged mob murders of two supporters of the Cannery and Agricultural Workers Industrial Union; these acts should subject him to impeachment. The IJA sent material to Bernard Ades to help him in the disbarment proceedings growing out of his unsuccessful representation of Euel Lee (Orphan Jones) for the ILD. Four lawyers prepared a brief on the right of New York City College students to a public disciplinary hearing for participating in anti-war demonstrations.

King maintained that she didn't know any law except deportation and contempt. On all other legal matters she claimed to be illiterate and in desperate need of someone's help. That is how she recruited a bright young lawyer named Leo Linder to become an expert on the emerging Social Security legislation. Soon she was telling people about Linder's expertise; colleagues turned to him for answers, and he indeed turned into a lifelong expert.

Justine Wise Tulin made her entry into IJA affairs by a circuitous route that was typical for the IJA. She had gone to the front lines for workers' rights, commuting from Yale Law School to help the textile workers on strike in Passaic, New Jersey, during her second year, along with Bertha Paret (who soon married Tom Emerson, also at Yale Law). This action led to a reprimand of Ms. Tulin from the president of the college, and created problems when she faced the character committee of the Connecticut Bar Association. It took letters of support from two of her father's friends (Chief Justice Taft and Judge Benjamin Cardozo) to overcome the political and very anti-Semitic bias of the committee members, she said later. Then she could not get a place in a New York law firm as a woman unless she agreed to work in a back room on wills and never see a client. These personal experiences confirmed her view of the state of human rights and her commitment to working people.

Tulin's husband, a young law professor at Columbia, had died in 1933. The young widowed mother had a rather rough year and decided to take two months off and go to the Soviet Union. On the tour, she met Henry Shapiro, the lawyer-journalist who had befriended King a few years before on her trip to the Soviet Union. Shapiro told Tulin about the IJA and suggested that on her return she get in touch with the American Section headed by Carol Weiss King.

When Tulin called, Mrs. King invited her to a meeting that night. "I went down and there was this small group in her room," Tulin recalled later, "and behind a little square card table was one Shad Polier, who was running the meeting. At the end of the session, he assigned jobs and he assigned me the subject of Brooklyn, the Injunction Reno. Carol was much amused, I learned later, when she saw him take my briefcase and start walking home with me."

Carol wrote to a friend:

> I feel as tho I had found a new person who, unless
> I am very much mistaken, will some day be a friend.
> Such an experience always excites me. It's like
> life pouring over you. And then our situations, or
> rather what we have lived thru, is very much alike.
> . . . So many problems are the same and both of us
> know it tho we haven't said a word about it.

Carol King's many personal friendships helped solidify the IJA–American Section. One summer she decided to combine business with pleasure when Abe Isserman of New Jersey said he had to go to Poland, New York, to try to get the Consumers Union to support a milk strike against the milk company monopoly. Carol and Joe Kovner joined Abe and his girlfriend on the trip. After his speech, Carol announced they were all going to her family's place in Maine, which she hadn't visited in some years. When they got off the steamboat near Lorac Lodge, Carol said, "Let's take a swim!" and quickly stripped off all her clothes and went skinny-dipping. The others followed suit.

On a much more formal level, in 1935 Charles H. Houston, dean of American Negro lawyers, joined the IJA executive committee and soon sent out a letter to "Fellow Members of the National Bar Association and Friends," praising the accurate and unbiased accounts of Negro cases in the *Bulletin* and suggesting that members of the association subscribe.

Nuddy Greene said the editors had committed themselves to try "to understand the day by day and month by month movements in freedom's tide, and to convey this understanding to others." Filing lawsuits and defending clients, the IJA lawyers developed "faith that . . . the masses of our people" care deeply about "human freedom." As editors, they discovered that exposés of rights violations often led to anger and popular action. They supported the organized labor movement and believed in its potential for social progress. Nuddy and some of the others had picked up their approach in the unlikely halls of Harvard and other Ivy League schools from an occasional, inspired Marxist professor, and from the daily news of unemployment rates and industrial strikes.

The IJA recruiting system remained informal and highly successful. When Walter Pollak's small office hired young Samuel Silverman to help on a big case, this led to an invitation to a New Year's Eve party at Pollak's home on Riverside Drive, where Silverman noticed a striking-looking woman. He made a smart crack; Carol King immediately introduced herself and took him up on it, and their conversation was launched. He found her colorful and a little bit belligerent. She certainly loved to upset the establishment, the people she delighted in labeling "the bourgeoisie." Soon Shad asked Silverman to do an article for the *Bulletin* on using the anti-riot act in labor disputes, and Silverman agreed. After that, one thing led to another.

Carol King loved and needed the warmth of the IJA and the panache with which it conducted its affairs. She was developing her own style as an individual, which soon led her back to the defense of the *Scottsboro* defendants.

13.
Saving the "Scottsboro Boys"

The U.S. Post Office informed the ILD that envelopes bearing "Save the Scottsboro Boys" stamps "on the front or back" would be treated as unmailable in March 1933. It was four months after the historic decision by the United States Supreme Court reversing the convictions at Scottsboro.

The state of Alabama tried Haywood Patterson again. The local judge granted a defense motion to transfer the trial to nearby Decatur because it would be impossible to select an impartial jury of twelve in Scottsboro. On retrial Samuel Leibowitz, famous New York trial lawyer, joined Chamlee of Tennessee and Brodsky and Schwarzbart of the New York ILD for the defense, with Carol King continuing "to sort of hold the fort in New York," Schwarzbart said, sending "short briefs" on the admissibility of various pieces of evidence on call. She apparently stayed out of the political in-fighting that marked the defense of this, and other, major cases.

By this time, Joe Brodsky told the story of what happened in March 1931 in graphic prose:

> . . . nine Negro lads, ranging in age from twelve to nineteen years, were riding a freight. Some southern white boys on the same train, seeking to invoke the law of jim-crowism, sought to force some of [them] to jump off . . . ; the Negro boys resisted, and won the fight that ensued. The defeated white boys complained to the telegrapher at the station at Paint Rock, and he telegraphed ahead to Scottsboro. There an armed posse stopped the train and combed it[, netting] the nine Negro lads, two white boys, and two white girls. . . . A grand jury was immediately called; rape indictments were found against all the Negro boys on the complaint of the two girls — Victoria Price and Ruby Bates.

Now one of the "two young white women victims" recanted her previous testimony and testified that she had not been raped by the defendant.

Nonetheless, the jury convicted Haywood Patterson for the second time. He was sentenced to death for the second time. But now the trial judge granted the defense motion to set aside the verdict on the ground that it was contrary to the evidence, becoming the second Southern judge to find the courage to face the fact that the Scottsboro defendants had not been fairly tried and convicted.

In August 1933, near Tuscaloosa, Alabama, a judge forbade ILD lawyers Irvin Schwab, Allan Taub, and Frank Irwin to see their clients, Dan Pippen and A. T. Harden, two Negro youths charged with the murder of a white woman. Judge Henry Foster said he didn't want another *Scottsboro* case or the "nigger on the jury question raised." After the militia "spirit[ed]" the lawyers away, white men in a mob took the prisoners from a sheriff's auto and lynched them. The *IJA Bulletin* reported this incident as "Nullification — 1933."

One of the earliest memories of many African Americans is helping their parents collect money "to save the Scottsboro Boys." What was happening at the other end of the spectrum has not been described as often or succinctly. John Caughlan remembers the Christmas holidays at Harvard Law School in 1933 when he invited a student friend from Alabama to have dinner with him and his wife. The Alabaman came from a family with a large plantation but very little cash during the Depression, not enough money to go home for Christmas.

Late in the afternoon after a pleasant dinner, to make conversation John's wife asked their guest, 'What do you think about the *Scottsboro* case?' Sally and John were not active in any political group and had no strong political feelings or understanding at this point. This simply seemed a natural question to ask of someone about a case arising in his state.

Winnie answered, 'Well, they should be hanged.'

Sally asked, 'You think they are guilty?'

Winnie replied, 'You simply don't understand the situation. It is irrelevant whether they are guilty. You know, on the plantation I live on there are three white families and five hundred niggers. If we didn't have

Stop the Murder of the Scottsboro Boys! Full-page plea in dramatic red and black ink. By Hof in *The Labor Defender,* July 1932.

a lynching every now and then, we wouldn't dare go to bed at night. We would be too frightened.'

John remembers that neither he nor his wife had the courage, understanding, or knowledge to do anything about this answer at the time, except to remember it.

In late 1933 Alabama tried Haywood Patterson and Clarence Norris for the third time. After their third conviction, the defense had to submit to the court a printed copy of the record on appeal within ten days. And under Alabama law, all of the testimony had to be paraphrased into narrative form. Eli Schwarzbart could not face this deadline alone. He quickly figured out that his only hope was to ask Carol King to help. She agreed. Leaving Jonathan with Mrs. Barkley for whatever time it took, she literally moved into the office of the printer, smiling sweetly at him and acting as if this were a common procedure. She calmly set up shop with typewriters and secretaries to work on the record, as Eli assembled it and rushed it to her by taxi from the offices of the numerous lawyers who had been working on pieces of it.

From Friday night until Monday morning they worked without interruption, except to gulp down sandwiches and coffee. The presses were running night and day; the copy had to keep up with them. Others came to assist from time to time and the marathon was run. On Monday morning the printed record of more than 1,500 pages was ready to airmail to Alabama, and Carol went home to sleep it off. But all that work did not win the case; it only got them into the appeals court, which, predictably, affirmed the convictions and held that the motion for new trial was filed late in the *Patterson* case so that the court had lost jurisdiction of his appeal.

The defendants appealed to the U.S. Supreme Court a second time. Walter H. Pollak, Carl Stern, and Osmond K. Fraenkel, another ACLU lawyer, were on the brief. They were under a terrible time-bind, so Carl called on Carol and they ended up at the printer again. She finished proofreading the brief and called to the attention of her brother-in-law small points that required last-minute decisions.

The Supreme Court agreed to hear the case, and in February 1935 Pollak argued for defendants Patterson and Norris, retained by the ILD; Samuel Leibowitz argued for Norris on retainer from him. The large question they raised was the exclusion of Negroes from the juries in both cases. But first they had to get over the narrow, procedural question of the alleged lateness of the filing of the exceptions in Patterson's case. Did the time limit run from December 6, 1933, when the defendant was sentenced, or from December 1, 1933, when the judgment was entered? On April 1, 1935, the Supreme Court handed down its opinions in both cases, written by Chief Justice Hughes. Now, writing for a unanimous court (8–0), he got right to the basic question of exclusion of Negroes from the jury. This was the issue the Supreme Court had refused to hear in the case of Orphan Jones, sending that Black man to his death in 1933. Now the Court made an independent study of the defense's claims that the names of Negroes eligible for jury duty, "and who had courageously stated that they would be willing to serve if called, had been forged on the jury rolls, long after the jury lists had been drawn and filled."

The Court reproduced the testimony of one jury commissioner on the statutory requirements for jury duty: "I do not know of any negro [sic] in Morgan County" over twenty-one "generally reputed to be honest and intelligent" and "esteemed in the community" who is "not an habitual drunkard," afflicted "with a permanent disease . . . which would render him unfit" to serve "and who can read English, and who had never been convicted of a crime involving moral turpitude."

The Court found that, for a generation or longer, no Negro had been called for service on any jury in the county, although the defendants presented evidence that there were Negroes qualified for jury service whose names appeared on the preliminary list of adult male citizens but were not placed on the jury roll. This finding "established the discrimination which the Constitution forbids."

The *Scottsboro* defense exulted — they had done it again! They had saved the life of their client, and they had made another tremendous gain in the constitutional rights of all defendants claiming deliberate exclusion of Blacks from juries.

Then the Court turned to the *Patterson* case and the alleged lateness of the defense's filing of the bill of exceptions, and held that "the state court was undoubtedly at liberty, without violating any federal right," to hold that the filing was late. But Chief Justice Hughes again went beyond this state's right to find that this failure did not end the matter because of "the exceptional features of the present case," and the fact that it raised an important question under the *federal* Constitution. Therefore, the

Court vacated Patterson's conviction and sent the case back to the Alabama Supreme Court so that it could confront the "anomalous and grave situation" that would arise if it sent Patterson to his death on the basis of the narrow, technical issue of late filing of his appeal after the Court had ruled *for* Norris.

By this time Anna Damon and Limey Colman of the ILD and a great many others had made the *Scottsboro* cases big news nationally. The media gave wide coverage to every aspect of the cases, including this new ruling. It meant the end of automatic Supreme Court acceptance of convictions by all-white juries in Southern states. It proved that mass defense can win.

But it did not free any of the nine young men in *Scottsboro,* who awaited another trial. Clarence Norris explained:

> The worst feeling about being locked up was it didn't seem real. It was akin to living in a dream. Thinking that it will end in a minute. . . . From the time I was taken off that train, I was a robot. I was told what to do, when to do it and how. Most of the time I tried not to think of anything. Thinking and hearing about the pleasures people in the outside world were having was something I couldn't stand.

Everyone knew that the Supreme Court ruling did not mean the automatic seating of Negroes on any jury in the South, and certainly not in the case of the young Negro Communist Party organizer, Angelo Herndon, in Atlanta. He was charged with violating the infamous Reconstruction era Black Codes by leading a massive, peaceful, integrated demand for government assistance.

At his trial in January 1933, Herndon was represented by two Negro Atlanta lawyers, Benjamin J. Davis, Jr., and John H. Geer. Davis, a native of Atlanta, was a very recent graduate of Harvard Law School and the son of the Black Republican leader of the area. As he prepared for trial, Benjamin Davis spent many hours with Herndon, learning about Herndon's political beliefs and activities in order to present them in court effectively. Herndon said he had joined the Communist Party "believing that he had found a scientific value system to replace the outmoded Christianity of his youth."

Davis realized the nature of his task when Assistant Solicitor Hudson told the local press, "As fast as Communists come here we shall indict them, and I shall demand the death penalty in every case."

Herndon and other, older Black Communists told Davis the Communist Party was operating legally in Georgia and had even been on the ballot. Under these circumstances, Davis and Geer filed a series of motions to have the indictment against Herndon dismissed: first, because the statute was too vague and uncertain to put a person on notice as to what political conduct would be held criminal under it; second, because it was based on the 1866 Black Codes, which violated the defendant's right to free speech; third, because (citing the Supreme Court decisions in *Scotttsboro*) the jury list did not include the names of Negro residents.

The judge denied each motion and opened the trial. During jury selection, the defense tried to question each prospective juror individually concerning their ability to try a Negro defendant without racial prejudice. The judge forbade such questions. Each group of twelve prospective white Georgia jurors then denied any bias against Blacks.

Solicitor Hudson told the jury, "This is not only a trial of Herndon, but of Lenin, Stalin, Trotsky and Kerensky." He introduced the state's only evidence against Herndon: the literature the police had seized from Herndon's room, admittedly illegally: *The Party Organizer* and *The Daily Worker,* published by the Communist Party; *The Liberator;* a book by Episcopal Bishop William Montgomery Brown, *Christianity and Communism,* and George Padmore's *Life and Struggles of the Negro Toilers.*

The case of Angelo Herndon was Ben Davis's first lesson in mass defense, and he wrote later that mass defense was "distinct from the reformist methods used by the NAACP, whose leaders saw the legal defense as the be-all and end-all of every struggle." They "would have 'defended' Herndon as an isolated individual victimized by the excesses of an otherwise sound capitalist order, thus objectively sustaining the lynch system of national oppression" and ignoring participation in the defense. Instead, the defense promulgated "a working class defense policy in the deep South," presenting the Herndon case as "an out-and-out frame-up that should never have been brought to trial" because the charge contravened the basic right of free speech and free assembly. The ILD saw the *Herndon* case "as an extension of the class struggle into the judicial arena and it sought to unmask the brutal nature of that struggle in all its dimensions."

To carry out this strategy, Davis tried to call as defense witnesses two white economists of standing, one from Emory University, to prove that the documents seized from Herndon did not violate the state statute. The prosecution asked one economist whether he would like his daughter to marry a Negro, then challenged the qualifications of both men as experts. The judge ruled they could not testify.

Finally Herndon took the stand. In a dramatic speech he told the jury and spectators, "No matter what you do with Angelo Herndon, [or] with the Angelo Herndons in the future this question of unemployment, the question of unity between Negro and white workers cannot be solved with hands that are stained with the blood of an innocent individual. . . . The present [capitalist] system . . . is on the verge of collapse."

Judge Wyatt quickly charged the jury to convict if it appeared "clearly by the evidence that immediate serious violence against the state of Georgia was to be expected or advocated" by the defendant. The jury voted Guilty and recommended mercy. The sentence was eighteen to twenty years. Judge Wyatt denied the defense motions for a new trial and for Herndon's release on bail pending further proceedings.

By this time, Ben Davis, defense lawyer, had become convinced that his client's political opinions were sound. He joined the Communist Party but delayed the announcement until a more auspicious moment. Right now he had to prepare the brief for the appeal to the state supreme court. "For about ten days I withdrew from all other activity except my law books and a mountain-high stack of paper. Geer and I completed the brief in about a week, but I felt that the case was too important to be left wholly in our inexperienced hands. I called the ILD national office and asked them for the assistance of an experienced practitioner in constitutional and civil rights cases to give our brief the once-over."

Carol and the IJA accepted the assignment and the record of the trial was turned over to an IJA member, who set to work. A few days later Carol discovered they had misunderstood the date for filing the appeal, an issue that had plagued them in the *Scottsboro* case. The deadline was imminent, and she started phoning Victor Whitehorn, the lawyer with the record.

She couldn't find him. He had just gotten married and had left on his honeymoon to Atlantic City — taking the record with him, of course, to work on in his spare time, but carefully concealing the identity of the hotel to spare him from phone calls. It was enough that he was taking the record with him on his honeymoon, yet.

Carol had to find him and she did not drive. She insisted that a friend drive her at once to Atlantic City. Jesse agreed, somewhat reluctantly, as Carol wrote to Jay when she described Jesse and the day:

*He is a curious bourgeois, very race conscious
wealthy young Jew, a new addition to the I.J.A. He
is just like hundreds of others of his kind only a
little decenter. Apparently never talked seriously
to a woman, only regards them as a means of sex
satisfaction. I could feel what a revelation I was
to him. So we talked dashing along madly at 60-70
miles an hour with a blistering sun shining in a
blue sky all swept with clouds. It was a strange
ride, half in deadly earnest and half in holiday
mood landing at the flag bedecked board walk of
Atlantic City.*

*The classified telephone book showed some 200
hotels. It seemed almost hopeless. . . . Finally
Jesse took it up with the soda clerk — what were
the leading hotels?*

"Jewish or Christian?" he snapped back.

"Both."

*So we learned the names of both but telephoned
only the Jewish. On the second try Victor Whitehorn
was discovered.*

When they drove to his hotel, Whitehorn was astonished to see them.

*Scarcely waiting to say thank you we headed home
like mad, and arrived at the office before 6. That
still left the problem of reading the record and
getting out the brief. It was another kind of race
but we did it, with short pauses for coffee and
sandwiches and cigarettes, finishing and locking up
the office at 4:30 A.M. Siegartel was an angel, even
produced a friend to do some of the typing.*

In the process of working on the appeal, Ben Davis found Carol King
to be "a woman of brilliant mind and pure heart" whose help was
"invaluable." The brief submitted to the Georgia Supreme Court "was
virtually her entire handiwork," containing all the points he had assembled "with much travail," but put into presentable and legally forceful
shape. More important, "the brief contained telling arguments I would
not have thought of in a million years." After the decision, one of the
Justices called Davis to commend it.

Nonetheless, in May 1934 the Georgia Supreme Court affirmed
Herndon's conviction, holding that the question of the exclusion of

Negroes from the jury had not been properly raised. And they cited *Gitlow v. New York* to affirm on the First Amendment question.

The defense immediately moved to get bail set for Herndon's release. Even deep in the Depression, the ILD raised the $15,000 set, and Herndon walked away from the threat of the chain gang after spending two years in jail.

At this point, Carol King really took hold of the case. Davis said she was "a remarkable personality — generous, warm, dynamic, self-sacrificing — yet objective. She was frank and jovial, brushing away attitudes of male supremacy with contempt. She was indefatigable, even though a chronic back ailment found her in frequent pain. Her mind was quick and penetrating in all phases of the law, particularly constitutional law." She saw that the federal question may not have been properly raised in the trial by the fearless, Harvard-trained, but inexperienced lawyers, and set to work. She found out that Professor Jerome Michael of Columbia Law School was a member of the Georgia bar. She found a way to meet him, but he was too busy to go to Georgia and suggested his young colleague, Walter Gellhorn, who undertook the assignment.

In her role as one of the editors of the *IJA Bulletin*, Carol wrote in the August 1934 issue a clear statement of the several ways in which a federal constitutional question can be raised in a state criminal case, and the several moments in a case when this *must be done,* concluding that it is ordinarily too late to raise such questions on a motion for rehearing.

But that is exactly what attorney King and her colleagues proceeded to do in *Herndon* in their petition for rehearing. The state supreme court obligingly denied the motion, so the federal questions were now securely embedded in the appeal to the U.S. Supreme Court, according to another article in the *Bulletin.*

Carol knew that they needed three kinds of lawyers in cases like this: pit lawyers like Davis and Geer to go into the trenches and try the cases to local juries, research lawyers to go into the libraries after work and stay there until they finished a brief, and conservative lawyers from prestigious firms committed to technically brilliant arguments in the appellate courts.

Carol asked Professor Herbert Wechsler of Columbia Law School to write the memo for the Court on its jurisdiction to hear the federal questions, and Wechsler did the job. She asked Professor Gellhorn if he knew anyone who might argue the case, preferably a noncommunist "leader of the bar" who could present the issues so they could be dealt with on their merits.

Gellhorn suggested Whitney North Seymour of the New York Bar, assistant solicitor general of the United States, 1931–1933, while Gellhorn and Wechsler were clerks to Supreme Court Justice Stone. Carol liked the idea, and when Gellhorn asked Seymour, he agreed, with the stipulation that there should be no defense publicity about the case unless he consented. He emphatically did not want the sort of mass rallies and letters to judges that had characterized the *Scottsboro* cases. But no good lawyer would reject the chance to make a national name for himself if he won on an important constitutional point, as Pollak had just done in *Scottsboro.*

Mrs. King readily accepted his stipulation, and at the time everyone agreed she "scrupulously adhered" to it. (In the cold war year of 1952, Seymour changed his memory of this incident.)

Having settled that matter, Mrs. King persuaded Wechsler and Gellhorn to do "the paper work" for the appeal and write the brief supporting the need for the U.S. Supreme Court to agree to hear this case. The lawyers indicated that she had a good grasp of the issues involved, and her name, which was known to the Court, appeared on the brief with theirs, although she did not help in the writing.

Carol, in her customary fashion, got to know more than these two Columbia law professors through the work on the case. She met their brightest and most socially conscious students, many of whom worked on the *Columbia Law Review.* Several came to work on the *Bulletin,* both before and after graduation. Howard Meyer said, "Carol King was a personality who defies classification." Her face framed with closely cropped curly hair, her bright eyes peering through heavy glasses, she persuaded, enticed, and cajoled him and other young lawyers into contributing to her cases and her publication. "She was a great-souled woman," he wrote later in describing the *Herndon* case.

By this time, the Joint Committee to Aid the Herndon Defense included the General Defense Committee of the IWW, the ILD, the League for Industrial Democracy, the League of Struggle for Negro Rights, the National Committee for the Defense of Political Prisoners, and the Non-Partisan Labor Defense. Although not a member of this committee, the ACLU cooperated by raising funds for the legal defense, and Carol turned to them in an emergency.

In May 1935 the U.S. Supreme Court, having heard Seymour's argument, dismissed the appeal by a vote of 6 to 3 on the very ground that Carol had predicted. Later Carol wrote about this decision for the ILD:

> Justice Cardozo wrote a scorching dissent for the minority [joined by Brandeis and Stone] . . . in which he showed that Herndon had fulfilled every necessary legal technicality, and had a right to a forthright opinion. The majority held that Herndon had not raised the question of constitutionality quite so soon in the case as he should. The minority said this was ridiculous.
>
> This raises the question: If three Justices of the United States Supreme Court think a technical legal procedure is proper, how can an ordinary lawyer know it's wrong? To those who have faith in the self-declared divinity of the Supreme Court, it's very confusing.

After this defeat, Carol and the rest of the IJA/ILD team of lawyers had to figure out their next move in *Herndon* while meeting deadlines in their other cases and causes.

14.
A New Deal for Aliens?

On March 4, 1933, Franklin Delano Roosevelt strode into Congress on paralyzed legs held up by guts, tradition, and braces to take over the reins of the paralyzed country. In his inaugural address, he immediately described the "host of unemployed citizens" facing "the grim problem of existence," and the "equally great number" who "toil with little return." He said, "Our greatest primary task is to put people to work." He quickly used the analogies of war and armies, saying, "We are, I know, ready and willing to submit our lives and property to such discipline" as "a trained and loyal army" would, "willing to sacrifice for the good" because of the "dark realities of the moment." He said he would ask Congress for emergency powers if it failed to act quickly so that he could "wage a war against the emergency as great as the power that would be given me if we were in fact invaded by a foreign foe."

The emergency was clear to everyone, rich and poor alike. The only disagreement in the Congress, in the country, and on Wall Street, was how to deal with it. In March 1930 the massive demonstrations for unemployment compensation had been part of a truly revolutionary mood on the part of millions of workers and unemployed in the United States. That was clear to Joe Brodsky, Carol King, and Isaac Shorr, as well as to leaders of the Democratic Party and Big Business. Now, three years later, no one knew how widespread that mood remained or where that mood would lead. No one knew how it could be turned aside or encouraged. It was common knowledge that citizens had formed block committees to put the furniture back in houses after evictions. As people walked through any major city, from Washington to Manhattan, they could see Hoovervilles of homeless shacks, sometimes stretching for miles. As lawyers entered their offices every morning, most of them worried much more about their rising debts than they did about the legal issues in the cases they were handling.

FDR soon made his jaunty cigarette holder part of the image of an activist President as his wife became the ubiquitous Eleanor. Roosevelt brought bright, creative people to Washington who helped him work out a series of emergency acts. Congress immediately began holding hearings on bills that would change forever the nature of the government's relationship with agriculture, industry, public utilities, railroads, workers, and gold. The actions in Washington were reported in the press like a military campaign, each week a new bill saving a new group or region of the country.

In April 1933 Roosevelt launched the Civilian Conservation Corps to employ 250,000 jobless young men to work to improve public lands.

On May 12, Congress passed the Agricultural Adjustment Act to give emergency relief to farmers by raising agricultural commodity prices to the pre-war level by voluntary crop reduction. In the face of widespread hunger, farmers would actually plow under crops and pour milk down the drain in order to raise prices enough for them to pay their bills.

Congress also authorized the President to devalue the gold dollar by not more than fifty cents.

On May 18, Congress passed the Tennessee Valley Act to construct dams and transmission lines, and to promote public health. The act meant thousands of jobs for workers, electricity for thousands of their homes, and a new concept of government responsibility. FDR also set up the Federal Emergency Relief Administration to distribute direct relief to the hungry.

On June 5, Congress, by joint resolution, abandoned the gold standard.

On June 16, Congress passed the Emergency Railroad Transportation Act to reorganize the railroads under the direction of a federal coordinator.

And on June 16, the last day of its first session under FDR, Congress passed the National Recovery Act (NRA). It provided for federal control of the entire industrial structure of the country through the mechanism of codes drawn by government administrators. Everyone agreed that it was the most extraordinary law ever passed by Congress. The new codes "of fair competition" for trades and industries were to provide that "employees shall have the right to organize and bargain collectively through representatives of their own choosing" for the first time in U.S. history. The Blue Eagle Codes were to be nonmonopolistic. The act also provided for emergency public works and construction projects that would mean millions of new jobs. And the act swept away constitutional restrictions on the right of states and cities to borrow money to carry forward local public works. Not less than $50 million was allotted for national forest highways and other roads, with a guarantee that prison labor would not be used — that ex-servicemen would get a preference, followed by citizens and aliens who had declared their intention of becoming citizens. The act provided a little money for slum clearance and low-cost housing construction.

As Congress passed and the President signed each of these emergency acts, the President quickly filled the administrative positions they created. Bright, liberal lawyers like Jerome Frank wrote to Professor Felix Frankfurter at Harvard that they wanted to get out of the Wall Street racket and "join up for the duration" of the crisis. In May 1933 Secretary of Agriculture Henry Wallace named Frank general counsel to the new Agricultural Adjustment Administration and to the new Federal Surplus Relief Corporation. IJA member Frank quickly surrounded himself with a remarkable group of lawyers: Thurman Arnold, Abe Fortas, Adlai Stevenson, John Abt, and IJA members Alger Hiss, Lee Pressman, and Nathan Witt. The group had in common the best legal training in asking hard questions, plus practical experience in big business firms in Chicago and New York. They shared a commitment to the craft of lawyering and the joy of planning a strategy to win a point before a court. Whether they supported the economic theories of Karl Marx or John Maynard Keynes, their job was to convince sitting federal judges to uphold New Deal economic legislation passed by Congress on the basis of well-worn constitutional principles.

Within one month of the adjournment of Congress on July 17, hardworking and creative New Dealers issued the Cotton Textile Code in accordance with the NRA.

Big Business, big banks, big agriculture immediately attacked each of the new laws in the media, fought them in the agencies, and sued to overturn them in the courts. Every lawyer wondered how the New Deal laws would work in practice and how they would fare in the old Supreme Court.

This made Washington the most exciting place for a lawyer to be. It drew Professor James M. Landis down from Harvard to head up the new Securities and Exchange Commission in 1934, and young IJA member Tom Emerson down from New York. He had worked with King on the *IJA Bulletin* at night while working days with Walter Pollak on the

Scottsboro appeal to the Supreme Court. He spent a year with the
National Recovery Administration (NRA).

John Abt came to Washington because "between 1929 and 1933, I
saw enough . . . to reject . . . [the capitalist system] as an acceptable social
system. So I welcomed the opportunity . . . to help in the fulfillment of
what I thought was Roosevelt's promise of fundamental reform. Those
were the heady days of the early New Deal when we young militants
thought that we had at least a finger on the levers of power as we set out
to curb the entrenched forces of monopoly."

The older IJA lawyers stayed in New York and struggled to keep
putting out the *IJA Bulletin* and to represent aliens, unemployed workers,
Unemployed Councils, organized workers, and their old and new organizations.

Carol's work with the American Association of Labor Legislation
after graduating from college served her in good stead in this exciting
period of pioneering legislation. She had learned that employers would
claim that any protective measure would destroy "freedom of contract,"
the freedom of each worker individually to contract with his employer.
Carol had not noticed any freedom of contract among the nonunion
members she met at the ILGWU in 1915, and even the union members
didn't feel free. How could there be freedom of contract when one side
could fire the other?

Even when unions and the association occasionally lobbied their bills
through a state legislature, the United States Supreme Court could be
relied on to strike them down as "unconstitutional violations of freedom
of contract" and "denials of substantive due process of law." Now, almost
twenty years later, the problem of Supreme Court opinions based on
denials of substantive due process persisted. But now the package of
far-out bills from the 1910s, long enforced in western European capitalist
countries, seemed perfectly rational, even necessary: workers' compensation for on-the-job injuries, protection of occupational health and safety,
one day's rest in seven, and especially compensation during periods of
unemployment. The IJA pushed for their passage.

In November 1933 the IJA research committee issued a summary of
the projects completed during 1933 through the joint efforts of twenty-
five attorneys. They included an amazing number and range of topics,
mostly efforts to pass new laws to right old wrongs: deficiency judgments
prepared for the Small Home Owners League of Staten Island, New York,
and for farmers' groups in Oklahoma, Iowa, and Nebraska; bills on milk

control drafted for the Farmers National Committee; a memo on the constitutionality of proposed statutes for indicting lynchers in counties other than those in which the crime was committed. They also prepared more traditional memos on the right of the government to intervene in a lynching in Tuscaloosa; opposing the government's asserted right to deport members of Left-wing unions under present law; and a memo supporting removal of a commissioner of conciliation at the Department of Labor who was considered "a notorious red-baiter."

It was not clear immediately how the Roosevelt administration was going to deal with the old problem of aliens. The administration changed the name of the Immigration Bureau to the Immigration and Naturalization Service (INS), but this change did not prove that the Service would really start "serving" immigrants at a time of massive unemployment among the native-born.

The first step of the INS was in the wrong direction. In May and June 1933, the Service arrested three people for deportation who were later shown to be U.S. citizens. And in May, INS officials went after unemployed sailors, as their predecessor would have done. The New York police arrested fifty-one seamen for resisting eviction from the Jane Street YMCA, the only shelter they could find while on the beach. The police turned the seamen over to the INS, which held them without bail. Carol noted in the *IJA Bulletin* that the Service also made arrests for deportation of striking granite workers in Maine and Vermont, of Commodore Hotel strikers in New York City, of berry pickers in El Monte, California, and of Food Workers Industrial Union members in Paterson, New Jersey.

In June 1933 FDR's Secretary of Labor, Frances Perkins, took an affirmative step for aliens. She appointed a committee of prominent citizens "to inquire impartially into conditions at Ellis Island and the welfare of immigrants generally and make recommendations for the guidance of the department." She acted after reading the Wickersham Report to President Hoover in 1931 and talking to its author. "Mr. Wickersham told me with his own mouth that he was sure that men had been run out of this country and deported by the immigration authorities on trumped up evidence that they were trying to overthrow the government by force and violence," she explained later in her oral history. "He didn't put that in his report because they could not specify chapter and verse, but their conversations with immigrant inspectors led them to that conclusion."

Mrs. King had been impressed by Miss Perkins's reputation as a fair, liberal administrator of social welfare programs in Governor Roosevelt's administration in New York State. Now she welcomed Perkins's appointment of the Ellis Island Committee and sent committee members a memo on abuses in the administration of the deportation laws, "chapter and verse," based on her own cases and those she had collected and described in the *IJA Bulletin*. She charged that the immigration laws were being used to interfere with trade union organization and to break strikes. This interference violated the declaration in Section 7a of the new National Industrial Recovery Act of 1933 that all workers were entitled to form and join unions of their own choice. She declared that the threat of deportation for trade union activity had "seriously interfered" with unionism, that its effects had been "far wider" than the number of persons actually arrested would indicate.

The Service was also arresting aliens who applied to public welfare agencies for relief and seeking their deportation on the ground that they had become public charges. Carol instead proposed that the Service expand its policies of referring aliens to social welfare agencies for assistance with personal problems. She recommended that all persons arrested for deportation because of their political and social views and activities be referred to the ILD and ACLU for advice and aid. Roger Baldwin of the ACLU made a similar suggestion. Turning to procedural abuses, Carol continued her indictment of the Service, listing the charges she had been compiling for years.

At the same time, she reported a series of deportations *to* the United States. James Gralton, born in Ireland and naturalized in the United States, had gone back to Ireland to take part in "the Irish revolutionary movement" and was deported for it. Walter Orloff, a U.S. citizen studying medicine in Germany for three years, was deported for alleged Communist activity at a German university. And Alexander Bruckman, a delegate to an anti-war congress in Shanghai, was arrested in Tokyo and deported for his "radical activities."

On August 19, 1933, in this early New Deal period, *Collier's* magazine reported on a long-standing problem in the United States: surveillance of leading Americans. Ray Tucker revealed that the FBI had shadowed Herbert Hoover as a "dangerous radical" after the World War when he was head of a foreign aid mission to Moscow, and "at one time or another the bureau's files have contained reports on such prominent Americans as Justice Stone, the late Senator Thomas, Senator Wheeler, Senator

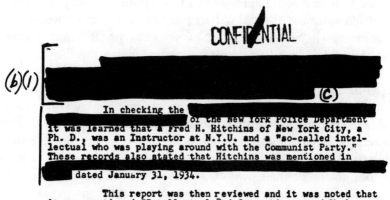

CONFIDENTIAL

(b)(1)

(C)

In checking the ▉▉▉▉▉▉▉▉▉▉ of the New York Police Department it was learned that a Fred H. Hitchins of New York City, a Ph. D., was an Instructor at N.Y.U. and a "so-called intellectual who was playing around with the Communist Party." These records also stated that Hitchins was mentioned in ▉▉▉▉▉▉ dated January 31, 1934.

This report was then reviewed and it was noted that it was captioned "Intellectual Red Sympathizers and Members of the Communist Party Show Their Hand at Last." Hitchin's name appeared on a list of people who were described as having given their money, names and efforts to secure the release of German Communists. It was noted that this list was quite long and included such names as Carol King and Arthur Garfield Hayes.

9-4-47, New York Report Re:"Fred Harvey Hitchins, was.

(b)(1)

(C)

62-84655-9 (73)

JW:mlb

FBI File: Carol King (9-4-47). 1934 FBI report on "intellectuals" seeking to secure the release of German Communists.

Borah, Dean Roscoe Pound, Professor Felix Frankfurter, Professor Zechariah Chaffee, Jr., Frank P. Walsh, and John L. Lewis."

In the fall Carol began reporting for the *IJA Bulletin* on the "Reichstag fire trial" in Leipzig. The German judges denied Dimitroff the right to be represented by the lawyers he selected, both German and foreign, including the American, Leo Gallagher. Dimitroff therefore represented himself. He called Hermann Goering to the stand, and in a blistering cross-examination, accused the Nazi leader of himself setting the fire. Dimitroff ridiculed the evidence against himself and the other Communist defendants, proudly stating his beliefs and leading the president of the court to exclaim, "To hear you, one would think that you are conducting these proceedings and not I." His closing speech in his own defense was a ringing denunciation of the Nazis, hurled at them in a courtroom the Nazis thought they controlled.

After four months of trial, deep in the furnace of fascism, the German judges in December 1933 acquitted all the defendants except the feeble-minded man who had confessed.

Dimitroff emerged a hero to anti-fascists everywhere. In a Depression city already ringed with liberal cowardice and racist hysteria, he had stuck to the issues in the case and in the country, using a straightforward approach. His victory opened a new phase in courtroom struggles. His defense became an instant international model for lawyers and potential clients.

The Nazi authorities refused to release Dimitroff after his acquittal by the court, and Carol and the IJA participated in the ensuing international campaign to free him. Finally the Germans released Dimitroff and quickly expelled him from the country. Then the Nazis arrested U.S. attorney Leo Gallagher for deportation. Carol appealed to the Bar Association of the City of New York to protest and asked Secretary of State Cordell Hull to inquire into the cause of Gallagher's detention. Gallagher was eventually permitted to leave Germany.

On November 16, 1933, President Roosevelt took the step of recognizing the government of the Union of Soviet Socialist Republics established after the Russian Revolution of 1917. Within a year the USSR had joined the League of Nations and started a campaign for a united front against Hitler's fascism. Roosevelt did not follow Stalin into the League of Nations. He was busy at home, moving from cash relief to work relief, establishing the Civilian Works Administration (CWA) to provide temporary jobs.

❧

In March 1934 Carol met a client whose case was to continue for decades. Isaac Shorr received a letter from the Immigration Service about Jack Schneider, originally from Romania. Two years before, Schneider had been arrested for deportation in connection with a strike while working as an organizer for the Needle Trades Workers Industrial Union, affiliated with Bill Foster's Trade Union Unity League. Now the Service asked Isaac to produce Schneider at Ellis Island for further questioning, after which, the letter said, "he will again be released in accordance with the terms of your bond."

Schneider was still active as an organizer for the union; he still did not want to be deported from the United States, and he especially did not want to be deported to his native Romania, where his politics would undoubtedly cause him to be harassed and perhaps imprisoned.

When Schneider and Shorr reported to Ellis Island, the Service took Schneider into custody.

Shorr demanded to know the reason.

The INS agent said that the surety company that had posted Schneider's bond two years earlier had gone out of business.

Shorr protested that this arrest violated the specific statement in the letter telling Schneider to appear. Besides, the surety company had been in liquidation for months, and Schneider would have produced a new bond if told to do so.

The agent insisted on holding Schneider nonetheless.

After some delay, Shorr secured a new bond.

The local INS authorities still refused to release Schneider, claiming that the new bond had to be approved by the Department of Labor in Washington.

Back and forth, back and forth went the ping-pong of administrative law. Finally Shorr had had enough. He went to a law court for a writ while Carol wrote to attorney George Ernst, a member of the Ellis Island Committee, describing the Schneider case and explaining that she was convinced that the hostility toward Schneider was the result of pressure on the Labor Department by the AFL. Edward McGrady, assistant secretary of labor, had been head of the International Fur Workers Association–AFL, and a rival of Schneider's Needle Trade Workers' Industrial Union.

Before the writ was scheduled to be heard, the INS released Schneider, as had happened so often when King and Shorr called their bluff by hailing them into court. Schneider's deportation case started pending.

Carol and Isaac welcomed this small victory for its own sake, but also as a counter to the very bad news from Europe. The nature of their practice brought them into confrontation with foreign fascism sooner than colleagues who specialized in other fields. Every German and Italian vessel docking in New York carried the fascist virus, and only inspired action could quarantine it on the docks.

One fast-paced case had all the elements of melodrama. Theodore Eggeling, a German, arrived in New York as a seaman aboard a ship of the Hamburg-American Line. While he was on shore leave, he participated in an anti-Nazi demonstration and broke a plate-glass window. He was arrested for disorderly conduct, found guilty of this charge, and required to pay for the window.

As Eggeling emerged from Magistrate's Court on June 12, 1934, special police of the Hamburg-American Line seized him and hurried him away in a taxicab.

His friends followed the taxi and slowly realized they were headed for New York harbor. There they watched with horror as the special police took Eggeling aboard a German ship. They learned the vessel was scheduled to sail the next day. Knowing Eggeling's fate in Hitler Germany, they rushed to a phone to call attorney Carol King.

She said she could do nothing at the moment because the federal courts had closed for the day, but she would go to work first thing tomorrow morning.

She did, hurrying to federal court in Foley Square with a habeas corpus petition while Sol Cohn went to keep watch over the ship. He paced up and down the docks until it seemed logical that Carol could have found a judge to sign a habeas corpus writ. He called his office but was told they had not heard from King. Fretting there on the docks, Sol repeated the process time after time all afternoon.

Nightfall came. No word.

Nine P.M. — sailing time — approached. Still no word.

Sol was frantic by the time Carol arrived in a taxi with the writ she had finally gotten a federal judge to sign. Cohn and King hurried onto the ship and handed the writ to a German ship officer. He said nothing about whether he would honor the court order. He had the lawyers deposited back on shore.

While they waited on the dock, Carol described her courthouse search, office by office, for one federal judge who would listen to her petition. Long after she finished her tale, a boat was lowered and came toward them. Eggeling was on it! He quickly vanished into the night. He was never heard from again. His attorneys presumed his friends had taken him to a safe place.

The next month the IJA gave a luncheon honoring Dr. Kurt Rosenfeld, former Prussian minister of justice, now an exile from Nazi Germany. He spoke on the status of labor and civil liberties in Germany, mourning the execution of German labor unions by act of the new Nazi government. Dr. Rosenfeld urged the lawyers to announce their readiness to defend in German courts Ernst Thaelmann, leader of the German Communist Party, and other political prisoners in the Reich. Another exile, Willi Muezenberg, had been elected to the Reichstag as a representative of the German Communist Party. The two men predicted the end of Hitler's rule in a few years, but only after a terrible bloodbath. Later Dr. Rosenfeld testified before an American inquiry commission studying Nazi activities in Germany. ILD publications began describing the quantity and quality of violations by the Nazis, indicating that fascism was a horror qualitatively different from capitalist democracies in a terrible Depression.

Carol continued to record the worst human rights violations in the United States in her "Recent Items" section of the *Bulletin,* indicating that violations of civil liberties and labor's rights were by no means confined to Germany.

In November 1934 the sheriff in Aliquippa, Pennsylvania, a Jones & Laughlin Steel Company stronghold, arrested George Issoki for handing out union literature and had him secretly committed to the state hospital for the insane. When his wife found out and the public protested, Governor Gifford Pinchot had to have an investigation, which found Issoki perfectly sane. Carol commented in the *IJA Bulletin* that this kind of incident "would explain why the company union still flourishes in the steel industry."

The next month she reported that a Chicago municipal court judge had Jane Emery Newton arrested and held for mental examination because she was a twenty-six-year-old white woman married to a Negro Communist. The judge had previously ordered the family evicted from a white neighborhood because of their activity in the ILD and the Communist Party. The case made news because Mrs. Newton was the daughter of the first commander of the American Legion. On December 19, 1934, the staff psychiatrist released Mrs. Newton, saying "This woman is not only sane but is an exceptionally brilliant person."

These cases were discussed at a conference on civil liberties under the New Deal sponsored by the ACLU in December. The representation was broad, including the IJA, American Federation of Teachers, Church League for Industrial Democracy, Fellowship of Reconciliation, League for Industrial Democracy, the Methodist Federation for Social Action, the NAACP, and organizations supporting the rights of farmers and students, as well as legislation for birth control.

At this point, FDR's administration was continuing to fashion its New Deal as Eleanor Roosevelt was continuing her pioneering work. In 1933, after holding the first press conference by a President's wife, she led a firsthand investigation of conditions resulting in the Reedsville, West Virginia, homestead experiments; the National Youth Administration and its summer camps; the Federal Surplus Relief Corps; the Public Works of Art Project; and clearance of Washington alley dwellings.

In this climate the subjects for discussion at the ACLU conference were equally broad: the rights of farmers and farm workers to organize and bargain collectively; the plight of sharecroppers; the right of the unemployed and relief workers to organize and demonstrate; whether Section 7a of the National Industrial Recovery Act protected the rights of Negro workers; whether birth control information sponsored by medical agencies should be permitted in the mails; the federal anti-lynching bill and what to do about lawless activities of fascist and semi-fascist organizations in the United States; new liberties for the American Indian; and rights for U.S. colonies like Puerto Rico.

Carol had, of course, added consideration of some of the special problems of aliens: whether bona fide alien political refugees should be admitted to the United States and whether alien conscientious objectors should be admitted to citizenship.

The chances for passage of social legislation had increased by far more than one vote when New Yorkers elected Vito Marcantonio, a protégé of Fiorello LaGuardia, as congressman in November 1934 on the Republican ticket. Marc had started his training in the firm of Hale, Nelles & Shorr, had translated for Italian-speaking witnesses in the *Greco-Carillo* case, and could be counted on for effective support of progressive bills through oratory and inspired knowledge of the parliamentary procedure practiced in the House.

In her practice Carol continued to concentrate on immigration cases and to describe them in such poignant detail to relatives and friends that they never forgot the names of her clients. John Ujich, for example, had complained about the local administration of relief in Tacoma, Washington. The INS promptly arrested him for deportation on the basis of statements *by others* as to his beliefs. The hearing officer nonetheless ordered him deported on the ground of *personal* belief in the violent overthrow of the government, and sent him to Ellis Island.

Carol lost habeas corpus petitions in the district court and in the circuit court of appeals; the Supreme Court would not hear her appeal. By this time several years had passed and the relief administrator who had instigated the deportation proceedings against Ujich had been indicted for misappropriation of relief funds. This new fact led Carol to apply for cancellation of the deportation warrant on the ground that Ujich's initial complaints were valid.

The board of review of the Labor Department refused to reverse the ruling, and Ujich faced deportation to Mussolini's fascist Italy, although his birthplace had been part of Austria when he came to the United States in 1906. Finally, to save himself from an Italian jail, Ujich sought and was granted voluntary departure to the Soviet Union in September 1935. The *IJA Bulletin* noted, "This is apparently the first case in which an order of deportation has been based solely on the opinion of others as to what an alien advocates or believes . . . or . . . his membership in a proscribed organization."

This case strengthened Carol's and Isaac's resolve to resist when the Service suggested in 1934 that their union organizer client, Jack Schneider, should "depart voluntarily" for another country because the INS still could not provide him with a Romanian passport. Schneider would not agree to leave. He had lived and worked in the United States for many years and he wanted to stay here. Besides, the Trade Union Unity League (TUUL) was being dissolved, in keeping with developments in the U.S. labor movement. Its leaders said it had served its purpose, and its members were struggling to join the new industrial unions that were emerging out of the craft structure of the AFL. They were not interested in retaining dual unions. Schneider's Needle Trades Workers' Industrial Union (NTWIU) joined the Fur Workers International Union, which had affiliated with the staid American Federation of Labor.

To Shorr and King, this chain of events marked a new chance to win a deportation case. Shorr immediately applied to the Labor Department for cancellation of the deportation warrant against Schneider, which was still based on his membership in the NTWIU and its affiliation with the TUUL, and *its* affiliation with the Red International of Labor Unions, and *its* affiliation with the Communist International. With the links all broken, logic required that the alien should be free of the threat of deportation.

In September 1935 the Department of Labor complied with Shorr's request. This action left open the question of whether an alien could be deported for membership in a union affiliated with the now defunct TUUL. The Supreme Court had agreed to hear argument on the *Boric* case in 1934, which raised this issue. But in what had now become a habit, the service immediately agreed to cancel the warrant if Frank Boric would withdraw his appeal, so the legal issue was not settled although that case was also won.

At this juncture, George Ernst showed Carol King a draft of the proposed report and recommendations of the Ellis Island Committee appointed by Secretary of Labor Perkins. Ernst had gotten "a lot of ideas and suggestions" from Carol, but almost all of his proposals were rejected by the committee. Even so, Carol saw that the "Report of the Ellis Island Committee" would have a salutary effect. It recommended that the Secretary of Labor be given broader power to extend discretionary relief, and said that it is "intolerable" to have the same official serve as investigator, prosecutor, and judge in the deportation process.

But the recommendations did not seem to change the day-to-day operation of the INS. For example, in May 1935, seventy-three hod carriers were picketing during a strike against a federal road project in New Jersey. Without warrants of any kind, the contractors piled the pickets into trucks and took them to a nearby fire station for questioning by immigration inspectors. Someone from the new American Committee for Protection of Foreign-Born got wind of the affair and sent over an attorney, who strenuously objected to the proceedings. All seventy-three were then released, as Carol gleefully reported in the next *IJA Bulletin*.

The American Committee for Protection of Foreign Born was the brainchild of Roger Baldwin of the ACLU and Joe Brodsky of the ILD, who had been working together on many cases and causes. In this Popular Front period of 1934, Baldwin's thinking was like Brodsky's on some basic issues. Baldwin wrote in *Soviet Russia Today* that when the "power of the working class is once achieved [as in Russia] I am for maintaining it by any means whatever." He talked ACLU leader John Haynes Holmes out of barring Communists from ACLU leadership. Now he and Brodsky could see that the ACLU and ILD had their hands full dealing with civil liberties cases. The government was always throwing curves in alien cases that required a roster of pinch hitters. Carol had been trying for years to increase the number of immigration lawyers, but this was no easy task. Dedicated criminal defense lawyers were willing to help in alien cases, but they had no idea at all about the particular and peculiar rules (and lack of rules) of the Immigration Service. The plan was to have the American Committee concentrate on all of the cases of noncitizens.

The American Committee began its work by publishing a few facts. According to the U.S. census for 1930, there were 14,204,149 persons of foreign birth in the United States. With their families they constituted one-third of the population. The best estimates were that fewer than 4,500,000 were noncitizens. The committee added another significant fact: more people had been leaving the United States than entering in the Depression years starting in 1931. Despite this, "the foreign-born, particularly the noncitizens, are being blamed for poverty, unemployment, and crime in this country."

The committee also began working with Carol, the IJA, ACLU, ILD, and others to propose several bills to stop the Labor Department from deporting people who claimed they would be subjected to political persecution in their native countries, and to permit them to remain in the United States indefinitely, even if they had entered illegally. But the temper of Congress was anti-alien, and the LaGuardia and Copeland bills got nowhere.

By this time, Carol King had established her own style. Sol Cohn said, "She had this magnetism." She walked down the street puffing on a cigarette, which other women simply did not do. But when she started to speak, you realized "she spoke like a book. And that's the way she dictated," using some poetic phrase from Shakespeare that left her secretary asking, "What was that again?"

Carol King had become one of the unquestioned leaders of the immigration bar in the country and while she could not report a New Deal for aliens emanating from Washington, she could demonstrate that aggressive representation brought victory, or at least forestalled defeat, in some cases in the United States.

15.
Representing Clients in Warsaw and Dixie

In June 1935 Anna Damon asked Carol King to become the United States representative on an international delegation to Poland. Damon said that it was critical that Carol go to try to save the lives of ILD members there as the situation in Poland deteriorated.

The ILD was affiliated with International Red Aid, which had taken up several big cases from the United States. Many U.S. speakers had gone to Europe to describe the *Sacco-Vanzetti* case; later, mothers of several *Scottsboro* defendants had attended conventions of International Red Aid in Europe. It was assumed the U.S. chapter would take up IRA cases from other countries in return, such as Japan, Lithuania, Hungary, and several African and Latin American countries. After the success of the Russian revolution, in January 1920, the U.S. government began targeting Russia's neighbor, Poland, as an area of U.S. concern. A U.S. delegation now might have some impact on Polish human rights practices.

Carol King was an obvious candidate for the delegation. She had visited the Soviet Union and Germany on her own a few years before, meeting legal/political people who had convinced her to participate directly in their struggles.

Anna Damon and Limey Colman, Carol's friend and drinking companion, had a clear picture of the seriousness of the situation in Poland from their work in the ILD and editing its *Labor Defender*. A new Polish constitution placed more arbitrary power in the hands of the government. This new constitution would not solve the basic problem of the government, Anna and Limey told Carol: the country could not feed the workers. But it would make it easier to silence their complaints.

The legal situation in Poland was quite different from the legal situation in the United States, although both were suffering from the same economic depression. In Poland the trade unions were illegal and it was a crime to be a member. It was also illegal to be a member of the Communist Party or of the Polish ILD. A person who, in connection with an attempt to influence government or its officers, "[came] to an understanding with other persons," was liable to imprisonment, as well as someone "seeking to overthrow the government." Under this vague provision of the code, many militant workers were being sent to jail and sentenced to six, eight, or ten years. Others were imprisoned for taking part in meetings that "result[ed] in injury to person or property."

The Polish ILD had urgently requested an international delegation to come, investigate conditions, and report their findings to the press in their countries on their return, demanding international censure of the undemocratic practices of the government. It was essential that the delegates be accepted as impartial; otherwise, they would create additional problems for the Polish ILD. A lawyer was a natural in this situation.

Carol apparently agreed she had the qualifications but was hesitant to accept this mission. Being a single parent constantly raised difficult questions about parental responsibilities versus political or social responsibilities. But this would be a quick trip, and Mrs. Barkley said she could manage ten-year-old Jonathan while Carol's partners said they could cover for her at home and the office. Carol finally agreed to go.

On the Paris-Warsaw express, she met the delegates from Canada and France, and her U.S. orientation began to drop away. The train puffed slowly into the Warsaw terminal on June 19, 1935, and she described how she stepped quietly from the train to observe the superficial peace and charm of the medieval city "with its beautiful buildings and cobbled streets, quite inappropriate to the modern taxi."

On their first day in Warsaw, thirteen delegations came to their hotel to meet with them, including trade union representatives, members of the Polish ILD, and other workers' groups. The most emotional meeting was with families of prisoners. They told about the outlawing of militant trade unions and the jailing of their leaders. They said factory workers in Warsaw received the equivalent of $2 to $4 a week in the face of high living costs, while members of the union of domestic servants made $3 a month and had to house themselves. In her subsequent report for the *Labor Defender,* Carol reported that "even pitiable jobs were sought after and many who spoke to us had no work. Unemployment was apparent everywhere."

The Polish delegations said there were 12,000 to 16,000 political prisoners in Polish jails. Carol translated: "This means that out of the total population of . . . 32,000,000, one out of every 2600 or 3000 is in jail for a political offense, and of course an even larger proportion of the adult population."

The international delegation was able to visit two prisoners in the L'Wow jail, who dared, in the presence of the warden and two jail guards, to tell their stories. The man was in jail for nine months without being permitted to see a printed word, receive a letter, or have a visit with his wife. He spent three weeks in solitary confinement in a cell dripping with moisture for protesting his prison clothes and his placement with ordinary criminals when he was in jail for a political offense — membership in the Communist Party — and for his refusal to stand when Catholic prayers were being said. The woman would be in jail eleven months before she even knew what the charge was.

The warden "admitted the prisoners got meat only once a week, only coffee and bread for breakfast, soup at noon, and bread and potatoes at the evening meal." The rules forbade solitary confinement for more than forty-eight hours, but no one denied the story of three weeks in solitary. "The Polish constitution forbids corporal punishment on prisoners, but when asked if the prisoners were beaten, the warden replied, 'sometimes the guards get nervous.' "

A cordon of police accompanied the international delegation on the train from Warsaw. Stepping off in Lodz, the delegates were acclaimed by a demonstration of workers when suddenly "the police charged with raised clubs, the crowd opened before the attack, reformed and marched behind us to our hotel in triumph shouting and clapping." Carol wrote that "great bunches of red peonies were thrown" to them. "It was apparently safe to present these in silence, but one young girl who shouted a greeting to the 'International Delegation, anti-fascist' was seized by the police."

Carol learned that the reception committee of twenty-two elected by the Lodz unions to greet them was jailed before the delegation arrived, and two were arrested as they left Carol's hotel, each having one or more family members already in jail. The secret service pursued the delegates wherever they went, one operative for each delegate.

When the delegation sought admission to a rubber factory to present their message of "international solidarity and encouragement," the workers were locked in after hours to prevent any contact. When a young girl passing in the street "asked if we were the International Delegation, not only she but her companion were locked up. The very next day, according to the figures even of one capitalist paper, 80% went out in the general political strike of June 25 to show hostility" to the new constitution.

The delegation spent eight days and nights in Poland, long enough for the stench of fascism to permeate their consciousness, along with another unforgettable sensation:

> On June 27 the delegation left Warsaw. It was night. The workers came to the station to say good-bye. They bore great bunches of red roses and peonies that glowed in the electric light. We separated the bunches and threw blossoms to our friends. They caught and saved them as remembrance of the International Delegation which had come to them as a token of the international solidarity of the workers.
>
> The police made no move to stop them or us. Perhaps even they for a moment felt their powerlessness against the courage of the Polish workers.

On Carol's return to New York, an ILD photographer came to her office to take a picture to go with her article in the *Labor Defender*. He snapped her thirty-nine-year-old face, open, clear-eyed, and certain, totally different from the Leyda photo three years before. Her sad sincerity was untouched by bravado or the practiced smile required of public figures.

After finishing her report for the ILD membership, Carol prepared a second piece for the lawyers. She had long admitted that there were political prisoners in her own country, despite protestations to the contrary by the liberal establishment. She could see no way to improve their lot by appealing to the courts, which she and other lawyers had been trying for years. In October 1935, the ILD held a conference on the status of political prisoners attended by Professors Karl Llewellyn, Walter Gellhorn, and Herbert Wechsler, and by attorneys Shorr, Brodsky, King, Whitney North Seymour, and fourteen other lawyers. In preparation for the conference, Carol drafted a model bill prescribing conditions and treatment of political prisoners in the United States. The *IJA Bulletin* published it, and the ILD started using it in its ongoing lobbying on the subject. As another aspect of the work, on April 4, 1936, Joe went to Brazil to assist Mr. and Mrs. Harry Berger, "political prisoners in Rio de Janeiro," according to Brodsky's FBI file.

However, the main work of the ILD, as Joe frequently pointed out, was to keep people from becoming political prisoners, not to ameliorate their lot after their cases were lost. Carol agreed, of course, and redoubled her efforts to bring additional people into their work. Her trip to Poland

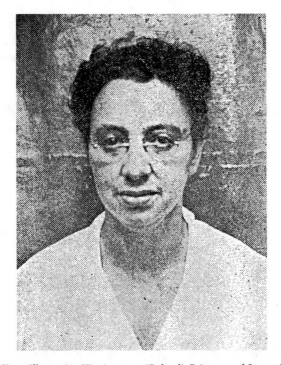

Carol King. Illustrating King's report "Poland's Prisoners of Starvation." In *The Labor Defender*, September 1935. (Photographer unknown.)

had sharpened her convictions and her tongue, which had different effects on different people. Her radical stance led a few to throw off their hesitancy and commit more time and thought to the movement.

To Samuel Silverman, at this point Carol seemed to "combine a very warm personality with a tendency to scorn for people who didn't see things as clearly as she thought they were. She shared what I thought was a characteristic of some Communists I knew, a sort of dogmatic assertiveness — 'this is black; that is white, with nothing in between.' I frequently had the feeling that she said to herself: 'These dumb, confused liberals! I can use them when I need them!' And she did get very good people to work on important cases. I assumed that the reason she was not a Communist Party member was that she thought she could be more effective that way."

❦

Carol always needed to combine business with family. The good news at this point was that her older brother, Billy, had just started a new career in the law from the wheelchair in his home. The idea for a neighborhood legal clinic for low-income people grew out of Weiss's experiences as a victim of multiple sclerosis. In order to get to various hospitals for tests and consultations, he hired a chauffeur who soon learned that his rider was a lawyer. The chauffeur tried out the lawyer, seeking advice on his own legal problems. The passenger always seemed to have the answers and they panned out. Weiss began to notice that the chauffeur was asking more and more questions about problems that did not seem to be his own, and he questioned the driver. The chauffeur admitted he had started getting free legal advice for some of his friends.

Weiss thought about it awhile and decided he didn't want to give legal advice for nothing because he assumed it would be valued at nothing. On the other hand, thinking about other people's problems certainly took his mind off his own and made him feel like a productive member of society again. He made a deal: when the driver obtained advice for other people, they should pay the lawyer $1 for it.

As the chauffeur and other satisfied clients spread the word, William Weiss began to have a stream of people coming to his apartment. Usually he knew the answers to their problems without resorting to the law books that had become inaccessible to him. On the rare occasions when he needed specific citations, he called his old law firm and they gladly supplied them. For problems requiring court action, he referred his clients to lawyers who agreed to charge fees appropriate under the circumstances. In 1934 he wrote an article on his unique legal clinic for the *New York Times,* which led some leaders of the Bar Association to criticize him for providing good legal services at low fees, although they were convinced to change their minds.

By this time Carol's other brother had become one of the liberal leaders of the bar in New York. Louis Weiss was a warm, sympathetic person who also had the patience to do the detailed financial work arising from a matrimonial case for someone like his new client, Marshall Field III. He had settled deep into the law, using his mythical trio — Bifkins, Trashbasket and Brokenbasin — to make some of his points on the law and life to friends and audiences. He had gotten involved in the New School for Social Research and, according to Samuel Silverman, who worked for the Weiss firm at this time, had almost become the legal father figure of the psychoanalytic movement, Freudian wing. He represented the

American Psychoanalytic Association and the New York Institute. He and his wife, Honi, had become friends of Justine Tulin through Carol. Honi was connected with slightly more Leftish causes than Louis, but of course they were both deeply concerned about the *Scottsboro* and *Herndon* cases. By now millions of others were also following the slow unfolding of the litigation.

In order to convince the Supreme Court Justices to change their minds and hear the case of Angelo Herndon, the ILD convinced a broad group of individuals and organizations to file an amicus brief on October 7, 1935, supporting this petition. Petitioners included the NAACP and National Bar Association (of Negro lawyers), and the Central Conference of American Rabbis, and the director of the Council for Social Action of the Congregational and Christian Churches of the United States. Each petitioner described the particular interests of his group in having justice done in this case. Evidently the ILD had outgrown the "sectarian" errors of which it had been self-critical in 1932.

But it was the foregone conclusion that this motion for reconsideration would be denied by the Court when it reconvened in the autumn. Unless some way could be found to raise the federal constitutional issues in a Georgia court, the case was lost and Herndon was en route to prison for a long time. At least eleven others had been indicted under the same statute in October 1934. They were Jews and Gentiles who had attended an anti-war meeting in an Atlanta suburb that was raided by local police. They might be headed for prison as well, although prominent Atlanta citizens had finally caused the prosecutors to suspend their anti-Communist crusade in the fall of 1934.

At this juncture, Carol King got an idea, dredging up a seemingly inconsequential fact and demonstrating that it was really the key to victory. She had never fallen for the theory that this is a government of laws and not of men. She knew that every case consists of both law and the people who decide the law, and she related to individual people and appealed to them as individuals. Her memory was loaded with trifles about specific people. In the summer of 1935 she recalled something about one Hugh Dorsey, the hard-driving solicitor general who convicted the Jewish defendant in the sensational Leo Frank murder case in Atlanta in 1913–1915, while she was growing up. This conviction led to Dorsey's election as governor of Georgia. Later he lost his campaign for the U.S. Senate and became a Fulton County judge in Atlanta, Georgia. Somewhere Carol had heard a rumor that the lynching of Frank after his conviction had brought Dorsey much personal grief and that he was ashamed of his part in the case. Now she reasoned that Judge Dorsey might welcome a chance to redeem himself. (On March 11, 1986, the State of Georgia finally sought redemption, officially pardoning Leo Frank posthumously and admitting that he had been denied justice.)

The defense put the question of Dorsey's redemption to the test in October 1935 when the U.S. Supreme Court denied its motion for rehearing, as expected. Herndon surrendered himself in Atlanta, and his lawyers filed a motion in the Fulton County court asking Judge Dorsey for a writ of habeas corpus on the ground that Herndon had been illegally convicted. Judge Dorsey ordered Herndon kept in Fulton County pending his decision. This kept Herndon off the chain gang.

In December 1935 Judge Dorsey issued his ruling. He sustained the contention of Herndon's lawyers that the application of the insurrection statute to Herndon had been in violation of the U.S. Constitution because the statute was "too vague and indefinite." He granted Herndon's petition and immediately released him on $8,000 bail, pending the state's appeal from his ruling. The ACLU hailed the decision as "the most important civil rights victory in the South for years," and Angelo Herndon left at once for New York, where his case had become so well known that Random House contracted to publish his autobiography, *Let Me Live.*

Carol knew her next step would come when the Georgia Supreme Court reversed Judge Dorsey's decision, which they were almost certain to do. This action would clear the way for a second appeal to the U.S. Supreme Court with the federal constitutional issues carefully preserved in the trial record.

As to Scottsboro, after two victories in the highest court in the land, all the defendants were still in prison. On November 14, 1935, the prosecutor had sought new indictments against all nine defendants from eighteen grand jurors, including one Negro man, the first to serve "in the memory of man." This great change had no effect on the jury's decision because it only took a two-thirds vote to indict. The court clerk called twelve Negroes for duty on the trial jury, a second great change, and then ordered them to sit in a Jim Crow–segregated section of the room until the prosecutor could use a peremptory challenge against each of them (saving him from having to state any reason for his challenges). The fourth all-white jury sat in judgment on Haywood Patterson and voted to convict, leaving him another year's wait for the decision on his appeal.

This wait left Carol and the other lawyers time and energy to deal with other problems. Their immediate problem was their survival as lawyers with few paying clients. The main problems their New York and Northern clients faced were similar: lack of jobs and miserable pay rates.

On December 1, 1935, all federal relief ended. The United Organization of Unemployed and Relief Workers charged that 7.5 million families of unemployed workers were left "stranded and at the mercy of bankrupt cities, counties and states." On July 1, 1936, the existing WPA program was scheduled to end. The United Organization put out a pamphlet urging militant action, listing the recent successful strikes of WPA workers. A six-week strike of 1,500 skilled workers in New York City won a 100 percent increase in wages, from $93.50 for 120 hours to $93.50 for 60 hours; the monthly take-home remained the same. In Walker County, Alabama, 2,500 unskilled WPA workers struck for three weeks against a cut from 30 cents to 15.5 cents per hour for 140 hours. They won 27 cents an hour for 116 hours, which was 90 percent of the union wage scale in that county.

WPA lawyers were part of the unemployed movement, demanding an "opportunity to be useful members of a society in which none need suffer poverty, hunger, want and misery in the midst of plenty."

In the spring of 1936 the crew of the *S. S. California* went out on strike for higher wages. The Secretary of Commerce immediately recommended that the 374 seamen be prosecuted for mutiny, a felony punishable by ten years in prison and a fine of $2,000.

Carol King and the IJA research committee rushed to work. It was outrageous to send workers to prison for ten years for striking for better pay, just because they worked on sea instead of on land! The lawyers quickly procured a number of affidavits concerning the deplorable conditions aboard ship. These affidavits became the basis of a report signed by Professors Brissenden, Gellhorn, Gifford, Michael, and Wechsler of Columbia, and by Whitney North Seymour and Bruce Bliven of the New York bar and the *Nation*.

Carol decided this situation called for the help of someone known to many leaders in FDR's Washington, so she called her brother Louis, whose representation of Simon & Schuster and his work on civic issues had built his reputation in the capitol. He agreed to take the IJA material to Washington, where he visited the Departments of Justice, Commerce, and

Labor, seeking a withdrawal of Secretary Daniel Roper's "mutiny" proposal and an investigation of conditions aboard ship.

Carol played her part by speaking on "Legislation and the Seamen" at the Town Hall Club under the auspices of The Woman Today. She concluded that "legislation is necessary to establish decent conditions of work and pay for seamen, . . . but in the final analysis the seamen must depend upon collective action to secure not only decent working conditions but also enforcement of the statutes enacted to protect them and the travelling public." In May 1936 the *Yale Law Journal* published an article called "The Right of Seamen to Strike" prepared by V. Henry Rothschild, an editor of the *IJA Bulletin* — a first for both periodicals. The *Bulletin* reprinted the piece and submitted it to the Commerce Department.

By then the government thought better of the "mutiny" charge and dropped it. Carol enjoyed this speedy victory but pointed out that "it remains to be seen whether anything will be done to improve the economic conditions of seamen, . . . with wages lower than those of any other group of skilled workers, . . . and provisions as to living conditions for crews practically unchanged since 1897." She got to know some of the seamen personally. Their style of life appealed to her and she picked up some of their colorful language to use on occasion.

Labor unions might be winning, but aliens kept losing in 1936. FDR was supporting one anti-alien bill after another. The Kerr bill proposed that any employee of the INS can arrest without warrant any alien "he has reason to believe is subject to deportation" and detain the person for twenty-four hours, and to deport for arrests during strikes. Another bill would transfer deportation cases from the Department of Labor to the Department of Justice, apparently to hasten and strengthen deportation proceedings against West Coast labor leader Harry Bridges. A 1936 bill reduced immigration quotas, flatly required the deportation of any alien found to be a member of any organization affiliated with the Communist International, and required every noncitizen resident in the United States to register every year with the government, be fingerprinted, and report all changes of address.

All the liberal and Left organizations fought hard against these bills, and none was adopted. But in 1936 Congress prohibited all noncitizens who had entered the country illegally from getting relief or working on any project supported by relief funds. "The effect of this provision," commented the *IJA Bulletin*, "is to doom to starvation a group estimated

"Aw, be a sport. Tell the newsreel audience you still have faith in the Lawd and good old Franklin D."   CROCKETT JOHNSON

Faith in Good Old Franklin D. "Aw, be a sport. Tell the newsreel audience you still have faith in the Lawd and good old Franklin D." By Crockett Johnson in *Redder than the Rose* by Robert Forsythe. New York: Covici-Friede Publishers 1935, p. 232.

at 120,000 persons!" And experience had taught Carol that the defeated bills would be filed for easy reintroduction at the proper time.

The IJA now appealed to the two major groups among its readers: "believers in civil liberties, . . . who regard the free expression of thought as essential to progress and to good government whether capitalist or soviet," and "those who have lost faith in democracy under a class society." Both groups should see that "exclusion and deportation of alien radicals stands as a serious menace and warrants unrelenting and active opposition."

During the Depression, the number of aliens deported fell from 19,246 in 1932 to 9,195 in 1936; one-tenth of the reported decisions involved Communists. The number of aliens "permitted to depart without warrant proceedings" also fell, from 10,775 in 1932 to 8,251 in 1936. In fact, more aliens left the United States in each year from 1930 to 1936 than arrived here, according to the annual reports of the Secretary of Labor.

In her "Recent Items" column in the *Bulletin,* Carol reported in October 1936 that the Department of Labor refused to grant a visa to a member of Parliament, William Gallacher, who represented the British Communist Party. In the same issue, she reported the convictions of Pedro Albizu Campos, president of the Nationalist Party of Puerto Rico, and seven others on a charge of conspiracy to overthrow the United States government.

Summing up the status of the foreign-born in 1935 and 1936, the ILD reported eleven persons deported for trade union activity in 1936 and thirty-five facing deportation for such activity, including nine to Nazi Germany and four to fascist Italy. However, due to the work of the American Committee for Protection of Foreign Born, "and the intensive campaign it has waged for the right of asylum, no anti-Nazi refugee has as yet been deported from the United States to face Hitler's axe."

The intensive campaigns of the American Committee and the ILD were touching many lives, especially in New York City. A young lawyer from Brooklyn might pick up a copy of the *New Masses,* enjoy the commentary (or the cartoons), and hear about the Communist Party. He might go to a club meeting, hear a speech by Joe Brodsky, and get fired up enough to take a can from the shelf at the end of the meeting and go out and stand on a street corner to collect money to save the *Scottsboro* boys or free Angelo Herndon. That is the way Victor Rabinowitz remembers this era as a young lawyer coming from a wealthy family with a Russian-Jewish anarchist background. He was working in a labor law firm with his partner, Leonard Boudin, and was intrigued by his clients and the law they were all trying to make. He was touched by the Marxist analysis of Leonard's uncle, the famous lawyer and scholar Louis B. Boudin, who boasted that V. I. Lenin had read his early writing.

People in other fields were also discovering Marxism. Louis Harap, a young instructor at Harvard interested in the philosophy of art, went with a group from Cambridge down to New York to meet with Lewis Corey, historian Louis Hacker, Bernhard Stern, and others to start a new magazine, *Science and Society,* and form its first editorial board.

Hallie Flanagan, as director of the WPA Federal Theatre, was declaring that although "the arts projects were being set up to deal with physical hunger" they also had to concern themselves with "another form of hunger . . . the hunger of millions of Americans for music, plays, pictures and books." The Federal Theatre put on *One Third of a Nation,* daring to name senators who had produced and even profited from slum

J. P. Morgan's Apple Cart. Untitled cartoon published during the congressional hearings about super profits of munitions makers during World War I. By William Gropper in *Redder than the Rose* by Robert Forsythe. New York: Covici-Friede Publishers 1935, facing the title page.

conditions. A group from the International Ladies Garment Workers Union soon pioneered a popular review, *Pins and Needles,* with its unforgettable ditty about "The Horse with the Union Label."

In the spring of 1936, the American Federation of Labor (AFL) suspended the unions affiliated with the Committee on Industrial Organization (CIO), which were trying to organize workers in steel, auto, and other mass-production industries. IJA lawyers quickly got caught up in what they called "The C.I.O. Controversy." The *IJA Bulletin* explained the background of the dispute, providing information not available in analytical form in any other legal journal or law review, as Carol constantly pointed out.

"Did you try reasoning with the officer?"

GARDNER REA

"Did you try reasoning with the officer?" Cartoon on the perennial topic of police misconduct. By Gardner Rea in *Redder than the Rose* by Robert Forsythe. New York: Covici-Friede Publishers 1935, p. 149.

On August 22, 1936, the editor of the *Bulletin* sent out a mimeo-graphed letter inviting lawyers to a meeting at Carol's apartment to undertake legal research for the Steel Workers Organizing Committee (SWOC) of the CIO. For the October issue the editors prepared "Steel and Law," describing the history of efforts to organize the steel industry since 1891. The *Bulletin* boasted about its extensive research project on defenses against arrests and on injunctions against organizing activity, working with the new general counsel to SWOC-CIO, Lee Pressman, who had moved from New Deal lawyer for the AAA to labor lawyer for the CIO. The IJA looked to actions for false arrest and false imprisonment and injunctions to prevent infringements of civil liberties. Out of the work on the mutiny case, Edward Malament and Herman Rosenfeld ultimately joined William L. Standard, general counsel for the National Maritime Union–CIO, and the two younger men soon found their way into the *IJA Bulletin* board and Carol's friendship.

The *Bulletin* described some of the problems arising on the local level, requiring the Southern Tenant Farmers Union, for example, to protect their members from long criminal sentences for union activity in eastern Arkansas.

The *Bulletin* continued to describe the law developing at the new National Labor Relations Board as lawyers moved from the failed AAA and NRA to the new NLRB, where Nat Witt soon organized the review section. Charles Fahy, as NLRB general counsel, showed a willingness to hire Jewish lawyers who "did not have good opportunities" in private practice, according to G. Warren Madden; Fahy also hired a few women lawyers. Many of these lawyers were members or friends of the IJA who kept the *Bulletin* informed of events in Washington that were building to a clash between the conservative Court and the New Deal President and Congress.

16.
Building a Guild of Lawyers

The great issue in the country was whether the U.S. Supreme Court would declare the new National Labor Relations Act unconstitutional. Carol and the other members of the IJA had been watching for some time the sharpening of the dispute, ranging the majority of the Justices of the Court on one side and Congress, the President, and the majority of men and women of the United States on the other. The pattern had become clear after the October 1929 stock market crash. Unemployed Councils, the Communist Party, Socialists, and other groups would call for nationwide marches and meetings on a particular day to demand unemployment compensation, government jobs for the unemployed, housing, and other reforms.

Masses of hungry, angry men and women would turn out. Many would be arrested; some would be clubbed; occasionally someone would be killed. The media would report the demonstrations. President Hoover would take no action because "prosperity is just around the corner." But after President Roosevelt's inauguration in March 1933, the script changed. FDR's brain trust would propose a bill to alleviate a particular problem caused by the Great Depression. Congress would pass a bill setting forth the need for the legislation, providing money to fund a new program, and establishing a new federal agency to police enforcement of the rights and regulations.

The Chamber of Commerce and the National Association of Manufacturers (NAM) would attack the bill in the press.

President Roosevelt would explain the bill to the voters in one of his fireside radio chats, defend it, sign it, and immediately appoint an administrator from outside the Washington beltway to get regulations written and enforced.

Instantly the chamber, the NAM, or individuals they supplied would file suit to have the act declared unconstitutional. The American Bar Association could be counted on to support this attack.

When the case reached the U.S. Supreme Court, a majority of the nine Justices would hold, in each case, that Congress could not pass such social legislation.

First, Congress in June 1933 rushed through the National Industrial Recovery Act, with its emergency provisions for the government to fix prices, wages, and hours. The Court struck it down unanimously in May 1935. Congress passed the Frazier-Lemke Act to relieve farm debtors. The Court struck it down unanimously in May 1935. Congress passed the Agricultural Adjustment Act in 1933 to regulate enough features of farming to permit some family farms to survive. A divided Court struck it down in 1936. Congress passed an act in 1934 establishing compulsory retirement and pensions for railroad workers. A divided Court struck it down in 1936. Next, Congress passed the Guffey Coal Act in 1935, regulating wages and hours of coal miners as well as regulating the production of coal. A divided Court struck it down in 1936. In each of these cases, the Court majority said it was acting in the name of states' rights: under the federal system, social legislation is solely up to the states.

At this point, Shad Polier, and some of his colleagues, had had enough. To him, the Depression was a great calamity, similar to slavery, and now events were paralleling the period after the Civil War when the President vetoed every bill passed by the Reconstruction Congress. Now the Supreme Court was overturning every bill passed by the New Deal Congress and signed by the President. As executive director of the IJA, Polier issued a press release charging that the decision on the Coal Act was "a second Dred Scott decision." In both cases the Court declared the federal government "impotent to deal with the major social problems presented," including the rights of workers to join unions and not to live in company-owned houses.

Chief Justice Hughes in a separate opinion in *Carter v. Carter Coal Company* suggested that the only method of dealing with the situation was by constitutional amendment, giving Congress power to enact labor legislation.

This opinion did not mollify Shad. He wanted an amendment "to deprive the Supreme Court of its veto power over legislation." Many Liberal, Left, and Communist lawyers agreed. They did not consider making the New Deal legislation permanent by adding an amendment to the Constitution, as the Radical Republican Congress had done when they were frustrated by the President and Supreme Court after the Civil War. But neither did they accept the distinction Justice Brandeis said he had been making: opposing those New Deal measures he felt would simply enlarge government bureaucracy without solving the underlying social problems, and supporting those New Deal measures he felt provided new, sound administrative methods of dealing with the rights of labor.

When New York State passed a law setting a minimum wage for women workers, employers challenged it immediately. The case put the Nine Old Men to the test. They could not find the legislation unconstitutional on the ground that it was up to the states to pass social legislation because the act *had* been passed by a state. And they *had* sustained two New Deal–like state laws in 1934 by a 5-to-4 vote. But now in 1936, the majority returned to the old theory that the state law violated the "substantive due process" of employers.

Carol and her colleagues had been fighting this concept every since the Court had said states could not pass laws limiting child labor in the twenties. The lawyers pointed out that when the "due process" clause was enacted into the Fourteenth Amendment after the Civil War to protect "persons," it was clearly intended to help one group of real *persons* — Negro ex-slaves. The Supreme Court recognized that intent until leaders of the new corporations began insisting in litigation that *corporations* were "persons" whose "property" was protected by the "due process" clause. They said corporate property included corporate profits. Corporate lobbyists fought every law passed by a state legislature to regulate rates for railroad freight or to set standards of safety, minimum wages, or maximum hours. They said these rules cut corporate profits and were not set by a fair system, thus denying corporations "due process."

The Court had agreed with the corporations on many of these issues from 1873 on, striking down one statute after another on the ground that it violated the "liberty of contract" or the "property" of corporate employers, railroad management, etc., although it had permitted the Interstate Commerce Commission (ICC) to continue to function.

Now Justice Harlan Stone dissented in the New York minimum wage case, *Morehead v. New York ex rel. Tipaldo*, saying:

> The Fourteenth Amendment has no more imbedded in the Constitution
> our preference for some particular set of economic beliefs, than it has
> adopted, in the name of liberty, the system of theology which we may
> happen to approve. . . . We should . . . leave the selection and the method

of the solution of the problems to which the statute is addressed where it seems to me the Constitution has left them, to the legislative branch of the government.

Carol and the IJA editors welcomed this opinion of Justice Stone (who had ruled against Carol's client, Vajtauer, in the 1927 deportation case). The IJAers saw the issue as a contest between the Court and the Congress for supremacy over legislation. In February 1936 the *IJA Bulletin* proposed a constitutional amendment taking from the courts the power to declare legislation unconstitutional — all legislation — saying it would be "absurd" to go to all the work required to amend the Constitution just to authorize states to pass minimum wage laws for women and children. After a lengthy discussion of the need to "Curb the Courts," the editors did give one final warning: "Vesting the legislature with supreme power does not guarantee truly democratic legislation. It at least makes it possible — if the people are organized and conscious of their wants." This stand made them natural allies of the lawyers in the New Deal and Democratic Party struggling to move forward in the face of a recalcitrant Republican majority on the Supreme Court and in the bar nationally.

Wherever Carol met with lawyers and clients, they gnawed at certain fundamental questions in this New Deal era of bitter strikes, arrests of demonstrators — and occasionally of lawyers — of labor spies, lynchings, and, at the same time, a new WPA Arts Project, National Labor Relations Board, and Social Security Act, and a vast increase in the number of government lawyers. In 1933 the anti-trust division of the Justice Department employed thirty-six lawyers, handling the bulk of federal government civil suits. Later in 1933, Jerome Frank hired ten lawyers for the Agricultural Adjustment Administration alone. The NLRB grew from fourteen lawyers to 226 by 1939. Each new agency repeated this pattern.

The labor and progressive lawyers in New York were largely from poor or middle-class families, many with parental roots in anarchism or socialism in the Old Country. Some were from intellectual upper-class families who had faced open anti-Semitism when they sought jobs in the big New York (Gentile) firms. Their clients were from a variety of nationalities and ethnic backgrounds including Irish, Negro, Italian, and Jewish.

By now, many who had followed John Abt and others to Washington had also followed his line of thought. Abt said later that he "quickly learned that while FDR was prepared to do as much as he thought necessary to save the system, he was not about to change it. . . . [T]he failure of the best that reformism had to offer sent me searching for alternatives and convinced me that the only alternative was the revolutionary path to socialism." This led Abt to join the Communist Party in Washington in 1934.

Some CP lawyers paid dues and attended a lot of meetings of their neighborhood clubs that concentrated on community issues. A very few CP lawyers and union leaders were members of so-called "secure," or secret, clubs, to protect their political privacy (and positions). Many more active lawyers were not CP members, did not pay dues, and attended fewer meetings. They all had a common worry about their office debts and a common language and set of understandings: capitalism is not working; socialism will be better; the working class is basic to the struggle for a better world; the rights of Negroes are being denied; sometimes FDR and Congress can be pushed into taking steps in the correct New Deal direction; and some capitalists can be made to see that unbridled capitalism cannot continue. They also agreed that the government must take responsibility for the basic needs of the people if the system is to continue to function, and that the Supreme Court's Nine Old Men will continue to stop whatever New Deal laws Congress enacts. They certainly agreed that the Soviet Union is a socialist country and that fascism and war are the main dangers.

Other lawyers were liberals, stalwart defenders of democratic rights for workers and political parties and of defendants' rights in criminal cases. Most were Democrats; a few were old-fashioned Lincoln Republicans. They followed the Ralph Waldo Emerson/William Lloyd Garrison/Wendell Phillips tradition. They wanted to defend the legal system, to lobby Congress and administrative agencies for good bills and regulations, and to enforce constitutional rights in the courts. They did not believe in socialism and they did not want to debate Left-wing ideology. They were prepared to provide vigorous representation to communists, socialists, anarchists, and other ideologists at low or sometimes no fees. They were absolutely opposed to fascism.

The largest group of progressive lawyers had a commitment to justice for their individual clients. They were pragmatists who went with the crowd on economic/political questions without any deep analysis or commitment to a particular ideology.

It was, then, the worst of times; it was the best of times. Certainly it was the Left of times. Millions were still homeless and hungry; millions were still unemployed. But many of these millions were also in motion politically — angry enough, determined enough, to try to change the system. How far would they go? Nobody knew for sure. Everybody knew there had been a revolution in Russia fifteen years before. Would it come to revolution in the United States? Sometimes it almost seemed possible, especially to those new to politics and political action.

A young worker in Portland, Oregon, spoke at a public meeting organized by the Communist Party to protest the shooting of striking longshoremen by the police and against illegal raids on workers' halls and homes. In 1934 Dirk DeJonge, an open CP member, stuck to these subjects, while urging his audience to obtain members for the Party and to purchase some Party literature. The police raided the meeting and arrested DeJonge and several others under the Oregon criminal syndical- ism act. ILD lawyers tried to defend them on the ground that the meeting was public and orderly and was held for a lawful purpose — that neither criminal syndicalism nor any unlawful conduct was taught or advocated at the meeting. They lost; the defendants were sentenced to seven years in prison, where they would join earlier Oregon criminal syndicalism defendants.

On appeal the Oregon Supreme Court held that mere participation in a meeting called by the CP was sufficient to violate the law, and affirmed the convictions.

The ILD lawyers in Portland sent a report on the case to Carol King in New York. She published it in the next *IJA Bulletin*. Then she began thinking about how to get a reversal in the U.S. Supreme Court. She talked to Osmond K. Fraenkel about the case. They had worked together on *Scottsboro* and other cases for the ILD and the IJA, and she had undoubtedly observed the inspired craftsmanship he added to every brief and argument he undertook.

They agreed that the best way to win *DeJonge* was to have the ACLU take over the appeal from the ILD and to have Osmond appear for the defendants in the Supreme Court. They also agreed "on the wisdom of

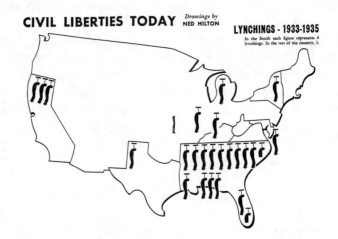

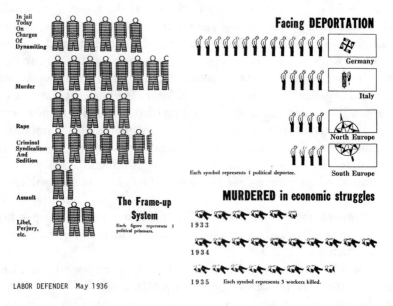

Civil Liberties Today. A graphic statistical report. By Ned Hilton in *The Labor Defender,* May 1936.

not challenging the state's contention that the Party advocated the forcible overthrow of the government," Fraenkel wrote later, "and that we should concentrate on the fact that he had not been charged with membership in the Party."

Carol and Osmond convinced the ACLU to take the case and to have Osmond undertake his first representation of the ACLU; this became a habit he continued for decades.

Their strategy worked. Fraenkel argued the case to the nine Justices in December 1936, soon after FDR's resounding re-election at the polls. He "spoke for about ten minutes outlining the bare facts and then said there was nothing more a lawyer could present. . . . Justice McReynolds tried to get the young lawyer [representing] Oregon to say they had made incendiary remarks, but he was honest and couldn't be led."

Everyone was mulling over these issues of economics and justice. Soon they sparked a new organization of lawyers as they had sparked *Science & Society* and a new type of theater. The impetus came from several sources. Maurice Sugar, IJA correspondent in Michigan and attorney for the new Auto Workers Union, wanted a national organization to overcome his political isolation in Detroit. He proposed the idea to IJA and ILD lawyers he knew in New York. Robert J. Silberstein liked the idea. He was president of the Lawyers Security League, whose members were unemployed lawyers who got jobs with the Works Progress Administration (WPA). Silberstein had learned how to be a political lawyer from working with Carol and others in the IJA and ILD. His members were certain to welcome a militant New Deal bar association. David Freedman of the ILD was another early supporter of the idea. At the same time Morris Ernst of the ACLU was urging lawyers to organize a union, as Heywood Broun and other journalists had just organized the American Newspaper Guild.

Bob Silberstein talked to Ernst, who agreed to proceed, understanding that the professional economic goals of the Lawyers Security League should be a part of the program of the new organization. Silberstein pledged that the league people would help do the day-to-day work.

Accordingly, on December 1, 1936, a small group gathered for dinner at the City Club. Ernst presided. Silberstein came from the Lawyers Security League, King and Polier from the IJA, along with Osmond K. Fraenkel. William L. Standard, longtime counsel to union sailors, and Abe Isserman were there, along with others who had been baptized in court fights for the IJA, ILD, CP, and the American Committee for

Protection of Foreign Born. Justine Tulin represented the lawyers hired by Mayor LaGuardia to try to cope with the massive breakdown in the economic system by working in new relief and regulatory agencies in the city. Louis Waldman attended, an older Socialist lawyer who had distrusted Carol King when he met her fifteen years before at the Civic Club, just after the Palmer Raids.

Everyone agreed to launch a National Lawyers Guild with a founding convention in February in Washington, where many lawyers were working for New Deal agencies. The group quickly put together an impressive executive committee, including Wisconsin governor Philip F. La Follette; Washington senator Homer T. Bone; retiring Chief Justice of the Minnesota Supreme Court John P. Devaney; Illinois federal District Court judge William H. Holly; state court judges from Missouri, California, and New York; and leading lawyers from one end of the country to the other, including the general counsel of the AFL.

After the dinner party, Waldman warned Ernst, "You've got too many Communists here," and he departed. Discussing the incident for an article on Carol King in 1951, entitled "The Communist's Dearest Friend," Ernst said he shrugged off Waldman's prophecy. Then "they sucked us in on a proposal to make dues one dollar. There were a lot of lawyers on WPA those days who could not afford more, and it seemed the democratic thing to do. Guild meetings thereafter took on more and more of a *Daily Worker* tone," Ernst wrote, referring to the Communist Party newspaper of that era.

Mortimer Riemer recalled the '30s as "a period of great unemployment, unrest, confusion, and indecision," when he "was particularly disturbed by those conditions domestically, and . . . by events abroad, particularly in Germany. As a Jew, I was deeply concerned. And it was represented to me that the Communist Party had a program, an effective one, to contribute to a solution of some of those ills, and I was solicited to join and I did so." He also joined the Lawyers Guild and became its first national executive secretary. (In 1955, in his testimony before the House Committee on Un-American Activities, Riemer was a friendly witness, naming the names of his former comrade lawyers.)

Martin Popper, an energetic, young, socially conscious lawyer from New York, moved quickly to the center of Guild work. He helped put together the first meeting of the New York City chapter of the new organization in early 1937. The legal and commercial press gave good coverage to the meeting, which was attended by 600 lawyers and addressed by Frank P. Walsh, chairman of the New York Power Commission. This longtime member of the American Bar Association said the ABA "has degenerated into a sort of lawyers' trust." Columbia professor Karl Llewellyn declared, "The abomination of abominations" of the ABA "is not that they have been completely blind on every public question, but that they have been . . . such incompetent advocates of the position they maintain." Ernst reported that he had refused for twenty years to join the ABA, ever since he learned that it elected a Negro to membership "by mistake."

But before its first convention, lawyers working for the new National Labor Relations Board strongly opposed Ernst's candidacy for Guild president. They said he was on the carpet for being an officer in some business that had fired its workers for union activity. They defeated his candidacy, which he never forgot or forgave.

In January 1937 the Supreme Court decided the case of *Dirk DeJonge,* unanimously (8–0) reversing his conviction. Chief Justice Hughes set forth the rule on the right of assembly cited in every constitutional law book from then on. The Court held that a Communist was "entitled to discuss the public issues of the day and in a lawful manner, without incitement to violence or crime, to seek redress of alleged grievances. That was of the essence of his guaranteed personal liberty":

> The greater the importance of safeguarding the community from incitements to the overthrow of our institutions by force and violence, the more imperative is the need to preserve inviolate the constitutional rights of free speech, free press and free assembly in order to maintain the opportunity for free political discussion, to the end that government may be responsive to the will of the people and that changes, if desired, may be obtained by peaceful means. Therein lies the security of the Republic, the very foundation of constitutional government.

The *IJA Bulletin* commented that this was also the time to reverse *Gitlow v. New York* — to make clear that criminal syndicalism statutes are unconstitutional — and for the Court to reaffirm the clear and present danger test. Perhaps the Court would take this step to further civil liberties protection in the pending *Herndon* case?

ॐ

In January 1937 the auto workers of Flint, Michigan, stunned the country by going on strike against General Motors. In the heart of the Middle West, white farmers' sons sat down at their machines and refused to move. GM could not bring in scabs to do the work and could not remove the machines to do the work elsewhere. Michigan's Democratic governor, Frank Murphy, listened to the plea by his University of Michigan classmate Maurice Sugar, representing the union, and refused to send in the National Guard to retake the plants in what would have been a bloodbath. GM was nudged by FDR to negotiate. It was threatened by dynamic support for the strike from John L. Lewis's coal miners and all the other members of the CIO who could just decide not to buy GM cars for a long time. The great corporation finally sat down with the new president of the new UAW-CIO. Sugar and other Detroit lawyers were infused with the power of the new labor movement as they headed for the founding convention of the National Lawyers Guild in Washington.

Carol could look forward to a reunion with IJAers who had already made their way into government jobs in Washington, joining the "plague of young lawyers" there. Some were with the Federal Communications Commission and the Securities and Exchange Commission. Others were with the NLRB and the new Social Security Administration, which faced extinction unless the Nine Old Men changed their minds about the constitutionality of social legislation, or lost their power to decide such questions.

The convention delegates supported FDR's proposal to "do something" about the recalcitrant Supreme Court by increasing the number of Justices, packing the Court by adding one for each sitting Justice who had reached seventy and served ten years. They also adopted a national constitution with a memorable preamble that Carol printed in the next *IJA Bulletin:*

> The National Lawyers Guild aims to unite the lawyers of America in a professional organization which shall function as an effective social force in the service of people to the end that human rights shall be regarded as more sacred than property rights.

The delegates voted to "welcome all lawyers who regard adjustments to new conditions as more important than the veneration of precedent, who recognize the importance of safeguarding and extending the rights of workers and farmers upon whom the welfare of the entire nation depends, of maintaining our civil rights and liberties and our democratic institutions, and who look upon the law as a living and flexible instrument; . . ."

Editor King also printed some of the objects of the Guild: "To aid in the establishment of governmental and professional agencies to supply adequate legal service to all who are in need or cannot obtain it; To aid in the adoption of laws for the economic and social welfare of the people; To keep the people informed upon legal matters affecting the public interest; To advance the economic well-being of members of the profession and the community at large."

The bylaws of the new Guild were to be drawn up by a committee of three leading Negro and white legal educators: Felix Cohen and Charles Houston of Washington, D.C., and Alexander H. Frey of Philadelphia. The delegates elected seven officers and thirty-six members of the National Executive Board, including two women, both from Chicago: Ruth Weyand, labor lawyer, and Pearl M. Hart, a large figure with an imposing style coming out of the strong, creative group of women who founded Hull House and later the Women's International League for Peace and Freedom. There was sharp competition for the seats from New York, and Carol King did not make it onto the list.

After the convention, Abe Isserman asked Carol to help him on his newest case, fighting judicial veto power in the face of runaway shops. She wrote an appellate brief against an anti-labor injunction, but the New Jersey appeals court ruled against them. The facts soon outstripped the law, however, which was happening all over the country. The employers who could still win in court had to sign a collective bargaining agreement with the union because it was the only way they could get any production. King immediately saw to it that the issue of runaway shops was fully explored in the next *Bulletin*, alongside the ceaseless recital of strikes, arrests for criminal syndicalism, beatings, and murder.

On March 11, 1937, Oregon repealed its criminal syndicalism law because the U.S. Supreme Court had struck down the conviction of Dirk DeJonge under that act. Then Washington State repealed its statute. And the Alabama Supreme Court reversed the conviction of Jack Barton, a Bessemer citizen under an ordinance prohibiting "seditious literature" and declared the ordinance unconstitutional. The U.S. Supreme Court decision of 1925 in *Gitlow,* upholding state criminal anarchy statutes, was finally overturned by federal and state courts, following the other rule in *Gitlow* that the federal government must protect people against violations of their rights by the states.

The IJA also held a meeting in April 1937 on "the legality of the sit-down strikes" going on all over the country, and especially the successful sit-down at the General Motors plant in Flint, Michigan.

It was a heady time to be a lawyer for labor and the Left as the New Deal legislation faced its most severe challenge. The big legal question was what the Supreme Court would do to the Wagner Labor Relations Act and the board it had established to protect the rights of workers to organize unions and bargain collectively with their employers. IJA members were intimately connected with the five cases challenging the NLRB. Tom Emerson, for one, went to work for the NLRB after he left the NRA, and he helped draft the NLRB brief in the *Jones & Laughlin Steel Corp.* case, using every technical skill he had learned from Walter Pollak and the IJA crowd.

Almost every legal scholar and Supreme Court watcher was sure the majority would declare this New Deal statute unconstitutional, as it had all the others. On April 12, 1937, Chief Justice Hughes announced the decision to a packed courtroom, sounding to Tom Emerson as if he were deciding an ordinary case about which there really was no dispute. By a vote of 5 to 4, the Justices upheld the act. They even sustained its application to *production* employees manufacturing steel, automobiles, and garments — i.e., workers who were not engaged in the traditional "commerce" or "transportation" of goods. The *Bulletin* reported in May that "the Supreme Court startled the country by sustaining the Act."

The IJA editors had to gloat at the extent of the victory: Jones & Laughlin Steel Corporation, "one of the mightiest in the country," must restore ten men to their jobs and award them back pay for over a year, and "for the first time, the Labor Board is in a position to enforce its rulings." As a result, International Harvester, Carnegie-Illinois Steel, American Steel & Wire, and Tennessee Coal and Iron announced withdrawal of support for their company unions.

The IJA editors faced a dilemma, or at least a contradiction. They wanted to welcome the decisions while condemning the reason the Court had made them. The editors insisted that "without doubt the outstanding feature of these decisions lies in the fact that they were brazenly political. . . . [C]ertain justices . . . must have been governed not by legal precedent but by political strategy," finally accepting the New Deal in order to save the ruling class from a revolt by workers and the unemployed. The IJA doubted that the Court's about-face seriously damaged its prestige, because "the Court's action, as usual, is concealed beneath a protective screen of legal formulae and the ultimate fact that the meaning of the Constitution changes under pressure is not readily made clear to the public. The basic myth which has made the Supreme Court sacrosanct in the middle-class mind is not so easily destroyed."

The Justices' action in 1937 saved the country from arguing about an amendment to the Constitution to give Congress more power over social legislation and the Supreme Court much less power. President Roosevelt's whole strategy had been to provide a series of quick Keynesian fixes to "solve" the "temporary" problems created by the Depression, which he had always painted as an aberration, not as the "cyclical phenomenon" the Communists termed it. As such, the country did not need a constitutional amendment enunciating basic economic rights. It only needed emergency measures proposed by a benevolent father figure in Washington, passed by a willing Congress, and declared constitutional by a realistic Supreme Court that was finally beginning to follow the election returns.

Having joined in putting a stop to the attack on the Court, Justice Harlan Stone soon started something that came to be known as a quiet revolution. He made his move in a footnote in another one of the cases attacking an act of Congress that regulated corporations. By now, Stone spoke for the majority of the Supreme Court in upholding a law regulating the interstate shipment of skimmed milk. For the Court, Stone held in *United States v. Carolene Products Co.* in 1938 that the Court could not overturn a statute regulating economic or commercial matters when the act had "a rational basis." He was building on his earlier dissenting opinion, lauded by the *IJA Bulletin* at the beginning of FDR's Supreme Court–packing fight, and thinking deeply about the appropriate legal response to the continuing crisis in the United States.

In Footnote Four, Stone went on to ask what courts should do when legislative bodies passed laws limiting voting rights for Negroes, interfering with the activities of minority political parties, or censoring newspapers. He based his question on Justice Holmes's opinion in *Gitlow,* on the decisions in *Herndon v. Lowry,* and the narrow string of cases setting forth strong First Amendment principles and protecting voting rights. He asked whether the courts should scrutinize more closely statutes threatening "prejudice against discrete and insular minorities" than statutes on economic questions.

Traditional civil libertarians quickly translated his difficult phrase, "discrete and insular minorities," into the "racial, religious, and political groups" Stone was referring to. They welcomed this proposal for a "double standard" of judicial review as a natural outcome of the cases Stone cited. Left-wing lawyers felt that their militant and aggressive defense of the *Scottsboro, Herndon, DeJonge,* and other cases was finally paying off. By raising the basic constitutional questions in those cases, in the media as well as in the courts, they had freed the defendants. They had also caused a liberal member of the judiciary to put a new gloss on the Constitution, based on the economic and social realities of the times.

Soon NLG, ILD, ACLU, CP, and other lawyers were insisting on a "yes" answer to the question posed by Justice Stone in Footnote Four. They said the courts *should* give closer scrutiny to statutes limiting human rights, while they should let Congress have freer reign to regulate the wages, hours, prices, and profits set by Big Business. In effect, the lawyers had decided that judges might be better protectors of the rights of racial, religious, and political minorities than state legislatures or Congress, while elected legislators and members of Congress might be quicker to regulate business than lifetime judges would be. The lawyers wrote and encouraged law review articles on the subject until Footnote Four achieved an honored place in constitutional law books and, at a later period, became the basis for majority opinions of the Supreme Court.

૨૬

The same month they handed down the Wagner Act decision in April 1937, the Justices of the Supreme Court decided *Lowry v. Herndon.* By a 5-to-4 vote, they freed Angelo Herndon.

Speaking for the majority, Justice Roberts unconditionally reaffirmed Justice Holmes's "clear and present danger" test. The Court pointed out that Angelo Herndon had been convicted because he was soliciting members for the Communist Party, which allegedly advocated unlawful doctrines. But to convict him for mere solicitation of members, without showing that he personally advocated a proscribed doctrine, was "an unwarranted invasion of the right of free speech." The Court also held that the statute as construed and applied in this case was so vague that it did "not furnish a sufficiently ascertainable standard of guilt" and it therefore violated the Fourteenth Amendment.

Carol King analyzed the decision for the ILD's *Labor Defender.* This was her second big win on the First Amendment after *DeJonge,* but she repeatedly attacked the vagueness of the majority opinion and the fact that only one vote stood between Herndon and the chain gang. She maintained that this victory was due to Roosevelt's proposal for reform of the Court, "bludgeon[ing]" it into a more decent point of view. She did conclude that "as a practical result of the Herndon decision Communist Party organizers should be able to carry on their work unimpeded in Georgia, and not only should this be true of party organizers but of persons active in behalf of left wing and trade union groups."

The *Labor Defender* followed her article with "We Salute the Lawyers," thanking trial lawyers Davis and Geer; Supreme Court lawyer Seymour; King, Wechsler, and Gellhorn, "who did brilliant work in preparing the case for argument"; W. A. Sutherland of Atlanta, counsel in the writ hearings and appeals; Charles Houston and Bethuel M. Webster, who filed an amicus brief in the Supreme Court in the rehearing proceedings with Arthur Garfield Hays and Morris Ernst; and the IJA, "which as an organization must be given credit for bringing together and coordinating the legal talent that was drawn upon from all sides to make this case a success." This was quite a different emphasis on the role of the lawyers than the quick paragraph after the victory in the *Greco-Carillo* case in the twenties. Whitney North Seymour told Walter Gellhorn that it was the most enjoyable moment in his legal career.

On May 24, 1937, in that remarkable spring of discontent with the old Supreme Court, the new Court, 5 to 4, upheld the Social Security Act in three decisions. It had taken more than four hard Depression years for the New Deal to break into the third branch of government after it was launched by the President and supported by the Congress.

Leo Linder, the lawyer Carol had recruited to become an expert on social security, discussed the decisions in detail in the *IJA Bulletin,* concluding, with what seemed a timely forecast, that soon health insurance would be provided under the same "public purpose" approach upholding payments of unemployment compensation and old-age benefits "for the general welfare." But the New Deal was, in fact, already over by the time the Court found it constitutional. Reform legislation from this time on faced major resistance in the Congress and was not proposed by the President.

By 1937 Carol had become a sole practitioner in the same suite as the deceased pioneering firm of Shorr, Brodsky & King. Joe also stayed; Isaac found other quarters.

After the demise of S.B.&K., King apparently never considered trying to establish a several-person firm to handle immigration and labor cases as she had successfully built the IJA to analyze and report on such cases. She avoided the complicated issues that would be raised by trying to find partners who would bring in enough paying cases to pay the overhead and who would agree on what cases to take at what fees, and what cases to take without fee. She loved the independence of sole practice and had learned to face the economic problems that went with it, although she was sorry to see Isaac move out.

Carol's phone rang repeatedly as lawyers sought her advice on difficult cases from coast to coast. It was common knowledge that Carol King often had a new idea, the name of a new expert, or the citation to a new decision. Everyone also seemed to know that she had built no ego barriers that were hard to breach and asked for no quid pro quo. If you would use her ideas for labor or civil rights clients, she would not even insist on your acknowledging that she was the source if you won.

Her friend Justine Wise Tulin, meanwhile, was building a legal career in the New Deal government, doing jobs that would help the working people who were her primary concern. She became a referee of the New York State Labor Department, which led first to her appointment as assistant corporation counsel of New York City in 1934 and on to Mayor LaGuardia's Committee on Relief as counsel and secretary. She continued what she called her "evening work" on the *IJA Bulletin*. In 1937, she was first sworn in as a justice of the New York Domestic Relations Court, then she invited Carol to celebrate her new domestic relation with Shad Polier. Carol particularly enjoyed attending this IJA wedding, as she had no hope of a second wedding for herself. King had little to celebrate in her own daily work. Paying cases remained scarce, so King accepted Abe Isserman's request to help on a different kind of problem involving a native ideology considered to be foreign. Mr. and Mrs. John Hering were working people with strong religious convictions whose children had just been expelled from public school for refusing to salute the flag in school or to pledge allegiance to the United States because these actions violated their religion. The Herings wanted the children reinstated in public school without violating their religious beliefs as Jehovah's Witnesses.

Isserman and King agreed that the New Jersey flag salute statute violated the First Amendment guarantee of religious freedom and the constitutional and statutory guarantees of free public schools for all children, although this issue had never been decided. Carol was soon digging into the history of religious freedom, finding cases and theories completely covering the subject. Abe nonetheless lost to the jury and in the New Jersey appellate court, which unanimously declared that the salute-and-pledge ceremony was patriotic in character, and ignored the stipulated agreement that the parents were too poor to send their children to private school.

Isserman and King took the case to the U.S. Supreme Court, where they could not find the four Justices needed to vote to hear the case in March 1938. Other lawyers for Jehovah's Witnesses around the country read about the brief in the *IJA Bulletin*, and it became the model in Witness litigation that continued to raise this issue in other states.

Despite this defeat, Carol was able to report some victories in this period. It was an exciting moment to join forces with the movement as a nonlawyer, and Clara Binswanger took this step about this time. She heard about the *IJA Bulletin* and applied for the rather ill-defined job of helping the editor and putting the subscription list in order. Mrs. Binswanger had a great deal in common with Mrs. King, although their differences were also pronounced. Her father had made a fortune in Philadelphia, where she married, started a family, and got divorced. Her mother was a Guggenheimer, a vigorous woman and a famous supporter of good causes. Sol Cohn remembers watching her signing affidavits with both hands, affidavits of support for innumerable refugees from Hitler's Germany so that they could enter the United States. Clara moved to New York with her children and followed her mother's tradition, putting in countless hours on the *Bulletin* every month — not for the remuneration, which was low, but for the principles, which were high.

Carol had one kind of relationship with Clara, a woman of similar age and situation. She had a different kind of relationship with her niece Peggy Stern and with a young woman law student, Marjorie Leonard, who met Carol through her husband, Norman, one of the Columbia Law School bunch around the *IJA Bulletin*. Both remember evenings with Carol ending on a subway, with Carol talking too loudly and attracting unwanted attention. Peggy recalls Carol "in evening dress, a shiny velvet affair, short in front and long in back, an expensive model in the fashion of several years before. One of the straps slipped off her shoulder as she was talking about sex in a loud voice." All eyes were turned their way, as Carol, ignoring her shoulder strap, continued talking.

When Peggy brought an instructor to meet Carol at her house, "Carol appeared in bare feet, a kind of Bohemian stock figure, making nothing but shocking and outrageous remarks." Peggy says it was typical of Carol to adopt a pose with people she didn't know, "like a child who wants you to love him despite the fact he is being impossible."

On Memorial Day 1937, Chicago police shot into a large peaceful crowd outside the Republic Steel plant. They killed ten unarmed workers. Carol King had been reporting the shooting and killing of unarmed strikers and unemployed demonstrators in the *IJA Bulletin* since 1932, usually one at a time in smaller towns in the South and West. This Memorial Day massacre shocked people throughout the country. In June, one of the strikers and an attending physician described the massacre to the delegates at a national conference called by the ILD in Washington. They said the cops acted brutally and without provocation and then prevented the union from aiding the wounded. The state practically admitted this statement was true when it reduced the charges against sixty-one defendant workers from conspiracy to unlawful assembly and fined them $1 to $10.

The conference delegates included representatives from the IJA. They considered many issues: criminal syndicalism and related repressive legislation, protection of the foreign born and the right of asylum, the current situation in Puerto Rico, prison conditions in the United States and recognition of the status of political prisoners, anti-lynching legislation, and civil rights in the United States today. In August, the ILD concluded that a significant feature of the year's fight had been "the cooperation of defense organizations in unified committees for work on single cases or situations" that helped produce "improved conditions." The cooperating organizations were the ACLU, American Committee, ILD, IJA, and the new National Lawyers Guild.

One of the first and most successful efforts at organizational cooperation had been work on the *Scottsboro* cases. And they were not over. In June 1937 they sprang back to life when the Alabama Supreme Court affirmed the fourth conviction of *Scottsboro* defendant Haywood Patterson. But the state of Alabama had had about enough of this case, which had broadcast the state's racist reputation internationally. The prosecution proposed a compromise. Judge Callahan blocked it. He held trials against three of the defendants one more time, at which he excluded evidence of the bias of the prosecutrix. He charged the jury for forty-eight minutes without once mentioning "reasonable doubt" or the possibility of acquittal. He did not mention the testimony of a physician who had examined the prosecutrix soon after the alleged rape and injuries but found no evidence of either. He assumed that all nine defendants present in the railroad car were guilty of rape, whether or not they had touched the two women. The three were convicted again, but this time the prosecutor did not even seek the death penalty against two of the defendants.

On July 24, 1937, the state wiped out (nolle prossed) the rape indictments against the remaining five of the nine "Scottsboro boys."

The defense committee immediately pointed out that logic now required wiping out charges against *all* the remaining defendants! By dropping charges against five of the nine, the prosecution had rejected Victoria Price's unconfirmed testimony as to the presence of two of the defendants in the car and her insistence that all nine took part in the alleged rape. Now that she was admittedly not credible, *none* should have been convicted on what was, in effect, her uncorroborated accusation.

The state immediately freed four of the defendants after more than eight years in prison. The fifth defendant, Ozie Powell, pleaded guilty to assaulting the deputy sheriff in prison and got the maximum: twenty years. The remaining four also stayed in prison: Clarence Norris under sentence of death, Haywood Patterson and Andy Wright for seventy-five years, and Charlie Weems for ninety-nine years.

On July 29, 1937, a gigantic victory meeting at the Hippodrome in New York City welcomed the four newly freed *Scottsboro* defendants. As Joe Brodsky spoke, many in the audience called up the image of this large Jewish lawyer from New York (and Russia) striding through the streets of Southern cities one step ahead of white mobs who thought lynching Negroes was right.

"Why do the bourbons of Alabama fear the Scottsboro case?" Brodsky asked. "Why have they felt it necessary to make this concession of freeing four of the boys? . . . Because they have come to see that Scottsboro symbolizes the growing unity of black and white in united defense against their common exploiters. They want to get rid of the Scottsboro case, so as to stop it from being a living issue."

Before Carol moved out of *Scottsboro,* she sat down to write a brief description of the litigation for the *IJA Bulletin,* setting forth the lessons learned to show to the next batch of lawyers she would recruit when the next hard case arose. She had a feeling that the remaining five would eventually be released, but only after another major effort. She knew the immediate value of the precedents set by the Supreme Court because she had begun to use them in her other cases to prove that poor defendants have a right to the effective assistance of counsel in felony cases, and that Negroes cannot be deliberately excluded from juries if convictions are to be upheld.

By this time, the labor movement was in high gear. Some former AFL chiefs of Right-wing trade unions had moved to the new CIO industrial unions. They were busily hiring as CIO organizers the very leaders of Unemployed Councils and Communist Party clubs whom they had ordered beaten up by their goons in the 1920s, according to Aaron Cohen (one of the beating recipients). The deep national economic crisis appeared to be responding to FDR's New Deal/Keynesian medicine, although close observers noted that the newly created jobs were usually related to armaments to be sold abroad and not to products and services needed by the people at home.

The National Lawyers Guild was well launched as FDR turned his attention overseas. Carol also faced new problems, international in scope, that would force her out of her backstage role and into the limelight.

17.
Uniting on Many Fronts

Clients constantly appeared at Carol King's office in the mid-thirties seeking help in solving a myriad of individual problems created by the rise of fascism in Europe and Asia. King's view of events was based on what she heard from these clients and from friends; from her own travels in Moscow, Berlin, and Warsaw; from what she read by Henri Barbusse, Albert Deutsch, John Dos Passos, Maxim Gorki, Lincoln Steffens, and others who wrote for the *Labor Defender;* and from articles in the other periodicals she read, from the *New York Times* to the *Daily Worker* and the *New Masses.*

Hitler, backed by the German industrial/military complex and its friends abroad, first led an attack on the German trade unions, the Communist Party, IJA lawyers, cultural and intellectual leaders, Social Democrats and other German democrats, and then specifically against gypsies, homosexuals, and Jews. The Nazis destroyed the elected government and the scientific and cultural heritage of Germany, and then threatened to destroy the democratic governments of every surrounding country. Some people in England and France feared socialist revolutions in their countries due to the economic crisis more than they feared German fascism. They supported Hitler openly or called for neutrality with Nazi Germany. The Soviet Union said it feared attack by fascist forces, and Stalin launched treason trials he said were needed to root out traitors. Opponents said he had become a ruthless dictator.

Spain was thrown into civil war by Generalissimo Franco and his Falangists, who were prepared to overthrow the first constitutionally elected government of that country. Communists, Socialists, anarchists, and other Leftists all over the world united on this issue. Thousands volunteered to go and fight for the Loyalist government of Spain, including lawyers from the United States like Max Krauthamar, a member of the IJA, Lawyers Guild, Lawyers Security League, and ILD legal staff. He was cited for exceptional bravery in defense of Madrid before he was killed. Twenty-five hundred lawyers and guests attended the memorial meeting for him in September 1937. Guild members Melvin Orsink and Daniel Hutner also died there in battle, as did Milton Herndon, brother of Angelo Herndon The War led to much soul-searching among fellow lawyers and activists about the need to put their bodies on the line.

In this period, progressives and Leftists all over Europe were seeking to escape, or at least preparing for quick departure if that became necessary. Some Asian radicals were in a parallel situation due to the Japanese invasion of China and to Chiang Kai-shek's attack on Mao Tse-tung and the Chinese Communist forces fighting the Japanese. Some saw the situation as reminiscent of the great migrations from Europe in 1848, when radical workers fled after defeat of their efforts to establish workers' socialist states envisioned by Marx and Engels in *The Communist Manifesto*. Now radical workers tried to get out of Europe and find a haven. To many, the United States seemed the best spot in which to settle until Hitler, Mussolini, and Tojo were defeated — and their defeat did not seem imminent. Some sought refuge in Central and South American countries.

In contrast to the migrations of 1848, the barbed wire of immigration forms and regulations was strung across the entryway to Ellis Island during the Red scare of the Great War and was still very much in evidence during the Depression. The wise course now was to try to find a U.S. lawyer to help cut the wire, or at least find a small tear through which one could enter.

On such a mission, one day in March 1937, a woman Carol King knew in the publishing business apparently brought her $7,000 in cash and asked her simply to deposit it and write a check for $7,000 to open an account for a writer presently in Holland. (This information appears in King's FBI file.) The friend was from Germany originally; she said the money came from the writer's account in an Amsterdam bank. Carol evidently wrote the check, which the friend deposited in an account in the Manufacturers Trust Company in the name of Stefan Brandt. The bank sent a deposit book to its new depositor in Europe.

Carol King would have had no reason to make any connection between this transaction and a *New York Times* headline on October 3, 1937: "THREE SEIZED AS SPIES ACCUSED OF KILLING." The *Times* reported the September murder of one Ignace Reiss of Switzerland, allegedly because of his denunciation of Stalin's policies in the European press. Carol probably thought no more about the transaction as she went on about her work. (The FBI ultimately established that Ignace Reiss was also known as Stefan Brandt; and after his widow came to the United States, they worked for months in 1943 to establish a connection between King and Mrs. Brandt and to discover some wrongdoing by King.)

In May 1937 seaman Johannes Wiegel faced deportation as the INS continued to arrest anti-Nazis for deportation, with German sailors their frequent prey. Wiegel pleaded that he would face persecution for his political beliefs if ordered back to his native Germany, and the lawyers argued that his life hung in the balance. At the last minute the American Committee for Protection of Foreign Born got the INS to permit him "voluntary departure" to another country.

More and more often, lawyers were asking Carol to help on hard cases. She knew the law cold, and the judges. And she knew how to think strategically — without insisting on taking credit, or a retainer. She had achieved a good part of the goal she had set herself fifteen years before: to have the authority to decide how to conduct the fight against the Immigration Service.

Joe Brodsky asked King to represent two IWO members in Cleveland who had applied for citizenship. The INS officials claimed that IWO membership, by itself, was a bar to the naturalization of Dominik Stevko and Paul Hanus. Carol took a train to Cleveland to help the local lawyers argue the case. They lost nonetheless. And the federal judge stressed that the lawyers "theoretically" representing the aliens were also frequently employed by the IWO and the ACLU. He characterized the ACLU as an organization revealed by the New York Lusk Committee of 1919–1920 and a congressional report of 1931 to be a supporter of subversive movements.

Client Dominic Sallitto sent Carol back to the INS to work with Isaac Shorr to prevent Sallitto's deportation as an anarchist. The only evidence in the record of Sallitto's membership in an anarchist group was the testimony of an immigration inspector who had made a "mental note" of an alleged public admission to that effect. Four citizens who had been present at the time of this alleged admission denied that Sallitto had made it. He also had a three-year-old child born in the United States, a U.S. citizen who would either lose his father if Sallitto were deported or his residence in this country if he left with his father.

The district court judge held Sallitto deportable and said he was without power to do anything about possible attacks on Sallitto after his deportation to Mussolini's Italy. The Second Circuit Court of Appeals sustained the deportation order against Carol's claim of insufficient evidence. But thirty months after Sallitto's arrest, in January 1938, his attorneys were notified that the Labor Department had canceled the warrant of deportation against him — on the ground that the evidence was insufficient! Having lost the companion case of Vincent Ferrero, who was deported to Italy, they savored this victory doubly.

This kind of action led the ACLU to consider King the appropriate person to prepare a memo for them on "Suggestions to Attorneys Handling Deportations Involving Political or Economic Views and Activities." She had been involved in each of the political deportation cases decided by the U.S. Supreme Court since 1920 — *Tisi, Mensevich, Bilokumsky, Mahler,* and *Vajtauer,* with or without her name being listed on the brief. She had been involved in hundreds of administrative proceedings and innumerable cases in the lower courts. Probably equally important, she had bothered to record hundreds of these cases, and the cases of other lawyers, first in the *Law and Freedom Bulletin* and then in the *IJA Bulletin.*

The IJA and Carol King chalked up another victory in May 1937, when the U.S. Supreme Court held that picketing in the absence of a strike is constitutional in *Senn v. Tile Layers Protective Union.* New Dealer Francis Biddle, ACLU lawyer Osmond K. Fraenkel, Professor Lloyd K. Garrison, and IJAers Nathan Greene and V. Henry Rothschild II had filed a brief on behalf of the IJA and the ACLU as amici curiae in support of this position. At the same time, King reported that a circuit judge in Kankakee, Illinois, was denying naturalization to any applicant who said "yes" to the question the judge had added to the traditional list: "Do you favor the sit-down strike?"

⁊⋲

When the Lawyers Guild held its second convention in February 1938, it boasted 2,000 members among the 175,000 lawyers in the country, including one each from Alabama, North Carolina, and Rhode Island; more than one-third were from New York. Carol and Isaac and Joe, Vito Marcantonio, Maurice Sugar, and a few others from the Palmer Raid days could consider these lawyers the professional descendants of the little band of willful lawyers from twenty years earlier. Some of them had begun to correspond with each other during the World War to stop the assault on conscientious objectors and union organizers, and had determined in 1920 and 1921 to stop the Attorney General's raids, to restore constitutional rights to citizens, to gain rights for aliens, and to achieve equal protection for Negroes. Now they had joined forces in 1938 with thousands of young lawyers on the side of democratic rights. This occasion turned out to mark the high point of joint work by New Dealers, Communists, Socialists, some Lincoln Republicans, some anarchists, and many less ideological lawyers for the underdog and people of color.

Time magazine reported very favorably on the convention of 605 Negro and white delegates that "was less pretentious than the convention of a moderately prosperous labor union [with] dinner jackets scarcer than paying clients." Guest speakers included solicitor-general designate Robert H. Jackson, Senator Robert M. La Follette, Jr. (Rep.-Wis.), University of Wisconsin Law School dean Lloyd K. Garrison, and Representative Maury Maverick (Dem.-Tex.). *Time* said the resolutions and program of the Guild "looked sufficiently Rooseveltian" to justify the "cordial greetings" sent by the President. With 350 New York members of the Guild "either on relief or working for the WPA," the Guild was still fighting for a WPA lawyers project as well as a radical new plan to set up 'legal clinics' throughout the country "to provide regular jobs for needy lawyers and justice for poor people with good cases."

New York Supreme Court Justice Ferdinand Pecora was the unanimous choice for Guild president. He was a natural, after his biting examination of J. Pierpont Morgan during the Senate investigation of the Stock Exchange four years before. The Guild's new National Executive Board of 64 included Governors Elmer A. Benson of Minnesota and Philip F. La Follette of Wisconsin, John P. Devaney of the Minnesota Supreme Court, brilliant CIO general counsel Lee Pressman, pudgy AFL general counsel Joseph Padway, and many other well-known labor lawyers.

Carol and her friends watched for the ABA's response to the upstart Guild. They noted with interest that the staid ABA House of Delegates established a special committee on the economic condition of the bar under the chair of Dean Garrison, an *IJA Bulletin* subscriber who had just addressed the Guild convention. In June 1938 the committee finally told the public the truth about lawyers in one of the interminable sentences for which such lawyers are famous:

[with] large numbers of lawyers . . . unable to earn a living in the practice;
. . . with innumerable young lawyers unable to find openings; with many
of the older men . . . scarcely able to keep going; with substandard
proprietary law schools turning out each year thousands of ill-prepared
. . . aspirants for admission; with lay agencies . . . encroaching . . . upon
the practice; . . . with people in the low income groups frequently go[ing]
without legal assistance because they cannot afford to pay for it, or because
they distrust lawyers, . . . or do not know when they need advice; with
evidence . . . that the public relations of the bar are defective; with . . . cost
of maintaining offices excessively high, . . . we think it imperative that the
bar should take action both to get at the facts more fully and to experiment
with remedies.

The New York County Lawyers Association issued a study that was
even more specific: almost half the lawyers in New York County earned
less than the respectable minimum family subsistence level of $2,500 per
year. One-third earned less than $2,000, one-sixth less than $1,000, and
almost one lawyer in ten earned less than $500. Substantial portions "are
on the edge of starvation, with close to 10 percent of the New York City
bar virtually confessed paupers."

This poverty among lawyers was still widespread among all workers
in 1938. Starting in the fall of 1937 and moving into the spring of 1938,
the economy had slumped disastrously. After the Great Depression of
1929 followed by the New Deal recovery starting in 1933, it was a
frightening prospect to see industrial production decline by 33 percent
and industrial stock prices go down by 50 percent. Worse than that, nearly
four million people lost their jobs, boosting total unemployment to 11.5
million. Once again some people started wondering: If the New Deal does
not work, is there really any answer short of revolution?

The INS had never stopped working to deport people who thought
about revolution. In 1938 their target was Joseph Strecker, who had
entered the country in 1912 from Austria and resided here continuously
thereafter. When he became her new, hot client, Carol humphed that he
was 'Some alien!' to anyone who would listen.

In 1933, after twenty-one years in this country, Strecker applied for
naturalization, and at his examination he admitted that he had been a
member of the Communist Party, having joined in 1932 and been dropped
from membership for nonpayment of dues six months before his arrest

for deportation. There was no contrary evidence. The Service ordered his deportation for having been a CP member after entry into this country, and assumed that the CP at all times advocated the violent overthrow of the U.S. government. But Austria refused him a passport because his birthplace was now part of Poland. Finally Poland, cooperating with the U.S. government, agreed to give him a passport.

Strecker's lawyers convinced the Fifth Circuit Court of Appeals that "a deportation order requires more than a mere fiating. There must be evidence in the record supporting the finding on which the order rests." The judges found that the record did not show that the Communist Party advocated the violent overthrow of the government in 1932–1933. Editor King reported in the *IJA Bulletin* that Judge Joseph Hutcheson went further than that, because it seemed to him "a kind of Pecksniffian righteousness, savoring strongly of hypocrisy and party bigotry, to assume and find that merely because Strecker joined the Communist Party of America, he is an advocate of, or belongs to, a party which advocates the overthrow of the government of the United States." The spokesman for the circuit court for the South expressed a strong commitment to the Jeffersonian tradition in his comment: "It seems to me, too, that the cause of liberalism is more retarded than advanced by forays for deportation on evidence like this." The court ordered the *Strecker* case sent back to the Immigration Service for new hearings.

The government appealed to the Supreme Court, and Strecker hired King to defend him. She convinced Whitney North Seymour and Herbert Wechsler to write the brief and argue the case, hoping for a repeat of their recent victory in *Herndon.*

Carol maintained that Strecker's fate would determine the tactics the Immigration Service would follow in going after bigger game — one Harry Renton Bridges, president of the International Longshoremen's and Warehousemen's Union (ILWU), California regional director of the Congress of Industrial Organizations (CIO), undisputed kingpin of the labor movement in California and on the West Coast docks, and inspiration to maritime workers on the Gulf and the East Coast. On March 2, 1938, Secretary of Labor Perkins issued a warrant for the arrest of Harry Bridges on four charges: having been a member of, or affiliated with, an organization advocating, teaching, and distributing literature advocating the overthrow of the U.S. government by force and violence.

Lee Pressman, Esq., general counsel to the CIO, soon retained Carol King to go to work on the case. She responded forthrightly:

The law in cases of this character is very simple. There are about twenty-five reported cases of deportation for membership in or affiliation with the Communist Party. I have already finished rereading and digesting them. As there are only a very few cases where membership was not admitted the cases do not throw much light on the situation.

The important questions are questions of fact, and it is quite impossible to deal with these at long distance. I hope that the lawyers in California have long been busy gathering evidence to discredit Arthur Kent. I believe that this is the crux of the whole case. If the government can prove the truth of the statements in that affidavit we are sunk. The end of the affidavit is clearly false, and that, together with Kent's criminal record, should make it possible to undermine him as a witness. . . .

Unless the West Coast is investigating the facts thoroughly *now,* I believe that my time could be much better spent out there directing the investigation than sitting in New York reading law which will prove of slight consequence. The law and facts should be coordinated and I don't know the facts.

Pressman and the West Coast lawyers agreed with King. She took the long train ride out to meet with young labor lawyers Richard Gladstein, Aubrey Grossman, and Ben Margolis, and young labor leader Harry Bridges. The client was a cocky sailor from Australia who was confident he could win his deportation case if he could maintain his strategic position. The U.S. government as a whole was not against him — only the INS, the FBI, assorted bureaucrats at all levels, and a large number of congressmen and senators. The President actually needed Bridges's support if he planned to win an unprecedented third term in 1940, and Bridges had been careful not to become an automatic Democrat.

Sitting in a meeting with her client, and his local counsel, Carol felt the San Franciscans were properly deferential to the expert from New York, and Carol was impressed by Harry Bridges. He would obviously make a good client, which was important in a hard case. She realized that if she got into this case she would have to put all her "little alien" cases on hold for a couple of months while she worked in San Francisco on this "big" one. She concluded that she could make this adjustment, and that handling a case in California would not be bad for her son because the hearing would probably be held in the summer, when Johnny would be in camp anyway.

On her return, Carol began corresponding with her new co-counsel, writing to Grossman that she felt "rather different about writing to you now" knowing "what the Mills Building is like, not to mention Gladstein, Grossman and Margolis, collectively and individually." She also enclosed a bill "which I trust you will find in good order." She added that she was "gradually beginning to clear my head about the case" and was "getting some ideas . . . the first and foremost and one that I shall never give up, is that there should be an open hearing." (She also asked him to tell Caroline Decker that "when my hat got lost on the train it would have broken her heart because it was finally discovered under the mattress in my berth.")

In light of the pendency of the *Strecker* case, the INS stayed proceedings against Bridges until that case was concluded.

ॐ

In the summer and fall of 1938, so many people were talking about communism and social change that it affected the climate in which King practiced law. When the Bronx County Communist Party put on a party in New York City to celebrate the seventy-sixth birthday of Ella Reeve Bloor, *Life* magazine published a full page of photos, reporting the Young Communist League's bathing beauty contest and Gay Nineties folk-dance contest as Mother Bloor greeted 10,000 friends under the slogan "COMMUNISM IS 20th CENTURY AMERICANISM."

In this political climate, Vito Marcantonio ran for re-election to Congress in the November 1938 election on the American Labor Party ticket, not as the red Republican heir of LaGuardia he had been when he won in 1934 and lost in 1936. Lawrence Lader remembers "the storm and emotional pitch prized by those of us who worked three, four, and five nights a week" for Marc. "You had to be young and strong and ferociously committed to climb those tenement stairs night after night canvassing the voters." You gained "an understanding of poverty's meaning" as you smelled the uncollected garbage and figured out what "devices . . . to employ to get an apartment door opened, and the lengthy talk, often half an hour, that it took to probe a voter's needs and interests and convince people that only Marc represented them."

Lader and thousands of others did their job. In November 1938 the voters returned Marcantonio to Congress, where he soon began writing and supporting economic and social legislation.

And in November, nineteen men returned from fighting with the Loyalists in Spain, where Franco's fascist forces had been gaining ground with the support of German and Italian troops. In September the Spanish government had announced to the League of Nations that it was withdrawing from combat everyone who was not a Spanish citizen, in the vain hope that this decision would cause the United States and other democratic nations to lend support to Spain. The nineteen men had long lived in the United States as resident aliens before going to Spain. Having no U.S. passports, they returned as stowaways. When Roosevelt's New Deal government agents found them, they held the men at Ellis Island.

Carol and other immigration lawyers fought for the men tenaciously, one by one. They convinced the Department of Labor to release four without posting bond, or on $500 bond conditioned on their not becoming public charges. The INS ordered one man deported to Germany. Carol had prepared a brief in a similar case setting forth the political conditions inside Germany, including the instructions to guards at the Esterwegen concentration camp to seize "political and intellectual demagogues by the throat and silence them." She quoted an official German government information sheet issued February 2, 1937, showing 1,936 political prisoners, including 1,203 Social Democrats, 898 Communists, and 157 Social Laborites. This defense finally convinced the Immigration Service to permit the German-Spanish Civil War veteran to take "voluntary departure" to a South American country. The lawyers sued out habeas corpus petitions to prevent the United States from returning twelve of the remaining fourteen men to France, where they would be imprisoned.

After hearing their allegations of political repression in their homelands, Judge William Bondy of the U.S. District Court in New York denied habeas petitions even to Stefanos Tsermegos, born in Greece, and to Mirko Markovich, born in Yugoslavia. But he did so with a heavy heart. On the back of each petition he wrote, "Under the unusual circumstances of this case the court suggests to the Secretary of Labor that she consider the advisability of permitting the subject to depart to a country where he may remain in safety."

The secretary granted voluntary departure in some cases but denied it in others. The reasons were not clear to Carol King, but she described the facts in each case fully in her "Recent Items" column. She also quoted from President Roosevelt's statement in the *New York Times* dated November 18, 1938, that he had instructed the Secretary of Labor to extend visas of German visitors for six months and for other like periods as long as necessary. The German government had announced its intention to cancel all passports of nationals who did not return to Germany before December 10, 1938. The President reported that between 12,000 and 15,000 political refugees from Germany had arrived in the United States, and noted that not all of them were Jews by any means.

Concentration camps, war, and killing were much closer to Carol's daily life in this period than they were to many of her colleagues and friends. They were totally immersed in representing the new industrial CIO unions in steel, rubber, auto, and electrical or were working in the busy NLRB or in various state agencies to help almost one-third of the nation still lacking food, clothing, shelter, and jobs. As respite from thinking, Carol would spend hours folding and sealing the wrappers to send out the *Bulletin,* sitting with her stenographer of the moment and with Clara Binswanger, blithely confiding that this was the kind of work she was cut out for.

Nineteen thirty-eight was a great year for the *Bulletin*. Its circulation jumped from 800 in 1937 to 1,450 in 1938, including the libraries of the U.S. Supreme Court, Department of Justice, twenty-eight state supreme courts, and numerous courts, bar associations, and universities across the country. The *Index to Legal Periodicals* began to index all *Bulletin* articles, which were also cited by several courts, including the U.S. Supreme Court. To get lawyers to complete the articles they promised to write for the *Bulletin,* Carol had developed a system of reminder letters to authors that she dubbed their diaper service. One sample to Philip Dunaway: "It's the only time you ever failed me. How about the I.J.A. piece? If I don't have it by tomorrow, you are going to have to send it to me by telegram, collect, and even if you only write two hundred words, that is quite expensive. Love to you and Lillian — that is, if the piece is en route; otherwise, you may both go to eternal damnation!"

The success of the *Bulletin* led to a repeated shortage of personnel lost to new agencies and unions. This turnover had its affirmative side, of course. Carol could look in her address book and call up the CIO, NLRB, New York State Labor Department, the American Jewish Congress, National Maritime Union, Social Security office, or an occasional law school, and talk to a lawyer who had gotten his or her start on the *Bulletin.*

The "IJA boys" all cherished the story they heard from an appellate lawyer who had recently visited one of the liberal Justices of the Supreme Court. The only thing he saw on the large judicial desk was the latest issue of the *Bulletin.* This kind of story encouraged Carol to continue to run her effective, if informal, employment agency for new lawyers. When she met a young lawyer looking for a job, she would start pestering her friends who were in established New York law offices or in government agencies in Albany or Washington. Remembering that she had performed the same service for them a few years before, and knowing they would meet her soon at some convention, they usually helped her succeed in her quest.

At this point, Carol's life was very full of people, at home and at the office. Sometimes she got away to her brother's place in Wilton, Connecticut, where Louis and Honi kept a sort of open house — nobody had keys. It was like a way station to young folksinger Tom Glazer. He knew one of the Weiss's daughters and was living at the place in Wilton because he was broke. He met Carol King at a party there while the senior Weisses were away. He heard her say to another guest, Stanley Edgar Hyman, 'What do you mean, you can't get married on $25 a week? Of course you can!' Hyman wanted to marry Shirley Jackson, a classmate at Syracuse, but his sole income was a job at the *New Republic* for the summer, which he had won as a prize in the magazine's essay contest. The two young writers did not have a nickel between them in the depth of the Depression.

But they were in love, and Carol talked them into it. She said, 'I can get you a judge who will marry you right here in this apartment. It won't cost anything!' Glazer recounted. "So they, with not inconsiderable reluctance, did it. There was a wedding at the apartment, much to my amazement. The entire staff of the *New Republic* came — Malcolm Cowley was editor, Bruce Bliven was a leading writer. They were trying to be jolly at the wedding, although it was one of the darkest moments in U.S. history, with Hitler overrunning Europe and Roosevelt preventing aid to the Spanish Republic." Glazer happily reported that the marriage lasted, as Hyman became a leading literary critic and Jackson a famous short-story writer.

Glazer remembers Carol as very strong looking, "stronger than most men care for a woman to look." She was feminine but a little tough, he thought, maybe too tough. She was somewhat forbidding although he wasn't frightened by her. She seemed absolutely dead sure of herself, he remembered forty years later, having met her only twice. She was not unattractive to him, "but firm and fully packed, like the Lucky Strike ads of the period."

Glazer remembers her enormous energy. No one told him Carol was an important lawyer, although he had been told that Louis was, but he realized "she was way ahead of her time."

His view, as a younger man, of Carol King as a woman, he kept to himself. It was not universally held, as Carol discovered to her dismay and recounted to Clara Binswanger, who was on vacation from her job on the *IJA Bulletin* in Westport, Canada. Carol wrote on September 1, 1938:

> *Did I tell you about my long lost friend from Texas who was hanging over me? He devoted Friday to me and I'm afraid his intentions were not of the most honorable. But somehow at the time I didn't get the drift and finally disposed of him by 3 a.m. Saturday. It was at least a 10-hour day.*
>
> *Jonathan arrived Saturday [from camp]. The Barkley end of his family picked him up at the station because I was still tied up at the office, — but we managed a movie in the afternoon. . . . He ended [up] with a good case of seasickness Sunday morning and since then has been angelic.*

Carol went on to describe her Sunday, which she had determined to spend on her "Recent Items" column (RIs) for the next *Bulletin*. First Jonathan and the Barkleys went off to the beach. Then some people came for breakfast. Then Arto Funduklian, her friend and tenant, returned from a trip, and they started breakfast all over again. They gossiped for hours. And it was he who "discovered the dishonorable intentions of the Friday gentleman." Then Sol Cohn came over with his new wife for a very, very late breakfast. "By that time J. K. had returned from the beach and the day was gone — he finished it up by licking me at chess." Carol concluded with a note on her constant preoccupation: "You'll be glad to know business is a little better, but nothing to boast about."

꙳

One piece of Carol's business had to do with the development of the law, even when there was no possibility of a fee for her. She was not puritanical about the nature of her clients if their rights had been denied, and the Supreme Court might make a good decision in their case that would help in the cases of clients who were more principled and socially useful. Carol was consulted when the ACLU was asked to come into the case of two run-of-the-mill accused counterfeiters named Bridwell and Johnson. They claimed they had been denied the right to counsel in their criminal trials in a city where they had no friends or family and no access to lawyers.

This was the issue that had won one of the *Scottsboro* cases. It was important to Carol because of the posture of the case. Bridwell and Johnson had exhausted their direct appeals; they were trying to get out of prison by raising issues in a petition for habeas corpus. If the Supreme Court would decide an important issue on a *citizen* prisoner's habeas petition, she could argue that an *alien* could also raise an important issue on a habeas petition.

The problem in what came to be known as *Johnson v. Zerbst* was money. The habeas appeal could not get to the Supreme Court unless money was found to pay for the printing of the record and brief, a total of $300. As Carol wrote to her ally in Westport, the lack of such a sum could spell the end of a good constitutional lawsuit:

> Dear Clara,
> I can't decide whether to pull out of it
> permanently or merely resign as Secretary of the
> I.J.A. All of which arises from a conference in the
> Bridwell & Johnson cases. . . . All arrangements
> were complete to go ahead with the appeals. The
> A.C.L.U. to pay $100, Bridwell to pay $100 and [X]
> to raise $100. So Bridwell went home. At which
> point [X] changed his mind (Nuddy having refused to
> pony up his quota) and has now ultimated that he
> won't go ahead. Somehow I can't get it out of my
> mind that the I.J.A. sticks by its word and I don't
> know what the hell to do. I haven't been so simply
> furious in years & in order not to blow up here I'm
> blowing up to you . . . till that happened life was
> not so bad.
>
>   * * *
>
> [Representing an interval of some four hours]
>   Life has become delightful again. I can't believe
> that it and I are the same and of course I'm not.
> All that has happened is that I waited hours in an
> office and got what I wanted: (the big gun
> recognized me as a friend of his wife's at college
> although he had only seen me once 15 years ago at a
> railroad station for 5 minutes); that [B] has sent
> [X] packing because he's such a selfish guy and
> essentially mean & untrustworthy (she did a much
> better character sketch of him than I could ever)
> and that Mr. [K] is arranging to get married again.

Such a mix of political and personal gossip about what became a famous constitutional case might have upset some of Carol's (male) lawyer friends; others enjoyed and understood it, as Clara certainly did.

The appeal went forward in *Johnson v. Zerbst;* the Court agreed to decide the issue raised in the habeas petition. In April 1938 it was argued by an eminent lawyer, Elbert P. Tuttle of Atlanta (who was headed for a distinguished career on the Fifth Circuit). Within six weeks the Court found for the defendants (7–2). Newly appointed New Deal Justice Hugo Black ruled that the Sixth Amendment right to trial would be meaningless if defendants were not represented by counsel (citing the *Scottsboro* opinion); for this reason, in order to find that defendants intended to waive the right to counsel, the facts must be very clear.

All of this fancy procedural footwork made Carol King the appropriate person to chair the Committee on American Citizenship, Immigration, and Nationality of the National Lawyers Guild. Soon after assuming that position, she contacted the State Department as attorney for the ILD in an effort to get a visa for William Gallacher, who was still a Communist member of the British Parliament, as he had been when he was denied a visa in 1936. This time Gallacher wanted to attend a convention of the U.S. Communist Party. His request was denied.

⁊₹

In December 1938 the New York City chapter of the Guild presented a conference on the economics of the legal profession addressed by Professor Harold J. Laski of the London School of Economics, Professor Karl N. Llewellyn, chair of the New York State Board of Law Examiners, and by the assistant attorney general of New York State. The assemblage affirmed that "the economic security of lawyers is a necessary condition to the maintenance" of a "fearless bar" to assure "real equality before the law."

This forthright approach to economic survival touched the problem Carol found more vexing and intractable than any other in her practice. Still, she was managing as one of the few women in practice and one of the handful in the Lawyers Guild, organized in part to support the President's Court-packing plan, which was well on its way to becoming a broad-based, effective, and permanent organization as the fever to pack the Supreme Court ended.

On Lincoln's birthday weekend in 1939, King took off for Chicago by train to be a delegate to the third convention of the Guild. A divisive issue surfaced at the first meeting of the National Executive Board (NEB) prior to the convention. Under "new business," founding member Morris Ernst told the NEB that he intended to propose an amendment to the bylaws and constitution of the Guild "making clear that we are for democracy[,] and the Bill of Rights and we are opposed to Communism, Fascism, and Nazism. . . . Short of such a declaration by us, we are going to have a hard time clearing our record before the public." He wanted convention action for his "own emotional comfort." (Ernst did not mention his blossoming friendship with FBI chief J. Edgar Hoover, which was revealed decades later.)

Ernst's proposal led to intense discussion of the issue by the diverse elements making up the Guild — from Hubert Delany, a leading liberal Negro lawyer, to Harry Sacher, a leading Communist labor lawyer, to Judge Ferdinand Pecora, outgoing Guild president, all of New York, to Justice Devaney of the Minnesota Supreme Court.

Fiery tempers were cooled as the NEB adjourned to attend the fancy convention banquet where President Pecora tried to bridge over the dispute, quoting Louis D. Brandeis in 1905:

> Instead of holding a position of independence, between the wealthy and the people, prepared to curb the excesses of either, able lawyers have, to a large extent, allowed themselves to become adjuncts of great corporations and have neglected the obligation to use their powers for the protection of the people. We hear much of the "corporation lawyer," and far too little of the "people's lawyer." The great opportunity of the American bar is and will be to stand again as it did in the past, ready to protect also the interests of the people.

Pecora said he supported the later Justice's view, and concluded with Ernst's formulation.

At 10:00 P.M. Saturday night, full of meat and drink and these words of Pecora, the National Executive Board members left the banquet to reconvene. Most of them were desperate to reach some consensus before the Ernst issue tore apart the whole convention. There were twenty-nine members present, surrounded by nonmembers including Carol King. Some labor lawyers and law professors immediately expressed concern about a phrase Pecora had used about rejecting both the tyranny of Big

Business and "the tyranny of . . . labor" at a time when labor and the new NLRB were being attacked from the Right.

George B. Leonard of Minnesota said that nobody had a greater admiration for Clarence Darrow than he had. Darrow was a philosophical anarchist, by Leonard's definition. Darrow's associate, Peter Sissman, was a socialist. Leonard did not know whether he could classify Judge Holly, but Holly had practiced law with both of them and been tolerant of their views (in the kind of political mix Carol King had experienced in Shorr, Brodsky & King). "You cannot go before the public," Leonard maintained, "whether as an individual or as the president of the National Lawyers Guild, to give any indication that we are for suppression of freedom of opinion. This sentence is susceptible to that charge."

Pecora replied that if his words were against freedom of conscience, he would buy another dictionary.

Judge Pat O'Brien of Michigan finally spoke up, a portly white-haired New Deal Irishman who said the Detroit Guild chapter had already faced down the same sort of proposition Ernst had just presented. He said that if the Guild "is going to be just another American Bar Association, I do not want to belong to it." Isidor Lazarus said that the Guild should "get down to business as a professional organization," united in action for the "pragmatic life in which we believe." The short, feisty Sacher entered the fray, speaking with the intensity that had won many jury trials for his labor clients (and brought one contempt citation): "Our fundamental concern is not really the resolution but appreciation on our part that we are not confined to purely professional problems." The Guild constitution contains no such limitation and one objective is "to protect and foster democratic processes and civil rights."

Some rose to warn against the idea that men would resign from the organization if their position on this motion did not prevail; others assured the body that this, of course, would not occur. It was a long, hot debate, sometimes vitriolic.

In the end, Pecora called for a vote on a compromise motion to publish his speech in the Guild *Quarterly.* Those in favor raised their hands: 28. Those opposed: 0. One lawyer abstained. The National Executive Board members returned to the convention, the matter seemingly settled without divisive debate on the floor. The delegates, in a spirit of unity, elected Municipal Court Judge John Gutnecht of Chicago president, and then elected several new members to the NEB, including Carol King of New York. But the Guild had been changed by the dispute, changed utterly.

In the first NEB meeting after the convention, only two issues were discussed: the filing of an amicus curiae brief in *Hague v. CIO,* which everyone favored, and the raising of money to pay the $3,020 deficit, which everyone also favored. But the Ernst controversy had resulted in Judge Pecora's failing to make the customary appeal to all of the delegates before the convention ended to pay up and meet the debt.

By the time Carol went down to Washington for her next NEB meeting, the mood was one of crisis. The NEB agreed to establish an executive council including Ernst to advise and confer with the Guild president. Treasurer George Leonard reported 3,250 paid-up members with a cash income of approximately $10,000 against expenditures of $14,000. The proposal to save money by ceasing publication of the *Quarterly* was unanimously defeated. Mortimer Riemer, national executive secretary, reported that the new Dies Committee on Un-American Activities had requested an examination of Guild records and membership lists, which had been furnished. The NEB proposed that a committee prepare an effective reply in the event of a public congressional committee hearing on the Guild.

Carol returned to New York and switched her attention temporarily to her son, Johnny. Although the precise role of women was changing, the problems of working mothers were constant. Women were strikers and strike leaders, organizers of unemployed councils and also, for the first time, one was a member of the cabinet of President Roosevelt. His wife had transformed the role of First Lady until "Eleanor" was a name known to every American, and known with a kind of affection and pride by most of the working people and aliens with whom Carol King associated.

But it was one thing for Eleanor Roosevelt to write a daily column about her life and to appear at the most unexpected times and places, such as checking out the working conditions of miners and their families. It must have been quite another to be Johnny King, an only child whose mother was gaining some national mention, often of a derogatory character. There were times when Carol asked Mrs. Barkley or Clara Binswanger to act in loco parentis when she was playing lawyer/mother instead of mother/lawyer.

Carol decided not to conform to another common parental attitude. She told a friend she had decided to give her teenager his entire annual clothing allowance at one time so he could select his own wardrobe, and do it all at once.

⅋

For many years, Carol's life had involved constant changing of hats. She had gotten quite good at it, even enjoyed it. Now she turned from concern about the Guild and Johnny to concern about the Supreme Court decision on the case of *Joseph Strecker*. In April 1939 Strecker won by a vote of 7 to 2. The Court rejected the INS deportation order, holding that the statute required proof of present membership in the CP whereas Strecker's membership had ceased before his arrest. The Court explicitly refused to rule on whether there was enough evidence in the record to decide whether the Communist Party advocated the violent overthrow of the government. It was a narrow victory, but it was a victory.

Since the Court had refused to deport Strecker for past membership, on June 12 the Immigration Service amended the deportation warrant against Harry Bridges to allege that "he *was and is* a member, or affiliated with, the Communist Party." This change opened the way for the hearing in his case, which would mark the beginning of a new era in the life of Carol King and in the development of free speech law in the United States.

PART III:
The War Forties, 1939–1945
Winning Cases in the Supreme Court

The Immigration Service and the FBI tried to deport Harry Bridges.
The President called for a democratic mobilization to win the war.
The army put 200,000 Japanese Americans into detention camps.
The Soviet Union became an ally against fascism.

The Constitution said:
"No person shall be . . . deprived of life, liberty, or property,
without due process of law, . . ."
— Fifth Amendment

On May 9, 1934, 15,000 longshoremen went on strike from San Francisco down the Coast to San Pedro and from Texas to New Orleans on the Gulf. The longshoremen had been quick to take advantage of Section 7a of the National Industrial Recovery Act passed by the Depression Congress in 1933. When the government for the first time guaranteed the legal right to organize unions in the United States, members of the International Longshoremen's Association (ILA) immediately stepped up their efforts to convince workers to join their weak American Federation of Labor locals and transform them into strong unions controlled by the rank and file.

Theirs was the seventh strike in 1934 involving 10,000 or more workers, and the fifty-fifth strike that year recorded by the young Labor Research Association. From Boston, Massachusetts, and Shelby, North Carolina, to Kenosha, Wisconsin — from Indianapolis to Des Moines to Butte, 280,000 workers had hit the bricks by May Day.

The ILA members in San Francisco demanded union control of hiring halls, an increase from $.85 an hour to $1 an hour as the basic wage, a five-day, thirty-hour week to spread the work, and recognition of the union. The next day the Marine Workers Industrial Union joined the walkout. That action was expected from this affiliate of the avowedly red Trade Union Unity League. Then the conservative International Seamen's Union–AFL joined the strike. This was unprecedented. Next came the Masters, Mates & Pilots–AFL. Then the Machinists Union–AFL refused to handle maritime work. Slowly every union working on or near the docks joined the concentric circles around the longshoremen, 25,000 strong. Within a month, the Pacific Coast maritime industry was at a standstill; not a single ship entered San Francisco Harbor.

The strike committee met nonstop, working out strategy and tactics. On June 16 the workers rejected an agreement that ILA president Joseph Ryan had signed with the Waterfront Employers' Association. It did not provide for a closed shop or the firing of strikebreakers.

On June 25 President Roosevelt appointed a board to investigate the strike and mediate. On July 3 the Industrial Association of San Francisco tried to open the port with strikebreakers and police assistance. They injured twenty-six workers, but the port remained closed.

The press kept mentioning one of the strike leaders, Harry Bridges, who stood out because of his militant speeches and his strong Australian accent. Bridges described the situation later. He said in the eighth week of the strike the ranks were holding firm. "Come July of 1934, the companies decided to open up the port. Of course the docks were piled high with cargo and we had to move them. So there was a big battle July 5, 1934. We lost two men, killed, shot down by the police, two to three hundred wounded, went to the hospital. That evening the governor of California called out the National Guard. It marched down the waterfront and took over."

Bridges remembers that his own committee met and said, "Now, what do we do? We've got to go back to work! We're licked."

Bridges said, "Oh, no, we're not! We can call a general strike!"

That doesn't mean he knew a hell of a lot, Bridges said. "I was only relying on experience I'd picked up in Australia. There was a general strike there in 1917 and tied up the whole darn country, for something like the same reason. There was a battle on the waterfront and the government called upon the Army."

Now Bridges own committee said, "Jesus, this cock-eyed Australian is nuts, talking about a general strike. How do you do it?"

"Well, you go and talk to the workers," Bridges answered. "Which we did. Didn't get turned down once. That included workers who were in unions in San Francisco, like the streetcar crews, and a big bunch of unaffiliated workers as well. Had a general strike which lasted four days, during which time we signed up 35,000 workers."

The mood in San Francisco moved journalist Lincoln Steffens to send an open letter to Secretary of Labor Frances Perkins:

> There is hysteria here, but the terror is white, not red. Businessmen are doing in this labor struggle what they would have liked to do against the old graft prosecution and other political reform movements, yours included; they are sicking on the mob, which, mark you well, is all theirs. It is the lawless tool of these righteous civic leaders who have always corrupted the law and the government. . . . It takes a Chamber of Commerce mentality to believe that these unhappy thousands of American workers on strike against conditions in American shipping and industry are merely misled by foreign Communist agitators.

The *New York Times* reported that vigilantes wrecked workers' halls and the offices of the *Western Worker,* leading the police to arrest 400 men and women and throw them into a crowded jail.

On July 19, by a vote of 191 to 174, the longshoremen called off the general strike. On the last day of July, 12,000 longshoremen and 13,000 other workers returned to work, agreeing to submit their demands to arbitration. In October, FDR's National Longshoremen's Board announced its award: $.95 an hour straight time, $1.40 overtime; joint control of hiring halls by union and management; and a thirty-hour week to spread the work (a unique condition then, and ever since).

The success of the general strike was momentous. It meant the whole West Coast was ripe for organization in solid, rank-and-file industrial unions. The longshoremen drafted a democratic union constitution with guarantees of referendum votes on contracts and practically everything else, and extremely easy methods of recalling officers. Harry Bridges, the "alien agitator," immediately became the storm center for attacks on the new industrial union movement on the West Coast. California governor Frank Merriam asked the federal government to rid the state of alien Reds. Secretary Perkins replied in 1934 that her department would "cooperate with California officials to the full extent authorized by law" and that the statutes authorized the deportation of anybody who "teaches Communism."

18.
Moving Onto Page One

When Carol King wasn't marveling at the sights she saw out the train windows on her long trip across the country in early July 1939, she was busy planning the best strategy for handling Harry Bridges's deportation hearing. In 1934 she had taken her first step in what became the *Bridges* case. She wrote in the *IJA Bulletin* that Secretary of Labor Perkins had made "a misstatement of the law" when she said the law permits the deportation of anyone who "teaches communism." King said this statement was a "positive encouragement to the lawless treatment of radicals" then underway. King made sure, through friends in Washington, that a copy of her article reached Perkins because she thought the Secretary might change her actions once she knew what the law really was.

Miss Perkins reported in 1934 that 373 persons were arrested during the longshoremen's strike on the West Coast; 101 were aliens, but only one could be deported for advocating or being a member of an organization advocating violent overthrow of the government, and only thirteen others were deportable for illegal entry or overstaying their legal time in the United States. The rest were legal residents.

Early in 1936 the commissioner of the Immigration Service testified before a subcommittee of the House Appropriations Committee that the San Francisco police department had followed Harry Bridges "unremittingly for years, and our men have also. He either is not a Communist, or has so carefully guarded his utterances that there is no legal ground for his deportation." A check on Bridges in Australia had turned up nothing about illegal activities prior to his departure in 1920. Three immigration agents appointed in 1936 to review the evidence against Bridges reported there was no legal basis for deportation proceedings.

By then the dockers had elected him president of their AFL local, and then had switched to the new Congress of Industrial Organizations and

The San Francisco General Strike. Longshoremen parade up and down the sidewalk in front of the docks. Police raid the Marine Workers Industrial Union hall. Harry Bridges addresses a mass meeting of striking longshoremen. Stores close in support of the strike. By Bits Hayden in *The Big Strike* by Mike Quin. Olema, California: Olema Publishing Co. 1949, pp. 3, 47, 91, 159.

elected him president of the new International Longshoremen's & Warehousemen's Union–CIO. When the fledgling California CIO named Bridges its regional director, anti-Red fear escalated: 'Now they can close down the whole state!' The feeling was that if Bridges were deported, things could get back to normal.

In January 1938, replying to congressional inquiries, Secretary Perkins stated the law again, this time correctly: "The various immigration acts do not forbid an alien to organize workers, lead strikes, induce fellow stevedores not to unload ships, or engage in other trade-union activities. Nor can such actions be regarded as attempts to overthrow the government." Attorney King had quietly won her point.

But by now Perkins had received numerous affidavits from the Seattle office of the INS alleging that Bridges had been a member of the U.S. Communist Party. On March 2, 1938, she issued a warrant for his arrest for deportation for past and present membership and affiliation. King had noted that because Bridges did not live in the Seattle district, this procedure was out of the ordinary.

The INS had to postpone the proceedings until the Supreme Court decided the *Strecker* case, leaving the Department of Labor to face the political dilemma posed by Bridges. The Roosevelt administration needed the CIO vote in the 1940 election, which was just around the corner, and the CIO was defending Bridges. Some members of Congress were demanding his immediate deportation; Representative J. Parnell Thomas (Rep.-N.J.) introduced a resolution to impeach the Secretary of Labor and two of her assistants for alleged failure to enforce the law against Bridges. (The fact that the Secretary was the first woman to serve in a President's cabinet made it much easier to make this proposal.)

In this situation, Secretary Perkins hit on an approach that would solve several problems at once. Pressured from the Right to 'get Bridges, and to hell with due process,' and from the Left and liberals to institute 'new, fair procedures in all alien cases,' Perkins went ahead with the *Bridges* case but appointed a special officer to conduct the hearings. This appointment marked a significant step toward due process: for the first time, the prosecutor would not also be the judge. Then Perkins selected as the special officer James M. Landis, new dean of Harvard Law School, author of *Cases on Labor Law* (1934) and *The Administrative Process* (1938), based in part on his experiences on the Federal Trade Commission and as chairman of the Securities and Exchange Commission. If Landis, the liberal Democrat, said Bridges was not deportable, he had the position and reputation to make the decision stick. And if he said Bridges should be deported, the New Dealers would take his word for it.

Carol told friends she was pleased with the Landis appointment. She had read his article on contempt of court in the twenties, and the *IJA Bulletin* had reported his statement that sitdown strikes may be legal. Her academic and establishment friends assured her that Landis was no cloistered professor. His years on the SEC had been spent trying to bring a measure of order to Wall Street after the debacle of the booming twenties, when corporate power had corrupted the free flow of the market. King thought Landis ought to be able to understand the defense argument that corporate power in San Francisco had tried to corrupt the free choice of dock workers to build unions. Certainly Landis would understand and respect the concept of due process of law in a deportation case.

When Dean Landis announced that the hearings would begin in San Francisco on July 12, 1939, Carol saw her thirteen-year-old son off for summer camp, left her household arrangements in the competent hands of Mrs. Barkley, and left the *IJA Bulletin* to her friend Clara Binswanger.

This was the first case Carol had worked on in which there would be a dispute about virtually every piece of evidence presented by either side since Greco and Carillo were charged with killing Mussolini supporters in 1927. But this time there would be no Clarence Darrow for the defense, no criminal court jury to play to, and no liberal Jewish judge. There would be, instead, an articulate Harry Bridges as client, represented by Carol King, Richard Gladstein, and Aubrey Grossman appearing before Dean James M. Landis, hearing officer.

The Bridges Defense Committee had planned Carol King's arrival in San Francisco as a newsworthy event. It had just publicized its big Saturday night dance at the Scottish Rite Auditorium featuring Hollywood stars Melvyn Douglas, John Garfield, and Lionel Stander, with journalist Herb Caen as master of ceremonies. Now Estolv Ward, executive secretary of the committee, planned King's first press conference carefully.

Local labor lawyers breathed her name with such reverence that Ward thought he knew exactly how to promote her and the case. He envisioned a New York career woman, attractive in a sophisticated sort of way, smartly dressed, retaining considerable youthful charm — and not averse to using it when necessary. He endowed his Carol King with brains, courage, and glamour and wanted her met by crowds of longshoremen and the press on the upper deck of the ferry crossing from the Oakland train terminal to San Francisco.

She brushed aside all his good intentions, taking a streamliner train to the middle of the desert east of Los Angeles and making the final 450 miles of her journey by bus.

Ward bemoaned this turn of events without understanding the reason for it. He switched his plans, calling all good longshoremen to greet the oncoming heroine at the San Francisco bus station at the ungodly hour of 9:30 on a Saturday night. When he learned that the bus would be an hour late, he decided to bring Mrs. King to San Francisco himself. Rushing onto the bus as it stood idling in the Oakland depot, Ward shouted, "Is Carol King here?"

Faces of weary travelers lifted up vacantly, until someone answered, "Yes." The voice sounded quite ordinary, and the sound led his eye to an ordinary-looking woman, middle-aged, rumpled, and dowdy. It was Ward's impression that she wore the queerest, most bedraggled wreck of a hat that had ever disgraced a human head.

He transferred Carol King and her luggage, without fuss or feathers, to his secondhand sedan. She quickly put him at ease, chatting about her son in New York and her experiences on the train and bus. She was obviously a motherly, neighborly widow. Her eyes were kindly, intelligent, busy. Ward saw immediately that she would have no patience with formality or pomp, and that external appearances mattered not a damn to her.

When they arrived at the bus terminal, Mrs. King was met by two longshoremen and one reporter. The longshoremen, complete with roses, mumbled embarrassed greetings, and the reporter asked silly provocative questions. She accepted the longshoremen and their flowers with warm smiles and laughter, making them glad they'd waited for her. She handled the reporter and his smart-aleck questions with an aplomb that disclosed the mettle beneath her kitchen-wrapper exterior. When Ward left her at her hotel, he was convinced that Carol King was a most unusual personality. He had never met such keen ability cushioned in such old-shoe comfort.

Carol delighted in having won her first battle against publicity. But her victory was short-lived. The next day's edition of the *San Francisco Examiner* reported:

Somehow, the rumor got around at the Bridges' hearing that Carol King, chief counsel for Bridges, was the daughter of Emma Goldman, one-time firebrand. The rumor sputtered along like a blazing fuse until it went right smack up to Carol King herself — and there was an explosive guffaw from her when she heard it.

Then Mrs. King, sputtering like a firecracker, proclaimed: "My father was Samuel Weiss, a corporation lawyer. My mother was Mrs. Samuel Weiss. They were an eminently respectable, middle class, bourgeois family." She paused and then suggested: "As a matter of fact, you might say I was the only black sheep."

Carol Weiss King was not amused by this encounter. She had to dispel the "Carol King" described in the press, which she did best with her pen. The minute she was alone she wrote a letter to her friend and ally Clara Binswanger, touching on a variety of concerns of a woman lawyer starting a big case.

> Sat. July 8, 6:00 a.m.
> Dear Clara:
>   Your package of IJA Bulletins arrived here O.K.
> and I have taken a few samples down to the office,
> but so far have had no one to sell them to other
> than witnesses in the case. If ever there is time,
> I'll turn out for a Lawyers Guild Wednesday
> luncheon meeting and go to town. But there just
> isn't time for anything, and I keep getting further
> and further behind. What I notice is that pressing
> inessentials have a way of taking precedence over
> essentials that have no time set for performance —
> so I guess the important things will never get done.
>   I keep seeing Harry all the time now. Even though
> he's a prima donna, I like the guy. He's the only
> prima donna with a sense of humor. . . . I really
> resented Harry's intrusion last night 'cause
> Caroline Decker had me to supper. I just felt
> pleasant and sociable and full of whiskey when we
> had to start on the evidence again.
>   Remember, I am avid for the N.Y. gossip. It's
> like going to the movies.
>   The hem is out of my new dress, and I have nei-
> ther a needle and thread nor Clara. Safety pins are
> a complete solution.
>   Love,
>   Carol

Carol admitted in her letters that she liked being at the center of things in a position to make a difference in the outcome. For almost twenty years she had been at the center, and for at least a decade she had helped make a difference, winning more often than she lost in several legal fields. Clearly the *Bridges* case would become the center of immigration law. And if the government could deport the president of the ILWU-CIO, no Left-led union was safe. Most of the industrial unions had some foreign-born workers among their leadership. They could be arrested for deportation, too, or their naturalization papers could be revoked if Bridges lost.

As to the law, it was eighteen years since the Palmer Raids arose out of the anti-alien hysteria of the Great War while a liberal Democrat, Woodrow Wilson, sat in the Oval Office. This was a new era in which war seemed imminent and the President was another liberal Democrat, Franklin Roosevelt. The *Bridges* case would determine which way the White House would handle the immigration policy in the coming period. So far, the record was bad for aliens.

Carol assumed she would be in charge of the strategy and tactics in the case in a legal sense and would be treated by the young lawyers in San Francisco as she was now treated by the young lawyers in New York. They would listen to her ideas, make them their own, and carry them out in the hearing, without being required to acknowledge their origin. At the first defense meeting, Carol avoided the customary jockeying among lawyers for the spotlight role. It was quickly agreed that the fiery Gladstein would cross-examine the government witnesses, based on material unearthed by the bulldog Grossman. If necessary, Ben Margolis could drop the firm's other cases to uncover friendly and unfriendly witnesses. King would simply listen and take notes. After each day's session, the lawyers would eat dinner together and return to their office to work. King agreed to summarize the transcript of the day's proceedings before the hearing opened the next day so the attorneys could trap a witness with his own previous words. She also wanted to analyze at the moment how each witness was stacking up, because she would have to write a brief for Landis when the hearing ended and another later for an appellate court if Landis ruled against Bridges.

By the end of their first week of working together, the older woman and the younger men had found a relationship in which they felt more comfortable than the unheard of idea of a woman senior partner with two men as juniors. Ward says Carol had become "Momma" and they had become her "boys," although there was less than a generation between them. As trial lawyers, Grossman and Gladstein thought about how they would stack up in the eyes of the hearing officer, and the press. They were good-looking young men who had put some money and thought into the suits and ties they planned to wear at the hearing. As the opening day of the hearing approached, they swore that "Momma" had to do something about her appearance before they would appear in the hearing room with her.

Finally the crisis came to center on her hat. Caroline Decker, whom Carol had befriended the year before, was designated to get her a new hat, and she did. Mrs. King good-naturedly wore the hat, which was charged to the defense committee expense account and put up to Estolv for inspection and approval. He was on the spot. Caroline wanted him to applaud the skypiece, while its wearer wanted him to laugh at it. He solved the problem by asserting that the hat was probably all right before Momma put it on, but once she wore the thing it was instantly transformed into a Carol King hat and looked the same as any other Carol King hat.

⁂

Dean Landis immediately asserted his style by announcing new rules for the hearings because of "the seriousness of the consequences of deportation to the alien." While "technically civil in character," deportation should be governed by "those constitutional standards of fairness in criminal administration set forth in the Sixth Amendment" — a breakthrough. The proceedings would be open to the press and the public — unusual. Counsel for the alien could buy a copy of the official transcript — never before allowed. The alien could subpoena witnesses — another first.

The defense was delighted that the government would have to parade its witnesses in full view of the public. Of course, the defense would also have to work harder. To win they would have to discredit thoroughly each government witness to the satisfaction of the press and the public attending the hearings, as well as to convince the hearing officer. Otherwise, Bridges's role as a union leader would be jeopardized.

Carol, Richie, Aubrey, and Harry worked out their strategy in long discussions in the defense office. Carol presented her plan for the hearings based on her successes in deportation hearings and habeas petitions to the federal courts. Most of her ideas were accepted. But the other lawyers

Carol King. An artist/journalist's ink sketch made during the first *Harry Bridges* hearing. By Pele DeLappe, 1939. Published with permission of the artist.

did not agree about the perimeter of the defense. They had brought Carol into the case because of her vast experience, but when she opposed their ideas based on that experience, they fought her tooth and nail.

They all wanted to win this case, but she thought the best method was to limit what the defense tried to prove, even under Landis's expansive rules. The younger men *also* wanted to prove that the government had conspired with anti-labor business interests to destroy Bridges and his union. She was afraid this tactic might backfire and warned them to limit the issues.

The Sunday before the hearing, the three lawyers and the client met in a small, warm room. The argument raged all day. Nobody won.

Finally the lawyers and the client agreed on three points. They had to smash every government witness to disprove the charge that Bridges had ever been a member of the Communist Party. They had to prove what Bridges had really said and done since he came to the United States. And they were also determined to prove that the charges against Bridges were based on an illegal conspiracy between some government officials, state officials, and powerful private interests. It was a tall order, and Carol left the meeting exhausted and down.

She woke up very early the next morning and started writing.

> 6:15 a.m., Mon., July 10, 1939
> Dear Clara:
>   I write letters the way some people play solitaire. If I weren't due at the office at 7:30, I could write interminably and this, believe it or not, is my seventh letter this morning. I do it to distract my mind or what passes for such.
>   Yesterday [we] fought all afternoon and evening. As human beings, we're cracking — I don't know what we'll do as lawyers. But, if we manage Major Milner [the first government witness] without suffering too great losses, the worst is over — .

A few hours later, the actors in this long-advertised play found their places on the launch running from San Francisco to the immigration station on Angel Island, thirty minutes away.

19.
Harry Bridges: Round One

In re Harry Bridges opened on a simple but dramatic note. The government called The Alien to the stand, and Landis permitted this procedure. Thomas B. Shoemaker, who had been sent from Washington to present the government's case against Bridges, examined him:

> Q. At this time I just wish to ask you but two questions. Are you an alien?
> A. I am.
> Q. Are you now a member of the Communist Party?
> A. No.
> Q. Or have you at any other time in the past been a member of the Communist Party?
> A. No.

As the cocky Bridges walked away from the stand, Mrs. King rose in her place, equally sure of herself. This was a forum she had long sought for all her alien clients. She explained that the defense theory of the case should be stated in advance so that Landis would be able to consider it in ruling on the admissibility of questions the defense asked the witnesses for the prosecution.

"This case is a product of employer plans and employer money," King began. "A conspiracy exists against Bridges. A key figure in it is Harper Knowles, chairman of the Commission on Subversive Activities of the American Legion in California. As a modern Voltaire might say, 'If there were no evidence against Bridges, Knowles would find it necessary to create some.' We shall show that blackmail was carried out with the active assistance of high public officials. The most prominent participants of this type are Captain Keegan, of the Portland Police, Lieutenant 'Red' Hynes, of the Los Angeles Police, Clarence Morrill, director of the

Harry Bridges. An artist/journalist's ink sketch made during one of the early days in the first *Harry Bridges* hearing. By Pele DeLappe, 1939. Published with permission of the artist.

California State Bureau of Criminal Identification, and Captain Odale, of the Portland Police Force."

The press corps rushed to take down her charges.

"This conspiracy needed and depended upon the cooperation of someone in [the] Immigration and Naturalization Service. We charge that R. P. Bonham [Seattle director of the Service] and his assistant, Mr. R. J. Norene, were also cogs in this complicated wheel." But the hub of the conspiracy was one Larry Morton Doyle, a free-lancing lawyer and investigator who claimed official ties with the governors of Oregon and California in pursuing Bridges. "It is he who does the dirty work in perjuring witnesses so that Mr. Bonham's hands may remain clean."

Dean Landis thought this went too far: "I do not like to interrupt you, Miss King, but the issues in this case . . ."

"I am coming to the issues," said Mrs. King.

"I trust so," Landis replied dryly.

She concluded directly, using the statement Nuddy Greene had worked over with her before she left New York. It accepted without argument the government's insistence that the alien had the burden of proving a negative:

> We finally shall prove that Harry Bridges is not a Communist, or affiliated with the Communist party; that those who testify he is a Communist do so falsely; that this false testimony was deliberately prepared outside of the Labor Department; that those who really prepared the case against Bridges hate Bridges, the CIO and the labor union movement; that, finally, the witnesses against Bridges are felons, or labor spies, or both, and their evidence is not credible; whereas Mr. Bridges is telling the exact truth when he says he is not, and never has been a member of the Communist Party.

Shoemaker rose to declare, for the Service, that her charges were "utterly silly."

Landis set everybody straight: "What will be tried in this case will be the issues in the case, to wit, whether or not Mr. Bridges is a member of the Communist party, and whether or not the Party advocates the overthrow by force or violence, [of] the government of the United States, so that he is deportable under the laws of the United States."

The moment had come for the prosecution to show its hand. They called as their first witness Laurence A. Milner, who testified on Monday that he had been employed by the military department of the state of Oregon to investigate subversive activities, making 1,400 reports between 1933 and 1937. He brought seventy-seven pages to the hearing and testified that he had seen Harry Bridges at secret meetings of leading Communist Party officials.

The local defense attorneys had prepared carefully for the hearing, assuming they would have to demolish every government witness "beyond a reasonable doubt" in the mind of the hearing officer, although they did not know who those witnesses would be. There was no "discovery" (a procedure now available in most cases) by which to force the government to reveal the witnesses' names before the hearing began so the defense could investigate them.

In this situation, the defense had taken no chances. Aubrey and the defense committee had compiled a file of names: every enemy of Bridges, trade union opponent, and person who had ever testified on Communism at any state or federal investigation. Then they prepared a comprehensive biography of everyone on the list and the substance of every statement he had ever made about Communism. They indexed and cross-indexed this catalog for quick use against a witness on the stand. The "Rat File" cost $20,000 and occupied six file drawers. The lawyers planned to bring it into the hearing every morning and remove it each night for safekeeping. Some of the ripest evidence came from Senator Robert La Follette's subcommittee on civil liberties of the Senate Labor Committee, concerning the hiring of labor spies to infiltrate unions on the West Coast. Another source included witnesses before the Dies (Un-American Activities) Committee.

As she thumbed through the file Carol assured her associates, "You people really have the finest lot of sons-of-bitches I ever saw."

Now, as the government's first witness testified, Grossman pulled cards from the "Rat File" on Laurence Milner and put them to good use when he began to cross-examine the witness a few days later. One card showed that Milner had testified in the trial of Dirk DeJonge, prosecuted in Oregon earlier under a state sedition statute that the U.S. Supreme Court had declared in 1937 was so broad that it violated the First Amendment.

Grossman asked whether Milner had told the truth in the *DeJonge* trial.

'Yes,' said Milner, he had.

'Are you positive?' Grossman asked (in somewhat more elaborate language).

'Absolutely,' Milner answered (in essence).

Grossman then pointed out contradictions between Milner's testimony in the *DeJonge* trial and his testimony against Bridges a few days before.

'Oh,' said Milner, 'I testified falsely in the *DeJonge* trial so that the Communists would think I was on their side.'

Dean Landis interjected:

You see, what worries me — you have given an explanation for the first time that you gave false testimony, to wit, your desire to do your job better, to build yourself up with the Communist party, and you said, as any decent human being would say, that you dislike to give false testimony, but you felt the interests of your country made it desirable for you to give false testimony. Now, when I come to the Monday giving of false testimony, I just say to myself, "Now, why did the major testify falsely on Monday with reference to that issue? How could that testimony help him to build himself up with the Communist party?" Maybe you can answer that.

Although Major Milner tried through half an hour of careful, close questioning by the dean, he could not explain why he had testified in this hearing a few days before that he had testified truly in *DeJonge* when he now admitted that he had lied in *DeJonge*.

During the lunch recess, one of the lawyers picked up a stone and skipped it over the waters of the bay. Some of the others followed. Carol described this strange picture in a letter to Clara — Angel Island, a beautiful and peaceful spot dotted with white houses, green palms, and flowers, set in the sparkling blue bay. It almost seemed like a picnic. She wasn't surprised when Commissioner McGrath, who was in charge of the island, told her he wanted to buy it for a summer resort when the Immigration Service moved out the next year.

After lunch the hearing resumed, and Carol started trying to hear the testimony with Dean Landis's ears. As to Major Milner, she wrote that "the first one up certainly struck out," and this turned out to be Landis's view. At the end of the hearing, Landis found that Milner's "spectrum provides no measurement for distinguishing labor-union activity from Communism" and dismissed him as "a self-confessed liar, a man who had admittedly tried twice — once successfully — to make falsehood parade as truth."

Tom Shoemaker quickly called his second witness, John Leech, an official in the Communist Party until his expulsion two years before. Leech also testified that he had attended secret Communist Party meetings with Bridges, so-called "top fraction meetings."

The defense lawyers could not agree on how to handle Leech and met for a discussion. Carol said she thought it would jeopardize the chances of convincing Landis not to deport Bridges if the defense seemed to be using the case to make propaganda for Bridges's views on unions, or the capitalist system, or anything else. Aubrey and Richie disagreed sharply. How could they fail to use the forum that had been thrust on them to prove not only that Bridges had a right to stay in the United States, but also that his enemies were evil, whether in government offices or corporate suites?

By this point, everyone in the *Bridges* case knew Carol King was not to be feared. She was helpful and easy to get along with. She supplied citations of unreported cases without any fuss, from the index to the *IJA Bulletin* or her own files. Looking at her, listening to her talk, going to dinner or breakfast with her, it was obvious she was not "the great Carol King."

Yet her colleagues, clients, and friends in New York knew as well as her enemies did that Carol King was someone to conjure with. However informal or even sloppy she might appear, her mind never lost its razor edge, and the only thing that stood between the thought and the sharp

Dean James M. Landis. An artist/journalist's ink sketch of the hearing officer in the first *Harry Bridges* hearing. By Pele DeLappe, 1939. Published with permission of the artist.

retort was her genuine liking for the other person. The progressive folks on the West Coast didn't know this trait yet. And they had never experienced the small-townishness of the Manhattan progressive bar. They were too few and transient to have established a pecking order. Carol wrote home that the West Coast lawyers lacked a sense of history, and of style. She apparently missed a sense of proportion and of possibilities based on precedent that they had developed at Shorr, Brodsky & King, with Isaac's slow pondering about the eternal equities, and Joe's suggestions based on his broad experiences in Albany, Scottsboro, and places in between.

Carol was not prepared for the noisy acrimony of her co-counsel. And finally they crossed her once too often. She threatened to resign from the case. She said it with some heat, although she didn't mean it.

Harry Bridges immediately offered to resign as well!

That ended the matter with a laugh, except that Carol, back in her hotel room, had to write her way to a reasonable perspective.

Dear Clara:
    Tom Shoemaker is beginning to expand with Leech
on the stand. But I have a hunch that that bastard
is overplaying his hand, and that we'll trip him
tomorrow. If he's laid low, it's going to have a

> tremendous psychological effect in discouraging
> government witnesses.
>   Just one more day to the weekend when we'll have
> time to pick up on ourselves. I think the
> government is putting on its best witnesses first.
> God knows I hope so.
>   Yesterday was the longest pull yet — from 3:30
> a.m. to 11:00 p.m.
>   The Hearst papers are nagging us, but the rest
> are pretty decent. I wish the damn papers would
> leave me in peace — I've got enough to do without
> them. I'm convinced that publicity means you ain't
> getting nothing done. The photographers are in my
> hair — especially Hearst which specializes
> deliberately in horrid Semitic-looking ones.
>   Outside of my old friend, Caroline Decker,
> there's just one person here I get on with like a
> house afire and that's H.B. (always referred to in
> that way in office memos.) He's got a swell sense
> of humor and we play up to each other marvelously.
>   . . . [When I threatened to resign] he picked up
> the expression and now we each resign regularly.
> Somehow the idea of his resigning from the case
> still tickles me. . . .
>   HB always refers to the Bridges' luck. Somehow I
> have faith — and the boys have worked like the
> devil getting the case ready. I'm really not doing
> a thing. It's mostly unexciting — just a hard
> grind. We've been saved twice by luck already. Hold
> your thumbs for us.

Carol was finding that the world of San Francisco was simply not the world of New York. It was wide open, exciting, full of action, fast-moving, healthy, young, and vigorous. But it did not include the art galleries she counted on back home, and the friends. She kept her perspective by writing home early in the morning while sitting up in bed or in the bathtub with a bottle of Coca-Cola and a board to write on. Carol told her correspondents a great deal more about the case than they got out of the daily stories in the *New York Times* or the *Daily Worker.*

Carol's glimpses of the day-to-day life of a lawyer in trial are unparalleled. Other trial lawyers have not needed, or managed, to record their daily brushes with their co-counsel, the client, the client's organization, the judge, opposing counsel, prospective witnesses, the press — and their own real selves. But Carol was surrounded in this hearing, all day every day, by men sitting as hearing officer, government lawyers, defense lawyers, and client. All major government witnesses and defense witnesses and all reporters were men. To associate with the women busy on the case, she had to work with the secretaries who were typing the transcript, and with the members of the ILWU Ladies Auxiliary who were putting on fund-raisers for the defense. In her spare time, she picked up her pen and wrote to her friend Clara.

> *Sunday*
> *It was such a beautiful sunny day that I really*
> *begrudged spending it indoors. I was looking*
> *forward to a walk home from the office, but Harry*
> *insisted on driving me. . . . [A]lthough it was*
> *gorgeous to sleep from 5:30 yesterday till this*
> *morning, I bemoan the waterfront drunk he was*
> *planning for me — he's a grand guy, but I can't*
> *quite understand why the ladies all fall for him —*
> *there is no intensity of emotion — just a good*
> *sport with a superlative sense of humor. Also no*
> *fool.*
> *   I did a swell job yesterday at a meeting of*
> *delegates from the maritime unions. I like talking*
> *to them much better than at the hearings.*
> *   Tomorrow is a terribly important day. Pray for us!*

The next day John Leech and his wife brought their baby to the hearing and Carol decided, "off the record, that she was a cute baby and that it must be damned hard to be born a fink." On the record, Leech testified not only about Bridges and his alleged Communist Party membership, but also about the teachings of the Party. He said that he studied at a Party school under an instructor from the Soviet Union, using *The History of the Communist Party of the U.S.S.R.* as a text. This was in 1938.

On cross-examination, the defense asked him to read the date on the flyleaf of that book. He read it aloud: "1939."

> *Tuesday a.m. July 14*
> *Dear Clara,*
> *   We didn't smash Leech as badly as we had hoped*
> *to, but one thing is sure, his cross-examination*
> *didn't serve to increase his credibility. Nor did*
> *the four-months-old Leech baby. . . . Right after*
> *the Leeches left the stand, we discovered that he'd*

> been lying like hell about his relief and that he'd
> been getting it while he had a job. . . .
> Sunday evening I went to Chinatown alone for
> supper. I'm alone so little that it's quite a
> treat. Chinese kids are completely fascinating to
> me and they swarmed all over the place in the best
> behaved manner in the world.

The next day the defense revealed that Leech had made false statements in order to secure public relief. The defense also produced an affidavit, signed with Leech's name, stating that he had no knowledge that Harry Bridges was a Communist. Leech denied he had written and signed it. Later in the hearing, the defense called an attorney and a secretary who testified that Leech had signed the affidavit. A handwriting expert gave his judgment that the signature had been written by Leech.

Landis had made up his mind about Leech on the basis of his testimony alone, writing in his findings at the end of the trial:

> It is impossible accurately even to summarize this day and a half of testimony by Leech. In evasion, qualification, and contradiction it is almost unique. . . . The evasions are truly labyrinthine in nature.

Carol had been watching Dean Landis intently throughout the hearing, and she concluded that the defense was making some points with him, but they could not afford to relax for a minute.

> Saturday a.m.
> Imagine, Clara, I've tucked more than 8 hours
> sleep in my belt and am not in a hurry this
> morning. I can't believe there is any higher bliss.
> Of course, I'll be getting to the office soon and
> everybody will be rowing and things won't look as
> rosy as they do from my present recumbent position.
> It was a just too gorgeous day yesterday — during
> the lunch recess I found a secluded spot and had a
> sun bath. It was broiling hot, but the kind of heat
> that's pleasant, as though one were a piece of
> bread being pleasantly toasted. . . .
> Landis's kids, 9 and 11, came over yesterday.
> They are exquisite, but too well brought up —
> scared to talk.
> The first two witnesses up definitely struck out.
> Harry suggests if we get the third that the next

STATE OF CALIFORNIA,   )
                        } ss
COUNTY OF LOS ANGELES   )

JOHN L. LEACH, being first duly sworn, deposes and
says:

My name is John L. Leach; I was formerly a member of
the Communist Party, occupying the position of Los
Angeles County Organizer and member of the California
State Committee until about November, 1936. The name
under which I held membership in the Communist Party was
John A. Lewis. I understand that I was expelled from
the Communist Party sometime in the Spring of 1937.

About June 23, 1937, I was approached by a man calling himself William E. Browne, who claimed to be a
United States officer, an Immigration Department officer,
a United States Intelligence Department officer and a
Portland, Oregon policeman. This man offered me the sum
of One Thousand Dollars to make an affidavit which would
state that Harry Bridges was a member of the Communist
Party, and would state that said Harry Bridges was present at certain meetings of the Communist Party at which
I was present. He explained that he wanted me so to
testify before a United States District Court and that
the affidavit would not be produced as long as I told
the same story. I refused because to my best knowledge
and belief Harry Bridges is not a Communist or a member
of the Communist Party, nor was he at any such meetings
where I was present. Later this man returned and offered me Two Thousand Dollars to make such an affidavit.
I likewise refused this offer.

Affidavit of John L. Leech. An affidavit introduced July 17, 1939, in
the first *Bridges* hearing describing an offer from a U.S. Intelligence
Department officer for testimony. Facsimile-reduced reproduction
from Richard Gladstein's oral history papers, University of California–
Berkeley (Bancroft).

inning should be put off a couple of years till
they gather some more evidence.

The third witness against Harry Bridges was John L. Leppold, a member of the Marine Cooks & Stewards Union, expelled in 1938 after two union trials for anti-union activity. Then the government called Frederick Allen, former secretary of the Fish Reduction Workers Union, expelled for taking the local's $4,000 when it decided to leave the AFL to join the CIO. The government called John R. Davis, on probation from his conviction for grand larceny of $1,800 from the Sailors Union of the Pacific local while acting as business agent. Arthur Kent, the witness Carol had focused on in 1938 as perhaps the government's key witness, played no role at all.

Carol just couldn't take these witnesses seriously. She thought one was "a complete phony," the next "completely crazy." And, she wrote to Clara, "to make it more absurd, Harry kept passing notes expressing his uncensored views."

Landis later scorched these government witnesses in his findings, calling one "a problem in contumacy;" another "a self-confessed liar." "[O]n occasion he lied, . . ." he wrote of a third. Others were "prejudiced, intemperate, overbearing"; "impossible to separate truth from fiction"; "corrupt . . . repudiated . . . truth matters little [to him]"; "pathological."

By this point in the trial, Carol lived for the weekends.

Sat. a.m. [July 22, 1939]
I have a most luxurious feeling this morning,
Clara. There is no 8:45 boat to make — I have some
lovely fresh marigolds in my room, a bunch of
grapes on which I'm nibbling and a half pound of
chocolates that don't taste nearly so delicious in
the morning. The sun is shining and I can lie
luxuriously for two hours and still be round by the
time Caroline and Richie come to breakfast. In
other words, I'm purring.
Yesterday's Examiner (Hearst), which is very
close to the government's case, explained that
there is one important government witness left and
the rest just fill in the picture. If that's true,
you can start in now taking bets. We win! But
there's many a slip you know. Only if anyone had
told me that we'd be in this good shape at the end
of two weeks, I wouldn't have believed them.

Harry Bridges. An artist/journalist's ink sketch made during one of the later days in the first *Harry Bridges* hearing. By Pele DeLappe, 1939. Published with permission of the artist.

    Life with a single aim is much simpler. I like
the simplification at least for a time.

By July 27, the government had put in most of its case and Carol "played hooky" one night, going out for a drink with friends from New York who had dropped in. "It was much the most frivolous thing I've done since I arrived," she wrote Clara, "and 'The Top of the Mark' where we went has a gorgeous view of the city and bay even at night, tho Harry has set his mind now on showing me how much better it is in the daytime."

When she got back to her hotel room she enjoyed reading letters from Whitney North Seymour and Herb Wechsler, her colleagues in *Herndon,* intimating that the case wasn't going too badly as reported in the New York press.

> *Dear Clara:*
>   *Yesterday I woke up feeling in the hell of a good mood . . . as if the government's case was over except for some more literature and that the important thing was to keep the boys from dragging out the defense too long. Ping! Two more witnesses (new ones we hadn't expected) placing HB at a top fraction meeting at Seattle. It was kind of a drop but after all the only proof that it was a top fraction meeting was their say so. . . .*
>   *I'm feeling fine. . . . Glad you sound so perky — your last was grand that way. . . . The arrival of the Bulletin Thursday was thrilling — envelope and all!*

The government's last witness, Engstrom, had been a member of the Marine Firemen's Union who learned about unionism from Earl King. King was serving time in what the defense said was a frame-up conviction for a strike-related death. He had urged Engstrom's election as president of the Maritime Federation. Later Engstrom was expelled from his union for nonpayment of dues for a year.

Landis had no difficulty in assessing his testimony:

Engstrom left a convincing impression that he was not telling the truth. . . . [He] emerged [as] a weak-willed, characterless individual from whose once promising hands the reins of leadership had slipped and who in desperation was now pursuing new hypocritical tactics in the hope that these might succor him from the loneliness of his failure and for a time again surround him once more with "friends."

The day after the government closed its main case, Carol King sat down to bring her friend, and herself, up to date. By now she knew quite a bit about her client.

> *Dear Clara:*
>   *Well, the government closed last night except for the testimony of HB, which will start on Wednesday.*
>   *If Harry does a good job, I feel as if the case were in the bag. But that poor guy is sick — stomach ulcers — and I don't quite know how he'll stand the strain. It's one thing to fight in the industrial field, but this damn court business is something quite otherwise. Harry is so cocky that I'm afraid he may snap if things go badly. And I want him to be magnificent — a complete contrast to*

their God-forsaken witnesses. So pray for us
Wednesday when HB goes on — so far you've done very
well.
I was up at Caroline and Richie's again for
supper last night. Richie was exhausted and went
sound asleep after a most voluptuous meal that
Caroline put on. So she and I talked along very
comfortably. I haven't seen two people as much in
love as that for a long, long time. I hope there is
no smash, not now of course, but ever.

After the hearing had been going on for three weeks, Carol decided she could take Sunday night off. It was such an unusual occasion that she wrote home about it.

Tuesday morning [August 1, 1939]
I have been to a movie! I went Sunday night and
the movie, "Goodbye Mr. Chips," was not too
wonderful though it had its points. But for two and
a half hours while I was awake I completely forgot
H.B. It was strange coming back to him with a thump
afterwards.
I am, believe it or not, an honorary member of
the International Longshoremen and Warehousemen's
Union, having been unanimously moved in at the
meeting last night. It was thrilling to walk into a
hall with thousands of longshoremen present and
have them rise and stand while I walked to the
platform — and they yelled and cheered their
enthusiasm. My speech — after a twelve-hour day at
the office — was lousy, but I think they liked me,
and I did a good job before the ladies auxiliary.

Carol had a compulsion to touch New York — and her reality — every morning before she went to the hearings on Angel Island, even when she admitted she was "really overworked." She wrote "a scrawny note" to Clara to acknowledge a letter from Maine that "was a great comfort" when she got back to her hotel room one night. She reported "an amusing letter" from Johnny about a canoe upset that he apparently took "with great nonchalance."

                                    ⚘

On Wednesday, August 2, Harry Bridges was sworn in. In three days on the witness stand under government cross-examination, Bridges didn't give an inch. The colloquy (slightly abbreviated) went this way:

'Do you know Communists?'

'Sure.'

'Associate with them?'

'Certainly.'

'What about your associations with the Communist Party during the 1934 longshore strike?'

'Look,' said Bridges, 'we took whatever help we could get, and we were grateful for all of it.'

'And how about the *Western Worker,* a Communist newspaper?'

'Well,' Bridges answered, 'we were afraid that the longshoremen would be confused by all the scare stories and back-to-work reports in the daily newspapers. Two newspapers, the *Western Worker* and the *Catholic Leader,* offered to publish daily strike bulletins put out by the strike committee. I advocated the acceptance of those offers, and they were accepted.'

'Did you meet and talk with Sam Darcy, Communist official in California, during the longshore strike?'

'Yes, I did.'

As the strike progressed, the newspapers published increasingly hysterical charges that the whole strike was a Communist plot. It became obvious to the strike committee that they would have to counter these charges. As Bridges said on the stand, "I didn't think it was fair, the action that we subsequently took, because amongst the only friends we had in that strike — at least in the beginning, . . . were the Communist Party and the Communist Party officials. However, there was such . . . an organized red scare raised . . . in the press that eventually we took certain actions in the union to . . . publicize in many ways that we had no dealings, contacts, or associations whatsoever with the Communist Party. It was only fair to tell them about this before it took place."

Carol told Clara that "HB was much better than the papers even show. It was grand — only I'm a little desensitized." And she complained that during one of Caroline's dinner parties, Estolv took the opportunity "to tell me that the press is down on me bad, which is probably true. But what am I to do? I've told the press (1) that I won't tell them anything of our case for fear of prejudicing it, (2) that they're a Goddamn nuisance and that I know I'm doing nothing when I find my name in the papers.

In addition, I associate with all the reds that come to the island and never conduct the hearing. Is it a wonder that I'm not in too strong?"

Weekends were to recover from one impossible week and to prepare for another. That Saturday night Carol finally just wandered the streets of San Francisco as she might have done at home in New York, eating at a joint with a counter instead of a decent restaurant, and ending up at the movies.

On August 8, the defense called Harper L. Knowles of San Francisco as its first hostile witness. Commentators agreed this was a gutsy move, since the defense could not then keep the witness from saying what he chose, within broad limits. Knowles testified that in 1935 he became chairman of the Subversive Activities Commission of the American Legion of California, which was reorganized in 1936 as the Legion's Radical Research Committee. Knowles described his hundreds of informants from the 530 California Legion posts, and the committee's close working arrangements with the army, navy, State Bureau of Criminal Identification, immigration inspectors, private detective agencies, the Industrial Association of San Francisco, the Waterfront Employers' Association, the Associated Farmers, chambers of commerce, civic and fraternal groups, sheriffs' offices, and the State Police Officers Association.

Gladstein was thoroughly prepared for Knowles. The defense had surreptitiously gotten possession of a cardboard carton of material from his office, including copies of correspondence, secret codes used by undercover agents in reporting on Bridges, etc. Gladstein's questions were based on this undercover material.

Knowles had not expected to be cross-examined on his intimate relations with employers and law enforcement agencies. He had to concede that he had supplied officials of the Industrial Association with the records of individuals in whom they were interested. Faced with his own documents, he had to admit he had also received information from a leader of the Waterfront Employers' Association, particularly reports from the undercover operator named Bakczy, a sea captain who had offered to sell his testimony to Carol and Aubrey a couple of weeks before. Knowles also admitted that the Portland police chief had officially instructed his men to cooperate with Knowles. One of the chief's detectives was Knowles's counterpart as chairman of the American Legion's subversive activities committee in Oregon. Knowles admitted that Larry M. Doyle, as special agent for Oregon, was ferreting out subversive activities under the special direction of Oregon's Governor Charles Martin, and using Knowles's office occasionally.

Carol began her letter to Clara describing these events like a single-minded advocate enjoying the kill:

> Despite screaming headlines in the Hearst press
> about our rifling of the American Legion files,
> it was fun to confront Knowles with his own
> correspondence when questioning him. He wriggled,
> and somehow I feel that he'll never quite be able
> to rehabilitate himself.

Carol could not hold this stance very long. She soon reverted to her awareness of Knowles as a human being who had gotten his job with the legion because he was a disabled veteran. Carol concluded, "poor guy, and he expected to make such mincemeat of us."

She went on to explain:

> All in all, I see no end, but when you get there at
> the moment victory awaits. Which, being translated,
> means that I figure on leaving about September 1st
> (when they say the weather gets warm and sunny) and
> on winning.
>   At the moment all my energies are devoted to
> stopping the boys from taking risks. It's O.K. with
> Aubrey home [with chicken pox], but he'll be back
> today or tomorrow and then it's all my life is
> worth to hold this down to a defense of HB and
> prevent it from becoming our private LaFollette
> [Senate] Committee [on civil liberties violations].
> They have a wonderful forum, but just suppose some
> witness (adverse) comes through with a scrap of
> evidence against HB. I'd pass out. HB has become
> one of my aliens and I'm becoming quite maternal
> and protective.
>   The hell with all their legal and political
> maneuvers.

Landis reached certain conclusions concerning the witness Knowles and his committee:

> There is abundant evidence to indicate that the work of Knowles' committee came perilously close to that of those organizations whose sole effort is to combat militant unionism. The spread of unionism was watched with

concern, particularly its spread into the unorganized agricultural areas of the State. A close differentiation was not always made between labor agitators and those truly engaged in subversive activities. Indeed, the close alliances that existed between Knowles' committee and the powerful employer associations lead to the conclusion that Knowles, whether wittingly or unwittingly, was frequently made the tool of their policies.

Knowles . . . was neither a candid nor a forthright witness. . . . Recollection, even when it existed, tended at times to be suspiciously faulty.

The defense followed with another hostile witness, Captain John J. Keegan, chief of detectives of Portland. His testimony filled in many details about the work of the Portland police on the *Bridges* case. For example, Keegan got reports concerning Bridges from one Arthur Scott, although the two never met. Later, when Scott was wanted for burglary in Beverly Hills, Keegan wrote to the Los Angeles police doubting Scott's guilt, "as you are well aware of what we are trying to do in regard to Harry Bridges." After Scott's conviction, Keegan filed an affidavit supporting commutation of the sentence, talking about his "personal observation" of Scott. And in June 1937 in Portland, Keegan "generally investigated" the annual convention of the Maritime Workers Federation while Stanley M. Doyle and Detective Browne concealed a dictaphone in Bridges's room, which was discovered.

Landis, in his findings, concluded that these incidents showed that Keegan was "one of the prime movers" in the effort to deport Bridges. "It illustrates also that his claim that the Bridges investigation was a normal, routine investigation is pure fiction":

Keegan's testimony from the beginning shows an effort to conceal his activities and the activities of his men. . . . A reason that could motivate such insistent concealment was that the means employed were in themselves disreputable, means that might discredit the evidence that had been adduced. . . .

He misled the examiner again and again only to be forced by documentary evidence and the testimony of others ultimately to reveal a wholly different story. . . . The picture that Keegan draws of himself is not one of a chief of detectives confident of the integrity of his office and the trustworthiness of his men and their tactics.

Keegan was such an unconvincing witness that the defense could relax a little. Aubrey, the workhorse, even urged everyone to take Sunday off entirely.

Friday evening [August 11, 1939]
   It's almost worth working so hard during the
week, Clara, in order to get to this point. I spent
60 cents for which I secured the most gorgeous
bundle of zinnias, six magnificent peaches, two
pounds of grapes, and a basket of tiny round
tomatoes. It's much the largest housekeeping job in
which I have become involved since my arrival. Only
I thought it would be nice to eat breakfast in bed
Saturday and Sunday.

Carol had often relied on Clara to act in loco parentis. Now it was natural to ask her friend to do "whatever is needed" to enroll Johnny properly to begin his career at the Bronx High School of Science. "Maybe nothing is necessary. But I'd rather the school didn't find out who I am and why I'm away." She confessed that "it will be weeks after I get to New York before I finish up on the brief. But somehow that's different and more normal. I don't like having Johnny come home to an empty house."

That Saturday night was a bright spot for Carol. Estolv Ward invited her over for supper at his place with Angela. Carol thought they were swell people, and they all ended up at the "Swing Mikado," full of joy and color. Afterward she invited them in for an impromptu meal at her hotel, as she would have invited them home if she'd been in New York. But it was after 6:00 P.M. and she got the whole hotel staff worrying about the raw filet steak she wanted to serve. Somehow, they rounded one up, and Carol was pleased with her efforts as a hostess.

One of the unspoken, or seldom mentioned, issues of fact in the *Bridges* case was the woman question. Marxists in the defense team accepted this phrase to cover what came to be known later as male chauvinism on one side and women's liberation on the other. The problem was that Harry Bridges was married, and some government witnesses had testified that Mrs. Nancy Bridges had said that Bridges was a member of the CP. If she never attended the hearing, it would appear that she did not support her husband and that such testimony might be accurate.

It was also widely rumored that Bridges, at this point, had had many relationships with women who were not his wife, as Carol delicately phrased it in another connection. Carol began alluding to this issue in letters to Clara almost as soon as the hearing began. On August 1 she had written:

Things have been happening outside the case. [Two
of the men in the defense team] *suddenly got scared
of public opinion on the subject of sex – each is
living with a lady not his wife. They got the
notion that the press was out looking for dirt –
S.F. is a Catholic town, you know. Well, there was
a flurry and now* [the two men are] *sleeping in a
big double bed and so* [are the two women]. *But this
really isn't outside the case, 'cause nobody would
have bothered except for the publicity attendant on
the case.*

*Anyway, four people are completely miserable and
I went out to supper with them just before the
smash-up and talked my head off trying to cover up.
Meanwhile, I've talked some with* [one of the
couples] *and the divorce is starting between* [him]
*and his wife as soon as the hearings are over and
his name consequently less in the limelight. S.F.
papers publish dirt religiously, by which I mean
divorce proceedings.*

Carol concluded, "I can't help feeling that all these domestic changes for
a guy with HB's reputation is slightly absurd, but then I have no
organizational sense in such matters."

By August 14, the issue had become acute. The defense concluded that
they must present Bridges as a man with a loyal wife. Carol described the
situation to Clara from her position as a lawyer wanting desperately to
win an important case:

*One reason I'm jumpy today, and about the press, is
that Mrs. HB is actually coming to the hearing. And
there'll be hell to pay. The press will be on her
tail and will want explanations of her alleged
admissions* [of Bridges's CP membership] *which have
been testified to. But all in all, I think it's
better for her to turn up than not. Only I wish HB
was a widower. I can just see things getting into a
jam.*

On Sunday the defense had its weekly meeting, which ended in
another row. Carol was so mad that she started to walk out in a huff, but
Aubrey piped down and she let herself be persuaded to stay. The curious
part of it was that there was no substantial disagreement. She concluded
it was just a mannerism of Aubrey's that she had decided she would not

tolerate any longer. Looking back, Ben Margolis thinks Carol's letters fail "to give sufficient credit" to Aubrey and Richie "since often in such conferences a great deal was achieved despite the manner in which they were conducted, which would certainly irritate most people." You did have "two keen minds often clashing but coming up with conclusions that were often brilliant."

Carol admitted to Clara that she was "generally in a cross mood at the moment derived . . . from too much Bridges and a sense that from here on everything's a little superfluous." She was also "sore at a guy from N.Y." with whom she and her husband had been intimate ten years before. "He went on to higher and better things when Gordon died and he remarried," and was bothering her now "just 'cause I'm in the papers and thus amount to something. . . ."

The second letter she wrote to Clara on August 14 had a Virginia Woolf quality:

> Monday p.m.
>
> I should do a lot of domestic things, Clara, like clean my shoes — but I can't open the [bottle] — and the week's washing — so I naturally turn to writing to you instead as a pleasant way to get away from Reality (spelled quite unconsciously with a capital R).
>
> Although I worked all day yesterday, I was less tired when I quit than when I began. . . . The trouble with the Law Library in the Mills Building (there is a public one for the whole building) is that the view over the bay is too beautiful. It makes work very difficult. . . .
>
> You must get a bit tired of the Bridges case, but really I have no other news. I'm getting a bit fed up myself.

20.
Proving a Government/Business Conspiracy

Carol King had insisted from the beginning of the *Bridges* case that she knew nothing about political theory and wasn't interested in it; she was a lawyer and didn't need to be interested. In fact, Aubrey Grossman felt that her assertion was not completely true; he says she frequently had very bad ideas about the handling of theoretical questions, and also frequently had good ideas.

Carol had never studied Marxism in college in the 1910s and had not attended classes on Marxist theory when they became popular in the 1930s (although she was impressed when her niece Peggy Stern expressed an understanding of dialectical materialism). Carol had heard government witnesses quote from "Marxist classics" they had selected to prove the illegality of such theory, and had studied government briefs based on this testimony. In defense of demonstrators and political deportees she had had to read many CP pronouncements on current issues, only to see them totally rejected and reversed later by their proponents because of changing events.

For years King had avoided meetings where only political theory would be discussed among her Communist and anarchist friends, and with colleagues in the Lawyers Guild. She enjoyed going to a law library "to dig for worms," as she put it, to find little-known cases that proved a point that might appeal to a judge in a case. And she enjoyed arguing out the constitutional law issues and moving people to act for constitutional rights in courtroom work, in congressional hearings, and in administrative agencies. She understood the need for popular support for changes in the law and frequently gave speeches to other experts in the law and to labor unions, nationality groups, and women's organizations.

But when she was not working, she preferred to go to a new show in an art gallery rather than to a meeting where polemical statements would be made and refuted by people whose views she respected no more than her own. She didn't like to "waste time hammering out a political line."

Since a large number of her clients were members of the Communist Party, former members, or believers in socialism or communism, King was constantly engaged in discussions about proper methods of defense of Communists and communist ideas against attacks by various agencies of the United States government. And she liked to win. It had become clear to her that to win the *Bridges* case required thinking about political theory. The problem arose because it was always possible that the government would produce a witness whose story would be believable to Dean Landis. If Bridges had been "affiliated with the Communist Party," even if he had not been a "member," the policies of the CP would become a major issue in the case. The government claimed that the Party had been distributing Marxist documents that "advocated" the "violent overthrow of government." The defense would have to answer this claim.

First they would have to prove that no hearing officer or court could take judicial notice of the aims of the Party. "Judicial notice" is a tricky concept that permits a court to accept the fact that a certain date in a certain year fell on a Monday (according to any calendar), or that the moon was full on a certain night (according to any official weather report). The lawyers do not have to prove such facts by means of witnesses; an almanac will do. Bridges's lawyers would contend that the nature of a political organization could not be determined without hearing testimony on the matter, as it was not a simple fact of nature and there was no political almanac. Then the defense would offer expert testimony on the Party's aims.

Carol, the non-Marxist, figured this out rather than Aubrey, the avowed Marxist. She argued that expert testimony in the *Bridges* case on the theory of communism would counterbalance the testimony of non-academic "stoolpigeon witnesses" who would be qualified as "experts on theory" by the government. This conflicting testimony might permit Landis to decide he did not to have to decide the question whether the Communist Party advocated violent overthrow. He might rule that the government had not proved this point by the requisite standard of proof and decide the case on other issues of fact. That was the minimum victory to be won by presenting expert witnesses on Marxist doctrine in the *Bridges* case.

The maximum victory that might be won was incredible. No court in the United States had ever heard expert academic testimony on the doctrines of the Communist Party and then held, on the basis of the evidence, that it was legal to advocate basic social changes in the economic system, from capitalism to socialism. If the defense presented such evidence in the *Bridges* deportation case, and won such a ruling, it would affect every political deportation and denaturalization case in the country, every state prosecution for criminal syndicalism, every effort to put the CP on the ballot.

King's legal perspective on this issue was based on her experiences from the Palmer Raids on. Judge Anderson had ruled in *Colyer v. Skeffington* that knowing membership in the new Communist Party was not ground for deportation; he had been overruled. The Supreme Court had ruled in 1925 that Left Wing Socialist doctrine was illegal. The Supreme Court had ruled in 1937 in *DeJonge* that a CP member could make a speech at a CP meeting on legal activities of the CP and could solicit memberships. The Supreme Court in 1937 had ruled in *Herndon* that it was not illegal to solicit memberships in the CP or to distribute CP literature as long as one did not personally advocate incitement to violent insurrection. The next step in this contest would be to win *Bridges* on the ground that membership in the CP was not a ground for deportation. Therefore, it seemed necessary and wise to present evidence in *Bridges* on the legality of the doctrine of the CP to a scholarly hearing officer.

After Carol convinced the rest of the defense team, the search went out for experts who could stand up under cross-examination, which was bound to be rigorous. Finally Ben Margolis located two professors who fitted the bill: "impartial," not members of the Communist or any other Marxist political party, but knowledgeable about what the CP was saying currently and what Marx and Engels had written ninety years before. They agreed to be subpoenaed to present evidence on what could become the key issue in the case, and what would make history as a departure from all previous political trials in this country.

Harold Chapman Brown took the stand and testified that he was a Harvard Ph.D. with a reading knowledge of seven languages, including Russian. He had taught at Columbia and Harvard before coming to Stanford University, where he was chairman of the philosophy department. "I come from an old New England family," he testified. "My ancestors came over, I think, somewhere in the 1600s. . . . Mostly lawyers, doctors, a few clergymen way back. My grandfather was Supreme Court Justice in Massachusetts." He testified that he had no sympathy with Marxism.

Shoemaker was not so sure.

LANDIS: He might be an authority on Communism and still be a good
American citizen.
SHOEMAKER: I think this is the basis for the questions which will after-
wards be propounded.
LANDIS: Well, I don't quite see why a man can't be an expert on Commu-
nism and yet have no sympathy with Communism as such.

Professor Brown testified to the recent increase in interest in Marxism
in universities, as evidenced by numerous doctoral dissertations, and for
the rest of the day interpreted Marxist theory based on Marxist classics,
over government objections of irrelevancy. Landis participated in the
examination, and the defense noted that his questions revealed a good
knowledge of the historical and theoretical problems at issue.

Next the defense called Walter Thompson, a Wisconsin Ph.D. who
had served as a Carnegie professor at Upsala, Sweden, and Oslo, Norway.
Since 1928 he had been on the political science faculty at Stanford.
Thompson discussed the issue that the Communist lawyers, in the interest
of unity, had skirted at the recent Lawyers Guild convention: whether
Marxists and Communist Party members oppose democracy and advocate dictatorship through violent revolutions. Thompson presented traditional Marxist theory: democracy and dictatorship are forms of
government, whereas capitalism and communism are forms of economic
organization. Belief in democracy does not assume belief in capitalism
any more than belief in communism assumes belief in dictatorship. A
person can believe in democratic communism achieved by the ballot,
while noting that throughout history those in power have never turned
over their reins without violence or revolution.

The government could not shake Dr. Thompson on cross-examination.

Carol wrote home that she was delighted with the success of her idea,
and the hearing ended early so that everyone rode back to the city on a
funny little launch instead of the customary one. Carol parked on top of
the cabin and enjoyed the wide-open spaces and the roll and the spray.
She wrote that she liked it better than anything that had happened so far,
and her opponent, Shoemaker, was so enchanted that he broke into song.

Back at her hotel, Carol decided to take the evening off, for the second
time in a row, and went out alone to a restaurant where she met up with
a young Newspaper Guild member who was a Bridges enthusiast. She
had apparently picked Carol out the minute she sat down at the counter

and finally got up the courage to speak to her. Carol wrote to Clara: "I decided it must be fun to be great if you can always be picked up by peppy kids who are so glad to see you when really they are much nicer and certainly more charming than you are."

With less to do in the case, Carol King began to act the least bit like a New York City tourist in San Francisco. At lunch one Saturday she bummed around the town and even bought a new book, John Steinbeck's *Of Mice and Men*. She read it that evening and enjoyed it so much that she wanted to get *The Grapes of Wrath*.

> Sunday morning, [August 20, 1939]
> The sun is beginning to come out and I can't quite stand it any longer just lazying around, so I guess I'll get up, kiss my roses good-bye and get out into the wide, wide world. You have no idea how little of S.F. I have really seen. I just wear a path from the Drake-Wilshire to the Mills Building and back again. To my amazement yesterday I discovered Twin Mountains at the end of Market Street. Imagine a real city street with peaks poking up at the end of it! S.F. is really a swell place and I'll be sorry to leave without getting better acquainted. . . .
> Thanks for everything and especially for being so nice and in fact for existing at all. I begin to look forward to seeing you.

A few days later, Carol reached the age of forty-four and wrote home about it.

> My birthday in the evening. [August 24, 1939]
> Somehow being alone out here made me much more birthday conscious than usual, Clara. I went out last night and bought myself fresh flowers — lovely yellow daisies — put on a clean nighty and woke up at 3:30 this a.m. with a couple of hundred pages of transcript to read and index before today's session. Of course, I'd waked up too early so I spent the first hour or so just being glad I was born.
> In other words, though war threatens and it's a hell of a world, I can still celebrate myself along with Walt Whitman.

Soon Carol met two convicted felons whose humanity she also insisted on celebrating, in defiance of their prosecutor, Earl Warren. She interviewed Earl King and Ernest Ramsay in further defense efforts to prove that a conspiracy existed against Bridges. They could testify to bribe offers by government officials, but their appearances posed critical problems.

Earl King was an official of the Marine Firemen's Union, Ramsay an active member. In March 1936 a chief engineer aboard a ship in San Pedro died after being beaten up in the course of a seamen's strike. Five months later King and Ramsay were arrested for the murder and prosecuted by a likeable and ambitious young DA, Earl Warren. His witnesses testified that King had sent Ramsay and two other men to attack the anti-union chief engineer and had killed him. King and Ramsay insisted they were innocent and that the testimony against them was perjured: some militant union members might have done the beating, but they were not the ones. The jury convicted them of second-degree murder, and they were sent to prison on indeterminate sentences of five to twenty years.

The version of events told on the waterfront then, and repeated years later by Harry Bridges, was that the dead man had been a first-class fink. The union's educational committee had visited him, as it had occasionally visited other anti-union bums in recent years. King and Ramsay were not on the committee. The engineer suffered a blow on the jaw that would have shaken up, but not killed, an average man. The autopsy revealed that the engineer had a "glass jaw," which he had never known and which the members of the educational committee obviously had not known. However, they left the state, and some said the country very quickly, and had not returned.

Now King and Ramsay were in San Quentin Prison, and their appearance as witnesses for Bridges might prejudice their pending applications for parole or executive clemency. Counsel for Bridges tried to solve this problem by getting favorable action on the clemency petitions before they testified. Earl Warren fought against parole tooth and nail. Finally a decision had to be made, and the prisoners decided to testify.

To set the stage, Garfield King, an attorney in Vancouver, Canada, testified that he was Earl King's brother. On February 26, 1938, he had been visited by an agent of the Immigration Service who read him a letter from R. P. Bonham, director of the Service in Seattle, intimating that there was some doubt as to Earl King's guilt, stating that he understood that Earl, because of a situation that had arisen in connection with Earl's wife, might no longer be on good terms with the Communist Party, and suggesting that if Garfield King would advise Earl to furnish evidence on Bridges, Bonham would use his influence to secure a pardon for Earl King. Garfield King said he had taken notes of the conversation and had immediately put it in the form of an affidavit before a Canadian notary.

Bonham sat in the hearing room as Garfield King testified. He did not contradict King's testimony. Neither did any other government witness. The government contented itself with the argument that the action of Bonham could not be truly criticized because Bonham had not *explicitly* suggested that Garfield King urge Earl King to testify falsely.

Dean Landis later came to a different conclusion:

> Obviously this inferentially admits the truth of Garfield King's testimony. The extraordinary nature, to say the least, of this conduct is patent. But expiation for guilt was not the issue here. No one would question the impropriety of a government official threatening to throw an innocent man into jail on a groundless charge unless he produced certain testimony. There is little substantial distinction between such conduct and that here involved — withholding action that might release an assumedly innocent man from jail unless he produced certain testimony.

Next Mrs. Ramsay testified for the defense. When her husband was sent to prison, she was eighteen years old and had been married a year. Now she testified that in 1937 Larry Doyle had taken her with him and a man named Ferguson to San Quentin to convince her husband to testify against Bridges.

Landis asked why she had not urged her husband to accept Doyle's offer.

She replied, "After all, my husband was framed, and I know what it is. And it isn't — well, I wouldn't want to see anybody else framed if it can be helped."

Shoemaker did not cross-examine Mrs. Ramsay.

The next day, the hearing was moved to the recreation hall of the California State Prison at San Quentin. Carol found "San Quentin . . . such a beautiful location that the prison seems particularly out of place. It's on the bay" and this day it was "gay and blue and sunny. They grow flowers so that the gray prison walls rise abruptly from the brilliant flower beds. The whole thing was unreal."

The defense called Ernest Ramsay. He testified that Doyle and Ferguson had come to see him in prison, bringing his wife along:

Ferguson thought that would be one way of me getting out of this place if I would sign the affidavit, that after all I was up here on perjured testimony anyhow, so what is the difference; it won't hurt to perjure a little bit now to get out of here.

Ramsay couldn't set the date of the conversation with Ferguson and Doyle: "The days are all the same here; you don't pay much attention to the time."

By this time, Carol had concluded, "Without being a bit sentimental, the prisoners looked like much better guys than the guards."

Next the defense called Earl King to the makeshift stand. He said Doyle came to see him and said that if King would testify that Bridges was in top-fraction meetings with King, Doyle would get King a parole to Canada because he was a Canadian citizen. Otherwise, Doyle said they would hang the "Cherbourg murder" on him. Doyle also said that he had spoken to Earl Warren, and Warren would put in a word against King when he appealed his case. Doyle told Earl King to "think it over awhile."

I says, "It won't make any difference how long I think it over. The answer will still be the same."

He said, "Don't you know what you are facing if you don't do as I ask you?"

I says, "Quite possible, yes."

He says, "Well, I don't understand you."

So I says, "Well, I am about 45 years of age. I have been to a lot of places, and done pretty near everything I wanted to do, had a good time, had good friends. Nobody can make me perjure myself."

[Witness visibly moved and sobbed audibly. Short recess taken.]

"Well," he says, "what is the matter with you?"

"Well," I says, "I told you. I am not going to lie," I says, "against Harry Bridges just to get out of here." I says, "I don't care what happens to me now," I says, "I have only got my self-respect left; I am going to keep that. Nobody is going to take it away."

So he left.

On cross-examination, Earl King was asked:

Q. If you thought Doyle was attempting to get a statement from you that he knew was false, you wouldn't have shaken hands with him, would you?

A. Well, just a mechanical handshake. I am a convict here and I can't be very uppity with people that are free.

Carol couldn't get Earl King out of her mind all weekend, writing to Clara: "This is just to tell you that I lost my heart to Earl King and don't believe he's any more of a murderer than Johnny is — which is neither here nor there."

When the *Examiner* reporter phoned her just as she was going to sleep Saturday night, she told him, "Go ahead and smear. I don't give a damn what you say." That was the way she felt, but she wrote Clara that "the C.P. and Aubrey and Richard get furious" when she let loose with the press that way. "Somehow it's all so funny — the better our case goes the more the papers fume. I'm beginning to think it's a good sign." She asked Clara to send her one article from the *New York Times* for purposes of comparison with the San Francisco papers.

Dean Landis, in his findings, said that he had to discount the testimony of King and Ramsay in part because they would naturally be vindictive against law-enforcement officials, because they claimed they had been convicted on perjured testimony. But before disregarding their testimony, he said that "it is wise to examine it." San Quentin records showed that Doyle, Ferguson, and Mrs. Ramsay called on Ramsay on July 31, 1937. They showed that Doyle called on King and that Doyle and Ferguson called on Ramsay on September 30, 1937. Obviously, Mr. and Mrs. Ramsay and King could not have known of the existence of such records when they testified.

⁂

As the trial wore on, Carol occasionally realized that the *Bridges* case was not the only thing going on in the world, but "Europe is much further away in S.F. because the newspaper coverage is lousy and I have no access to a radio," she wrote. She struggled for perspective, and finally found it the day Germany invaded Poland and World War II began. She wrote home that "it seems absurd with the world in such a turmoil for all this time and money to be going into the problem of ascertaining if a particular individual is in a particular organization which functions all over the country."

As to the case itself, it had convinced her "that the government could deport any alien in the country by producing one witness who could say, without being discredited, 'I sat in a Communist meeting with X.' It's all crazy." She wanted to "get around sometime to making this clear to folks as it is clear to me."

The daily pressure was on again, and Carol reflected it in a long letter home.

Friday morning [September 1, 1939]
I'm in one of those sunny states where the only pleasure there is left in life is the enjoyment of one's own misery. But as I have a considerable capacity for enjoyment, I'm not having such a bad time of it. In addition to the worst mess (i.e., the failure of this case ever to end) I have two subordinate complaints against life: (1) I am all broken out with hives — which I believe is a nervous disorder with me because it occurs whenever the government is pounding us; (2) I have to go to the Press Club to dinner tonight where everyone is supposed to get tight and have a wonderful time — I don't dare get tight for fear of talking too much and when sober such affairs are dreadful.
As a subordinate complaint against life, someone else or perhaps my own sweet self has burned my black dress (the one with flowers embroidered on it that I got for the [Lawyers] Guild convention) full of cigarette holes and somehow it's all I have to wear. So I am actively and enjoyably miserable. . . . I want sun, but I don't want all these thoroughly nice and intellectual people. I want to let down and be stupid and stodgy and most of all I want to come home where I fit better.

After putting down on paper several other problems in the *Bridges* case, Carol concluded, "I'm afraid I feel better and I'd better get up."

Carol constantly thought about some of the facts in the case that might determine the outcome but would probably not be officially considered as facts, for example, the personalities of the participants, particularly the personality of The Alien. As the defense considered what Bridges should say in his third appearance on the stand, Carol wrote her uncensored views to Clara:

One thing that disturbs me a bit — HB is crazy, but a delightful and extremely effective person. Aubrey and Richie say "He shouldn't talk so much." "Quite right, but he wouldn't be Harry if he stopped," is my answer. I don't know the answer to that one — HB must communicate — everything, and he must be admired and feel himself great in a funny

*proletarian way. Then he can function. I'm not
trying to establish anything only HB is a curiously
pertinent example of my thesis that folks have to
be themselves come what may.*

A few days later, the external world forced its way to the forefront of
Carol's consciousness, and she wrote that she found "actual war instead
of its threat a relief." She felt much better than after Munich, and
confident Hitler would finally be eliminated and "maybe even Communism set up in Germany." The results of war were very clear to her as she
cautioned, "Only I hope there's anything left to be fixed up afterwards."

⚸

A major trial tries each of the participants as well as the legal issues
raised in the formal proceedings. The daily deadlines and media coverage
of every aspect of the lives of the major figures test each individual's
fundamental philosophy. Carol described to Clara how all of this affected
her at this point:

*The weekend was a strange interlude. The most
satisfactory episode was my acquaintance with Pete
Steffens, a boy of 14 who goes after what he wants
in a quiet and effective way* [the son of Lincoln
Steffens and of Ella Winter, who married Donald
Ogden Stewart after Steffens died]. *He drives a car
competently, his conversation is intelligent and
stimulating, his social poise is extraordinary.
Briefly: I like Pete Steffens — he's a complete
article.*

*For some reason — one that I have never under-
stood but have come to accept as inevitable —
everybody got started on how much better person I
would be if I was just different in this respect or
that. One of the things for which I've always been
grateful to you is that you didn't do this. I've
never paid much attention to this indoor sport
since I was a kid, when I was completely
disorganized by it and developed a capacity for
resisting criticism and relying on my own judgment
which has served me well.*

D.O.S. [Donald Ogden Stewart] *wanted me to give
up my sentimental attachment for little aliens and
become openly the important force which I am.*

Caroline and Richie were for making me over into a
lady with fine clothes and lipstick. Pete only
wanted my hair set in Jonathan's interest. It was
all very good natured, but I was a bit bored.

Only I couldn't help being highly entertained
when yesterday at lunch Pete, on being importuned
to eat his lunch, remarked coolly that it was quite
foreign to his nature to consume his mackerel and
consequently he was afraid he couldn't do so. I
felt that the argument might have been worthwhile
in the end.

Once or twice I got into an interesting impasse
with D.O.S., as when I suggested that he shouldn't
devote his life to making enough money to pay the
premiums on his life insurance. I went a step
further and suggested that his kids might be better
off if they didn't each get $100,000 from him than
if they did — an idea which had apparently never
occurred to him.

When the weekend ended, the defense jumped back into total immersion in the trial. It was quick: Bridges again, then the errant Larry Doyle at last. The press reported that Doyle had played hide-and-seek with subpoena servers in Minnesota for several weeks, and then came to San Francisco "ready to tell all." There was a dispute over his expense money, which ended after the hearing was adjourned when defense attorneys refused to pay the amount Doyle claimed he should receive; he, in turn, pocketed the money already advanced and said he would say nothing.

Suddenly, with a gasp, the deportation hearing of Harry Bridges died. Carol lost no time in taking a train back to what she called "the relative peace and quiet of New York," where she could chat with her son Johnny about high school, eat dry sandwiches for lunch, and write the defense brief for Dean Landis.

At least that was her plan during her long train trip home. But the first day she walked into her office after three months in California, she realized she faced a financial crisis. For several years her law practice had involved more principle than pay. And the *Bridges* case, in spite of the large sums collected for the defense, had cost a lot of money in investigation and witness costs, for stenographers and public relations. None of the lawyers was well paid, but Gladstein, Grossman, and Margolis came from a firm where their young associate, Norman Leonard, could take on new cases throughout the hearing, so they could go back afterward to pick up their share of the work — and the fees. As a sole practitioner, Carol King took in no new clients when she was out of the office, and no fees came in until several weeks or months after she returned and new clients heard of her availability.

In fact, if she had been solely dependent on her legal fees, Carol would have been destitute. The apartment house on Twenty-second Street made possible a comfortable standard of living in normal times, but her total earned income in 1939 was barely $3,000, which did not balance her expenditures. Fortunately, the United Shoe Workers–CIO approached her to handle a case involving aliens. She said she would get back to them when she finished the *Bridges* brief. She submitted the brief in October after terrible struggles with co-counsel to get them to send the summary of the evidence they had promised to produce. Her October 5 letter was addressed "Gentlemen?" and warned: "If it is not in my hands by Wednesday of next week . . . I shall fly out to San Francisco . . . C.O.D. to collect it. So watch your step." She needed it quickly because she proposed "to send one copy to Herbert Wechsler, the genius behind the *Herndon* and *Strecker* cases, and get his views on it. I reserve the right to do considerable alteration after that." By October 23, she was able to send a copy of the finished brief to "Dear Folks," but she had to mention their failure to supply the citations to the record, "something I will not discuss with you because it was an unforgivable offense and caused me to lose five pounds and three nights' sleep." She proceeded to criticize every aspect of her and their portions of the brief in detached detail.

But at least the job was done! Now all they had to do was wait for Landis's decision. By late December, the anticipation was almost unbearable.

Finally, on December 28, 1939, Secretary of Labor Perkins released the 150-page "Findings of James M. Landis" and his letter to Perkins:

> These Findings are, perhaps, unusually long and detailed, but I have thought it desirable to state in full the bases which underlie my conclusions. I have, therefore, set forth substantially every item of evidence contained in the long and voluminous record [7,724 pages of transcript plus 274 exhibits concerning 59 witnesses] and attempted to give it that weight that it deserved . . . after painstaking and minute analysis. . . . That process alone permits a fleeting doubt to be dismissed or to ripen into the conviction that what is paraded as truth bears the unmistakable mark of falsehood.

Landis held that the record of the hearings contained no valid evidence that Harry Bridges was a member of or affiliated with the Communist Party. Therefore, it was unnecessary to consider the question of whether that organization advocated the violent overthrow of the government. "Opposition to 'red' baiting is not the equivalent of proof of Communist membership," he concluded.

And he found that a conspiracy had existed against Bridges. The participants included Larry Doyle, Harper Knowles, Captain Keegan of the Portland police, and R. P. Bonham of the Immigration Service, who had ventured far beyond their pretended duty of enforcing the law. Keegan's testimony in the hearings was "far from reliable." Doyle was "a problem in contumacy," who tried in every way to "avoid truthfully detailing his relationship to the facts put in issue." Knowles was "neither a candid nor a forthright witness."

Landis characterized the defendant immigrant in relation to these government officials:

> Bridges himself was undoubtedly his own best witness. . . . Bridges's own statement of his political beliefs and disbeliefs is important. It was given not only without reserve but vigorously as dogma and faiths of which the man was proud and which represented in his mind the aims of his existence. It was a fighting apologia that refused to temper itself to the winds of caution. That Bridges' aims are energetically radical may be admitted, but the proof fails to establish that the methods he seeks to employ to realize them are other than those that the framework of democratic and constitutional government permits.

Landis had gnawed and worried over every incident and witness, pondered his reasons for appearing, his manner of testifying, his idiosyncrasies and their relationship to the truth or falsity of his testimony. What Landis couldn't discuss and illustrate completely in the text of his findings, he forced into the footnotes and appendices.

From his administrative and academic background, Landis had somehow walked into the wilderness of the Western waterfront with enough understanding to plumb the witnesses and their ambitions. He had faced directly the facts about two kins of institutions: law-enforcement agencies and labor unions, with their friendships and enmities, their bitter struggles for power, their pervasive effects on the people in the large areas in which they operated, and their frequently haphazard and anarchistic methods of operation. Landis, like Carol King, had lived with the *Bridges* case until he not only understood it, but could diagram it in legalistic and canny prose.

His opinion proved that Aubrey and Richie had been right about using the hearing to prove the conspiracy against Bridges and his union by employers, an INS official, and city police. Carol had been wrong; her fears would have narrowed the evidence and the decision. His opinion also inferentially proved Carol had been right to put in the expert testimony on the nature of what the Communist Party advocated. By presenting this evidence, Landis had been prevented from taking judicial notice of the nature of CP policy as presented by the government. He had been permitted not to reach the question of CP policy but to decide simply on the question of Bridges's alleged membership. Like so many of Carol's contributions to cases, this one was unstated.

On January 8, 1940, Secretary of Labor Perkins made Landis's conclusion official when she canceled the warrant of arrest for Bridges.

By then, Carol had received copies of the San Francisco papers for December 30. The *News* gave the case a full eight-column page, with photos of the leading figures: Perkins, Landis, Doyle, and counsel on both sides, under the headline: BRIDGES CASE MOST BITTERLY FOUGHT IN NA-TION'S HISTORY. The subheads told the story: Anti-Bridges Witnesses Denounced; Proceedings Brought General Airing of Labor Troubles; Defense Sought to Prove Action was Anti-Labor Plot.

The *News* contrasted the elusive Mr. Doyle with the expansive Mr. Bridges:

> Occasionally [Bridges's] own answers were so frank that his own counsel blinked.
> Did he believe in a capitalistic form of government?
> "If you mean the capitalistic form of society, which to me means the exploitation of a lot of people for profit and a complete disregard of their interests for that profit, I haven't much use for it," he said.
> "Would you believe in the abolition of private property for reasons stated by the Communists?"
> "When they talk of private property," said Mr. Bridges, "they don't mean somebody's two-by-four piece of land. I take it to mean the big utilities, the big factories, the various heavy industries. I am in favor of government ownership of those things, yes, and if the government can't do a better job of running them, I would say give it back to private industry again."
> At another time [he said]: "Sometimes I get a little irritated when my views are ascribed to the Communist Party, because I had them before the Communist Party came into being."

While local defense lawyers hailed the decision, Captain John J. Keegan, Portland chief of detectives, told the press, "Landis was sent out here for a whitewash. We expected nothing else with that kind of a setup."

Carol wrote her own estimate of the significance of the case for the February issue of the *IJA Bulletin:*

> The Secretary's order and the Landis report mark the termination, for the present at least, of an episode the sordid background of which is to some extent outlined in Dean Landis's summary of the testimony. The episode has ended, however, in a proceeding which sets a standard of intelligent procedure and judicious deliberation epitomized in Dean Landis' scholarly report — a standard unique in deportation annals but hailed as a possible harbinger of reform in a field notorious for lack of definition.

Now why did she have to add that qualification "for the present at least"?

21.
Fighting Fascism and the FBI

Ending the Bridges case for Carol was like saying good-bye to a relative who has recovered from a serious illness and getting back into the movement in New York, where she could work comfortably with all the Left and liberal activists, attorneys, union leaders, and friends she had known for years. They would bring her a mixture of labor and immigration cases she would have to handle without losing her footing in the maelstrom of U.S. politics at the beginning of the Second World War.

In October 1939 that meant digging into the charges of the native United Shoe Workers–CIO against the alien Bata Shoe Company under the Contract Labor Law. King asked the union to pay her $50 "if possible" before she made the trip to Washington for them, because she was short of funds and Congressman Smith's committee would not pay her fare. The committee was investigating the International Juridical Association as part of an investigation of the NLRB.

While waiting for the advance, Carol finished the major work on the brief to the Labor Department based on numerous studies on Bata by the International Labour Organization of the League of Nations and the U.S. Department of Commerce. Bata, with headquarters in Czechoslovakia, was the most important firm in international footwear, exporting six million pairs of shoes a year to the United States. When Hitler took over Czechoslovakia in 1938, imposing Nazi rule, President Roosevelt responded with economic sanctions, setting countervailing tariff duties on German products, including Czechoslovak shoes. Bata countered by establishing a factory in the United States that would eventually employ 2,000 workers, and sought permission to bring in 100 people for a year on visitor permits to instruct U.S. workers in unique Bata techniques. The government granted these permits over strenuous objections from U.S. shoe companies that the industry was already suffering from overcapacity.

The United Shoe Workers immediately protested because thousands of their members were unemployed, and these men would not be temporary instructors. The company was notorious the world over for its anti-union practices. Later it would try to employ teenagers at low wages and keep out the union.

Two weeks after Carol sent her first statement to Leo Goodman, the union's research director, she dictated a short letter saying she had no intention of coming to Washington until she heard about funds. This may have startled Goodman, a salaried union employee with an expense account and no cash-flow problems.

When he got her brief, Goodman praised "the swell job you did," (adding news about a mutual friend who had suffered a nervous breakdown, having hallucinations that the FBI was trailing him and that congressional committees were passing resolutions to reduce his pay).

Prodded by the King brief and union delegations, the Department of Labor sent investigators to the Bata plant. The day Landis decided for Bridges, the commissioner of immigration decided for the shoe workers at Belcamp, Maryland. Only ten of the seventy-two people imported under visitor permits could continue to be employed at Belcamp because the others were competing unfairly with skilled U.S. shoe workers.

Immediately immigration lawyer King started worrying about the fate of sixty-two discharged alien employees, but wrote to Goodman, "I guess you're right that there were larger issues." Goodman replied with documentary proof that the aliens had been commuting in and out of Nazi Germany at will.

Carol turned immediately to the Congressional investigation of the International Juridical Association and the *IJA Bulletin*. She was outraged!

The day Congress adopted the Wagner National Labor Relations Act in 1935, anti-labor Congressmen started demanding broad amendments. This chorus swelled after the Supreme Court made NLRB a permanent agency by upholding the constitutionality of the act in 1937 in the *Jones & Laughlin Steel* case, and the 1939 report of the Dies Committee on Un-American Activities suggested "that the 'communist activities' and beliefs of the National Labor Relations Board be investigated."

The NLRB prepared testimony opposing amendments they considered destructive of the Wagner Act and its bill of rights for workers seeking to organize their own unions. They cited articles in the *IJA Bulletin* among other sources.

In retaliation, anti-labor Representative Howard Smith (Dem.-Va.) got himself appointed to investigate these efforts by employees of an administrative agency to influence legislation. Smith charged those employees with a violation of the separation of powers. Representative Smith and his staff soon leaked the story that the NLRB was linked to the Communist Party via the IJA, intimating broadly that Joe Brodsky had had a hand in running the NLRB through his secret domination of the IJA. Cloaked in all the unusual initials and with proper fanfare, this rumor sounded like a choice morsel at a time when support for the Communist Party was at a very low ebb due to events in Europe.

At the same time, a federal judge in Seattle granted a temporary injunction sought by ship owners against ILWU pickets who had successfully halted loading of vessels with scrap iron for Japan; the ILWU's actions were protesting Japan's violation of the nine-power peace pact by invading China. The judge said he was "unable to run ahead of the executive branch of government and Congress in naming enemies or near enemies."

Early in August 1939, President Roosevelt established the War Resources Board of the War and Navy Departments. FDR was primarily concerned about the war in Europe and ordered the board to cooperate in the mobilization of the economic resources of the United States to meet any "emergency" that might arise. Organized labor immediately criticized the board: its six members included the chief executive officers of U.S. Steel, American Telephone & Telegraph, General Motors, and Sears, and no representative of the AFL or CIO.

All domestic news paled into insignificance when Hitler and Stalin signed a nonaggression pact on August 23, 1939. The U.S. Left was totally unprepared for this event, according to Margaret Nowak in her joint biography of herself and her husband, Stanley, a leader of the American Committee for Protection of Foreign Born and of the Polish-American community. But "[we] soon recognized it as an attempt by the Soviet Union to buy time to prepare for what they knew would inevitably happen, an attack on the Soviet Union by Nazi Germany."

Carol King had many clients, friends, and colleagues who came to the same conclusion in this period. Her own opinion was affected by her experience with Poland's detention of political prisoners in 1935, when she was part of the international ILD delegation.

According to Nowak, the Polish community in Detroit, where she lived, represented "every ideological viewpoint from left to right," and "was split wide open, . . . However, as international developments occurred, the controversy died down. Poland had been offered a mutual assistance pact by the Soviet Union earlier but rejected it out of hand and made such a pact instead with England and France. We saw Poland attacked by Nazi Germany on 1 September and a very tardy response from England and France" in the period called the "sitzkrieg" or sitting war in Europe; the U.S. Left began calling it the phony war. The Soviet Union entered Poland from the east on September 17.

By the end of September, President Roosevelt disbanded his new War Resources Board in response to all the criticism. Popular New Deal Senator Wagner (Dem.-N.Y.) opposed "millions of our fellow men" being "offered up as sacrifices to the gods of war" in Europe and the Pacific. Over NBC radio he instead called for adoption of a national health program to "demonstrate to all the world that America places human resources first among the assets of an enlightened civilization." The *IJA Bulletin* headlined this statement in its January 1940 issue.

So the New Deal was over; the United States was not at war, but it certainly was moving into war production as the declared war in Europe seemed to stand still.

One of the complex questions in this period was the proper role for the U.S. Communist Party in response to events abroad and in the United States. An equally complex question was the proper attitude of the U.S. government toward the CPUS in light of these events. Both questions were epitomized in the status and cases of Earl and Raissa Browder in 1939.

Their cases had begun innocently enough when a native-born citizen decided to regularize the status of his Russian-born wife after they had been married for thirteen years. She had entered the United States in 1933 without a visa — that is, illegally — and had borne three U.S.–citizen sons. The couple retained Carol King, who advised them to follow a customary procedure to regularize their status, with the husband filing a petition and a citizen filing an affidavit of support for the wife, as required on such applications. Mrs. King herself filed the affidavit for Mrs. Browder.

Earl Browder, native-born general secretary of the Communist Party of the United States, was pursuing in his own life the line he had gotten the CP to adopt: to clean up its image in the United States as having a "foreign ideology." According to Jean Kramer, loyal active CP members

who had been arrested for political deportation were quietly being asked
to leave the Party so that any headlines about their cases would not repeat
this "alien" image of the Party at a time of rising hysteria against all aliens.

After Browder filed his petition, he was first subpoenaed and then
arrested in the fall of 1939 for using a 1934 passport he had secured by
making a false statement. The three-year statute of limitations had run
on other violations of using false names on earlier passports.

While he was awaiting trial, Browder was nominated by petition to
be a candidate for Congress at a special election to be held in February
1940 in New York City's Fourteenth District.

⊱

War broke out between the Soviet Union and Finland on November
30, 1939. This fact affected many of Carol's cases and clients, especially
a series of Red Finns she had represented in deportation cases. They
considered Mannerheim's Finnish government a pro-fascist dictatorship.
They said that was why Mannerheim had rejected a Soviet offer to
exchange land. They said the Soviets wanted to gain a strategic advantage
in the coming inevitable clash with Nazi Germany, despite the nonaggression pact. This view was sharply contested by many who supported the
"small democracy" against the "giant dictatorship."

The Soviet-Nazi pact, the invasion of Poland, and the Soviet-Finnish
War really split the Liberals and the Left in the United States. Thousands
left the Communist Party; Liberals attacked the CP. A handful even began
to make their peace with J. Edgar Hoover and the tactics of the FBI. The
unity built in support of New Deal legislation and of Loyalist Spain was
permanently broken.

In this climate, Carol King, secretary of the International Juridical
Association, was called to testify before the Smith Committee on December 14, 1939. She was in an argumentative frame of mind. She became
more so as the committee's counsel, Edmund M. Toland, began developing his line of questioning.

First, where was her office and where did she practice law?

MISS KING: My office is at 100 Fifth Avenue, and I practice law wherever
my cases are.
MR. TOLAND: That even extends to San Francisco, does it not?
MISS KING: I think that is irrelevant, but it does.

MR. TOLAND: Did you represent Mr. Bridges in his hearing in San
  Francisco?
MISS KING: I was one of the attorneys for Harry Bridges, engaged because
  I am a specialist in the law of immigration.
MR. TOLAND: Is your office connected with or adjacent to any other
  member of the bar? . . .
MISS KING: I will answer that question if the chairman tells me to, but I
  think it is quite irrelevant. [The chairman did, and she did.]
MISS KING: There are a group of attorneys with whom I share a library,
  who have no connection with my office, and those attorneys are: Arthur
  P. Wendorf, George Barnett, Joseph R. Brodsky, and Sol H. Cohn.

Miss King said she had been officially connected for a number of years
with Brodsky, and later they worked on cases together. Several lawyers
got involved in the IJA at its first or second meeting, including four from
her office — Brodsky, Schwartzbart, Cohn, and herself — and Osmond
Fraenkel of the ACLU.

Mr. Toland then read into the record the report by the Education and
Labor Committee containing a statement by the NLRB concerning proposed amendments to the NLRA, including several references to the *IJA
Bulletin*. (King was anxious to explain that these were actually footnote
references to *Bulletin* articles.) Next Toland waved in his hand an
advertisement for the *IJA Bulletin*, stating that the IJA had worked with
the CIO to solve the legal problems involved in the CIO organizing
campaign. It was admissible, according to Toland, because the NLRB had
quoted material from the *IJA Bulletin*; Brodsky was on the IJA Executive
Committee and had represented Communist Party leaders before the Dies
Committee. Toland thus exposed a conspiratorial plot: the board "referred to and relied upon" the IJA in its presentation of its cases,
employees of the board "contributed information or articles" to the IJA,
and members and employees of the board "contributed to its upkeep."

Congressman John Murdock (Dem.-Utah) was concerned that the
committee was encroaching on the jurisdiction of the Dies Committee on
Un-American Activities by going into "these communistic matters."
Congressman Charles Halleck (Rep. Ind.) had a different concern: when
the advertisement for the *IJA Bulletin* was written was "there was nothing
secret about it?"

Mrs. King broke in heatedly, "There is nothing secret about the entire
organization." She objected to intimations that Joseph Brodsky had
mysteriously controlled the IJA. One purpose of the IJA was to provide
legal research in cases involving civil liberties and labor. To carry out this

purpose, the IJA needed close contact with the defense organizations active in these areas. The presence on the IJA board of Brodsky of the ILD had the same cause, and the same significance, as the presence of Osmond K. Fraenkel of the ACLU and the other seven members. Brodsky did not control the organization, and he had never written a single word for the *IJA Bulletin* (which must have irritated a hardworking editor):

> MISS KING: It seems to me this business of smearing is something not fair either to this investigation or to the organization I represent. . . . Mr. Chairman, I feel it is unfair to this organization not to bring out its connection with the American Federation of Labor.

The chairman admitted the record showed that the IJA had some connection with the AFL. With that he excused the witness.

Congress took no action against the IJA, King, Brodsky — or the NLRB at that session. But Congressman Martin Dies (Dem.-Tex.) assured the country that if his Un-American Activities Committee were permitted to continue, "the investigation would result in the deportation of 7,000,000 aliens." King was quick to note in the *IJA Bulletin* that there were only 3,838,928 aliens in the United States, according to the Secretary of Labor.

After her testimony about the IJA, Carol King returned to her customary concerns about the IJA — the need for authors and money. The attack by the Smith committee certainly did not help on either count. As of January 1, 1940, the bank account held $211.99. In 1939 the *Bulletin* took in 376 new subscriptions, but 402 expired and were not renewed, leaving about 1,200 subscribers. Expenses and income were running around $4,000 a year.

```
[FBI File]
THE DEPARTMENT OF JUSTICE ISSUED A PRESS RELEASE AT
WASHINGTON, D.C., IN JANUARY 1940, TO THE EFFECT
THAT A SPECIAL GRAND JURY WOULD INQUIRE INTO THE
COMMUNIST PARTY AND SEVERAL OTHER ORGANIZATIONS.
THE STATEMENT INCLUDED THE FACT THAT JOSEPH BRODSKY
WOULD BE SUBJECT TO INQUIRY BY THE SAID GRAND JURY.
```

Early in 1940 Carol was busy with all three Browder cases. She lost her petition for Mrs. Browder to go to Canada to regularize her status on technical grounds. After a four-day jury trial in federal court, the jury voted Earl Browder guilty on the passport charge, and the judge sentenced him to four years in prison, then released him on $7,500 bail pending appeal. In February, New York State Supreme Court Justice Bernstein heard the suit by two local politicians objecting to Browder's name on the ballot. The judge ruled that Browder was qualified to run for Congress: to require "that he alter his philosophy of government or abandon his advocacy of international Communism or abdicate his position in the Communist Party of America, as a condition of being permitted to run for office, would in itself constitute a violation of our own law." On the same day, the Board of Elections upheld the sufficiency of the petition filed in Browder's behalf, so New York State citizens could vote for this convicted federal criminal.

The day before this special election, the American Civil Liberties Union adopted the Ernst-type resolution the Lawyers Guild had defeated the year before. Carol printed the ACLU resolution in full under the heading: *Quis Custodiet Ipsos Custodes?*

The ACLU Board of Directors and National Committee said it should be "subject to the test of consistency in the defense of civil liberties" and, therefore, held it "inappropriate" for any person to serve as an officer or staff member "who is a member of any political organization" that supports "the totalitarian governments of the Soviet Union and of the Fascist and Nazi countries, (such as the Communist Party, the German-American Bund and others); as well as native organizations with obvious anti-democratic objectives or practices." However, it would not require *members* to pass "any test of opinion on political or economic questions."

Every ACLU board member did not agree — philosopher Corliss Lamont for one, attorney Osmond K. Fraenkel for another. Harry F. Ward, for twenty years chairman of the ACLU board, resigned from the board and the ACLU. He charged the ACLU with using guilt by association, which it had always opposed. He said the board was really only anti-Communist because no fascist or Bund member had come near the ACLU, let alone had become an officer. No one had challenged the record in defense of civil liberties of the one open Communist member of the board, who was also a charter member of the ACLU. (Carol printed Ward's letter without comment in the *Bulletin,* furnishing a footnote indicating that the member referred to was Elizabeth Gurley Flynn, Irish-American union organizer and orator who had started out with the Wobblies in the 1910s and had long been a member and leader of the

Communist Party and the ACLU. Her "trial" by the ACLU would be reported in a later issue.)

Ward concluded, "In thus penalizing opinions, the Union is doing in its own sphere what it has always opposed the government for doing in law or administration." It is "attempting to create an orthodoxy" in "political judgment upon events outside the United States, in situations of differing degrees of democratic development." The majority, "acting under the pressure of wartime public opinion," tells the minority "to conform to its views or get out. What kind of civil liberties is this?"

On February 6, 1940, 3,080 New Yorkers voted for Communist Browder for Congress; 6,665 voted for Republican Louis J. Lefkowitz, and 12,962 for Democrat Michael Edelstein. The Communist candidate got one out of every seven-plus votes.

The saga of Communist leader Earl Browder, candidate and convict, was not unique. In this changeling time, bright graduates of City College of New York could find no positions of any kind in New York. Several took jobs as clerks in the FBI in Washington in the late thirties. They proceeded to exercise their First Amendment rights and their Marxist principles by organizing an industrial club of the Communist Party based on their workplace. They carried out typical CP club tasks — reading the *Daily Worker*, raising money to help political defendants, etc. — until they were found out. Hoover was apoplectic but had no grounds for firing them, let alone charging them with any crime. They were quietly transferred to other government jobs; Hoover hushed up what would have been a hilarious tidbit and intensified his public attacks on Reds in government. (During the postwar congressional investigations, one of the group told this story to his attorney Morton Stavis, Carol's friend from early IJA days.)

Soon after the election, Carol King found herself near the center of events on another revolving stage. Someone called from Detroit to report that the FBI had raided the homes of eleven people — two doctors; the Wayne County secretary of the Workers Alliance; leaders of the ILD, CP, and Young Communist League; and veterans of the Lincoln Brigade in the Spanish Civil War. The FBI staged the raids simultaneously, using force to enter and ransack. They also raided the Detroit office of the Communist Party, jimmied open cabinets, and removed papers. (The FBI in Milwaukee conducted a similar raid on a doctor's office and arrested him.) The FBI took its Detroit victims to FBI headquarters and grilled them for hours.

Those arrested asked to see their relatives and consult their attorney, Ernest Goodman, a young partner of Maurice Sugar, founder of the Lawyers Guild and general counsel of the United Auto Workers–CIO.

The FBI denied both requests, and then refused to let Goodman and another attorney see their clients or the indictments prior to arraignment. The government sought and got unusually high bail set for these longtime residents, from $2,000 to $20,000. They held the one woman in solitary confinement and denied the men privileges usually accorded persons awaiting trial. Finally the charges were revealed: violation of the Neutrality Act, which prohibits recruiting, in the United States, people to act against any foreign government with which the United States is at peace. In this case, the recruits were going to defend the first democratically elected government of Spain, with which the United States was at peace, against Franco, who was seeking to overthrow the government by force and violence.

The Michigan Civil Rights Federation, the ACLU, and the ILD sent telegrams to President Roosevelt protesting the flagrant violations of civil rights in the raids, arrests, and excessive bail. In the *IJA Bulletin,* Carol emphasized the startling similarity to the postwar Palmer Raids in 1919–1920 conducted by the same J. Edgar Hoover — although, of course, on a much larger scale.

On February 15, she wrote to a handful of lawyers around the country whom she knew: Richard Gladstein in San Francisco, Duke Avnet in Baltimore, Leo Gallagher in Los Angeles, Arthur Goldberg in Chicago, Ed Lamb in Toledo, John Caughlan in Seattle, Maurice Sugar in Detroit, and Louis McCabe in Philadelphia. She enclosed galley proofs of an article to appear that week in the *New Republic,* entitled "American OGPU," about recent actions of the FBI against "Reds." She urged the lawyers to ask the organizations and unions they represented to urge their congressmen to use their influence on the Department of Justice or the FBI to have the proceedings in Detroit dropped because "just a little more pressure should be able to put a finish to this mistake." In fact, O. John Rogge, head of the Justice Department's Criminal Division, said the whole incident was being studied.

The same day, the new Attorney General, Robert Jackson, ordered dismissal of the Detroit indictments. He said he could see no good in reviving the "animosities" of the recent "Spanish conflict." (He failed to mention another relevant factor noted by King: Right-wing Finns and others who supported Hitler were openly recruiting soldiers for the

Finnish War against the Soviet Union, with which the United States was at peace, but no indictments had been issued against them.)

Having won a victory for the Detroit defendants, Carol tried to take the offensive. Carol King, lobbyist, wrote to her group of lawyers from Seattle to Philadelphia that "if appropriate demands" were made to senators and congressmen, "there may be an investigation about the F.B.I." In the March issue of the *Bulletin,* Carol King, editor, reported that "public indignation aroused by the nature of the prosecution and the means employed by the government officials . . . seems likely to result in an official investigation."

Meanwhile Carol King, banker, was reconsidering her $150 contribution to "the public campaign." On March 13, she wrote to Ernest Goodman: "On balancing my bank account this morning I found I was broke. Is there any chance of getting anything back? In other words my heart is always larger than my pocketbook. . . . What ho?" Goodman answered promptly that the Michigan Civil Rights Federation was "broker" than she was because of the printing and mailing of a pamphlet on the incident, costing $300: "I think when you see it you will almost be willing to forget the $150."

Later Carol's first lawyer employer entered the scene. Max Lowenthal approached Goodman to ask whether he would be interested in meeting with Senator George Norris (Rep.-Neb.). Lowenthal had been working for Senator Burton K. Wheeler (Dem.-Mont.) and Senator Harry Truman (Dem.-Mo.) on their Senate Committee investigating chicanery with railroad securities and holding companies before the crash. Lowenthal thought the Detroit cases represented a real opportunity to expose the FBI, as he was doing in a book he was writing. Goodman agreed and described to Carol his meeting with Norris, the last of the great liberal-radical senatorial triumvirate of the past decades — Borah, La Follette, and Norris. With his "deep-lined face, white flowing hair, large loose body," Norris represented to Goodman "more of a legend than a living being. He listened to our accounts with patience and concern, more of sadness at what he was hearing, at what his government had been doing. He asked few questions."

Finally Senator Norris said, "I am an old man. I don't have the energy left to take on a new fight — especially with someone as powerful as Hoover. But, he's a dangerous man for our country. Someone has to do something."

Senator Norris wrote to Attorney General Jackson requesting an investigation, and the Attorney General appointed a special assistant to look into the matter. Henry Schweinhaut's report admitted illegal searches and seizures by FBI agents making the arrests, and stated that FBI headquarters in Washington had approved the plan for prohibiting the defendants from calling their lawyers after they were arrested. Nonetheless, Jackson sent a letter to Norris praising the "vigorous and effective work for law enforcement" of the FBI, "conducted with a fundamental purpose to observe the rights of defendants."

Soon Senator Norris took the floor of the Senate to present his last major address. He disagreed with "whitewashing" what had happened in Detroit: "I think a fair conclusion from the evidence taken by Mr. Schweinhaut must bear out the charge that the Federal Bureau of Investigation was guilty of conduct which ought not to be approved by the Attorney General." He continued:

> Mr. President, it is my humble judgment that Mr. Hoover is doing more injury to honest law enforcement in this country by his publicity-seeking feats than is being done by any other one thing connected with his organization. Unless we do something to stop this furor of adulation we shall have an organization — the FBI — which, instead of protecting our people from the evil acts of criminals, will itself in the end direct the Government by tyrannical force. [U]nless this procedure is stopped, there will [soon] be a spy behind every stump and a detective in every closet.

As Goodman and King toasted their victory, some questions remained. Why had outgoing Attorney General Frank Murphy, New Deal Democrat from Michigan, sanctioned the FBI raids and arrests? Was it to appease the Catholic hierarchy so it would not oppose FDR when he elevated Murphy to the United States Supreme Court? And why had incoming Attorney General Robert Jackson, an early member of the Lawyers Guild, first done the right thing by dropping the indictments, and then done the wrong thing by whitewashing the FBI?

These questions were soon lost in the next crisis in this period of turbulent political maneuvers in the United States. Leaders of business, government, and unions — isolationists, One-Worlders, liberals, progressives, and Communists — tried to respond to events as Hitler's Nazi armies marched up and down at the borders of Germany and imperial Japan menaced the Soviet Union's eastern flank, as the Nazi-Soviet pact held and the Soviet-Finnish war continued.

This was a seesaw period. Win *Bridges,* lose *Browder.* Face criminal charges for recruiting anti-fascist soldiers for democratic Spain; get the charges dropped as "that man in the White House" begins fishing for support for an unprecedented third term. And out in Hollywood, Carol's liberal friend from the *Bridges* case, Donald Ogden Stewart, started writing the screenplay for *Philadelphia Story,* starring Katherine Hepburn, Cary Grant, and James Stewart.

It seemed a good omen in early March 1940 when the chairman of the INS Board of Review agreed to speak at the conference of the American Committee for Protection of Foreign Born, chaired by Representative Vito Marcantonio (American Labor Party-N.Y.). Seven others from Capitol Hill addressed the conference, from Senator Claude Pepper (Dem.-Fla.) to John M. Coffee (Dem.-Wash.), as well as Stanley Nowak, Polish-born Michigan state senator; Archibald MacLeish, Librarian of Congress and friend of Louis Weiss; Dean William Hastie of Howard University Law School; and Charles H. Houston of the NAACP.

The executive director of the National Institute of Immigrant Welfare set the stage. Before 1919, he reported, deportations numbered no more than 1,500 a year. As a result of the Palmer Raids, this figure doubled in 1919. After the quota restrictions in 1921, deportations mounted steadily to over 1,500 *every month.* Between 1933 and 1938, 45,000 men, women, and children were deported. The chairman of the American Committee then reported that in the past year it had defended people threatened with deportation, assisted those seeking naturalization, and also secured 50,000 signatures on petitions requesting defeat of anti-alien legislation. This work was done on a budget of approximately $12,000, which was obviously inadequate.

When Ralph T. Seward spoke, as chairman of the Board of Review of the Department of Labor, he expressed concern about the broad powers in the hands of the Immigration Service: an order of deportation could not be fully reviewed in the courts; there was a presumption that it was valid, and it could not be appealed on all issues. It could only be attacked collaterally by means of a petition for habeas corpus. These rules placed "great responsibility" on the Service, and it was studying ways of improving its procedures. If these reforms were adopted in the future, an alien arrested for deportation would be "fully apprised of the charges against him" and would have "adequate opportunity to prepare his case" and to file exceptions to the initial decision. The prosecuting and the judicial functions would be separated in the deportation hearings.

Carol King, speaking as secretary of the IJA, agreed that the Labor Department "has recently been very cooperative in trying to give the alien a fair deal. Nevertheless, it is also true that we cannot let the Department go unwatched." She thought the *Bridges* case was "an excellent example of how, under fair conditions, it is possible for the alien to show that the case against him is a frame-up." In most strike situations, an alien who is leading the strike is arrested for deportation. "For this the Labor Department is not solely to blame. The boss will probably keep running to the Department and report such an individual. The Labor Department must eventually investigate. With a fair hearing, however, the case can be blown up." She insisted that "the fair procedure in the Bridges case" is "the right of every alien."

⁊

Carol King gladly put on her best dress to hear Carey McWilliams, chief of the Division of Immigration and Housing of the California Department of Industrial Relations, and her good friend Nuddy Greene talk about civil liberties and the NLRB at the annual fund-raising dinner of her favorite organization, the IJA. In planning the dinner at the Hotel Murray Hill ($2 per person including tip), the IJA Bulletin hoped to net a little toward printing costs.

By now the *Bulletin* was full of long articles analyzing every aspect of labor law as it continued to report on civil rights and alien cases. It was appropriate for Wall Street lawyer Greene to talk about the steelworkers at Jones & Laughlin before April 12, 1937, when the Supreme Court upheld the Wagner Act as constitutional; the conditions at Republic Steel and in Harlan County, Kentucky, and at a Ford plant in Somerville, Massachusetts. In each instance, Greene explained, the liberty of the employers to run their businesses exactly as they wished had been struck down, first by the act, then by the NLRB, and finally by a court. He concluded with a "fair summary of what the Act and the Board have done *to* liberty and *for* liberty":

> *To liberty:* they have . . . narrowed the employer's freedom to be irresponsible in the use of his economic power. *For liberty:* they have raised millions of workingmen to the dignity of free human beings; they have given millions of workingmen access to freedoms about which they had become deeply cynical; . . .

> I have heard an important person in this City defend what he called
> Henry Ford's right of free speech in the cases I have discussed. He said, "I
> am for free speech though the universe shall smash."
> Forgive the IJA. We are for free speech in an unsmashed . . . world. We
> believe speech and the other civil liberties are meaningful only to men who
> dare to use them. And that before "daring" come bread and water, come
> roots in the community, come respite from fear. Only a reasonably whole
> world, not a "smashed" world, will ever tolerate free speech.

Carol immediately agreed to print Greene's speech in the next *Bulletin,*
and then sold reprints for 5 cents per copy.

But Greene's view had faded on Capitol Hill as Congress was being
pushed and pulled out of concern for U.S. workers and the economic
problems of the United States into international questions raised by the
Second World War and opportunities for U.S. industry in the arms race.

On April 9, 1940, the German Nazis occupied Norway and Denmark.
The Sitzkrieg was over. On May 1, Germany invaded Holland, Belgium,
Luxembourg, and France. On June 10, Italy entered the war and invaded
France. The world soon discovered there was no invincible Maginot Line;
there were traitors in high offices in Paris who preferred German fascism
to the possibility of French communism. On June 22, France surrendered
to the Nazi-Fascist Axis. Suddenly Germany controlled all of Europe
outside the Soviet Union. England stood alone, and Germany began its
bombing raids on civilian targets in London. World War II turned hot and
bloody.

President Roosevelt had been pursuing a public policy of noninterven-
tion while planning his campaign for a third term. He watched these
international events closely, as he also watched the mood of Congress.

The year before, Representative T. F. Ford of California had declared,
"The mood of this House is such that if you brought in the Ten Com-
mandments today and asked for their repeal, and attached to that request
an alien law you could get it." For many congressmen, the special target
continued to be Harry Bridges. Representative Howard Smith's committee proposed an amendment to the Wagner Act to exempt employers from
the requirement to bargain collectively with the representative of their
employees if that representative was not a citizen. Another bill was
specific: "That the Secretary of Labor be, and is hereby, authorized and
directed to take into custody and deport to Australia, . . . the alien, Harry
Bridges."

The IJA promptly submitted a brief showing that the bill was unconstitutional. Solicitor General Francis Biddle told the Pennsylvania Bar Association that the bill was "directed against a single individual, what amounts to a bill of attainder. And yet I have heard no bar association protest." His speech did not change this situation. In June, the House full of lawyers passed the bill 330 to 42. Carol rushed to help develop opposition in the national press and among key senators. The bill died in the Senate.

In May the President had asked Congress to transfer the Immigration Service from the Labor Department to the Department of Justice in the interests of "national safety." This was symbolic and contradictory — the purpose of Labor was to protect wage earners; the purpose of Justice was to prosecute criminals, and even *illegal* aliens were not criminals. But no aliens were entitled, under existing law, to the due process protections prescribed for criminal defendants. The ILD sent out a strong letter opposing this transfer, with Congressman Marcantonio's name on the letterhead as national president: "The Department of Justice will be the greatest spying, union-busting organization in the history of the United States."

After the shift, Henry Hart and others in Justice worked over the machinery and improved it somewhat, in Tom Emerson's opinion, establishing a Board of Immigration Appeals to exercise the attorney general's judicial functions in immigration matters.

Very soon the House set about amending the deportation law and soon passed a bill sponsored by Representative Smith (Dem.-Va.) that was known as "Smith's Alien Registration Act of 1940." It wiped out the results of the Supreme Court decision in *Strecker* by providing that an alien could be deported if he had, *in the past,* belonged to an organization that advocated the violent overthrow of the government. "It is my joy," chortled Representative Samuel Hobbs (Dem.-Ala.), "to announce that this bill will do, in a perfectly legal and constitutional manner, what the bill specifically aimed at the deportation of Harry Bridges seeks to accomplish. . . . The Department of Justice should now have little trouble in deporting Harry Bridges and all others of similar ilk." The act also provided that each noncitizen in the United States must register with the federal government, notify it of every change of address, and state under oath the activities in which he or she had engaged and expected to engage in the future.

In addition, Smith's bill contained provisions that did not relate to aliens. The *IJA Bulletin* and the ILD called attention to these other sections, applicable to citizens and noncitizens alike. They included a federal sedition and military disaffection law that the IJA said was "of a type long successfully resisted as unneeded and dangerous," making it a crime *to conspire to advocate* the overthrow of the government of the United States by force and violence. The House was consumed with concern about Harry Bridges and other "dangerous aliens." They debated this totally new provision for barely half an hour, and then passed the bill 384 to 4; the Senate followed and sent the Smith Act to the White House. President Roosevelt vetoed it. Congress overrode his veto by the necessary two/thirds vote, and Smith's Alien Registration (and citizen seditious conspiracy) Act became law.

⁂

King reported in the *IJA Bulletin* for the summer of 1940 a few of the "Recent Items" on the road that seemed to lead to U.S. involvement in World War II. Congress passed a peacetime conscription bill. The House passed a bill permitting some wiretapping by the government. The University of Michigan expelled six students for political activity in the American Student Union. Oklahoma City police used terror against CP leaders. People in twenty-one states committed forty-two acts of violence against Jehovah's Witnesses after the Supreme Court held that Witnesses could be expelled from public school for refusing to salute the flag. The *Bulletin* warned that civil liberties were in trouble in wartime Canada and spelled out the dangerous provisions of the Defense of Canada Regulations.

The only really good piece of news to report was the U.S. Supreme Court decision that peaceful picketing is a form of free speech in *Thornhill v. Alabama*.

In this climate, the "Ernst issue" arose in the Lawyers Guild in a new form. At the summer 1940 Guild convention in Washington, D.C., liberal New Deal lawyers proposed a resolution equating Germany and the Soviet Union. Delegates listened to Justice William O. Douglas, guest of honor at the annual banquet, and Dean Landis of Harvard Law School, and then voted down the Ernst-type resolution.

When the new Guild president, Robert W. Kenny, walked into the Guild's Washington office after the convention, he faced a mountain of telegrams of resignation. This Democratic state senator from California went back to his hotel room with Martin Popper to try to cool off. Popper recalled that they were interrupted by a phone call from a lawyer representing the leading Guild lawyers in the Roosevelt Administration: Robert Jackson (later Supreme Court Justice), Jerome Frank, and Adolf Berle. At first they proposed resigning from the Washington, D.C., chapter while remaining members-at-large, because they did not have time to deal with "the problems in the Chapter," including "Communist domination." Kenny accepted this proposal. Then the group reconsidered and upped the ante. They called Kenny back to demand that certain named lawyers resign from the National Executive Board because they were "too Left."

Kenny and Popper saw the group's demand as the end of the uneasy United Front in the legal community that had started in 1933 and made possible the effective work of the Lawyers Guild at the national level. The Guild had appealed to Lincoln Republicans, New Deal Democrats, Communists, and independents, emphasizing the importance of labor unions and the rights of Negroes, providing plenty of room for lawyer egos, incipient loners, and anarchists.

Now Roosevelt Democrats like Frank and Berle were distancing themselves from those still focusing on the rights of labor and the need to improve the economic system in this country. They were following FDR as he was moving the country away from isolationism to support imperial England, which had moved from its nonaggression Munich treaty with Germany to defense against Nazi bombing, while the Soviet Union was busily producing arms and living under its nonaggression treaty with Germany.

Kenny, as president of the Guild, rejected this old New Dealer's demand to purge Leftists from Guild leadership. He told the group, "We couldn't do anything like that," and went home to become Attorney General of California and to preside over a somewhat smaller Lawyers Guild for eight years.

Many friendships were strained and some were broken in this period, as were some organizational ties. Herbert Wechsler, a leading figure in the early IJA, recalled in 1952 that his personal relations with Carol King had been quite hostile since he had prepared the brief for the Department of Justice that sent Earl Browder to jail in 1940. Professor Wechsler said King was undoubtedly "a clever woman," especially at "dissembling," during the United Front period, but that later events showed her to be closer to Communist operations than she had admitted in the 1930s. Tom Glazer, the folk singer who had met King at her brother's home in 1939, had not agreed with her politically. In 1982 he commented that "She was in a position I had given up years before. She said something to me which indicated that she was very very pro-Soviet. I had become disenchanted and was down because of the world situation, knowing what the USSR was like because of the Moscow [treason] trials and all that had been investigated by John Dewey. After Trotsky was murdered it was very easy to be critical about politics. She still believed in certainties that had been exploded for me."

In June, Carol received word that the U.S. Court of Appeals had affirmed the conviction of Earl Browder for violating the Passport Act. Two months later the Immigration Service, now part of the Justice Department, issued an arrest warrant for the deportation of Raissa Browder, apparently triggered by Earl Browder's petition to legalize his wife's status.

Carol continued to work on this case, although the only forums remaining to her were very difficult. She tried to influence public opinion and finally she went to the top, sending a long message to the President. She argued that, as head of the executive department, he had the power to take the actions the Attorney General refused to take. She supplied several pages of citations in support of this principle, and the provisions of law "especially intended" to relieve the hardship of separating an American family. President Roosevelt did not act, and the Board of Immigration Appeals soon upheld the deportation order against Raissa Browder.

In August 1940 the *IJA Bulletin* ran a long and thoughtful discussion of the Burke-Wadsworth Conscription Bill, including its provisions for conscientious objectors. The article sought some basis for unity among "minds at conflict on defense needs" at this point. It assumed agreement that a "mounting popular tension . . . has produced disturbing trends in local vigilantism and government lawlessness" and "that forces which have always fought against labor and social legislation have returned to battle with a new technique, under a new banner, and with far greater chance of success." The editors asked, "What dangers to free public discussion and to a sane national temperament are inherent in the injection of the virus of martial spirit into the current of peace-time life" by requiring 12,000,000 men to register for the draft?

Wartime life became more global in September when Germany, Italy, and Japan signed their Tri-Partite Pact in Berlin as Japanese forces invaded Vietnam. In October, German troops entered Romania and Italian troops entered Greece. Carol described the mood toward aliens as one in which "the press seeks to identify the alien with the fifth column and Congress has gone on a debauch of alien-baiting legislation."

But when Attorney General Jackson refused the appeal of Mrs. Browder, the wife of and assistant to a leading Communist, the *New York Daily News* responded editorially that the United States should not follow Russia's example of making it hard for Russian wives to come to the United States with American engineers they married while the men were working on the Dnieprostroy Dam. Nothing was proved against Mrs. Browder concerning espionage or sedition, and "it is far wiser to let the Communist Party remain a legal party in this country, blow off what steam it pleases, and lose out consistently by overwhelming majorities in our free and open elections." Even Westbrook Pegler, the reactionary columnist on the *World-Telegram,* opposed the deportation order.

In this difficult period, Walter Pollak died suddenly. He had been one of Carol's earliest, closest friends, as well as a colleague she could count on to win impossible cases in the Supreme Court. Carol mourned with her friend Marion Pollak, who became closer than ever as the two women shared their roles as widows and single parents. Carol wrote succinctly in the next *Bulletin* that Walter Pollak's "gifts were freely given to freedom's cause."

One of Pollak's and King's causes was still in great jeopardy. Their Supreme Court victories in the *Scottsboro* cases had won the principle of trial by a jury from which people like the defendant had not been systematically excluded on account of race. But the Alabama Parole Board refused parole to the five *Scottsboro* defendants still serving terms from twenty years to life. And Black sharecroppers still could not pay poll taxes, so a Virginia sharecropper, Odell Waller, was tried for murder by an all-white jury. Waller claimed he shot his landlord in self-defense after being refused his share of the crop. The twelve white taxpayers rejected this defense, as Carol reported in the November 1940 *Bulletin.*

In November, voters went to the polls to choose between Franklin Roosevelt and Wendell Willkie. The Republican candidate had rejected isolationism and supported the concept that the United States is part of

"One World." Roosevelt won, bringing into the White House as Vice President his progressive former Secretary of Agriculture, Henry A. Wallace, who had employed many IJAers in the early New Deal days.

After the election, J. Edgar Hoover was still very much in the saddle at the FBI. The Left claimed that his number-one enemy continued to be U.S. labor, not German Nazis or Italian or Japanese fascists. According to an FBI report, on September 13, 1940, the FBI received information alleging that a field examiner for the NLRB in St. Louis "had radical tendencies leading toward Communism and was educated to be an anthropologist and so forth." The FBI wrote to the chairman of the NLRB on November 14, 1940, furnishing this information. The National Federation for Constitutional Liberties condemned this investigation, which Senator Pat McCarran (Dem.-Nev.) mentioned in a report he submitted at the time.

In this climate, on November 14, the Harry Bridges Defense Committee (which included Communists, anthropologists, and so forth) sent out a warning that the FBI "has offered improper inducements and used intimidation" to secure false evidence against Bridges from trade unionists and liberals. "TELL THE FBI ABSOLUTELY NOTHING. If FBI agents approach you at home or at work, turn them away."

Carol King saw 1940 ending with a string of defeats for citizens Earl Browder and Odell Waller, for noncitizen Raissa Browder, and for legislative reform of the alien and sedition statutes. In this anti-communist and anti-Soviet climate, what would 1941 bring as Attorney General Robert H. Jackson and the Department of Justice took jurisdiction over the Immigration Service, and the Axis fought to take over the world?

22.
Harry Bridges: Round Two

On August 24, 1940, Attorney General Jackson directed the FBI to investigate whether, under the new Smith Alien Registration Act, grounds existed for reopening deportation proceedings against Harry Bridges. Other clients of Carol King were suddenly rearrested. As aliens, they could not plead double jeopardy or complain about ex post facto laws. On November 28, Jackson announced in a press release that FBI Director J. Edgar Hoover had transmitted his report on Bridges, comprising 2,500 pages.

The next day the FBI completed, but did not announce, a new five-page report on one of Bridges's lawyers:

The following is quoted from this report:

re <u>CAROL KING</u>

"The information contained in instant file as well as associated files has been reviewed for any and all pertinent information concerning CAROL KING who was an associate counsel in the deportation hearing for HARRY BRIDGES held at Angel Island in July, 1939.

In addition to the Bureau files which were reviewed, the files of the Immigration and Naturalization Service were likewise perused for any information concerning CAROL KING, inasmuch as there are strong indications that she is closely connected with the Communist Party.

The files of the Immigration and Naturalization Service
contain a copy of a letter dated July 8, 1939, to CAPTAIN JOHN J.
KEEGAN, Chief of Detectives, Portland, Oregon, Police Department,
over the signature of JOSEPH P. RYAN, President of the International
Longshoremen's Association, New York City, which contains the following information pertaining to a check of the registration of
voters in New York City and which indicates that CAROL U. KING had
the following registrations:

        1929 - 32   Not registered
        1933 - 34   Communist
        1935 - 36   ---------------
        1937 - 38   American Labor Party

In addition to the foregoing information relative to

                    159   CONFIDENTIAL

                    CONFIDENTIAL

CAROL KING, there is the following summation of her activities
which appears in the files of the Immigration and Naturalization
Service:

CAROL KING, New York Jewish Attorney.
Subscriber to Certificate of Incorporation. Comprodaily Publish-
            ing Co. Inc., 50 East 13th Street, New York City, which
            published "daily except Sunday, the Daily Worker, Central
            Organ, Communist Party of U.S.A."

Member Legal Advisory Committee, International Labor Defense, es-
            tablished by the Communist Party in America during the
            summer of 1925, as the United States Section of the Inter-
            national Red Air, headquarters in Moscow and under the
            complete control of the Third International (Comintern).
            The Central Committee of the Communist Party, U.S.A. is
            the subordinate arm of the Comintern and, as such, con-
            trols the I.L.D.

Gold Book Signer, signature appearing in facsimile in the Special
            November edition, "Soviet Russia Today", official organ
            of the Friends of the Soviet Union. depicting the beau-
            ties of Communism and its superiority over the Government
            of the U.S.A. The "Golden Book of American Friendship"
            for the Soviet Union was signed by hundreds of thousands
            of Americans at outings and picnics held by the Communist
            Party, the Young Communist League, The International Work-
            ers Order, and various other United Front organizations
            allied therewith in commemoration of, and presented to
            the President of the Soviet Union at the Twentieth Anni-
            versary Celebration in Moscow at the end of 1937.

Listed in the Sherman Report in that connection as Attorney for the
            International Labor Defense and the Garland Fund whose
            trustees were "leading members of the Communist Party and
            which had contributed $1,500,000.00 all to the further-
            ance and support of Left-wing and Marxist projects, much
            of it through the International Labor Defense". The Gar-
            land Fund was also one of the principal financial sponsors

                    160   CONFIDENTIAL

CONFIDENTIAL

of the American League for Peace and Democracy shown by,
the Sherman Report also to have been in turn a heavy
contributor to the Communist Party.

Author, Monthly Law Bulletin, American Civil Liberties Union,
1923-25, which, according to the Congressional Fish
Report, investigating Communism in the United States
"is closely affiliated with the Communist movement in
the United States and fully 90 percent of its efforts
are in behalf of Communists who have come into conflict
with the law", and which, according to the Committee of
the New York State Legislature investigating subversive
organizations in that State "is the supporter of all
subversive movements".

Member, National Committee to Aid Striking Miners Facing Starvation, an intellectual communistic group formed to aid
the Communist National Miners' Union operating in Pineville and Harlan Counties, Kentucky, in 1931.

Member, National Committee to Aid Victims of German Fascism, organized by the Communist Workers International Relief
in 1933, with an affiliated membership, according to the
Daily Worker (September 29, 1933) of 400,000 and which
listed among its supporting organizations the International Labor Defense, International Workers Order
(Jewish), Communist Party, Jewish Workers Party, the
Communist Trade Union Unity Leage, etc.

Petitioner for the Communist Hunger March on Washington, D.C. 1932.

Secretary of the International Judicial Association which, in July,
1937, issue of the "Labor Defender" (official organ of
the I.L.D.) is named as one of the thirteen organizations
represented by the United Front Conference and by the
International Labor Defense at Washington, D. C. in June,
1937, which was addressed by EARL BROWDER, Executive
Secretary of the Communist Party, U.S.A. and VITO MAR-
CANTONIO, International Labor Defense, and which was
mentioned in the July, 1937, issue of the "New Order",
along with the American Civil Liberties Union, and the
National Association for the Advancement of Colored
People, as one of the thirteen well-known national organizations which participated to make the conference
one of the "most important conferences held in the recent period."

Presiding Officer, International Labor Defense Conference held at
New York City in December, 1935."

161 Y

*FBI File: Carol King (11-29-40). Excerpts from a long summary of the voting
record, presumed religion, and political activities of one of Harry Bridges's
attorneys. Facsimile-reduced reproduction.*

On December 16, Director Hoover gave an interview concerning the
FBI report, although the *Washington Post* reported that officials at the
Department of Justice "privately expressed embarrassment" at his "pre-
mature" statement.

On January 10, 1941, the FBI rearrested Joseph Strecker for deportation, after his 1939 victory in the Supreme Court under the old deportation law that required proof of *present* membership. Now he was arrested
for *past* membership under the new Smith Act.

Meanwhile, Hoover's statement on Bridges had provoked the *Nation*
to editorialize that the FBI director "has already shown that he can't tell
a red from an anthropologist and his index [of 'subversives'] is a great
potential menace to liberty in war time." And why hadn't he made a
thorough investigation into Bridges's documented charges of Nazi 'plants'
in West Coast aviation factories?

The government's answer was to rearrest Harry Bridges on February
14 on the same ground as Strecker, past membership in the Communist
Party.

Bridges had jested in 1939 that the government should wait to try him
again until it got some more witnesses. The jest had become reality; the
new witnesses were scheduled to start appearing in San Francisco six
weeks later.

The time for preparation was very short. Carol King would have to
skip the Fourth Annual Conference of the American Youth Congress at
the Annapolis Hotel in Washington, although she had agreed to be a
sponsor for the group, along with Eleanor Roosevelt (who was also under
covert FBI surveillance). Carol would also have to skip the Fifth National
Conference of the American Committee for Protection of Foreign Born
slated for March in Atlantic City. The committee reported that they
expected the attendance of 227 delegates from 142 organizations, including thirty-seven delegates from CIO unions representing 1,043,375 workers, sixteen delegates from AFL unions representing 62,890 workers, and
two delegates from an independent union representing 30,000 workers.
They also expected delegates from numerous language, fraternal, civil
rights, professional, Negro, youth, welfare, and service organizations.

Obviously, Carol didn't need to worry about neglecting the American
Committee. Her son, Johnny, presented a different situation. She never
felt entirely comfortable in her work, knowing that she could get totally
engrossed in a way her own mother, and most of her women friends, had
never done. Of course, she was always available by phone, she went home

for dinner almost every night, and Mrs. Barkley was always there. But she didn't like the idea of leaving Johnny for another stretch of several months during HB-II and asking Clara Binswanger to take over again, as on so many other occasions.

Before she figured out a satisfactory solution to the perpetual, insoluble puzzle of the single parent, the Department of Justice named the hearing officer for the second trial. Carol's careful investigation of his career indicated that Judge Charles Sears of New York was no Dean Landis of Harvard. He had served with comfortable mediocrity on the New York State trial bench and briefly on the New York Court of Appeals before his retirement. Her informant, who knew nothing about his activities during the Palmer Raids, said he was "seldom analytical; allows himself to be convinced by prima facie case."

That was not a good sign. The government ought to be able to put on something like a prima facie case by now — evidence that superficially proved Bridges's past membership. It would require some of the analytical skills Landis had displayed in the first hearing to separate truth from falsehood.

Carol filed a motion to dismiss the charges against Bridges on the ground of double jeopardy. She filed a second motion to dismiss on the ground that the Smith Alien Registration Act was unconstitutional as an ex post facto law because it added "past" membership as a basis for deportation. She filed a third motion that the defense be furnished with a copy of the FBI's 2,500-page report on Bridges.

Finally she decided to go with the flow as to her son. Since Johnny did not seem to be totally committed to school, he had never really seen his mother in action in a hearing, and the *Bridges* hearing would undoubtedly teach many lessons in history and government, she concluded that Johnny could miss a few weeks and come with her to San Francisco. He was fifteen and thoroughly enjoyed the three and a half days on the train.

There was no joy in the Bridges Defense Committee the second time around, although they did have a new song by Pete Seeger, Lee Hays, and Millard Lampell:

Let me tell you of a sailor, Harry Bridges is his name.
An honest union leader that the bosses tried to frame.
He left home in Australia to sail the seas around.
He sailed across the ocean to land in 'Frisco town.

The story of Bridges's life unfolded between rousing choruses:

> Oh, the FBI is worried, the bosses they are scared;
> They can't deport six million men, they know.
> And we're not a-goin' to let them send Harry o'er the sea.
> We'll fight for Harry Bridges, and build the CIO.

The defense knew the FBI had worked feverishly on the case this time. "The country had been scoured for witnesses," a circuit court judge said later; "every circumstance of Bridges' active life had been subject to scrutiny, and presumably no stone had been left unturned which might conceal evidence of the truth of the charges which are so flatly denied." Everyone could feel a nastiness in the Justice approach that had not been present when Labor ran the case in 1939. The role of the American Legion came to light when its chronology of the case was published in the appendix to the *Congressional Record* on March 18. The Legion file contained long quotations from letters by officials of the Immigration Service in Washington to Service officials in San Francisco. One was a "gentle reprimand" that was explicitly supposed to be destroyed after it was read. How these letters got into the American Legion file was not explained.

Justice, the FBI, and the Legion assembled a large cast of new characters for this rerun. The hearings began March 31. Carol King "was especially caustic," the *New York Times* reported, about the basis for the new hearings, in light of the thirty-two government witnesses and their 8,000 pages of testimony in the first hearing. "The defense spent more than $28,000" then. "A national campaign to raise money for the present defense is now under way," she said.

The defense team was both the same and different from the team in the first hearing. Gladstein and Grossman were two years older and had grown massively in local prestige due to the victory in the first *Bridges* hearing. They were learning the folk wisdom of scrappy lawyers, like wearing shirts with taller shirt collars and longer cuffs during trials because the whiteness impressed jurors with the lawyers' uprightness. King scorned any costume or behavior in court or before the media that was different than her true self. Her comments suggest she would have preferred that her colleagues pack up their egos along with their high collars and briefs when they left the courtroom so they could have better conversations out of court about the case and on general topics.

Jonathan King went to the hearings regularly and quickly made his own assessments of some of the leading figures. Albert Del Guercio, the chief prosecutor, came from the Immigration Service in Los Angeles.

Johnny thought he was more or less of a thug, he recalled later. Del Guercio boasted often (with considerable accuracy) about his physical resemblance to Benito Mussolini, fascist leader of Italy. Finally he was told this was not smart in the anti-fascist atmosphere of spring 1941, and he stopped. Johnny thought Richard Gladstein, his mother's co-counsel, was a little too much of a sharpie personally for her to accept him entirely, although she respected his ability at examining witnesses, which she was not good at. Of the lawyers, Carol seemed to like Hal Sawyer better than anybody else in the labor law office of Gladstein, Grossman, Margolis, and Sawyer, although, or perhaps because, Sawyer had little to do with the case.

Johnny always liked Harry Bridges, but he wasn't sure how his mother felt. He knew she resented Bridges's apparent attitude that the only reason for having women on earth was so they could sleep with Harry Bridges. All through the hearing, the defense lawyers seemed terrified by the idea that a half-dozen of Bridges's women might appear as government witnesses against him, but none of them ever did.

Johnny saw that Judge Sears was upset by the ill-mannered conduct of the other participants. He was a rather abstracted "gentleman" who disliked all the talk about strikes, class warfare, etc. Carol apparently had decided to try out her feminine wiles on this elderly man, and she did some of the direct cross-examination this time.

The site of these hearings was the Federal Building in San Francisco, blanketed with FBI men and uniformed members of the Immigration Border Patrols. Del Guercio said they were needed to protect government witnesses from intimidation by the defense. The defense challenged him to substantiate his concern; he simply repeated it.

Then the defense requested Del Guercio to provide a bill of particulars under the INS rule allowing the alien to inspect "all the evidence" on which the warrant was issued.

Del Guercio refused as the government made repeated attacks on the conduct of the first hearing by Dean Landis. On April 3, J. Edgar Hoover testified before the House Appropriations Committee in Washington that Landis had had no authority to administer oaths to witnesses and, as a result, "the Department of Justice could not follow the FBI director's recommendation to prosecute some of the witnesses for perjury." A government brief argued that "Landis's so-called opinion was based upon misinformation" and was "meaningless" and "naive."

And the government tried a new tactic. On April 3 it called to the stand Benjamin Gitlow, defendant in *Gitlow v. New York* in 1925, based on his circulation of the *Manifesto* of the Left-Wing of the Socialist Party with John Reed after World War I. His case had established the important principle that the Fourteenth Amendment incorporates First Amendment liberties and in the intervening years, the *Gitlow* case had helped get acquittals for thousands of pickets, street-corner speakers, and others exercising their freedom of speech and press. Now the government qualified Gitlow as an expert on Marxism because of his leadership in the Communist Party in the early twenties and his later open break with the Left. The prosecutor asked him to identify *The Communist Manifesto* written by Marx and Engels in 1848. Then the prosecutor introduced a certified copy of the incorporation papers for several Communist publications, including the *Daily Worker,* and asked him if he could identify the "Carol Weissking" who was listed as the owner of one share of stock in each.

Gitlow pointed to the chief defense counsel at the defense table and testified that Mrs. King's former law partner, Joseph R. Brodsky, was a Communist Party member and had been its chief legal adviser for years. He did not identify Mrs. King "as a party member," the *New York Times* reported. But two days later, defense counsel Gladstein started cross-examining government witness Chase.

"Your hand is trembling, Mr. Del Guercio," said Mr. Gladstein.

"That's because I'm not a communist like you are," the inspector replied.

"Did the court hear that remark?" defense counsel asked.

"No, I am blind and deaf today," Judge Sears replied.

The defense brought out in cross-examination that Gitlow had been interviewed and made a statement to the Service in August 1939 (near the end of the first *Bridges* hearing), but had not been called as a witness. Carol made a motion that the government be required to produce that statement, and pre-trial statements of all government witnesses, to check for variations from what the witness now testified to. (Release of pre-trial statements was finally required by the Supreme Court in the *Jencks* case in 1957.) Judge Sears denied the motion but did recess the hearing so that The Alien, in his capacity as president of the ILWU, could preside over the ILWU Convention in Los Angeles.

While in Washington testifying before a Senate subcommittee on pending immigration legislation, Major Lemuel B. Schofield, special

On April 9, 1941, at 10:40 A.M., Major L.C. Schofield
called the Director and advised him that he had returned from
San Fransisco the previous day and that the case (apparently the
Harry Bridges case) was going along almost perfectly. Major Schofield
said that, "It has already been proved through exhibits and
testimony that Carroll King is a Communist and that before they are
through they expect to prove that the other lawyers are Communist
also." The Director stated that, "This would have a very good
effect on the point of view of the whole case."

~~Source as stated.~~
Memorandum from the
Director for Mr. Tolson,
Mr. Tamm, and Mr. Foxworth;
4-9-41
39-915-1071
(113)

FBI File: Carol King (4-9-41). Report of an Immigration Service official to
the FBI director on efforts to prove that Bridges's lawyers were Communists
during the deportation hearing.

assistant to the Attorney General in charge of the INS, stated that the
Bridges defense intended "to concoct false alibis, false testimony, and
endeavor to falsely and corruptly to meet the evidence." Later, on
cross-examination in the hearing, the defense asked Schofield to substantiate the charge. He did not do so.

Within two weeks the government's tactic of publicly calling defense
counsel "Communists," plus the "horrid Semitic-looking" photos Carol
King feared from the press, had had an effect.

The following letter, dated April 21, 1941, with a
picture of Carol King enclosed, was sent to President Roosevelt
by a Miss Sarah E. Dunne, 7 Rexford Street, Norwich, New York:

"My dear Mr. President -

Enclosed is a clipping from Sunday's New York
Times.

If the enclosure is a fair likeness of 'Bridges
Counsel' I would suggest that she be placed under
secret service investigation. Any woman with the
appearance of Mrs. King is not normal and I feel,
must be a Communist to defend Bridges. Also, her
husband if she has one. I don't believe she has.
No normal man would marry a woman of her type, but
should one make such a mistake and continue to live
with it, he should be investigated as well."

4-21-41
Letter to President Roosevelt
from Miss Sarah E. Dunne
39-915-1093X
(50)

FBI File: Carol King (4-21-41). One woman's response to a newspaper
photograph of Harry Bridges's woman lawyer.

On April 29, the *New York Times* daily story reported that chief government counsel Albert Del Guercio had said that Richard Gladstein, Aubrey Grossman, and Carol King were all Communists.

For their part, the defense did not pass up opportunities to prove the anti-labor bias of the prosecution, although the brief pro-labor moment had passed as the country veered toward war. Later Carol applied for a subpoena to get records of the Los Angeles police department showing communication between a government witness and police officer "Red" Hynes about a strike, based on testimony on strikebreaking in the U.S. Senate report of the La Follette Civil Liberties Committee. Hynes was a red-headed cop who had long headed the LAPD Red Squad.

Sam Darcy, the head of the CP in California in the early thirties, told a story to Pete Steffens about Hynes's encyclopedic knowledge of his chosen field. It may have been apocryphal; it certainly was amusing. He said that in 1931, during a long strike in Long Beach, for the first time people were charged with distributing the doctrine of dialectical materialism. When defense counsel Leo Gallagher called "Red" Hynes to the stand as his first defense witness, the crowd in the courtroom expressed surprise and then outrage. According to Darcy, the ensuing colloquy went something like this:

> GALLAGHER: The defendants are charged with the crime of teaching dialectical materialism. Please tell the court what is "dialectical materialism."
> HYNES: You have to take it apart. There is dialectics and there is materialism.
> GALLAGHER: Can you explain it?
> HYNES: Yeah, I can explain it. Now, "dialectics," that's from dialect — that's what foreigners speak. And "materialism," that's guys out for everything they can get. So foreigners out for everything they can get, that's "dialectical materialism!"

The courtroom broke up in laughter.

⁂

But the climate during this hearing was not that of 1931. The defense found it deeply anti-alien. For the first time in U.S. history, people born abroad were required to register as aliens under the Smith Act, and they were subject to prison terms for failure to do so. In April the Department of Justice announced it had begun searching the records of five million people who had registered under the new Alien Registration Act, "prepared to act sternly . . . where deliberate violations" showed up on their forms.

In its action against one alien in 1939, the government had produced thirty-two witnesses. In 1941 the government did not call one of these witnesses. All but two of its new witnesses testified about different episodes.

The defense maintained that the new cast of characters could claim legitimately to be the blood-brother of its predecessor: Bridges's enemies from the labor movement. People expelled from trade unions were brought to San Francisco from as far away as Pennsylvania. Some of the testimony was patently absurd, according to the defense, and none was substantiated on any basis beyond the unsupported word of a single government witness.

On April 28, the government called James D. O'Neil as its last substantive witness. It immediately claimed he was a hostile witness, so they would actually cross-examine him and would not be bound by his testimony. Their reason? O'Neil had allegedly made two contradictory statements in interviews with FBI agents and Major Schofield. In one he said he had seen Bridges pasting dues stamps into a CP membership book in 1937. Then he was quoted as saying, "It is my belief that Bridges never at any time attended any Communist Party meetings." Neither statement read to O'Neil was written in his handwriting, signed, dictated under oath, or notarized.

The defense moved to have the statements stricken from the record under the Immigration Service rules requiring oaths, signatures, and notarization.

Judge Sears reserved decision until the end of O'Neil's testimony.

The government then asked O'Neil whether he had made the statements. He denied it. He denied he had ever seen a Communist Party membership book for Harry Bridges. He denied he had personal knowledge that Bridges was a Communist. He testified that these statements were hopelessly garbled distortions of what he had said when he had been questioned six times by the FBI. He testified that there was only one true sentence in the two statements: "It is my belief that Bridges never at any time attended any Communist Party meetings." He explained that some of the meetings the FBI asked him about were really meetings of Labor's Non-Partisan League, the Maritime Federation of the Pacific, and the CIO Council.

Del Guercio then called Major Schofield to the stand. Schofield had been acting as co-prosecutor. Now he became a witness, testifying that O'Neil had actually made the statements ascribed to him. An FBI stenographer supported his testimony.

The defense moved to have all of O'Neil's testimony, *and* his alleged statements, stricken. They had a new reason. Even if O'Neil had made the statements attributed to him, they said, he denies them now so we can't cross-examine him. Who can know when, if ever, he was telling the truth?

Judge Sears ruled that he *would* admit the testimony of Schofield and the FBI stenographer, but only to impeach or challenge O'Neil's testimony, *not* as affirmative proof that the unsigned statements were true (since they were hearsay). On this basis, the defense did not press its objections because now the statements could not be used to prove that Bridges was a member of the CP, only that O'Neil was a liar in general.

Episodes like this took their toll among the defense lawyers. They engaged in sharp arguments to decide on the best tactic, and then used quick thinking to protect the record so that every issue could be raised on appeal if Sears ruled against them.

Carol had another gnawing concern. She was not at all sure Johnny was getting as much of her time and attention as he deserved. She kept trying to find nonexistent hours to spend with him. Aubrey and Richie were no help on this; none had teenage children, and in fact, Aubrey was just expecting his first child. He was sure that the quality of the time Carol spent with Johnny was wrong and therefore wasted, because she was trying to bring him up according to middle-class standards that decreed that mothers have limitless time to spend with their children. Carol couldn't possibly meet this standard and still work in an important case like *Bridges,* so she felt guilty and spoiled her son, according to Aubrey. Toward the end of the hearing, Carol sent Johnny back East.

On April 17, 1941, the government called Maurice J. Cannalonga to the stand as a government witness.

Bridges was astonished. Cannalonga wasn't in the same class with the other government witnesses. He was known as a militant member of the Marine Firemen's Union in Seattle with a good record — definitely not a stool pigeon. The defense figured there must be something wrong.

Del Guercio ran into the contradiction immediately.

Q. Did you make a statement to any FBI agents?
A. Yes, sir.
Q. Was it made voluntarily?
A. Yes and no.
Q. What do you mean "Yes and no"?
A. Just what I said.
Q. Were you threatened?
A. Well —
PRESIDING INSPECTOR: You can answer these questions; . . . Were you
  threatened?
THE WITNESS: I don't know. . . . No, I don't believe I was.

Bridges told Gladstein to go easy on Cannalonga on cross-examination because he was a very nice guy, Norman Leonard remembers. On cross-examination, Cannalonga said he had been approached by a government agent during the 1939 deportation hearing and had refused to testify. Now he testified, however reluctantly, that he had attended CP fraction meetings with Bridges and CP leader William Schneiderman.

Del Guercio said Cannalonga was a "hostile witness" who had taken him by surprise.

The defense couldn't afford surprises like that. They sent Richie Gladstein to Seattle early in May to see Cannalonga, who was working on a ship there. On May 4, Cannalonga went with Gladstein to the office of a local attorney and answered Gladstein's questions. Another attorney, a court reporter for the Oregon circuit courts for fifteen years, recorded the interview. Cannalonga said on this occasion that he had lied at the hearing in April; he had never been at a Communist meeting with Bridges and Schneiderman. In the presence of still another man, Cannalonga said that he had been intimidated into testifying against Bridges: the FBI had threatened to prosecute him under the Mann Act for transporting a woman across state lines for immoral purposes. On Gladstein's return to the hearing, the defense put on two witnesses to testify to this Seattle episode involving Cannalonga.

Judge Sears promptly authorized the issuance of a subpoena for Cannalonga's immediate appearance. He could not be found, and the hearing ground on. On June 4, the government called Cannalonga back to the stand. The defense soon learned that the government had kept him in custody for four days before producing him at the hearing, ignoring the order in the subpoena.

Cannalonga held the stand for three full days. He now testified that on May 3 and 4, when he talked to Gladstein in Seattle, he had been so drunk he could not recall a single thing he had done or said. He also denied that he had been intimidated by government agents. The government put on two of its agents who testified to the same effect.

The defense found several people who would testify that Cannalonga was not drunk at all on those days. His worksheet showed that he had worked seventy-nine hours in the week ending May 3, and another thirty-nine hours between Sunday, May 4, and Wednesday, May 7. The defense was prepared to use this material in rebuttal.

Nearing the end of its case, the government finally produced Harry Lundeberg. The defense had learned from scuttlebutt that government agents had been after him for more than two years. Lundeberg was a longtime leader of the Sailors Union of the Pacific. In 1934 he had cooperated with the brash young Bridges; as he watched Bridges's rise to leadership, he became one of his bitterest enemies on the West Coast. But three times, in 1939, in 1940, and in 1941, Lundeberg had told government agents that he did not have any personal knowledge that Bridges had ever been a Communist.

On the witness stand, he described on direct examination a dinner he had attended at Bridges's home along with Sam Darcy (the Communist official with the story about Red Hynes). Three times the government lawyer led Lundeberg over the story of this dinner; the third time Lundeberg finally mentioned that Bridges had said orally that he was a member of the Communist Party. On cross-examination, the defense asked Lundeberg when he had first told this story to the government.

Lundeberg said "Last night." He left the witness stand in less than an hour, making no splash in the long string of witnesses because there was another distraction.

The Alien, Harry Bridges, could not be limited to that role very long. Events kept requiring him to do his jobs as president of the ILWU and regional director of the CIO. His leadership was needed again when members of the United Auto Workers–CIO in Los Angeles struck North American Aircraft, which was building planes for the war raging in Europe.

Immediately, government officials denounced the strike on the ground that it was interfering with national defense. Many CIO leaders agreed in print and condemned the anti-war stand of the Communists and the Left. Bridges said nothing publicly. Del Guercio considered Bridges's obvious support for the strike as additional evidence that Bridges was a Communist, for the strike had been widely condemned as a Communist maneuver to impede war preparations. Del Guercio was so sure of himself that he subpoenaed Richard Frankensteen without interviewing him first as to the nature of his testimony.

Frankensteen was national director of the Aviation Department of the UAW-CIO. He came to California from UAW headquarters in Detroit to get the North American strikers back to work. He testified for the Government on June 11, the day Bridges finally sent his telegram to the leaders of the strike declaring that the strike had been started for just and legitimate reasons but that it should now be called off because the opposition of the government had made victory impossible.

Frankensteen testified he had fired several leaders of the UAW local at the plant for supporting the strike, which was solid among the 12,000 workers, and that Communists were behind the strike. He did not mention Bridges in his testimony. Del Guercio turned Frankensteen over to the defense for cross-examination.

MR. GLADSTEIN: I don't think we have any questions at all.
PRESIDING INSPECTOR: You are excused, Mr. Frankensteen. You may go.
. . .
THE WITNESS: I want to make a statement regarding my appearance here.
. . . That it is my considered judgment that some of the patterns set in this hearing are ominous ones for the future —
MR. DEL GUERCIO: [interposing] We object to the statement being made.
THE WITNESS: [continuing] — of legal action in the United States. After one exhaustive trial in which Mr. Bridges was completely cleared of charges against him, there is a hollow — [renewed objections by Del Guercio].
PRESIDING INSPECTOR: We will take it in the record. You have called the witness and I think you have gone far afield. I will take the statement . . . [reserving judgment on admissibility].
THE WITNESS: . . . After one exhaustive trial in which Mr. Bridges was completely cleared of the charges against him, there is a hollow mockery in this hearing and a double jeopardy which cannot but prejudice American working men against their government. They resent obvious unfairness and discriminatory practice whether it is practiced by the manufacturers for whom they work, or the government which they respect. Attacks such as this one, aimed at a militant leader of labor who has made outstanding gains for the members of his union . . . exhaust the patience of citizens.

Having had his say, Frankensteen left the stand.

Del Guercio was so nettled that he recalled Harry Bridges to the stand and began questioning him about the North American strike:

Q. Isn't this what actually happened: You had received orders from the Communist Party to support this strike, and when you realized the asinine mistake you had made you tried to retract, but it was too late, isn't that what actually happened?

A. You are just a fool.

Q. [reading Bridges's telegram] Did you also state: "There can be no question that their strike was for a just and reasonable demand"?

A. Right. . . .

Q. Did you also state: "The striking workers should know that they have demonstrated solidarity, —"?

A. They have to.

Q. You got that in the *Communist Manifesto,* "Solidarity," didn't you? [laughter from spectators]

A. [no answer] . . .

Q. Why did you not publicly denounce this strike as soon as it started?

A. When a group of workers are on strike, at least, they think they are right. When you are going to change their mind you don't want to kick them around the ears, but to handle them decently, and because we have always done that they listen to us.

Bridges also testified concerning voting for a political candidate known to be a Communist: "If he is a bad unionist, we don't care what he is, we are against him; if he is a good one, we don't care what he is, we are for him."

On that kind of note, the hearing ended on Thursday, June 12.

But that was not the end of the story. Friday morning's papers carried a page-3 item on an automobile collision in Oregon involving Cannalonga and two other government witnesses. Cannalonga was killed in the crash; the others were injured. No one knew how this event would affect the outcome of the case.

The responsibility for the fate of Harry Bridges now resided in the uncertain hands of Judge Charles B. Sears.

Carol hurried back to New York, telling correspondents that she felt confident that none of the testimony had really damaged Bridges. She believed Sears would reach the same decision Landis had reached before him: the government had not proved that Bridges had been a member of the Communist Party. But after hearing Del Guercio's tone and watching Schofield at close range, she was far from sure that such a decision would settle the matter once and for all. Their venom had been too strong to accept defeat.

But the defense team could not take the time to worry much about this. Carol had to turn immediately to defend her next client, William Schneiderman of San Francisco, the head of the California Communist Party. The government was trying to take away his U.S. citizenship. Aubrey and Richie were busy in San Francisco preparing for reargument in the U.S. Supreme Court of a case in which their client was again one Harry Renton Bridges, this time charged with contempt of court for sending a telegram to the Secretary of Labor in 1937 condemning a San Pedro Superior Court decision against his union. Carol told them it was crucial to have this case out of the way — and won — before Sears decided the deportation case. It would not do to have Bridges labeled a law violator while Judge Sears was deciding whether he should be deported.

23.
The Cumulative Effect of Five Liars

Carol King began to settle into her New York office again and to catch up on the major news she had largely ignored during the second *Bridges* hearing in San Francisco. In May 1941 the Lawyers Guild Convention had met in Detroit and resolved that "the activities of the Guild must be directed to the end that neither new millionaires nor new paupers shall be created by military preparation." The convention opposed the administration's excess-profits tax proposal as inadequate because it would permit armament makers "to reap exorbitant profits," making war "a very profitable enterprise" and "imperiling our national security by failing to aid in the preservation of peace." The convention also dealt with a bakers' dozen of perennial problems exacerbated by the war preparation, from attacks on academic freedom to unemployment compensation.

These resolutions reflected the mood of many clients and acquaintances of King in this period. William Z. Foster wrote in a pamphlet in March 1941: "Our Government, as a great capitalist power, . . . bears a heavy responsibility for . . . [World War II]. Its betrayal of republican Spain; its failure to support the international peace front proposed by the Soviet Union; its sale of munitions to Japan with which to wage war against Nationalist China; its imperialist policy generally, have contributed decisively to the outbreak of this new orgy of organized mass murder. Of all the great countries, only the socialist Soviet Union follows a policy of peace."

This anti-war sentiment led the new Attorney General, Francis Biddle, to discuss "the whole question of subversive activities" in September, so it would be "handled promptly." He "talked to the President about it." With FDR's approval, Biddle changed the system, taking from each agency its duty to investigate charges of subversion if it found them worthy of investigation. He told the House subcommittee of the Committee on Appropriations that under the new procedure, the FBI would "inaugurate investigations on complaints received without referring them to the Department or to the agency employing the various individuals."

In 1941 the Senate and House approved a new provision for the FBI budget, so that "at least $100,000 shall be available exclusively to investigate the employees of every Department, agency, and independent establishment of the Federal government who are members of subversive organizations or advocate the overthrow of the Federal government and report its findings to Congress." The Appropriations Act also forbade paying wages to any person "who advocates, or who was a member of an organization that advocated" the proscribed doctrine.

❧

Carol King got busy in the defense of Professor Morris U. Schappes from anti-Communist attacks by the New York State Rapp-Coudert Committee, fueled by CP opposition to war preparation.

Suddenly, on July 22, 1941, the Nazi government in Germany launched a massive military attack on the Soviet Union. Hitler broke his 1939 nonaggression pact with the socialist government. This event changed the political climate in the United States at least 180 degrees.

Carol King had to figure out how this would affect the case of her current number-one client, Schneiderman, as well as her perennial number-one client, Bridges.

A couple of weeks later, Harry Bridges came to New York on union business and settled into a room in the Edison Hotel. Within a few days he concluded that someone had been there before him. He had had his telephone tapped on the West Coast in preparation for the 1939 hearing and had been able to prove to Dean Landis that Larry Doyle and an assistant of Portland Police Captain Keegan had planted a dictaphone in his hotel room during a union convention, so he knew the proper response to such electronic surveillance. He called the liberal daily paper, *PM*, got a couple of other people who would make good witnesses, and let the man who was operating the dictaphone know that he had been seen. The man fled, leaving his equipment in plain sight.

PM ran the story with photographs of the tap and the tapper. This was big news! Wiretapping was prohibited by the Federal Communications Act. The U.S. Supreme Court had called it a "dirty business" and decided that evidence secured by wiretapping could not be used in federal courts. The *IJA Bulletin* had devoted its entire issue in March 1941 to alleged wiretapping by the Department of Justice, and Carol King had written letters to lawyers all over the country, urging them to help defeat a bill to legalize the practice. Now the daily paper represented by her brother Louis had brought the issue to national attention.

After breaking the story, Bridges got around to asking an associate to call his New York lawyer. Carol's immediate response was to dictate a series of letters to the Bridges Defense Committee and to co-counsel in San Francisco. She said she didn't know exactly what the facts were as she had not been consulted; she had heard that Harry was too busy to talk to her, "but that I am to get ready to sue out a warrant against the FBI agent or whoever he is." She was not at all sure this was the wisest course, although the publicity on the wiretap was good. She also felt that if there were to be extensive litigation by Harry against the FBI, it should not be handled by her.

She couldn't administer such a large lawsuit while pursuing the appeal of William Schneiderman in the Supreme Court against an order taking away his citizenship. This was particularly true because suing the FBI was a totally new concept that would require endless thought and work. But her lawyer's caution did not diminish her pleasure at the prospect of discomfiting Del Guercio and the other government officials who had been running the deportation case in San Francisco. More than that. A government that would wiretap an enemy in New York would probably have wiretapped him in San Francisco — before or during the hearing. If so, it might be possible to get the whole government case against Bridges thrown out!

Actually, there was much more surveillance going on than Carol King or her most cynical colleagues dreamed. Documents made available in 1988 show that in 1940 or 1941, FBI agents entered the offices of the American Peace Mobilization and the Washington Committee for Democratic Action covertly and made copies of their membership lists, which included old IJAers Herbert Wechsler and Thomas Emerson, as well as Charles Fahy, then assistant solicitor general of the Department of Justice where all three worked. J. Edgar Hoover saw to it that reports were made on these and other lawyers.

As to the wiretapping of which she was aware, Carol began an extensive correspondence with co-counsel about how to use this information. One of her first steps was to seek an interview for "distinguished

supporters" of Bridges with the liberal Acting Attorney General, Francis
Biddle, who had spoken out against the Bridges deportation bill, "in view
of the fact that this seems to be a violation of the law." Later she and
Bridges filed a complaint with the criminal division of the U.S. Attorney's
Office in New York, presenting affidavits executed by three witnesses to
the wiretapping.

```
CONFIDENTIAL August 28, 1941
CONCERNING THE HARRY BRIDGES MATTER, MR. BRIDGES,
ACCOMPANIED BY HIS ATTORNEY, CAROL KING, CALLED AT
THE UNITED STATES ATTORNEY'S OFFICE IN NEW YORK
THIS MORNING. MR. CORREA, THE UNITED STATES ATTOR-
NEY, DID NOT PARTICIPATE IN THE INTERVIEW, BELIEV-
ING IT UNDESIRABLE TO ATTRIBUTE THAT MUCH
IMPORTANCE TO IT. THE ASSISTANT UNITED STATES ATTOR-
NEYS TOOK THE COMPLAINT, HAVING A STENOGRAPHER IN
THE ROOM TO RECORD THE DETAILS. THE TRANSCRIPT IS
BEING TYPED BY THE UNITED STATES ATTORNEY AT A
RATHER SLOW PACE AT THE PRESENT TIME. . . .
    MR. CORREA IS OF THE OPINION THAT NO FURTHER AC-
TION IS REQUIRED BY HIS OFFICE IN THIS MATTER AT
THIS TIME. BRIDGES AND THE KING WOMAN DID NOT ASK
WHAT ACTION WOULD BE TAKEN. AS BRIDGES AND CAROL
KING LEFT THE UNITED STATES ATTORNEY'S OFFICE, THE
KING WOMAN WAS HEARD TO EXCLAIM, "WE HAVE MADE OUR
COMPLAINT. THE MATTER IS NOW UP TO THE GOVERNMENT."
```

On August 28, Carol King wired Richie: "IF YOU CAN SECURE AFFIDA-
VIT FROM WITNESS INDICATING THAT HIS WIRES MAY HAVE BEEN TAPPED BY
THE FBI SAME WOULD BE GRATEFULLY RECEIVED."

The relationship between counsel on the two coasts had changed since
the first *Bridges* case. Victory in that case had boosted the reputations,
and accordingly the egos, of the young West Coast lawyers, who had
never been self-effacing. And they had learned many procedural niceties,
some from their labor cases and some from Carol King. Now Aubrey
replied to Carol, approving her general approach to raising the wiretapping issue but setting forth certain conditions, and concluding: ". . .
REASON FOR SUGGESTED PROCEDURE IS MAKING PROPER RECORD FOR USE
BEFORE REVIEW BOARD AND COURTS. ABSOLUTELY ESSENTIAL YOU READ US
PROPOSED APPLICATION AND AFFIDAVITS OVER TELEPHONE BEFORE FILING."

By September 2, Carol had discussed, drafted, edited, and completed
a motion and affidavit for Judge Sears that were as unprecedented in

content as they were long in title. Form books had been useless. She couldn't even turn to other practitioners for copies of similar pleadings; there were none. She was plowing new ground, and she had to be right. She finally laid it all out in the title of her innovative pleading, asking Sears for an "Order Directing a Hearing for the Examination of Witnesses Concerning the Use of Wiretapping in the Preparation or Presentation of Evidence in the 1941 Bridges Deportation Hearings, and the Use Made, Directly or Indirectly, of Intercepted Telephone Messages and Facts Ascertained as the Result of Such Wiretapping." She attached the affidavits of HB, Leon Goodelman, Lawrence Kammet, and herself, spelling out the facts of the New York tapping and the law.

As a team player, Carol sent copies of the completed motion and affidavits west, with a letter:

> Dear Folks:
>   Consultation with all the experts in the entire
> city of New York, convinces me that you can't put
> in this newly discovered evidence point in your
> [proposed] motion. . . . Also, your bias and
> prejudice of the FBI has no place in a notice of
> motion.
>   As a special concession, I am putting in the
> application to strike evidence secured directly or
> indirectly from intercepted telephone messages.
> I can't go any further, even for you guys, much as
> I love you. I am getting advice from all the best
> lawyers and I refuse to take any more advice from
> any more sources lest I go off my nut.

The response from Grossman and Gladstein was a wire: "WE THINK YOU SHOULD GIVE FULL PRESS RELEASE TO APPLICATION YOU FILED WITH SEARS IF NOT ALREADY DONE PLEASE DO SO."

That did it! Carol called in her secretary and dictated a letter, with feeling:

> Dear Children:
>   Your telegram filled me with amusement. The
> Citizens Committee got out an elaborate press
> release on the motion which, as far as I can
> ascertain, received no publicity at all from the
> regular (I almost slipped into the error of saying
> "capitalist") press. . . . I have just heard that
> the Immigration Service is very much embarrassed

> by the motion and that it is regarded as a very
> good move on our part. Undoubtedly, if I had
> redrawn all the papers, I could have done a better
> job, but time was of the essence.
>
>   Mother

On September 10, Carol wrote west again to say that she had seen Del Guercio at the office of an INS official and was happy to report on the effect of their work on him as an individual:

> Poor Del! He is distraught. So, by the way, is the
> government of the United States. They have been
> working steadily on the motion for days and have
> just about decided that it is necessary that there
> should be a hearing — at least [Edward] Ennis
> [another government lawyer] asked me when I wanted
> the hearing, and I said at his convenience, and
> that is the way we left it.
>   Ennis likewise told me that he has assurances
> from Del that none of the evidence, either used or
> unused, at the hearing was secured by wiretapping.
> I wish we could turn up something to the contrary
> and offer you that little job.
>   . . . Our client's isolationist stand [as to the
> war in Europe] is raising general Ned in these
> parts. I haven't spoken to him about it because I
> decided I ain't influential and might just as well
> act as if I wasn't.

Carol interested Nuddy Greene in the wiretap question and as a result, virtually his whole office began working on it, "at no expense to the Bridges Defense Committee." She pointed out to her colleagues in San Francisco that Judge Sears would probably hold a hearing on the alleged wiretapping in Washington, D.C., and that she would have to pay travel expenses there for herself and several witnesses. She did not have the required $150 and could get it only by selling some of her small amount of stock. Could they get some money from the Bridges Defense Committee? And, "Don't get me too upset by directions, orders, suggestions, law, etc., and for Christ's sake get the Bridges contempt situation out from under foot," she admonished Gladstein and Grossman.

The young lawyers had been letting the contempt case pend while they worked on more pressing issues. Thinking strategically, Carol insisted there was no more pressing issue facing them at the moment than Bridges's seeming penchant for getting into constitutional law cases that ended up in the U.S. Supreme Court.

This case arose out of the shift of the West Coast longshoremen from the AFL to the CIO in the fall of 1937, as described in the *IJA Bulletin*. In the large San Pedro local, the officers and 3,000 members sought to change their allegiance to the CIO. The fifteen who remained with the AFL obtained a decree from the local superior court restraining the officers from shifting and appointing receivers to continue to operate the local and its hiring hall on behalf of the AFL. The day the CIO moved for a new trial, Bridges sent a telegram to Secretary of Labor Perkins. As president of the CIO Longshoremen and West Coast director of the CIO, he characterized the court decree as "outrageous" and said the CIO did "not intend to allow state courts to override the majority vote of members in choosing its officers and representatives and to override the National Labor Relations Board" in favor of an AFL local reduced to fifteen members. Bridges warned that attempted enforcement of the court decree would result in a West Coast strike because 11,000 of the 12,000 longshoremen had chosen the CIO. Bridges approved publication of the telegram in the newspapers. For this action he was charged with contempt of court, tried, convicted, and fined $125.

Bridges's appeal had been argued in the Supreme Court in October 1939, but in June 1940 the Justices restored the case to the docket for reargument for reasons known only to themselves.

Carol wanted it reargued now, in 1941, before the Bridges deportation case went any further.

But King could not dally over the contempt case very long. She had to concentrate on the new wiretap situation. She soon learned Judge Sears's attitude on the wiretap from his reply to a minister's query to him. The judge wrote Reverend William Howard Melish saying that he could not credit the thought that responsible officials of the FBI or other departments of our government would engage in illegal enterprises of such a character. He conducted the hearing on the wiretap; it was short.

Just one week later, on September 26, 1941, Judge Sears issued his opinion. But it was not limited to the question of wiretapping. He began by saying that he was convinced, by the affidavits and testimony before him, that the FBI had tapped the telephone in Bridges's hotel room in New York from August 5 to August 22, 1941, but he found no evidence that the FBI had tapped any telephones before or during the deportation

NATIONAL AND STATE WITCH-HUNT COMMITTEES 1939-1941

National and State Witch-Hunt Committees 1939–1941. Illustration in booklet *Equal Justice: The Bill of Rights 1939–1941: A survey of civil and democratic rights in the U.S.A.* prepared by the International Labor Defense. Devoted to the preservation and extension of democracy and aid to labor's prisoners. Winter 1941, p. 42. (Artist unknown.)

hearing. The issue of wiretapping was, therefore, irrelevant to the deportation proceeding, which he proceeded to decide.

Carol was amazed. She told friends she had thought Sears would eventually decide for Bridges due to the international situation, which had played a part in the entire case. Everything had changed when the German armies invaded the Soviet Union on July 22, 1941, putting the Communists on the same side as England and the other allies and, unofficially, the United States. She had heard "that all Red cases have been put on ice by the Immigration Service."

The gossip was obviously mistaken. Sears had decided the *Bridges* case, and his analysis of the evidence not only surprised the defense, they learned; it also amazed the government. The total government case had taken twenty-two days. Sears ignored the testimony given in 21.5 of those days. He rested his decision on two quite unremarkable witnesses: Harry Lundeberg and James D. O'Neil. Lundeberg was on the witness stand less than an hour; O'Neil's testimony took about two hours. The nature of their testimony was more significant than its duration. Lundeberg, ancient union competitor of Bridges, had not been forthcoming when he took the stand, finally mentioning that Bridges had told him orally that he was a member of the Party at a dinner party in 1935.

O'Neil raised a different problem. The statement attributed to him by the government was clear-cut: he had seen Harry Bridges pasting dues stamps into a Party membership book in 1937. The problem was that on the witness stand, O'Neil had denied he had made the statement. It was not dictated under oath, written in his handwriting, signed, or notarized — all required under the INS's own rules. And he had also made a contradictory statement.

Sears found that the Party advocated the violent overthrow of the government, that Bridges had been a member of and affiliated with the Party, and that Bridges was therefore deportable.

The judge included a section on "Bridges as a Good Labor Leader," saying "proof as to the character" of his role as a labor leader was "without probative value." Sears said Bridges's leadership "was good in the eyes of his fellow unionists. He helped to establish better employment and working conditions as a result of the 1934 strike. . . . He may well have shown . . . wisdom in negotiations and in determining for or against strikes or mediation or arbitration. On the other hand . . . in 1937 he worked against his superiors in the AF of L and he and his union were expelled therefor"; they favored strikes the AFL leadership disapproved. "Even while a high official of the CIO he sent encouraging messages to men engaged in a strike disapproved by the CIO National leaders."

Unionists guffawed at Sears's total ignorance of the labor movement, both AFL and CIO. Certainly Bridges and his fellow CIO members had not considered the AFL bureaucrats their "superiors." Neither did Bridges consider himself automatically bound by an anti-strike policy of national CIO leaders.

Carol said she found Sears's opinion totally unjudicial. She filed a notice of appeal to the new Board of Immigration Appeals and got busy writing the defense brief. The more she worked on each separate issue, the more she found herself returning to the underlying legal problem in immigration law: "just how badly we are handicapped by the fact that this is a civil and not a criminal proceeding. . . . In fact, I am beginning to consider raising another question of the same general character — that there is no showing of personal knowledge of Bridges as to the character of the Party, and that a deportation for guilt by association is unconstitutional as a denial of due process." (This became one of the first winning arguments for citizen-victims of repression in the cold war fifties.)

King heard again later that the INS had finally "put all the Communist cases on ice," this time meaning they were "ready to deport all Reds for technical violations of the immigration laws but do not want to face the issue squarely" of Communist ideology and membership being illegal.

⁂

During this period, Carol's co-counsel were hard at work on the underlying legal/political problem: how to fight against abuses by the FBI in cases like Harry Bridges while supporting prosecutions of alleged Nazi spies in Brooklyn. Should the Left approve of the use of wiretapped evidence against the spies? Framed more broadly: how should they support the Roosevelt administration in its aid to the Allies and the Soviet Union against the fascist axis while continuing to oppose the anti-Communist, anti-labor actions of that same administration, as shown especially in the continued persecution and prosecution of Harry Bridges?

The ACLU apparently had a different problem: how to make peace with the FBI and its investigation of "subversive" government employees at this juncture. According to the FBI, Roger Baldwin called to see J. Edgar Hoover on October 17, 1941, "and discussed at some length the Bureau's activities in investigating Government employees," and the bureau's policy of inviting each employee being investigated "to come to the local field office after working hours" for an interview.

The FBI says Hoover told Baldwin that such an employee did not have to make any statement. The bureau would then submit its report to the government agency involved, which would hold a hearing at which the employee might be represented by counsel. "The Director specifically advised Baldwin that it was the Bureau's belief that the employee should not be represented by counsel when being interviewed at the FBI office since this was not a hearing but merely a chance for the employee to state his situation. Baldwin specifically stated that he agreed it would not be desirable to have the employee represented by counsel at this time." Carol King was not aware of this kind of ACLU/FBI contact as she continued to seek the ACLU's support in the *Bridges* case.

The second side of the administration's policies was apparent in the characterization of The Alien in the government's reply brief in *Bridges:*

Bridges was and is a serpent, slithering into the trade union movement from a dark, unwholesome den of the past, to practice in the movement the treacherous tactic of hypocrisy and deceit, and to form with his "comrades" a tyranny therein that might compare in its exercise of power with that most vicious one Soviet Russia, where 9,000,000 human beings were slaughtered as a single project in the most cruel and inhuman program in the history of the world.

This approach led the Justice Department to push the Roosevelt administration's "emergency" alien bill, which provided for the deportation of any alien who had acted in the United States "in behalf of any foreign government or foreign political party or group." It expressly listed, as coming under this definition, the Communist Party, Nazi Party, Fascist Party, and German-American Bund. As one of his final acts before being elevated to the Supreme Court, Attorney General Jackson urged passage of this bill to relieve the Service of the burden of proving in each deportation case that the organization to which the alien allegedly belonged had illegal objectives. Moreover, the bill provided that aliens who were ordered deported but could not be sent to their native country for any reason could be confined for fifteen months in the United States, subjected to parole conditions, and required to submit to psychiatric examinations and to file sworn statements on their "circumstances, habits, associations and activities."

The House of Representatives voted down this bill on November 19, 1941. The *Bridges* defense saw this vote as a good omen going into the November 24 hearing before the Board of Immigration Appeals. Two weeks later they saw another good omen when California governor Cuthbert Olson paroled the witnesses Earl King and Ernest Ramsay of the Marine Cooks and Stewards Union, men who had appealed so strongly to Carol in the first *Bridges* hearing.

But as these two witnesses in HB-I stepped out of jail, a key government witness in HB-II whose testimony had helped the defense, James O'Neil, stepped into federal prison on a three-year sentence for perjury in that equivocal testimony. And Thomas A. Imper paid for his testimony as a character witness for Bridges by being discharged by the Oregon State Department of Geology and Mineral Industries on his return to Portland from the hearing.

Then, on a quiet Sunday in early December, the radio announced that the Japanese had attacked the United States at Pearl Harbor, Hawaii! The base had been totally unprepared. The losses were devastating. Within hours, President Roosevelt asked Congress to declare war on the Axis powers — Japan, Germany, and Italy. Congress immediately complied, and all other news became insignificant.

The next day the Supreme Court handed down its decision on the *Bridges* contempt of court charge, joining it with a contempt charge against the anti-labor newspaper, the *Los Angeles Times*. The Justices had divided closely on the issues, with Justice Hugo Black writing for the five-man majority reversing Bridges's conviction. Black's opinion declared that Bridges's telegram to the Secretary of Labor in Washington had had a negligible effect on the administration of justice in a California state court. Moreover, ever since the *Gitlow* case in 1925, the Court had agreed that the First Amendment guarantees of free speech were incorporated in the Fourteenth Amendment. This meant that no *state* could limit the free speech of one of its residents.

The opinion was based on Bridges having rights under the First Amendment. It did not mention that Bridges was not a citizen. The opinion, therefore, meant that aliens as well as citizens have rights under the First Amendment. The opinion calmly set forth this broad principle of human rights law without any fanfare. But what a victory!

Frankfurter's sharp dissent, joined by three Justices, maintained that only the due process clause of the Fourteenth Amendment was applicable to aliens, not the free-speech guarantees. Besides, Bridges's telegram *had* interfered with the administration of justice, according to this Harvard liberal. Both Justice Black and Justice Frankfurter in their opinions cited the article by Nelles and King, "Contempt by Publication," *Columbia Law Review*, 1927.

With this victory at hand, Carol wrote to Gladstein, her "putative son":

> Dear Rich:
>   I feel very much more personal than business-like today. In fact if your letter had not come requiring an objective answer I would have in my own inimitable handwriting . . . written to you about the many things which I had on my chest — which passes in a he-woman for a heart.
>   First of all, about the baby: I am all in a dither about my grandchild. You don't even tell me what she looks like. You don't tell me if Caroline is feeling fine. . . . You don't even give me a

```
character sketch of Nancy Robin. What kind of a
child is she? What is she going to do with her
life? What are her political views? Is she well
behaved? Does she already know that she is my
grandchild, and does she act with the dignity that
that situation requires? These are matters of
importance and the hell with reply memoranda.
```

Richie replied in kind:

Immediately upon birth she looked around her with a look which has been interpreted by one wag around here to mean to say, "What! Isn't socialism here yet?", and not receiving an affirmative reply, immediately proceeded to piddle all over the table, Caroline, the doctor, and all and sundry. There, I think, lies the answer to your question, although I admit that a person who has no profound understanding of such events might well dismiss the whole thing as an evidence of Nancy's uncontrolled plumbing facilities.

The December 1941 issue of the *IJA Bulletin,* written after the United States entered the war, continued to emphasize problems of workers: "Now that the country is faced with a war on all fronts, it is essential that attacks on labor cease, that the basic problems of production be faced and that intelligent action by taken toward eliminating basic obstacles to the prosecution of a successful war." Mobilization of industrial production must plan to minimize the displacement of skilled and unskilled workers.

The December *Bulletin* also reported with grave concern the first conviction under the new Federal Sedition (Smith) Act of eighteen members of the Socialist Workers Party in Minneapolis. They were obviously indicted because of their participation in the effort of the Teamsters Union local to disaffiliate from the AFL and to join the CIO. Having heard evidence on the doctrines of the SWP, the jury acquitted all defendants on the charge of "conspiracy to overthrow the Government," convicted eighteen defendants of "advocating the desirability of overthrow," and recommended leniency in punishment.

During these early days of the war, Carol's friend, Justine Wise Polier, was working as counsel to Eleanor Roosevelt in setting up the Office of Civilian Defense, having taken a leave of absence from the Domestic Relations Court. She was staying with Tom and Bert Emerson, old friends from the Passaic strike and Yale Law School. One night Emerson brought home a report stating that he should be dropped from government as a subversive. "In those days, right after Pearl Harbor, by executive order all security clearances were divided among three agencies — Treasury, Civil Service, and the FBI," Polier recounts. Emerson was not supposed to see the report about himself, but someone gave it to him. Polier said the charges against Emerson were that he "had three books on the Soviet Union within reach of his favorite armchair; that his wife believes in health insurance; that he is a friend of those two radicals, Justine and Shad Polier and that he is a member of a Communist cell in Seattle, Washington." The report mentioned that Emerson was six foot one and also said that "Morris Ernst told J. Edgar Hoover that Emerson was not to be trusted."

Polier went to Mrs. Roosevelt in the morning, described the "outrageous report," and said she would like to see Secretary of the Treasury Henry Morgenthau but assumed he had a few other things to do right after Pearl Harbor. "Mrs. Roosevelt said no, she thought I should see him right away and called him to make the appointment.

"I went over at lunchtime and told him about the report," Mrs. Polier recalled. "Among other things I told Mr. Morgenthau, 'Emerson has never been west of Chicago in his life, and he is not a tall man.'

"Morgenthau was very decent and called in some assistant and said, 'I want this report recalled and a thorough investigation made.'" It turned out that only a man Emerson had fired for incompetence had been interviewed — none of the responsible people with whom Emerson had worked. He was cleared in the end, but Polier found it "quite an experience," which Emerson described in *Young Lawyer for the New Deal* and Polier shared later with Carol and her brother Louis.

Mrs. Polier remembers Louis Weiss as "one of the most cultivated human beings I have ever known, gracious in manner, very gentle, very generous in being willing to drop anything and work for anybody who was being unjustly treated. He attracted the top echelons of intellectual society, . . . Dean Acheson, Archibald MacLeish, and Marshall Field."

Throughout the war, Carol knew that her brother continued to have ties in Washington with the liberal administrators left over from the New Deal. He was close to the power of the press as well, through his representation of the newspaper *PM* and of various book publishing companies. Through him, she had entrée to this group that might augment whatever legal precedents she could find through hard work.

꣠

Early in 1942 the second *Bridges* deportation case was decided for the second time by the Board of Immigrant Appeals (BIA). One of its members was a highly respected immigration lawyer, Jack Wasserman. The BIA overturned Sears's opinion and ruled that the evidence did not sustain Sears's order of deportation against Bridges. This decision would go to the Attorney General for approval, but everyone knew this was mere routine. The Attorney General never overruled the BIA. Besides, Attorney General Biddle, while solicitor general in 1940, had strongly criticized lawyers for not attacking the proposed bill of attainder to deport Bridges. And he had made a statement when his nomination for Attorney General was before the Senate that he intended "to see that civil liberties in this country are protected; that we do not again fall into the disgraceful hysteria of witch hunts, strike-breakings and minority persecutions which were such a dark chapter in our record of the last World War."

Edward J. Ennis had just been appointed to the new position of general counsel to the INS. His office was set up to take all the deportation cases out of the criminal division of the Justice Department and to handle all INS appeals to the Supreme Court. "Our job was to help these people [aliens] get straightened out and not to go after them," Ennis said later. After he read the BIA decision in favor of Bridges, Ennis advised Attorney General Biddle that this appeared to be "the correct decision . . . on the merits of the case and he should not pursue it any further." Ennis proved himself to be another in the long line of government officials following Louis F. Post after the Palmer Raids, people who wanted to enforce the U.S. Constitution. Ennis told Biddle that if he reversed Ennis's recommendation to support the BIA decision, Ennis would not handle the appeal to the Supreme Court.

While the government could go into the courts for review of the BIA decision, Carol assumed they could not succeed in reversing it. This meant that Bridges was free.

And the United States was at war against fascism, on the side of imperial Britain and the Socialist USSR after all the alleged "neutrality" of recent years. Political activists were busy trying to respond to the tremendous changes in U.S. foreign and domestic policy. It had all happened very fast: the New Deal, the attempted United Front against fascism, the Munich deal, the invasion of Poland, the phony war, the

Nazi/Soviet pact, the battle of Britain, the Nazi attack on the USSR, and now the Japanese attack on Pearl Harbor.

The declaration of war did not automatically bring unity at home. In February some whites in Detroit became violent when sixty-five Negro families were finally scheduled to move into Sojourner Truth Homes, a new federally supported housing project. The Lawyers Guild joined many other organizations in demanding action by the U.S. Attorney General and local officials.

On March 29, 1942, the Dies Un-American Activities Committee attacked Vice President Henry A. Wallace, chairman of the Board of Economic Warfare, and on May 14 let it be known that it was 'investigating' the Vice President, according to *PM* on that date.

```
                                    March 23, 1942
Richard Gladstein, Esq.
Dear Richie:
   Some weeks ago H.B. arrived in New York and on
reaching me by telephone he stated, "Hello, Mama.
This is the guy who keeps you in furs." He then
went on to state that he was going to Washington to
try and straighten out the problem of finances.
After that he disappeared to the West Coast and
nothing more was heard from him. I am wondering
whether from your end you have learned anything
about whether the finances in this case are likely
to be straightened out. Like everyone else I have
troubles about money and I would like to know the
worst, if the worst has got to be known.
                                    Yours,
                                    Carol
```

World War II brought new threats to the rights of the foreign-born. The first, and most serious, was the forced relocation of all Japanese-American residents of the West Coast, about two-thirds of whom were U.S. citizens. FDR's Executive Order 9960 embroiled Carol King in a dispute with Louis Goldblatt, secretary-treasurer of the ILWU whom she had met in San Francisco on the *Bridges* case. In testimony before the Tolan Committee of Congress, Goldblatt, while supporting the relocation policy, decried racial discrimination, demanded protection of the real and personal property of the people relocated, and charged that families had been disrupted and evacuees victimized by "land grabbing, raiding of homes or racketeering." He also denounced the concentration of the

Japanese-Americans in work camps and demanded prompt measures to separate the loyal from the disloyal residents of these camps. His attitude was based on the ILWU's intimate knowledge of West Coast life and the frequent successful appeals to fear of "the yellow peril" that had besmirched the history of the region.

Carol King had no experience with the treatment of Asian immigrants in agricultural California by agribusiness interests, and she had no specific clients telling their stories and asking for her help. She was deeply concerned about defeating fascism and unusually single-minded on this issue. From this vantage point, she wrote Goldblatt that he was "screwy on the Japanese work camps. That is the only way you are going to avoid having the Japanese work at substandard wages for private employers. My hunch is that the Japanese cause is a lost cause. . . . The emphasis will have to be on the Italians and Germans." She even wrote "that what you say may be true enough, but . . . the emphasis is too much on protecting individual rights and too little on the protection of the U.S. against the possibility of fifth column activity."

Her views reflected the news that many young Japanese-American citizens, including those in the Longshoremen's Union, the Communist Party, and other militant groups, had decided not to contest the evacuation order but to demonstrate their anti-fascism by volunteering to fight in the U.S. Army. They were soon sent to Italy, where they fought heroically against fascist forces and became the most decorated unit in history.

The U.S. entry into the War did change the relationship between the Left and the government. In the spirit of unity to defeat fascism, numerous dignitaries starting with FDR himself sent greetings to the Sixth National Conference of the American Committee for Protection of Foreign Born, which convened in Cleveland on May 9, 1942. The President maintained that there are no foreigners now that we are United Nations. He encouraged the foreign-born to work for victory so that they could be accorded the right to go on as a free people. Wendell Willkie, his 1940 Republican presidential opponent, also sent a message to the conference. Secretary of the Interior Ickes, the U.S. commissioner of education, U.S. Senators Elbert D. Thomas (Dem.-Utah) and James E. Murray (Dem.-Mont.), and church and union leaders also sent greetings. Special assistants to the secretaries of state and treasury spoke to the conference (pushing bonds as a way of financing the War) and Dr. Malcolm S. MacLean, president of Hampton Institute spoke as chairman of the President's new Committee on Fair Employment Practices. The mayor of Cleveland and several local judges welcomed the conference in person.

The important address was the one made by Earl G. Harrison, special assistant to the Attorney General and Roosevelt's nominee for U.S. commissioner of immigration and naturalization. Harrison reminded his audience of largely foreign-born citizens and noncitizens that 24,000,000 people had arrived in this country in the past fifty years. More immigrants from European countries "have perished here in industrial accidents than early American colonists were killed in subduing the wilderness and in the War for Independence." Harrison expressed concern about the relocation centers for Japanese-Americans. He quoted with approval a San Francisco newspaper that exhorted its readers to be fair, so that "by the process of individual justice the mass injustice of an emergency war measure will be abated."

The American Committee applauded his speech, soon reprinting it in pamphlet form along with its own program "to facilitate the complete mobilization of Americans of foreign birth for victory in 1942." The committee would encourage fair employment practices in order "to enable Americans of foreign birth to contribute to [the] war effort" and "to eliminate Axis agents and fifth-column elements from their ranks." It would help noncitizens become naturalized so that they could "assume greater responsibilities as citizens" while bolstering the status of naturalized citizens "by preventing the establishment of two kinds of American citizenship," And it would work to prevent the enactment of "anti-alien" legislation by Congress.

Carol could take the train back to New York after the conference with Harrison's policy statement in mind, feeling some sense of security for her "little aliens," and even her two "big aliens."

This mood lasted barely a fortnight. On May 28, without a hearing, Attorney General Biddle exercised his discretion to reject the decision of the Board of Immigration Appeals in the *Bridges* case. He ruled that Bridges was deportable because he had been, after entering the United States, a member of, and affiliated with, an organization advocating violent overthrow of the government and circulating printed matter so advocating. Biddle found that Bridges had been a member of the Communist Party and affiliated with it, and also found that he had been affiliated with the Marine Workers Industrial Union, which, Biddle found, was a Communist organization. He based his conclusion on a broader range of witnesses than Judge Sears. Neither Sears nor the BIA had placed any credence in the testimony of Thomas Lawrence, Maurice J. Cannalonga, Richard A. St. Clair, Robert P. Wilmot, or John Oliver Thompson. Now Biddle said that their testimony "taken as whole . . . cannot, because of its volume, be completely disregarded."

Bridges, when he got the news, dictated a telegram to war production chief Donald Nelson:

> I WISH TO ASSURE THAT DESPITE THE OUTRAGEOUS DECISION OF ATTORNEY GENERAL BIDDLE, AND NUMEROUS PROTESTS ALREADY POURING IN FROM WORKERS, I WILL DO ALL POSSIBLE TO OFFSET ANY EFFECT IT MIGHT HAVE ON THE PRODUCTION PROGRAMS AND LABOR-MANAGEMENT UNITY, AND WILL URGE ALL WORKERS AND UNIONS I CAN INFLUENCE TO REDOUBLE THEIR EFFORTS IN SPEEDING PRODUCTION TO WIN THE MAIN FIGHT AGAINST THE AXIS.

On May 30, Radio Berlin commented:

> Attorney General Biddle gave a very good resume of the Communist Party's policy to overthrow the U.S. Government. . . . By the remarks of the attorney general, Roosevelt's Moscow policy is brought into a peculiar light.

Sen. Robert Reynolds (Dem.-N.C.) told Hearst International News Service: "Bridges should not be permitted to make the trip out of the country alone. There are thousands of others who ought to be deported or put into concentration camps and held there until we can get rid of them. . . ." The Biddle decision led the Ohio secretary of state to rule the Communist Party off the Ohio ballot.

The Bridges Defense Committee used all of these quotations to prove that the government had made a terrible mistake in coming to this decision. They also quoted several newspapers and magazines attacking the Biddle opinion.

Carol's response to Biddle was a petition for a hearing with the Attorney General that she filed within three days. It was probably the angriest document she ever wrote. She pointed out that this was an administrative proceeding and the hearing officer's deportation order could only be attacked collaterally on a writ of habeas corpus. The issues of fact wrongly decided by Sears would have to be corrected by the Attorney General, or not all. She ridiculed the liberal Biddle mercilessly. In regard to the additional five witnesses whose testimony he felt he could not completely disregard: ". . . the Attorney General . . . accepts as having probative value testimony of witnesses not believed even by the Presiding Inspector [Sears]. Thus each individual liar's evidence apparently has no probative value but the cumulative effect of testimony of five liars 'taken as a whole . . . cannot . . . be completely disregarded.' "

Her fury availed nothing. The Attorney General refused to grant a hearing or to reconsider his deportation order. However, as a result of the position taken by Edward Ennis as general counsel to the INS, the Attorney General had to turn to the criminal division to handle the defense of his order in the Supreme Court, an unusual procedure that would be noted by the Justices, since deportation is not a criminal proceeding.

On Friday, May 29, Carol went to Washington to find out from the Department of Justice how much time Bridges had before surrendering under Biddle's order. She was assured that he would be allowed the customary time, thirty to ninety days. When she called Gladstein in San Francisco with this information, she learned that she had been diddled. At the very time she was being told Bridges had thirty to ninety days, Major Schofield, head of the INS, was telephoning Gladstein to surrender HB immediately. Of course Gladstein refused, so a telegraphic warrant was transmitted to San Francisco in an effort to hustle Bridges out of the country before his lawyers could file a habeas petition in federal court to test Biddle's order.

This effort failed; bail was arranged and the habeas petition filed.

In the White House, Eleanor Roosevelt was sending a memo to FDR describing Harry Bridges in very different terms from those used by the Attorney General, adding, "Please read this and if you think worth passing on to the AG you may do so." President Roosevelt responded to his wife, "I have checked twelve statements in two pages which are questionable as to their correctness — and that is a pretty high average." Presumably he did not forward his wife's memo to the Attorney General, and presumably she continued campaigning on this issue in other ways.

Carol continued to have trouble with another customary ally in regard to Bridges. She wrote to co-counsel on June 2, 1942: "Look out for the ACLU in this case. They are always wanting decisions on matters of principle where the principle has, in the specific case, been badly developed. I feel a little groggy and can think of nothing more at the minute."

Carol then turned from the problems in the *Bridges* case to those in the case of William Schneiderman, which were, like the two men, totally distinct yet legally interconnected.

24.
Getting a Republican to Represent
a Communist

Carol King had learned how to administer a law case. She sometimes got in, at, or near the beginning, as in *Bridges,* although she usually was called in when a case had gotten into a seemingly hopeless quagmire. She would read the record, and the parties, very carefully, mindful of the quirks and characteristics of client, co-counsel, opposing counsel, judge, and friendly and opposing witnesses. Then she would sit offstage — advising, introducing people, furnishing an idea about a legal point or procedure or a fact about a person that might lead to victory.

She had become a broker of low-fee and pro bono political cases, inserting herself in cases that raised important legal points. She would start telling bright lawyers that this case could be won in the Supreme Court if the right lawyer took hold of it and worked out the fine points of law in a creative manner. Then she would start telling the clients, the trial lawyers, and the defense committee that such-and-such a lawyer would be perfect on appeal. Fame was the spur.

Having been raised in New York in a family conscious of class and status, she understood a great deal about social class, and about power — who has it, how they got it, and from whom — and especially what chinks the powerful themselves perceive in their armor. She used this understanding in planning every aspect of each case.

She also had a larger perspective than the lawyers among her friends, who were often called "brilliant." They concentrated on the legal issues in a case, which they had learned to do in law school. A few rose to the level of understanding the importance of the specific facts in a case, which they did not even hear about in law school and had to learn from older lawyers or from experience. Some lawyers, like Bill Patterson, activist in *Sacco-Vanzetti* and *Scottsboro,* quit practicing law altogether and concentrated on building a mass movement around a case (and raising money to pay for bail, transcripts, briefs, and other litigation costs). Paul Robeson, like Edgar Lee Masters, moved out of law into the arts to contribute to and change the culture of the nation. Others, like Vito Marcantonio of the American Labor Party and Ben Davis of the Communist Party, quit practicing law in the courts in order to make law in Congress and the New York City Council. Still other lawyers, like Carol's brother Louis spent a lot of time behind the scenes seeking to influence the influential to modify an outrageous action or to compromise in the face of conflict with a constitutional principle.

Carol knew many lawyers in each of these categories. She called each lawyer by name, pulling him into her symphony of litigation like the master conductor she had become, although she sat in the pit, not at center stage. She never acted as if she had a completed score, always saying she "desperately needed your particular talents" at this particular moment. At her best, she placed every aspect in proper perspective — the close relationship with the client needed to bring out all the helpful facts; the meticulous following of court rules (as in *Scottsboro*); the endless check-ing of legal citations; the personal history of a judge (as in *Herndon*); the careful phrasing of a broad legal issue (as in *Johnson v. Zerbst*); the limitation of issues (as in *DeJonge*); the occasional genius of a new legal idea (as in *Gitlow*); the aura of a big name (like Landis in the first *Bridges* hearing); the feeding of news to the press (as long as she didn't have to be the spokesperson).

She was at her best in the case of William Schneiderman. She wasn't overly cautious, as she had been early in *Bridges*. She tried to win on the broadest issue while carefully briefing the narrower ones. She did not put off a wealthy liberal lawyer, as she sometimes seemed to want to put off her brother Louis.

King heard about the case when she reached San Francisco in July 1939 to mastermind the first *Bridges* case. Schneiderman was born in Russia in 1905. Three years later he was brought to the United States, and his family located in Los Angeles. He grew up poor. He had to help support his family while he went to high school at night and had to quit college after two years. He applied for naturalization and in 1927 became a citizen of the United States. In 1930 he became an official in the Communist Party and thereafter held several posts in California, where he met Bridges and other longshoremen and participated in many strikes, demonstrations of the unemployed, and political rallies.

He lived and acted like a citizen until 1939, when an attorney for the Immigration Service filed an affidavit for the revocation of his citizenship on the ground that it was "fraudulently and illegally procured." This was the short, sharp era after the start of World War II when the U.S. Communist Party was condemning the "phony imperialist war" because no Nazis were being killed, and the C.P. was being isolated and attacked for not supporting Poland or Finland. Roosevelt was arming the United States against Germany while the Soviet Union was living under its nonaggression pact with Hitler.

The immigration law provided that no alien could be naturalized unless, for the preceding five years, "he has behaved as a person of good moral character, attached to the principles of the Constitution of the United States, and well disposed to the good order and happiness of the United States." The affidavit stated that Schneiderman had not met this requirement in 1927 at the time of his naturalization because he was then a member of the Workers Party of America, which later combined with the Communist Party.

Schneiderman was brought to trial in the federal district court in San Francisco in December 1939. A man with a modest manner, he was represented by high-powered counsel, including Communist labor lawyer George Andersen of San Francisco and popular New Deal lawyer Robert W. Kenny of Los Angeles, now president of the National Lawyers Guild. The defense showed that Schneiderman had not been asked, at the time of his naturalization, whether he was a member of the Workers Party.

Two government witnesses testified that membership in the CP was incompatible with attachment to the Constitution. William F. Hynes was the cop who had defined "dialectical materialism" to the amusement of the courtroom in the 1931 Long Beach case and later headed the subversive squad of the Los Angeles police department. On cross-examination of the short, wiry red-head, attorney Kenny developed the fact that Hynes had taken an eight-month leave of absence from the LAPD to work for the railway company during the Los Angeles street railway strike. Later, the police department had disbanded the Red Squad, long under attack by labor and civil liberties groups.

The second government expert witness, Miles G. Humphreys, had testified against Bridges in the first deportation hearing. Dean Landis had found that his testimony revealed an inability to distinguish a Communist meeting from a CIO meeting.

The Schneiderman defense replied to this testimony on Communist Party theory by reading into the record the interpretations of Marxist philosophy given by professors Walter Thompson and Harold C. Brown in the first *Bridges* hearing. Schneiderman was a low-budget case, and this procedure saved time and money by not having the professors appear personally, while saving the record if an appeal became necessary.

Then Schneiderman testified in his own behalf. He said he had been and was now a Communist, that the Communist Party did not advocate the forceful overthrow of the government, that he personally held no such belief, and that membership in the Party was not in any way incompatible with attachment to the principles of the Constitution. He considered membership in the Party compatible with the obligations of American citizenship. He stated that he believed in retention of personal property for personal use but advocated social ownership of the means of production and exchange, with compensation to the owners. He believed and hoped that socialization could be achieved here by democratic processes, but history showed that the ruling minority has always used force against the majority before surrendering power. By "dictatorship of the proletariat" Schneiderman meant that the "majority of the people shall really direct their own destinies and use the instrument of the state for these truly democratic ends." He stated that he would bear arms against his native Russia if necessary.

The district judge decided against Schneiderman, revoking his citizenship on the ground that it was "illegally obtained." In April 1941 that decision was upheld by the court of appeals.

Six weeks later, Carol finished the second *Bridges* deportation hearing before Judge Sears, and Schneiderman immediately retained her to handle his appeal to the U.S. Supreme Court.

Wanting to get acquainted with her new client quickly, Carol invited him and his wife to pick her up at the hotel where she was staying and spend the day together. Leah Schneiderman was a very good legal secretary, but on the shy side. As she and her husband approached Mrs. King's door, Mrs. Schneiderman felt overawed and could not imagine how she could talk with this great lawyer.

Mrs. King answered their knock with a question, "When are we going to tear apart a herring?"

"I suddenly realized 'this is a beautiful human being,' " Leah Schneiderman recalled later. " 'She's famous and no one can equal her in her field!' After that crack, we spent the whole day at the beach — eating hot dogs and popcorn, riding the rides, you name it. It was just a glorious day."

King, as a constitutional lawyer, wanted to develop the First Amendment doctrine on freedom of political association through the *Schneiderman* case to add to the limited doctrine set forth in *Herndon* and *DeJonge*. But as in those cases, King, as a careful lawyer, wanted to win, so she included narrow traditional issues that could garner conservative judicial votes.

In her petition to the Court to hear *Schneiderman* she raised several due process points. First, the petitioner had fully and strictly complied with the statutory requirements for naturalization, and he had committed no fraud, which was the customary basis for denaturalization. Second, the only basis for setting aside his naturalization was his membership in the Communist Party, although Congress had expressly refused to provide that membership in the Party was a bar to naturalization. Third, he was losing his citizenship for failing to reveal his membership, which no one had asked him about. Fourth, the lower courts had deprived him of the benefit of evidence that he had behaved "as a man of good moral character attached to the principles of the Constitution, and that he had renounced all foreign allegiances" during the five years preceding his naturalization. This exclusion of evidence also denied due process. And the government was violating the First Amendment by canceling his citizenship for political beliefs and affiliations that were not prohibited by statute at the time of naturalization.

King added a prescient warning "concerning the dangers that this decision holds not only for naturalized but for native citizens who take oaths as lawyers, notaries, public and civil servants:

> If the doctrine of this case is permitted to stand, a person's professional status or position may be infused with insecurity, subject to a potential adjudication that years before he took a false oath. The oath may be held false because views were expressed of political beliefs which some displeased official has later concluded are inconsistent with a pledge to support the Constitution. Or what is infinitely worse, . . . falsity may be attributed from association with a party and from a selection of interpretations of party doctrine that do not represent the views of the affiant.

The Supreme Court decided to hear Schneiderman's case. Carol was certain the case could be won if the issues were properly put before the Supreme Court. But who could do it? Walter H. Pollak would have been her automatic first choice. Now she had to cast about for a replacement. She apparently let her mind wander at first, unconcerned about practical difficulties. She reasoned that since Schneiderman was a leader of the Communist Party, the appropriate person to represent him would be a leader of another political party. He would need to have a tremendous commitment to the democratic process and no fear of being labeled a Communist. Wendell Willkie popped into mind. He was a Lincoln Republican who resembled Harold Ickes (except that Ickes had actually shifted from a Republican to a New Dealer under FDR, administering his Interior Department with an environmental fervor). When Willkie ran for President on the Republican ticket in 1940, he campaigned on a "One World" platform that showed a remarkable understanding of world economic and political realities. Lately he had been making strong statements about civil rights within the country, and he had sent a greeting to the American Committee Conference. Willkie would bring enormous prestige to the case.

Checking around, Carol found that Willkie had never argued a case in the Supreme Court. This meant he might be very tempted to say Yes. It also meant he had no experience in that difficult forum. And of course he was far from a specialist on questions of naturalization and civil liberties. Still . . .

King began pondering the best way to approach Willkie to take the case. She pestered everybody she knew with questions about whether they knew anybody who knew him. No one did. Then Nuddy Greene, for whose judgment she had great respect, suggested she send Willkie a simple letter asking him to handle the case along with the brief she had used to convince the Supreme Court to hear it. She did so, but with no expectation of success. When she got no answer she began to consider alternative choices.

At this point, on October 28, 1941, unbeknownst to Carol King, her colleagues, or her clients, J. Edgar Hoover, director of the FBI, transmitted to Mr. L.M.C. Smith, chief of the Special Defense Unit, "a dossier showing the information presently available in the files of this Bureau with respect to *Mrs. Carol Weiss King with alias*" together with a form letter that could send her to a detention center not unlike the "relocation camps" that would soon house Japanese Americans on the West Coast:

IT IS RECOMMENDED THAT THIS INDIVIDUAL BE CONSID-
ERED FOR CUSTODIAL DETENTION IN THE EVENT OF

NATIONAL EMERGENCY. THE INFORMATION CONTAINED ON
THE ATTACHED DOSSIER CONSTITUTES THE BASIS FOR AP-
PROPRIATE CONSIDERATION IN THIS REGARD.

IT SHOULD BE UNDERSTOOD, OF COURSE, THAT ADDI-
TIONAL INFORMATION MAY BE RECEIVED FROM TIME TO
TIME SUPPLEMENTING THAT ALREADY AVAILABLE IN THE BU-
REAU'S FILES, AND AS SUCH DATA ARE RECEIVED THEY
WILL BE MADE AVAILABLE TO YOU SO THAT THE DOSSIER
IN YOUR POSSESSION MAY BE SUPPLEMENTED THEREBY.

IT WILL BE GREATLY APPRECIATED IF YOU WILL ADVISE
THE BUREAU AT YOUR EARLIEST CONVENIENCE AS TO THE
DECISION REACHED IN THIS CASE.

One Saturday afternoon some time after sending the letter to Willkie, Carol's telephone rang. Her secretary said it was Wendell Willkie.

Carol was so amazed that she fell over in her chair.

Willkie asked Carol to send him the record in *Schneiderman*. She wasted no time in complying.

A few days later, she was summoned by Willkie. "His gloomy outer office, with its wooden panels and hexagonal shape more like a church than a law office, had depressed and scared me. His smile and his handshake put me instantly at ease," she wrote later in the *New Masses*.

He thought she might be interested in how he came to accept the case after putting it aside till he had time to read the brief. "I read it on a Saturday morning. I reread it. After that, I could not with my beliefs have remained satisfied with myself if I refused to accept the case if two conditions were true — (1) that Schneiderman was a decent fellow personally, and (2) that the record sustained the brief. That was the reason for my making inquiries about Schneiderman and asking you to send me the record." Like any prudent lawyer, Willkie had asked a California colleague, Bartley Crum, to see what kind of reputation Bill Schneiderman had before taking him on as a client. Crum found that Schneiderman had never been arrested or been in any trouble; he had been a good citizen.

Willkie made it clear that in his judgment the *Schneiderman* case involved "the individual liberties of an American citizen, and not the Communist Party." He would represent Schneiderman but he would accept no fee in the case, from the Communist Party or anyone else.

Carol King readily agreed to this condition.

The two attorneys conferred together several times, and Carol liked his style. "Willkie had an informal and not too neat manner of working," she wrote later. "He generally leaned back in his desk chair with his feet on the desk. Only at our first conference had he managed to keep his feet on the floor. I would probably never have noticed that his shoes were rarely shined except for the fact that they were always in the immediate foreground. When he was busy, he would go right on talking as he ate a ham sandwich and swallowed coffee out of a container from the corner drug store." She did not mention, and may not have known, that Willkie's mother had been a lawyer, the first woman admitted in Indiana; this may have helped prepare him to work in tandem with Carol King.

The announcement on November 29, 1941, that Wendell Willkie would appear in the Supreme Court for Schneiderman created much comment. The solicitor general allowed himself a dry "splendid" for the *New York Times*. But Arthur Garfield Hays, general counsel of the ACLU, wrote Willkie a letter of praise. "The injustice" in *Schneiderman,* said Hays, "calls to high heaven and it is about time that the principle involved is made clear to the American people."

A week later, the Japanese air force bombed Pearl Harbor, and the United States entered the war as an ally of the socialist Soviet Union. While this fact had no legal bearing, it certainly did no harm to Communist Schneiderman's cause, although the U.S. press did not expect the Russian Communists to win. The media were predicting that Hitler would make mincemeat of the Russian army within six weeks, as he had walked over all the armies of the Western European democracies except England.

King and Willkie did expect to win, and in an effort to help Willkie, King wrote a draft of what she thought might become the Supreme Court brief on the merits and sent it to Willkie. His response, Carol wrote later, was "gentle but firm."

> He didn't want to be a "shirt front." The brief had to be completely his, a part of his very being, his own expression of the political injustice he had agreed to combat. But he did not regard himself as above criticism or suggestion. "Don't pull your punches," he would say and mean. Willkie didn't want to be treated as some superior being to whom others had to toady. He treated everyone as an equal.

By mid-January 1942 Willkie, Carl M. Owens, and Howard C. Wood, both of his office, had completed their brief and filed it in the Supreme Court. Although it contained Carol's name, it did not contain her thoughts. Nuddy Greene, somewhat of a connoisseur on such matters, thought the brief showed its origins. From his Wall Street associates he had heard that one of Willkie's partners had been assigned to protect Willkie from having radical ideas injected into the brief, including all of Carol's proposals. As a result, Nuddy thought it wasn't a very good brief.

The *New York Herald Tribune* reported that Willkie's brief declared that the "real question" in the case was "whether our free institutions are to be preserved by totalitarian methods or whether there is to remain that basic fundamental of our constitutional growth, freedom of political thought and belief, with the inherent corollary of freedom of advocacy, so long as that advocacy does not suggest the use of force or violence."

⅔

While Willkie was writing in this vein, J. Edgar Hoover was authorizing a break-in at the law office of Willkie's co-counsel. In March 1942 FBI agents entered Carol King's domain and photocopied three volumes of what they called "material" and "various items," as revealed in 1988 by Theoharis and Cox in *The Boss.* The FBI then prepared summaries on the lawyers whose names were found (perhaps in Carol's address book), including Arthur Goldberg (later CIO general counsel and U.S. Supreme Court Justice), labor lawyer Edward Lamb of Toledo, and Columbia University law professor Herbert Wechsler. These reports could be used against them for the rest of their lives. It has now been revealed that the FBI used similar methods in 1941–1943 raids on the Veterans of the Abraham Lincoln Brigade, the Joint Anti-Fascist Refugee Committee, and the League of American Writers. Later in the war, FBI agents raided the offices of other organizations whose members turned to Carol King, including Russian War Relief, the IWO, and the Negro Labor Victory Committee.

In ignorance of all such actions, Willkie pursued his role as advocate. He wanted to meet his client and Schneiderman wanted to meet him. Such a meeting is not required in an appellate case because the client cannot testify in the Supreme Court and usually does not even attend the argument there. The meeting was held shortly after Pearl Harbor, and Carol described it: "They liked each other as human beings. Willkie explained to his client that nobody with a 'lively intellect' in Schneiderman's situation could have been anything but curious about the world of economics. When Willkie was at college he had organized a Socialist

Club. Throughout the case, Willkie maintained the attitude that what Schneiderman had done was normal and to be expected, that he was a better than average citizen because study and speculation had brought him to the conclusion that social change was necessary."

King's collaboration with Willkie on *Schneiderman* led her to refer to him as a person with an infinite capacity for learning. She decided to ask him to help her on another one of her difficult cases, involving another Communist Party leader. Earl Browder was still serving time at Lewisburg Federal Penitentiary at Atlanta on the passport fraud charge arising out of his attempt to get his wife's immigration status regularized during the difficult Nazi-Soviet pact period. Carl Stern had lost the case in the Supreme Court in early 1941 (and had lost many of his own clients for his courage in taking the case). Now Carol told Estolv Ward, veteran of the Bridges Defense Committee, "in a manner indicating unusual pride of performance, that she had persuaded Willkie, after considerable argument, to use his influence with FDR to free Earl Browder. When he agreed to act, she told me, she lost control and burst into tears.

"Willkie said to her, 'Why, my dear, you seem to be personally involved in this matter; you seem to have more than the ordinary attitude of attorney to client.' And she replied, 'Yes, Mr. Willkie, you are quite right.' " She apparently did not explain that she seldom had a client for whom she had the "ordinary" attorney-client attitude.

And she undoubtedly did not explain another significant background fact of the times: that most of the leading American politicians then in power had known most of the leading Left political activists never in power. They had met at picket lines, demonstrations, election rallies, and had worked on many common causes. This shared history made it easy for Mayor LaGuardia, for example, to call in a reporter he knew for the *Daily Worker*, Harry Raymond, and tell him, "The Boss [FDR] is going to spring Browder but he doesn't want any demonstrations. Tell Elizabeth [Gurley Flynn] about it, but don't tell Bob [Minor]. He would mess it up." Journalist Sender Garlin tells this story.

On May 16, 1942, President Roosevelt did commute the sentence of Earl Browder, head of the CPUSA, "in the interest of national security." The CP celebrated but did not demonstrate.

❦

Carol continued to be intimately involved in life on many levels simultaneously, like the First Lady of the land. Carol participated in family affairs by phone and in person, and must have savored publication of the first book by her brother Billy in 1942. *How To Keep Out of Trouble* was based on the common problems he dealt with for the low-income clients who made use of the legal clinic he ran out of his home. Dale Carnegie's foreword made the book more popular, and the book enlarged his clientele. William Weiss conducted much of his counseling now by correspondence, which he could manage during the hours when the ravages of multiple sclerosis were not interrupting his work.

Carol's own work load shifted when the Supreme Court postponed the *Schneiderman* argument until the fall term. In late summer, FDR asked Willkie to go to the Soviet Union and China as a special envoy of the United States while the Russians were making their heroic stand at Stalingrad. (Carol must have savored reading the byline, "Henry Shapiro" in United Press reports from Stalingrad about the dramatic accounts of that fateful battle. Shapiro had introduced her to the IJA during her meeting with him in Moscow in 1931.)

Even the *Schneiderman* case and the war could not keep the *Bridges* case from Carol King's mind for very long. In July 1942 she wrote to Aubrey and Richie about their draft of the amended petition in that case. Their relationship was not at a high ebb:

> I have almost recovered my temper sufficiently
> since the receipt of the amended petition to settle
> down and try to find out what we are going to do
> about it. Your document is, of course, a much more
> finished product than anything I created. The only
> difficulty with it is that it fails to protect many
> of our constitutional rights. The problem in my
> mind now is not a problem of placing blame, but of
> trying to figure out some way of fixing up the situ-
> ation so that if this case goes up we are not out
> of court merely because of the faulty allegations
> in our amended petition.
>   . . . I should like to be kept informed exactly
> what you are about to do, as I have said a number
> of times. I don't like to be put in a position of
> having the United States Supreme Court say that
> they have no jurisdiction because we did not raise
> constitutional issues. I don't like it for Harry's
> sake and I don't like it for the sake of my own
> reputation. . . .

She then ticked off the narrow legal issues in six numbered paragraphs.

Meanwhile Richie was trying to get Wendell Willkie involved in the *Bridges* case via Willkie's friend Bartley Crum. Willkie wanted to get the Civil Liberties Committee of the American Bar Association to file an amicus brief at the proper time. Crum also talked to Professor Max Radin at the University of California-Boalt Hall Law School, and defense counsel worked to get other prominent amici.

As Carol had predicted, the ACLU was not prepared to come into *Bridges* while ACLU leader Roger Baldwin was perhaps seeking a rapprochement with J. Edgar Hoover. Baldwin recommended in a letter to Harry that they bring in "somebody of prominence not associated in the public mind with Left or labor cases, who can be persuasive not only in the courts but as to public opinion." By October, Carol had to report that she wasn't making much headway on getting friend of the court briefs "because everyone who might become involved in them seems to be taking a government job and is unavailable for this project."

By November, Carol's major concern about *Bridges* had to do with getting the legal bills paid, as she wrote to "the Folks" in Mills Tower:

> On Wednesday, I attended a Bridges luncheon in
> Boston . . . at the CIO Convention. [David J.]
> McDonald, of the CIO Defense Committee, . . .
> explained to the gathered antique females of Boston
> that the case was being financed by the CIO, and
> the CIO was going to fight it up to the Supreme
> Court if necessary and pay all the way. He added,
> seeing [my] withering look upon him, that some of
> the bills had not yet been paid.
>   I had just gotten over the shock of his
> enthusiastic talk of Harry — and by the way at the
> luncheon he mentioned each and every one of us by
> name and harangued the multitude on what remarkable
> lawyers we were — when I arrived the next morning
> at the Convention to hear some more guff on the
> wonders not again of HB but again of his attorneys.
> . . . [F]inally Phil Murray delivered a
> considerable speech not only praising Harry but ask-
> ing each and every international union to answer
> the plea for funds that had already been sent them.

Meantime, J. Edgar Hoover directed the SAC (Special Agent in Charge) office in New York to the closing report of special agent S. P.

Ferrin dated August 18, 1942, concerning "Mrs. Carol Weiss King — Internal Security (c)":

```
IN VIEW OF THE SUBJECT'S IMPORTANCE IN CONNECTION
WITH COMMUNIST ACTIVITIES, YOU ARE INSTRUCTED TO RE-
OPEN THE INSTANT CASE AND TO ASSIGN THE SAME SO
THAT THE INVESTIGATION CONCERNING THIS SUBJECT WILL
BE KEPT CURRENT AT ALL TIMES.
```

~

In view of Wendell Willkie's importance, the FBI's "subject," Carol King, enjoyed writing and talking about him and *Schneiderman*. She did so in some detail later for the *New Masses*, explaining that Willkie was hardly rested from his global trip when he argued the case in early November 1942.

"Two days before, he buried himself at the Carlton Hotel in Washington with a large slice of his law library, an assistant from his office, and his secretary. He knew what he wanted to say. The process of preparation was one of working out ways and means." Willkie called Carol and asked her to go down to brief him in Washington as he was nervous, although he knew that was silly, etc.

Carol was very pleased. She had bought a new dress for the occasion and quickly packed for the trip. (The dress was black and quickly became her "Schneiderman dress," hung in her closet next to her black "Bridges dress.") Carol called her friend Lillian Dunaway about ten o'clock in the evening and asked her to call back in fifteen minutes. Carol had to take a nap but didn't want to miss her train. She arrived at the Carlton that night ready to talk about the case.

Willkie talked — with great charm, she admitted later — about everything else. Only once did he show that he had ever heard of William Schneiderman. Referring to his client's birthplace, he asked, "Where is Romanoff, Russia?" Nobody knew. But Willkie found out by the next morning, and while his countrymen were marveling at the long Russian stand against the Nazi encirclement on the Volga, he told the Supreme Court, "Mr. Schneiderman was born near Stalingrad, in 1905." This remark undoubtedly reminded the Justices that the lawyer *against* the government had just *served* the government as the President's special ambassador to the Soviet Union.

CONFIDENTIAL

A report from Confidential Informant
~~from the New York Office.~~

described her attitude as "very clever, intelligent and
cagey."

Mrs. King represented the "moderate" party line

b7D

9-12-42, Letter to Director
from SAC, New York
Re: "Harbim"
39-915-2090
(51)

JW:nck:mlb

CONFIDENTIAL

295

FBI File: Carol King (9-12-42). A report on the lawyer for Harry Bridges
("Harbim") during the war against fascism.

Willkie liked to mark the things on which he was working himself,
saying, "I can follow my own tracks." According to King, he came to the
argument in the Supreme Court "with a much tracked-up record, a sheaf
of quotations and a page of notes scrawled in pencil. There wasn't much
on the sheet either. He obviously talked from the heart and not from his
notes."

King sat next to Willkie at counsel table for the *Schneiderman* argument. The great courtroom was crowded; the bench was not. There was one vacancy on the Court, and Justice Jackson had disqualified himself because he had been Attorney General when the proceedings against Schneiderman were started in 1939. He came in toward the end to listen. The government was represented by Charles Fahy, who had moved from general counsel to the National Labor Relations Board to solicitor general. The seven Justices frequently interrupted Fahy and Willkie during the two-hour argument.

The atmosphere was unique in U.S. history. The Communist Party of the United States had ties with the Communist Party of the Soviet Union, which ran the USSR. The U.S. and Soviet governments were allies. The Marxist ideology of the USSR was the same as the ideology of the Communist Party of the United States. This ideology was inspiring heroism in the USSR and among Communists in the U.S. armed forces. The U.S. court must decide whether a person could lose his U.S. citizenship for believing in the Marxist ideology and being a member of the Communist Party of the United States.

In this setting, the Republican lawyer characterized his Communist client as a "highly intelligent citizen" and a man of "exemplary honor" who had lived "an exemplary life" during the five years preceding his naturalization. "There was not a blot on his record." Willkie said that Schneiderman had a "strong social urge" and became interested in social and economic theories while still a youth. Willkie said, in an aside, that he had organized a Socialist Club himself while he was in college, and "if my client can understand [all those social and economic theories], he's a better man than I am."

That got a good laugh from the audience of lawyers, and some of the Justices smiled.

Willkie said *The Communist Manifesto* of 1848 recommended such terrible things as a progressive income tax and universal education. This got a real laugh from several Justices. "Why, I have no doubt that every member of this court probably read that when he was 16 to 21 and had his thinking on social matters affected by it. Whether one believes in it or disbelieves in it, the 'Communist Manifesto' is a tremendously important social document." Willkie quoted from the *Manifesto* and declared that Schneiderman believed in it as "applicable to the period in which it was written." Willkie drew the picture of Europe in 1848, when Marx and Engels wrote the *Manifesto*. His own grandfather had fled to the United

States from Germany as a refugee from the 1848 revolution, along with Carl Schurz and others who contributed "much" to the United States. In fact, repressions in Europe "accounted for some of the finest strains that came here to make the great melting pot that is America."

Willkie said that at Schneiderman's naturalization hearing, nobody had asked whether he belonged to the Workers Party.

Justice Frankfurter interrupted, "So the charge of fraud is one of failure to volunteer information not requested?"

Willkie replied, "That's right." He added that the government had never said that Schneiderman personally advocated the violent overthrow of the government. It had merely ascribed that doctrine to the Communist Party, and then imputed the views of the party to Schneiderman. "All the proof in this case is by imputation." This method of proof violates the basic precept that guilt must be personal. "You might as well prove my belief by showing the beliefs of Ham Fish," Willkie said, referring to the ultraconservative Republican congressman from New York.

Several Justices smiled, and the defense hoped they would remember the point.

During the solicitor general's argument, Justice Douglas asked him "whether the Communist Party in the period in question was passing out the ammunition." Fahy could not simply say "yes." Douglas seemed dissatisfied with his response.

During Willkie's argument, as Carol reported later, he met questions put to him by the Justices "with enthusiasm," except when Justice Murphy asked how the *Schneiderman* case happened to be started.

Willkie replied, with a trace of embarrassment, that he didn't like to go outside the record (which is against the rules in all cases), "but it was in 1939." When Murphy looked puzzled, Willkie continued, "And Mr. Schneiderman was born in Russia," using these "cryptic phrases" to suggest the frigid political climate during the Soviet-German nonaggression pact.

Throughout his argument, Willkie relied on his wide knowledge of history and political philosophy, Carol reported. "He recognized the 'Communist Manifesto' as a dignified historical document and the foundation of the economic interpretation of history. Thus it ceased to be the collection of disconnected sentences advocating violence relied upon by government counsel."

In fact, the government had not been able to reach a consistent interpretation of certain Communist documents. In its brief opposing certiorari, the government declared that the 1938 constitution of the U.S. Communist Party "contains nothing inconsistent with a peaceful accomplishment of the party objectives." In a later brief, the government said that "further consideration leads us to the belief that this statement was in error," and they quoted "revolutionary" language in the acceptance speech by William Z. Foster, CP candidate for President.

Willkie played on the Justices' deep personal knowledge of the game of politics and got several chuckles from them as he referred to his own role as a defeated candidate for President against an unbeatable incumbent. He said his client admitted that he had not read the acceptance speech by Foster, the head of his party. He added reflectively, "I doubt that any presidential candidate's acceptance speeches are ever read."

The Court recessed for lunch, and defense counsel went to the cafeteria together. Carol suggested that Willkie sit down at the table and she would bring him lunch. Willkie declined her offer. Carol could see him in Moscow "telling a ditch digger or Joseph Stalin not to pull his punches. And I'm sure he gave both the feeling not only of being on equal terms with them but of being genuinely interested in what they had to say."

After the recess, Willkie picked up his argument, talking easily, vigorously. Finally he raised a note and read from it: "This country, with its institutions, belongs to the people who inhabit it. Whenever they shall grow weary of the existing government, they can exercise their constitutional right of amending it, or their revolutionary right to dismember or overthrow it."

Justice Roberts was smiling even before Willkie said that the quotation was from Lincoln's second inaugural address. "This is from the founder of my party," the Republican Party. Willkie went on: "God forbid that we should ever be twenty years without such a rebellion. . . . The tree of liberty must be refreshed from time to time with the blood of patriots and tyrants." He paused. "That," he said, "is from Thomas Jefferson, the founder of the party of many of you gentlemen — the Democratic Party."

What did it mean? "The formulated doctrine of the founder of the Republican Party, the founder of the Democratic Party and the founder of the Communist Party all talk of revolution under certain circumstances, [and] the mildest of the three by far was Karl Marx."

As he sat down, Carol "had the notion that Mr. Willkie never enjoyed an argument more and had never argued a case he thought more important." Members of the Supreme Court Bar who packed the courtroom "looked surprised at such directness, but the marble pillars did not tremble before the breath of life to which they were exposed."

The *New York Herald Tribune* ran a long story on the case the next day, saying Willkie's conclusion was "as forceful as any he ever made on a campaign platform. . . . Some observers thought the court seemed about 4 to 3 for Willkie, but they wouldn't bet on it."

Seemingly the case was over, and counsel exchanged letters. Willkie wrote to "My dear Carol" to say, "I don't know when our paths will cross again but whenever that is, soon or late, I shall always remember with great satisfaction my association with you in the Schneiderman case. As a co-worker you are great. Good luck in all you undertake."

But Nuddy Greene had been right. The issues had not been stated clearly enough, in narrow legal language, for the Justices to write an opinion citing other opinions based on a clear line of precedent or doctrine. On February 12, 1943, the seven sitting Justices ordered the case reargued, as they had the *Bridges* contempt case. This was a real disappointment. On the other hand, such a case had never been won in the U.S. Supreme Court. And they had not lost it.

Everyone would simply have to wait till the Court heard the case argued again. In the meantime, the law, the war, and life, went on. When her client announced the birth of Helen Schneiderman in San Francisco, Carol jollied her New York friends into finding dozens of diapers to send to Leah Schneiderman because diapers were a scarce item in wartime.

25.
Folks Have to Be Themselves

Finally the rumor Carol King had heard after Germany attacked the Soviet Union in 1941 came true. The U.S. government stopped arresting U.S. Reds for deportation; instead it drafted them or permitted them to volunteer for the armed forces or the merchant marine. Carol heard from her friends that some radical GIs were being sent to the areas of greatest military activity where they could fight and die as heroes. Others were sent to isolated spots and assigned to menial work where they were separated from the troops. The army sent Dashiell Hammett, creator of *The Thin Man,* to a remote camp in Alaska for his politics.

But the Reds were on the same side as the government, as some of their lawyers had been in the New Deal days; they were not fighting the government in the courts. A second wave of Carol's colleagues on the *IJA Bulletin* began leaving New York for jobs in Washington. The first wave in the thirties had gone from poverty in private practice into New Deal agencies — AAA, NLRB, Social Security. Now many went with new wartime agencies — the Office of Price Administration, the War Labor Board. Every day several of the younger men went into the armed forces, serving in various ranks; Norman Leonard went into the navy and took action against racial discrimination in the Service. Some committed older Guild lawyers, like Bob Silberstein, also volunteered for military service.

As the country moved from Depression to World War, the IJA editors described how New Deal methods of dealing with social problems were being transformed into ways to increase military production to defeat the fascist powers. They insisted that civil liberties must be protected in wartime, and race discrimination must be forbidden. They opposed the conscription of workers into defense industries and the awarding of defense contracts to monopolies and anti-labor employers.

Nathan Greene, who remained the intellectual senior partner on the *Bulletin,* summed up their work at the *Bulletin*'s annual dinner in April 1942. He took this always festive occasion to talk about their work in the past ten years, about the "anxious times — occasionally, despairing times. But . . . anxiety was always tempered by one great elixir. . . . It was — and is — an abiding faith that for the masses of our people in America the principle of human freedom is deeply rooted and staunchly held. . . . [T]hat whenever the full glare of knowledge centers upon and exposes violations of human freedom . . . there wells up in our people shame and, also, terrible anger."

Greene expressed the faith of the IJA editors in the people of the United States. "But entwined with this faith has been a sure belief that faith without effort was sterile, that faith without work was a ghost." And he described the particular group in whom the IJA editors had faith: "the stable, responsible organized labor movement comprising some 11,000,000 men and women. . . . On the ground-work of unionism the American worker has developed informed and able leaders [with] vision and authority."

The *Bulletin* reported that part of FDR's brain trust still had the American workers and their love of freedom very much in mind as the country continued to gear up to defeat Hitler. Britain and the Soviet Union needed the United States to play the decisive role in producing the weapons of war and in transporting them where they were needed. U.S. government agencies were estimating this work would require Negroes and women to enter the industrial work force in unprecedented numbers. Thirteen million war production workers were needed, mostly people who had spent their lives working on small farms in the South and Midwest and as housewives all over the country. Arms production would require terrible disruption of daily lives, causing people to move to new areas where housing would be short, traffic congested, and overtime heavy. This mobilization would require massive centralized planning by the government, and inducements to enter the work force.

In November 1942 the *IJA Bulletin* described the National Resources Planning Board, appointed by Roosevelt and chaired by his uncle, city planner Frederick Delano, to do long-range national economic planning. The board proposed a new Bill of Rights including economic rights: the right to work usefully and creatively through the productive years; to fair pay; to security with freedom from fear of old age, want, dependency, sickness, unemployment, and accident; and to education for work, for citizenship, and for personal growth and happiness. It included "the right to live in a system of free enterprise, free from compulsory labor, irresponsible private power, arbitrary public authority and unregulated monopolies"; and it included King's concern, "the right to come and go, to speak or to be silent, free from the spyings of secret political police."

A group of practical visionaries had finally put the individual emergency New Deal bills passed by Congress into a constitutional framework, although the group proposed postponing adoption of the bills until after the war. The goal of their "womb to tomb" social security plan was to stabilize capitalism and reduce profit rates. (Their list of rights was pulled out at San Francisco in 1945 when the United Nations Charter was being written. Eleanor Roosevelt used it again at the United Nations in 1948 when the Universal Declaration of Human Rights was being drafted.)

Carol King began noting another of those contradictions she and the country had been experiencing for some time. The government had stopped arresting her clients, which cut down her case load. When she wasn't working on or worrying about *Bridges* or *Schneiderman,* she had relatively little to do as an immigration lawyer. She told her friends that she began to envy other lawyers who had not specialized in what was becoming a moribund field of law. Life became more leisurely. She could schmooze with Marion Pollak on weekends, now that her friend had completed her degree in social work following Walter's death and was working as a medical social worker.

But during the week, Carol was not only able, but eager, to take any client who entered her office — for example, a friend from the first *Bridges* case who had moved to New York. The friend and an art dealer had sponsored an art show for British, Chinese, and Russian war relief. Some of the liberal anger at the Soviet Union for signing the pact with Hitler in 1939 was melting in the face of heroic Soviet resistance to Hitler's invasion of Russia. The show was an artistic success, but there were no proceeds and the art dealer lost more than $1,000. (When Carol made notes on the case later, she used the names "Mrs. Smith" and "Q" for her client and the art dealer.) Q threatened to sue Mrs. Smith for obligations incurred while acting as her agent and wrote letters attacking Mrs. Smith's reputation. Carol managed to calm Q down considerably. Then Mrs. Smith wrote Q another letter, and Q hit the ceiling again. Mrs. Smith also carelessly overdrew her bank account, leaving Carol to cover the deficits for her. Finally Carol dictated a letter to her difficult client that epitomizes how bilingual she had become in providing simultaneous translations from legal principles to lay English, and making them palatable to clients.

> Now, I am a person of a very sloppy exterior and
> generally messy, but I have learned from hard
> experience that if you are in a ticklish situation
> you have to be careful and precise. By my crossness
> I tried to convey to you the idea that I wanted
> just such accurateness and precision from you. If
> you are careful and watchful and ask my advice
> before you do anything, I can be the most charming
> woman in the world, but God help you if you go off
> half-cocked when I am your lawyer. It is a
> dangerous process and I thought I might just as
> well tell you first as last. . . . NO MATTER WHAT
> HAPPENS DON'T SAY ANYTHING OR DO ANYTHING WHILE I
> AM GONE. I will be back Wednesday.

During this period, Carol won some points, if not cases, for one of her favorite relations. Her niece Peggy Stern (the one Carol had said "did not have a Weiss mind") was just beginning to get around again after a serious operation. Carol took her out to dinner and pointed out that now Peggy, like Carol, "must have the courage of your difference from other people." Peggy had not thought of her situation in just that way, and the advice helped, as well as the "sheltering and flattering identification" with Carol in the comment.

By this time Peggy was going to college at the University of Chicago, and Carol "became the symbol of New York: the talent for living, the unconventional conviviality, the search for identity, the analysis, the probing. Always the ritual and institution of Barkley." When Peggy was languishing for a lost love, she complained to Carol, "But time passes so slowly." Carol replied drily, "Well, you should get a lot done."

Peggy was getting interested in political action and was studying Marxist theory, which Carol had never done. Carol's son, Johnny, did not seem interested in either political theory or action at this point, instead following his own bent. Carol herself was full of contradictions. While reiterating her aim to be "inconspicuously badly dressed," she insisted that her niece should take more interest in her clothes and was always going with her to buy dresses. Peggy later recalled a shopping trip with Carol.

Immediately she heard I was engaged . . . she wanted to buy my wedding dress. She bought three. While we were shopping, she decided she should have something appropriate for such a special occasion. But each thing she tried on was more unbecoming than the last. The salesgirl at length brought her a creation all net and taffeta.

Carol surveyed herself in the mirror and remarked, "I look like a madam," which indeed she did. The salesgirl was highly diverted and voiced the hope that Carol would come back and that whenever she did, she must, of course, ask for her. This happened over and over — typical of the devotion of those in casual relationships to her.

❧

Carol's relationship to publications was never casual. She had been editor, first of the ACLU *Law and Freedom Bulletin* in the twenties, then of the *IJA Bulletin* in the thirties. The *IJA Bulletin* had given her space to record all the significant cases that would never be reported in the traditional law reports, and had provided a forum for discussion of her ideas about immigration, constitutional, and labor law. It had also provided her with a simple, reasonably respectable citation when she needed support for an innovative idea in a brief.

The *Bulletin*s had also brought her into contact with some of the brightest young law students and lawyers in New York, among whom she had made many warm friends. Ruth Roemer remembers the marvelous, sophisticated discussions of the issues involved in the cases they were writing up. "Carol led the pack. She had a mind like a razor blade." Taking a walk with Ruth in downtown New York, Carol said something about the fact that she might be looking for a job.

Roemer said, "Well, with your expertise in immigration law, all kinds of people would want you!"

"You think the government would want me?" she asked, and let out a big belly laugh.

Carol King, IJA editor, had gotten to know lawyers throughout the country by mail and by phone, although the IJA as an organization had been fading into inaction as its key members had become leaders in the National Lawyers Guild, or had moved from New York, or both. Since 1937 the New York City chapter of the Guild had undertaken many of the activities of the IJA, particularly the jobs of holding forums and working on cases of social concern.

The Guild had established the *National Lawyers Guild Quarterly* in 1937, a more traditional law review than the *IJA Bulletin,* although the

Quarterly included notes on Guild activities. By late 1942 the *Quarterly* was feeling the pinch caused by the war. The nature of the legal innovations that epitomized the New Deal had slowed down and changed character. The creative work was being done largely in the new agencies established to gear up for the anti-fascist war. In time, the excess-profits tax, war rationing, the Office of Price Administration, and the War Labor Board gobbled up the available legal talent. Lawyers embarked on an all-out war effort run from Washington on government time, with no access to monthly fat-chewing sessions at Carol King's. Another thousand Guild lawyers were serving in the armed forces, and a few had been lost during the Nazi/Soviet pact.

The Guild editors proposed to combine the two publications, to change the name to *Lawyers Guild Review* and publish six times a year, to introduce the popular "Recent Items" section Carol had long prepared for the *IJA Bulletin,* and to welcome the whole IJA board onto its board.

Carol, Nuddy, and the other IJA members remaining in New York saw this invitation as a way out of their own difficulty. In the December 1942 issue, they announced the end of the *IJA Bulletin,* "[n]ot because of financial reasons and not because of diminution of reader interest," they were quick to explain, but due to staffing losses and the opportunity to join forces with the Guild, which should "greatly widen the area of our influence."

"What of the *IJA Bulletin?*" they asked. "Its work will go on. We pray it will go on to greater glory."

Such immodesty was not unbecoming under the circumstances. The IJAers had worked until many of their great cases ended in victory: *Scottsboro* (twice); *Herndon, Bridges* (once); *Strecker, DeJonge,* and *Leader v. Apex Hosiery, NLRB v. Jones & Laughlin Steel Corp., Senn v. Tile Layers Protective Union;* and *Hague v. CIO* — all found in law school casebooks decades later. Tom Mooney and Warren Billings had been released from prison. So had Georgi Dimitroff. The IJA had supported many great new acts of Congress: Social Security, Wagner Labor Relations Act, Norris-LaGuardia Anti-Injunction Act, Tennessee Valley Authority, Fair Labor Standards Act. They had supported the new administrative agency to enforce fair employment practices for Negroes, and had applauded when Chicago Negro Guild member Earl Dickerson had been appointed to head the agency. They had argued persuasively that these acts must be upheld in the courts for the system to endure. Causes they could not win they had at least recorded, from silicosis to group health plans, from runaway shops to the Puerto Rican independence movement.

The editors were endlessly intrigued with the possibility that the ideas in their articles would become history by being incorporated in an important bill, administrative regulation, or Supreme Court opinion. Although the *Bulletin* had been as much like a traditional law review as the Wobblies had been like a traditional labor union, the *Bulletin* had occasionally achieved respectability by being cited in opinions and other reviews. Many lawyers and judges had cribbed from it without attribution.

The ten-year file of *Bulletin*s reported no neat epochs in fact, only in scholarly overview, and a few clear-cut people's victories. And yet changes had occurred, if not in the basic struggle for human rights versus the property rights of Big Business, then in the legality of certain forms of struggle. Congress had finally declared that it was legal to join a labor union and strike for certain rights. The President had finally issued Executive Order 8802 forbidding racial discrimination in defense industries. The Court had finally declared that peaceful picketing is a form of free speech protected by the Constitution, and that Congress has the power to pass social legislation that has a "rational basis." The Court had declared that the police could not arrest someone for legal speech and advocacy at public meetings called by the Communist Party, and the states had begun repealing criminal syndicalism laws. The Court had declared that a poor person has a right to an attorney in a capital case, and the right to a jury from which Blacks have not been deliberately excluded. The Court had suggested that it would protect "discrete and insular minorities" from congressional attack. But FDR had forestalled any constitutional amendments setting forth economic rights by getting Congress to pass statutes, like the Social Security Act, that sounded as if they could never be repealed without Congress actually proposing that they become constitutional amendments.

In a sense, the IJAers had been so successful that they had made themselves dispensable. Their coverage of labor cases and labor legislation in the *Bulletin,* unique in 1932, had been taken up by the traditional law reviews; commercial law publishing companies now sold looseleaf reporter services in this area of law, as they long had done in areas of commercial law, although the new editorial "we" did not demand a patriotic tax on excess profits, an end to racial discrimination in industry and the armed forces, or even a war against fascists at home, as the IJAers had done.

As the editors moved from their *Bulletin* to the Guild *Review*, they realized an era was ending in each of their lives. There would be no more monthly editorial board meetings at Carol's apartment. The Guild was a much larger organization, with many more talkers who would not come through on paper. And some political lines had been drawn that would not survive the organizational shift. Carol, too, moved from her monthly hassle with IJA "Recent Items" to the more leisurely quarterly *Review*.

⅋

In 1942 INS commissioner Earl Harrison took the lead in pressing for legislative reforms of immigration law. He even challenged the existing racial barriers to immigration and naturalization, saying, "The only other country in the world that observes such racial discrimination in matters relating to naturalization is Nazi Germany, and all will agree that this is not very desirable company." In March 1942 INS provisions went into effect for the naturalization of any person who had served three months or more in the U.S. armed forces.

The War Convention of the National Lawyers Guild in Chicago, held on Presidents' weekend in February 1943, was greeted by Mayor Edward J. Kelly; Fowler Harper, who had become deputy chairman of the War Manpower Commission; the general counsels of the Federal Security Agency and Office of Price Administration; as well as by federal judge William H. Holly and a U.S. Army lieutenant colonel. The Guild had just issued a pamphlet on inflation as the main domestic problem and supported the President as Commander-in-Chief "and for his policy of the firmest coalition of the United Nations for an offensive prosecution of the war." The Guild said that "the greatest contribution towards the development of uninterrupted and maximum production was labor's waiver, for the duration, of the strike" and supported regional NLRBs to speed the processing of grievances.

The U.S. government did not speak with one voice, even during the war against fascism. The Federal Communications Commission refused to dismiss three employees: William F. Dodd, Robert Morss Lovett, and Goodwin Watson as directed by the repressive Kerr Committee, but ultimately FDR signed the budget from which their names had been deleted, an act declared unconstitutional by the Supreme Court as a bill of attainder.

And in New York, on December 19, 1943, Dr. Morris U. Schappes of City College of New York surrendered himself at Sing Sing prison to start serving more than thirteen months in jail for refusing to be an informer in 1941 before the Rapp-Coudert Committee investigating "Communists in higher education." Carol King had been one of the lawyers who had counseled him and other professors during that witch-hunt leading to Schappes's conviction for perjury.

During 1943 and 1944 and after the official ending of the Communist International, the FBI was hot on the trail of one Carol Weiss King, trying to discover her relationship to a Soviet spy murder plot in Europe in which the Russian secret police were allegedly involved. The FBI file on King contains forty pages on this matter. The material that has not been blacked out indicates that the FBI obtained information from two books on Soviet espionage, *New York Times* news stories, interviews with the murdered man's widow, and the widow's attorney. The file does not explain why this issue had ever been important or why it was important at this juncture, but King had defeated Hoover in public in the first *Bridges* case and was putting up a strong challenge to basic FBI ideology in *Schneiderman*.

The spy story that emerges concerns a European who was allegedly a Soviet military intelligence operative in Western Europe. Born Ignacy Poretsky in Polish Galicia, he had allegedly become a high officer in the NKVD operating in Switzerland. He set up a network allegedly including an American, Noel Field. (Field moved to Hungary in the late 1940s at the time his friend Alger Hiss came under attack.) Using the name Ignace Reiss, Poretsky married, had a son, and assumed several aliases. In December 1936, he obtained Austrian passports. In March 1937 a literary friend of his in New York went to see Mrs. King. (This woman, Hedda Massing, had been the first wife of a German Communist named Gerhart Eisler, and she had remarried and found new politics.) She brought $7,000 to Mrs. King and asked her to write an exchange check in that amount to open an account at the Manufacturers Trust Company in the name of Stefan Brandt of Paris, which King did.

In July 1937 Reiss/Brandt allegedly sent a blistering letter to Stalin opposing attacks on the POUM, a Trotskyist Marxist party, and then went underground. On September 4, 1937, two men and a woman whom he had known took him for a ride in Lausanne, Switzerland, and killed

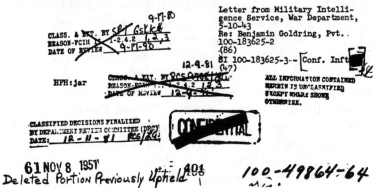

A MID Report, dated April 30, 1943 was forwarded to the Bureau by the War Department, Military Intelligence Service on May 10, 1943. This report reflected that an examination of the April 16, 1940 issue of the "Daily Worker" revealed that the appeal of the Browder case was handled by the Defense Committee for Civil Rights for Communists. Oral arguments in the Circuit Court were presented by Attorney Walter H. Pollak. Cooperating with him were Carol Weiss King and Benjamin Goldring.

It was noted that James P. Gifford, assistant to the Dean of Columbia Law School, Columbia University, advised on April 1, 1943 that Goldring was formerly "connected in law with Carol King."

On April 1, 1943, Elliott Evans Cheatham, professor of law at Columbia Law School, Columbia University, stated that Goldring allegedly was "connected in law work with Carol King, a female Communist attorney" for Earl Browder and associated in some respect with the American Civil Liberties Union.

G-2 files contained an F. B. I. report dated January 7, 1943, on Mrs. Carol Weiss King. Goldring was allegedly reported to have been "connected in law work" with Carol King, who, according to the F. B. I report, had been "active in the defense of Harry Bridges and well-known radicals. Confidential informants reported her as a Communist".

Letter from Military Intelligence Service, War Department, 5-10-43
Re: Benjamin Goldring, Pvt.. 100-183625-2 (86)
BI 100-183625-3-- [Conf. Inft
(47)

ALL INFORMATION CONTAINED HEREIN IS UNCLASSIFIED EXCEPT WHERE SHOWN OTHERWISE.

61 NOV 8 1951 Deleted Portion Previously Upheld

100-49864-64

FBI File: Carol King (5-10-43). A Columbia Law School assistant dean and professor advised Military Intelligence that a Columbia graduate had worked with other lawyers on the case of a Communist Party leader in the Supreme Court.

him. The murderers were found; one confessed that she was a member of a secret organization. Leon Trotsky, from his refuge in Mexico City, warned that the man's widow might also be attacked for her knowledge of details related to the Moscow treason trials.

Four years later, early in 1941, a woman and her son left Lisbon for New York. After arrival, she filed a declaration of intention to become a

U.S. citizen using the last name Brandt. Two months later she filed a petition to become administratrix of the estate of Stefan Brandt, which consisted of one asset — the $7,000 deposited in Manufacturers Trust Company by Carol King. In February 1942 the money was distributed to her as Brandt's widow, and to their son. When asked, Mrs. Brandt said she did not know attorney Carol King.

This is the end of the story, according to the partially declassified FBI files.

I heard of Carol King about this time, and benefitted from the fact that she was answering her mail even more promptly than usual. I was in my junior year at college when my mother sent me a clipping about the *Schneiderman* case that mentioned his lawyers, Wendell Willkie and Carol King. I decided to ask Mrs. King her opinion about my becoming a labor lawyer, but I also wanted to check out my impression that the law was a dirty business, a feeling that arose while I was working half-time as secretary to a traditional Ann Arbor attorney during my freshman year. She answered in an unforgettable style:

```
Dear Miss Fagan:
    It is difficult for me to answer your letter . . .
because, although you tell me some things about
yourself, the individual situation makes much more
difference than the general pattern.
    I am sure that if you are going to be very
fastidious, you had better stop thinking about
being a lawyer. It is not a ladylike occupation
either for men or women. It is hard for anyone to
make a living at the law — and even more difficult
for a woman. I had an easy time making out because
I had enough money to carry me over, so I could do
pretty much what I pleased, but if you are going to
make a living practicing law, it is going to be
dirty, and you can make up your mind to it.
    I can't quite figure out why that is so dreadful
as you seem to think it is. When a picket knocks
out a scab on a picket line, it isn't so pretty
either; sometimes it is effective, sometimes it
isn't.
    To sum up, if you want to practice law, go ahead
and practice law, but if you are going to be
```

> *fastidious, you had better get a job teaching*
> *economics in some workers' school and starve to*
> *death.*

I loved her straightforward answer, her easy reference to the scabs and picket lines on which I had been raised, and I accepted her puncturing of my "fastidiousness."

Carol dictated letters like this to Shirley Lerman, who paints the picture she saw as a legal stenographer in the office Carol shared with two lawyers. According to Lerman, working for Carol "was different in almost every way from working in any other law office. Her clients varied from the poor unknown immigrants with naturalization and immigration problems, to people like Harry Bridges, Earl Browder, and William Schneiderman. All were treated with concern, warmth, and some degree of informality."

Carol was certainly not the typical boss. Ms. Lerman said she didn't believe she ever called her Mrs. King. "Unless she was actually in court, we had tea in her office every afternoon. Even the physical outlay of her office was informal — a huge Mexican rug on one wall; a comfortable couch with a long coffee table in front of it; an electric percolator; milk outside on the ledge during the colder months. When Carol walked to the Fulton Fish Market at lunchtime, we always had something different at teatime — I remember learning to eat raw mushrooms sitting on her couch!"

Attorney Carol King, from the beginning of her career, had made strong relationships with the women who worked as her secretaries, as well as with the men who worked, in fact if not in title or pay, as her law clerks and juniors. In her era, legal secretaries made or broke a law firm by their degree of attention to detail: knowing dates of court appearances, when briefs were due, whether the account was overdrawn, and what large fees were unpaid. These women who ran the offices determined the degree to which clients felt comfortable waiting for their lawyers, who were often held up in court or even went out of town unexpectedly and missed appointments. Years later, these secretaries continued to tell stories about King's unique warmth and style.

As the war progressed, the American Committee got busy correcting one of its worst errors. On February 13, 1943, it sponsored a forum in New York on "Japanese-Americans in the Victory Program," at which Louis Goldblatt of the ILWU was the key speaker. The FBI made an extensive report on his speech, in which he maintained that the Japanese had two great propaganda weapons to use against the United States: "we do not permit Asiatics to become American citizens," and we discriminate against American citizens by birth, "evacuating them to relocation centers, without even a trial." The FBI reported that King stated that she was in complete agreement with Goldblatt, "and stated that an amendment of the naturalization laws permitting the granting of American citizenship to Asiatics was to be brought up, presumably through her efforts in the next few days."

Carol had time for writing and legislative work early in 1943 because everything was quite peaceful in her office — except, of course, for the *Bridges* case, which was proving to be an exception to every rule. But the review of the deportation order in the district court would be handled entirely by the West Coast lawyers, so it would not concern her unduly.

Not having to appear in district court turned out to be fortunate for Carol's equanimity because she would have been faced with her own past — the losing cases of Nelles, Shorr, King, and Pollak in the wake of the Palmer Raids. On February 8, 1943, federal district court judge Martin Welsh followed these precedents not with a bang, but a whimper: ". . . better administrative practice might dictate a policy of disclosure of prior statements by witnesses. But I cannot say that the Government's refusal to disclose such prior statements rendered the hearing so essentially unfair as to result in a want of due process," citing *Mensevich* (1924). "I cannot say, as a matter of law, that the testimony of Harry Lundeberg is so unsubstantial as to lend no support to a finding based thereon of past Communist Party membership and affiliation by petitioner." With the help of *Vajtauer* (1927), and a triple negative, the judge found some evidence to sustain the deportation order against Bridges.

Carol found the opinion "really charming" and predicted "that some day we will win the Bridges case, and when we do, the chief credit will go to Martin I. Welsh, J." She asked co-counsel for 100 or 150 copies of the opinion because "I'll go nuts if everybody in the City of New York and environs lives over in the office trying to read it. Remember, I have moved into smaller quarters."

In a footnote to her letter she asked a narrow, procedural question of her highly political co-counsel: "Had you ever thought of the answer to this question: If the Court should not interfere with the determination of the administrative tribunal, can it properly sustain a warrant of deportation on evidence which does not constitute the same evidence on which the administrative tribunal acted?" She spelled out what she meant: "Being translated, can the Court sustain Biddle, who acted on the testimony of a half-dozen witnesses, and especially O'Neil, by saying that Lundeberg alone proved the case[?]" (This narrow issue became the precise point on which the Supreme Court ultimately based its decision in the case.)

Carol's co-counsel were concerned with a different kind of narrow, procedural problem: how to get paid by their client. They had been charging $25 per day and had been paid $42,000 since the first case began in 1939. Of this, Aubrey Grossman assumed each lawyer had actually received about $15/day, the rest going to the office. He wrote: "If we don't get paid now or very soon there is a grave chance that we will never get our money. Should the unlikely occur by victory in the Circuit Court, it might be difficult for the Defense Committee to raise funds merely for the purpose of liquidating the Committee's debts."

While awaiting the next steps in *Bridges* and *Schneiderman,* Carol spent some time with her son, and some in the galleries immersed in modern painting, and some in the studio of artist Ellis Wilson, whose work she liked and purchased early. She also found time to spend with her niece Peggy Stern, who recalls:

> There was always the haven of Carol, her half-humorous wisdom, her enjoyment of herself and of you, her complete indulgence except of self-indulgence. Her sudden anger with injustice. And all the realms of her political and social convictions where she was so much more emotional than in the matters of a more personal nature.
>
> Except where Gordon was concerned. Once we had a picture of him displayed in our house on an occasion when she came to supper. She removed it and stuck it into a drawer. Now I was in college, which was roughly 15 years after his death. Carol asked suddenly if I would like to go up to the studio and help her arrange his books. She had not been able to look at them in all that time!

Over the years, Carol would occasionally comment during a conversation that "Gordon would say" such-and-such, but she never talked directly to her niece about her relationship with her husband. He had been shrouded in the past.

Now Jay Leyda stepped back into her life. On his return to New York in 1936, he had become assistant curator of the new film department at the Museum of Modern Art and editor, with Lee Strasberg and Lincoln Kirstein, of its journal, *Films*. He kept trying to "conjoin . . . the scholarly vocation with an active involvement in history," according to his peers in art and film history (who honored him in 1979 with a special issue of *October* magazine). In 1942 he and his wife moved to Hollywood where he worked as a technical advisor for Warner Brothers and MGM on *Mission to Moscow, Song of Russia*, and *The Bridge of San Luis Rey*. He was inducted into the army in 1943, became ill during basic training, and was honorably discharged. Back in Hollywood, his wife, Si-Lan, could continue to find paying work as a choreographer. Due to his Left politics, he could only find nonpaying work teaching East Coast emigrées like John Garfield at the Actor's Lab. Down on his uppers, he stayed at Carol's apartment on his way to Boston to do further research on his new interest, Herman Melville. He had learned to be frustrated but not defeated, as Carol had hoped. When he moved without sending his forwarding address to Sergei Eisenstein, the Soviet film master called a Boston radio station to find Leyda. They spoke by transcontinental telephone about the release in this country of Eisenstein's *Ivan the Terrible*, but Leyda couldn't bear to tell his mentor that film work was impossible for Leyda due to rising anti-Soviet sentiment.

Once again Carol saw a friend through a crisis and then let go when he was back in shape to face the world, as she, like Leyda, tried to conjoin scholarly legal work with the active practice of social-change law.

Some women in King's era suffered so deeply from discrimination in their lives and in their work that they became hostile to men. Carol King never went this route. She had had a great romance with Gordon. She had borne and raised a son. At the same time, she never seems to have flirted with the male lawyers with whom she worked, never dressed for or played up to them as men. Some of the men expected this kind of attention from the other women in their lives — mothers, sisters, wives, girlfriends, secretaries, female clients. This aspect of Carol's style may have led Abe Isserman to describe her almost as if she were disfigured, rather than as she appeared to me: plump and usually careless about her personal appearance.

But not when this stance might affect her legal appearances. For each big case Carol King, Esquire, bought a new black dress to wear to the Supreme Court.

Carol King went down to Washington to hear Wendell Willkie argue *Schneiderman* for the second time in March 1943. It was old-issues week for Carol. The day before, the Court had heard argument on another effort by Jehovah's Witnesses to win the right not to salute the flag in school, the issue she and Abe Isserman had lost in 1937.

Willkie's second brief for *Schneiderman* was forthright and legalistic. One of his arguments was that the belief in or advocacy of changes in the Constitution, even those involving fundamental social and economic changes, does not preclude a citizen or an applicant for citizenship from truthfully taking an oath to support the Constitution if one follows the method of amendment prescribed in the Constitution. To support this proposition, Willkie cited the *National Prohibition Cases,* which many observers thought was a nice touch. His reargument before the Justices was more legalistic than the first argument had been. But it was still impossible to gauge who would win.

Within a week, Carol was back in New York appearing before the Second Service Command of the U.S. Armed Forces, which was considering excluding her client, Shuji Fujii, from the Eastern Military Area. The FBI reported on the hearing of Fujii, the former editor of *Doho,* "a pro-Communist newspaper in Los Angeles, and an alleged Communist Party member in 1938," before the Exclusion Hearing Board comprised of military officers. The report said that his "advisor" was "Carol King, a prominent attorney for Communists in the New York area," who made a very personal argument, stating that she had known her client nearly a year and "felt that he was a most loyal American citizen." In December 1943 she won this case.

After the hearing, Jonathan said he wanted to discuss with her a poem he had been writing. To friends who were also striving to work out their relationships with their teenage offspring, Carol wrote, "I was quite pleased to be cooperating instead of fighting his views." In this period, Carol's line to her son was that there were terrible "injustices occurring in this country" but "that we have to beat Hitler first of all, and that the fight for democracy and freedom must go on at home as well as abroad."

In early 1943 the U.S. government suddenly indicted and arrested Michigan state senator Stanley Nowak, a leader in the American Committee for Protection of Foreign Born and in the Polish community in

Detroit. He was charged with perjury for swearing falsely on his application for citizenship that he believed in organized government when he did not so believe because he was a member of the Communist Party. The National Lawyers Guild and many other organizations raised a ruckus; the charge was withdrawn but filed away; the Attorney General publicly acknowledged his error, and the Guild complained that "time and efforts had been expended which might otherwise have been more usefully utilized in direct war activity."

King and Willkie may have seen this public outcry as a good omen for the forthcoming decision in the *Schneiderman* case.

26.
Winning in the Highest Court

Near the end of the Supreme Court term, Justice Robert Jackson announced the decision of the Supreme Court in the Jehovah's Witnesses' case, *West Virginia State Board of Education v. Barnette*. By a vote of 6 to 3, with the help of some changes on the bench, the Justices reversed their pre-war decision and held that Witnesses *could* exercise their religion by not saluting the flag in public schools. In the midst of the world war against fascism, Jackson wrote a memorable passage on the scope of civil liberties:

> If there is any fixed star in our constitutional constellation, it is that no official, high or petty, can prescribe what shall be orthodox in politics, nationalism, religion, or other matters of opinion or force citizens to confess by word or act their faith therein. If there are any circumstances which permit an exception, they do not now occur to us.

Abe Fortas and Zechariah Chafee had signed the amicus brief supporting this position filed by the ABA Committee on the Bill of Rights, as Osmond K. Fraenkel had signed for the ACLU. This was a personal victory for King and Isserman because of their pioneering work in *Hering*. The next week, on June 21, 1943, Justice Frank Murphy announced the Court's decision in *Schneiderman*. By a 5 to 3 majority, the Court reversed the lower courts and decided that Schneiderman's citizenship could not be canceled. They held that the issue of Schneiderman's 'attachment to the Constitution' in 1927, and his behavior for five years before 1927, could not be tried anew (de novo) twelve years after he had been naturalized. The government could have presented witnesses against Schneiderman in 1927, asked questions, and appealed his naturalization if it had not liked the judgment. The government had not done so. Therefore, the decision to naturalize Schneiderman could only be set aside now if Schneiderman had concealed facts in 1927. There was no evidence he had done so. Guilt must be personal; it cannot be shown by mere association, and the evidence must be clear, unequivocal, and convincing because taking away U.S. citizenship "is more serious than a taking of one's property, or the imposition of a fine." The government had not carried that burden successfully.

Did the Communist Party in 1927 advocate the violent overthrow of the government? The Justices found it unnecessary to rule on that question, but Justice Murphy did discuss it for sixteen pages in the majority opinion. He commented, "With commendable candor the Government admits the presence of sharply conflicting views on the issue of force and violence as a Party principle, . . ." Schneiderman had "testified that he believed in the nationalization of the means of production and exchange with compensation, and the preservation and utilization of our 'democratic structure . . . as far as possible for the advantage of the working classes.' He stated that the 'dictatorship of the proletariat' to him meant ' . . . a state of things' in which 'the majority of the people shall really direct their own destinies and use the instrument of the state for these truly democratic ends.' " Justice Murphy found, for the Court, that "none of this is necessarily incompatible with the 'general political philosophy' of the Constitution. . . ." He said, "Lenin . . . wrote that depriving the 'class enemies' of their political rights 'was not necessary to realize the dictatorship of the proletariat.' "

Murphy wrote as a man who had debated Marxists (including my father) at the University of Michigan before World War I around the Inter-Collegiate Socialist Society, who had negotiated with Communists as mayor of Detroit during the hunger marches of the Great Depression and as governor of Michigan during the sit-down strikes in Flint. He wrote as a Catholic who knew the roots of what has come to be known as liberation theology.

The CP platform of 1928 advocated the abolition of the U.S. Senate and the Supreme Court and of veto power by the President, and replacing them with 'councils of workers' with legislative and executive power. Murphy held that "these would indeed be significant changes in our present governmental structure — . . . but . . . as judges we cannot say that a person who advocates their adoption through peaceful and constitutional means is not in fact attached to the Constitution." Murphy accepted the legality of Schneiderman's "possible belief in the creation of some form of world union of soviet republics" as he accepted "those who believe in Pan-Americanism, the League of Nations, Union Now, or some other form of international collaboration or collective security which may grow out of the present holocaust."

Four of the Justices signed on to Murphy's broad opinion rather than Rutledge's much narrower one. Murphy's majority opinion provided the first lengthy analysis in any Supreme Court opinion of the nature of Marxist theory and the Communist Party's attachment to it, based on quotations from the documents themselves presented in historic context.

Justice Rutledge, in a concurring opinion, summed up neatly and narrowly:

> If, seventeen years after a federal court adjudged him entitled to be a citizen, that judgment can be nullified and he can be stripped of this most precious right, by nothing more than reexamination upon the merits of the very facts the judgment established, no naturalized person's citizenship is or can be secure. . . . It may be doubted that the framers of the Constitution intended to create two classes of citizens, one free and independent, one haltered with a lifetime string tied to its status.

Chief Justice Stone wrote a long dissenting opinion supporting denaturalization because "the evidence shows and it is not denied that the Communist Party . . . at the time . . . was a revolutionary party having as its ultimate aim . . . in . . . the United States, the overthrow of capitalistic government, and the substitution . . . of the dictatorship of the proletariat. It sought to accomplish this through persistent indoctrination by . . . systematic teaching of Party principles, . . . and by the publication and distribution of Communist literature." Justice Roberts joined this dissent, as did Justice Frankfurter.

Justice Jackson, who had disqualified himself because he had been Attorney General when the case began, summed up the Court's holding in *Schneiderman* later (in the *Dennis* case):

> Schneiderman . . . overruled earlier holdings that the courts could take judicial notice that the Communist Party does advocate violent overthrow of the Government by force and violence. This Court reviewed much of the basic Communist literature that is before us now, and held that it was within "the area of allowable thought," . . . and that success of the Communist Party would not necessarily mean the end of representative government. The Court declared further that "A tenable conclusion from the foregoing is that the Party in 1927 desired to achieve its purpose by peaceful and democratic means," . . . Moreover, the Court considered that this "mere doctrinal justification or prediction of the use of force under

hypothetical conditions at some indefinite future time — prediction that is not calculated or intended to be presently acted upon" was within the realm of free speech.

In other words, Marxism does not equal conspiracy to overthrow the government by force and violence. Active membership in the Communist Party is protected by the Constitution. (Jackson added in 1951 that, in his opinion, Chief Justice Stone "challenged these naive conclusions" in his dissent in *Schneiderman*.)

The same day, the Justices unanimously upheld the curfew order against Japanese Americans on the West Coast in *Hirabayashi v. United States*. The *Lawyers Guild Review* commented that all the opinions in the case "recognized the danger . . . to civil rights, but condoned it in view of the necessities of the military situation." The decision in *Schneiderman*, then, was no harbinger of broad democratic rights even during the war against fascism.

Still, they all felt it was a great victory. Wendell visited Carol's office to celebrate. She introduced him to the other lawyers in the suite; then, as they sat around her large coffee table, she pulled out a bottle of champagne, which they drank out of paper cups. (One of her associates, far to the left of Willkie politically, couldn't get over his reaction to Willkie: "It seems strange for me to feel so deep an admiration for the titular head of the Republican Party.")

Wendell declared, "I have always felt confident as to how the Supreme Court would decide a case involving such fundamental rights. My bafflement has been as to why the administration started and prosecuted a case in which, if they had prevailed, a thoroughly illiberal precedent would have been established." What did Carol think?

Carol's answer is not recorded, but later she wrote, "to the man in the street — and to the future of our democracy" the significance of Murphy's opinion "is crystallized in one sentence of the Court's opinion: 'The constitutional fathers, fresh from a revolution, did not forge a political strait-jacket for the generations to come.' " This was her introduction to the American Committee's pamphlet containing the text of the decision, printed in 20,000 copies.

Within a month of the Supreme Court's decision in *Schneiderman*, Attorney General Biddle took a major step to enforce it by abolishing the government's secret custodial detention list.

There is no statutory authorization or other present justification for keeping a "custodial detention" list of citizens. The Department fulfills its proper functions by investigating the activities of persons who may have violated the law. It is not aided in this work by classifying persons as to dangerousness. . . . [I]t is now clear to me that this classification system is inherently unreliable. The evidence used [to make] the classifications was inadequate; the standards applied . . . were defective; and finally, the notion that it is possible to make a valid determination as to how dangerous a person is in the abstract and without reference to time, environment, and other relevant circumstances, is impractical, unwise, and dangerous.

Carol obviously did not know she had been on the custodial detention list. She did know that the spirit of the *Schneiderman* decision affected the media. The *New York Herald Tribune* published a comment about the decision by Earl Browder. After his (quiet) release from prison by President Roosevelt, Browder had convinced his comrades to change the name and policies of the Communist Party. As head of the nonrevolutionary U.S. Communist Political Association, Browder called the Schneiderman decision a "body-blow against the 'bogy of Communism,' in the same line as the dissolution of the Communist International . . . [was] in its international aspects." The *New Yorker* published articles critical of the FBI during the summer, which led to lengthy correspondence between the FBI and editor Harold Ross concerning allegations that an FBI man called to inquire about playwright Robert Sherwood.

The *Nation* published "Washington Gestapo," an attack on the practices of the FBI and the Civil Service Commission in handling complaints of "disloyalty" by "XXX, a minor Government executive." Charles Malcomson, the director of public relations in the Department of Justice, answered with an eight-page letter to the *Nation,* characterizing himself as "a one-time contributor." Malcolmson quoted Attorney General Biddle's testimony in the House Appropriations Hearings on the 1944 budget that he did "not know . . . what 'subversive' is. . . . I do not think anyone knows definitely. I think you meant the Communist Party and . . . the Bund. But . . . I have had only a terrible headache in enforcing the 1941 Congressional authorization for investigating federal employees."

Then the FBI learned that someone had asked Carol King to prepare a brief to demolish each of the points made by Malcolmson. The FBI began preparing a sixty-eight-page "Memorandum Re: Carol King Material" (undated) alleging that her brief was the basis for a fourth article in the *Nation* by I. F. Stone. The FBI obtained a copy of King's twenty-

> It is to be noted that on October 16, 1943, the New York
> Office submitted to the Bureau a 22-page brief obtained from an
> extremely confidential source. According to the information received
> by the New York Office the brief was prepared by Carol King. From the
> content of the 22-page brief it would appear that it was used to some
> extent by I. F. Stone, Washington correspondent of "The Nation" in
> his article dated September 25, 1943, entitled "XXX and the FBI."
> The true name of I. F. Stone is Isidore Feinstein. The July 17
> and July 24, 1943 issues of "The Nation" contained articles
> entitled "Washington Gestapo" which were very critical of the
> FBI and the Civil Service Commission primarily with regard to
> the investigation of Government employees. The articles were
> purportedly written by a minor Government executive who was
> referred to as "XXX." In addition to these two articles there was
> a third article on July 21, 1943, written by Freda Kirchwey, Editor
> of "The Nation" and entitled "End the Inquisition!." This article
> defended the two previous ones signed "XXX" and reaffirmed some of
> the allegations contained therein.
>
> The September 25, 1943 issue of "The Nation" contained
> an article entitled "XXX and the FBI," by I. F. Stone, the
> Washington correspondent of the magazine. A headnote of this
> particular article alleged that the articles submitted by
> "XXX" were anonymous by necessity and that since Stone vouched
> for the author he was asked to do a "round-up" reply. Stone,
> it will be recalled, has been particularly critical of the
> FBI in the past. During 1935, he applied for a position in the
> Bureau and was not accepted since he was not qualified. This
> individual was at one time rebuked by the Secretary of State
> at one of the State Department press conferences because of his
> failure to keep a confidence.

FBI File: Carol King (11-29-40). FBI reports on a brief by Carol King used by "Isidore Feinstein," who wrote under the name I. F. Stone, about FBI investigations of government employees. Ann Marie Buitrago, expert on FBI reports received under the Freedom of Information Act, says that "extremely confidential source" means "black bag," i.e., stealing and making a copy of the document.

two-page brief "from an extremely confidential source." (Experts on FBI terminology and practices say this means a copy was stolen by the FBI.) The FBI memo contains extensive verbatim quotes from King's brief and the text of numerous letters to and from King on the FBI, which indicate that King was treating this brief like any major brief in a case she was handling.

King attacked the practice instituted in 1941 of FBI investigations of "suspected" government employees, quoting Attorney General (now Justice) Jackson as stating that "the use of particular or selected reports might constitute the grossest injustice, and we all know that a correction never catches up with an accusation." He mentioned "the statements of malicious or misinformed people."

To counter this attack, the FBI memo quoted a "typical letter" to a government agency:

AS YOU ARE AWARE, THE FEDERAL BUREAU OF INVESTIGA-
TION HAS BEEN SPECIFICALLY INSTRUCTED BY CONGRESS
TO INVESTIGATE ANY GOVERNMENT EMPLOYEE WHO IS THE
SUBJECT OF A COMPLAINT COMING WITHIN THE PURVIEW OF
PUBLIC LAW NO. 135, 77TH CONGRESS, AND TO MAKE A
COMPLETE REPORT OF ITS FINDINGS TO CONGRESS.
    IN COMPLIANCE WITH THIS DIRECTIVE AN INVESTIGA-
TION HAS BEEN CONDUCTED CONCERNING [S. F.] AND I AM
TRANSMITTING HEREWITH ONE COPY OF THE FOLLOWING IN-
VESTIGATIVE REPORTS REFLECTING THE RESULTS OF THIS
INQUIRY: . . . INASMUCH AS OUR FINAL REPORT TO CON-
GRESS MUST BE COMPLETE IN EVERY RESPECT I WOULD AP-
PRECIATE RECEIVING YOUR OFFICIAL COMMENT AS TO THE
ULTIMATE DISPOSITION OF THIS CASE EITHER BY EXONERA-
TION, DISMISSAL OR OTHER ADMINISTRATIVE ACTION.

The Bureau maintained that this kind of letter would have no adverse effect on the constitutional rights of the employee. Carol King's brief ridiculed this stance. She maintained that a letter from the FBI had the following effect:

Here is a report on a rascal who is working for you. We can't fire him, that's your job — you do your own dirty work. But — if you don't fire him pronto — we'll tell Congress on you when we file our annual report and then you'll have to have a pretty good alibi to tell [congressmen and senators] Dies, Cox, Hobbs, Rankin, Smith, and their colleagues. You'd better get rid of Jones quietly or face the consequences.

King asked:

Would you fire Jones under these circumstances, with this big stick held over your unsteady head? It is not surprising that many government executives have yielded, and are still yielding, to the FBI's pressure to take the easy, Congress-appeasing, FBI-appeasing step. Hoover wins, Dies wins, the public service loses many a Jones.

Carol King also took the opportunity to attack a longstanding nemesis of her clients, Mrs. Shipley, "who presides over the Passport Division" of the State Department. The FBI quoted the King brief as stating, "although

FBI reports are said to be kept under lock and key they have a surprising currency in Washington"; snippets "keep turning up in speeches of anti-labor and anti-administration Congressmen" and in the *Washington Times-Herald*. They "find their way into the hands of A. A. Berle" in the State Department and reach Ruth Bielaski Shipley, "a sister of two former FBI men . . . who turned labor spies and wiretappers according to the Senate investigation of wiretapping against political figures in . . . Rhode Island."

⁂

Within a few months, the decision in *Schneiderman* led to interesting comments in other cases. In a denaturalization case against a German-American, Paul Bante, New York federal judge Knox declared in late February that the present defendant was motivated by a desire to "serve the ends of Germany," whereas Schneiderman was "law-abiding, reserved and philosophic in nature."

Harry Bridges still did not fit into the same category, and Carol wrote to San Francisco: "In re briefs amicus, I am stuck. [Zechariah] Chafee wired me 'TOO BUSY TO PLAY BRIDGE EVEN FOR MONEY,' and I became so furious that I stopped cold." The Bridges Victory Committee was having trouble raising funds to meet its obligations to lawyers.

The political climate got cooler when the House Committee on Un-American Activities issued its report citing the National Lawyers Guild as a "Communist front" on March 29, 1944, at a time when a number of Guild lawyers were holding very responsible positions in the federal government, and more than 1,000 were in the armed forces. The *Lawyers Guild Review* also noted that in 1944, one McWilliams and twenty-seven other alleged pro-Nazis were finally indicted for conspiracy to violate the sedition sections of the 1940 Smith Act after considerable pressure from the Guild and other anti-fascist organizations. But when their trial judge died after seven months of trial, the men were never retried, and their indictment was ultimately dismissed for failure to prosecute.

In the spirit of the *Schneiderman* victory, Carol wrote that she hoped "to lick the pants off" the FBI when they argued *Bridges* in the Ninth Circuit Court of Appeals in February 1944. In her first letter back from California to Clara Binswanger, who was in the hospital in New York, Carol began by discussing the political future of her most prominent political friend, Wendell Willkie. Carol heard from Bartley Crum, Willkie's California representative, that Willkie "is building up a record on issues (as see his statement on higher taxes) and not worrying about the nomination [for President in 1944]. I almost told Crum that apparently Wendell is quite unconsciously taking Earl [Browder's] advice and holding off till '48. Meanwhile he (this time I mean Wendell and not Earl) plans . . . 'an attack on the soft underbelly of the Republican Party.' "

Carol obviously relished the fact that she was on a first-name basis with the titular heads of the Republican and Communist Parties and could mention them in the same sentence. She also explained that she was "feeling very set up 'cause all my underwear is washed and blowing in the breeze. Thought of you all across the country 'cause the sleeve lining of my corduroy was out. Don't worry, I won't bring it back to you."

Carol wrote that on the appeal, Richie Gladstein would argue the evidence and she the law. "I'd rather have our side of the argument than the government's but from what they say hereabouts concerning the court I don't guess we have too good a chance. . . . Funny I'm always hopeful in the Bridges case — it's too raw for a case that's in the public eye."

But after the argument Carol sent home a brief note that contained none of this sentiment: "This is just a line to say the argument is over and I've been out to get drunk and am going to get drunker. It didn't go well. Judge Matthews took Richie for a terrible ride. The government was lousy and ought to lose but it won't. I was better than I've ever been."

Within a week, Carol had moved down to Hollywood to act as a great-aunt. She wrote home that "life is a little strange because it has become a curious combination of taking over [baby] Jon and going Hollywood." She slept with the "brat," and saw him through a nightmare one night, and in the morning had to change his dirty diapers "while he howled miserably for food. By that time I was nervous and dropped the last and only sterilized nipple on the floor. So I resterilized it in a rather superficial manner and had just gotten the kid going when your telegram arrived. . . . The kid kind of eats into my time but I like being useful even though I never cease to be amazed at my own awkwardness —"

A couple of weeks later, Carol started writing to Clara about financial and family affairs, which, as in all families, were often intertwined:

> First of all I beg to state that my stay out here
> is likely to be foreshortened by lack of funds.
> Uncle M— did die, but he cut me off without a
> penny — the only really smart and politically

> conscious thing the dope ever did. Louis writes me
> a very solemn personal letter hoping this won't
> interfere with our relationship. He quotes Uncle M
> as having delivered himself of the following:
> "Carol wouldn't even spit at me", "and I don't see
> why I should leave her son anything when I don't
> even know him." I think my independence in this
> matter and the humor of it may be worth the
> financial loss — in fact I'm sure they were.
>   But anyway L.A. has given me about all it has to
> offer, except an Hanns Eisler case. I'm hoping to
> know today just when that will happen. But I don't
> look forward to getting back home — too much to do.
> I have gotten used to basking and afternoon naps,
> etc.

As she was writing, she got news that the *Hanns Eisler* case was never coming on for hearing. He was a famous composer and refugee from Hitler Germany who had been working on Hollywood movies since his arrival in the United States, along with Bertold Brecht and other anti-fascists. "So quite suddenly, in fact in the middle of this communication, I decided to pull out and quick. I have set my heart on starting mandamus against the A.G. [Attorney General]. So I'll probably move permanently to Washington as soon as I get back to N.Y. . . . [T]he situation has outraged me speechless, if you know what I mean."

Even in the midst of the anti-fascist war, contradictions abounded. President Roosevelt sent greetings to Robert Kenny, President of the National Lawyers Guild, in March 1944, saying he was "glad to learn" that the Guild will be meeting "to lay plans for helping to initiate forms of permanent collaboration between associations of lawyers of the various members of the United Nations to work for international cooperation." Soon Kenny and Martin Popper and nineteen other Guild members were on their way to the third conference of the Inter-American Bar Association in Mexico City. And the first Chinese ever were admitted to U.S. citizenship. But FDR's chairman of the War Manpower Commission postponed indefinitely hearings on fair employment practices on the railroads. And as of August 1, Commissioner of Immigration Harrison said he was disappointed at the slow pace of congressional approval for aliens serving in the armed forces to be able to follow a simplified naturalization proceeding. As he resigned, he said, "The only other country in the world that observes racial discrimination similar to that reflected in our [naturalization] laws . . . is Nazi Germany."

ॐ

Soon after her return to New York after arguing *Bridges,* Carol's draft-age son announced his intention to follow in his mother's footsteps in one aspect of her private life. Carol, married at twenty-two during World War I, had always argued for young marriages. Now facing action in World War II, Jonathan, eighteen, announced his intention to marry Cynthia Bregman. His mother and Cynthia became good friends, and Carol found spare interludes to include Cynthia in her busy life.

ॐ

On June 26, 1944, Carol's dire prediction about the Ninth Circuit Court in *Bridges* proved correct. They voted 3 to 2 against Bridges, interpreting strictly the rule in *Vajtauer.* As a concurring judge said: "In no case have I given the evidence more careful attention than in this one. However, such attention has not left in my mind the pleasurable satisfaction that barring a very slight possibility of error, the truth has been revealed. Such satisfaction is beside the point here. The simple question this court must answer is: Is there some evidence to sustain the charges? There is." Even while sustaining Bridges's deportation, the majority of the West Coast court felt called upon to add that in his management of the 1934 strike, Bridges "was attacking most vicious and inhumane practices" and "that he was justified in accepting help from any quarter."

Two judges dissented from the decision; Judge Healy reviewed the nationwide search for witnesses by the FBI and then commented caustically on "the paucity of the evidentiary result." The O'Neil statements, crucial to the decision, were inherently infirm: "No amount of philosophizing can serve to make a silk purse out of this obvious sow's ear. Rather than deport the alien on evidence which would be condemned and proscribed without hesitation by any American court it would seem a more forthright procedure to do what was proposed in the first place, deport him by legislative resolution 'notwithstanding the provisions of any other law.' "

Carol began to think about how to win *Bridges* in the Supreme Court.

At the same time, Carol was interested in Wendell Willkie's campaign to win reform of the Republican Party. She had become very fond of Willkie personally. He was her kind of man. And it was not a little exhilarating for someone who understood power as well as she did to be so near someone who just might become President of the United States. If he couldn't win in 1944 — an unlikely moment to defeat "That Man in the White House" — then perhaps in 1948?

Later Carol wrote very frankly about her chats and correspondence with Willkie. She saw his disappointment at losing in the Wisconsin primaries to Tom Dewey. Willkie had made the issue clear — internationalism against isolationism. "After that defeat, he gave up the personal fight for the Republican nomination, but not the fight for his principles. Between 1940 and 1944 he had grown from a partisan politician to a statesman." After the convention, he invited Carol to drop in for a chat, and when Carol took him up on it, told her he was not really invited to the Republican national convention. Carol said, "Willkie was outraged at who was managing it — he outlined the tie-up" with "the McCormick interests" of the reactionary *Chicago Tribune*. "When things got too hot for Dewey as a result of his sniping" at the Dumbarton Oaks conference, which laid the basis for a United Nations organization, "he ran to Willkie for cover. The latter was amused."

Busy as she was in this period, Carol King remained easily approachable, as I learned from Private first class Louis Pollak on my first trip to New York with my new husband, Private first class Ray Ginger. Lou was the soldier-student son of Carol's friends Walter and Marion Pollak, and he was absolutely sure Carol would want to meet us and that no advance notice was necessary. This seemed a little strange to me, but Lou turned out to be quite right. Carol King, Esq., appeared to have all the time in the world to talk to Lou and to any number of his friends.

She made us feel quite at home and reminded me a little of my mother, although I was immediately aware of major differences. My mother was a schoolteacher who got married and moved to East Lansing, Michigan, in 1918 and was barred from teaching under local board of education rules against married teachers. Her only power lay in her sharp intellect and forceful tongue, plus whatever groups she and my father could organize. Carol, on the other hand, was a leading force in a going concern of constitutional lawyers who knew what they were doing and could afford to do it in style. Carol recounted conversations with people we just read about in the newspapers, and she retained and established contacts with people some of her clients called "members of the ruling class."

What amazed me was that she asked us what we were doing, and actually listened to and remembered what we said, making us seem more important by her interest in our affairs.

I remember her merry eyes in a round face, her dark-rimmed glasses and dark, tightly-curled hair. Somehow she conveyed the idea that she not only had infinite time, but space, and that of course Ray and I should always plan to stay with her whenever we visited New York thereafter. It would be no bother whatever, she assured us, because Mrs. Barkley could see to everything. We did as she suggested, without realizing how many other people had the same arrangement with her.

ᕲ

Suddenly, on October 8, 1944, Wendell Willkie died. Carol was deeply affected, as she wrote in the *New Masses:*

> Willkie dead. It is unbelievable, as if the light had suddenly gone out of the sun. His handshake was so warm, his laugh so full of fun; he had been so very much alive and loved living.
>   His death was a great personal loss to me. Even now it is hard to write of him. But I found in the few days after the public learned of his death how personal that loss was not only to me but to people who had just met him, or seen him, or even to those who only knew there was a Willkie, a great democratic American with a love for humanity and for the principles in which he believed. . . . Willkie helped unify the country, Republican and Democrat alike, behind the broad vision which made him see contending international forces as "One World."

That issue of the *New Masses* reported another international event of contending forces when Pablo Picasso joined the French Communist Party, saying "While I wait for the time when Spain can take me back again, the French Communist Party is a fatherland for me . . . [with] the great scientists Paul Langevin and Frederick Joliot-Curie, the great writers Louis Aragon and Paul Eluard, and so many of the beautiful faces of the insurgents of Paris. I am again among my brothers." The *New Masses* juxtaposed this item with the One World envisioned by Wendell Willkie.

On December 30, 1944, the War Department issued a special order granting commissions and making certain other appointments to members of the armed forces who had been Communist Party members or sympathizers to its views. The *Lawyers Guild Review* quoted the army directive: "the basic consideration is not the propriety of the individual's opinion, but his loyalty to the United States." In the subsequent special congressional investigation, Major General Clayton Dissell testified that as a practical matter, Communists were "defending this country with force and violence."

27.
Winning in the Highest Court, Doubled

The *Bridges* case forced Carol to turn her attention immediately to a very practical question: how could she convince the best possible brief writer to write the brief soon due in the Supreme Court? The person was obviously Nuddy Greene, and she convinced him. He set aside the several previous briefs and started from scratch to tell the facts and explain the law. He was a master craftsman, and in her judgment, it was the finest brief she had ever read. It stayed clearly within the bounds she had set in a memo to co-counsel: in no more than thirty to fifty pages, it should "unify the whole argument and just take the position that Bridges has been denied due process of law, with everything else subordinate to that" because the defense is "technically in much too good a position to start making a great speech about foreign policy, etc." Greene's name on the brief had the added merit of stirring memories in at least one key Justice of the acclaimed history of U.S. labor law, *The Labor Injunction*, by Professor Felix Frankfurter and student Nathan Greene, published in 1930.

Carol and Richie also wanted Greene to participate in the oral argument. Richie didn't think Lee Pressman could spend the time to become sufficiently familiar with the facts, although his position as CIO general counsel would seem to make him a natural to argue before the high court. Richie wrote to Carol that if Greene could not be convinced, Carol should share the argument with Richie because of her intimate knowledge of the case.

Carol disagreed. She also didn't think, at first, that Lee fitted the bill; he was too personally ambitious. But Nuddy declined to argue and said, "You have to give the devil his due, and Pressman is an excellent lawyer." (Greene had noticed that King never liked people she thought didn't like her, and Pressman fell into this category.) In the end it was agreed that Gladstein and Pressman should share the argument.

Counsel faced a curious problem at this juncture: their politically astute client had become terribly sensitive about the case and did not want to talk about it or to discuss the public campaign. But by January 12, 1945, Richie Gladstein wrote to Carol that Bridges "suddenly had a flash of intelligence. The realization came over him that if the Supreme Court turned down our petition, he was as good as on his way to Australia." On that great day, Elinor Kahn began "doing a dynamic job," getting publicity from Hollywood people and unions announcing that they would vote money. San Francisco Mayor Roger Lapham virtually committed himself to take a trip to Washington to tell the President "that the waterfront employers do not want Bridges deported." The defense was working on a delegation of four western senators and fourteen western congressmen to descend on FDR in a body and demand the dropping of the case. This did not happen, but the Court did decide to hear the case.

Meanwhile, Carol was receiving periodic reports that her son, Johnny, was on the verge of being shipped to a combat area. Her need to relax prompted her to follow Willkie's example; she read the six volumes of Sandburg's biography of Lincoln. She also joined the Museum of Modern Art and attended more art shows than she had in some time.

The *Bridges* case finally reached the Supreme Court on April 2–3, 1945, four years after the hearing before Judge Sears, six years after the hearing before Dean Landis, eleven years after the San Francisco general strike, and twenty-five years after Bridges landed in the United States. On one side of the argument, Charles Fahy represented the government, as he had in *Schneiderman*. On the other side, representing Bridges, were Lee Pressman, another early New Deal lawyer, Richard Gladstein, and Carol King. She carried the heavy briefcases full of law books up the many steps to the Supreme Court for the two men, but would not share in the oral argument.

For the defense, the proceedings had their amusing moments, as when Solicitor General Fahy declared that "this petitioner has had more due process of law than perhaps any one of the numerous ones who have been deported in the past, including the Chinese labor, the prostitutes and others."

> JUSTICE REED [interrupting]: I am unable to understand that. Did you mean he has had more hearings? They tried him more times?

MR. FAHY: Yes, Your Honor.

The defense also found an ambiguity in the government's case that was ominous. It emerged clearly in a colloquy:

> JUSTICE RUTLEDGE: Suppose fifty years ago X came to the United States. He then joined a party which advocated at that time the overthrow of the government by violence.
> MR. FAHY: Yes.
> JUSTICE RUTLEDGE: Three years later he renounces the party and becomes a good citizen, and remained so all the rest of his life. Now, in 1944, Congress passes a law which says because he was a member forty years ago he must be deported, notwithstanding all the balance of the time he complied with the law.
> MR. FAHY: Well, I don't know, Your Honor —.
> JUSTICE RUTLEDGE: You are not advocating that?
> MR. FAHY: I think not, in this case.

Not "in this case," said the solicitor general, formerly head of the National Labor Relations Board in the New Deal. But Carol noted that his tone and argument did not indicate that he had officially and decisively rejected such an approach for the future.

The defense attorneys placed several issues before the Court. They argued that there was no evidence to show that Bridges had been affiliated with the Communist Party. They invoked the doctrines Carol had explained to Clara during the court of appeals argument: *res judicata* and double jeopardy ("or in simple language, trying the guy twice"), and *ex post facto* (the 1940 amendment was "passed after HB was found not to be a member or affiliated"). They argued that Bridges had been denied due process of law. They urged that under the contempt of court decision in *Bridges v. California* (1941), an alien has the full protection of the First Amendment, and cannot be deported for exercising rights guaranteed to him specifically by a decision of the U.S. Supreme Court.

Nine days after the argument, President Roosevelt died suddenly. Harry Truman was instantly sworn in as Chief Executive. Carol King joined millions in the United States and around the world in wondering how Roosevelt's death would affect the outcome of the war, and the peace. Her own personal concern was for her soldier son and innumerable friends and colleagues in the armed forces.

Early in May, while she was in the Federal Building in New York finishing up a case, word broke that the war in Europe had ended. She described the scene in a letter to her brother-in-law Howard King:

> I guess everybody that knew anybody on the European
> front had the same sense of personal relief as well
> as an objective sense of being glad that the thing
> came out right. I found that the people who were
> the closest did the least merry-making on Monday.
> But it was a spectacular sight. I enjoyed it from
> the 17th floor of the Federal Court Building. The
> snowstorm of paper was quite a sight. And I enjoyed
> it particularly as it just served as a background
> for a victory in a naturalization case which had no
> great importance but which was very close to my
> heart.

She wrote that she kept "trying to convince myself that an early end of the war with Japan is not to be expected" and shared some of her concerns about her soldier son, which snuggled near the surface of her consciousness and made a bond with her clients, colleagues, and friends who had relatives in the Service:

> Jonathan has just emerged from a long silence
> period from which he was aroused by the
> indications, a recurring disease with him, that
> he was going to be shipped. So we have been writing
> furiously all about what he needs, etc., etc. Now
> we have resumed our usual delinquency because it
> appears that this was yet another false alarm and
> that he is staying in Texas a few more weeks.

Carol's letter writing to Howard King was interrupted briefly, but she was determined to get back to it:

> A few minutes ago one of my favorite old clients
> whom I nursed along from the point where he was in
> the country illegally as an unregistered alien to
> where he is an honest to God citizen dropped in to
> say hello. He was just back from Antwerp where he
> must have seen quite a lot, including robot bombs.
> Present indications are that we are going out
> drinking, and I rather hope that term includes at
> least some food on a refund check from the federal

> government for overpayment of income tax. He is an
> interesting guy, an American born in Turkey, who
> has been sailing all of his life. He has seen just
> about everything and has taken a good deal of it
> in. His demands on my ability to hold liquor are
> pretty high.
>   I am planning a lazy summer. . . . Of course I
> know that I make great plans about taking it easy
> that never materialize. Only it's fun to dream
> about. Actually I'd probably get the jitters if
> there wasn't too much to do. You sound as if you
> were up to your neck.

During this period, Carol's brother also had an important case pending in the Supreme Court. Louis Weiss continued to represent Field Enterprises, Inc., which published *PM*. Weiss, Carl Stern, and Samuel Silverman filed a brief for Field as friends of the court in support of the position of the U.S. government in *Associated Press v. United States*. They claimed the AP was violating the anti-trust laws by prohibiting nonmember newspapers from using its news.

Finally, on June 18, 1945, the Supreme Court decided the cases of the brother and the sister. They both won. The Court held that the government was right and that the AP had been violating the anti-trust laws. And the Court held that the government was wrong and that Bridges could not be deported.

The Court decided the fate of Harry Bridges on one narrow issue. Justice Douglas, speaking for five Justices, ruled that the evidence did not establish that Bridges had been a member of or affiliated with the Communist Party. The Attorney General had based his order of deportation on the combined testimony of O'Neil and Lundeberg. The "unsworn" "ex parte statements" of O'Neil were "highly prejudicial" and they were inadmissible. The language of the Attorney General's order did not make clear whether he would have based an order of deportation on the testimony of Lundeberg alone, which was all that was left of the government proof. "[S]ince [the issue of membership] was so close," the Court was "unable to say that the order of deportation may be sustained without [O'Neil's] unsworn statements"; therefore, it reversed Judge

Union Hiring Hall. An illustration of one of the long-range victories of the International Longshoremen's and Warehousemen's Union: a union-run hiring hall. By Bits Hayden in *The Big Strike* by Mike Quin. Olema, California; Olema Publishing Co. 1949, p. 196.

Sears, Attorney General Biddle, the District Court, and the Ninth Circuit Court majority.

This was the precise point Carol had predicted would be decisive years before. In reaching this point, Douglas referred to the political time of day:

> Common sense indicates that the term "affiliation" in this setting should be construed more narrowly. Individuals, like nations, may cooperate in a common cause over a period of months or years though their ultimate aims do not coincide. Alliances for limited objectives are well known. Certainly those who joined forces with Russia to defeat the Nazis may not be said to have made an alliance to spread the cause of Communism. An individual who makes contributions to feed hungry men does not become "affiliated" with the Communist cause because those men are Communists.

Douglas quoted Dean Landis's 1939 decision for Bridges on the definition of "affiliation." He held that "when we turn to the facts of this case we have little more than a course of conduct which reveals cooperation with

Communist groups for the attainment of wholly lawful objectives. . . . [Bridges's] advice to support for office certain candidates said to be Communists was based entirely on the platform on which they ran — cash relief; abolition of vagrancy laws; no evictions; gas, water and electricity for the unemployed; and unemployment relief."

In a nice touch, Douglas set forth the law covering Bridges's conduct, with the appropriate single-shot citation: "Freedom of speech and of press is accorded aliens residing in this country. *Bridges v. California,* 314 U.S. 252."

Chief Justice Stone, speaking in dissent again for himself and Justices Frankfurter and Roberts, declared that the O'Neil testimony was admissible; therefore, the record contained *some* evidence against Bridges, and the order of deportation should be sustained. This strict application of the *Vajtauer* rule was not surprising since Justice Stone had written the decision in that case in 1927 and the Justice Stone who had written Footnote Four in 1937 had been transformed into the Chief Justice Stone of the 1940s.

Justice Murphy wrote a stirring opinion dealing with the broader issues in *Bridges,* but it did not garner the majority of votes as his similar opinion in *Schneiderman* had done in 1943, leaving Murphy to file it as a concurring opinion:

> The record in this case will stand forever as a monument of man's intolerance of man. Seldom if ever in the history of this nation has there been such a concentrated and relentless crusade to deport an individual because he dared to exercise the freedom that belongs to him as a human being and that is guaranteed to him by the Constitution.
>
> For more than a decade powerful economic and social forces have combined with public and private agencies to seek the deportation of Harry Bridges. . . . Emerging from the Pacific Coast maritime strike of 1934 as a recognized labor leader in that area, Bridges incurred the hatred and hostility of those whose interests coincided directly or indirectly with the "vicious and inhumane practices toward longshoremen" . . . that Bridges was combatting.

Murphy had felt the massive power of those interests when he was governor of Michigan during the sit-down strikes of 1937. He had refused to order the National Guard to go into the GM plants in Flint to blast out the thousands of workers sitting down at their machines, thus avoiding a mighty bloodbath. Only FDR's intervention had saved him from oblivion and put him in a position to present an authoritative review of the campaign against Bridges.

Murphy mentioned that "wiretapping, searches and seizures without warrants and other forms of invasion of the right of privacy have been widely employed in this deportation drive." He pointed out that recognizing the free-speech rights of an alien and then deporting the alien for exercising those rights "would make our constitutional safeguards transitory and discriminatory in nature. . . . The alien would be fully clothed with his constitutional rights when defending himself in a court of law, but he would be stripped of those rights when deportation officials encircle him. I cannot agree that the framers of the Constitution meant to make such an empty mockery of human freedom."

He then pointed out "several constitutional infirmities" apparent in the deportation law, and waxed eloquent about the Constitution as a priest might declaim about the Bible:

> But the Constitution has been more than a silent, anemic witness to this proceeding. It has not stood idly by while one of its subjects is being excommunicated from this nation without the slightest proof that his presence constitutes a clear and present danger to the public welfare. Nor has it remained aloof while this individual is being deported, resulting in the loss "of all that makes life worth living," . . . on a finding that, regardless of his personal beliefs, he was a member and an affiliate of an organization advocating the forceful overthrow of the Government. When the immutable freedoms guaranteed by the Bill of Rights have been so openly and concededly ignored, the full wrath of constitutional condemnation descends upon the action taken by the Government. And only by expressing that wrath can we give form and substance to "the great, the indispensable democratic freedoms," . . . to which this nation is dedicated.

Justice Murphy concluded:

> Our concern in this case does not halt with the fate of Harry Bridges, an alien whose constitutional rights have been grossly violated. The significance of this case is far-reaching. The liberties of 3,500,000 other aliens in this nation are also at stake. Many of these aliens, like many of our forebears, were driven from their original homelands by bigoted authorities who denied the existence of freedom and tolerance. It would be a dismal prospect for them to discover that their freedom in the United States is dependent upon their conformity to the popular notions of the moment.
>
> But they need not make that discovery. The Bill of Rights belongs to them as well as to all citizens. . . . It protects them in the exercise of the great individual rights necessary to a sound political and economic

democracy. Neither injunction, fine, imprisonment nor deportation can be utilized to restrict or prevent the exercise of intellectual freedom.

Congressmen Henry H. Jackson (Dem.-Wash.), Charles R. Savage (Dem.-Wash.), and Hugh De Lacy (Dem.-Wash.), Bertram W. Gearhart (Rep.-Calif.), and Ed V. Izak (Dem.-Calif.), William J. Gallagher (Dem.-Minn.), and Vito Marcantonio (ALP-N.Y.) all hailed the Court decision, along with Senator Glenn H. Taylor (Dem.-Idaho). The American Committee quickly published 50,000 copies of the opinions. And Carol began a successful campaign to get Nathan Greene an honorary membership in Bridges's union for writing the brief she felt had won the case.

Just five days after the Supreme Court decision, Harry Bridges filed his final naturalization forms in San Francisco. Carol had been very much opposed to his taking this step. She felt he was perfectly safe after the Supreme Court's decision and that trying to become a naturalized citizen would only create difficulties for him later.

But the mood in New York was not the mood in San Francisco. Richard Gladstein summed up the euphoric feeling: "The military forces of fascism had been overthrown [by the] triumphant political alliance . . . between men of goodwill extend[ing] across the face of the entire earth." This alliance "joined peoples of diverse tradition, culture and faith — our capitalist system in America; Russia's communist system; China's semi-communist country; Britain's half-socialist society, embarking on its program to end colonialism; France's United Front of mixed socialist-and-communist and liberal-democratic orientation; and numerous variations." The United Nations had been constructed "in our City of San Francisco" out of a United Nations Conference on International Organization in which IJA member Alger Hiss had acted as secretary general. Robert Kenny and Martin Popper attended as representatives of the National Lawyers Guild because they would fully support a strong UN at a time when the American Bar Association would not. The UN would "mobilize the collective resources of mankind for the culmination of the war: to erase, for all time, and in all places, the scourge of poverty, exploitation, bigotry, and violence."

ə⟡

Once Harry Bridges's naturalization papers were filed, Carol asked questions about his naturalization when she went to the Service office in

Philadelphia, trying to get the officials to be gentlemanly and forget the whole thing and shake hands. She wrote to Gladstein that "the Service officials said they didn't bring the second deportation case without thinking they could prove it," so they would not recommend his naturalization.

Gladstein responded that at the last minute the Service tried to block HB's naturalization with an affidavit from Mrs. Bridges, whom he had recently divorced. Her affidavit listed dates and places indicating that HB was a CP member. However, during the divorce proceedings Gladstein had prudently gotten Mrs. Bridges to reiterate her 1943 affidavit to the contrary, so her 1945 affidavit meant nothing.

On September 17, Harry Bridges appeared in Superior Court in San Francisco for the naturalization hearing with two ILWU officials who testified they had known him for five years or longer and vouched for his loyalty to the United States. Under oath, Bridges said he had never belonged to an organization that advocated the overthrow of the government by force or violence and had never been a member of the Communist Party.

```
Sept. 17, 1945
To Harry Bridges:
    YOU MAY BE A GOOD CLIENT, BUT YOUR LAWYERS ARE NO
SLOUCHES. CONGRATS. CAROL.
```

A few days later, Richie described Bridges's naturalization proceeding in the federal district court in San Francisco: "For the record, even though you may not believe it, it was the first time I have seen Harry so flustered, nervous and excited. There were real tears in his eyes as he took the oath. It even made me feel like a young bride again. . . . Got any other little aliens who can be grown into big ones?"

Carol King, sitting in her New York office surrounded by pending case files, probably thought that she did.

PART IV:
The Cold War Forties And Fifties, 1945–1952
Holding The Line

The Attorney General issued a list of "subversive organizations."
The Immigration Service rearrested hundreds of political deportees.
The courts upheld the execution of Julius and Ethel Rosenberg.
The President sent troops into a hot war in Korea.

The Constitution still said
"Congress shall make no law . . .
abridging the freedom of speech, or of the press;
or the right of the people peaceably to assemble,
and to petition the government for a redress of grievances."
— First Amendment

Now the UN Charter added
"All members pledge . . . to . . . promote:
. . . full employment, . . . and . . . universal . . . observance of human rights
and fundamental freedoms for all
without distinction as to race, sex, language or religion."
— Articles 55 and 56

For one brief, shining moment starting on June 26, 1945, the United States committed this nation to being one united nation among many, promising to respect the sovereignty of each other nation, small and large, and pledging "to promote . . . full employment, higher standards of living, [and] the solution of economic problems." President Truman signed the United Nations Charter containing these solemn commitments and sent it to the Senate for its consent. After brief debate, the Senate voted 89 to 2 to sign this treaty, making it part of "the supreme law of the land."

Five weeks later, on August 6, 1945, the United States dropped an atomic bomb on the civilian city of Hiroshima, Japan. The U.S. acted after notifying its British and French allies but without consulting its Soviet ally or the new United Nations, without warning to the government of Japan. One hundred twenty thousand civilians died immediately in the inferno that crystallized into the cold war.

Two days later, the United States signed a historic agreement with the Soviet Union, Great Britain, and France to try the defeated leaders of the Nazi German government, not simply to execute them because they had lost the war. A similar effort after World War I had failed, but now the Nazis would be tried at Nuremburg for committing crimes against peace, crimes against humanity, and war crimes.

The next day, the United States dropped its second atomic bomb on the civilian city of Nagasaki, Japan. The bombing was done with no warning or clear knowledge of its long-range disastrous effects, and without awaiting the results of its first atomic bomb on the willingness of Japan to surrender. On the same day, the Soviet Union entered the war against Japan, according to the plan made by the Allies on the day Germany surrendered.

These historic events shook the lives of everyone in the world in ways we are still studying. On September 2, Japan signed an unconditional surrender.

The U.S. Armed Forces immediately began to demobilize. Veterans returned to work, determined to get more out of life than before they went to fight. Soon they joined defense workers in facing lower incomes because of the end of overtime. On December 15, 1945, 200,000 General Motors workers in ninety-two plants in the United States went out on strike demanding a 30 percent raise ($.33 an hour). One month later, 200,000 electrical workers went on strike against General Electric, Westinghouse, and GM for a $.25 an-hour or $2-a-day increase. The next week, 750,00 steelworkers in thirty states went on strike for the first time since the United Steel Workers Union was organized in 1937. President Harry Truman's fact-finding board recommended that GM settle with its workers for a 17.4 percent increase. GM refused to comply. Soon more workers were on strike in the United States than at any time since the end of World War I.

Early in March 1946, in the new era of One World and United Nations, President Truman invited Sir Winston Churchill to make a major speech in Fulton, Missouri, which the former British prime minister entitled "Alliance of English-speaking People." The man who had just been rejected by the voters of his own country clearly relished laying out the foreign policy another nation should follow. Churchill said it would be "wrong and imprudent to intrust the secret . . . of the atomic bomb" to the United Nations. Instead he proposed "the joint use of all naval and air force bases in the possession of" the United States and Great Britain based on their common heritage and language. He proclaimed that "from Stettin in the Baltic to Triest in the Adriatic, an iron curtain has descended across the Continent." He described "Communist fifth columns" established "in a great number of countries, far from the Russian frontiers." He concluded that "the old doctrine of a balance of power" would not be strong enough and that "our Russian friends and allies during the war" must face a clearly superior military force. Otherwise, he threatened, we would face a repeat of the problem created by Hitler's Germany in the 1930s.

By June, Churchill's "iron curtain" speech had been applauded widely in the media, and the phrase "cold war" (which the *London Times* said was coined by Hitler's minister of finance and used by his minister of propaganda) was becoming part of the English language.

Attorney General Tom Clark went before the Chicago Bar Association in June to attack strikers and civil rights activists. Specifically Clark attacked the demands of the National Lawyers Guild and the NAACP's demands that the government do much more to protect civil rights. Clark said the federal government could not step in unless someone proved that a state or federal government official had *willfully* misused his power to deprive people of their civil rights.

Clark then charged that this country is the target of a sinister and deep-seated "plot" on the part of "communists," "outside ideologists," and "small groups of radicals" directed at the seizure of our country through a division of national unity. He said they work by capturing important offices in labor unions, fomenting strikes, raising barriers to efforts of lawful authorities to maintain civil peace, and by protesting that civil rights are being abridged. Clark cautioned lawyers: "We must be alert as officers of the court to see the difference between sincere and honest protest of groups of our citizens against injustice and the effort of these outside ideologists to stir up trouble according to the old plan of 'divide and rule.' " Only one year after the defeat of the fascist powers, the Attorney General said bluntly of fascism and communism: "I see no difference in them."

In light of the Attorney General's defeat in *Schneiderman* and *Bridges*, Clark concluded:

> I do not think there is anyone more subject to censure in our profession than the revolutionary who enters our ranks, takes the solemn oath of our calling, and then uses every device in the legal category to further the interests of those who would destroy our government by force, if necessary.
>
> I do not believe in purges because they bespeak the dark and hideous deeds of communism and fascism, but I do believe that our bar associations, with a strong hand, should take those too brilliant brothers of ours to the legal woodshed for a definite and well-deserved admonition.

28.
The Attorney General Threatens Revenge

Between Prime Minister Churchill's "iron curtain" speech and Attorney General Clark's "woodshed" speech, Carol King had to figure out how to stop Clark's new deportation orders against 300 Indonesian seamen imprisoned on Ellis Island by the immigration authorities since November 1945. The seamen had refused to work on Dutch or British ships taking men and munitions to war on their families in Indonesia. The Left launched a nationwide campaign to prevent the deportation of the seamen while Carol appealed to the Board of Immigration Appeals. In April 1946 Attorney General Clark made the final decision, ordering immediate deportation of the seamen to the Dutch government in Indonesia.

Carol and their other attorneys asked federal courts in New York, Los Angeles, and San Francisco for writs of habeas corpus, explaining that the Australian government, faced with a similar group of 821 Indonesian seamen, deported them not to the Dutch but to the new Republican government of Indonesia where they wanted to go. The Dutch government was forced to reassure the district courts that the Indonesian seamen need not fear prosecution or reprisals for their refusal to man Dutch ships.

By the order of the U.S. government, the seamen in New York started for Java by way of San Francisco, where they were joined by the seamen on the West Coast. Just as their ship was about to sail out of the bay, their lawyers got a judge to order removal of the whole group from the ship so they could appear for a hearing on their habeas petition. Then the judge dismissed the petition, but the men were not sent back to the ship; they were sent to the immigration camp at Crystal City, Texas, until their appeal could be heard. To the uninitiated, this did not look like a victory, and it would not be dissected in the law reviews. But it would save some seamen from deportation, and it might mean that none would ever be deported. The situation in Indonesia might change during the appeal so that deportation would no longer mean imprisonment or death. The lawyers argued in the appeal that "the Constitution forbids the imposition of cruel or unusual punishment," and people should not be deported "to a place where they will suffer persecution because of race, desecration of property, unemployment or death."

⁂

As the Lawyers Guild convened in Cleveland on July 4, Clark's woodshed speech overshadowed Churchill's iron curtain in discussions in the lobby by some of the "too brilliant" lawyers who had been defeating Clark in the Supreme Court.

At the Guild's opening session, Carol King and the other delegates listened to the chairman read messages from four of the nine Justices of the Supreme Court who had decided *Schneiderman, Barnette,* and *Bridges.* Justice Wiley Rutledge regretted that he could not attend because "the forward-looking and progressive spirit which characterizes your outlook upon the law no doubt will be evident in all of your proceedings." Justice Black trusted that the Guild would "continue to fight for those things which its members deem to be for the best interests of the people of the United States as a whole" and wished us "a successful meeting." Justice Stanley Reed wrote that "this meeting of the Guild is of great importance" and that "much good" would come from it. Justice Murphy sent "every good wish for the success" of the meeting.

The delegates enjoyed the speech by Guild president Robert W. Kenny, one of Schneiderman's trial lawyers and now the Attorney General of California. He was a wise and very witty commentator on civil rights in the postwar era. He was followed by Democratic senators Claude Pepper of Florida talking about Roosevelt and the future of liberalism and James E. Murray of Montana explaining that restrictive labor legislation was an attack on civil liberties. Congressman Glen H. Taylor (Dem.-Idaho) discussed "Monopolies: Their Program for Disaster and War." Shad Polier gave an incisive short speech on "Law, Conscience, and Society." Drawing on his experiences as editor of the *IJA Bulletin* and as a leader of the American Jewish Congress, he argued convincingly that laws can, indeed, change how people behave. Therefore, it is worthwhile to pass laws requiring "moral" behavior, especially in the treatment of racial and religious minorities. Leo Linder, Carol's thirties recruit on social security law, presented "A Program of Basic Social Protection for Americans," making the subject exciting to the novice. Later delegates discussed the legal problems of the new United Nations and the status of prosecutions against German and Japanese war criminals.

At one point, Carol invited me to join her and some of her friends who were playing hooky to look at the paintings in the Cleveland Art Museum, a tradition of hers during conventions. I was having such an exciting time as a law student attending my first Guild convention that I respectfully declined. The minute any of her resolutions came up, I noticed Carol in the middle of the floor making sure they got full discussion and weren't amended into meaninglessness by someone more concerned about syntax than principle.

Finally the delegates passed a resolution committing themselves "to protect and assist" any member of the bar "against whom an effort is made by Tom C. Clark or any person or organization acting at his instance, to take any such lawyers 'to the legal woodshed.' " They would send a committee asking President Truman to reject Clark's explanation for his failure to protect the civil liberties of Negroes seeking to vote in the South. They demanded "the immediate strengthening" of the Department of Justice and the FBI by the addition of liberals, both Negro and white, "in positions of high responsibility," and "the immediate reorganization of the FBI." The convention also passed resolutions on the problem of full production and employment in the postwar economy, American foreign policy, utilization and control of atomic energy, and extension of legal services to low-income groups.

Carol King talked to the 1946 Guild convention about "the general deterioration in the position of aliens" since the end of the war, after some hopeful steps had been taken in the heat of the battle against fascism. She had written a piece for the *Lawyers Guild Review* in 1945 to help ensure against a rerun of the Palmer Raids. She commended INS commissioner Earl Harrison for enforcing the Alien Registration Act in a fair manner, for making registration "as easy as an unpleasant duty could be made," and for starting proceedings "one by one in a lawful and quiet manner" against illegal aliens. She applauded the virtual end to deportations during the war, and was shocked when the *Gripsholm* sailed with a large group of deportable aliens right after V-Day in Europe in 1945, including Italian seamen interned just before the declaration of war between the United States and Italy in 1941.

She also applauded the teaching of foreign languages in our schools during World War II (unlike World War I) and praised the lack of "enemy alien-baiting." In fact, the INS helped German refugees get naturalized. She contrasted William Schneiderman's victory over denaturalization with the government's efforts to denaturalize during World War I. She concluded that "Attorney General Palmer would have been surprised if he could have lived to see the complete controls that were imposed on aliens without a fanfare of publicity, and without terrorizing this section of our population." But she felt compelled to provide a final footnote: new INS commissioner Ugo Carusi had stated that 16,000 aliens from Europe would be deported at the end of the European war under outstanding warrants.

The ambivalence of the period touched Carol's colleague Joe Brodsky, who was launching the new People's Radio Foundation, Inc., "to reach a large radio audience with Democratic education, truthful news reports, together with exciting entertainment and good music." At the same time a temporary confidential informant was advising the FBI that the chairman of the Virginia State Corporation Commission had advised Brodsky that the IWO should not be licensed by the Bureau of Insurance of Virginia. In response, the Jewish People's Fraternal Order-IWO held a successful concert in Norfolk with Brodsky as the main speaker.

Within a few months of the end of the war and the founding of the United Nations, King had written again about deterioration in the treatment of noncitizens. Contract laborers, mostly West Indians and Mexicans, brought to the United States to do agricultural and industrial work during the War, were now being subjected to mass deportation "to take them out of competition with American labor." The INS held thousands in Florida for many months, "insufficiently housed and fed, awaiting transportation home." The INS would not permit married men to remain with their U.S.–citizen wives. The INS would not permit them voluntary departure and pre-examination, which was allowed to others. Carol reported, also, that deportations of Italians and Greeks were proceeding at a rapid pace, with Italy "serving as a dumping group" for people without travel documents.

At the same time, the treatment of West Coast citizens of Japanese ancestry was finally emerging as a national issue. One thousand Japanese at the Tule Lake segregation camp sued to regain U.S. citizenship and to block their immediate deportation to Japan under the Alien Enemy Act of 1789. They claimed that three 'fanatically pro-Japanese' organizations were able to operate within the camps, conducting a campaign of 'violence, terrorism, and sedition' to force Japanese-American citizens to

renounce their U.S. citizenship. In a three-month period, 4,300 suc-
cumbed under duress. The most tragic cases to Carol were minor children
scheduled to be deported, and U.S. soldiers of Japanese ancestry returning
as anti-fascist war heroes to find that their interned relatives were
scheduled for deportation.

Carol had these problems in mind during the Guild convention, as
many individuals and institutions were returning to their original styles
after wartime shifts. In July 1945 U.S. Communists who had followed
Earl Browder's line and turned the "Communist Party" into the "Communist Political Association" were stung by the sharp criticism of French
Communist Jacques Duclos. He called Browderism "class collaboration."
Now the CPA returned William Z. Foster to leadership and soon reorganized the CPUS. Others with different politics were returning to their
original lines. Robert Jackson had started out as a liberal government
official who had joined the National Lawyers Guild, becoming a sometimes repressive Attorney General just before the War and his appointment to the U.S. Supreme Court. Now he would become one of the
prosecutors in the first trial of a defeated World War II enemy at
Nuremberg. He would help prove the allied case against Goering, Hess,
and the other Nazi government, military, and financial leaders. Francis
Biddle had started out a liberal, New Deal Attorney General, becoming
the author of one decision against Harry Bridges in 1942, and then
stopping the FBI-type political "detention" list during the War. Now he
would become one of the judges on the International Military Tribunal
in the historic multinational Nuremberg trials.

In this climate, Carol and some of her colleagues thought it would be
a good idea for her to join the Association of the Bar of the City of New
York. It had an excellent private law library for the exclusive use of its
members; it was a nice place to meet; and it certainly seemed appropriate
for someone of her stature at the bar to be a member. (Besides, she was
finally making enough money to afford the annual dues.) Admission to
this selective organization depends on nomination by several members
and approval by the admission committee. After her nomination, Mrs.
King received a summons from this committee.

Of course, the members knew she had represented Bridges, Schneiderman, and Browder, whose cases and activities were reported in the *New
York Times* (including Browder's recent expulsion from the Communist
Party for rejecting the new/old militant Party line). How much more they
knew about her she wasn't sure. She understood that many lawyers, like

many laymen, assume that other lawyers usually have something in common with their clients — although they reject this guilt by association when it is applied to themselves. Carol had always disdained to placate this sentiment by dissociating herself from her clients. A lawyer who does this, she said, loses effectiveness and prejudices the case against the client as well. So she went to the admission committee meeting somewhat curious about what would happen when Nathan Greene's colleagues from Wall Street had a chance to question her qualifications to join their bar association.

She found out soon enough. The members asked her, more or less tactfully, whether she was a member of the Communist Party.

Partly amused, partly annoyed, she objected to the question.

They would not withdraw it.

She finally said that she was not. 'However,' she added, 'I wish I were, just so I could tell you "yes." '

Her questioners were not amused by her response. Many weeks later she heard that one of them had asked her sponsor to withdraw her nomination.

He refused to do so, saying he felt the committee should be forced to make a decision. Eventually the Association of the Bar of the City of New York admitted Carol Weiss King to membership.

❧

Carol decided that Congress was the important forum for protection of foreign born in 1945. There were several friends of the foreign-born in Congress, from Vito Marcantonio (ALP-N.Y.) and Hugh DeLacy (Dem.-Wash.) to Claude Pepper (Dem.-Fla.). The Lawyers Guild national office in Washington was busy networking and lobbying on all kinds of bills and could count some successes. Carol also had friends from New York and the IJA still working in government agencies in the postwar period, but that era was quickly drawing to an end. As chairman of the Guild committee on immigration law or as general counsel to the American Committee, she enjoyed several trips to Washington to testify on pending legislation before the House committee chaired by Samuel Dickstein (Dem.-N.Y.). She urged that the deportation law be altered to limit deportation for illegal entry to ten years after entry and to give the Service discretion to grant suspension of deportation for people who had belonged

to certain "proscribed" organizations like the Communist Party, or had
been convicted of a crime before entering the United States.

MR. MASON: . . . The present Congress, I am quite satisfied, would refuse
overwhelmingly to strike that out of the law at the present time.

MRS. KING: You didn't ask for views on what could be done, but what it
is advisable to do. I believe I can't compete with you in my knowledge
of the Congress of the United States. It seems to me that if the thing is
presented in a logical way, with certain exceptions, it might be considered.

Mr. DICKSTEIN (chairman): You couldn't talk logic with the Bilbos, Rank-
ins, and Coxes [Dixiecrats in Congress].

MRS. KING: I said with some exceptions. I am not an associate of theirs.

Carol continued lobbying on the high road, using logic in opposing a
pending bill that would exclude as immigrants all members of certain
Nazi organizations in Germany because "there is no such thing as group
liability . . . it is an individual question." Later she applauded the
conclusions of the Dickstein committee.

But in December 1945 a federal judge in Oregon had denied naturalization to Mrs. Lena Halverson because of her refusal to reply to questions
by the naturalization examiner as to her "affiliation with organizations
alleged to be subsidiary to the Communist Party." By this time, twenty-
five similar cases had come to Mrs. King's attention. She recognized some
names from the Palmer Raid days, people who had been saved from
deportation in the early twenties, and again in the thirties when they led
Unemployed Councils and TUEL unions — Jack Schneider, Fred Fierstein.
Some had fought in Spain and many in World War II. The third time
around, their cases might finally settle the constitutional question left
undecided in *Bridges:* "We may learn whether, as the Government argues,
aliens in deportation and naturalization cases have no substantive constitutional rights, or whether Mr. Justice Murphy was correct that noncitizens cannot be deported or denied citizenship in violation of the free
speech and association and clear and present danger test applicable in
criminal cases."

She was hopeful that she could win these cases in light of the decisions
in *Schneiderman* and *Bridges.* Many came to her through the American
Committee for Protection of Foreign Born. She had gotten very active in
the committee during the War and now, as its general counsel, she finally
had a perfect professional setup, similar to Joe Brodsky's relationship with
the ILD. The staff knew when to contact her for advice on a legal question

and when to handle something on their own. They had become expert on public relations and fund-raising. They trained their own experts on immigration law, who came to know more about specific immigration procedures and forms than most lawyers, solving problems for thousands of individuals each year. They also knew what they did not know — how to solve impossible problems. For these issues, they called on their general counsel.

The staff was headed up by an indefatigable executive secretary, Abner Green. He was a tall, lean Marxist with a Lincolnesque face. Abner never seemed to be impatient or in a hurry, crisscrossing the country every year to attend meetings of each foreign-born group affiliated with the committee, welding them into a national network of people knowledgeable about their rights and determined to fight for their protection. He knew enough about national pride, cultural differences, and minor points of tension to walk wisely among groups that were determined to maintain their separate identities in the patchwork United States. Abner's style was like Carol's — businesslike, professional, personal, friendly — a combination that felt comradely. Harriet Barron, the administrative secretary, was likewise efficient and consistent, providing the kind of no-nonsense backup on which lawyers and clients could rely absolutely.

Carol said, "I've learned to work with Abner because, as a lawyer, I have my job and as an executive secretary he has his job to do and they are inseparably connected. So when I get into a jam, I would call Abner and say 'Abner, I'm suing out a writ. Do something.' " And he would.

The committee concentrated on the problems of the foreign-born as a new defense organization was put together, the Civil Rights Congress. In April 1946 the International Labor Defense and the National Federation for Constitutional Liberties had decided to meet the new era by merging. The initiating committee for the new CRC included names often seen on progressive letterheads at that point (and later on lists of witnesses called before un-American activities committees): actor John Garfield; historian Arthur M. Schlesinger; dancer Katherine Dunham; attorney Raymond Pace Alexander; poet Langston Hughes; Reverend Adam Clayton Powell; Elizabeth Gurley Flynn; and labor lawyers Nathan Witt, Frank Donner, Abe Isserman, and David Scribner. Carol King had quickly accepted membership on the national board.

Soon she was meeting every month with the new Civil Rights Congress legal committee, and then with the New York chapter CRC legal staff pulled together by Ralph Powe. The lawyers were old standbys: Emanuel Bloch, Abe Isserman, Herman Rosenfeld, Nat Witt, and David Scribner.

Like many of Carol's deportation clients, Peter Harisiades had started out as an applicant for citizenship. He told her he was born in Greece in 1901 and came to the United States when he was fifteen. About 1922 he took out his first citizenship papers but did not complete the process. In 1928 he became an organizer for the Communist Party in the textile centers of Massachusetts. By 1930 he had been arrested eight times for his activities in strikes, but never brought to trial. On March 6, 1930, he was questioned in a police station in New Bedford, and a record was kept of the interrogation:

Q. Do you believe in Socialism?
A. I do believe in Socialism. . . .
Q. Are you a member of the Communist Party?
A. Yes. . . .
Q. Do you believe in the overthrow of the present government of the United States?
A. Our purpose is to overthrow the present form of government and establish a worker's government.
Q. Do you believe in force or violence or destruction of government?
A. We do not believe in violence. We believe in establishing a government by the organized working class . . . building up their political power; . . . Only then will we be able to take the power away from the capitalist.

Harisiades signed his name to the statement, and a warrant was issued for his arrest for deportation but it was never served. In 1937 he married. In 1939, as fear of aliens swept the country and Congress tried to make Communist Party membership a ground for deportation, the Party convinced him and others arrested for deportation to cease their memberships quietly and changed its constitution to limit membership to citizens. Many noncitizens resented this decision, according to San Franciscan Jean Kramer. The CP dropped Harisiades's name in October 1939. He was now the editor of a Greek-language radical newspaper in New York City and had two U.S.–citizen children born in 1939 and 1944. In December 1944 he filed a petition for naturalization and hired Carol King as his lawyer.

Two years later, just after the war ended, he received a letter asking him to come to the offices of the Immigration Service. He casually notified Carol, who said that she would accompany him, although he protested that it was not necessary.

The INS official arrested him the minute he arrived.

Carol demanded to see the warrant. It was dated 1930. She turned to Harisiades. "See," she said, "it's a good idea I came with you." Then she demanded to know why the immigration agent had waited sixteen years to serve the warrant.

We couldn't find Harisiades, he told her.

She snorted; Harisiades had registered each year under the 1940 Alien Registration Act, and he was listed in the Manhattan telephone directory.

The agent told Harisiades to post $1,000 bail.

She objected strenuously. Her client had no desire to run away; he worked every day and spent evenings with his wife and children.

Faced with her outrage, the Service released Harisiades on his own recognizance — on his word to appear without putting up any bond.

In 1946, the government scheduled a deportation hearing on the *Harisiades* case under his 1930 arrest warrant. It became clear that the postwar government was going to focus on one pre-war issue: that the Communist Party from 1928 to 1939 advocated the violent overthrow of the government of the United States. It would seek to overturn the historical basis for the Supreme Court's decision in *Schneiderman* on this issue by using extracts from Marxist documents, like the ones the government had used in *Bridges* that Justice Murphy had countered. They would also call several ex-Communists as experts to counter the professorial experts Carol had brought before Dean Landis in the first *Bridges* hearing, who had provided some of the basis for Murphy's opinions in *Schneiderman* and *Bridges*.

Carol got the Service to agree that the testimony on the issue of Communist Party doctrine in *Harisiades* would be used in all future cases on that issue. Then she tried to get the Party to produce an authoritative statement as to what Marxist documents had been official Party doctrine during specific years. The Party leadership, as usual, was busy with nine other things that seemed more urgent than the preparation of a lawsuit. It took Carol a mixture of patience and annoyance to get the list of publications she wanted. There was just one catch. The Party no longer used many of the pamphlets and leaflets it had printed years before, and did not have a single copy of many of them. ('What is as useless as an outdated political tract?' one of the CP leaders asked Carol rhetorically.) So Carol either had to ask the government for copies, or do without. While she was pondering that little problem, she went ahead with other work on the case.

❧

Peggy Kahn attests that when Carol was especially under the gun at work, she could turn to her large circle of intimate friends and relatives for sustenance. Nothing really explains King's choice of "friends, art or bric-a-brac," according to Kahn. Clearly King took her art selections seriously, at her home and her office. By now the walls of both were filled. She looked at the paintings, moving them around, putting up new ones. Only her father's picture, her honorary membership in the ILWU, a montage of defense counsel headlines on The Alien in the *Bridges* case, and a photo of a bust of Willkie stayed in their places.

"There was a characteristic irrationality in her affections," according to her niece. "She liked those she liked with a fierce loyalty and an absolute generosity — she took pleasure in their very eccentricities." Peggy remembers that often, "before the fire in Carol's front room, conversation was good, illuminated by the warmth of her humor, by the wisdom and insight of her analysis, by her enjoyment of people and things. But sometimes it wasn't, too, and then she would curl up comfortably in front of the little grate and say happily 'It's so nice being with someone you like even if you just talk nonsense.' "

Carol always served meals off individual stools and tables, and the food again helped to individualize and identify the guest. "Whether it was chicken and ripe olives for breakfast, or slightly burned toast, Carol always considered it a mark of friendship to know just how you took your coffee or your Scotch."

Carol had made another new friend in the Christmas season of 1945, on her return trip on the Pacemaker from Chicago where she had been handling a hard case. She found a seat next to a rather forlorn and scrawny-looking girl. As Carol settled into her seat, it was obvious that her seatmate was feeling miserable, so she soon struck up a conversation.

Her fourteen-year-old companion said her name was Barbara and that she was on her way to New York to live with her aunt and uncle because her mother had died the month before, following the death of her father four years earlier. Barbara was miserable at leaving all of her friends behind in Chicago, and had looked forward to meeting other youngsters or families with children on her journey. Spending an overnight trip next to a distinctly uninteresting-looking middle-aged lady doubled her unhappiness, but she obviously couldn't let her companion know this.

Carol started telling Barbara stories about her extensive travels and experiences. "She encouraged me to talk about my own anxieties," Barbara Rubenstein recalled in 1982. "I had never met a professional woman before, except perhaps for my schoolteachers (who were not thought of as professionals in those days by their students), and the fact that a woman could be a lawyer made an enormous impression. Carol King opened up a whole new perspective on the future for me. I didn't have to think only of getting a secretarial job until some man claimed me. I could possibly have a far more interesting life with a profession, and opportunities to travel and work with people to better their own lives."

The two sat up all night talking. Almost forty years later, Mrs. Rubenstein could still "conjure up an image of a plain (almost frumpy) looking middle-aged woman, dressed in plain dark clothes." When they reached New York, Barbara's relatives were there to meet her and she made introductions. "I didn't understand at the time why my aunt and uncle were so terribly impressed by my travelling companion, but in time I came to appreciate Carol King's reputation among socially and politically concerned people." This encounter changed the life of Barbara Rubenstein, leading her to become a psychologist working with underprivileged children.

Carol was hard at work on the hearing in *Harisiades* when her brother William Weiss died in the fall of 1946 at the age of fifty-eight. Carol had always remained close to Billy. His death ended one instance of the majestic tragedy of multiple sclerosis attacking at random an individual and his family. The general director of the Community Service System wrote in the *Times* that attorney William Weiss would be sorely missed, and this fact could be attested by the 5,000 people he had provided with legal advice from his wheelchair in the past eleven years, charging fees of $1 to $10.

⁊⧸

When the *Harisiades* hearing opened on October 15, 1946, Carol King was ready. The defense introduced two expert witnesses, Harisiades and William Schneiderman. They were not the impartial Stanford professors who had been her witnesses in *Bridges,* but Schneiderman carried with him the aura of his victory in the Supreme Court. The presiding inspector, Gilbert Zimmerman, was not the dean of the Harvard Law School who had heard *Bridges,* but he gave the witnesses a reasonable chance to present their rebuttal evidence and then adjourned the hearing. Toward the end of 1946 Zimmerman prepared a tentative memorandum opinion in which he decided against the noncitizen.

This postwar era saw other tragic events. One of the former "Scottsboro boys" decided he had had enough of Southern justice. Clarence Norris fled the repressive Alabama parole system. He would live outside the law until he could get his sentence overturned — which might take the rest of his life.

For herself, Carol King could see that the new year would require a sharp shift in tactics simply to hold the line, let alone to win any cases in 1947.

29.
Making a Noise Like a Lawyer

INS presiding inspector Zimmerman ruled against Peter Harisiades in a sixty-five-page memo late in 1946. Carol King's strategy in the case had failed. She had carefully constructed her defense in order to build on the specific victories in *Schneiderman* and *Bridges,* decided by a liberal majority in the Supreme Court during a world war against fascism. Suddenly the United States had a new international enemy, its wartime socialist ally, the Soviet Union. The new internal enemy seemed to be the old bogeymen Carol had encountered in 1921 — Reds, Aliens, Labor. The new leadership of the Department of Justice and the INS embraced these old enemies. The ground on which she had built the Harisiades defense had shifted.

King wasn't sure what to do now except to follow the advice she had given to countless colleagues in hard cases — "Make a noise like a lawyer!" She sat down and dictated her exceptions to the Zimmerman memo, pointing out, in forty-eight pages, all the weaknesses in the case the government had presented.

In January 1947 the American Committee for Protection of Foreign Born decided to undertake the defense of Harisiades and proved that the Left/Progressive network was working well. By March, forty of Harisiades's neighbors in Brooklyn had formed a neighbors support committee. A Los Angeles local of the United Electrical Workers announced its support. So did the Tacoma local of the Building Service Employees Union, a Boston local of the United Furniture Workers, and a New York local of the United Hospital Workers. This militance in the labor movement, and the felt need to fight the bosses and the government, paralleled the recent fight in the Communist Party and its expulsion of Earl Browder for being soft on capitalism.

```
[1/9/47 FBI file on JOSEPH BRODSKY]
THE BUREAU DESIRES THAT YOUR OFFICE PREPARE A RE-
PORT IN SUMMARY FORM IN THIS CASE SETTING FORTH BY
WITNESSES ONLY SUCH INFORMATION OF A LEGALLY ADMIS-
SIBLE CHARACTER AS WILL TEND TO PROVE, DIRECTLY OR
CIRCUMSTANTIALLY, MEMBERSHIP IN OR AFFILIATION WITH
THE COMMUNIST PARTY, AND KNOWLEDGE OF THE REVOLU-
TIONARY AIMS AND PURPOSES OF THAT ORGANIZATION.
```

The unions were feeling the political heat from the fight in Congress to force all union leaders to sign non-Communist oaths. If the Taft-Hartley bill became law, a union could not go to the National Labor Relations Board and charge a company with an unfair labor practice, or seek an election to decide whether the workers wanted a union, unless its leaders had signed this oath. This bill would unleash an attack on all Left/Progressives in unions.

The deportation of Harisiades would likewise provide a field day for attacks on all Left/progressives who were foreign-born. In April 1947 representatives of 112 organizations met in New York for an action conference. The committee issued 50,000 copies of a protest postcard on the case, and scores of organizations of the foreign born went on record in support of this Greek-American Communist whose fate might determine the future of some of their members.

At the end of July, Joe Brodsky died suddenly. "There was never a fighter less afraid and less grim," the *Daily Worker* reported. "Laughter, wit and the sheer delight in living were inseparable from him. He was — and he wore the honor with unshakable pride — an American Communist." Two thousand people attended his funeral, including hundreds of lawyers with whom he had worked over the decades, in and out of the CP. Three members of the New York city council spoke, led by Benjamin Davis, trial lawyer for Angelo Herndon, now a Communist Party member of the City Council. Davis couldn't forget "Joe Brodsky walking down the streets of Georgia and Alabama towns and defying the Ku Kluxers . . . and 'white supremacy' lynchers. When others trembled Brodsky fought on — and won." Congressman Vito Marcantonio spoke. William Z. Foster spoke for the Communist Party, and Paul Robeson for the world. Representative Benjamin Radin (Dem.-N.Y.) attended, along with leaders and rank-and-file members of scores of unions whom Brodsky had counseled, and Roy Wright, one of the *Scottsboro* defendants. Artist Rockwell Kent presided as the current president of the International Workers Order, which Brodsky had founded. Elizabeth Gurley Flynn gave a moving Irish/Marxist farewell.

Carol was not good at losing the people she loved, but she was very good at working on the causes they had shared. In October 1947 the Service issued an order reopening the *Harisiades* hearing to take additional evidence to meet her complaints. To make its success doubly certain, the Service removed Zimmerman from the case and designated Arthur J. Phelan as presiding inspector and John P. Boyd as examining inspector, both of whom were involved in what Dean Landis had found to be a conspiracy against Bridges in 1939.

Carol objected bitterly on both counts. The Service could not be given a second chance to present its evidence just because its opponent had done a careful job as a lawyer and pointed out innumerable weaknesses in the record! The government was not permitted to reopen a criminal case unless there was newly discovered evidence. How could a different rule be followed in a *noncriminal* case? Moreover, she charged that Zimmerman had been removed because he had been too fair to her client; he had permitted Harisiades to state his case.

Her protests had some effect. The Service scheduled reopened hearings for February 18, 1948, but they left Zimmerman in charge.

Carol worked on her next move in *Harisiades* on her way to Cleveland in late October 1947, where the American Committee was holding its national conference. The credentials committee reported that 37 delegates represented labor unions and 295 represented fraternal and national groups. William Green, president of the AFL, sent a strong message of support for the foreign-born, an unusual type of expression for him. Messages also came from many unions and from Henry A. Wallace, who had served as Vice President of the United States in Roosevelt's third term and as Secretary of Commerce under President Truman, until Truman fired him for opposing the cold war.

The convention gave Peter Harisiades a chance to explain the fundamental flaw in the attack on his right to remain in the United States:

> I came to this country from Greece as a young boy 31 years ago. . . . I worked with my hands in railroads, in shops and factories. I joined unions and helped to organize unions. I participated in strike struggles. I faced and actually I felt the club and the brutality of the police in different

industrial towns and I was thrown into jails. I helped to organize unemployed workers and participated in hunger marches for relief and for
unemployment insurance.

This is the way that my ideas were formed, that I began to understand
America and to become an American. It was the period of Harding,
Coolidge, and Hoover. What is my "crime"? As a result of these experiences, at the time when . . . Sacco and Vanzetti . . . were framed and
murdered by the State of Massachusetts, I joined the Communist Party and
continued my membership until 1939, when non-citizens were dropped.

This conference caused Abner Green to seek new levels of eloquence
in his report on the new attacks on the foreign-born:

Reaction tried the same thing with the Alien and Sedition laws of 1798. It
did not succeed. Reaction tried the same thing in 1870 with the Ku Klux
Klan. It did not succeed. Reaction tried the same thing in 1920 with the
Palmer Raids. It, too, failed. Reaction tried the same thing in 1930 with
the Black Legion [midwestern anti-union/anti-Negro gang]. In each instance, the forces that were seeking to prevent progress and to wipe out
human rights in this country tried first to divide the people by promoting
prejudice and hysteria. In each instance, reaction tried to get into power,
or to stay in power, behind a smokescreen of alien-baiting, Negro-baiting,
Catholic-baiting, red-baiting. They never succeeded. In each instance, the
American people united in defense of their liberties.

Today, we must stimulate the kind of national movement that, in 1800,
resulted in the repeal of the Alien and Sedition Act.

Carol enjoyed meeting with other immigration lawyers at the conference. As she started home, prepared to broaden her response to the latest
attacks on the foreign-born, certain other events were occurring of which
she had no knowledge.

DATE: AUGUST 12, 1947
TO: DIRECTOR, FBI
FROM: SAC, PHILADELPHIA
SUBJECT: CAROL WEISS KING
SECURITY MATTER — C
   REFERENCE IS MADE TO BUREAU LETTER DATED JUNE 27,
1947 WHEREIN PERMISSION WAS GRANTED TO EXAMINE THE
IMMIGRATION AND NATURALIZATION FILES IN WHICH CAROL
KING HAS BEEN INTERESTED. INASMUCH AS KING IS A
PROMINENT COMMUNIST PARTY LAWYER, IT IS BELIEVED
THAT SOME OF THESE INDIVIDUALS MAY BE ENGAGED IN
COMMUNISTIC ACTIVITIES WHICH HAVE NOT AS YET BEEN
BROUGHT TO THE ATTENTION OF THE BUREAU OR BUREAU
FIELD OFFICES. ALL FIELD OFFICES RECEIVING COPIES

BILL MAULDIN

Red in 1947. "I ain't goin' near ol' [Senator] McKellar's office. If he didn't call me red on accounta my hair, he'd say I'm left-wing 'cause I'm a southpaw." By Bill Mauldin, Printed March 17, 1947, in newspapers throughout the United States.

```
OF THIS LETTER, ARE REQUESTED TO CHECK THEIR
INDICES AGAINST THE NAMES OF THE FOLLOWING INDIVIDU-
ALS AND AN APPROPRIATE INVESTIGATION SHOULD BE CON-
DUCTED IF DEEMED ADVISABLE. . . .
     FERDINAND CHRISTOPHER SMITH — NEGRO, BORN AT LA-
MAR, SAVANNAH, WESTMORELAND, JAMAICA, BRITISH WEST
INDIES ON MAY 3, 1893. THIS INDIVIDUAL IS A SUBJECT
OF AN INTERNAL SECURITY - C CASE NOW PENDING IN THE
NEW YORK DIVISION, THEIR FILE 100-14347. INVESTIGA-
TION PRESENTLY BEING CONDUCTED BY THE IMMIGRATION
AND NATURALIZATION SERVICE IN NEW YORK CITY, HAS
NOT AS YET BEEN COMPLETED IN CONNECTION WITH POSSI-
BLE INSTITUTION OF DEPORTATION PROCEEDINGS.
```

The FBI memo continues for eleven single-spaced pages detailing the facts about some of King's clients. Of the eleven aliens described, three were seamen who had allegedly jumped ship between 1923 and 1942; two were Blacks from the British West Indies; three were women; Ferdinand Smith's case was clearly political, and three others might have been politically motivated; two involved allegations of narcotics use. (In one case a nonpolitical deportee was in trouble for lying to immigration authorities in 1940 based solely on his getting drunk in 1918 and stealing a camera and women's apparel.)

On September 15, 1947, Attorney General Clark called for an intensified drive against the foreign-born in an address to the National Conference of United States Attorneys. "If any alien in your district engaged in Communist activity, there is no place for him in the United States," he said. And on October 1, 1947, the Immigration Service finally issued a warrant of arrest for Hanns Eisler, the world-renowned musician and composer who had fled Nazi Europe to go on living and making music, and had been threatened with deportation in 1943.

Carol King explained to the press that her new client had entered the United States legally in 1940 and landed in Hollywood, where he wrote music for the movies until the end of World War II. His problems arose because his brother, Gerhart, a veteran of the German brigade in the Spanish civil war, insisted on proclaiming with pride his membership in the German Communist Party. Hanns Eisler refused to testify against his brother and suddenly found all avenues of employment closed to him in this country. He tried to go to Europe to fulfill contracts for his musical compositions, but the State Department refused him an exit permit and the INS refused him a re-entry permit.

While Carol King had no way of knowing that the Immigration Service was permitting the FBI to intervene, informally but effectively, in all of her cases — political and nonpolitical — she began to suspect that something fishy was going on. She protested immediately, as the Service promptly reported to its unseen ally:

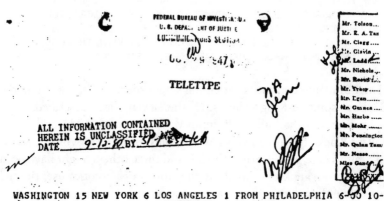

WASHINGTON 15 NEW YORK 6 LOS ANGELES 1 FROM PHILADELPHIA 6-50 10-
DIRECTOR AND SACS
CAROL KING, WAS., SMC. SUBJECT APPEARED AT CENTRAL OFFICE,
AND NS THIS DATE AND REQUESTED TO SEE FOUR FILES, AMONG WHICH WAS
FILE OF HANS EISLER. WHEN KING WAS ADVISED EISLER-S FILE WAS IN
LOS ANGELES SHE SEEMED TO THINK SHE WAS GETTING THE "RUN AROUND"
AND LEFT WITHOUT WAITING TO REVIEW THE OTHER FILES. SUBMITTED FOR
YOUR INFO.
          BOARDMAN
WA PH R 15 WA
ALSO RELAY FOR LOSA   WA
NY PH R6 NY
END

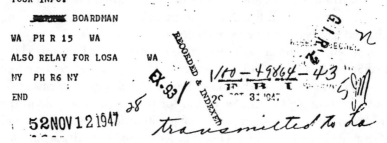

FBI File: Carol King (10-31-47). A report from one side of several lawsuits to the FBI about the opposing counsel's effort to review INS files of her clients.

At this point, the House Un-American Activities Committee subpoenaed Hanns Eisler, but he had nothing to say to them. His refusal led the service to arrest him in October 1947 for deportation and to schedule deportation hearings in Los Angeles in January 1948.

These events marked the political shifts in the fall of 1947. The liberal Walter Reuther defeated the Left-wing triumvirate in the United Auto Workers–CIO. His first act as undisputed leader was to fire Carol's old friend Maurice Sugar as general counsel. Within six months Lee Pressman was out as general counsel to the National CIO in Washington, the post he had created on the founding of the CIO. Some "liberal" union leaders were splitting from the Left, which had often helped them to power, seven years after some "liberals" in the New Deal had split from the Lawyers Guild. The Left urged everyone to fight the non-Communist oath required under the new Taft-Hartley Labor Relations Act, but some unionists were agreeing to sign. These unionists also accepted the Marshall Plan, which the Left/Communists said would hurt the common people of Europe because the aid was going to the industries still owned by fascists, and would hurt the common people of the United States because old U.S. factory systems would not be replaced with modern technology.

These events meant that suddenly Carol King could no longer call the general counsels of many CIO unions and reach friends from IJA days who would go out of their way to help defend militant foreign-born members. Lawyers low on these labor law totem poles also lost their jobs and turned to King for help, rather than the reverse. (I lost my toehold in Maurice Sugar's Detroit labor law office at this point.)

To sharpen the cold war, the Attorney General issued a list of over 250 organizations having "significance in connection with the national security." For the first time in United States history, membership in a "disapproved" group would lead automatically to the loss of employment in the federal government and to many other civil penalties: inability to obtain a passport, public housing, licenses to practice law or teaching credentials, even to loss of veterans' benefits, unemployment compensation, and social security benefits for deported employees of the Communist Party. The list of "subversive organizations" included the Communist Party, the IWO, and most of the organizations to which Carol King and her clients related that worked on civil rights, labor issues, peace, and defense of individual deportees or other political defendants. The list also included many cultural, national, and women's groups from the Depression and World War II, as well as many organizations like the

International Juridical Association that had been defunct for years. Only 15 percent of the organizations were from the far Right (KKK, German-American Bund, etc.)

The progressive Left decided to try to take the offensive against Democratic President Harry Truman and his cold war attacks. They founded a third party to make a major splash in the electoral arena for the first time since the 1924 Progressive Party campaign of Bob La Follette. They ran Henry Wallace for President on his record as FDR's Secretary of Agriculture and Vice President during World War II. The Party platform was for negotiated peace with the Soviet Union abroad and advances for labor and civil rights at home, and was against the cold war and the Marshall Plan as foreign policy and the Taft-Hartley Act as domestic policy.

On the defensive side, in December 1947 Pablo Picasso, Henri Matisse, Jean Cocteau, and twenty other world-famous artists filed a petition at the U.S. Embassy in Paris protesting attempts to deport Hanns Eisler from the United States. Carol made the long train trip to California to represent him at his deportation hearing in January, only to have the Service postpone it, first temporarily, then indefinitely.

On February 2, 1948, after Carol's angry return to New York, the Justice Department made a series of arrests that marked the heightening of the new cold war against noncitizens. They arrested Hanns Eisler's brother, Gerhart Eisler, on a deportation warrant. King said that Gerhart Eisler had hired her in 1947. Because she was already overburdened, she recommended that her old associate Abe Isserman take charge of this case. Now the Justice Department refused to set bail for Gerhart's release pending his deportation hearing; they promptly sent him to the prison at Ellis Island.

On February 10, 1948, the Justice Department arrested for deportation John Williamson, a leader of the U.S. Communist Party. They refused to set bail for his release pending his hearing and promptly sent him to the prison at Ellis Island. He retained David Freedman, whom Carol had known for years in the ILD, National Lawyers Guild, etc.

On February 12, the Service ordered Hanns Eisler deported after a hearing in which he did not defend himself because he wanted to leave.

On February 16, the Justice Department arrested Ferdinand C. Smith, age fifty-four, top leader of the National Maritime Union–CIO and of many organizations concerned about Negro rights, and one of Carol's clients mentioned in the earlier FBI report. He had come to New York from the British West Indies thirty years before; his wife and daughter were U.S. citizens, and he had applied for citizenship in 1945. The Service refused to set bail and shipped him off to the prison at Ellis Island to join Eisler and Williamson. He was represented by William L. Standard, longtime general counsel of NMU, who had known Carol for decades through labor and other cases, and through the Guild.

The National Lawyers Guild held its annual convention in Chicago in this grim period, February 20–23, 1948. Carol King attended but refused to get into the proper mood. She joshed to Julius Cohen as the train headed into Chicago, "You know, maybe I ought to join the CP and then resign and make a lot of money."

On February 20, the Justice Department arrested Charles A. Doyle, age forty-four, international vice president of the United Chemical Workers Union–CIO. He had entered the United States legally in 1924, and was married and the father of four U.S.–citizen children. The Service refused to set bail and shipped him off to the prison at Ellis Island, although he lived in Niagara Falls. Ira Gollobin became his attorney, an immigration law specialist who had known Carol since the 1930s and was her close associate in the American Committee.

Smith, Eisler, Williamson, and Doyle were not permitted to visit the library or to eat with the other detainees on Ellis Island. They were only allowed thirty minutes of exercise daily outside their solitary cells. It took two weeks of fighting, on the inside and on the outside, to get the four put into one large cell and permitted one hour of exercise daily on the roof, from which they could see, very appropriately, the back of the Statue of Liberty.

Throughout February, Carol and Abner received calls from around the country reporting more arrests for deportation: in San Francisco, John Voich, secretary of the All Slavic Council; William Heikkila, leader of the Finnish Benevolent Society–IWO; Per Eriksson, head of the Swedish Seamen's Union; and Nat Yanish, advertising manager of the *Daily People's World;* in Seattle, Julius Blichfeldt, who had entered the United States from Denmark in 1915, and William Bigelow, who had arrived from Canada in 1912; in Milwaukee, John Hilty, a member of the Hod Carriers Union–AFL.

On February 18, the director of the FBI sent a PERSONAL AND CONFIDENTIAL message concerning Carol Weiss King, with copies going to the Assistant Attorney General for the criminal division and to the commissioner of the Immigration Service.

FBI File: Carol King (2-18-48). A report during the tense period of arrests of longtime resident union and political leaders, who were then held without bail.

Forty years later the FBI claimed that the document's contents still must not be revealed. (See p. 450.)

This wave of political/labor deportation arrests, followed by denials of bail, was unprecedented in this era. Nonetheless, Abner and the American Committee knew what to do in its wake. The unions, fraternal organizations, and political parties to which the deportees belonged all went into the streets. They sent wires to Attorney General Clark and President Truman demanding that bail be set promptly so that the deportees could be released.

The lawyers for the deportees knew what to do next. They asked Carol King to serve in all five New York cases as general counsel of the American Committee, and she got David Rein and Joseph Forer of Washington, D.C., to come in with her. They had to go to the federal district courts as quickly as possible to get their clients out of jail.

Carol reminded the labor lawyers, who were not immigration specialists, that their goal was not simply to get their clients out on bail bonds, but on treasury bonds. The bond unit of the Service in New York had added a new requirement in late 1947, requiring a private citizen to prove personal ownership of the treasury bonds offered as bail, and that the bonds were bought with the citizen's own money. In many cases, the second point was impossible to prove, even though it was true. Carol took the time to explain the point because bail bonds involved a lot of money going to bondsmen that otherwise could go to the defense of the cases.

The labor lawyers concealed their impatience as best they could. Their sole aim was to get their clients out of jail promptly. The question of bail bonds or treasury bonds was not that critical in the total scheme of things. And frankly they admitted that they felt acutely uncomfortable in the role of immigration lawyers. They couldn't get a handle on the procedures. They knew criminal law and practiced it when their clients got arrested on picket lines. Some of their partners specialized in taking workers' compensation cases before state administrative agencies. And they were accustomed to appearing before the National Labor Relations Board, which was also an administrative agency. However, it had been established in the New Deal to administer the pro-labor Wagner Act, and its first board members had established clear-cut rules and a procedure very much like a court where lawyers could make arguments and write briefs with some hope of winning.

Immigration law was murky at best, and this business of having a client incarcerated in something that was not called a jail for something that was not called a crime leading to an appearance in something that was not called a court before someone who was not called a judge — this was frustrating in the extreme, to say nothing of the lack of a jury that might be swayed by law, logic, or emotion.

When Carol started talking about what should go into the petitions for writs of habeas corpus, the other lawyers were with her 100 percent. Habeas was an old and trusted friend. The New York lawyers went into federal court on February 17 seeking the release of Williamson and Eisler, because the Attorney General had abused his discretion in refusing to fix bail for these longtime, legally resident noncitizens who were not charged with any crime or wrongdoing.

The government replied that the Attorney General had absolute discretion in such instances, and that the courts could not review his denial of bail. Judge Edward A. Conger agreed with the government and refused to set bail pending appeal from his ruling. Three days later, federal judge Harold R. Medina repeated the process in the case of Ferdinand Smith, whose lawyer promptly appealed to the Court of Appeals. The others lawyers tried another approach, filing new applications for bail with the Attorney General for Eisler, Williamson, and Doyle on expanded grounds. It was understood that a victory by any route would benefit all four deportees.

At this point, the four on Ellis Island figured out what *they* had to do. They had been incarcerated on Ellis Island now from seven to twenty-four days and faced indefinite imprisonment, which would lead to a wave of fear throughout their communities unless they took drastic action. Each was a leading figure in his union or in the Communist Party. They couldn't waste time in a prison while their lawyers tried to get them out by strictly legal arguments. They knew the lessons in the old ILD pamphlet published in the thirties, the one with Bill Gropper's cartoon on the cover about how workers should defend themselves in court. Eisler well knew the militant tactics Georgi Dimitroff had used successfully in the Reichstag fire trial in 1933. All the deportees knew they could not depend on the courts to provide justice to labor leaders and Communists, especially in a period of economic uncertainty caused by a wave of strikes for higher wages and problems of conversion from war production to peace.

The four agreed that leaders had a duty to lead, not simply to rely on their members to march and on their lawyers to argue in court. They wrote a letter to Attorney General Clark charging that he was trying to bury them alive and that no one was safe if his action succeeded. They concluded, "We notify you that as of the morning of Monday, March 1, we are starting a protest hunger strike."

Clark did not release their letter to the press.

On Monday morning, March 1, Eisler, Smith, Williamson, and Doyle refused to leave their cells for breakfast. They would not eat any lunch.

During the afternoon another political deportee was incarcerated with them — Irvish Potash, age forty-five, vice president of the International Fur and Leather Workers Union–CIO, arrested in the middle of collective bargaining negotiations with the Furriers Joint Council of New York. Potash not only worked for the 110,000 members of IFLWU, but he was also vice president of the Greater New York CIO Council, representing 615,000 workers in many fields and a member of the executive board of the New York State CIO Council, representing 1,000,000 New York workers. Potash had left Russia thirty-two years before. He could never be deported to the country from which he came, so he faced possible imprisonment for life. The next morning, he joined the hunger strike.

During the next three days, as Williamson later recalled, the INS tried every maneuver to break the hunger strike. "We were taken out individually and offered food; big, savory meals were brought to our cells. We were suffering from hunger pangs but we ordered them to remove the food, threatening to throw it at the guards."

When politically active people heard about the hunger strike, they knew what they had to do. More than 500 delegates to a Congress of American Women meeting in New York called for an end to the deportation drive. Charles Doyle's four children marched on a picket line in Buffalo. The *New York Post, PM,* the *Nation, Chicago Star, Furniture Workers Press, Daily Worker,* and *Daily People's World* all condemned in editorials the denial of bail. Ten thousand New Yorkers circled the Immigration Service building and then marched down Broadway demanding release of the five on bail. Five hundred pickets marched in front of the Justice Department building in Chicago. The 1,000-member UE-CIO Local 163 in Pulaski, Virginia, wired President Truman condemning the denial of bail. Trade unions in San Francisco conducted a week-long mass picket line in front of the Immigration Service. Charles P. Lucas, executive secretary of the Cleveland NAACP, wired Clark asking him to permit release on bail.

The government did not budge.

Now it was up to the defense lawyers. They had to come up with something new, or their clients would sit on Ellis Island for a long, long time.

Carol King was clearly the expert among them on immigration law, and she could never stand it when a client was in jail. Now she had five jailed in New York, and as general counsel for the American Committee, more than a dozen more around the country. She wracked her brain to come up with a new line of attack.

It was her custom to stand back and try to see a situation in perspective so that a new avenue might open up in her mind, a new basis for litigation. Ira Gollobin and Isidore Englander, fellow lawyers for the American Committee, recognized this ability; it was what set her apart from other good lawyers.

Carol knew that on the deepest level, law is based on power, but on another level, it is a chess game. She had been playing a kind of procedural game against the Immigration Service since 1921. The INS had most of the advantages: a large budget, a sizable permanent staff, Ellis Island and a series of other "islands" at its disposal with bars on the windows. The Service also had easy access to the media. It could play on anti-alien sentiments, on fears — rational and irrational — for the "national security." Because it was a national agency, it could launch an innovation in any area and could then cite that instance as a precedent for using the same procedure elsewhere. Finally, when it was defeated on a point in court, it could ask Congress to change the law (as it had done successfully after the *Strecker* decision in 1939, paving the way for the second *Bridges* case).

Although the legal conflict between aliens and the Immigration Service often became complicated and technical, it still revolved around the same simple questions Carol had faced in 1921 along with Hale, Nelles, Shorr, and Brodsky: (1) To what extent does the U.S. Constitution protect the civil liberties of noncitizens? (2) What are the requirements of "due process of law" in dealing with noncitizens? What is a "fair hearing" before the Service? (3) Do aliens arrested for deportation have the right to be released on bail until a final decision is made, or can the Attorney General deny bail at his absolute discretion without the possibility of court review? (4) When can the deportees get a court to listen to their cases?

So far in 1948, the Immigration Service had managed to take the offensive on every one of these issues, and the stream of deportation cases threatened to become a flood. Carol was searching for the right material to construct a legal dike. She left to others the political strategy to fight the broader cold war.

Her search finally came to rest on the Administrative Procedure Act, proposed in a report by FDR and prepared under Walter Gellhorn's supervision in 1941, before the war. The *IJA Bulletin* had discussed the proposal at that time. Congress finally pased the act in 1946 after countless amendments. The act (known popularly as the APA) was adopted to bring more fairness into the procedures of the Federal Communications Commission, the Securities and Exchange Commission, and all federal agencies — especially the New Deal bureaus established in a hurry by FDR to meet the economic crisis of the thirties. Judges in traditional courts must have no interest in the decision in the cases they hear. To ensure this basic right, the government provides two different individuals to work for it in a criminal case: a prosecutor to present the evidence and a judge to decide whether the evidence is convincing.

Big Business interests demanded the same rights in hearings on million-dollar issues of licensing and stock market deals gone sour. They finally won the APA, which requires that the official who acts as judge in an administrative hearing must not have an interest in the outcome of the case. In deportation hearings, presiding inspectors were still deciding whether the aliens should be deported based on the evidence they themselves had often found as investigators and that they had presented, acting as prosecutors.

The Ellis Island Committee had recommended this reform in the 1930s, but Congress had never implemented it. And Carol and her colleagues had never been able to convince a judge that this combination of three functions in one person violated the due process rights of an alien. But it clearly violated the APA requirement for impartial judges, and the APA was now the law of Congress and the country. The Service was violating the APA every time it held a hearing. If the APA applied to the Service, the deportees and their lawyers were home free. All the lawyers had to do was to convince the judges that the APA did apply.

Carol called a meeting of the lawyers to tell them her great new idea. As I heard the story from Carol's viewpoint, her idea went over like a lead balloon. The men said she was wrong; the APA obviously did not cover the Service. She said she asked them to show her where in the act it said it did not cover the Service. It specifically exempted the armed forces. If the Service were exempt, why didn't the act say so? The men purportedly said that Congress obviously did not intend to include the Service, and they would look foolish if they made this argument, even if there were no explicit exemption.

Carol had never worried too much about looking foolish for raising a novel issue. Now she waited a while, and then asked whether any of them had any other bright ideas that might get their clients out of jail by May Day. None of them did, and they finally gave in.

Carol quickly dictated a paragraph for a new petition for habeas corpus, charging that no date could be set for a hearing "by reason of the fact that there is no one competent to conduct such a hearing as presiding officer in accordance with the Administrative Procedure Act, inasmuch as the Immigration and Naturalization Service has not appointed or designated any of its inspectors to act as presiding inspectors in accordance with the rules and regulations set forth in the said [APA]."

The next day the government replied that the APA "is not applicable to deportation hearings," and in any event, an alien can not seek judicial review on that issue until after the deportation hearing.

At this point Congressman Adolph J. Sabath, a Chicago Democrat, condemned the denial of bail. Sam Sage, secretary-treasurer of the Wayne County CIO Council, went on a solidarity hunger strike in Detroit. Courtney Ward, secretary of Painters District Council 6 in Cleveland, called on all members of his union to protest the deportations. Twenty-four labor leaders in St. Louis and the American Slav Congress in Pittsburgh wired Attorney General Clark. Creator of *The Thin Man* Dashiell Hammett, actress Uta Hagen, and seventeen other prominent Americans sent Clark a telegram demanding bail for the hunger strikers. CIO president Philip Murray publicly protested on behalf of Smith, Doyle, and Potash. Pickets demonstrated in various cities in front of federal buildings. NMU vice president Frederick Myers, Food Workers Union leader Charles Collins, singer Lena Horne, and artist Rockwell Kent spoke at a protest meeting in New York. The Left was involved and knew how to organize an effective public campaign.

On March 3, Carol King argued the bail case before district judge William Bondy, who wrote later that he "always regarded her as a very good lawyer and as an expert on immigration matters." Judge Bondy dismissed the writ in the case of Irving Potash: he would not overrule the Service and set bail for Potash's release on his deportation warrant. At the same time, he set bail of $5,000 for Potash's release pending his appeal on the bail question to the U.S. Court of Appeals. This legal nicety was not lost on King and company. This judge would not cross the Service by reversing its denial of release on bail, but he would accomplish the same result by granting bail pending appeal from his decision denying bail.

This was their first break.

By March 4, the remaining four hunger strikers were in a weakened condition. They had to be moved by the Immigration Service to the U.S. Marine Hospital. On Friday, March 5, they were brought from their hospital beds into Judge Bondy's courtroom to hear arguments on their new petitions. The room was packed with the press, friends, and families who spontaneously rose in their honor when they entered, altering the tradition of rising in honor of the judge. The lawyers argued for five hours. This was an ordeal for the four detainees because for some reason the bailiffs denied them water, the only thing that had passed their lips for the preceding 110 hours. Finally the judge adjourned court for the night, sending the four back to the hospital until he made up his mind what to do.

Friday, March 5, 1948, had turned into one of the bleakest days in the career of Carol King, lawyer for the foreign born and other minorities with minds of their own. She emerged from the courthouse glum and depressed. She could not stand to have basic legal principles ignored by judges. She could not stand to have clients in jail. Now she had four in that fix. She felt like going home and having a few stiff drinks. Instead, she had to take the evening off to go out and celebrate. It seemed highly inappropriate, under the circumstances, but it was a command performance. A testimonial dinner had been scheduled for that evening at the Hotel Astor in honor of attorney Carol King.

30.
"The Hell With You! Love, Carol"

Abner Green had gotten up the scheme to raise money for the American Committee for Protection of Foreign Born by honoring its general counsel on her twenty-fifth anniversary as an attorney, March 5, 1948. In fact, it was her twenty-eighth, but Abner had a preference for round numbers.

Carol King had never been honored with a dinner or an award by the IJA or the Guild, and she wasn't sure she liked the idea. But she agreed that raising money for the committee was a worthy objective.

The Saturday Evening Post put a very different spin on the affair in an article by Craig Thompson:

> Now Carol King has put mass defense on a mass production basis. In a typical deportation case, for example, her first effort is to get the arrested person out on bail. Then she has either the American Committee for the Protection of Foreign Born or the Civil Rights Congress — as general counsel for each, she virtually runs both — turn out a red-hot pamphlet using the case as a springboard to denounce United States justice. Invariably the pamphlets end by instructing the reader to "Write the Attorney General. Have your friends and neighbors write. Write to your local newspaper. Order a quantity of this pamphlet. Send a contribution to this organization."
>
> This Moscow-prescribed method of trying a case explains the 1948 accounting of income and expenses of the American Committee . . . From collections totaling $42,300, it had spent $12,075.80 on wages, $655.38 on printing, $2635.69 on postage, $1081.52 on telegrams and $2108.51 in promoting a fund-raising testimonial dinner to Carol King.
>
> Since the committee publicly claims to be a legal-aid bureau for oppressed aliens, there was also an item of "deportee expense" amounting to $7691.47. Apparently, for every dollar spent on actual legal aid, more than $3.18 was spent for anti–United States propaganda. During the year the committee undertook the defense of sixty-seven cases, but one was dropped. By a strange coincidence, that defendant was not a communist.
>
> *Satevepost 2/17/51*

Carol King was always a little amazed at how much work the committee could do on its budget with its small staff of Abner Green, administrative secretary Harriet Barron, and some volunteers. The committee report showed that 3,000 people or more came to the committee every year for advice on naturalization problems. The staff also raised funds to pay attorneys' fees and court costs. Abner constantly worked on legislation favorable to the foreign born and frequently asked Carol to do some lobbying in Washington. He and Harriet distributed mimeographed copies of the text of every important immigration decision to attorneys and other interested people all over the country. This function was vital because the Service still did not publish its decisions and even some court opinions were not carried in the regular law reports.

So Carol King went home from court, put on the new dress she had bought for the occasion, and set out for the Hotel Astor. She had suffered through an occasional stuffy Guild dinner but knew that at worst hers would be over fairly soon so she could go home and to bed (to wonder what Judge Bondy would decide — and when).

The minute she walked into the banquet room, she was surrounded by friends, clients, fellow lawyers, and relatives; the count was 275. Donald Ogden Stewart had agreed to come from Hollywood to be toastmaster. This was a nice touch, considering their long, bantering relationship. Nuddy Greene was co-chair with Charles H. Houston, with whom Carol had worked on so many good cases and causes since the thirties. And the festivities began.

Isaac Shorr spoke about Carol's early years at the bar. He and she were the sole survivors — Swinburne Hale, Walter Nelles, Walter Pollak, Joseph Brodsky were all gone. Stewart read a message from Henry Wallace, the Progressive Party candidate for President in November, and one from Bartley Crum, Willkie's friend. Remembering Wendell Willkie's warm words of praise, Crum wrote: "She has carried out the tradition of the American Bar in the highest terms. No lawyer in my memory or recollection has done so much to give validity and substance to the Bill of Rights."

As the program unfolded, it was clear that the committee and Carol's friends had planned well. Suddenly someone in the audience stood up and insisted on having his say. Toastmaster Stewart seemed a little nonplussed, and the audience was embarrassed for him. What a shame to have this kind of disturbance on this kind of occasion. Finally Stewart relinquished the floor.

The man said his name was Stanley Van Eyck, and he started telling the story of his life. He said he had worked as a waiter in Nyack after coming to this country from Holland. He got arrested for deportation and was denied bail on the ground that he was a seaman who had overstayed his leave. He contacted a Nyack judge whom he knew, but "the judge did not know the difference between immigration and personal property and so was not much help."

By now, Carol knew what was happening. The man wasn't Van Eyck, of course, but whoever he was, he had memorized the words Carol had dictated the other day when someone from the arrangements committee had insisted that she describe a few of her clients and their curious legal problems. Abner had added a few details she had not thought worth mentioning — like her fee arrangements. But it made a good story as the actor continued:

> My wife lived on a houseboat in the Harlem River. The adjoining houseboat was inhabited by a Yugoslav who was a client of Carol King's. The Yugoslav sent my wife to Mrs. King. Soon she came to see me at Ellis Island. From there she went to the Immigration Service. She explained that I had lived in this country for many years. I was in Holland for a visit when the German armies invaded that country. In order to get back to the U.S., I took a job as a seaman, but I despised the ocean; it made me seasick. I don't care if I never see the ocean again; in fact, I would prefer it that way. Carol King and I convinced the Service that I was not a seaman, so they granted me bail. Later they suspended the deportation order.
>
> And the next time the Nyack judge got a deportation case, he sent the client directly to Mrs. King.

"Van Eyck" sat down to an outburst of applause as Stewart returned to the formal program, reading a statement from the great anti-fascist novelist, Thomas Mann: "A Testimonial Dinner . . . is only too desirable in times when all sorts of reactionary shadows are darkening the American mind and when threats of war, persecution of beliefs and declining legal security are the order of the day. A personality like Carol King, who unflinchingly is defending the true nature and the traditional ideals of this nation, deserves our greatest admiration." Author Lion Feuchtwanger wrote that it was "a great comfort to witness the enthusiasm and intensity of people like Carol King who are continuing the fight of Benjamin Franklin and Thomas Jefferson. He who, like the undersigned, had twice to bear the brunt of the overthrow of democratic institutions, doubly appreciates such activities for the preservation of freedom." Robert Morss

Lovett sent a message as a long-time liberal and recent victim of the first bill of attainder in modern U.S. history — a statute passed by Congress specifically firing him and two others from the positions to which FDR had appointed them.

Then another actor told the story of another client. There was a hush in the hall, a straining to hear. Finally Irving Potash rose, the one hunger striker free on bail. In this dramatic setting, he read the speech prepared by Lee Pressman, who had been forced out of his position as general counsel to the CIO and was now a partner in Pressman, Witt and Cammer, and a Progressive Party candidate for Congress. Pressman had argued the bail question in federal court that afternoon for the labor leaders. He had written: "No sooner had this case been dumped in my lap than I found myself almost automatically picking up the phone and calling Carol. Her work with me in this case only served to remind me that this experience of mine had been duplicated by other lawyers on hundreds of occasions over the last 25 years. Suddenly, some harassed general practitioner or bewildered labor lawyer finds himself entrusted with an immigration or deportation matter. There's only one way out — get Carol King! May we continue to have that way out for at least 25 more years!"

Those in the audience who knew Lee Pressman could not think of another lawyer, or another woman, to whom this self-confident professional would have turned — or could have admitted it.

Pressman concluded his remarks by contrasting this period with the Palmer Raids: "It is to the glory of the American Bar" that in 1920 they "called forth some of the most honored voices in our profession" — Charles Evans Hughes and the twelve who issued the "scathing Report upon the Illegal Activities of the U.S. Department of Justice. Other outstanding lawyers served" in cases "at a great financial sacrifice and at considerable risk to their political or professional futures." Pressman testified from personal experience that today "there has been practically no response from the so-called leaders of the American bar to the crying demand that they share with us in the defense of the basic civil liberties of the American people."

The gala had also drawn a true leader of the Chicago bar, Pearl Hart, who, like Carol, befriended young women lawyers in particular, and all progressive lawyers in general, as chair of the Midwest Committee for Protection of Foreign Born, a leader in the Lawyers Guild, and a presence in Chicago civic affairs.

The evening was full of Carol King stories, letters, smart remarks. One Los Angeles attorney reported that the Immigration Service had begun its annual roundup in the Southwest of thousands of migratory workers from Mexico; he had written to Carol to find out where he could go for guidance on the law? She replied: "There is no literature on how to handle deportations. That is how I made my reputation. My advice to you is to fight every one of the 250,000 cases. You will find that if a fight is put up the Immigration Service gets discouraged. If no fight is put up they start deporting everybody in sight, citizen and alien alike. . . . But the main thing is to fight and fight like hell."

A San Francisco lawyer wrote that the government had tried to deport an aged, invalid woman with two resident children. He had written to Carol, wondering if it might not be a good idea to have a private bill introduced in Congress to prevent her deportation. Mrs. King advised against it because her experience was that it was virtually impossible to get such a bill passed. When the lawyer wrote back, unconvinced, Mrs. King replied: "I wish that you would stop wasting money writing letters to me asking my advice and then doing what you goddam please. I am of the same opinion still. You are of the same opinion still. She is your client. Do what you please and the hell with you. Love, Carol."

Many times Carol had confessed that she was baffled about the best course. In one case, she sent an attorney a detailed analysis of the possible courses of action, said that none of them was promising, and concluded, "If you can't do anything else, make a lot of noise and holler." The case was lost, even with the noise and holler.

All of this led one astute political leader to remark that Carol King was "a new kind of woman." Claudia Jones had met Carol in the course of her work as secretary of the Women's Commission of the Communist Party. When she was arrested for deportation to the British West Indies, she retained Carol and Ira Gollobin to fight for her.

Jones did not spell out what she meant by "a new kind of woman," and no one spoke about it. Certainly Carol King had become a lawyer woman. She had fused her professional concerns and skills with her personality and individual style so that anyone who met her knew almost at the same instant that she was a woman and that she was a lawyer.

Having had no women lawyer role models, King had followed the styles of several of the men lawyers she respected as to the practice of constitutional law, while developing a motherly role in the personal relationships that surrounded her law practice. Mothering, in turn, powerless clients, secretaries, and young colleagues — many of whom were present to honor her — she was what she once called herself: a he-woman with a heart.

Clients in Local 1 of the Bakers Union in New York baked an enormous cake for the occasion. Others came to pay tribute to Carol King because at her greatest she had also come to mother legal principles, nurturing them until they moved from appellant's brief to dissenting opinion to a 5-to-4 majority opinion that would affect all cases — until the next precedent was set. In the process, the crowd contributed $3,000 to the American Committee.

At least two in the audience had other reasons for attending the banquet. Their reports to the FBI indicate that neither of them managed to get the real name of the lawyer who read the speech prepared by O. John Rogge, former Assistant U.S. Attorney General. One report said "Golderman," the other "Goldman" — apparently any Jewish-sounding name would suffice for Ira Gollobin. Rogge's remarks were reported at some length.

```
CONFIDENTIAL March 10, 1948
EXCEPT FOR THE PALMER RAIDS, "SECRET AGENTS OF
CLARK AND HOOVER" HAVE BECOME INCREASINGLY ACTIVE
IN RAIDING HOMES, ONE AT A TIME AND HOLDING THOSE
ARRESTED WITHOUT BAIL; THIS MIGHT CONTINUE FOR SEV-
ERAL YEARS. THOSE ARRESTED ARE AT THE MERCY OF ONE
PERSON, CLARK. THAT JUSTICE DOUGLAS OF THE SUPREME
COURT HAS HAD THE COURAGE TO OPPOSE MAJORITY OPIN-
ION. HE WAS QUOTED AS HAVING SAID, "A PEOPLE INDIF-
FERENT TO THEIR CIVIL LIBERTIES MAY SOON NOT HAVE
THEM." HE ALSO REFERRED TO A STATEMENT OF OLIVER W.
HOLMES TO THE EFFECT THAT THE ULTIMATE GOOD IS
REACHED BY THE FREE TRADE OF IDEAS, AND THAT WAS
THE THEORY BEHIND OUR CONSTITUTION.
```

Late in the evening, the honoree was permitted to say a few words. Carol did not relish making speeches. They forced her to say specific things she sometimes preferred to leave unsaid and simply to demonstrate. But on this occasion she had a few choice things she did want to spit out. According to the FBI report:

```
DURING THE SPEECH GIVEN BY CAROL WEISS KING SHE
DENOUNCED THE DEPARTMENT OF JUSTICE AND SAID THAT
IT WAS ITS PLAN TO "PICK OFF" OFFICIALS OF THE
```

COMMUNIST PARTY ONE AT A TIME AND THE ARRESTS WERE
A PART OF A PLAN OF "STAGED TERRORISM" AGAINST
ALIEN COMMUNISTS.

The celebration finally came to an end, and Carol predictably wended her way home and to bed in a rosy glow.

The next morning she woke even earlier than usual, restless, conscious of four men in the hospital on Ellis Island. Nothing could be done about them at that hour, so she passed the time replying to many letters of congratulations she had received. To one friend: "Very few people listen to their funeral orations and while alive discover what wonderful folks they are. That seems to be my fate." To another: "Dinners are always bad, but as such things go, I must admit that I enjoyed this one. I guess everybody likes to hear nice things about themselves." To a third: "I did send your check to Abner Green rather than convert it to my own use. I thought that was quite generous of me, particularly as my finances get worse the more work I do."

Finally, at noon, she got a call.

Judge Bondy had dismissed the petitions for writs of habeas corpus in the cases of *Potash, et al.,* deciding that the Attorney General had not abused his discretion in denying bail to the four. He had also ordered each of the four petitioners released on $3,500 bail pending appeal from his decision, with the proviso that the appeals must be filed by Monday, March 8, repeating his order releasing Potash.

King knew that the Immigration Service customarily closed at noon on Saturday. She called and insisted they stay open long enough to complete arrangements for the immediate release of the four men on Ellis Island.

At 3:30 officials placed the prisoners on stretchers. Ferdinand Smith, a tall, slender man, had lost twenty-seven pounds in his hunger strike. Chunky Johnny Williamson was down eighteen pounds, Gerhart Eisler and Charles Doyle ten and twelve pounds each. The men were brought back to Manhattan to their families.

Carol spent the rest of Saturday and all day Sunday working feverishly to prepare the papers for the appeal by Monday.

31.
A New Kind of Woman Fights
the Cold War

As soon as the five hunger strikers were released from Ellis Island on March 6, 1948, their nine attorneys met in New York to decide what to do. Of course they would carry forward their appeal from Judge Bondy's contradictory order denying bail pending deportation hearings and at the same time granting release on bail pending appeal from this denial.

But Carol said they should do more. They should take the offensive. They should seek an injunction in federal court to prevent the Immigration Service from proceeding in any way with the deportation cases against the five unless the Service complied with the provisions of the Administrative Procedure Act and hired impartial hearing officers. This goal seemed completely logical to her. She had always wanted to establish that a deportation order could be attacked directly on the issues, like any other case. The courts had always said no, it could only be attacked *collaterally* by filing a habeas petition in which only *some* aspects of the deportation process could be challenged. She wanted to use the APA as a catalyst to raise this issue, and called another meeting of the lawyers to discuss her proposal.

The other lawyers objected. So far they had lost on the simple question of whether the APA really applied to the Service. Even if they could ultimately prove that it did apply, no judge would agree to hear their argument until Potash and the others had used up all of their administrative remedies. The rule about "exhaustion of remedies" clearly applied to the Service, and no judge would grant an injunction to prevent the holding of a hearing. Later a judge might rule that the hearing had been conducted in an unfair manner, but no judge would condemn it in advance.

Carol finally asked, in her shrill, tense voice, what they proposed to do while waiting for the appeal court to decide on the bail question. Were they willing to go forward with deportation hearings before immigration hearing officers who would continue to act as investigators, prosecutors, and judges all at once?

The others agreed that would be a futile gesture.

Then how would they stop the deportation hearings?

The men had no answer. One reluctantly agreed to write a brief on the right to an injunction against a hearing in this situation. After a fortnight of research and pondering, he quit.

By this point Carol's attention had been forcibly turned again to the musician Hanns Eisler. He was not a political activist like his brother, Gerhart. Having seen the web in which Gerhart had been trapped, Hanns's main wish was to depart from this country. He asked his attorney to try to arrange his departure. She thought it should be quite possible, as his goal and the goal of the United States government seemed to be the same: to get him out of the country.

But the Service refused to permit a "voluntary departure" by Hanns Eisler under the customary procedure, insisting he must be deported so that he could never re-enter the United States. Then they did not schedule a deportation hearing. Carol publicly offered the Service an opportunity to issue an order for his deportation, to which he would consent. The Service then called a hearing. Before the hearing, Carol plea-bargained that Hanns Eisler would give up his right to appeal from any part of the deportation order in return for having thirty days after the hearing in which to find a country to which he could go. The Service informed the press of this deal. Then the Service changed its mind.

At his hearing, the INS called Hanns Eisler to the stand so they could ask him whether he was a member of the German Communist Party because they had no proof. He said he had nothing to say. This refusal to answer finally became the sole ground on which the Service ordered him deported.

On March 26, Hanns Eisler left for Austria, expressing his gratitude to the many American friends who had stood by him, especially the American composers. To him the House Un-American Activities Committee members represented "only one thing — fascism." To Carol King, the *Hanns Eisler* case represented a defeat, but at least he was free to live and compose music and she could move on to her next case.

The INS quickly scheduled a deportation hearing in the case of Charles Doyle, one of the five hunger strikers. King wrote a memorandum to the Service repeating her contention that Doyle's hearing had to be conducted in accordance with the APA.

The Service sent a prompt reply denying such a hearing because the APA governed only those administrative hearings "required by statute." Deportation hearings were not required by statute.

Carol did not bother to consult again with all the other lawyers in New York. Many were busy campaigning for the Progressive Party presidential ticket and for Lee Pressman for Congress. Carol wrote to the law firm of Forer and Rein in Washington asking them to write a brief showing that the district court had authority to grant an injunction against the Immigration Service. They would and did.

According to a confidential informant (blacked out, but probably a wiretap on Joe Forer's phone), the FBI learned that on March 17, King "informed" Forer that the five hunger strikers were going to bring suit against the INS, and explained the basis of the suit.

Carol King supplied her co-counsel with an affidavit to prove that it was unfair to make a deportee wait until the administrative process was concluded before he could have judicial review. In none of her cases in twenty-five years had "the administrative proceeding been completed in less than two years," citing *Harry Bridges:* arrested March 2, 1938, case ended June 18, 1945; *Peter Harisiades:* warrant issued in 1930, administrative proceedings still going on in 1948; *Zusman Fierstein/Fred Firestone:* arrested October 15, 1928, reopened hearings still going on.

The APA case came first before Judge F. Dickinson Letts in district court. On March 26, 1948, he decided not to grant a temporary restraining order. Six weeks later Doyle's petition for a temporary injunction came before Judge Thomas Goldsborough in Washington, who happened to be hearing motions at the time. The immigration lawyers thought this was a mixed blessing: the judge was notoriously fond of granting injunctions, but he was also a former FBI agent and most of his actions were consistent with his past employment.

King did not even bother to go to Washington for the argument by Forer and Pressman. It was a foregone conclusion that they would lose. Joe Forer began his argument in his customary style — a mixture of New Jersey cockiness and sound research, quickly putting his opponent on the defensive. He had scarcely talked for five minutes when the judge interrupted him.

'Oh, if the Administrative Procedure Act applies to the Immigration Service I'll enjoin them, all right,' he said.

Forer saw a tremor sweep over the U.S. Attorney and hurriedly finished his argument, knowing the old adage about a lawyer who talked so long he lost a winning case.

Judge Goldsborough did not stand on ceremony. He said that "the Courts have read due process into the Act, and due process means a hearing"; therefore, "hearing is an integral part of the Deportation Act" as much as if the act stated so in words. And "it is more or less ridiculous to say that a matter of this importance, which can be decided now just as well as it can at the end of a long proceeding, should await the end of the proceedings." Two days later, he signed an order forbidding the Service from conducting hearings against any of the five hunger strikers unless the hearing officers satisfied the requirements of the APA.

The American Committee gleefully reported that, "Although the injunction technically applied only in these five cases, all deportation hearings in the country were supposed to be postponed by the Justice Department. No hearings . . . have been held since May 5."

The Justice Department was nonetheless quite sure of itself. The House had just passed a bill co-sponsored by the new Republican congressman from California, Richard Nixon, and Congressman Mundt (Rep.-S.D.) initiating major "internal security" measures to deal with "the menace of communism." Late in May, Attorney General Clark stated that he supported a law under which he could jail indefinitely noncitizens ordered deported but who could not actually be sent out of the country because their countries of origin no longer considered them citizens. This group would include 427 people facing deportation to the Soviet Union, twenty-seven for their political opinions. The American Committee dubbed this the "Hobbs Concentration Camp Bill" because it permitted lifetime imprisonment for many noncitizens.

The following day, Clark added the American Committee to his new list of "subversive organizations."

Abner Green, executive secretary of the committee, responded immediately: "In 1940, President Franklin Delano Roosevelt greeted the American Committee for Protection of Foreign Born and stated, in part, 'We welcome the work to maintain the rights of the foreign born.' " Abner and Carol saw this action as another move in their unending contest with the Service, which could easily overpower each individual noncitizen. Without a national organization of individuals and national groups that could coordinate their legal defense, the Service would easily have its own way with the foreign-born.

Carol did not sue the Attorney General, but the Joint Anti-Fascist Refugee Committee did, challenging his right to establish such a list and to place their organization on it. If they won, the American Committee would benefit as well.

Soon other attorneys caught the APA idea. Some nonpolitical lawyers asked the federal district court to free their client Wong Yang Sung from deportation because his hearing had not been conducted by an impartial judge under the APA. Sung had already finished all administrative steps and had been ordered deported. But in July 1948 Judge Alexander Holtzoff held that the Service was not required to conduct hearings in accordance with the provisions of the APA in the *Sung* case, making it a test case.

Carol heard that *Sung* might not be appealed for lack of funds, but this problem was solved somehow and the *Sung* appeal got ahead of the *Potash* appeal due to "the ineptitude and slowness of the government," according to Joe Forer. The government made the mistake of entering an appeal as of right at a time when they could only petition for leave to appeal. After the government realized its mistake, it took other steps that led *Potash* to the court of appeals while *Sung* was in the Supreme Court. King and Forer asked the Supreme Court to hear them with *Sung*, skipping the court of appeals. The Court refused, which was fine with Carol, for *Sung* did not involve tricky problems of exhaustion of remedies or Left-wing politics.

So many things were happening in a radical lawyer's office that it was difficult to keep track of the larger picture in 1948. Ira Gollobin remembers the period only as a busy blur. He does remember worrying about Carol — she was smoking and drinking too much for her own good.

❧

Then the U.S. government decided to make the first ever frontal attack on the U.S. Communist Party. In July 1948 the Attorney General asked a federal grand jury to indict William Z. Foster, Benjamin Davis, Eugene Dennis, and nine other national leaders of the CPUS for violating sections of what had been known as the Alien Registration Act sponsored by Representative Smith. In the anti-alien days of 1940, the discussion in Congress was all on the need to protect our national security from enemy aliens, and there had been less than half an hour of debate on the act's provisions relating to *citizens,* although a few civil libertarians had warned that they amounted to a new sedition bill as unconstitutional as the Alien and Sedition Act of 1798. The government had used the act successfully against the Socialist Workers Party leaders during the War. Now the anti-citizen sections would be used against Communist leaders just five years after the Supreme Court upheld the right of Communist leader William Schneiderman to remain a citizen and three years after the Court upheld the right of Left-wing labor leader Bridges to remain in this country against a charge of "membership or affiliation" with the Communist Party.

The federal government also began enforcing President Truman's "loyalty order" (Executive Order 9835), calling people before administrative agencies to justify firing them for conduct that the employees said had always been considered the exercise of one's rights under the First Amendment until only yesterday. Each labor leader had to decide what to do about the non-Communist oath provisions of the 1947 Taft-Hartley Act. Every Hollywood actor and actress who had taken a political stand on the Left started to worry about a subpoena from the House Committee on Un-American Activities and the blacklisting that might follow. The government did not conduct any midnight raids on workers' classes and homes across the country as it had in 1919 and 1920. It engaged, instead, in daily assaults on an ever-widening list of individuals, organizations, and activities. These assaults led to the daily loosening of links in the network of Left/Progressives, New Deal Democrats, and Willkie Republicans in the unions, the arts, the schools, churches and nationality groups, and in the professions.

Each of the committed New Dealers still in Washington was feeling the chill of the cold war as the federal government began moving against the people whose names they had found in Carol King's office in their raid in 1942. The once brash editors of the *IJA Bulletin* now faced "loyalty/security" problems based on their connections with the *Bulletin* and Carol King. The list included Donald M. Murtha, assistant solicitor of the Department of Labor; Alger Hiss, director of the Office of Special Political Affairs of the State Department; Arthur D. Eggleston of the U.S. army; and David K. Niles, administrative assistant to the President.

The people Carol and Shad Polier had drawn into their endeavors were now forced, one by one, to make the terrible choice. They could stand by their past beliefs and activities, or they could refuse to discuss them because they were protected by the First Amendment. Either stand would lead to loss of livelihood and loss of the chance to continue to play important roles near the center of things in government. Or they could deny their past beliefs, or admit and now reject them, hoping either of these stances would pass muster in the new climate. The tie with one Carol Weiss King was enough to get you a job in the Depression/New Deal thirties; it was enough to ruin your career in the Truman forties.

The press reported few lawyers denying or rejecting their pasts at this point. But few were heard to stand and shout their defiance.

⁂

Carol King and the lawyers defending the CP leaders in Foley Square concluded that the *Schneiderman* and *Bridges* decisions would not hold up without a terrific fight in the new cold war climate. Justice Murphy in his concurring opinion in *Bridges* had explained: "Proof that the Communist Party advocates the theoretical or ultimate overthrow of the Government by force was demonstrated by resort to some rather ancient party documents, certain other general communist literature and oral corroborating testimony of Government witnesses. Not the slightest evidence was introduced to show that either Bridges or the Communist Party seriously and imminently threatens to uproot the Government by force or violence." Carol hoped that the Justices who had voted with Murphy would stand together despite the cold war climate.

It was obvious that the major struggle over the legality of the Communist Party must be waged in the *criminal* Smith Act case against current *citizen* Communist Party leaders, not in the *administrative* deportation case against Harisiades, a *non*citizen *former* Communist Party leader. The ultimate decision in the Smith Act case would therefore control several issues in *Harisiades*. And the courts would not rule on constitutional grounds *for* the alien Harisiades if they ruled *against* citizens Eugene Dennis and Benjamin Davis and their citizen comrades. The *Harisiades* case still had to be fought, but on less basic grounds, which removed some of the pressure from his lawyers.

When the Service decided not to comply with the APA, it could not schedule a single hearing until it won the case in the Supreme Court. This gave Carol King a little time to turn around for the first time since the cold war had begun and led to her friendship with an attorney from Seattle, John Caughlan. In July the Canwell Committee of the Washington state legislature held hearings on "un-American activities" at the University of Washington while similar committees were meeting in California and other states, copying the tactics of the House Un-American Activities Committee nationally.

Without consulting anyone, Barry Hatton, a Washington lawyer, advised his client, Professor Joe Butterworth, to refuse to answer questions about membership in the Communist Party on the ground that the answers might tend to incriminate him; therefore, he could claim the constitutional privilege.

John Caughlan went to New York to a national conference of CP lawyers to discuss the propriety of this new idea of claiming the Fifth Amendment privilege to keep people from being sent to jail for contempt or for perjury. Should a witness use the privilege? Should a lawyer advise a client to do so? Should lawyers claim the privilege if they were called to the stand?

John was told that he could stay at Carol's apartment to save a hotel bill. John knew Carol only by her reputation in *Bridges* and other cases. In their first conversation, Carol asked John if he were a member of the Party.

John gave his stock denial in this period.

Carol said, 'That's not the way I heard it.'

John admitted she was right. "I immediately knew that Carol King was not in the Party but knew everything that went on in the Party because people totally trusted her and needed her."

In the course of the visit, John and Carol had a pleasant, person-to-person talk about their offspring and "she became a human being instead of a figure."

Carol's many old friends quickly discovered her new accessibility in this period. They had long known they could go to her "at the bad moments," according to Peggy Kahn, who found Carol's interest in people "because they were just themselves" reassuring and maturing. "She would help them rebuild their egos and their dreams, there before the fire in the winter, or sipping a long iced drink in the summer. Always the relationship assumed a special quality flavored by the expansiveness of her hospitality. She used to say, 'X must be doing well, I haven't seem him lately.' "

Carol's brief respite ended with another victory. On August 3, 1948, the circuit court of appeals overruled Judge Bondy in the case of the five hunger strikers. The appeals court held that courts *could* review the action of the Attorney General when he denied bail to deportees. It sent the case back to the district court so the Attorney General could prove that he had valid reasons for denying bail to the five men. Meanwhile the five remained at liberty on bail.

The case never did come to trial. In court, the INS would have to state the reasons why the Attorney General had refused to fix bail for each deportee and to present valid proof for each decision. Ultimately the Service would have to convince a majority of the Supreme Court Justices that its actions were constitutional. The INS decided instead to release the five on administrative bail of $3,500 each. Release on bail would permit the Service and the FBI to keep their eyes on the actions of the men, thereby frightening their customary contacts while avoiding a constitutional challenge.

The FBI was also keeping its eyes on the lawyer for the five men, according to an FBI report of a speech by CP leader Elizabeth Gurley Flynn at a CP meeting in San Francisco. (See p. 474.) Flynn said that King was not happy about the way the movement was dealing with — and not paying — its attorneys, including King.

⁂

For some time Carol King had been searching for an answer to her impossible case load. She finally found a suitable law partner. In the spring of 1948, on a trip to southern California, she became acquainted with another New Yorker, Blanch Freedman, who was vacationing with her young son, Michael. Michael Freedman learned from Carol King that the best things to eat in a bathtub are potato chips, soda pop, and oranges. In spite of this corruption of her son, Mrs. Freedman found it easy to like Mrs. King, who was an old friend and colleague of her husband, David. Blanch Freedman, an attractive blond somewhat younger than Carol, was a member of the New York bar who had decided years ago that it was more important to work for the Women's Trade Union League than as a lawyer. Now she wanted to go into private practice.

Both women could see the advantages of a partnership, and the firm of Carol King and Blanch Freedman was launched on September 1, 1948. While Carol and Blanch never mentioned it, the founding of a female law firm was a singular event in 1948. Even more unusual, King & Freedman shared a suite with another firm, Freedman & Unger, which consisted of Blanch's husband and Abraham Unger, who was known both for his

(b)(1) ~~C~~ furnished (date not given) a copy of a speech
entitled, "Communist Party Defense Campaign", given on September
23, 1948, by Elizabeth Gurley Flynn before the State Board Meeting
of the Communist Party of California which was held at the Communist Party headquarters in San Francisco. (V)U

    In her speech Flynn stated that the Civil Rights Congress
had been delegated to undertake to raise money for the Defense Fund
of the 12 indicted Communist Party leaders. She stated that one
of their difficulties however, had been that the American Committee
for the Protection of Foreign Born would not merge with the Civil
Rights Congress as had been suggested in order to strengthen the
Civil Rights Congress. Flynn stated that Carol King in particular
had resisted the merger because King had stated "that this is her
baby, and she had to organize it all by herself and more or less
runs the legal end of it!" Flynn also stated that "we haven't a
common policy, unfortunately on the deportation cases, as a result
of this." (V)U

    Flynn further stated in part: (V)U

    "This (CPFB) is just a committee, it is not a mass move-
ment but it is just a committee of top people, very broad and very
capable people, but what happened in that when people get arrested
like _____ SANTOS and OGOMEYER (ph) and then they set up their
own defense committee in their union. (V)U

    "Now let's take OGOMEYER. They paid PAUL TYLER fifty
thousand bucks and he didn't do a damn thing but lend his name and
CAROL (KING) had to do all the work and then CAROL didn't get paid
and then CAROL got sore and then you always have this feeling of
frustration on her part because she did not get paid but this is
partly due to this set up and partly due to this situation where
you have each case working from a separate Committee and try as we
will, we have not yet been able to solve this problem to try and
merge all these committees and try to tie it up as a branch of the
C.R.C. ABNER GREEN's original argument was that they have relationships with the Immigration Department, friendly relationships, where
by they can get people to go out to Canada, and re-enter legally,
and all that sort of thing. Well, that kind of guy has long past
where they don't have any friendly relationships and a little pressure can be brought to bear on this committee from all parts of the
country to push them into the C.R.C. because they have no machinery

FBI File: Carol King (4-23-48). A report of a report by Elizabeth Gurley Flynn
at a Communist Party meeting about Carol King's complaints against the
overpayment of other lawyers and the importance of the American Committee
for Protection of Foreign Born. Flynn's oral report was either taken down or
recorded by an undercover agent, or obtained by a wiretap of the closed
Communist Party meeting, as indicated by the names spelled phonetically
("ph").

commitment and for his doctrinaire style. Freedman & Unger handled some political cases and had many political clients in a general practice.

The new partnership worked out, but it had its trying moments as Carol found herself involved in cases at all levels on the same day, from an administrative hearing in the morning based on one kind of procedures, to a court appearance in the afternoon, followed by a long evening writing an appellate brief in quite a different style. She had never written down the dates of appointments or noted when pleadings had to be filed; she just remembered them. She had never bothered to keep her files in order; she just stacked up the folders on the sofa or in the corners of her office. Now, with responsibilities divided, Carol grudgingly modified some of her habits. Others remained. Blanch was quiet and methodical, reassuring worried clients by her calm in the midst of the political storm, while Carol continued to be flamboyant, addicted to her own hunches, disrupting the office with shrill anecdotes and frequent laughter.

Carol swept through many of her personal relations with the same gusto. She said she was trying to follow a policy of scrupulous noninterference in the affairs of her son Johnny and his wife, who lived only a few blocks from her. She saw them about once a week and remained intimate with Marion Pollak, who also lived nearby, and with her sister Nina. They all knew she liked to shock them, and she did. Carl Stern said, "Her big, tolerant nature kept her from seeking to impose her views on others. Except in the field of civil rights. There, if views were expressed at variance with those she held, she frequently became emotional and intolerant . . . feeling . . . she was being scoffed at."

But her friends also knew her as a sensitive person who could be kindly beyond all understanding. During one hectic period when she was trying to juggle a dozen cases simultaneously, she somehow found time to cook dinner for a family the day after the wife returned from the hospital. On another occasion she noticed that her friends, the Dunaways, looked haggard from staying up with their baby, who couldn't sleep at night. Carol took their infant away to Twenty-second Street for a week so the parents could get some rest while she and Mrs. Barkley cared for the baby. A neighbor somehow got on Carol's list, and she credits Carol with helping her through a lonely and otherwise depressing time while her husband spent every evening working for the American Labor Party.

Then the case of Benjamin Saltzman made Carol's life so hectic that her family and nonlawyer friends protested. They could not stand one more desperate story of injustice.

~~CONFIDENTIAL~~

(b)(1)
C

Confidential Informant████ advised (date not given, probably October, 1948) that "Carol King.is reported to have been working on the defense of the 12 indicted Communist leaders but is unable to get along with Abe Unger and, therefore, has not appeared in court or figured prominently in the publicity given the defense of this instant case."

New York letter 10-19-48
Re: "CP USA-Brief; IS-C"
100-3-74-2058
(100)

CLA:men   ~~CONFIDENTIAL~~

846

FBI File: Carol King (10-19-48). A report probably based on a wiretap indicating government knowledge of the internal relationships among defense attorneys in the Smith Act trial.

Carol insisted they had to hear the latest about her favorite client, who had come to her in 1944. She had taken an instant liking to this stocky man with grey hair and a habit of gesturing widely with both arms as he talked. She liked his friendly wife, who exuded a quiet pride in her husband and their three sons.

Saltzman and his wife had told Carol their story at their first meeting. He was a painter born in Lithuania in 1895, the year Carol was born. He was admitted to the United States in 1913 at the age of eighteen. In 1924 he married and the next year became the father of twin sons. About 1930 he joined the AFL Painters Union and soon assisted the effort to purge the union of racketeers, a difficult campaign that included moments of violence. In 1934 a third son was born. During World War II, his twin sons, Bernard and Isidore, went into the army. Saltzman and his wife participated in civil defense, donated blood, bought War bonds, and persuaded their friends to buy them.

In 1942 Saltzman applied for naturalization. In his interview, he volunteered the information that he had been a member of the Communist Party in 1936–1937 for about a year. In 1944 the Immigration Service summoned him back and questioned him at length. Then they summoned him again.

Mrs. Saltzman finally said he should find a lawyer. The Saltzmans had never been to a lawyer in their lives, but they had read in the newspapers about the *Bridges* case and Carol King, and they came to her for advice. Having written down the facts on her yellow pad, Carol told them, "Sure, I'll take care of your case, for nothing."

Soon Saltzman's petition for naturalization came before district judge John Bright. An agent of the Service stood up in court, called attention to Saltzman's admitted past membership in the Communist Party, and asked the judge to take judicial notice of the proscribed character of that organization. King followed with her description of the character of her client, and the law. Judge Bright postponed action and instructed the Department of Justice to schedule a court hearing on the naturalization petition.

Bernard and Isidore Saltzman were fighting in the Battle of the Bulge at this time. Isidore was killed there; Bernard was wounded. He recovered and went back to the front to earn five battle stars.

Carol tried repeatedly to get the INS or the Justice Department to schedule the naturalization hearing as the judge had ordered. In four years she could not budge them.

Now, early in the morning on September 28, 1948, Mrs. Saltzman phoned Carol. She had already been awake an hour or two, but her caller did not know her habits and had waited till a decent hour to call the lawyer.

Mrs. Saltzman said she had been fixing breakfast the day before for their thirteen-year-old son when she heard a knock on their apartment door. Two men stood in the hall. They said they were agents of the Immigration Service, and they wanted to know where her husband was.

'At work already,' she told them. 'Will you leave a message?'

'No, no,' they answered.

That evening, just as Saltzman got home from work, the two men returned and arrested him for deportation. They took him away to Ellis Island, but Mrs. Saltzman couldn't call the lawyer so late at night so she waited till first thing next morning.

Mrs. King was speechless with outrage — arresting a man like Benjamin Saltzman for deportation because he had applied for citizenship! She rushed to the office to draw up the habeas corpus papers and quickly took them to federal court. She found a judge to listen to the facts about her client and got Saltzman out on bail by nightfall.

At the deportation hearing against Saltzman, the government presented all its evidence against the alien: Saltzman's voluntary statement, then called George Hewitt and Charles Baxter to testify to the character of the Party. Hewitt and Baxter were former members of the CP who had been testifying as expert witnesses in numerous deportation hearings. (King reported to her network of lawyers that soon after the *Saltzman* hearing, Hewitt was indicted for perjury in the state of Washington for his testimony before a legislative committee there, although he never got to Washington for trial. Before that date he was confined in the mental ward of a New York hospital.)

King introduced evidence of the military records of Saltzman's sons, and of his activities as a civilian during the war. She put on Saltzman's witnesses: his wife and his employer, who testified under oath that Saltzman was honest and conscientious. This testimony took more courage in 1948 and 1949 than many other employers were exhibiting, from college presidents to Hollywood producers, as Carol was quick to mention.

When the hearing officer ordered Saltzman deported, Carol filed an immediate appeal with the Board of Immigration Appeals, and from the fall of 1948 on, the problems of Benjamin Saltzman were never very far from her mind. He became one of the "little aliens" she was determined to defend without turning his case into a "big" one.

Her "big alien" was still Peter Harisiades. She had made his case a test, but it still involved a specific human being — the secretary of the Hellenic American Brotherhood of the IWO and the husband and father of U.S. citizens. On June 24, 1948, the Immigration Service announced the 300-page decision by Gilbert Zimmerman proposing that Harisiades be deported.

Carol appealed from Zimmerman's proposed deportation order, and she and the American Committee convinced the commissioner of the INS to appoint a special three-man board to hear the appeal. In October, Carol argued to this board in the presence of Irene Harisiades, age nine, George Harisiades, age three, Mrs. Harisiades, and representatives of the United Electrical Workers–CIO, ILWU–CIO, and the Civil Rights Congress, each of which had leaders facing deportation, denaturalization, or both.

The INS conducted deportation hearings in several cases without complying with the APA. In one of these hearings they subpoenaed a new witness. In the deportation hearing of the young Negro leader of the CP, Claudia Jones, the INS called Angelo Herndon to the stand, knowing that this African-American leader had long since quit the Communist Party. Carol looked at the man whose case she had helped win fifteen years earlier, wondering what he would say.

Herndon refused to say anything at all on the witness stand. Later he explained, "I cannot allow myself to be used as a cog in the wheel of a machine that will grind people to death." After Jones's hearing, her lawyers decided to await the decision in the nonpolitical *Sung* case to determine their next steps in this political case.

☙

The lawyers and clients were also awaiting the political decision of the voters in November. The Progressive Party had conducted a spirited campaign in many states. Activists had been amused when Harry Truman, in the closing days, started using some of their rhetoric as the polls showed his likely defeat. When the votes were counted, Truman had won a close victory over Dewey. The Progressive Party garnered just over 1,000,000 votes, almost half of them in New York. This was a disaster to the activists, some of whom had convinced themselves that they might win some local offices; most expected to get a big enough vote to remain a political force. Lee Pressman lost his campaign for Congress.

The day after Truman's unexpected victory, Osmond Fraenkel had to go to Washington to testify as a character witness in a Truman loyalty board hearing for a young lawyer he had known in New York when he was active in both the ACLU and the Lawyers Guild. Fraenkel had become one of the leading appellate lawyers in New York, widely respected for his professional skill and for his commitment to constitutional liberties. Much to his astonishment, the lawyer conducting the government inquiry had a file about Fraenkel in front of him and cross-examined Fraenkel at length about various activities, including the 1940 election in the New York chapter of the Guild in which Fraenkel had defeated Paul Hays (then professor at Columbia Law School, later on the U.S. Court of Appeals for the Second Circuit). As Fraenkel wrote later, the board also asked "about my association with Consumers Union and about meetings, many of which I could not recall. Evidently the government lawyer was reading from reports in the *Daily Worker*. It was not a pleasant experience. But I am glad to say that the young lawyer kept his job in the Department of Justice."

The press daily reported proof that the Left was on the run. Where was there to run to? Carol King, her colleagues, and clients began looking for a place to make a stand in their part of the forest. She evidently found hers in the *Eisler* case.

32.
An Incredible Case

One Sunday in November 1948, Carol King attended a large family gathering in the country. She found these occasions refreshing. Her relatives, apart from her brother Louis, were comfortable people quite far from the headlines and events that wrenched the lives of her clients and kept her in a state of furious activity.

Louis Weiss had a great deal of respect for his sister Carol, "but no human beings could have been externally more different," according to their mutual friend Justine Polier, who described them, "he with his fastidious taste and she with her pretense of not caring, although she knew what was lovely and what was not. And she would rib him, and he would take it graciously as he did everything. So, it was a strange brother and sister relationship but I think with a great deal of love."

Weiss and his firm at this point were getting ready to integrate by hiring up-and-coming Negro attorney William Coleman (later President Ford's Secretary of Transportation). Like every liberal intellectual, Weiss was deeply worried about the steps the government was taking away from the New Deal and even the old Constitution with its new cold war at home and abroad. He told an audience at the New School for Social Research that "in the crisis threatening this land" we must seek "fruitful answers" and "without fear" seek "to convert those answers into action." Now Alger Hiss of the State Department had become embroiled in charges by Whittaker Chambers that in the New Deal thirties, Hiss had been a member of an underground group in the Communist Party. Weiss began doing what he could behind the scenes to quell the hysteria and make possible a rational approach to the charges.

His sister's law practice was very public and so completely intertwined with her private life that she had long ago gotten into the habit of talking about her latest case to any of her relatives who would listen.

They in turn had picked up from her an awareness of some of the realities of life on the other side of the tracks of power. King said that her clients were powerless but for her, and her many stories illustrated this point persuasively. The plot of almost every drama she unfolded was her effort to find a tool powerful enough to force the U.S. government to obey its own laws. She fought so hard, and recounted her battles so joyously, that her nonlawyer relatives were amazed later to discover how seldom she had actually won a case in court.

On this occasion, Carol got into a long discussion with Thomas L. Stix, her cousin on her mother's side, about her latest improbable front-page client. Stix was intrigued with the inside story of the seven cases of the "Number One International Communist Agent, Gerhart Eisler." Carol set them all down for him in a long letter on November 24, 1948.

When I was kidding with you on Sunday, you thought perhaps I exaggerated the humorous aspects of the Government's proceedings against my client, Gerhart Eisler. Actually I understated them. Only a James M. Thurber could do justice to this situation. Obviously after years of litigation, I cannot give you in detail all of the absurdities that the Government has indulged in, but I am giving you a summary.

[Gerhart] Eisler came to this country in 1941 . . . with a transit visa for Mexico, which he had managed to secure while in a Nazi concentration camp. He was unable to go directly from France to Mexico [due to the War] and so came to the United States. . . . He was ordered excluded at that time and, when asked whether he wanted to take an appeal from the order of exclusion, he assured the Government that he did not. He stayed at Ellis Island quietly and unobtrusively until the Government insisted on his leaving because they did not want to spend any more Government funds. . . . At that time Gerhart Eisler and [his wife] Brunhilde were together released on the nominal bail of $1000.

Gerhart Eisler first came to my office late in January of 1947. He was accompanied at that time by four F.B.I. agents who had the courtesy, I may say, to remain outside the office and marched up and down while Eisler retained me. I couldn't leave their presence unchallenged, so I took some sheets of yellow paper, walked out of my office, and took

*myself to the ladies' room and dropped them down
the toilet, to the consternation of the F.B.I.
agents, who didn't care to go beyond the portals of
the sacred precinct.*

*Shortly after that, I wrote both J. Edgar Hoover,
Chief of the F.B.I., and Tom Clark, the Attorney
General of the United States, suggesting that they
could make better use of the F.B.I. than wasting
that number to follow my client. I also suggested
that it was quite difficult for my client to live a
normal life with four F.B.I. agents always on his
tail.*

*I never got an answer to my communication, but
the F.B.I. vanished. I pride myself on being one of
the few people in this country who have ever driven
the F.B.I. underground.*

*The occasion for Gerhart Eisler's retaining me
was that he had been served with a subpoena by the
House Un-American Activities Committee for his
appearance on February 6.*

*By the time I reached Philadelphia . . . Gerhart
Eisler had been arrested with a fanfare all over
the papers about his being Communist Agent Number
1. I found it difficult to understand just what
grounds that was for arresting a person.
Consultation in Washington established that he was
arrested as an enemy alien.*

[Eisler Case One]

*Although 1) he was an Austrian and not a German and
there had been a ruling that Austrians were not
enemy aliens, and 2) he had gone through the entire
[World War II] apparently without any supervision
and certainly without any arrest. In fact he had
acted as an air raid warden and his Communist blood
had on a variety of occasions been given to the Red
Cross.*

[On February 6, flanked by two U.S. security
officers, Eisler stated that he would not be sworn
by the Un-American Activities Committee unless he
were given an opportunity to make the following
three-minute statement objecting to his being
brought into the presence of the Committee under
arrest:

"I am not a free man at present. I am an
antifascist, political prisoner in the United
States. . . .

As a German Communist, I always had only contempt for my jailers. And the more so when they
do their dirty business behind the hypocritical
mask of so-called democrats.

Let the American people and the world beware of
American reaction so cynically represented by the
Un-American Activities Committee and their
obedient servants in high authority."]

[The Committee denied his request to read the
statement.]

*I was Eisler's counsel at the Committee hearing.
I arose and said, "May I be heard?"*

*The report of that hearing bears out the fact
that I was not given the courtesy of a reply.* [The
chairman of the House committee, J. Parnell]
Thomas, merely shouted, "Take the witness out."

*When we returned to New York, I sued out a writ
of habeas corpus to determine the validity of his
arrest as an enemy alien. The case came on to be
heard before a totally deaf and rather senile judge
in New York. It took him some weeks before he
finally dismissed the writ and I was able to take
an appeal.*

*The appeal was never heard, because on the very
eve of the hearing and after the record and brief
in the habeas corpus had been printed, Gerhart
Eisler was indicted: 1) for contempt of the
Un-American Activities Committee,*

[Eisler Case Two]

*and 2) for making a false statement in an
application for an exit permit.*

[Eisler Case Three]

*He was released on those two indictments on $20,000
bail and apparently that established that he was
not a dangerous enemy alien because he was
immediately released without any further ado in the
enemy alien proceeding* [Case One].

[At Eisler's trial for contempt of the Un-
American Activities Committee, Case Two, Eisler
again was not allowed to say why he had refused to
be sworn.] *We got in an offer of proof on what he
would have testified if he had been allowed to
testify (that is,) his three-minute statement.*

*J. Parnell Thomas, on the other hand, was a
witness against Eisler* [at the contempt trial]. *He
testified that he did not know what Eisler was
going to say, and that the proper thing for him to
have done was to have stated a legal objection if*

he had such objection, and in any event Eisler's counsel should certainly have made objection if there was such objection [which is exactly what King said she had tried to do].

The contempt trial is about to be reviewed by the United States Supreme Court, which agreed to review Eisler's conviction. As one of the attorneys in the case, it seems to me inappropriate at this time for me to give an unexpurgated picture of my views of the trial judge. It is enough that my client is being held in contempt.

The trial [of Case Three: making a false statement on the application for an exit permit] *was conducted in somewhat more orderly fashion as the judge stated in his opinion that —*

"There can absolutely be no doubt that, when the notice was sent to the defendant which was tantamount to an approval of [his] application [for an exit permit], the Department of State had substantially all, if not all, of the critical information which the defendant is charged with having concealed."

After [this] *notice . . . had been sent to Eisler, such approval was hurriedly canceled — without notice to him — on the eve of his departure.*

Some of the alleged false statements which Eisler made in his application included such farcical matter as that he had failed to state in the application that he had used and been known by the name of "Gerhart."

Another name which he is alleged to have used . . . was "Julius Eisman," the name of a German infantryman who had fought with the Spanish Loyalists and had been killed. A fund for German refugees in this country was established under the name of Julius Eisman and the Joint Anti-Fascist Refugee Committee issued checks in that name [to refugees who were in particular need]. *. . . . Once he went down with their representative to the bank when they did not have cash on hand.*

Julius Eisman reappears in a proceeding by the income tax authorities
[Eisler Case Four]
which, after the second trial, charged Eisler with having failed to correctly state his income tax on account of his not reporting the $1200 which

*everybody admits he got, and much of which was
distributed to other German refugees who had
participated in the Spanish Loyalist movement.
Eisler himself, when he was sick, had used part of
this donation by the Committee. But none of it was
earned and none of it was income, a fact which the
income tax authorities apparently overlooked.*

*. . . After all the indictments against him had
been tried, Gerhart Eisler was finally served with
a warrant of arrest in deportation proceedings.*

[Eisler Case Five]

On this occasion he was held without bail.

*He suggested there was no reason to order his
deportation. He was trying very hard to get out of
the country! In fact, he was willing to stipulate
all the facts which the Government sought to prove
in his deportation proceeding.*

*Never daunted, the Government insisted on
deportation and insisted, although he was already
released on nominal bail and $20,000 bail in the
criminal cases, in holding him at this point
without bail. He became one of the five who went on
a hunger strike because of their detention at Ellis
Island without bail.*

He sought and secured a writ of habeas corpus.

[Eisler Case Six]

*This writ was dismissed and he took an appeal.
During the appeal from the denial of bail, he was
released on bail. . . .*

*Eisler claimed the deportation proceedings were
being improperly conducted* [by] *immigration
inspectors not appointed in accordance with a new
law, the Administrative Procedure Act. . . . Eisler
applied to Judge Goldsborough in the District Court
of the District of Columbia to enjoin the
Government.*

[Eisler Case Seven]

*The injunction was issued and the deportation
proceedings have been stayed* [pending the
Government's appeal from the injunction]. *No effort
on Eisler's part to stipulate the result* [that he
should leave the country] *can move those
proceedings forward one inch.*

. . . [T]*he Government . . . thereupon introduced
a bill in Congress to exempt the Immigration
Service from the operation of the Administrative
Procedure Act. You thus have a situation where they
say they are not covered, but in order to take no*

> chance against the determined attack of Gerhart
> Eisler, they seek reinsurance by legislation
> determining that the Act does not apply [to them].
> Nowhere in all this long list of proceedings
> against Gerhart Eisler has there been any charge at
> any time that he was an agent of the Communist
> International or that he is a Communist Agent
> Number 1, or any kind of agent. For that he is not
> being and never has been tried.
> Only Lewis Carroll or James Thurber could really
> tell this incredible tale in appropriate fashion.
> The one is dead. I wish the other would try.

Thomas Stix forwarded his cousin's letter to James Thurber, who replied:

> I enjoyed reading Carol King's letter but there is definitely nothing in it for me and *The New Yorker* at this late date. It is just one item in a bucketful of terror and travesty, and somebody should do a comprehensive story or book on the whole subject.

This avenue of redress having been closed to the lawyer, the client sought another — the United Nations. In January 1949 Gerhart Eisler announced in Washington that he was preparing to appeal to the United Nations to force the United States to return him immediately to his native Germany under the provisions of the new Universal Declaration of Human Rights adopted unanimously by the General Assembly on December 10, 1948. The declaration proclaimed that "everyone has the right to leave any country, including his own, and return to his country." Keeping him going around in a circle of trips to Ellis Island, jail, the courts, and the Un-American Committee, Eisler pointed out, was "a diplomatic way of kidnapping a man," a political refugee, and preventing him from returning to his native land. Eisler's action may have been the first effort of an individual in the United States to seek assistance from the UN on a human rights issue. It was another indication that Eisler had learned a great deal about United States history and heroes and how to make use of them.

The Universal Declaration had been drafted by the UN Human Rights Commission chaired by Eleanor Roosevelt, widow of the New Deal President. Mrs. Roosevelt was another new kind of woman, born into the established East Coast upper class, and then forged into a strong, independent humanist and internationalist by many forces, including the horrors and possibilities arising from the Great Depression and World War II. The Universal Declaration contained all the subjects covered in the U.S. Bill of Rights and in New Deal legislation, plus the broad rights spelled out by the National Resources Planning Board in its 1942 proposal for a postwar Bill of Economic Rights. But it contained no enforcement provisions, and Eisler's appeal was only a small media victory.

On February 17, 1949, U.S. District judge Goldsborough granted a permanent injunction against Attorney General Clark and Commissioner of Immigration Miller holding deportation hearings in Eisler's and the other hunger strikers' cases until the Attorney General and the commissioner complied with the APA.

U.S. Circuit judge Henry J. Edgerton pointed out in the *Eisler* case that the government was involved in "something of a paradox," having taken the position that "it is adverse to the government to allow Communists to enter the country, and adverse to the government to allow Communists to leave the country."

⅔

By the time *Eisler* Case Two, the contempt of Congress charge, was argued in the Supreme Court, Carol's young friend Louis H. Pollak had graduated from Yale Law School and was clerking for Justice Wiley Rutledge. His mother told him about one preliminary to the argument.

Carol was not arguing the case, but she had carefully purchased a new outfit for the occasion, which joined the (black) *Schneiderman* dress and the (black) *Bridges* dress in her closet. She arrived at Court at a quarter to twelve in her new suit and elegant blouse. She promptly took off her jacket and put it over the back of her chair at counsel table, next to the chairs to be occupied by co-counsel Abe Isserman and David Rein.

The court marshal immediately came up to her. "Mrs. King," he said, "Court is about to convene. You will have to put your jacket on."

Carol said, "I beg your pardon?"

The marshal repeated himself.

Carol asked why she must put on her jacket.

The marshal said, "Counsel must wear jackets in the presence of the Court," and pulled out of his pocket a copy of the Supreme Court rules.

Carol looked at the rule and replied, "Obviously that's an instruction with relation to male counsel!"

The marshal pointed out that the rule said nothing about men or women.

Carol insisted that it made no sense as a direction to women.

The marshal said, "Mrs. King, I don't know about that. My job is to administer the rules. That's what the rule says. If you want to take it up with the Chief Justice? . . ."

At two minutes to twelve, Mrs. King put her jacket on over her elegant new blouse and ended the incident, one of the few in her life at the bar in which she was treated exactly like a man.

Her proper behavior was matched by the very procedurally proper arguments by Rein and Isserman. They made two specific points: first, that the Un-American Committee was illegally constituted because it had adopted the role of a censor of thought, speech, and writing instead of that of a legislative fact-finding body; second, that Eisler did not have a fair trial inasmuch as Judge Holtzoff should have disqualified himself from trying the case due to his prejudice. They contended that before his appointment to the bench in September 1945, Judge Holtzoff was a special assistant to the Attorney General and in almost daily contact with J. Edgar Hoover, chief of the FBI, which had investigated Eisler.

Solicitor General Philip Perlman responded that Eisler's refusal to testify until after he had made a statement amounted to a refusal to testify except on conditions that he had no right to impose.

This statement aroused the interest of Justice Rutledge, who asked Mr. Perlman a number of questions concerning the right of a prospective witness to speak before taking an oath. The defense considered these questions a good sign because the record showed that Eisler had demanded the right to protest being forced to appear before the committee *in custody* before taking the oath. But, of course, there was no way to gauge from the argument how the Justices would vote on this case.

Eisler's notoriety had begun to rub off on his attorneys. Photographs of Carol with her client appeared frequently in the daily papers. At the height of the publicity, Mrs. Barkley told Mrs. King one evening that somebody in the grocery store that day had asked her if Mrs. King was a Communist. "I'm not sure you'll like my answer," continued Mrs. Barkley.

"Why, what did you say?"

"Well," Mrs. Barkley said, "I told her that I'd been living in the same house with you for thirty years and I'd just never thought to inquire."

Mrs. King assured her that was the perfect response, as she told me the story later. And soon the New York mail was carrying invitations "to join with a group of her friends in celebrating Mrs. Barkley's thirty years at Twenty-second Street. The more nuisance you have been to her, the more important is your presence. The jamboree will be at the Port Arthur restaurant . . . on Saturday, May 7 (she really started on May Day but some of us were marching), at 1:30. At 1:45 we'll start eating whether you have arrived or not."

⅌

Before the party convened, Carol's name hit the headlines again, bigger than ever. On May 6, 1949, the press reported that Gerhart Eisler had left the United States as a stowaway on the *SS Batory,* a Polish ship.

Attorney General Clark tried to find a way to bring Eisler back to this country from England but his effort failed.

Carol King was quoted in the *New York Times* as "chagrined" by Eisler's action. " 'I feel that jumping bail put him in an absurd light,' she said. His was a unique case of political persecution, she charged, with the government holding him, an anti-Nazi, as a Nazi when real Nazis were not being held, trying him for his political beliefs and activities rather than his actions as charged. . . . 'But a man of his political experience had no business to do it,' she said. 'I suppose his nerves were affected.' "

The American Committee prudently indicated in the next issue of *The Lamp:* "Eisler's departure was . . . a personal decision and his flight from the U.S. a personal act."

I remember Carol's anger when we discussed Eisler's act. I do not know which factor upset her the most. Obviously Eisler's departure meant that he forfeited his bail of $20,000 in his cases on contempt of Congress and making false statements on his exit permit, and his bail of $3,500 as one of the five hunger strikers up for deportation. In a sense, Carol felt that breaking his word to appear for trial implied that *her* word was also not to be trusted because she was his lawyer.

And this was forfeiture of bail that Carol and his other attorneys had fought for. His forfeitures meant that the government would now argue that no deportees should be released on bail because, like Eisler, they might also fail to appear for deportation hearings and skip the country. The same argument could be made for *citizens* out on bail pending trials for contempt of Congress for refusing to answer questions before the

House Committee on Un-American Activities, as Eisler also had such a case pending.

The lawyers knew this was not a valid argument. Almost every deportee except Gerhart Eisler and his brother Hanns fought for the right to stay in this country where their families had taken root, where they had jobs and were engaged in important political work. Other HUAC witnesses were struggling to remain in their communities. This rational argument, however, would fall on the deaf ears of many judges in the fearful period of anti-communism sweeping the country.

Another effect of Eisler's action would be to discourage citizens from putting up bail for deportees, fearing they would lose the money and become involved in court hearings concerning a missing person. As general counsel to the American Committee, Carol had to be concerned about this problem.

Then there was the problem of the cases Eisler had left behind. How could his lawyers go forward with them? On the other hand, they could not afford to lose them by default, because this would jeopardize the chance to win cases for other (nonfleeing) clients on the same issues.

Deeper than all the practical problems was Carol's disagreement with Eisler on the value of constitutional rights in the United States. She believed that she could use the U.S. Constitution and Bill of Rights to achieve justice sometimes. She knew that the judicial system often did not work properly for her clients. But she believed that people must learn to use this system, to seek to win good decisions from fair judges, and to win standoffs or delays from bad judges. Eisler's action clearly showed he did not believe she could win his cases for him in the lower courts or in the Supreme Court. And, in fact, his departure would mean that she would lose them all, ignominiously.

She had to admit that Eisler might have been right. She had lost a great many cases in a great many courts, and her percentage was going down. But to leave without giving it a fair try — especially with one case pending in the Supreme Court after argument on the merits — this must have disturbed her deepest faith in her own ability as a lawyer and her judgment that some political cases could still be won.

She was not haunted by the time factor, as Eisler was. He had sacrificed a great deal and had worked very hard in order to be in on the ground floor of building socialism in Germany. Even if his attorney could win eventually, it would not be soon enough to achieve this goal. For that he had taken the only path.

She did not claim to be a dialectical materialist, like Gerhart Eisler. She was not a member of the Communist Party–USA as he was a member of the German Communist Party. She did not participate in discussions at Party club meetings and was not subject to the discipline of Party decisions. She was an independent spirit committed to the use of the U.S. democratic system to win rights and reverse wrongs in the United States. If Eisler were right — she could *not* win any more cases for her clients in this cold war climate — that still left a question: Was it better to take individual action outside the judicial system in order to avoid years on Ellis Island or in prison on some political charge, or to become a political prisoner in the United States, like Sacco and Vanzetti (who were ultimately executed), or like Tom Mooney, the *Scottsboro* defendants, and Herndon (who were ultimately released)?

When she calmed down, Carol began discussing with friends and colleagues in the U.S. Communist Party the sharp debates going on throughout the Party, not only about Eisler's action, but also about the proper line for the defense to take in the trial of twelve leaders of the Party charged with violating the Smith Act. Benjamin Davis was one of the defendants. He was the lawyer in *Herndon* who had, until recently, been an elected member of the New York City Council.

Should the Communist Party leaders simply stand mute before the court and let their lawyers cite the string of cases from *Herndon* and *DeJonge* to *Schneiderman* and *Bridges* to prove that the Smith Act was unconstitutional on its face under the First Amendment and, therefore, the charges must be dismissed without the defense putting in any evidence? This was Abe Unger's absolute position. Would the trial judge agree? If not and the leaders were convicted, would the Supreme Court ultimately reverse its convictions under these precedents, or would it affirm in response to the political/military climate? Would this demonstrate that the country had turned toward fascism?

Should the CP leadership put in a First Amendment defense and *also* *attack* denials of due process by the grand jury and throughout the trial under the due process clause of the Fifth Amendment? Or should the defense make both points *and also* cross-examine government witnesses and put on their own witnesses to prove that they had not conspired to advocate the future violent overthrow of the U.S. government?

There was no way to know at that moment which of these positions was correct. Only time would tell whether further work in the courts would ultimately help turn the tide and return this country to a commitment to what Marxists insisted on calling "the bourgeois democratic principles won in the American Revolution," or whether fascism was inevitable in the United States, and Communists should deport themselves or go into hiding. Richard Gladstein, Abe Isserman, Harry Sacher, George Crockett, and Louis McCabe, trial counsel, argued these issues with their clients, who decided to follow the last alternative, not emphasizing due process issues but presenting a full statement and defense of CP doctrine.

There was actually very little time to ponder such questions at this juncture. One did well to respond spontaneously in a fairly professional manner. On May 13, 1949, the INS suddenly arrested Hilde Eisler, Polish-born wife of Gerhart, took her to Ellis Island, and denied her bail. On June 1, her deportation hearing was held there. At the hearing, Mrs. Eisler made clear that her sole desire was to leave the U.S. as soon as possible to join her husband in Europe. The presiding inspector on that day recommended her deportation. But Attorney General Clark made no move.

Ira Gollobin promptly filed a habeas petition to get his client out on bail. On June 14, Judge Bondy denied Mrs. Eisler's petition for a writ.

On June 22, after Hilde Eisler had been held without bail at the island for forty-two days, the government flew her out of the United States. She had offered to pay her own fare to Europe, but the Justice Department denied her "voluntary departure" and flew her out at U.S. government expense. This would make it virtually impossible for her to re-enter the United States if she ever wanted to, which, she assured her lawyer, was doubtful.

The Supreme Court played its expected role: on Case Two, Eisler's appeal from conviction for contempt of Congress, the Court removed the case from its docket due to the petitioner's flight from the United States after hearing oral argument. On Case Three, Eisler's appeal from conviction for making false statements on his application for departure, the Court denied certiorari. The Court also refused to hear Case Seven, the appeal of Eisler and the other hunger strikers in the APA-injunction case. In Case One, the enemy alien case, the district court held that Eisler had forfeited his bail.

These actions marked the formal end of the incredible cases of Gerhart Eisler, his brother Hanns, and their wives. Carol knew it marked the beginning of new attacks on her other deportation clients, on the American Committee, and on the Civil Rights Congress. And she was afraid the repercussions would not stop there.

33.
Once in a Lifetime!

Gerhart Eisler left the United States as a stowaway on May 6, 1949, to signal that the U.S. Immigration Service had turned a corner to retrace its past. Other progressive aliens responded in a variety of ways. On May 8, Alexander Stevens, labeled a "mysterious international red agent" by the press, left the country under "voluntary departure" so he could choose his country of exile. In Los Angeles, Abe Ozeran told fellow members of the executive board of News Vendors Union Local 75 that the FBI had been questioning him, threatening deportation proceedings. Later in May, Ozeran left the country in his own way, by suicide.

On May 25, a federal grand jury in San Francisco did as it was bidden by Attorney General Clark. They indicted citizen Harry Bridges on charges of conspiracy and perjury in obtaining his citizenship in 1945 after he won his deportation case in the U.S. Supreme Court. And they indicted two officials of the ILWU-CIO who had been his witnesses in the naturalization proceeding. Still, Clark didn't have everything his own way. In July, federal judge Guy Bard in Philadelphia enjoined the Attorney General from requiring deportees to report weekly to the INS, saying, "I think you are throwing your weight around a little too much [in this] newspaper created hysteria."

In total, the Service had arrested fifty people for deportation on political grounds in 1948, adding to a previous twenty-one. And on December 7, 1948, anniversary of the Pearl Harbor attack, the U.S. Department of Justice announced plans to revert to the Palmer Raid psychology. They would arrest 482 more aliens on political grounds, hold up applications for citizenship by 498 people charged with political or union activity, and revoke the citizenship of 228 naturalized citizens like Harry Bridges for alleged Communist Party membership.

On the other hand, the Bill of Rights, and the people who relied on it, had won some victories in 1948. King's wins had been really big: the release of the five hunger strikers and Judge Goldsborough's unprecedented injunction against the Service for holding improper hearings. She had also convinced the First Circuit Court of Appeals that Philip Stasiukevich of Maynard, Massachusetts, should not be denied citizenship because of his membership in the International Workers Order.

Carol and Is Englander worked strenuously on their argument before the Board of Immigration Appeals in the *Harisiades* case. In May the BIA agreed that Peter Harisiades did not personally believe in violent overthrow of the government. The BIA nonetheless sustained his deportation on the ground that he had been a member of the CP, an organization they found had advocated the illegal doctrine. A week later, the INS picked up Harisiades and sent him to Ellis Island, where it held him without bail.

Then the INS rearrested another client, George Pirinsky, and told him to post $25,000 bail.

Carol could not convince the court of appeals to grant bail pending appeal because Eisler had jumped bail. So she tried to get an individual judge to grant bail until the appeal could be heard, arguing that the Eighth Amendment prohibited "excessive bail." Judge Charles E. Clark of the circuit court and Justice Jackson of the U.S. Supreme Court both replied that Pirinsky seemed to be entitled to bail on the merits of his case, but they lacked authority to grant bail pending the appeal. Carol kept trying and finally the judges of the Second Circuit Court agreed to meet at New Haven, Connecticut, to hear the appeal.

What gave her the power to cause judges to convene a special session of the court during its recess? Guilt, pride, and history. Holding noncriminals in jail-like rooms just because they were not citizens had never sat well with judges. And by this time, the name "Carol King" on a brief reminded the judges of the 1920 "Report on Illegal Practices" ending the abuses of the Palmer Raids, and of her victories over the Service in *Schneiderman* and *Bridges*. Nuddy Greene pointed out that "judges knew when Carol was before them that the case would be appealed if it went against her. Therefore, any friendship they had with the prosecution, personally or in principle, went by the boards and so did any predilection against Carol's client or his views in the face of the desire not to be reversed on appeal. The judges wrote and decided carefully in her cases because they knew all adverse decisions would go on up to the Supreme

Court, if necessary. This . . . obliterated the problem of not being from a big downtown firm."

After Carol's argument, the appellate judges ruled that on the basis of the record before them, bail of more than $5,000 would seem an abuse of discretion by the Attorney General, who had held Pirinsky in custody for ten weeks by this time.

This decision was certainly out of step with the times.

The Justice Department had announced in May 1949 that it planned to deport more than 250,000 Mexicans. The American Committee charged that this decision had led to a "wave of terror" in southern California, where thousands of people were being shipped across the border. Carol urged lawyers in California to try to "fight every case," as the only way to stop the Service from further trampling on the Constitution. Then she rushed from the victory for Pirinsky back to the *Harisiades* case.

She sued the Service in federal district court to force them to set bail for Harisiades. She lost. She and Is Englander then filed a habeas petition to test the deportation order. By now it was July 22, and Harisiades had been in custody more than two months.

Judge Vincent Leibell ordered the Service to release Harisiades on $5,000 bail pending his decision on the merits, which would take him some time to prepare because by now the record was enormous and the case also involved a difficult new question: Could the Service require a deportee to report regularly, pending a final deportation order, as well as require the deportee to put up bail in order to be released?

This reporting requirement was the latest wrinkle in the attack by the Service on the freedom of a person during a deportation case. When deportees "reported," they were asked questions about themselves, their organizations, and other individuals.

Benjamin Saltzman was one of the first to face this new requirement. He had been free on $500 bail since September 1948. He had appeared for all deportation proceedings. Now the Service demanded that he should also report to them at intervals. Saltzman refused and Carol went to the federal district court for an injunction to stop this requirement. In August 1949 Judge Samuel H. Kaufman restrained the Service from re-arresting Saltzman, altering his bail, or forcing him to report.

In some other parts of the country, deportees and their attorneys quietly accepted the reporting requirement. Carol wrote to one such lawyer: "We think you people are taking it lying down and just as long as you take it lying down you make it harder not only for yourselves in future cases, but for all the rest of us."

But in one case in that long hot summer, Carol's client accepted the reporting requirement with Carol's unhappy acquiescence. Beatrice Siskind Johnson, sister of deportee George Siskind, had been arrested first in February 1948 for deportation and released on $1,000 bail. At the time of her deportation hearing in September 1948, Carol King was ill. Mrs. Johnson objected to proceeding without her attorney, but the hearing officer overruled her objection, conducted the hearing alone, and ordered her deported on June 6, 1949.

While Carol's appeal to the Board of Immigration Appeals was pending, the Service told Mrs. Johnson to post higher bail and also to report regularly.

She refused.

The Service arrested her and sent her to Ellis Island. Luckily, her young daughter was going away to a camp for the summer, so Beatrice Johnson remained on Ellis Island for forty-nine summer days. But she knew that when her daughter returned from camp, there would be nobody to care for her.

Beatrice Johnson, single parent, talked over with Carol King, single parent, what was to be done. In terms of the political/legal battle, Mrs. Johnson should continue to refuse to post bail or to report. In personal terms, Mrs. Johnson should not do anything that could irreparably damage her daughter's right to a reasonably happy and secure childhood. Mrs. Johnson reluctantly agreed to post $10,000 bail and to report regularly. The Service then released her.

A month later, the Board of Immigration Appeals ruled that her deportation hearing was improper because she had been deprived of counsel. Carol was vindicated by the outcome and outraged that her client had been in custody for forty-nine days under a deportation order based on an unfair hearing. A second hearing was held. (In February 1950 this hearing was also rendered invalid on other grounds, making necessary a third hearing.)

On August 3, the Service lost the hunger strikers' bail case in the court of appeals, and quietly dropped the case. The Attorney General then asked a federal grand jury in Buffalo to indict one of the five hunger strikers, union leader Charles Doyle. In January 1948 he had gone to Canada legally for a union meeting of the CIO Chemical Workers; the U.S. government canceled his re-entry permit. Now he was charged with illegal re-entry into this country, where he had lived legally for twenty-four years, had married and raised a family of four children. He was quickly tried, convicted, and sentenced to one year in jail. Ira Gollobin filed an appeal.

The sweltering political summer of 1949 was not yet over. On July 27, a mob of white townspeople prevented Paul Robeson, giant of the concert stage and an unforgettable Othello, from singing in Peekskill, New York, a summer resort. On August 4, Paul Robeson returned to Peekskill. This time the great Negro artist sang to a tremendous crowd. On their way out of town after the concert, the police stood by as a white mob threw rocks at the audience and their cars, injuring 200 people.

In this raucous period, with the Left under attack and fighting furiously, the American Labor Party asked Carol to run for the municipal court in New York City and she agreed. She had long been an ALP supporter and she could see the value in having a strong ALP ticket, even though she had no desire to stop practicing law in order to become a judge and realized she had no hope of winning. Her candidacy forced the Association of the Bar of the City of New York to confront the candidacy of one of its own members. The association always published its opinions on judicial candidates. Their action in this instance amused the candidate. The association declared, "Notwithstanding doubts as to her judicial temperament, the Committee, by a divided vote, finds her to be 'Qualified' because of her unquestioned ability and experience."

Candidate King did not have much time to counter this faint praise because the burden of work at King & Freedman was frightening. But as Carol got busier at work, she seemed to have more time for her friends — that is, for clients and lawyers and legal defense people with whom she worked. She often had people over for a meal while she was in the midst of preparing for a hearing. The people she met at meetings, conventions, and hearings around the country were always invited to call when they were in the City. She gave the invitations so warmly that a great many people took her up on them — and ended up eating some of Carol's (and Mrs. Barkley's) good cooking. Many spent the night and stayed for breakfast. None of this seemed to fluster Carol. It was just part of a week's work and fun. To other lawyers, it often seemed that there were no lines drawn between work and relaxation. But Carol King still retained a private side, a family and a group of nonlegal friends, including artists and writers she had met through Gordon, or later through her own frequent visits to the galleries.

She always told her colleagues what she was doing, asking for comments and suggestions as if they might have an answer she had not been able to figure out. She seemed to have plenty of time to listen to the legal — and personal — problems her young friends described. For example, in the midst of her crowded calendar, she somehow remembered to convince her friend Elizabeth Gurley Flynn that it was really important for her to answer a letter from Ray Ginger in Cleveland seeking information for his biography of Eugene V. Debs. At the time, I did not fully comprehend the level of organization this act required of Carol. She also found time to give counsel to a woman lawyer who was having difficulty with another woman lawyer who was sharing a suite of offices. Carol told Mary Kaufman to solve the problem quickly and peacefully. This was no time for women lawyers on the Left to get into a petty dispute.

ॐ

In October 1949 Judge Medina gave instructions to the jury leading to the conviction under the Smith Act of Eugene Dennis, Ben Davis, John Williamson, and the other Communist Party leaders, while Judge Leibell was still pondering the issues in the *Harisiades* case. Judge Medina also found all the defense lawyers guilty of contempt of court, and ordered Harry Sacher, Richie Gladstein, George Crockett, and Abe Isserman to federal prison for one to six months. The contempt citations of all defense counsel were unprecedented, the prison terms shocking.

Sacher promptly asked Osmond Fraenkel to represent him and the other Smith Act lawyers on their contempt appeals.

Fraenkel was willing to do so, he wrote later, "believing that Medina's own conduct had contributed to that of the lawyers, that the charge he made against them of conspiring to obstruct justice was baseless and that the sentences were too severe." He had attended several of the sessions and got the impression that "the judge and the lawyers were engaged in a baiting contest — unjustified in my opinion on both sides, but not deserving proceedings against the lawyers."

Fraenkel told Arthur Garfield Hays, who headed the firm with which Fraenkel had long been associated. Hays was still a leader of the ACLU, as he had been when he convinced Darrow to represent Greco and Carillo in the 1920s. He agreed that Fraenkel should take on the appeal. But the next day, after he had spoken to some of his partners about it, Hays changed his mind. Fraenkel was called into conference with the senior members — William Abramson, "Teddy" St. John, John Schulman, Sidney Struble, Seymour Heilbron, and Alan Hays. They stated their objection, "so serious that if I took the appeal I couldn't stay with the firm. . . . I was much upset." Before deciding what to do, he discussed the problem with his wife and daughters. "Regretfully we all agreed that it would be quixotic for me to go ahead. I told Sacher of my predicament the next day. His only answer was that they all loved me anyway. I was much moved."

Somewhat to relieve his feelings of frustration, Fraenkel wrote to a number of prominent lawyers asking if they would join him in a brief amicus to the court of appeals on the immediately pressing issue: bail pending appeal. "But the response was so overwhelmingly negative that I abandoned the project."

At this time the mighty CIO began efforts to expel eleven international unions with 1,000,000 members. Two grounds were stated: the Left-wing unions had refused to support the Marshall Plan after World War II, under which, among other things, the United States planned to rebuild private industries in West Germany and Italy, industries owned by former Nazis and Fascists; and the unions had supported Henry Wallace for president in 1948 on the Progressive Party ticket instead of supporting the CIO's man, Harry Truman. Carol's friends Eddy Malament and Herman Rosenfeld, lawyers for the National Maritime Union, and Victor Rabinowitz, lawyer for one of the eleven ousted unions, complained bitterly about the CIO's unseemly haste in taking this action — similar to the expulsion of the Left/progressive CIO unions from the AFL fourteen years before.

Rabinowitz, with other lawyers in the Communist Party, had developed a strong legal attack on the Taft-Hartley Act that he used in *American Communications Association (ACA) v. Douds.* They argued that the new act's non-Communist oath was unconstitutional, that is, that Congress had no power under the First Amendment to require union leaders to swear they were not Communists in order to be able to use the NLRB for union representation elections and other services. The lawyers cited, among other cases, *Schneiderman* and *Bridges.*

In this period, when the fact of membership or nonmembership in the Communist Party was becoming a litmus test in so many fields, Victor Rabinowitz recalls that he seldom thought about it. He says he attended many strategy meetings with lawyers and labor leaders where the topic of discussion was what to do about the non-Communist oaths required under the Taft-Hartley Act and Executive Orders. He assumed that everyone in the room was a CP member; but in fact, he did not know whether they were or were not, and it did not occur to him to ask or to consider this a problem. Everyone seemed to understand everyone else and to argue for his position within a broad set of common values and sense of history.

A problem did arise when the President of the CIO, Philip Murray, requested that Rabinowitz's *ACA* case be adjourned until early in the next term because the Steel Workers' similar case was not yet ready for argument, and the delay would enable both cases to be argued together. Murray advised the ACA "that President Truman had suggested a postponement of the argument because he expected a Congressional effort to amend the Taft-Hartley Act by striking out" the non-Communist oaths or modifying them substantially. "Truman thought it would be impossible to amend Taft-Hartley if the Supreme Court ruled in our case that it was constitutional," Rabinowitz reported in *The Cold War Against Labor*. Rabinowitz favored immediate argument but was voted down, and *ACA* was set for argument with *Steel Workers* in October 1949. "Disaster struck in the summer of 1949. Justice Murphy died in July. Justice Rutledge died in September. A few days before the argument, Justice Douglas fell off a horse . . . and . . . could not participate in the case. Of our stalwart band of four on whom we counted to support our attack on the constitutionality of the Act, only Justice Black was left."

At this point, Carol King's lawyer friends in the Communist Party were continuing to meet and work in two ways in New York. Some were still members of lawyers' clubs that worked primarily on the legal aspect of issues, doing their "mass work" in the National Lawyers Guild and legal defense organizations, and a couple worked in the American Bar Association. More lawyers were still members of Communist Party neighborhood clubs that concentrated on community issues, including work for local candidates. Most of the lawyers were busy more than forty hours a week representing labor unions, injured workers, and other traditional clients of small firms. The two types of Party lawyers met at an occasional large gathering of the Guild or the American Labor Party or at large political rallies. One might notice that another lawyer "sounded solid on the issues" without knowing whether the person was currently a Party member, and it was not the sort of question one asked.Carol always knew both kinds of Party lawyers.

King divided her own time between national (and international) legal issues and personal relationships, omitting the neighborhood/community issues that built a base for political campaign work. This predilection did not help her ability to campaign for the judgeship in New York in November 1949, although it is clear a woman could not have won in that climate in any event.

⅔

At this point, Carol King's opinion of the U.S. Department of Justice had touched bottom. There was little justice, and what little there was did not result from the actions of the department of that name. Carol revolted when President Truman nominated Attorney General Tom Clark of Texas to become a Justice of the Supreme Court to sit in the seat left vacant by the untimely death of Frank Murphy of Michigan, author of the humanist opinion in *Schneiderman* and the memorable concurring opinion in *Bridges*. Carol appeared before the Senate Judiciary Committee on August 9 to oppose Clark's nomination on behalf of the American Committee.

Clark was a different kind of Attorney General from his recent predecessors. He had never been in or near the National Lawyers Guild, unlike Frank Murphy, Robert Jackson, and Francis Biddle. His background included no close working relationship with leading militant Negro lawyers, and he had insisted the federal government could play only a limited role under his interpretation of the 1870 Anti-Klan Act and the recent Supreme Court decision in *Screws v. United States.*

Now King charged that Clark had tried to deny the protection of the Bill of Rights to non-citizens. He had tried to deny bail, and in *Potash* had refused to justify his actions before a judge in open court. He had tried to force deportees who were free on bail to report periodically to the Immigration Service until this practice was enjoined in two cases by district court judges. He had hired as clerks in the Immigration Service several ex-Communists who were used as traveling witnesses in deportation cases. One, George Hewitt, had been indicted for perjury in the state of Washington, and the Attorney General had "encouraged or aided" him in his successful resistance to extradition. Another, David C. De Leon, "admitted to committing perjury on five occasions" and was not proceeded against because he had testified at the request of the Department of Justice.

The Service had failed to abide by the Administrative Procedure Act. It had conducted mass raids and mass deportations. It had tried to deport an alien without giving him a chance for a hearing on his application for naturalization. Clark had acted illegally in the *Eisler* case, and had "exposed the United States to disrepute and ridicule in other countries." He had used his high office to engage in a ceaseless and improper propaganda campaign.

The Senate was not swayed by these charges. They swiftly approved the nomination, and Mr. Clark became Mr. Justice Clark.

In November 1949 the United States government brought Harry Bridges and two other ILWU union officials to trial in San Francisco on conspiracy and perjury charges based on Bridges's naturalization proceeding in 1945. Philip Murray had fired Harry Bridges as CIO regional director for Northern California for supporting Henry Wallace in 1948. Then ILWU Local 6 went out in a 110-day strike and won a wage hike up to a base rate of $1.475 per hour in a recession year when most unions were getting no increases. The defense found a connection among these events.

Although Carol was not involved in the case, she followed the trial closely, and in December wrote to one of Harry's lawyers: "I notice that Manning Johnson testified in the Bridges case and placed Bridges at certain Communist Party meetings. You may or may not recall that in the second Eisler case Manning Johnson placed Eisler (under the name of Brown) at a meeting in Buffalo, at which he placed Tim Buck and Sam Carr at the time they were both in jail in Canada." Johnson, a former Communist, had become a clerk in the Immigration Service and a frequent witness in deportation cases. The lawyers were grateful for Carol's information, but in that climate they could not convince the jury. The trial judge sentenced Bridges to seven years and canceled his citizenship. Everyone wondered whether "the Bridges's luck" would hold on his third trip to the Supreme Court.

❦

In late 1949 the U.S. government brought Alger Hiss to trial for perjury for the second time. Louis Weiss, seeking to help ensure a fair trial and to stem the reactionary tide, acted as counsel behind the scenes for the psychiatrist Carl Binger, whom the defense planned to call as an expert witness on Whittaker Chambers's strange psychological state. As so often happened at this point in his career, Louis Weiss found that his sister's name cropped up as the *Hiss* trial hit page one. This time it appeared by an indirect route. Hedda Massing testified about events involving Hiss in 1935 after she had moved to this country and married a sociology professor. But her first husband, in Germany, had been Gerhart Eisler. Eisler's name always had the name of his lawyer attached to it in the press. As expected, on January 21, 1950, the jury convicted Hiss.

I conducted my first deportation hearing about this time on a Tuesday. Out of habit I took down in shorthand the questions and answers of the government's witnesses against my client, Joe Lukas. Another lawyer asked me to handle the deportation hearing of his client two days later because he was afraid one of the government witnesses would identify the lawyer as a Communist Party member, which was happening around the country at that time. It could not possibly help the client and certainly would hurt the lawyer as well.

I brought the notes from my Tuesday hearing to the Thursday hearing, where the same witnesses testified against the second noncitizen. I began noticing that the witness, Charles Baxter, was being asked the same questions he had been asked on Tuesday, but that he was giving different answers, tailoring dates to prove the case against the Thursday client. On cross-examination, I asked him why he had given different answers to the same questions in the hearing on Tuesday.

The hearing officer immediately objected and we had some fun. Baxter had testified about his daughter, and I asked him if his daughter knew that her father was a stool pigeon witness for the government. The question was ruled out of order, but Baxter was flustered.

Of course I wrote to Carol immediately and sent her my transcribed notes of both hearings showing the discrepancies. Carol quickly notified all the lawyers doing deportation work. She said she was delighted with my work and made me feel that I had made a significant contribution to the fight against deportation. Thereafter, whenever Baxter testified anywhere, he had to face this discrepancy, and Carol let me know each time. She wrote that "in the Bennie Saltzman case we had the Service so scared that they terminated the direct examination of Baxter before its conclusion."

᠈᠊

On February 9, 1950, Carol lost the *Harisiades* case; Judge Leibell found him deportable. Carol realized that the court of appeals would probably decide the CP leadership's Smith Act case before the *Harisiades* case, so she carefully broadened the issues in *Harisiades* beyond the single question of what the Communist Party advocated. She found a purely technical issue to present to the court in the hope of a victory, however narrow. She claimed that Harisiades should have had the kind of hearing required by the Administrative Procedure Act. It was true that the warrant for his arrest was issued in 1930 and the arrest was made on May 2, 1946, before the APA was passed on June 11, 1946. But she claimed that the proceedings in the case hadn't really started until Harisiades got the notice of the deportation hearing in August 1946, and that was after passage of the APA.

Carol also found a strong human issue in the *Harisiades* case, a question of life or death. She asked the court whether deporting an anti-fascist like Harisiades to fascist Greece, where death might be the price of his views, did not constitute "cruel and unusual punishment." She also asked whether a deportation law for past membership "isn't an undue interference" with the right of free speech and association "because it is not needed to protect the government." She concluded by simply asking whether it makes any sense, "or in legal terminology, whether there is any 'reasonable relation' " between such a law "and the purpose for which Congress is given the power of regulation over non-citizens."

On the morning of February 20, 1950, Judge Leibell ordered Peter Harisiades to surrender for deportation.

Carol promptly went down to the courthouse to file the appeal she had been working on and a motion for continuation of Harisiades' release on bail. She felt that she and Englander had done a good job on the appeal, but she had little joy in the filing. She had lost too many cases recently. She returned to the office and the day wore on.

At three o'clock someone called her with amazing news. They had just heard on the radio that the United States Supreme Court had decided the *Sung* case. The Court held that deportation hearings by the Immigration Service must be conducted in accordance with the provisions of the Administrative Procedure Act.

Carol was jubilant. She had been right from the beginning: the APA covered the Service. Then it hit her. 'My God! Under this decision *all* deportation hearings in the country would have to be called off!' The Service would have to find new — impartial — hearing officers.

Soon the district director of the Service in New York City himself admitted the scope of its defeat: all deportation hearings since June 3, 1947 were invalid and would have to be retried. He added that further hearings had been "temporarily" postponed because of the decision. In the country as a whole, it was estimated that 14,000 invalid hearings would have to be retried. And of course, this time impartial hearing officers were bound to decide for the aliens in some of those cases.

Carol was exuberant when she wrote to Joseph Forer, her co-counsel in the APA case that had set the stage for *Sung*. Even though new business was at a halt, she was

> busy as a bee on the Harisiades appeal and in fil-
> ing everything that has remained unfiled all the
> time the Immigration office was open.
>
> Just the same it was a pleasure to go up there
> the other day and look at the elevator, which was
> marked with a big sign, "Closed."
>
> Only once in a lifetime, and sometimes not that
> often, does a lawyer have such pleasure as I got
> when the Sung decision rippled over the A.P. wires.

34.
A Big Fraud in a Little Palmer Raid

The cold winds of McCarthyism pursued Carol King from the heights of the Supreme Court victory in *Sung* down to the administrative proceedings facing the majority of her clients.

In January 1950 the Immigration Service reported that it was actively investigating about a thousand naturalized citizens, looking toward cancellation of their citizenship because at the time of naturalization they were or had been members of the Communist Party. Two months later, the new Attorney General, J. Howard McGrath, publicly criticized the decision Wendell Willkie and Carol King had won from the Supreme Court in the *Schneiderman* case in 1943 that rejected this kind of second-guessing and second-class citizenship. Carol King responded in her new column, "Legal Aspects," in the American Committee's monthly, *The Lamp:*

> For the first time since the United States Supreme Court handed down the *Schneiderman* decision in 1943, an official of the United States — Attorney General McGrath — saw fit to criticize that decision and take the position that it was an incorrect decision. The Supreme Court made sense and very good sense in the *Schneiderman* decision. [And] [t]he Attorney General's views are clearly motivated by political, rather than legal, considerations.

When she and her colleagues could get into a court, they could still win on a "technicality." In 1950 the Fifth Circuit Court of Appeals held that the Immigration Service had no jurisdiction to subpoena a U.S. citizen (*Estes*). In *Kamaiko* the INS finally admitted it had made a mistake; Jacob Kamaiko was still a citizen, and, therefore, could not be deported.

The screaming headlines of 1950 spelled an end to such victories on technical grounds. On May 8, the Supreme Court, for the first time in history, held that a loyalty oath could be required of a citizen in order to use a government agency. In *ACA v. Douds* five members of the Court upheld the Taft-Hartley Act, requiring a union leader to file an oath that he was not a member of the CP, and had not been for five years, if the union wanted to use the NLRB in any way. Chief Justice Vinson wrote the majority opinion. Justice Jackson, fresh from prosecuting the Nazi leaders in Nuremberg, wrote a long opinion concurring in the decision. Only Justice Black dissented, condemning this repression of political associations among workers as unconstitutional. (As Rabinowitz had noted, Douglas did not sit, and two seats had been vacant.)

The next month, on June 25, war broke out in Korea. The Soviet Union had absented itself from the UN Security Council to protest the refusal to seat Red China. The remaining members cast a unanimous vote to go to the aid of South Korea. By June 30, U.S. troops were commanding a "police action" in Korea under the banner of the United Nations, fighting North Korean troops. Fear in and near the Left was tangible.

In July, Julius Rosenberg, a progressive Jewish engineer, was arrested on charges of conspiracy to commit espionage by giving "atomic secrets" to the Soviets. He had been fired from a government job on allegations of Communist Party membership. He ridiculed the charges and maintained his innocence. In August, his wife, Ethel Rosenberg, and a friend, Morton Sobell, were arrested on related charges. In San Francisco, federal judge George Harris revoked bail for Harry Bridges, and the ILWU leader spent three weeks in jail before the Ninth Circuit released him, pending his appeal.

Yet early in August, people thronged Union Square to protest the start of the Korean War. New York City police dispersed the demonstrators brutally, according to some. In the same month, U.S. peace activists completed the collection of 2,500,000 signatures on the Stockholm Peace Appeal, demanding the "outlawing" of atomic weapons.

Two weeks later, Lee Pressman publicly resigned from the American Labor Party, blasting it as a "Communist front" because it was condoning and supporting Communist aggression in Korea, according to a story in the *New York Times*. Congressman Marcantonio, state chairman of the ALP in New York, said: "It is obvious that Mr. Pressman is disappointed in the amount of fees he expected to get from the progressive movement when he left the C.I.O. Not having received such fees, he has now joined the parade of fakirs." Marc charged that Pressman had not "lifted a finger in the day-to-day activities of the A.L.P." for peace, fair employment practices, social security, or repeal of Taft-Hartley. The timing of

Pressman's resignation was soon explained. He appeared before the House Committee on Un-American Activities, where he admitted he had joined the Communist Party in 1934 while working in the New Deal Agricultural Adjustment Administration under Henry Wallace. Pressman said he had joined because of the "blackness of [the] future" when he finished law school, and that he had remained a member for one year. He named three in the New Deal as Reds with him — John Abt, Nathan Witt, and Charles Kramer. They had all been listed by Whittaker Chambers as Communists in government. Pressman denied that Alger Hiss was in the Communist Party when he was.

The anti-Communist steamroller began working overtime as the United States faced the Korean War abroad and a nationwide railroad strike at home. The top headlines reported that United States troops had retaken a North Korean city as the British landed in Korea, Truman told General Douglas MacArthur to withdraw, and the Soviet ambassador to the UN tried to overcome the actions taken by that body during the Soviet walkout.

Not wanting to be outdone, a television network postponed "The Aldrich Family" because "Anti-Communists Oppose Jean Muir in Cast." A resort hotel banned a talk by foreign policy specialist Owen Lattimore after a poll showed that guests protested his talk. And the House Committee on Un-American Activities cited the National Lawyers Guild "as a Communist front which 'is the foremost legal bulwark of the Communist party, its front organizations, and controlled unions' and which 'since its inception has never failed to rally to the legal defense of the Communist party and individual members thereof, including known espionage agents.' "

In September 1950 much of the case law Carol King had been making was nullified by Congress. So Carol wrote to Forer that she "was busy in the library scratching for worms. After I found enough I went fishing and have just returned." Then the Immigration Service got a member of Congress to attach a rider to the appropriation act for the Department of Justice explicitly exempting the Service from the Administrative Procedure Act requirement of disinterested hearing officers. With no serious discussion or debate, Congress adopted the rider. This decision wiped out the great victory for administrative fairness in deportation hearings, and relegated *Wong Yang Sung v. McGrath* to an honored but dated place in administrative and constitutional law casebooks.

With Joe McCarthy and J. Edgar Hoover breathing down their necks, congressmen went on to pass the (McCarran) Internal Security Act, requiring the registration of the Communist Party and its members, and "Red fronts," increasing the discretionary powers of the passport division and providing that no court could take final action on a petition for naturalization if deportation proceedings had been started against the applicant.

President Truman agreed with Democratic senators Harley Kilgore (W.Va.) and Frank Graham (N.C.) and Republican senator William Langer (N.D.), who said the bill was "obviously unconstitutional" and "thoroughly impracticable," and vetoed the bill. Congress passed it over his veto.

The passage of the Internal Security Act brought Carol right back into a frenzied legal controversy over the right of a deportee to bail. The act provided that pending final determination of deportability, the Attorney General could exercise his discretion in deciding whether to free the alien on conditional parole or under bond of $500 or more, or to continue the alien in custody. On October 20, 1950, the Justice Department announced that it was ready to seize 3,400 noncitizens for deportation. It sounded like the Palmer Raids all over again.

Two days later, on October 22, Carol phoned Abner Green at home and asked him to come down to her office at once. Sunday or not, there was work to be done. At 3:00 A.M. that Sunday morning, the Service had arrested thirteen people in simultaneous sweeps in five cities from New York to Los Angeles. Abner left his wife and two children, arriving about 10:00 A.M. Carol had already written out in long hand a sample petition for a writ of habeas corpus to be used in any case in which the Attorney General carried out his threat. She went on working furiously on a skeleton brief any harried lawyer could use to support the petition. By nightfall, dedicated staff members had typed these documents, mimeographed them neatly, collated and stapled them, and put them in the mail to attorneys all over the country who worked with the American Committee. I received my copies in the Monday morning mail in Cleveland, and filed them for future reference. The next day, I needed them for my client, Joe Lukas.

By mid-November, the Service had arrested forty-eight people in eleven states — all of them longtime residents. The arrests did not match the Palmer Raids in scale, but the terror was there: aliens were rearrested on deportation warrants issued years earlier on which they had already been arrested once and then later released on bail. Now the Service denied bail to each alien, claiming again that the Attorney General had absolute discretion to deny bail to deportees and that his decisions could not be reviewed by the courts. The Service claimed the Attorney General had been granted this authority explicitly by the 1950 McCarran Internal Security Act. John Abt considered Morris Ernst the ideological father of the act, with his proposal for "an SEC [Securities & Exchange Commission] over ideas."

Carol rejected the Service argument. She contended that the courts had an inherent right to review discretionary acts by any administrative official to determine if he had abused his discretion, and this applied to the Attorney General as well as to other administrative officials.

This issue was raised by every one of the forty-eight aliens when they applied to the federal courts for release on habeas corpus, saying, through their lawyers, that the Attorney General had abused his discretion. Attorneys for the aliens were able to show judges that in some cases the Attorney General had not even exercised his discretion. A subordinate in Washington had sent a telegram to branch offices of the Service: "APPREHEND AND DETAIN IMMEDIATELY ALL ACTIVE COMMUNISTS UNDER PROCEEDINGS IN YOUR DISTRICT. . . ." The local officials had then decided who was an "active communist." The Service now declared that the courts had no power to review their judgment.

These forty-eight cases, added to the cases she had been handling before October 22, put a staggering burden on Carol King. She was involved in seventeen cases in New York City. Before they were finished, she had to try a case in Detroit, then catch a plane back to New York to participate in the second day of the argument. The judge granted the writs in *Klig, et al. v. Shaughnessy,* an outstanding victory.

King had never been able to relax as long as a client was in jail. Now she and co-counsel across the country labored feverishly to get all forty-eight out of jail. She prepared papers, argued motions, rode airplanes as often as she rode subways in normal times. Carol and Blanch conferred with attorneys by mail, telegraph, telephone, and in person. She consulted, advised, goaded, cajoled, swore. Then the INS made her life even more hectic by scheduling dozens of deportation hearings for the exact period when they knew she would be occupied in court with the

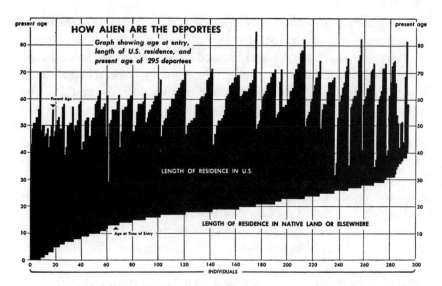

How Alien Are the Deportees. A graph in which each vertical line represents one of the 295 people arrested for deportation on political grounds during the Truman/McCarthy period for whom facts were available, showing their length of residence in the United States. By Ann Fagan Ginger, submitted in *Rowoldt v. Perfetto* brief for appellant in U.S. Supreme Court, 1957.

bail proceedings, including ten in ten days in November; six more in December.

And in November she and her cause watched a giant struck down in his prime. After several tries, the Republicans, Democrats, and Liberals ganged up on Vito Marcantonio, running on the American Labor Party ticket, and defeated him in his ninth campaign for Congress. It was not the quick strikes of the Palmer Raids, but for Carol King it had the same flavor. Francis Fisher Kane, the U.S. Attorney who had resigned his position in 1920 in a blast at Attorney General A. Mitchell Palmer, had no hesitation on December 1, 1950, in saying that "the violations of the constitutional rights of aliens thereby committed . . . were much less serious than the attacks on such rights made in recent months by Attorney General McGrath [which] . . . have continued month to month, if not from year to year."

Harassed on every hand by professional duties, Carol was struck by personal loss. Her brother Louis Weiss died suddenly at age fifty-six. He and Carol had actually shared a great many qualities while being very different in style. The tribute to him by the president of the New School for Social Research might almost have been written about her. Hans Simon said that Weiss's help was "always . . . personal, his interest direct, and his concern . . . wonderfully exclusive and complete. He did not spare himself. With his sense of public responsibility he was his own most exacting solicitor."

Louis Weiss had differed from his sister in the way he divided his time. Much of his professional life was spent on law-firm business, although with clients like Marshall Field III, he represented the progressive newspapers *PM* and the *New York Star*, whose viewpoints he generally shared. In the time he carved out for his private life, he had been chairman of the Board of Trustees of the New School, chairman of the Legal Defense Committee of the NAACP, a director of the American Council on Race Relations, and vice president of the U.S. Committee for the Care of European Children. Behind the scenes, he demonstrated concern for the rape of the First Amendment currently going on in congressional committees and other hearings. Simon wrote of Weiss: "His charity was fundamental, a matter of conviction and ensuing action, never limited to the routine of the tax return." In this, too, he differed from his sister. By 1950 the word "charity" did not accurately describe the activity that had become her life.

Gordon's brother, Howard King, sent his condolences, and Carol replied: "The fact that there have been so many men I could love in my life is a great satisfaction despite the void left behind them. Perhaps it is their loss that makes me cling all the more to those who are left to me. . . . I keep being busy about political cases but really the only thing that matters to me in this world are human beings."

The march of McCarthyism left her no time for grief and memories. In January 1951 she went to St. Paul to argue that longtime resident alien Knut Heikkinen should be released on bail. The judge denied the writ but freed Heikkinen on bail pending the appeal. In February she went to Cincinnati to argue that longtime resident alien John Zydok should be released on bail by the Sixth Circuit. In May she went to St. Louis to argue *Heikkinen* before the Eighth Circuit Court.

This woman lawyer who had decided in the twenties that she would never be a good courtroom lawyer was now spending more time in court than most of the younger men she had helped train. This woman who told everyone she wasn't really much of a lawyer was now consulted by leaders of the civil liberties bar like Arthur Garfield Hays, although in this era, they were quick to point out that they were "not in sympathy" with her "views or associations." But they were still great admirers of her "fighting spirit and of her ability as a lawyer." Hays said, "For years, whenever I had any difficult problem in immigration matters, I called on Carol as an authority to straighten me out, and she would always do so freely and willingly." He knew that her ability "was recognized not only by lawyers but by courts."

In this period, Carol was dipping deep into her memory of how she and her colleagues fought back during the Palmer Raids, coming up with a series of narrow points that might win a series of particular cases while searching for broad grounds that might win the whole class of cases.

And the points had become winners. Of forty-eight people arrested in the raids of 1950, forty-two were released by district court judges (including my two clients in Cleveland), victories based on the papers Carol had sent out from New York, shaped by local lawyers to the facts in their clients' cases. Two others were freed by circuit courts: Heikkinen and Zydok. Only four, in Los Angeles, had to seek relief from the U.S. Supreme Court. In all of these cases, including the "Terminal Island Four" in Los Angeles, the courts held they had power to review the discretionary acts of the Attorney General. With the exception of the Los Angeles cases, the judges found that the Service had abused its discretion.

The decision by the Sixth Circuit in *Zydok* was typical. The government tried to hold Zydok without bail on the basis of the sole uncontested fact that he had been a member of the Communist Party. The appeals court ruled: "Discretion does not mean decision upon one particular fact or set of facts. It means rather a just and proper decision in view of all the attending circumstances." In granting the writ to Zydok, the Court found that his past membership in the CP was outweighed by other considerations: John Zydok had lived in Detroit for thirty-seven years, had worked as a waiter and head waiter at the same restaurant for seventeen years, owned his home, and was the head of a family (wife, two sons, daughter, five grandchildren, all U.S. citizens). He had sold $50,000 in U.S. bonds during World War II and had donated blood for the war effort. Since his original arrest and deportation order and release on bail, Zydok had reported regularly to the Service. The Court also noted that the "record fails to disclose that he has violated any law or that he is engaged or is likely to engage in any subversive activities."

In the district court, Zydok had taken the witness stand but had refused to answer certain questions about the Communist Party on the basis of the Fifth Amendment. The district court judge, following the rule in the old *Vajtauer* case (1927), had drawn inferences unfavorable to Zydok. But the circuit court now ruled that "his failure to so testify should not have operated against him." The government appealed the decision to the Supreme Court, which agreed to hear it.

As Carol was rushing from courtroom to office to Ellis Island, the cold war was raging hot and heavy on the floor of the American Bar Association's House of Delegates at its midyear meeting in February 1951. The ABA had recently established a special committee on Communist tactics, strategy, and objectives, which sponsored a resolution calling on state and local bar associations to ferret out communist lawyers from their ranks. As a first step, the panel chairman proposed that "if it can be ascertained that any Communist lawyer, or one who has been a Communist lawyer and has not repudiated the party . . . is a member of the ABA, the committee feels that he should be forthwith relieved of his membership." The ABA swiftly approved the resolution.

That same month, as Washington's and Lincoln's birthdays were being celebrated, the U.S. government indicted the world-famous leader of African-Americans, W.E.B. DuBois, and other leaders of the Peace Information Center for failure to register as agents of a foreign principal for their work in successfully circulating the Stockholm Peace Appeal against nuclear weapons.

And in the same climate, the trial of the Rosenbergs for allegedly giving "atomic secrets" to the Russians was scheduled for March 8, 1951, with Emanuel Bloch as lead counsel, a lawyer Carol had worked with recently on the *Estes* case, in which a Texas citizen was called to testify before the Immigration Service about the politics of an alien, and refused. Dalton Trumbo, one of the Hollywood ten who refused to answer questions and name names for the House Un-American Activities Committee, began calling it "the time of the toad."

35.
"The Communist's Dearest Friend"

The popular weekly magazine, the *Saturday Evening Post,* published a major story about Carol Weiss King on February 17, 1951. Under the subhead "Look Where The 'Little Rich Girl' Is Now!" the author, Craig Thompson, maintained: "Carol King has probably defended more Reds than any other lawyer in the United States. Her tactics follow Moscow's edicts — and often succeed. Why has this well-off woman spent so much time acting for enemies of America?"

The article referred to "a lifetime" of "triumphs," which Carol must have enjoyed, as she must have cringed at the description of her appearance:

> At fifty-five, Carol Weiss King is a stubby, stoutish woman with a gift of invective and a fine disdain for fashion. She lives unostentatiously in an old house in Manhattan's Chelsea section and carries on her business from a plain lower Broadway office. . . . On gala occasions, such as fundraising dinners for one or another of the many communist fronts with which she is associated, she dons a black hat with a train of feathers which swirls down the back of her head and over her shoulder. Together with her heavily rimmed glasses, the hat makes her look like an owl in a cowl — an altogether unforgettable figure.

Thompson ticked off the names of Carol's best-known clients, calling them "an almost inexhaustible variety of communists and near communists," including "a man known to the United States Immigration authorities as Alexander Stevens and to the Whittaker Chambers espionage group as Jay Peters." The author emphasized: "Her name is known to every lawyer at the New York bar, but not one in a hundred knows anything more about her. She has remained essentially a figure of mystery." Her "two major activities" involve the "creation of a legal machine to serve the interests of communism" and "efforts to keep real or would-be subversives out of jail and busy at their prescribed mischief."

Apart from its cloak-and-dagger, sinister tone and some clear factual errors, the author presents a partially accurate picture of the significance of the work of Carol Weiss King during her legal career. For example:

> Next to money, lawyers are the Communist Party's indispensable necessity. The party lives in a twilight area between legality and illegality. It is staffed by literally hundreds of aliens who either entered the country illegally or have forfeited their chances of citizenship by communist activity. With one hand it seeks to make law by influencing legislatures and courts, with the other it seeks to destroy respect for law by making martyrs, however spuriously, out of those the law entoils. For all these operations the party needs not one lawyer, but a network of them criss-crossing the country, and such a network does in fact exist. Carol King not only had a major hand in setting it up, she is the core around which it revolves.

The article alleged: "During the late '20's the London police uncovered documentary evidence that [Joe] Brodsky was the United States receiver of party funds from Moscow. Not many years after that, communist couriers from Europe, so one of them now says, delivered Party money to Carol." No source was stated. The author lingered over what he called the "Brodsky-King collaboration," which he said led to the formation of the International Labor Defense as part of International Red Aid. The IRA "laid down strict rules to govern communists and their lawyers, particularly in the courts. 'Defense,' it directed, 'must be, above all, political. Transform the prisoners' bench into a revolutionary platform. From the defendant become the accuser. Organize mass defense (to) mobilize the masses against bourgeois fascist justice.' "

The author maintained:

> If all lawyers followed these rules, all legal process would become a shambles and courtrooms propaganda rostrums, which is, of course, what Red Aid wanted. . . . Georgi Dimitroff used them in the Reichstag fire trial in the early '30s, and they explain the behavior of at least some of the lawyers and defendants in the trial of eleven United States communist leaders in New York in 1949. Carol King has long been, and still is, a most skillful practitioner of "mass defense." It was under her direction that the rules were given wide distribution in the United States by the ILD.

This sentence is probably a reference to the ILD's "Workers' Self-Defense in the Courts" described earlier, which contained two or three paragraphs by King about the special problems of alien defendants. The author then discussed a series of cases on which Carol worked, starting with *Scottsboro*. He said that "it has been conservatively estimated that Brodsky and King spent $1,000,000 to create [the] impression" that that trial was "typical of the United Stated judicial system" with most of the money "coming from the pockets of excited innocents."

After a lengthy discussion of the *IJA Bulletin*, the article became a list of the names of every important person Carol King knew or worked with in any of her activities, at a time when being on such a list often resulted in harassment, discharge, or worse.

The author spent much space on the cases of Gerhart and Hanns Eisler. He claimed that "it was Carol who got" both Eislers "into the country in the first place," using this example to prepare for his conclusion:

> In view of her long association with communism and her close association with the Eislers, Carol could not conceivably have been ignorant of the fact that both Eislers were internationally important communists. Nor, in view of her long experience in immigration law, could she have been ignorant of the statute which forbade their entry.

Finally, the kicker:

> She must have forgotten her canons of professional ethics which bind all New York lawyers to remember: "No client, corporate or individual, however powerful, nor any cause, civil or political, however important, is entitled to receive, nor should any lawyer render, any service or advice involving disloyalty to the law whose ministers we are."

A study of the FBI's file on Carol King makes clear that the author of the article either spent many months painstakingly finding the facts, names, incidents, stories, innuendos, rumors, inaccuracies, and the final charge in his article, or else he spent several hours going through the FBI file where all of them are set forth in the 1,450 pages that the FBI released from its central office in response to a request under the Freedom of Information Act. If this is the strongest case the FBI had built against Carol Weiss King after twenty-seven years of surveillance, it may explain why she was not subpoenaed and charged with contempt of court or Congress and convicted, which was the fate of many of her colleagues in this time of the toad — ultimately including Harry Sacher, Abe Isserman, Nat Witt, Martin Popper, and Abe Unger of New York, and her old friend Richard Gladstein of San Francisco. (Most of these lawyers won their cases on appeal.)

Carol King's special relationship with the civil liberties establishment increased her invulnerability in this period. This was reflected in comments by her colleague of many years and battles, the ACLU's Roger Baldwin, who could never forget her inspired editorship of the little mimeographed *Law and Freedom Bulletin* that nurtured the ACLU and its lawyers in the twenties and early thirties. He said, "No more careful analysis of civil liberties law has been done than in her trenchant comments during those critical years when the courts were faced with so many novel issues."

❧

In the same month the *Saturday Evening Post* article appeared, February 1951, the Immigration Service lost so many bail cases in court that it became hesitant about pressing any more cases to a judicial decision.

Carol rejoiced, of course. But her eye was glued to events on Capitol Hill, and there the worst was yet to come. In both the Senate and the House, committees were considering drastic revisions of the immigration laws. After a careful study of these "God forsaken bills," she concluded that "you had better be dead than be an alien." The proposals were combined into the Walter-McCarran bill, which she condemned for: (1) perpetuating racial discrimination in the immigration quotas, and containing even some new discriminatory features; (2) extending political discrimination to all aspects of immigration, naturalization, and cancellation of citizenship; (3) preventing a conscientious objector from being eligible for naturalization; (4) preventing naturalization from proceeding while deportation was pending; and (5) specifically providing that no court could review any discretionary act of the Attorney General.

While Carol was working and worrying about legislation, many of her cases were going to the Board of Immigration Appeals in the spring of 1951, and she often made the trek to Washington and back. On one occasion she had to argue vigorously just to permit forty-five members of the families of several deportees to attend a session of the BIA.

Two days later, the Rosenberg/Sobell "atomic secrets" trial ended in federal district court in New York. The jury convicted the Rosenbergs. After conferring privately with the FBI, Judge Irving Kaufman sentenced Julius and Ethel Rosenberg to death and Morton Sobell to thirty years.

Across the street from that frightening courtroom drama, the superintendent of insurance for New York was demanding that the International Workers Order lose its right to continue to insure workers. IWO lawyers introduced *Dunne's Insurance Report* in evidence, rating IWO insurance "A plus" (Excellent) and concluding that the IWO of New York was "worthy of public confidence." Nonetheless, the state court sustained the right of the Insurance Department to liquidate the assets of the insurance benefit society founded by Joe Brodsky twenty-some years before, even though the U.S. Supreme Court had just agreed with the IWO that the Attorney General's effort to list the IWO as "subversive" violated its due process rights.

It had become difficult to win the simplest case before any of the administrative bodies under existing statutes, and the situation was likely to get worse. When I wrote to Carol for advice on one of my deportation cases, she blurted out, "All I can say it's a hell of a world."

But she went on working every day and half the night on her own cases, and cases that were not her own. She taught many younger lawyers that you almost never 'win' a deportation case in the customary law school sense. When your client dies a natural death in this country, that's a victory. And on May 5, the U.S. Supreme Court did free the "Terminal Island Four," the only remaining jailed deportees from the little Palmer Raid of October 22, 1950. However, this was only an interim decision until the Court decided whether to hear their case on the merits.

Carol King still achieved some victories, even before the Board of Immigration Appeals, and insisted on describing them to her relatives, who wanted to protest that they did not care to listen to one more such tale. Carol persisted because, to her, each client was special. And decades later, her relations could still recall the names of the clients whose cases she had won, like IWO member Clara Dainoff, who had entered the United States illegally twenty-five years before.

King hoped and worked for the same kind of victory for Benjamin Saltzman. By now she and her client had held back his banishment for eight years, taking advantage of every change in the law. The APA-*Sung* case had meant that his first deportation hearing had been fatally defective. In his new hearing on the same evidence, the Service asked Saltzman to what country he would prefer to be deported. He answered: "To the country where I have worked and lived most of my life. To the country where I have spent 38 of my 56 years. To the country where my wife and two sons live. To the country where my third son lies buried in a hero's grave. To the United States of America."

At the end of the hearing, the hearing officer again ordered him deported.

But by now Carol King and Benjamin Saltzman had found a new ally. The best of the press could not stomach this treatment of a gold star father. In 1951 the *New York Post* editorially called on President Truman "to intervene in Saltzman's behalf" if "nothing else can stop this infamous proceeding. . . . This verdict is cruel and inhuman punishment."

Carol was delighted with the *Post* and rejoiced that she and some of her clients had survived the little Palmer Raids of 1950. But the INS reported that it had deported fifty times as many aliens in 1950 as in 1940: 580,000 people. And it had excluded 470,000 people in 1950, including French actor Maurice Chevalier (for signing the Stockholm Peace Appeal).

Carol's side was losing in the summer of 1951, and she was very tired, very often. She had no time to go to a doctor and be told to take it easy when there was so much to do. Fortunately, Blanch Freedman could help her take a respite from the pressure of work, competently handling the most difficult, multifaceted cases in a calm manner that steadied the frightened clients. Finally Carol faced the kind of problem she delighted in. The doors in the studio apartment on Twenty-second Street needed to be replaced, and she cheerfully spent the extra money required to have the old doors duplicated exactly so that the style of the rooms would not be marred. She spent time with family and friends as she approached her fifty-sixth birthday in August.

36.
Finally, the Supreme Court

If Carol had found life hectic in the autumn of 1950, it became impossible in the summer of 1951. The roof fell in.

On June 4, before its summer recess, the United States Supreme Court, by a vote of 6 to 2, upheld the convictions of the eleven Communist Party leaders under the Smith Act for conspiring to advocate, in the future, the forceful overthrow of the U.S. government. Chief Justice Vinson had not agonized over the decision in the *Dennis* case, which he placed in a political rather than a juridical setting:

> To those who would paralyze our Government in the face of impending threat by encasing it in a semantic straitjacket we must reply that all concepts are relative. . . . [Courts in the past] were not confronted with any situation comparable to the instant one — the development of an apparatus designed and dedicated to the overthrow of the government, in the context of world crisis after crisis.

As Justice Jackson made clear in his long concurrence, this was not a denaturalization case like *Schneiderman* or a deportation case like *Bridges,* in which the individual defendants would lose citizenship or residence rights because of their beliefs or actions, which were admittedly legal. And this was not a free speech case like *DeJonge* or a freedom of assembly case like *Herndon,* in which the Court had looked at the facts and found that the defendants had not individually gone beyond the exercise of their First Amendment rights although they were admittedly leaders of the Communist Party.

This was a case based on conspiracy law, on what twelve individuals might do as leaders of a political party committed to Marxism/Leninism, which might threaten the internal security of the United States in the future — although the party had only 60,000 members in the country, according to the FBI, and could not win at the polls. The *individual* actions and ideas of the *individual* defendants did not emerge in the trial and were not discussed on appeal. The concepts behind their theories were not plumbed, as in Murphy's opinion in *Bridges*. The Justices discussed and cited *ACA v. Douds* and other cases on the need to curb the militancy of the unionists at home.

Justice Black, in dissent, pointed out that the Communist defendants were "not charged with non-verbal acts of any kind" and were "not even charged with saying or writing anything designed to overthrow the government." Justice Douglas wrote, "I repeat that we deal here with speech alone."

On the same day, the Court also refused to hear the appeals of attorneys Gladstein, Sacher, Crockett, McCabe, and Isserman, summarily convicted of contempt of court by the trial judge at the conclusion of the Smith Act trial. On that day, the Court refused to hear the appeal of attorney Vincent Hallinan from an income tax conviction that arose after his vigorous representation of Harry Bridges in the government's third attempt to get rid of that fiery West Coast labor leader, this time on criminal charges. And on that day, the Court failed to decide whether it would grant the petitions for certiorari and hear the cases of the Terminal Island Four and Peter Harisiades.

Even the *New York Times* said editorially that "this undoing of the Communist party [in the Smith Act case] has been achieved only by a violent upheaval in our judicial concepts."

The Communist Party leadership decided on a major upheaval in its response to these "judicial concepts." Early in July, the *Times* reported that Gus Hall, Henry Winston, Gil Green, and Robert Thompson failed to report to begin their five-year prison terms for conspiracy to violate the Smith Act. The other seven Communist leaders did appear. The CPUS said it had assessed the situation in the United States, considering it close to fascism, and had decided that the Party should follow two paths simultaneously. Seven leaders would submit to the authority of the federal courts while protesting that they had been illegally tried and sentenced under an unconstitutional law by a biased judge. The other four leaders would seek to return to their roots, as Gerhart Eisler had done, although for them this meant working underground in the United States to help end the cold war repression that had led to their trial and conviction. (After World War I, Big Bill Haywood, assessing the situation, had fled to the Soviet Union.) This decision immediately created a whole new set of problems for the four, their families and acquaintances, for their political party, and for people who had supported the Party's rights up to this point.

For Carol King, this decision posed a specific problem because bond for the four had been posted by the Civil Rights Congress Bail Fund. This fund had also posted bond for several deportees, and Abner Green, executive secretary of the American Committee, was a trustee of the CRC Bail Fund.

The day after the four failed to appear, a federal grand jury launched an investigation seeking to find them. The investigation quickly turned to the CRC Bail Fund. The grand jury subpoenaed the trustees: Green, millionaire Frederick V. Field, *The Thin Man* author Dashiell Hammett, and Black scholar Alpheus Hunton. They were ordered to produce the records of the CRC Bail Fund.

Each refused. Abner replied that he did not have the records, had never had them, and could not find them. The others gave the same answer.

Then O. John Rogge stepped forward as an adversary of his former colleagues. In 1948, after being fired by Attorney General Tom Clark for seeking further prosecutions of Americans with connections to German Nazi industrialists, he had cast his lot with the Progressive Party. The low vote for Wallace had left him without the large political base to which he had been accustomed. And he had lost a big criminal case when labor leader Harold Christoffel was convicted of perjury for denying before a congressional committee that he was a Communist. Christoffel had not been able to pay Rogge his fee. So this former Assistant Attorney General and former leader of the Progressive Party sued to get his hands on the list of names of contributors to the CRC Bail Fund so that he could collect his fee. Attorney Mary Kaufman successfully defended the fund against the renegade Rogge, and the scene shifted back to the grand jury.

That body now demanded that Abner produce the records of the American Committee for Protection of Foreign Born.

He refused again, saying that the records had nothing to do with the present investigation of the CRC Bail Fund.

Green was hauled before district judge John F.X. McGohey, who repeated the order and got the same answer from Green.

McGohey sentenced Green to jail for six months for contempt of court, and the same sentence was meted out to Field, Hammett, and Hunton. McGohey denied Carol's motion for a stay pending appeal, and the four promptly reported to begin their sentences. (The story about the surrender of Field soon made the rounds, one of the few uproarious jokes told in that parlous time. It is said that when the guards started their routine medical inspection of Frederick Vanderbilt Field prior to his incarceration, and searched his private parts, Field quipped, "You won't find the four CP leaders up there!")

Carol started working on Green's appeal, but was interrupted by an order from another federal district court judge, Sylvester Ryan. A second federal grand jury had indicted another group of Communist Party leaders in New York for violation of the Smith Act, including Elizabeth Gurley Flynn. These so-called "second-string leaders" had trouble securing counsel, which was not strange since each of the five lawyers who had represented the first-string CP leaders had ended up in contempt of court; four of the five had been ordered to prison, and two faced disbarment from practicing law in the state courts for their vigorous defense of their clients' cause. In addition to the possible prospect of contempt and disbarment at the end of the trial, lawyers like Harold Cammer knew the trial itself would be a long and arduous battle in the courtroom during the day, with preparation each night and with no hope of salvaging paying clients during or after the conclusion of the trial.

In this situation, Judge Ryan took the unprecedented step of appointing eight lawyers to defend the CP leaders, all members of the National Lawyers Guild. One of the lawyers he appointed was Carol King.

In a hearing before Judge Ryan, each of the eight attorneys asked to be relieved of the assignment. Harry Sacher was present at the hearing to explain that he could not represent the defendants because he was still occupied with the first-string cases and their aftermath (which had sent him to prison for six months). Ever the orator, Sacher pleaded for the defendants' rights to select their own attorneys: "Your honor, paraphrasing a 17th century poet, these defendants feel 'What care I how fair she be/If she be not fair to me?' "

Judge Ryan was not mollified in any way.

Counsel requested that Jack Stachel be released on the ground that he had a bad heart condition. Ryan replied, 'I am not going to release anyone on that ground because I think that the treatment one gets in federal prison is the best treatment you can get for a bad heart. It's quiet; you don't have to worry about anything; there is no anxiety, and you get good food.'

In that climate, Carol King explained that she had dozens of cases that required her immediate and personal attention, and that she could not engage herself in a trial that was certain to last for months. Moreover, she said she was ill, and "I don't propose to shorten my life to defend these people." She presented a corroborating letter from her doctor.

The judge replied that he had never seen her look better in her life. He added that she had for years been "more or less identified with the associations these defendants are alleged to have been —"

Carol King angrily interrupted to accuse the judge of prejudice and of committing an impropriety.

The judge demanded an apology.

King rose at counsel table. "I will apologize," she replied, "but I think it most improper —"

Now Judge Ryan interrupted: "We will have no more, and you will sit down."

She sat down.

"I do not propose to listen to impertinent, scandalous remarks," the judge added.

Recognizing that she was in danger of being cited for contempt, Carol King subsided, but she did not lose her sense of outrage at the episode. Imagine a judge in one sentence abolishing the line between client and lawyer, and with it the right of a client with an unpopular cause to obtain the effective assistance of counsel guaranteed in the Sixth Amendment!

In fact, Carol knew that the "second-string" Communist leaders were trying to retain "broad" counsel, lawyers with a respect for the Bill of Rights and a desire to conserve the Constitution, who were not Communists or Leftists, who could not be "more or less identified with the associations" of the defendants. This effort to find conscientious leaders of the bar, like Willkie in *Schneiderman,* was being made virtually impossible by the view expressed by Ryan.

As to Carol, aside from the fact that she was not a Communist Party member and was neither a trial lawyer nor a criminal defense lawyer, and that, for the first time in her life, she had no energy, what were the cases that she claimed were fully occupying her time? *Butterfield v. Zydok:* on appeal to the U.S. Supreme Court; *Harisiades v. Shaughnessy:* on appeal to the U.S. Supreme Court; *United States ex rel. Chew v. Colding:* on appeal to the Second Circuit Court of Appeals; plus innumerable deportation cases pending hearings and administrative appeals.

While Judge Ryan was deciding how to enforce his order requiring the eight unwilling lawyers to represent the unwilling defendants, Carol had to figure out how to deal with the problems created for deportees whose bond had been posted by the CRC Bail Fund before the four CP leaders had failed to appear for incarceration. In July the Service rearrested Peter Harisiades and held him on Ellis Island because the court of appeals had turned down his appeal and canceled his bail. Carol sought a writ from the district court, which turned her down. Carol sought a writ before the U.S. Supreme Court, which was in recess. No individual Justice would grant bail in this procedural situation. And in August, the Service rearrested thirty-nine more deportees whose bail had been posted by the CRC Bail Fund.

Now the Attorney General imposed the same conditions on anybody who tried to post bond in a deportation matter already imposed in the New York office. In California Harry Bridges's bail was lifted, and the president of the ILWU spent time in federal prison until this decision was reversed, as his third case headed for the Supreme Court.

Nonetheless, Carol was determined to win for Alexander Bittelman. The U.S. Attorney argued that the Attorney General had the right to reject any bail that might be offered by a deportee. The bondsman who had offered himself for Bittelman testified that he had never been a member of the Communist Party, and although he had belonged to the IWO for thirteen years, he was not an officer.

The U.S. Attorney said he was disqualified because the IWO was on the Attorney General's list of subversive organizations.

Carol replied with considerable heat that the Supreme Court had ruled that the Attorney General's list was not constitutionally valid in *IWO v. McGrath,* because no hearings had been held to determine whether each organization should be listed.

Judge Edward Weinfeld was impressed by the argument. He ruled that if the Service did not accept the bond that had been offered within twenty-four hours, he would accept it as court bond and release Bittelman.

The Service did as it was told, as to Bittelman. But it canceled the bond posted for Manuel Tarazona by the CRC Bail Fund in New York. Mrs. Tarazona converted their savings into U.S. bonds to post new bail, but she was still short, so she pawned her engagement ring. The Service rejected the bond because Mrs. Tarazona would not testify about her political views. She then transferred the U.S. bonds to her daughter, who tried to post them as bail. The Service rejected them because the daughter had not herself earned the money to buy them.

When the case came before him, Judge Weinfeld said:

> I think it is the most natural thing in the world for a woman to come
> forward and offer her life's earnings in order to release her husband on
> bail, and I do not see that it becomes material to inquire as to her political
> identification, political affiliations or political or economic philosophy.
> And assuming you had a right to do that, she conveyed a perfectly good
> title to the daughter, who was American born, a member of the Young
> Women's Christian Association, a member of the Civil Air Patrol, with
> every indication that she is a law-abiding, decent citizen believing in the
> traditions of our country and entirely unidentified with any subversive
> group.

He gave the Service twenty-four hours to accept the bail offered or he
would accept it as court bail and free Tarazona himself.

Again the Service had to accept the bail offered, and Carol could
momentarily escape the feeling of imminent doom. Nonetheless, in August when she wrote to me about the article we were preparing on the
McCarran Internal Security Act, she added: "If I should go behind bars
before this goes to the printer, please see to it that it is published in some
form or other. It must be a relief not to be involved with only people in
the Federal penitentiary."

Tom Emerson, Carol's old friend from IJA days, was now a law
professor at Yale and had just completed a term as president of the
National Lawyers Guild. He says he heard a rumor in the summer of 1951
that a federal grand jury in New York was investigating a batch of lawyers
who had been representing Communists and other dissenters. Perhaps
Carol had heard the same rumor.

In the midst of these events, Carol somehow found the time and energy
to continue her roles as editor and mentor. She transformed my outraged
chronological account of the little Palmer Raid cases into a well-organized
article on the fundamental changes contained in the 1950 act that
explained how the Justice Department and the Service were using them
to destroy the rights of people caught in their administrative meshes. She
made her total rewrite acceptable to my young ego by sending notes on
her reasons: "I think the stuff is all there but there is too much propaganda
and you don't make enough noise like a lawyer." And later, "I hope you
are not displeased with our joint effort. I felt that your piece was too much
like an instruction sheet for American Committee lawyers; and now most
of them are going to be in jail so we don't need exactly that kind of piece."
She enclosed a neatly typed manuscript that did not show the innumerable
changes she had made and did supply all the missing citations to unreported cases. She even permitted me some small pride in authorship by

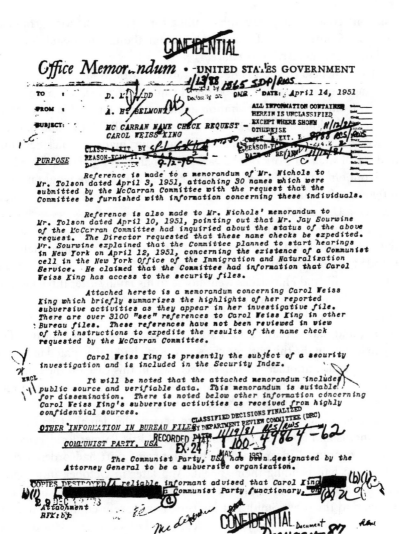

CONFIDENTIAL

Office Memorandum • UNITED STATES GOVERNMENT

TO :	D. M. LADD	DATE: April 14, 1951
FROM :	A. H. BELMONT	
SUBJECT:	MC CARRAN NAME CHECK REQUEST — CAROL WEISS KING	

ALL INFORMATION CONTAINED
HEREIN IS UNCLASSIFIED
EXCEPT WHERE SHOWN
OTHERWISE

PURPOSE

Reference is made to a memorandum of Mr. Nichols to Mr. Tolson dated April 3, 1951, attaching 30 names which were submitted by the McCarran Committee with the request that the Committee be furnished with information concerning these individuals.

Reference is also made to Mr. Nichols' memorandum to Mr. Tolson dated April 10, 1951, pointing out that Mr. Jay Sourwine of the McCarran Committee had inquired about the status of the above request. The Director requested that these name checks be expedited. Mr. Sourwine explained that the Committee planned to start hearings in New York on April 12, 1951, concerning the existence of a Communist cell in the New York Office of the Immigration and Naturalization Service. He claimed that the Committee had information that Carol Weiss King has access to the security files.

Attached hereto is a memorandum concerning Carol Weiss King which briefly summarizes the highlights of her reported subversive activities as they appear in her investigative file. There are over 3100 "see" references to Carol Weiss King in other Bureau files. These references have not been reviewed in view of the instructions to expedite the results of the name check requested by the McCarran Committee.

Carol Weiss King is presently the subject of a security investigation and is included in the Security Index.

It will be noted that the attached memorandum includes public source and verifiable data. This memorandum is suitable for dissemination. There is noted below other information concerning Carol Weiss King's subversive activities as received from highly confidential sources.

OTHER INFORMATION IN BUREAU FILES

COMMUNIST PARTY, USA

The Communist Party, USA has been designated by the Attorney General to be a subversive organization.

A reliable informant advised that Carol King [ ] Communist Party functionary,

Attachment
RFK:bjb

CONFIDENTIAL

FBI File: Carol King (4-14-51). A request from the McCarran (Senate Internal Security) Subcommittee to the FBI for information to use in a hearing on an alleged Communist cell in the Immigration Service allegedly giving Carol King access to security files.

using my concluding paragraphs, calling for repeal of the McCarran Act because "Court review of each Service action, though successful, is a slow and often inconclusive procedure."

The slowness of success in court forced Carol to jump from case to case more quickly than ever before. In mid-September, she argued the appeal from the contempt citation against Abner Green for refusing to answer questions and turn over records of the CRC Bail Fund and the American Committee. The Second Circuit Court made no quick decision, and Carol went to work on the case of seaman Kwong Hai Chew, which Ira Gollobin had asked her to argue, hoping her prestige would make a difference. It didn't, then. (He won the case finally in 1969, and Chew became a U.S. citizen.)

In October 1951 the United States Supreme Court agreed to review the deportation order against Peter Harisiades. King immediately demanded his release on bail, and this time she won. The family put up $10,000 bail, and Harisiades went home to his family after three months on Ellis Island. Carol asked Eugene Cotton to argue the case in the Supreme Court. He had worked with her on the *IJA Bulletin* twenty years before, and had developed into a leading labor lawyer in Chicago. For the first time in the thirty-three cases that King had participated in before the high court, another woman lawyer was in this case on the opposite side. Beatrice Rosenberg assisted the Assistant Attorney General in representing the Immigration Service.

The Supreme Court also agreed to review the denial of bail to the Terminal Island Four, the remaining jailed "Little Palmer Raid" victims. After six months' incarceration, the Supreme Court had ordered their release on bail pending their appeal. And later in October, in a highly unusual action, the Court granted the petition for rehearing by Harry Sacher and the other Smith Act lawyers, having refused in June to hear their case. But in an ominous minor decision, the Court denied the petition of the Lawyers Guild to file an amicus brief supporting the lawyers' position.

Then the Sixth Circuit Court of Appeals released John Zydok after the INS had held him for five months. The American Committee announced in *The Lamp* that Carol King would argue all these cases, plus the Knut Heikkinen case, in the Supreme Court in the next several months.

But the Second Circuit Court of Appeals decided against Abner Green. He was transferred to the Danbury House of Corrections to finish out his six-month term for contempt, while Carol arranged a thousand details about deportation hearings and arguments before the BIA.

By now her health was failing badly. Friends convinced her to get a medical opinion. One doctor suggested she needed a psychiatrist to help her learn how to deal with stress.

Instead, Blanch Freedman filled in for her as she made a hurried, 800-mile trip to Wisconsin to spend a few days with her niece and her family. She had a case in Detroit and arranged to be with them the weekend before she went to the hospital. Peggy Kahn said she did and did not realize that there was "something haunted, another dimension" to Carol's "always appreciative appraisal of what we said and did." Despite the fact Carol did not know she was going to die, "she seemed to feel this might be the last time she would see us." As Peggy recalled later,

> She had apparently suffered a serious attack before landing and when I saw her in the glare of the arc-light as she came off the plane I had the momentary impression of a death's head with the features of all the Stixes. But except for the faded rose in her bosom, the impression was completely dispelled as we sat at our special window in the airport restaurant. She always came and went via stratocruiser, "putting on a good show," as she said. And neither of us ever tired watching the planes take off and land for all the times she must have seen them. This night she was full of tales of what had happened on the plane and we sat talking until around 11 p.m.

They went home to the Kahns, and Carol stayed up "until all the fireworks were over, and I had given the baby her late feeding. But as was her wont, she was up at six the next morning making her inimitable Wheatena for the boys." She brought her slacks so she would be ready for anything that came up, and showed her enjoyment of the kids' pleasure in the ordinary things of life, like "sunshine clouds," and "how they would ring the bell to call our attention to the fact that the leaves were falling."

The day she returned to New York, Carol entered the hospital for observation. She stayed for ten days.

A month later, on November 26, Carol King, Esquire, slowly walked up the steps of the United States Supreme Court building to argue the Zydok case. In her thirty years of practicing law, this was her first argument before the highest tribunal. Always before, she had been convinced that another lawyer could make a better argument. This time it was clearly her turn, and no other lawyers were clamoring for the honor of losing a big case. She had, in fact, run out of the kinds of narrow, technical defenses she had uncovered and developed in *Bridges* and the hunger strikers' cases. Congress had specifically authorized the Attorney General to exercise broad discretion in the arrest and detention of noncitizens in this hot war era.

Her face was drawn, her manner tense. Friends in the courtroom thought her voice was shrill. And they worried that she didn't sound much like a lawyer. She insisted on talking about John Zydok, the man.

But Carol King said that was the whole point of her argument, the man John Zydok. It was the basic point she had been trying to make throughout her years of practice as a lawyer woman. It was what distinguished her from most of her male colleagues. She was perfectly comfortable with this argument. It fitted precisely her own interest in individuals and their right to be individuals. And her years as an immigration lawyer gave her the stature to argue for the fundamental principles of fairness that must govern our treatment of the strangers admitted to our gates, both for their own sakes and for the protection of the rights of the native-born put in jeopardy by repression. But she was not sanguine of winning before the cold war Vinson court (as she would have been before the Warren court that was not yet even a mote in General Eisenhower's eye).

The circuit court had said in releasing Zydok: "Discretion . . . means rather a just and proper decision in view of all the attending circumstances." The chief circumstance in the *Zydok* case was the man John Zydok, not simply his alleged political affiliations and beliefs. She argued that this human being did not belong in jail indefinitely under the new federal law. She emphasized that courts had freed all of the forty-eight arrested with such fanfare a year ago, except for the five now before the high court.

John McTernan of Los Angeles presented the case of the Terminal Island Four after Carol finished her presentation on *Zydok*. The issues in the two cases were as similar as the styles of the lawyers were different. Long John McTernan, an Irish American originally from New York, looked and sounded as everyone thought a lawyer should look and sound. His mind and manner had been honed in the NLRB and in private practice in Los Angeles. Carol King, intellectual Manhattan Jewish woman, looked and sounded like attorney King/"the King woman" and, at the same time, like Carol King. John and Carol faced the same lawyer for the government in both cases, veteran constitutional lawyer John F. Davis, who had never been an advocate of the First Amendment or the rights of aliens. They faced quite a different bench from the one that had reversed the deportation order against Bridges six years before. Roberts, Murphy, and Rutledge were gone; Harold Burton, Tom Clark, and Sherman Minton sat in their judicial seats. And the Frankfurter and Jackson of 1951 were not their former (or their future Warren court) selves.

After the arguments, Carol King slowly put her massive file into her large briefcase. She did not feel that she had won the five votes she needed, although she could count on Justices Black and Douglas, and may have had some flickering of hope of Frankfurter and even Burton. She was utterly exhausted, and it showed. The attorneys for the INS thought she would not make it back to New York without help. In an unparalleled move, they had Carol King driven to the railroad station in their car, an indication of the respect in which they held their opponent.

Carol went back into the hospital as the *Harisiades* deportation case was argued in December by Gene Cotton's partner, Richard F. Watt, former law professor at the University of Chicago. David Rein, of Forer and Rein in Washington, argued the companion case for Dora Coleman, and Jack Wasserman, who had worked for the INS in the early forties, argued for Luigi Mascitti. There was no sign during the argument that they had won any votes beyond Black and Douglas.

Carol had two major cancer operations in December.

Following the custom of the time, Carol's condition was not revealed by the American Committee, which went ahead with its traditional annual meeting in Chicago, knowing that both Carol King and Abner Green would have to miss it. The committee drew delegates again from all the national groups concerned about deportation and immigrant rights, but the mood was somber. Blanch represented Carol at the meeting, both as a partner in Freedman & King and as an attorney for the American Committee. Her stature was such that she could double for Carol, as she had been doing in court, and her clear reports on all the pending cases demonstrated both her strength and warmth as she promised to take back many personal and legal messages to Carol. But all of us missed watching Carol's face light up into an enormous smile on first sight and her asking just the right questions about the kids and spouses.

On December 25, the authorities released Abner Green from prison. He promptly visited Carol in the hospital and announced that he would soon make a national tour for the American Committee.

After Christmas, Carol came home to Twenty-second Street. She took pen in hand to write to her niece: "I am sitting in the front room, the fire is crackling on the hearth and the sun was shining until it got too late. Not a sound except the fire and the dim background of New York traffic. There hasn't been a human voice. . . . This room with Barkley to minister to your needs is pretty nearly perfect." Jonathan and Cynthia told her she would become a grandmother the following summer, and she wrote: "I don't have the feeling that some people do of wanting my blood to go forward into the next generation. But I love kids and there has to be some reason to get close to them. If it takes the grandmother myth to effect that result, well, it's all right to me."

Her friends and family came to Twenty-second Street to talk to Carol. Lawyers she had met over the years and had brought into her expanding network called to chat. One described later how "she refused to permit her illness to damper the cheerful fire of her personality."

After New Year's, Carol King went back to the hospital. She died there on January 22, 1952. She was fifty-six.

Afterword

CAROL KING, 56, NOTED LAWYER, DIES
Expert on Deportation and Civil Rights Cases
Had Defended Bridges, Browder, Eisler

In an unusual full-column obituary, the *New York Times* listed the famous Supreme Court cases Carol King had handled, including *Schneiderman* and the '*Scottsboro boys*,' "but her role was to prepare the briefs more often than to make the final argument." The *Times* emphasized: "She also handled thousands of inconspicuous cases involving what she considered improper interpretation or oppressive application of the immigration and naturalization laws. Throughout her long career she insisted she was not a member of the Communist party, and no evidence of such affiliation ever was produced."

Friends surmised that this respectful obituary was written by Alden Whitman, the *Times*'s "prince of death." It described her work in the *Bridges* case in which Dean James M. Landis of Harvard Law School had "cleared" Bridges of "Communist charges." It quoted the Civil Rights Congress statement that "no foreign born worker's case was ever too unimportant, nor was she ever too busy to help them with their many problems," and a similar tribute by the International Fur and Leather Workers Union.

Describing her as "a short, stocky woman of great energy" who "cared little for fashionable appearance," the *Times* said, "She earned professional respect for her brilliant mind and her last-ditch fighting spirit." This description was demonstrated for the *Times* by the "qualified" rating given King by the New York County Lawyers Association and the Bar Association of the City of New York when she ran for judge on the American Labor Party ticket in 1949. And the *Times* repeated the story about the INS attorney loaning the government car to his opponent after the Supreme Court argument in *Zydok* when King was seriously ill.

The *Times* did not mention her greatest victory — forcing the Immigration and Naturalization Service to shut down all deportation hearings until it could convince Congress to specifically exempt it from the Administrative Procedure Act covering almost all other government agencies.

Elizabeth Gurley Flynn in her column in the *Daily Worker* agreed that "no, my dear longtime friend, Carol King, was not a member of the Communist Party." Describing her major, and some of her minor cases, Flynn said "this brilliant, tireless and devoted woman lawyer . . . fought not only 'improper interpretations or oppressive application of the . . . laws,' as the *Times* concedes, but she also fought the basic injustices and discrimination of these very laws — the Smith and McCarran Acts and others which preceded them."

In his column in the *Daily Compass*, I. F. Stone assessed the *Schneiderman* case, "in which she enlisted Wendell Willkie," and the *Bridges* deportation case, "in which she bested David-and-Goliath odds," as "her most splendid successes." King waged "almost hopeless battles in the musty obscurity of the law courts with lovably cynical good cheer and incredible stamina."

Carol King had provided in her will that no service be held for her, but when Mrs. Barkley asked the family if it would be all right to have a mass said at the local church attended by Mrs. Barkley and some of the neighbors, of course the family agreed. They wanted a small, close service for themselves; her political colleagues, friends, and clients insisted on a large memorial meeting at the Hotel Astor. As happened repeatedly during her life, the solution was a compromise among nonpolitical relatives, political liberals, and active Communists. Thomas Emerson, friend and colleague since the IJA days, now a law professor at Yale, delivered the main address. Brother-in-law Carl Stern, colleague Abner Green, client Claudia Jones, and media friend I. F. Stone delivered their eulogies.

The *Guild Lawyer* summed up the life of one of its founding members, saying: "Her professional achievements are such that in retrospect we are likely to forget the wholeness of her personality. In the midst of her devotion to her work, she maintained an . . . excitement in the process of living; she . . . had a zest for all that gives pleasure and interest to life — for literature, for the arts, for good food, for furniture, for lively conversation. . . . And, of course, her passion for people explains in very large measure her success in her profession."

Carol King was also honored by respectful tributes from federal court judges before whom King had appeared: John C. Knox and William Bondy, and New York City Domestic Relations Court justices Jane M. Bolin and Dudley F. Sicher. John Raeburn Green, general counsel of the *St. Louis Post-Dispatch,* referred to Nelles's and King's article on contempt by publication, calling it a "magnificent study" that had been "of the utmost value to every lawyer who has engaged in that field . . . in protecting freedom of the press against arbitrary exercise of judicial power. If Mrs. King had done nothing else, she should be honored for her part in this."

Carol King had lived to see her colleague and client Abner Green released from jail for contempt. Now he conducted memorial meetings for her all across the country. The people who attended knew they had lost a great lawyer. Recalling some conversation or incident, they also felt, one after another, that they had lost a close personal friend. The National Women's Appeal for the Rights of Foreign Born Americans observed International Woman's Day in 1952 with a tribute to Carol King.

Carol King died in the midst of the busy season for constitutional lawyers, during the savage attacks on constitutional rights unleashed by the government and Big Business in the cold war, which were fueled by the hot war in Korea. When she died, certain principles for which she had fought were firmly entrenched in the minds of clients and lawyers, a few in landmark Supreme Court opinions, more in ringing concurrences and dissents.

But human rights law develops slowly, by accretion, and clear-cut victories are few. Most principles of law have to be won again in each generation, and King's cases and causes continued to make headlines long after her funeral.

On March 10, 1952, the Supreme Court ruled against Carol King (5–4) in the only case she had argued before it, holding that the Attorney General could arrest John Zydok and the Terminal Island Four for deportation and hold them indefinitely without bail. But Justice Frankfurter finally felt compelled to dissent because these deportees were denied bail for mere membership in the Communist Party, while the Court had held that CP leaders indicted under the Smith Act for criminal conspiracy to overthrow the government could not be denied bail automatically.

Justice Burton joined Frankfurter, as Justices Black and Douglas filed broader dissents. And the Court ruled against King (6–2) on all aspects of the *Harisiades* case, holding him deportable for membership in the Communist Party prior to 1939 under the 1940 Smith Act, with no consideration of his lack of criminal record, length of residence, family ties, or probable political persecution in his native Greece. In its third opinion that day, the Court (5–3) upheld Judge Medina's contempt citations against the Smith Act case attorneys who were her friends. Justice Black dissented, citing, among other authority, Nelles and King, "Contempt by Publication in the United States," *Columbia Law Review* (1928).

On June 27, 1952, Congress passed the McCarran-Walter Immigration Act, one of King's "God-forsaken anti-alien bills," over the veto of President Truman. On October 8, the Department of Justice suddenly granted bail of $5,000 to each of the Terminal Island Four after winning the Court's approval to hold them indefinitely, and then canceled bail of eight other political deportees and sent them to Ellis Island. It also announced plans to attempt for a second time to denaturalize William Schneiderman after his conviction as a Communist Party leader in the California Smith Act trial (*Yates v. U.S.*). And on November 12 that year, Peter Harisiades left with his U.S.–citizen wife and children for Socialist Poland, which had granted him asylum from possible death in Greece, now run by the generals. At the same time, the Progressive Party ran its last candidate for president, Harry Bridges's lawyer, Vincent Hallinan.

On January 1, 1953, the Justice Department announced plans to take away the citizenship of more than 1,500 naturalized citizens on political grounds under the new McCarran-Walter Act. But on February 9, Carl Stern won a case for Carol King when the Supreme Court held (8–1) that after two years' imprisonment, Harry/Kwong Hai Chew had the right to a hearing on the charges causing his exclusion from the United States. As the INS released him from Ellis Island, Attorney General Brownell had him arrested for perjury for falsely denying CP membership in his exclusion hearing.

In March, Brownell announced that 22,000 "Reds" face deportation because "snakes" must be driven out. By April, Brownell's deportation drive was focusing on thirty-eight, with "racketeers" joining "Red Big Shots" on the list.

On June 15, 1953, luck held for the third time for Carol's long-standing client. The Supreme Court reversed (6–3) convictions of Harry Bridges and two other leaders of the International Longshoremen's and Warehousemen's Union for conspiracy to make false statements in Bridges's 1945 naturalization proceeding, on the narrow ground that the statute of limitations had run before the 1949 indictment. But in an unprecedented move, Chief Justice Vinson called the Court back into session after Justice Douglas had issued a stay in the *Rosenberg* case. The Court denied the stay. The government executed Julius and Ethel Rosenberg on June 19, 1953.

By July the INS was boasting 290 political deportation arrests and the deportation of 480,000 Mexicans in six months, equal to the total number deported in 1950. On November 23, union leader Charles Doyle, one of Carol's hunger-striking clients in 1948, was deported to Scotland, accompanied by his U.S. citizen wife.

In the spring of 1954, as its political deportation arrests rose to 335, the Justice Department moved to denaturalize Harry Bridges. But in 1955 federal judge Louis E. Goodman in San Francisco dismissed the suit, finally ending the twenty-year drive to "get Bridges."

In 1955 the Supreme Court upheld the constitutionality of the act of Congress exempting the Immigration Service from the Administrative Procedure Act, and held the less strict standard constitutional in *Marcello v. Bonds*. The INS could continue to have one person act as investigator, prosecutor, and judge if it wanted to. And in 1955 what was left of the once vibrant CIO crawled slowly into the AFL-CIO.

Finally, on June 17, 1957, which the pundits came to call "Red Monday," the Supreme Court reversed (8–1) the Smith Act convictions of William Schneiderman and the other California Communist Party leaders because the statute of limitations had run before the charges were brought, and because the judge had given bad instructions to the jury on the type of evidence needed to convict in *Yates v. U.S.* It was no broad, ringing Murphy opinion in *Schneiderman v. U.S.*, but it spelled the end of the enforcement of the Smith Act, although the act remains on the books. (Later the INS dropped its second effort to denaturalize Schneiderman.) The Court that day also reversed the convictions of John Watkins (6–1) and of Paul Sweezy (6–2) for contempt of the House Committee on Un-American Activities and its New Hampshire state counterpart.

In December 1957 and January 1958, the Supreme Court (5–4) canceled deportation proceedings against Charles Rowoldt because he had only been a "nominal" member of the Communist Party in 1936 and (9–0) reversed the conviction and five-year sentence of Knut Heikkinen for failing to facilitate his own deportation by applying for travel documents.

These decisions marked the end of the successful cold war assaults on aliens and Reds by the INS and Department of Justice, although defensive clean-up actions continued for years, and decades. The United States had succeeded in jailing 150 Communist Party leaders, in destroying most of the 275 organizations it listed as "subversive," in causing the loss of tens of thousands of jobs and reputations, the loss of history itself as many people frantically destroyed files that can never be re-created now that the terror of blacklisting has abated. The United States had also succeeded in imprisoning twenty-eight Communist Party leaders on five- and ten-year sentences, and in expelling a handful of political deportees to Western Europe, the Caribbean, and Mexico, including Ferdinand Smith, Claudia Jones, and John Williamson. Another handful, facing persecution in South Korea, Portugal, Greece, and Spain, reluctantly accepted asylum in socialist Eastern European countries and the Soviet Union, including Carol's clients Peter Harisiades, Beatrice Johnson, and George Siskind, while hundreds continued to fight for their right to live out their lives in the United States, including Fred Fierstein, who was first arrested in the Depression.

In 1987 a court of appeals judge concluded in *Cynthia King v. U.S. Department of Justice:* "the FBI reports that its investigation [of King] was devoted exclusively to determining whether Carol King was guilty of political sedition. . . . While the eleven-year investigation amassed a file of 1,665 pages, . . . no charge was ever made."

Carol King and her colleagues practiced law within the system, although some felt it had to be overthrown and built anew. At their best they worked together with their clients — organized radicals, anarchists, liberals, and civil libertarians — to make the legal system live up to its constitutional promise. They did appeal to the wellspring of democratic values in the American people to stop the worst abuses against aliens and citizens — some by employers, some by the Congress, some by the courts. They did blunt the attacks of the Immigration and Naturalization Service, the Federal Bureau of Investigation, and the Department of Justice, who often worked in collaboration with industrial espionage firms, forcing these powerful agencies to refine their procedures or to do a better job of covering them up. They did make public the murders of many striking workers, union organizers, and militant African-Americans, and the deaths of many more men, women, and children from occupational accidents and diseases. They did participate in bringing to public attention the evil face of racism — first in the South, later in the North — and learned how to fight successfully in the streets and in the courts against the worst racist abuses and attacks on labor. They did welcome women and blacks, and tried to relate to them as equals.

They did initiate the shift from states' rights to federal power over civil liberties violations in the 1925 *Gitlow* case, which blossomed into Justice Hugo Black's "incorporation theory" in 1947 and was attacked by Reagan's Attorney General Meese in the 1980s. They did develop civil liberties case law to guarantee First Amendment rights through *DeJonge v. Oregon, Herndon v. Lowry, Bridges v. California, Schneiderman v. United States,* and *Bridges v. Wixon.* They did develop civil rights law to guarantee Fourteenth Amendment rights through the two *Scottsboro* cases. They did develop due process rights through *Johnson v. Zerbst* and *Wong Yang Sung v. McGrath.* They did develop labor law through *Hague v. CIO* and *Senn v. Tile Layers Protective Union* and countless other cases. Columbia Professor Walter Gellhorn, in testimony before the House Un-American Activities Committee in 1950, concluded that winning the right to picket in the absence of a strike in *Senn* and saving the seamen from the charge of mutiny in 1936 had been very significant victories of the IJA specifically. All of these became landmark constitutional law cases — the building blocks that have survived through the decades.

These lawyers and activists did blunt the attack on organizations unleashed by the Attorney General's list of subversive organizations in *Joint Anti-Fascist Refugee Committee v. Brownell.* They did prevent a Supreme Court decision finding that the Communist Party was an illegal organization, that its members must be registered and its publications stamped "subversive." These negative victories made the ending of the cold war much easier, with fewer restrictions to stop the flowering of the student, civil rights, and anti-war movements of the 1960s.

This group did develop the spirit of internationalism in *Sacco and Vanzetti* that proved significant in freeing *Dimitroff* in 1934. They did support the first efforts to turn to the United Nations to stop human rights abuses by the United States, a step that is becoming a movement in the 1990s. Their outrage at violations of the privacy and expression rights of their clients did fuel passage of the Freedom of Information Act in 1966, which ultimately led to the disclosure of many secrets and scandals, although many remained blacked out.

They did work successfully in Congress — as witnesses before congressional committees, sometimes as committee staffers, occasionally as candidates for Congress or as members — learning how to combine street demonstrations with effective lobbying for the underdog on specific issues. They did develop administrative law with due process built in during the New Deal, as they demanded the expansion of due process to cover the INS during the cold war.

FBI files make clear that these litigants and lawyers faced two opponents in every case. One they could face openly in the courtroom and sometimes defeat. The other, unseen, worked in the shadows — tapping telephones, ransacking offices, talking to judges, meddling with witnesses, not only in the big cases like *Bridges* but in the little cases as well. On Capitol Hill and in administrative hearings, Left/Progressives and New Dealers faced both opponents again as J. Edgar Hoover let it be known that it was dangerous to get in his way from 1920 until his death in 1972.

Carol King and the lawyers on her side studied the democratic system. They proved that the judicial system works sometimes — or rather, that it can be worked successfully with an enormous effort by a mass movement, creative and dedicated clients and lawyers, good media coverage, and a little luck in the appointment of a judge from the Wilson or New Deal era. Carol King proved that it is possible to manage the point and counterpoint of little and big cases to make precedents, and of equal importance to her, to turn immigrants into legally resident aliens and sometimes even into citizens. She called herself "a he-woman with a heart," and her typical lawyer-client relationship mocked the 1990s portrayal of Old Leftists as uncaring propagandists. At the same time, she and her colleagues proved that the legislative branch can be convinced to listen to the voters, although they also learned that in times of hysteria, congressional investigating committees can destroy lives.

Carol King and her crowd did build a permanent structure to counter the bureaucracy of the INS, the perpetual violations of constitutional rights endemic to the FBI, and other basic wrongs. The National Lawyers Guild, which they founded in 1937, proved strong enough to survive attacks and defeats. The Guild Immigration Project continues to be a gathering point for lawyers and legal workers specializing in immigration law, and every year gives the Carol King Award to an outstanding person or defense team.

Carol King did not fight openly for the rights of women and women lawyers — she assumed and exercised them. Her victories commanded respect — sometimes open, often grudging — and frequent efforts at emulation.

Carol King left behind a son and daughter-in-law with a grandchild on the way, a sister, brother-in-law, sisters-in-law, countless nieces, nephews, and close personal friends. She also left thousands of satisfied clients, and tens of thousands of citizens and noncitizens who continued to believe in social changes in the United States and continued to advocate their beliefs with a confidence gained, in part, they said, from their lawyer, Carol King. She left behind a few clients forced to live abroad, and lawyers around the world with whom she had worked. She left behind a handful of women lawyers and clients who had watched and learned from her struggles against male chauvinism, and thousands of lawyers touched by her training. She left the files of the ACLU *Law and Freedom Bulletin,* the *IJA Bulletin,* and the *Lawyers Guild Review,* and digests of the thousands of cases she had faithfully chronicled therein. Her familiarity with all the "little" cases had strengthened her capacity to supervise the field and to nudge certain cases into a position to go to the Supreme Court as potential winners. But she prepared no statistical study and no theoretical analysis of the meaning of these cases in relation to the operation of the formal judicial system in a democracy. She preferred personalities to political lines, and personalized both her friends and her enemies in trying to win specific victories and to prevent personal defeats.

She and her colleagues did not leave behind a theoretical work analyzing the conflicting forces they faced that some attributed to the status of the law as part of the super-structure of society, limited by the economic base on which it rested. Others saw liberty and law as the columns decorating but not supporting the developing military/industrial complex. They did not publish an analysis describing their approaches, and explaining why some of their efforts paid off and why others failed. They left behind no coherent critique of their sectarianism at some points or their lack of sufficient skepticism at others — about Stalin's violations of human rights; the failure of the United States to act against Hitler's "final solution" for European Jews, gypsies, and homosexuals; and the racism behind relocation camps for Japanese-Americans. Few of these lawyers left oral or written histories, so their busyness and their right to privacy have partially defeated the people's right to history. They saved their best writing for the briefs they filed, causing a few judges to immortalize their most telling phrases and concepts in opinions. They bequeathed their briefs to their legal heirs, along with a few fundamental principles, procedures, continuing organizations, and periodicals.

To these King added her share of legends, hope, and laughter. Her life reveals the reality behind the image of the great trial lawyer striding into court to best the government single-handed. It dispels the image of the studious civil liberties lawyer convincing a majority of the Supreme Court to enunciate a new clear rule of law solely on the basis of logic and precedent. Her life makes clear that great people's lawyers lose most of their appellate cases, their greatness being based on how they fought for their clients and their principles, on how many people they brought into the struggle and kept with them after defeats.

At her memorial, Tom Emerson emphasized Carol King's great zest for life, her willingness to tackle anything, her overpowering honesty and dislike of sham, and her unillusioned but joyful feeling when anything at all was accomplished. He summed up her credo very simply:

> Carol King really believed the things so many of us only talk about. She really believed a democracy must be bold, dynamic and advancing.

General Sources/Specific References

Carol Weiss King Collection

At Meiklejohn Civil Liberties Institute, Berkeley, California
All items in CWK Collection on pp. 545–576 are labelled ‡

Carol King Files

‡Typed notes from CWK office files (obtained 1952–1954).

‡Typed copies of CWK personal correspondence with Clara Binswanger, Gordon King.

‡Typed copies of minutes of IJA meetings by Sol Cohn.

‡Newspaper clippings (New York, San Francisco, other).

‡CWK notes for banquet honoring King, 1948.

‡Case materials: briefs, motions, affidavits, transcripts, etc., and notes typed from these materials.

‡Photocopies of CWK correspondence with Jay Leyda from Jay Leyda/Si-Lan Chen papers, Tamiment Institute Library, New York University.

Publications/Columns Edited by Carol Weiss King

Citations to IJA Bulletin articles are to volume, number, page — e.g., I, 9, 1
citations to Lawyers Guild Review articles are to volume: number, page — e.g., I: 1, 1

ACLU Law and Freedom Bulletin (1924–1931).

"Recent Items" (monthly columns). The International Juridical Association Bulletin, 1932–1942, 3 vols. Introduction and supplementary index by Ann Fagan Ginger. New York: Da Capo Press, 1982 (reprint).

IJA Bulletin Section. Lawyers Guild Rev. III: 1, 32 (1943)–V: 6, 378 (1945).

"Recent Items" editor, Lawyers Guild Rev. VI: 3, 561 (1946)–VIII: 4, 465 (1948).

Legal Briefs by Carol Weiss King

(see Cases with * in Parts I–IV)

Writings by Carol Weiss King

(see items in Parts I–IV)

Writings Probably by Carol Weiss King

(see also bracketed items in Parts I–IV)

[King, Carol]. NLG Resolutions on Immigration & Naturalization Laws & Procedures: 1 *National Lawyers Guild Quarterly* 144 (1938), 2 *NLGQ* 89 (1939), 3 NLGQ 119 (1940); *Lawyers Guild Review* I:4, 64 (1941); III: 2, 40 (1943); VI: 2, 521 (1946); VIII: 1, 320 (1948); IX: 1, 53 (1949); X: 2, 41 (1950); XI: 4, 182 (1951).

[King, Carol]. "NLG Resolution on Tom Clark." *Lawyers Guild Rev.* VI: 2, 518 (1946).

Writings About Carol Weiss King

Emerson, Thomas I. "In Memoriam: Carol King." *Lawyers Guild Rev.* XII: 1, 55 (1952).

Ginger, Ann Fagan. "Carol Weiss King." In *Notable American Women: The Modern Period.* Edited by Barbara Sicherman and Carol Hurd Green with Ilene Kantrov and Harriette Walker. Cambridge: Belknap Press of Harvard University Press, 1980, pp. 397–98.

‡Kahn, Peggy Stern. "Recollections," March 10, 1953.

‡King, Howard L. "Notes on Gordon King, His Early Years and His Married Life by His Brother Howard L. King," Feb. 16, 1953.

Larrowe, Charles P. "King, Carol Weiss." In *Dictionary of American Biography.* Edited by John A. Garraty. Supp. 5: 1951–1955. New York: Scribner, 1977, pp. 389–90.

‡*New York Guild Lawyer* (Feb. 1952).

‡Obituary. *New York Times* (Jan. 23, 1952) 27:1.

‡Running, Elizabeth. "In Memoriam." (Minneapolis, 1952). Poem reprinted in *The Lamp* (Apr.–May 1952).

‡Stern, Carl S. "Carol King." In *Memorial Book,* Association of the Bar of the City of New York, p. 52 (1952).

‡Stone, I. F., *Daily Compass* (Feb. 1952), quoted in Samuel Handleman letter to Cleveland memorial meeting for King (Feb. 6, 1952).

Writings About Relatives and Colleagues of Carol King

Obituary, Joe Brodsky, and tributes. *Daily Worker* (July 31, 1947) 5:1–5, (Aug. 3, 1947) 5:1–5; *NYT* (July 29, 1947) 21:4, (Aug. 1, 1947) 17:5.

Obituary, Gordon Congdon King. *NYT* (July 12, 1930) 13:6.

Obituary, Walter Nelles. *NYT* (Apr. 1, 1937) 23:5. Norman L. Meyers, "Walter Nelles." 46 *Yale L. Jour.* 1279 (1937).

Obituary, Mary Goldburt Siegel. *NYT* (Jan. 25, 1991) A, 19:4.

Obituary, Louis S. Weiss. *Time* (Nov. 27, 1950) 97; *NYT* (Nov. 15, 1950) 31:3, (Nov. 21, 1950) 30:6.

Obituary, William Weiss. *NYT* (Sept. 30, 1946) 24:7, (Sept. 24, 1946) 29:5.

Ginger Correspondents and Interviewees on King

The King Collection includes correspondence, shorthand notes, tapes, and transcriptions of interviews on King with relatives, friends, colleagues, and acquaintances who supplied information in interviews and/or correspondence in 1952–1954 and/or 1979–1992. Their names appear in bold type in the Index.

The following also supplied helpful information in correspondence or brief interviews: Noriko Bridges, Robert Cherny, Ramsey Clark, Ruby Darrow, Lincoln Fairley, Joseph A. Fanelli, Millie McIntire Franklin, Conrad Friberg, Harold Fruchtbaum, Bernard A. Golding, Marcus I. Goldman, Lottie Gordon, Bertram Gross, Bernard Jaffe, Alec Jones, Joe Joseph, Sonia Kaross, Sam Krieger, Martin Kurash, Lupe Martinez, Tuz Mende, Ginnie Muir, Sam Neuberger, Merle Richmond, Sam Rosenwein, Henry Silver, George C. Vournas, Karl Yoneda, Leo E. Ypsilanti.

Bridges Case Files
(also available on microfilm)

In the Matter of Harry R. Bridges (1939), (1941–1942). ‡Typed notes from transcripts of Landis and Sears hearings; all legal documents on Sears hearing (not transcript of hearing); proceedings before Attorney General.

Ex parte Bridges (1942–1943), *Bridges v. Wixon* (1943–1945). ‡Briefs, memos, motions in federal district court, court of appeals, United States Supreme Court.

U.S. v. Bridges (1949). ‡Record of proceedings in district court on charge of perjury in naturalization proceedings.

Federal Bureau of Investigation Files

‡On Carol Weiss King (1927–1952): 1,665 pp.

‡On Carol Weiss King, released after litigation with some deletions removed, entitled *Cynthia King v. U.S. Dept. of Justice*, Exhibit A to Declaration of Susan Delia Prust and Angus B. Llewellyn (1988): 133 pp.

‡Files on Joseph R. Brodsky (1927–1947).

National Lawyers Guild Collection
At Meiklejohn Civil Liberties Institute

Minutes of National Executive Board meetings.

Complete files of *National Lawyers Guild Quarterly* (1937–1940), *Lawyers Guild Review* (1940-1960), *Law in Transition* (1961–1963), *National Lawyers Guild Practitioner* (1965–1992).

International Labor Defense Collection
At Meiklejohn Civil Liberties Institute
(also available on microfilm)

Scattered reports, articles, minutes of meetings and conferences on criminal syndicalism, political and labor prisoners in United States, courts martial of Negro servicemen, *Herndon v. Lowry* (1933–1945).

Files of *Labor Defender* (1927–1938). Incomplete.

Files of *Equal Justice* (1939–1941). Incomplete.

American Committee for Protection of Foreign Born
At Meiklejohn Civil Liberties Institute
(also available on microfilm)

Complete file of *Bulletin* (1953–1959). Published irregularly.

Complete file of *The Lamp* (1944–1959) nos. 1–104.

Review of the Year. Annual. (1947–1950).

Surveillance Papers Collection
At Meiklejohn Civil Liberties Institute
(also available on microfilm)

Reports of undercover informants in San Francisco and elsewhere in California (1930s).

General Books
(see also Parts I–IV to follow)

Page numbers following "....." at the end of citations refer to page references in this book.

Cardozo, Benjamin Nathan. *Selected Writings of Benjamin Nathan Cardozo.* In *The Choice of Tycho Brahe.* Edited by Margaret E. Hall. New York: Fallon Law Book Co., 1947.

Chafee, Zechariah, Jr. *Free Speech in the United States.* Cambridge: Harvard University Press, 1920 edition; 1946 edition, pp. 36–228. 30

Draper, Theodore. *Roots of American Communism: The Untold Story of the Formative Years of the Communist Party in America.* New York: Viking Press, 1957.

Flynn, Elizabeth Gurley. *The Rebel Girl. An Autobiography. My First Life (1906–1926).* New York: International Publishers, 1955, 1973, p. 244. 17

Foner, Philip S. *History of the Labor Movement in the United States* vols. 4, 5. New York: International Publishers, 1965, 1979.

Foner, Philip S. *Women and the American Labor Movement: From World War I to the Present.* New York: Free Press, 1980.

Frankfurter, Felix, and Nathan Greene. *The Labor Injunction.* New York: Macmillan, 1930). 146

Ginger, Ann Fagan, and Eugene M. Tobin, eds. *The National Lawyers Guild: From Roosevelt through Reagan.* Philadelphia: Temple University Press, 1988.

Hoover, J. Edgar. *Masters of Deceit.* New York: Henry Holt and Co., 1958.

Katz, Richard N. *The National Lawyers Guild: An Inventory of Records 1936–1976, An Index to Periodicals 1937–1979.* Berkeley: Meiklejohn Civil Liberties Institute, 1980.

Labor Research Association. *Labor Fact Books 1–9.* New York: International Publishers, 1931–1949.

Le Sueur, Meridel. *Crusaders.* New York: Blue Heron Press, 1955.

Manfred, A. Z., ed. *A Short History of the World.* 2 vols. Moscow: Progress Publishers, 1974.

Mason, Alpheus Thomas. *Brandeis: A Free Man's Life.* New York: Viking Press, 1946.

Rubinstein, Annette T., and Associates, eds. *Marcantonio, Vito, I Vote My Conscience: Debates, Speeches and Writings.* New York: The Vito Marcantonio Memorial, 1956.

Smith, Louise Pettibone. *Torch of Liberty: 25 Years in the Life of the Foreign Born in the U.S.* New York: Dwight-King Publishers, Inc., 1959.

Theoharis, Athan G., and John Stuart Cox. *The Boss: J. Edgar Hoover and the Great American Inquisition.* Philadelphia: Temple University Press, 1988. (King is mentioned on page 14, Eleanor Roosevelt on pp. 191, 192.) 328, 371

Zinn, Howard. *A People's History of the United States.* New York: Harper & Row, 1980.

Cases Discussed

(see also cases in Parts I–IV)

The name of the person in whom Carol King was interested is given in capitalized letters in each instance. Cases are also listed by popular names; e.g., SCOTTSBORO CASES. Cases in which the United States or a state was one party are alphabetized under the name of the other party. The pages on which each case is discussed in the text are given.

All formal citations are given for cases reported in federal and state law reporters. Citations of Immigration Service case numbers are given where available. Descriptions of cases in the *IJA Bulletin, Lawyers Guild Review,* and *Labor Defender,* many of which King probably wrote or edited, are also given here.

* indicates cases in which King's name is listed in one or more official reports.

[ ] indicate the parts of the case in which King's name did not appear.

‡ indicates cases in which additional material is available in the Carol Weiss King (CWK) Collection, Meiklejohn Civil Liberties Institute, Berkeley, California. (For a virtually complete list of the cases in which Carol King participated that are reported in law reporters,

see CWK Collection.)

[Ginger, Ann Fagan], for the Committee on Immigration & Naturalization of National Lawyers Guild. "Political Deportations in the United States: A Study in the Enforcement Procedures: 1919–1952." 14 *Lawyers Guild Rev.* 93 (1954) (a heavily footnoted study used in chapters 1–5, 14–17, 32–36, with names of each deportee and citations to INS and court cases).

Sources of material on 6,000–10,000 political deportation cases: 1919–1920, 14 *Lawyers Guild Rev.* 93, Appendix A, 124 (1954).

Sources of material on fifty-three political deportation cases: 1930–1937, 14 *Lawyers Guild Rev.* 93, Appendix B, 124 (1954).

Sources of material on 219 political deportation cases: 1944–1952, 14 *Lawyers Guild Rev.* 93, Appendix C, 125–27 (1954).

Part I

Cases

JACOB ABRAMS v. U.S. (distributing pamphlet against U.S. expeditionary force to Soviet Russia), *aff'd*, 250 U.S. 616, at 624 (Holmes, J., joined by Brandeis, J., dissenting) (1919). 23–25

‡* Pennsylvania v. SALVATORE ACCORSI (murder at demonstration). 5 *Labor Defender* no. 1(1930), p. 6. . . . . 88–89, 90

AMERICAN SOCIALIST SOCIETY v. U.S. (Scott Nearing's anti–World War I pamphlet case), 260 F. 885 (S.D. N.Y. 1919), *aff'd*, 266 F. 212 (2d Cir. 1920). (Of counsel: Walter Nelles). 16

U.S. v. VICTOR BERGER (Espionage Act prosecution), 255 U.S. 22 (1921). 16

MICHAEL BILOKUMSKY v. Tod (deportation), [263 U.S. 149 (1923)]. 60–61, 65, 236

U.S. ex rel. RICHARD BRAZIER, Joseph Oates, et al. v. Commissioner (deportation despite presidential pardon), 5 F.2d 162 (2d Cir. 1924) (Hand, J., dissenting). 61–62

Petition of LAWRENCE BROOKS (cannot deport to USSR w/o diplomatic relations), 5 F.2d 238 (D.C. Mass. 1925). 42–43

BUGAJEWITZ v. Adams (deportation of prostitute is not punishment), Holmes, J., 228 U.S. 585 (1913). 60–61

CHINESE EXCLUSION CASE (Chae Chan Ping v. U.S.), 130 U.S. 581 (1889). 54

WILLIAM COLYER v. Skeffington (Palmer Raid case, Boston), 265 F. 17 (D. Mass. 1920); *Skeffington v. Katzeff, rev'd on limited grounds,* 277 F. 129 (1st Cir. 1922); Petition of BROOKS, Bonder v. Johnson, Commr. (released from deportation arrest), 5 F.2d 238 (D. Mass. 1925). 30, 33, 290

EUGENE DEBS v. U.S. (opposition to U.S. entry into WWI speech — Espionage Act), *aff'd*, 249 U.S. 211 (1919). 16, 24

ISSAC FERGUSON v. N.Y. (criminal anarchy), 199 N.Y. App. Div. 642 (1922), *rev'd,* 234 N.Y. 159 (N.Y. Ct. of App. 1922). 63

Michigan v. WILLIAM Z. FOSTER (criminal syndicalism) (arrested after 1922 CP National Convention; tried in 1933), *IJA Bull.* I, 9, 4 (1933); *see* II, 11, 4 (1934); *see Michigan v. Ruthenberg.* 81

LEO FRANK v. Mangum (murder), *aff'd,* 237 U.S. 309, at 345 (Holmes, J. dissenting) (1914); "A Lynching on His Conscience for 70 Years," *San Francisco Examiner* (Mar. 8, 1982), p. A7: 1–4. Ga. awarded posthumous pardon: *San Francisco Chronicle* (Mar. 12, 1986), p. 10. . . . . 13, 203–204

JACOB FROHWERK v. U.S. (conspiracy/Espionage Act), *aff'd,* 249 U.S. 204 (1919). 60–61

*U.S. ex rel. MARIO GILETTI v. Commissioner (deportation to Italy), *aff'd,* 35 F.2d 687 (2d Cir. 1929). 89–90

BENJAMIN GITLOW v. N.Y. (N.Y. criminal anarchy statute constitutional) [*aff'd,* 187 N.Y.S. 783 (1921); 136 N.E. 317 (N.Y. Ct. of App. 1922); 138 N.E. 438; *aff'd,* 268 U.S. 652 (1925). (Of counsel: Clarence S. Darrow, Walter Nelles, Walter H. Pollak)]. Weinberg, Arthur, and Lila Weinberg. *Clarence Darrow: A Sentimental Rebel.* New York: Putnam's, 1980, pp. 290–95; Gitlow, Benjamin. *I Confess: The Truth about American Communism.* New York: Dutton, 1940. 62–68

EMMA GOLDMAN v. Caminetti (deportation), 251 U.S. 565 (1919). 3–4

*New York v. CALOGERO GRECO and DONATO CARILLO (murder): 3 *Labor Defender* no. 1, p. 3–no. 2, p. 29 (1928); Ginger, Ann Fagan. "Watching Darrow Work a Jury." 8 *Criminal Justice Journal* 29 (1985) (including many footnote references); Hays, Arthur Garfield. *Let Freedom Ring.* New York: Liveright Publishing Corp., 1937; Weinberg, Arthur, and Lila Weinberg. *Clarence Darrow: A Sentimental Rebel.* New York: Putnam's, 1980, pp. 355–65. . . . . 80–88, 90

THOMAS HAMMERSCHMIDT v. U.S. (conspiracy to defraud/anti-draft), 265 U.S. 182 (1924). 66

NG FUNG HO v. White (deportation for fraudulent entry), 259 U.S. 276 (1922). 60–61

JAPANESE IMMIGRANT CASES (deportation of illegal entrants), 189 U.S. 86 (1903). 54

JOHANESSEN v. U.S. (ex post facto does not bar revocation of citizenship procured by fraud), 225 U.S. 227 (1912). 60–61

KELLER v. U.S. (deportation of illegal entrants), 213 U.S. 138 (1909). 54

New York v. JAMES LARKIN (criminal anarchy), 200 A.D. 858 (App. Div. 1921), *aff'd,* 234 N.Y. 530 (1922). (Clarence Darrow, trial lawyer). 62

Illinois v. WILLIAM BROSS LLOYD (state sedition law conviction), 136 N.E. 505 (1922). (Clarence Darrow, trial lawyer). 36

LOW WAH SUEY v. Backus (sustained statute expelling aliens practicing prostitution within three years of entry), 225 U.S. 460 (1912). 60–61

U.S. ex rel. OMAR MACKLEM v. Commr. of Immigration (bail for nonpolitical deportee), 268 U.S. 679 (1925). 75

*HERBERT MAHLER, et al. v. Eby (deportation), *aff'd,* [264 U.S. 32 (1924)]. 60–61, 236

Prentiss v. MANOOGIAN (bail on arrest granted), *aff'd*, 16 F.2d 422 (6th Cir. 1926). . . . .
75

MASSES PUBLISHING CO. v. Patten (injunction against postmaster), *granted*, 244 F. 535
(S.D. N.Y. 1917), *stayed*, 245 F. 102 (2d Cir. 1917), *rev'd*, 246 F. 24 (2d Cir. 1917). . .
. . 16, 24, 27, 28, 63

*NICOLAI MENSEVICH v. Tod (deportation), *aff'd*, [264 U.S. 134 (1924)]. 60–61,
236

MOORE v. Dempsey (murder convictions in lynch atmosphere), 261 U.S. 86 (1923). . . . .
65

JOSEPH OATES, *see U.S. ex re. Brazier v. Commissioner*

*†U.S. ex rel. OKOLITENKO v. Commissioner (deportation) (unrep.) (Nos. M 9-235, M
9-344, M 9-398 S.D. N.Y. 192); *see* brief for appellant, *Chew v. Colding*, 16 (decision
in 192 F.2d 1009 (2d Cir. 1952)). 42–43

Michigan v. CHARLES RUTHENBERG (criminal syndicalism), 201 N.W. 358 (Mich. Sup.
Ct. 1925); *IJA Bull.* II, 11, 4 (1934). 81

CHARLES RUTHENBERG v. N.Y. (criminal anarchy), *rev'd*, 199 N.Y. App. Div. 642
(1922), 234 N.Y. 159 (1925). 62

Massachusetts v. NICOLA SACCO and BARTOLOMEO VANZETTI (murder), 151 N.E.
839 (1926); *appeal denied*, 156 N.E. 57 (1927); SACCO and VANZETTI v. Common-
wealth of Massachusetts, *appeal denied*, 158 N.E. 167 (1927); *dismissed w/o consideration by Court*, 275 U.S. 574 (1927); *The Sacco-Vanzetti Case: Transcript of the
Record of the Trial 1920–1927*, vol. II. N.Y.: Henry Holt, 1928–1929, pp. 1806, 1809,
1848; Fraenkel, Osmond K. *The Sacco-Vanzetti Case*. New York: Alfred A. Knopf,
1931. . . . . 3, 29, 37, 69, 84, 88, 89

ANDREA SALSEDO v. Palmer (wrongful death suit against Attorney General), 278 F. 92
(2d Cir. 1921); Post, Louis F. *The Deportations Delirium of Nineteen-Twenty; AN-
DREA SALSEDO . . . Nineteen-Twenty*. Chicago: C. H. Kerr, 1923, pp. 220, 279–281;
Nat'l. Popular Gov't. League. "To the American People: Report Upon the Illegal
Practices . . ." Washington, D.C., 1920, pp. 21–22. 28–29

CHARLES T. SCHENCK v. U.S. (conspiracy to violate Espionage Act), 249 U.S. 47 (1919).
. . . . 24

FONG YUE TING v. U.S. (deportation is not punishment), 149 U.S. 698, at 744 (Brewer,
J., dissenting). (1893). 60–61

U.S. ex rel. CATONI TISI v. Tod (deportation), *aff'd*, 264 U.S. 131 (1924). 60–61, 236

U.S. ex rel. TURNER v. Williams (alien seeking admission has no constitutional protections),
194 U.S. 279 (1904). 54

*U.S. ex rel. EMANUEL VAJTAUER v. Commissioner (deportation order) [15 F.2d 127
(S.D. N.Y. 1925),] 273 U.S. 103 (1926). 75–76, 215, 236

*MILOS VOJNOVIC v. Curran (deportation order), 11 F.2d 683 (2d Cir. 1926), *cert.
denied*, 271 U.S. 683 (1926). 75

YICK WO v. Hopkins (deportation), 118 U.S. 356 (1886). 54

ZAKONAITE v. Wolf (sustained statute expelling aliens practicing prostitution within three
years of entry), 226 U.S. 272 (1912). 60–61

WONG WING v. U.S. (aliens have some due process rights) 163 U.S. 228 (1896).

Books, Articles, Pamphlets, Government Documents
‡In Carol Weiss King Collection at Meiklejohn Civil Liberties Institute

Allen, Frederick Lane. *Only Yesterday: An Informal History of the Nineteen-Twenties.* New York: Harper & Bros., 1931.

Bart, Phil. *Working Class Unity: The Role of Communists in the Chicago Federation of Labor, 1919–1923.* New York: New Outlook Publishers, 1975.

Bimba, Anthony. *The History of the American Working Class.* New York: International Publishers, 1927.

Broun, Heywood. *Encyclopedia Americana.* [by Robert W. Desmond].

Chaplin, Ralph. *Wobbly, The Rough-&-Tumble Story of an American Radical.* Chicago: University of Chicago Press, 1948.

Cohen, Stanley. *A. Mitchell Palmer, Politician.* New York: Columbia University Press, 1963.

Damon, Allan L. "The Great Red Scare." *American Heritage,* Feb. 1968, p. 22.

Darrow, Clarence. *The Story of My Life.* New York: Grosset & Dunlap, 1932.

DeCaux, Len. *The Living Spirit of the Wobblies.* New York: International Publishers, 1978.

‡deSilver, *Since the* Buford *Sailed: A Summary of Developments in the Deportation Situation.* New York: American Civil Liberties Union, 1920.

Dunn, Robert W., ed. *The Palmer Raids.* Prepared by the Labor Research Association. New York: International Publishers, 1948.

Foster, William Z. *Pages from a Worker's Life.* New York: International Publishers, 1939.

Fowler, Gene. *The Great Mouthpiece: A Life Story of William J. Fallon.* New York: Grosset & Dunlap, 1931. 62

Fraenkel, Osmond. *The Sacco-Vanzetti Case.* New York: Alfred A. Knopf, 1931.

‡Gengarelly, W. Anthony. "Opponents of the Red Scare, 1919–1921: An Exercise in Democratic Conservation." A paper presented at the Great Lakes History Conference, Apr. 23, 1976.

Gengarelly, W. Anthony. *Resistance Spokesmen: Opponents of the Red Scare, 1919–1921.* Ann Arbor: University Microfilms, 1972.

Ginger, Ann Fagan. "Watching Darrow Work a Jury." 8 *Criminal Justice Journal* 29 (1985) (a footnoted and longer version of Chapter 7).

Ginger, Ray. *The Bending Cross: A Biography of Eugene Victor Debs.* New Brunswick: Rutgers, 1949.

Gunther, Gerald. "Learned Hand and the Origins of Modern First Amendment Doctrine: Some Fragments of History." Appendix. 27 *Stanford L. Rev.* 719, 755–61 (1975). 24

Hale, Swinburne. "The Force and Violence Joker." *The New Republic* (Jan. 12, 1920), p. 25. 26

Hand, Learned. *The Spirit of Liberty: Papers and Addresses of Learned Hand.* Edited by Irving Dilliard. New York: Alfred A. Knopf, 1960. 24

Hays, Arthur Garfield. *Let Freedom Ring.* New York: Liveright Publishing Corp., 1937.

Haywood, William D. *Bill Haywood's Book: The Autobiography of William D. Haywood.* Westport, Conn.: Greenwood Press, 1983, c. 1929.

Holmes, Oliver Wendell. *The Common Law.* Boston: Little, Brown, 1881.

‡Hughes, Charles Evans. Memorial of the Special Comm. Appointed by the Assn. of the Bar of the City of New York, N.Y. Legislative Docs, vol. 5, 143rd Session (1920), no. 30, p. 4. 32

Johnson, Donald. *The Challenge to American Freedoms — World War I and the Rise of the American Civil Liberties Union.* Lexington: University Press of Kentucky, 1963.

Jones, Sarah. "Sacco and Vanzetti — Immortal Victims of Union-Busters." *People's Daily World* (Aug. 22, 1987), p. A9.

Joughin, Louis, and Edmund L. Morgan. *The Legacy of Sacco and Vanzetti.* Princeton, N.J.: Princeton University Press, 1978, c. 1948.

Kennedy, Stetson. *Southern Exposure.* Garden City, N.Y.: Doubleday & Co., 1946, pp. 163–65. 13

‡King, Carol. "Speech on History of Immigration and Exclusion Laws" (no date). CWK files. 91–92

‡King, Carol. *State Laws Against Free Speech.* New York: American Civil Liberties Union, 1925. 66

King, Gordon. *Horatio's Story.* New York: Boni and Liveright, 1923. . . . . 55–57, 94, 156

King, Gordon. *The Rise of Rome.* New York: Doubleday, Doran & Co., 1932. Junior Literary Guild Selection. 94

Kornbluh, Joyce L., ed. *Rebel Voices, An IWW Anthology.* Ann Arbor: University of Michigan, 1964.

"Left Wing Manifesto." Published in *Revolutionary Age* (1919) and "Revolutionary Radicalism . . . Report of the Joint Legislature Committee Investigating Seditions Activities," vol. 1. Albany, 1920, p. 706. . . . . 62, 332

Lerner, Max, ed. *The Mind and Faith of Justice Holmes: His Speeches, Essays, Letters and Judicial Opinions.* Boston: Little, Brown, 1943.

‡Moreau, Albert. "The Iron Heel Steps on Nicaragua." 3 *Labor Defender* no. 12 (Dec. 1928), p. 268.

Murray, Robert. *Red Scare: A Study in National Hysteria, 1919–1920.* Minneapolis: University of Minnesota Press, 1955.

‡National Popular Government League. *To the American People: Report Upon the Illegal Practices of the United States Department of Justice.* Washington, D.C.: National Popular Government League, 1920. . . . . 30–31, 461, 494, 495

‡Nearing, Scott. *The American Empire.* New York: The Rand School of Social Science, 1921.

Nelles, Walter, and Carol King. "Contempt by Publication in the United States." 28 *Columbia Law Rev.* 401, 525 (1928). 77–78, 159, 537

Pollak, Louis H. "Advocating Civil Liberties: A Young Lawyer Before the Old Court." 17 *Harv. Civil Rights — Civil Liberties Law Rev.* 1 (1982). 64–65

Post, Louis F. *The Deportations Delirium of Nineteen-Twenty: A personal narrative of an historic official experience.* Chicago: C. H. Kerr, 1923. 27

‡Poyntz, Juliet Stuart. "International Women's Day — March Eighth in the United States." 4 *Labor Defender* no. 3 (Mar. 1929), p. 56.

Preston, William, Jr. *Aliens & Dissenters: Federal Suppression of Radicals, 1903–1933*. New York: Harper & Row, 1966.

Quigley, John. "The Transformation of Eastern Europe and the Convergence of Socialist and Capitalist Law." 26 *Willamette L. Rev.* 937 (1990).

‡Sankari, Hjalmar, "Fascist Terror Reigns in Finland," 5 *Labor Defender,* no. 10 (Oct. 1930), p. 207.

Steffens, Lincoln. *The World of Lincoln Steffens*. Edited by Ella Winter and Herbert Shapiro. New York: Hill and Wang, 1962. 86

Tuttle, William M., Jr. Race Riot: Chicago in the Red Summer of 1919. *Studies in American Negro Life*. New York: Atheneum, 1972. 18

U.S. Congress. House. Committee on Rules. *Attorney General A. Mitchell Palmer on Charges Made Against Department of Justice by Louis F. Post and Others*. Hearings. Washington: Government Printing Office, 1920. 32

"Who Was Who": on Bouck White. v. 5, p. 773. Chicago: Marquis Who's Who, 1969–1973. 8

Williams, David, " 'Sowing the Wind': The Deportation Raids of 1920 in New Hampshire." 34 *Historical New Hampshire* (1979).

Young, Art. *Art Young: His Life and Times*. New York: Sheridan House, 1939. 17

Part II

Cases

In re BERNARD ADES (disbarment), *IJA Bull.* II, 7, 1 (1933); II, 10, 1; II, 11, 1; II, 12, 4; III, 7, 5 (1934); 6 F. Supp. 467 (D. Md. 1934). 167

Germany v. ALFRED APFEL, *IJA Bull.* I, 11, 2 (1933). 150

Ex parte JACK BARTON v. City of Bessemer (seditious literature unconstitutional), (Ala. Ct. of App. 1936). *IJA Bull.* V, 6, 60 (1936). 223

U.S., ex rel. FRANK BORIC v. Marshall (deportation), 4 F. Supp. 956 (W.D. Pa. 1933), *affd,* 67 F.2d 1020 (3d Cir. 1933), *cert. granted,* 290 U.S. 623 (1933); withdrawn; *IJA Bull.* II, 8, 5 (1934); rearrested, *The Lamp,* no. 62 (Aug.–Sept. 1952), p. 1. 195

PAUL BROWN v. O'Neil, Bayonne Chief of Police (beating CP applicant for parade permit), "A Communist in Court," (and see *New Jersey v. John Kasper*) *IJA Bull.* I, 8, 3 (1932). 147

U.S. v. PEDRO ALBIZU CAMPOS (conspiracy for Puerto Rican independence effort at U.S. Capitol), 88 F.2d 138 (1st Cir. 1937), *cert. denied,* 301 U.S. 707 (1937). *IJA Bull.* V, 3, 29 (1936); VI, 1, 10 (1937). 208

U.S. v. Carolene Products Co. [FOOTNOTE FOUR] (judicial scrutiny of civil rights statutes), 304 U.S. 144 (1938). 225–226

Re CITIZENSHIP APPLICATIONS (sitdown strikers prohibited), Hunter, Cir. J., Kankakee, Ill., *IJA Bull.* V, 12, 142 (1937). 236

DIRK DEJONGE v. Oregon (conviction under Oregon criminal syndicalist statute), [*rev'd*, 299 U.S. 353 (1937)]; ‡Fraenkel, Osmond K. "Some Recollections of Youth and the Law" (unpublished), pp. 43–44. . . . . 217, 219, 221, 223, 226, 270, 290, 364

Germany v. GEORGE DIMITROFF (arson of Reichstag), documents from statement to police inquiry magistrates (Mar. 20, 1933) through interview with representatives of Soviet and foreign press (Feb. 27, 1934), Georgi Dimitrov. *Selected Works,* vol. 1, (Sofia Press n.d.), pp. 332–419; *IJA Bull.* II, 3, 2 (1933). 150, 188–189

DUMAS v. Oklahoma (rape), 16 P.2d 886 (Okla. Crim. App. 1932); *IJA Bull.* I, 9, 3 (Jan. 1933). 141

In re THEODORE EGGELING (anti-Nazi German — disorderly conduct). *IJA Bull.* III, 1, 2 (1934); Sol Cohn interview (July 1952). 191

Re ALBERT EINSTEIN (U.S. visa), *World Almanac & Book of Facts* (Dec. 5, 1933), p. 123; *NYT Index* (1933), p. 2466. 143

*Feller, et al. v. LOCAL 144, I.L.G.W.U. (conspiracy), 191 A. 111 (1937), [*rev'd. unanimously,* 19 A.2d 784 (1941)]. 223

*VINCENZO FERRERO v. Commissioner of Immigration (deportation), 86 F.2d 1021 (2d Cir. 1936), *cert. denied,* 300 U.S. 653 (1937); *IJA Bull.* VI, 8, 101 (1938). 236

Ex parte (ZUSMAN) FIERSTEIN (FIERSTEIN v. Conaty) (political deportation), 41 F.2d 53 (9th Cir. 1930); A 4-663-283. FRED FIRESTONE v. Howerton (INS wrongfully denied registration application as a permanent resident), 671 F.2d 217 (9th Cir. 1982). 138, 467

Re WILLIAM GALLACHER (exclusion), *IJA Bull.* V, 3, 27 (1936); VI, 12, 147 (1938). 208

LEO GALLAGHER, et al. v. Porter (damage suit for police misconduct), Los Angeles Municipal Court, No. 305052, Aug. 1933 (Scheinman, J.), *IJA Bull.* I, 10, 4, (1933); II, 3, 2 (1933). 150

Germany v. LEO GALLAGHER (deportation), *IJA Bull.* II, 8, 1 (1934). 189

ANTON GOEPELS (private bill stopped deportation to Nazi Germany), *IJA Bull.* VI, 8, 101 (1938). 242

Ireland v. JAMES GRALTON; Germany v. WALTER ORLOFF; Japan v. ALEXANDER BRUCKMAN (deportations), *IJA Bull.* II, 3, 1 (1933). 187

Hague v. CIO (injunction against organizing unconstitutional), 307 U.S. 496 (1939). Isserman, Abraham J. "CIO v. Hague: The Battle of Jersey City." 36 *Nat'l Lawyers Guild Practitioner* 14 (1979). 250

*JOHN and ELLA HERING v. State Board of Education (Jehovah's Witness flag salute refusal), 189 A. 629 (1937); 194 A. 177 (N.J. Sup. Ct. 1937); *appeal dism'd,* 303 U.S. 624 (1938). 228–229

*ANGELO HERNDON v. Georgia (insurrection), [174 S.E. 597 (1934); *reh'g. denied,* 176 S.E. 620 (1934); *appeal dism'd,* 295 U.S. 441 (1935);] *reh'g. denied,* 296 U.S. 661 (1935); Herndon v. Lowry [186 S.E. 429 (1936); *rev'd,* 301 U.S. 242 (1937); 192 S.E. 387 (1937)]. ‡King, Carol. "Dictators of the Country's Fate." 11 *Labor Defender* no. 5 (1937); Herndon, Angelo. *Let Me Live.* Preface by Howard N. Meyer. New York:

Arno Press and the New York Times, 1969, p. xii. Davis, Benjamin J. *Communist Councilman from Harlem.* New York: International Publishers, 1969, pp. 91, 53–101. . . . . 136–137, 165, 175–181, 203–204, 208, 221, 225, 226–227, 239, 278, 290, 364

HOD CARRIERS (arrests, immigration inspections), *IJA Bull.* III, 12, 3 (1935). 195

Illinois v. MEMORIAL DAY MASSACRE DEFENDANTS (unlawful assembly), *IJA Bull.* VI, 1, 5; VI, 2, 17; VI, 3, 37; VI, 7, 84 (1937–1938); *NYT* July 23, 1937. 230

Pennsylvania v. GEORGE ISSOKI (distributing union literature/insanity), *IJA Bull.* III, 6, 3 (1934). 192

JOHN JOHNSON v. Zerbst (BRIDWELL v. Aderhold) [Bridwell and Johnson](habeas/right to counsel), 13 F. Supp 253 (D. Ga. 1935), 92 F.2d 748 (5th Cir. 1937), *rev'd,* 304 U.S. 458 (1938); *IJA Bull.* IV, 11, 4 (1936); VI, 12, 153 (1938). 245–247, 364

New Jersey v. JOHN KASPER, *IJA Bull.* I, 8, 3 (1932). 147

KENTUCKY COAL MINERS (strike-related felonies), *Civil Liberties Quarterly* July 1932. New York: American Civil Liberties Union, *IJA Bull.* I, 1, 1 (1932). 124–125

*EUEL LEE (ORPHAN JONES) v. Maryland (murder); [(change of venue), 157 A. 723 (1931); (method of selecting jury), 161 A. 284 (1932); (exclusion of Negroes from jury), 165 A. 614 (1933);] *cert. denied,* 290 U.S. 639 (1933); *IJA Bull.* II, 5, 4 (1933). 120–121, 167

LOCHNER v. New York (regulation of wages/hours), 198 U.S. 45 (1905). 213

*U.S. ex rel. LOUCAS A. LOUCAS v. Commissioner (deportation), 49 F.2d 473 (S.D. N.Y. 1931). 104–105

‡California v. J. B. McNAMARA (murder in dynamiting *Los Angeles Times* in 1910). *See* 9 *Labor Defender* no. 5 (1933), p 45. 81

‡New York v. ROBERT MINOR, WILLIAM Z. FOSTER (demonstration arrest), 5 *Labor Defender* no. 7 (1930), p. 144. 98–100

TOM MOONEY v. Holohan (murder), 7 F. Supp. 385 (N.D. Cal. 1934), *app. denied,* 72 F.2d 503 (9th Cir.), *leave to file habeas corpus denied,* 294 U.S. 103 (1935), *reh'g. denied,* 294 U.S. 732 (1935); *IJA Bull.* I, 11, 2 (1932)–IV, 5, 1 (1935). 9 *Labor Defender* no. 5 (1933), p. 44. . . . . 81, 146

MOREHEAD v. New York ex rel. Tipaldo (state minimum-wage law unconstitutional), 298 U.S. 587 (1936). 214–215

New Deal Legislation

Nat'l. Industrial Recovery Act *unconstitutional:* Schechter Poultry Corp. v. U.S. 295 U.S. 495 (1935). 213

Agricultural Adjustment Act *unconstitutional:* U.S. v. Butler, 297 U.S. 1 (1936). 213

Guffey Coal Act *unconstitutional:* Carter v. Carter Coal Co., 298 U.S. 238 (1936). 213

Nat'l Labor Relations Act *constitutional:* NLRB v. Jones & Laughlin Steel Corp., 301 U.S. 1 (1937). 224–225, 305

Social Security Act *constitutional:* Steward Machine Co. v. Davis, 301 U.S. 548 (1937); Helvering v. Davis, 301 U.S. 619 (1937). 227

Re JANE EMORY NEWTON (sanity hearing), *IJA Bull.* III, 7, 4 (1934). 192

NLRB v. Jones & Laughlin Steel Corp. (NLR Act constitutional), 301 U.S. 1 (1937). . . . .
224–225, 305

‡*SPIRO PIERATOS (deportation): Ellis Island 99205/792. . . . . 105, 107

Alabama v. DAN PIPPEN (Tuscaloosa lynching), *IJA Bull.* II, 3, 1 (Aug. 1933). 171

Georgia v. ALEX RACOLIN, et al. (sedition), *IJA Bull.* III, 5, 2; III, 6, 1 (1934). 203

IDA ROTHSTEIN v. Hynes (damages for illegal police search of CP hqtrs) (Los Angeles
Muni. Ct. #309794), *L.A. Daily Jour.* (Sept. 21, 1933), *IJA Bull.* II, 4, 2 (Sept. 1933).
. . . . 150

*U.S. ex rel. DOMINIC SALLITTO v. Commissioner (deportation), 85 F.2d 1021 (2d Cir.
1936); *IJA Bull.* VI, 8, 101 (1938). 235–236

*Re JACK SCHNEIDER (deportation); *IJA Bull.* II, 10, 4 (1934); IV, 4, 7 (1935). ‡King-
George O. Ernst correspondence (Mar. 9, 1943). 189–190, 194–195

DRED SCOTT v. Sandford (slavery legal), 60 U.S. 393 (1856). 213

*SCOTTSBORO CASES (rape):

[HAYWOOD PATTERSON v. State, 141 S. 195 (1932); OZIE POWELL v. State, 141 S.
201 (1932); CHARLIE WEEMS v. State, 141 S. 215 (1932); *rev'd.* re inadequate
counsel, POWELL, et al. v. Alabama, PATTERSON v. Alabama, WEEMS, et al. v.
Alabama, 287 U.S. 45 (1932)]. 139–141, 170

CLARENCE NORRIS v. Alabama, 156 S. 556 (1934), [*rev'd.* re exclusion of Negroes from
jury, 294 U.S. 587 (1935);] PATTERSON v. Alabama, 156 S. 567 (1934), [*rev'd.* on
technical grounds, 294 U.S. 600 (1935)]. 170–175

[PATTERSON v. Alabama, 175 S. 371 (1937), *cert. denied,* 302 U.S. 733 (1937)]. Patterson,
Haywood, and Earl Conrad. *Scottsboro Boy,* New York: Bantam Books, 1950. . . . .
204–205

[NORRIS v. Alabama, 182 S. 69 (1938); WEEMS v. Alabama, 182 S. 3 (1938); ROY
WRIGHT v. Alabama, 182 S. 5 (1938)]. 204–205, 230–232

IJA Bull. I, 1, 1 (1932)–VIII, 10, 102, 103 (1937); Hutchins, Grace. "Sacco-Vanzetti —
Scottsboro." 8 *Labor Defender* no. 7 (1937), pp. 123, 135; Brodsky, Joseph R. "A
Battle Has Been Won." 9 *Labor Defender* no. 8 (1937), pp. 8, 18; Alabama attorney
general re-examined evidence; found Norris innocent (1976) *in* Norris, Clarence, and
Sybil D. Washington. *The Last of the Scottsboro Boys.* New York: Putnam's, 1979. . . .
. . 97, 111–113, 119, 121–122, 124, 129, 146, 149, 162, 165, 169, 180, 208, 246, 323,
363, 364

‡SEAMEN'S MUTINY; IJA minutes by Sol Cohn (July 24, 1936). 205–206

Senn v. TILE LAYERS PROTECTIVE UNION (picketing in the absence of a strike is
constitutional), 301 U.S. 468 (1937). 236, 386

Matter of ELMER SMITH (disbarment), 233 P. 971 (Wash. Sup. Ct. 1925), *IJA Bull.* I, 1,
2 (1932). 124

Re Petition for Naturalization of DOMINIK STEVKO and PAUL HANUS, Jr. (IWO
membership bar to citizenship); *IJA Bull.* VI, 2, 20 (1937). 235

*JOSEPH STRECKER v. Kessler (deportation), [90 F.2d 1021 (8th Cir. 1937); *rev'd.,* 95
F.2d 976 (5th Cir. 1938), *reh'g. denied,* 96 F.2d 1020 (5th Cir. 1938),] 305 U.S. 587

(1938); *reversal aff'd*, Kessler v. STRECKER, 307 U.S. 22 (1939). *IJA Bull.* VI, 11, 134; VI, 12, 148; VII, 3, 28; VII, 5, 50 (1938); VII, 11, 125 (1939); IX, 8, 90 (1941). 238–239, 241, 251, 319, 328

*U.S. ex rel. TSERMEGOS and MIRKO MARKOVICH v. District Director (resident aliens returning from Spanish Civil War ordered deported), (unrep.) (E.D. N.Y. Nov. 25, 1938) (Bondy J.); *IJA Bull.* VII, 6, 63 (1938). *NYT* (Nov. 16, 1938) 3:5. 242

*JOHN UJICH v. Commissioner (deportation), 75 F.2d 1022 (2d Cir. 1935), *cert. denied*, 295 U.S. 746 (1935). *IJA Bull.* III, 9, 4 (1935)–IV, 4, 8 (1935). 193–194

U.S. ex rel. AUGUST YOKINEN v. Commissioner (deportation after Communist Party expulsion for racism), 57 F.2d 707 (2d Cir. 1932), *IJA Bull.* I, 1, 2; I, 6, 2 (1932); I, 9, 1 (1933); *cert. denied*, 287 U.S. 607 (1932); *Race Hatred on Trial: Yokinen White Chauvinist Trial*. N.Y.: Int'l Publishers, 1932; *Documentary History of the Negro People in the United States 1910–1932*, vol. 3. Edited by Herbert Aptheker. New York: Citadel Press, 1977, pp. 674–76. 121

Books, Articles, Pamphlets, Government Documents
‡In Carol Weiss King Collection at Meiklejohn Civil Liberties Institute

‡Abt, John. "My 80 May Days." *Political Affairs* 32 (July 1984). 123, 185

"Analysis of the National Industrial Recovery Act." *IJA Bull.* II, 2, 1 (July 1933).

‡Bank, Martin. "You Arrest! We Defend Ourselves!" 8 *Labor Defender* no. 6 (1932), p. 113. 132–135

‡Bell, Fred. "We Defend Ourselves." 8 *Labor Defender* no. 4 (1932), p. 91. 132–135

‡Benjamin, Herbert. *A Handbook for Project Workers*. [No publisher listed]. Available from list of National Unemployed Organizations and Unaffiliated State Organizations including National Unemployment Council of U.S., New York: January 1936; 2d printing February 1936.

‡Brown, Rt. Rev. William Montgomery, D.D. *Heresy: "Bad Bishop Brown's Quarterly Lectures" No. II, The Pope's Crusade Against the Soviet Union*. Galion, Ohio: The Bradford-Brown Education Co., April 1930. 176

Carter, Dan T. *Scottsboro: A Tragedy of the American South*. Baton Rouge: Louisiana State University Press, 1969 (rev. ed. 1979), pp. 312–19.

‡Colman, Louis. *Equal Justice: Year Book of the Fight for Democratic Rights 1936–1937*. New York: International Labor Defense, 1937.

‡Communist Election Platform 1938 for Jobs, Security, Democracy and Peace. New York: Workers Library Publishers, Inc., 1938.

‡Communist Party of the United States. *Southern Worker*. Birmingham, Ala., (Sept. 13, 1930) I:4. Reproduced in 5 *Labor Defender* no. 10 (Oct. 1930), p. 197.

‡"Constitution of the International Labor Defense": as adopted June 11, 1937 and amended July 9, 1939.

Davies, Joseph E. *Mission to Moscow*. New York: Simon & Schuster, 1941. pp. 272–79.

Democratic Party Platform of 1932, in Commager, Henry Steele, ed. *Documents of American History*, vol. 2. New York: F. S. Crofts & Co., 1940, p. 417. 137

Dimitroff, Georgi. *United Front Against Fascism.* 6th ed. New York: New Century Publishers, 1947.

Einstein, Albert. *The Fight Against War.* Edited by Alfred Lief. New York: The John Day Company, 1933.

Eisenstein, Sergei M., *The Film Sense.* Translated and edited by Jay Leyda. London: Faber and Faber, 1943.

Emerson, Thomas I. *Young Lawyer for the New Deal.* Savage, Md.: Rowman & Littlefield, Inc., 1991.

‡Engdahl, Louis. "Workers Defense Around the World." 7 *Labor Defender* no. 9 (1931), p. 177.

‡Executive Committee of the Communist International. ‡*Guide to the XII Plenum of E.C.C.I.: Hand Book for Propagandists.* No publisher, no date (late 1932/early 1933).

Folsom, Franklin. *Impatient Armies of the Poor: The Story of Collective Action of the Unemployed, 1808–1942.* Boulder: University Press of Colorado, 1991, pp. 242–43, 251–71. 98–99

Foner, Philip S. *The Fur and Leather Workers Union.* Newark: Nordan Press, 1950.

Foster, William Z. *From Bryan to Stalin.* New York: International Publishers, 1937.

‡Foster, William Z. *Industrial Unionism.* New York: Workers Library Publishers, April 1936.

‡Fraenkel, Osmond K. "Some Recollections of Youth and of the Law." Unpublished, p. 104. 217–219

Ginger, Ann Fagan. "Founding the International Juridical Association: American Section." 41 *National Lawyers Guild Practitioner* 73 (1984) (an earlier version of Chapter 10).

Ginger, Ann Fagan. "Workers' Self-Defense in the Courts," 47 *Science & Society* 257 (1983) (a footnoted earlier verson of chapter 11.)

Harap, Louis. "The Time Was Ripe." *Science & Society* vol. 50, no. 3 (1986), pp. 323–25. . . . . 208, 219

Herndon, Angelo. *Let Me Live.* 2d ed. Revised with a new preface by Howard N. Meyer. New York: Arno Press and The *New York Times,* 1969. 180

H.R. Hearings on H. Res. 282, 75th Cong., 3rd Sess. (Investigation of Un-American Propaganda Activities in the United States. Hearings before a Special Comm. on Un-American Activities. Aug. 12–23, 1938, at Washington, D.C.). *See* lists at pp. 268, 278–80, 328–37, 587–90, 875–76; ILD with lists pp. 493–507; ACLU with lists pp. 519–37; CIO with lists pp. 632–48; American Labor Party with lists pp. 648–53.

‡IJA. "Curbing the Courts." New York: IJA, 1937. 215

‡ILD. "Report of Arrests for the Month of April 1933."

‡ILD. "Information Material on Long-Term Political Prisoners in America." Prepared by the ILD for the delegates to the 3rd Congress Against War and Fascism, Cleveland, Ohio, January 3–5, 1936.

Investigations of the [La Follette] Senate Committee on Education & Labor into Violations of Free Speech & Rights of Labor, 74th Cong., 2d Sess. (1936) and 75th Cong., 1st Sess. (1937).

Irons, Peter. *The New Deal Lawyers*. Princeton University Press, 1982, pp. 120–25,134, 146–47, 158, 175–180, 234–37, 274–300.

Jackson, Robert H. "The Call for a Liberal Bar." 1 *National Lawyers Guild Quarterly* 1 (1937).

"Judicial Nominees." *IJA Bull.* I, 4, 2 (Aug. 1932); I, 8, 2 (Dec. 1932).

Keeran, Roger. *The Communist Party and the Auto Workers Unions*. Bloomington: Indiana University Press, 1980.

‡King, Carol. *Deportations — Suggestions to attorneys handling deportations involving political or economic views and activities, prepared for the American Civil Liberties Union*. New York: American Civil Liberties Union, February 1936. 236

‡King, Carol. "Dictators of the Country's Fate: A keen analysis of the Supreme Court's decision in the Herndon case. . ." 9 *Labor Defender* no. 5 (June 1937), p. 8. 227

‡King, Carol. *Injunctions to Protect Civil Rights. Model Memorandum of Law in Support of Application for Injunctions*. Assisted by George Heitler and Martin Kolovsky. New York: American Civil Liberties Union, April 1937.

‡King, Carol. "Memorandum on the Administration of the Deportation Laws." Submitted to Ellis Island Committee for International Labor Defense. Sept. 20, 1933. 195

[King, Carol]. "Deportation for Membership in the Communist Party." *IJA Bull.* VII, 11, 135 (1938).

[King, Carol]. "Likely to Become a Public Charge" (statistics on immigration, departures). *IJA Bull.* I, 5, 3 (1932).

‡Komorowski, Conrad. "The Reichstag Fire." 9 *The Labor Defender* no. 7 (July 1933), p. 5. 188–189

Lader, Lawrence. "A Radical from East Harlem." *Rights* 9 (June–Aug. 1990). 241

‡League of Professional Groups for Foster and Ford. Culture and the Crisis: An Open Letter to the Writers, Artists, Teachers, Physicians, Engineers, Scientists and other Professional Workers of America. New York: Workers Library Publishers, October 1932.

"The Legal Left." 31 *TIME* 16 (Mar. 7, 1938). 237

‡Leyda, Jay. Photograph of Carol King. From "A Portfolio of Photographs New York 1931–33:" *October* (1981). 126

‡"Jay Leyda: A Life's Work." Photography Dept. Gallery, Tisch School of the Arts, New York University, Jan. 29–Feb. 27, 1988. Guest curated by Elena Pinto Simon and David B. Stirk.

‡Max, Alan. *May Day 1938 for Democracy Jobs Security Peace!* New York: Workers Library Publishers, April 1938.

"Mother Bloor Is 76." *Life* (Aug. 15, 1938), p. 25. 241

National Commission on Law Observance & Enforcement (Wickersham Commission). "Report on the Enforcement of the Deportation Laws of the United States." Washington, D.C.: Government Printing Office, 1931. 108

National Commission on Law Observance & Enforcement (Wickersham Commission). "The Mooney-Billings Report." Sub-committee of Zechariah Chafee, Walter H. Pollak, and Carl Stern. New York: Gotham House. 1932. *See* Commager, Henry Steele, ed.

"The Mooney-Billings Case (Conclusions)." No. 471. *Documents of American History*, vol. 2. New York: F. S. Crofts & Co., 1940, p. 408.

Nordmann, Joë. "L'Association Juridique International: 1931–1944 — Predecessor of the International Association of Democratic Lawyers." 41 *Nat'l Lawyers Guild Practitioner* 69 (1984).

Obituary, Henry Shapiro. *NYT* (Apr. 9, 1991), D, 19:5.

"Jay Leyda." *October* no. 11 (Winter 1979).

Oppenheimer, Reuben. "The Administration of the Deportation Laws of the United States." 5 Nat'l [Wickersham] Commission on Law Observance and Enforcement. Washington, D.C.: GPO, 1931. 108

Oppenheimer, Reuben. "Recent Developments in the Deportation Process." 36 *Mich. L. Rev.* 355 (1938).

‡Patterson, William. "How We Organize: The ILD and Courtroom Technicians." 9 *Labor Defender* no. 5 (1933), p. 54. 130–132

Patterson, William. *The Man Who Cried Genocide: An Autobiography.* New York: International Publishers, 1971.

‡Piatnitsky, O. *Unemployment and the Tasks of the Communists: A world survey and detailed guide to work in this winter of crisis.* New York: Workers Library Publishers, August 1931 (printed in England).

‡"Poland — Land of Terror." 8 *Labor Defender* no. 7 (1932), p. 134.

Popper, Martin. "Oral History: Influential Black Lawyers in the Guild." 40 *Nat'l Lawyers Guild Practitioner* 55 (1983).

‡Program of the American Labor Party, adopted October 1936.

‡"Red 'Hunger March' Gets Gay Send-Off." *NYT* (Dec. 1, 1932), 3:1; "Capital Police Ban 'Hunger' Parades." *NYT* (Dec. 1, 1932), 3:2; "'Hunger Marchers' Arrive at Capital; Police Hem Bivouac." *NYT* (Dec. 5, 1932), 1:4; "Marchers Jeered by Capital Police." *NYT* (Dec. 6, 1932), 46:2. 141–143

‡Report of the Ellis Island Committee, 1934. . . . . 187, 195

‡Report of proceedings of the Status of Political Prisoners Conference held in New York, December 8, 1935. [C.W. King elected chairman.] 200

Roosevelt, James, and Sidney Shalett. *Affectionately, F.D.R.: A Son's Story of a Lonely Man.* New York: Harcourt, Brace & Co, 1959.

Rosenberg, J. Mitchell. *Jerome Frank: Jurist and Philosopher.* New York: Philosophical Library, 1970, p. xiv.

Rothschild, V. Henry. "The Right of Seamen to Strike," 49 *Yale L.J.* 1181 (May 1936). 205–206

Rubinstein, Annette. "The Radical American Theatre of the Thirties." *Science & Society* vol. 50 no. 3 (Fall 1986), pp. 300–20. 208

‡Schitsby, Marian. "Report of the Ellis Island Committee." Interpreter Release Clip Sheet II, no. 5. New York: Foreign Language Information Service (Mar. 26, 1934), pp. 25–29. 195

"Scottsboro Stamps & the Post Office." *IJA Bull.* I, 11, 2 (1933). 170

"Seamen Request Relief of Hoover." *NYT* (Oct. 25, 1932), 2:3.

‡Small, Sasha. *You've Got a Right.* New York: International Labor Defense, 1938.

‡Souvenir journal. From the fifth annual ball of the legal staff of the International Labor Defense, January 14, 1938.

‡Spector, Frank. "How We Organize: The Problems of United Front Against Boss Terror." 9 *Labor Defender* no. 2 (1933), p. 14-B.

‡Spector, Frank. "Keynotes of the Convention: Broaden the Base of the . . . I.L.D." 8 *Labor Defender* no. 11 (1932), p. 207. 132

"Steel and Law." *IJA Bull.* V, 4, 35 (1936).

Strong, Anna Louise. *I Change Worlds.* New York: Garden City Publishing Co., 1937. 115

Sugar, Maurice. "The Good Old Days — Lawyers Guild Banquet Detroit Sept 16, 1960." 37 *National Lawyers Guild Practitioner* 45 (1980).

"Three National Lawyers Guild Members Died in Spain." *Lawyers Guild Rev.* III: 2, 4 (1943). 233–234

Walker, Samuel. *In Defense of American Liberties: A History of the American Civil Liberties Union.* New York: Oxford Univerity Press, 1990. 195

‡"What To Do When Arrested." 9 *Labor Defender* no. 2 (1933), p. 35. 132–135

‡World Committee for the Victims of German Fascism. *The Brown Book of the Hilter Terror & the Burning of the Reichstag.* New York: Alfred A. Knopf, 1933. . . . . 150, 188–189

Part III

Cases

ASSOCIATED PRESS v. U.S. (anti-trust laws), 326 U.S. 1 (1945). 416

In the Matter of the Estate of STEFAN BRANDT, Surrogate's Court, County of New York (1941). ‡Report of Special Guardian, p. 789. (Sept. 4, 1943); Brandt a/k/a Ignace Porecki-Reiss. *See* Glotzer, Albert. *Trotsky: Memoir and Critique.* Buffalo: Prometheus Books, 1989, p. 80; Obituary, Mark Zborowski. *S.F. Chronicle* (May 12, 1990) C-10; Kaplan, Karel. *Report on the Murder of the General Secretary.* Translated by Karel Kovanda. Columbus: Ohio State University Press, 1990. . . . . 234–235, 389–391

HARRY BRIDGES v. California (contempt case), 94 P.2d 983 (1939); *rev'd,* 314 U.S. 252 (1941); *IJA Bull.* VII, 5, 51 (1938); X, 11, 115 (1942). 341, 347–348, 353

*HARRY BRIDGES v. Wixon (Ex parte Bridges) (deportation), File Nos. 55874/896 (1935), 55973/217; ‡Testimony of Thomas B. Shoemaker, H.R. hearings of H. Res. 282, 75th Cong., 3rd Sess. (1938) (Investigation of Un-American Propoganda Activities in the United States. Hearings before a Special Comm. on Un-American Activities. Aug. 18, 1938, at Washington, D.C.), pp. 707–12. ‡Excerpts from transcripts of 1939, 1941 deportation hearings, BIA opinion; 49 F. Supp. 292, 303 (N.D. Cal. 1943), 144 F.2d 927 (9th Cir. 1944); *rev'd,* 326 U.S. 135 (1945); ‡Bridges in the Supreme Court, vol. v, transcript of proceedings in U.S. Sup. Ct. (Apr. 3, 1945), pp. 66–69. [King, Carol.] *IJA*

Bull. III, 2, 1 (1934); VI 6, 71 (1937); VII, 10, 115 (1939); VIII, 1, 1; VIII, 8, 77; IX, 3, 23; IX, 8, 90; X, 9, 93, 97–104; XI, 1, 15; XI, 4, 43 (1942). *Lawyers Guild Rev.* [King, Carol.] III: 2:57 (1943); IV: 3:25 (1944); VI: 1:424 (1946). Perkins, Frances. Oral History, Book 6. Columbia University, pp. 338–42, 397–99. *San Francisco News* (Dec. 12, 1939), pp. 1, 4. . . . . 239–241, 256–303; 304, 309, 316, 317, 319–320, 324; 325–342; 343–362, 364, 366, 374, 383, 393–394, 405–406, 408, 412–414, 416–420

Alien Bill (to investigate and deport HARRY RENTON BRIDGES), H.R. 9766, 76th Cong., 3rd Sess. (passed by House June 13, 1940); "Harry Bridges Again Under Fire." *IJA Bull.* IX, 3, 23 (1940). 318–319

In re Application of O'Connor, et al. v. Cohen, Pres., Bd of Elections (BROWDER election case), NYC Spec. Term, Part I, *NYT* (Feb. 3–7, 1940); *IJA Bull.* VIII, 8, 87 (1940). 308, 310–312

*EARL BROWDER v. U.S. (false statement on passport application), *aff'd,* 113 F.2d 97 (2d Cir. 1940), *aff'd,* 312 U.S. 335 (1941); *IJA Bull.* VIII, 5, 42; IX, 1, 6 (1939); IX, 3, 22 (1940); X, 12, 126 (1942). 308, 310–312, 316, 322, 324, 372

*In re RAISSA BROWDER (regularizing entry), 56042/24; *IJA Bull.* IX, 5, 45 (1940). 307, 310–312, 323, 324

EUGENE DENNIS v. U.S. (Smith Act constitutional), 341 U.S. 494, at 561, 568 n. 12 (Jackson, J., concurring) (1951). 400–401

MILES E. DUNNE, et al. v. U.S. (first Smith Act sedition case/SWP), *affd,* 138 F.2d 137 (8th Cir. 1943), *cert. denied,* 320 U.S. 790 (1943); *IJA Bull.* X, 6, 60 (1941). ‡Fraenkel, Osmond K. "Some Recollections of Youth and of the Law" (unpublished), pp. 47–48. 354

The Trial of Elizabeth Gurley Flynn by the American Civil Liberties Union. Edited by Corliss Lamont. New York: Horizon Press, 1968. 311–312

‡*†SHUJI FUJII (exclusion of Japanese-American from Eastern [U.S.] Military Area), Second Service Command, U.S. Armed Forces (March 1943). FBI file on Carol King, pp. 412, 448, 449. 396

GORDON HIRABAYASHI v. U.S. (curfew valid for Japanese-Americans), *aff'd,* 320 U.S. 81 (1943). 401

CLINTON JENCKS v. U.S. (right to pretrial discovery of government witness statements), 353 U.S. 657 (1957). 332

‡California v. EARL KING, E. G. RAMSAY, and FRANK CONNER (murder), Calif. Dist. Ct. of App., 1 Cr. No. 1947 (1937). Appellants' opening brief; *released, IJA Bull.* X, 7, 69 (1942). 293–296, 352

*LEADER v. Apex Hosiery Co. (anti-trust charge against union rev'd), 108 F.2d 71 (3d Cir. 1939); 310 U.S. 469 (1940). 386

U.S. v. ROBERT MORSS LOVETT, GOODWIN B. WATSON, WILLIAM E. DODD, Jr. (unconstitutional bills of attainder against government employees), 328 U.S. 303 (1946). Fraenkel, Osmond K. *Our Civil Liberties.* New York: Viking Press, 1944, pp. 252–53. 388

U.S. v. McWilliams (Smith Act prosecution of pro-Nazis), 54 F. Supp. 791 (D.D.C. 1944); *dism'd for failure to prosecute,* 163 F.2d 695 (D.C. Cir. 1947); *Lawyers Guild Rev.* III: 1, 37 and III: 2, 4, 13 (1943). 405

NATIONAL PROHIBITION CASES, Rhode Island v. Palmer, 253 U.S. 350 (1920). 396

U.S. v. STANLEY NOWAK (denaturalization), *Lawyers Guild Rev.* III: 2, 4, 15 (1943); 356 U.S. 660 (1958). Nowak, Margaret Collingwood. *Two Who Were There: A Biography of Stanley Nowak.* Detroit: Wayne State University Press, 1989. 396–397

OLMSTEAD v. U.S. (wiretapping illegal), 277 U.S. 438 (1929). 343–344

H. Res. 67 to Impeach Secretary of Labor FRANCES PERKINS, H.R. Reps. Nos. 67 and 311, 76th Cong., 1st Sess. (1939); Proceedings tabled, *IJA Bull.* VII, 10, 115 (1939). 259

New York v. MORRIS U. SCHAPPES (perjury in hearings on "subversive activities"), 264 A.D. 917 (1942); 291 N.Y. 575 (Lehman, CJ, dissenting) (N.Y. Ct. of App. 1943); *cert. denied,* 320 U.S. 790 (1943). *IJA Bull.* X, 12, 1 (1942); *Daily Worker* (July 31, 1943); *People's Voice* (July 31, 1943). Schappes, Morris U. "Personal and Political (Cont.)" *Jewish Currents* (Sept. 1982), pp. 4–6. . . . . 343, 389

*WILLIAM SCHNEIDERMAN v. U.S. (denaturalization), [33 F. Supp. 510 (N.D. Cal. 1940), 119 F.2d 500 (9th Cir. 1941),] *rev'd,* 320 U.S. 118 (1943); *Daily Worker* (Nov. 10, 1942, June 22, 1943); *Lawyers Guild Rev.* III: 4, 42 (1943). *NY Herald Tribune* (Jan. 17, 1942, Nov. 11, 1942, June 22, 1943); *NY Post* (Nov. 9, 1942); *NYT* (Nov. 28, 1941, Nov. 29, 1941, Nov. 30, 1941, Nov. 10, 1942). ‡King, Carol. *The Schneiderman Case: U.S. Supreme Court Opinion,*with introduction by Carol King. New York: American Committee for Protection of Foreign Born, 1943. . . . . 341, 343, 344, 362–380, 398–401

Shipowners v. PICKETS (stopping scrap iron for Japan) (D.C. Wash. 1939), *IJA Bull.* VIII, 2, 9 (1939). 306

‡U.S. v. RUTH CLARK (SPANISH CIVIL WAR RECRUITERS) Detroit: Goodman, Ernest. "The Spanish Loyalist Indictments: Skirmish in Detroit." 36 *Nat'l Lawyers Guild Practitioner* 1 (1979); *IJA Bull.* VIII, 9, 90 (1940). 312–314

BYRON THORNHILL v. Alabama (picketing is a form of free speech), 310 U.S. 88 (1940). 320

Ashwander v. TVA, (Tennessee Valley Authority Act constitutional), 297 U.S. 288 (1936). 386

U.S. v. Bante (cancellation of citizenship of German American Bund member) (unrep.) S.D. N.Y. (Dec. 21, 1943); *Lawyers Guild Rev.* IV, 2, 40 (1944). 405

Virginia v. ODELL WALLER (murder), Pyttsylvania County Cir. Ct., *Waller v. Youell, cert. denied,* 316 U.S. 679 (1942); *IJA Bull.* IX, 5, 46 (1940); X, 12, 1 (1942). 323, 324

West Virginia State Board of Education v. WALTER BARNETTE (Jehovah's Witnesses flag salute case), 319 U.S. 624 (1943), *reversing* Minersville School District v. Gobitis, 310 U.S. 586 (1940). 320, 398

MINORU YASUI v. U.S. (wartime curfew for Japanese-Americans), 48 F. Supp. 40 (D.C. Ore. 1942), *aff'd,* 320 U.S. 115 (1943); *Lawyers Guild Rev.* III: 1, 39 (1943). 401

Books, Articles, Pamphlets, Government Documents
‡In Carol Weiss King Collection at Meiklejohn Civil Liberties Institute

"American OGPU." *The New Republic* (Feb. 19, 1940), p. 230. 313

Barnes, Joseph. *Willkie.* New York: Simon & Schuster, 1952.

Beard, Charles A. and Mary R. Beard. "A Basic History of the United States." New York: The New Home Library, 1944.

‡Biddle, Francis. "Leadership and Democracy." Pennsylvania Bar Assn, June 19, 1940. 319

Bridges, Harry. Foreword. In *The Cold War Against Labor,* by Ann Fagan Ginger and David Christiano, Vol. 1 Berkeley: Meiklejohn Civil Liberties Institute, 1987, pp. xx–xxii. 254–255

‡"Harry Bridges and Victory." San Francisco: Harry Bridges Victory Committee, 1942.

‡"Harry Bridges, the Guild, & the FBI." *Guild Lawyer* (June 1942).

Cook, Blanche Wiesen. "The Impact of Anti-Communism in American Life." 53 *Science & Society* 470 (1989–1990). 326

"Discrimination in Employment — The F.E.P.C." IJA Bulletin Section, *Lawyers Guild Rev.* III: 1, 32 (1943).

"FBI Conducts Night Raids in Detroit." *IJA Bull.* VIII, 9, 89 (1940). 312–314

‡Foster, William Z. "Socialism: The Road to Peace, Prosperity and Freedom." New York: March 1941. 342

Fraenkel, Osmond. *Our Civil Liberties.* New York: Viking Press, 1944.

Gladstein, Richard. Papers. Berkeley: University of California (Bancroft). Box 5, f. 4; Box 7, f. 5; Box 9, f. 6; Box 11, f. 6; Bx 19, f. 1, 3, 14; Box 20, f. 1, 2. . . . . 272, 283, 286, 300, 330, 353, 357

Goldblatt, Louis. "Working Class Leader in the ILWU, 1935–1977: Oral History Transcript." Interview by Estolv Ward. Berkeley: University of California (Bancroft), c. 1980.

Greene, Nathan. "Civil Liberties & the NLRB-1940." 38 *National Lawyers Guild Practitioner* 4 (1981). 317

Greene, Nathan. "Introductory Remarks." *IJA Bull.* X, 10, 105 (1942). 382

H.R. Rep. No. 1902, 76th Cong. 3rd Sess. (1941) (House Committee to Investigate the Nat'l Labor Relations Board Special Comm.) (Jan. 3, 1940–Jan. 3, 1941).

Huberman, Leo. *The Labor Spy Racket.* New York: Modern Age Books, Inc., 1937.

‡"Issei/Nisei/Kibei: *Fortune* magazine reviews the program of the War Relocation Authority and the Problems Created by the Evacuation from the West Coast of 110,000 People of Japanese Descent." *Fortune* (April 1944). Revised by *Fortune,* (October 1944).

‡Jones, Claudia. *Jim-Crow in Uniform.* New York: New Age Publishers, July 1940.

Keller, William W. *The Liberals and J. Edgar Hoover.* Princeton, N.J.: Princeton University Press, 1989.

King, Carol. "The Willkie I Knew." *New Masses* (Oct. 24, 1944), p. 10. . . . . 370, 410

‡King, Carol. Testimony before Smith Comm. to Investigate National Labor Relations Board, 76th Cong., 3rd Sess. (Dec. 14, 1939), pp. 464–69. *See* "The Smith and Norton Amendments to the Wagner Act." *IJA Bull.* VIII, 11, 116 (1940). 308–310

King, Carol. Book review of *Aliens & the Law,* by William Marion Gibson. *Lawyers Guild Rev.* I: 1, 32 (1940).

[King, Carol]. "Communists and Army Commissions." Recent Items. *Lawyers Guild Rev.* V: 2, 114 (1945).

[King, Carol]. "The Concentration Camp Bill Refurbished." *IJA Bull.* IX, 11, 124 (1941).

[King, Carol]. "Immigration and Naturalization." *Lawyers Guild Rev.* I: 4, 46 (1941).

[King, Carol]. "Pre-War Curbs on Aliens — The Alien Registration Act." *IJA Bull.* IX, 1, 6 at 8 (1940).

[King, Carol]. "Relocation of 'Enemy Aliens' and Others." *IJA Bull.* X, 12, 125 (June 1942).

[King, Carol]. "The Second Bridges Hearing." *IJA Bull.* X, 9, 93 (1942).

[King, Carol]. "Un-American Legislation against Aliens." *IJA Bull.* VIII, 7, 67 (1940).

[King, Carol]. "War Regulations and Aliens." *IJA Bull.* X, 8, 82 (Feb. 1942).

Kirchway, Freda. "End the Inquisition." *The Nation* (July 21, 1943).

Krinsky, Michael, Jonathan Moore, and Ann Mari Buitrago. "FBI Operations, 1940–1941." In *The National Lawyers Guild,* by Ann Fagan Ginger and Eugene M. Tobin. Philadelphia: Temple University Press, 1988, p. 36–37.

Larrowe, Charles P. *Harry Bridges: The Rise and Fall of Radical Labor in the U.S.* New York: Lawrence Hill & Co., 1972.

Leonard, Norman. "Life of a Leftist Labor Lawyer: Oral History Transcript." Interview by Estolv Ward. Berkeley: University of California (Bancroft), c. 1986.

Lowenthal, Max. *The Federal Bureau of Investigation.* New York: Wm. Sloane Assoc., 1950.

‡Meister, Dick. "Requiem for a Heavyweight: Louis Goldblatt." *San Francisco Bay Guardian* (May 18, 1983), pp. 4, 11.

‡National Federation for Constitutional Liberties. "Investigating Committees and Civil Rights," March 1941.

‡"Nazi Justice Exposed in the Sam Darcy Case." [California: Schneiderman-Darcy Defense Committee, c. 1940].

‡New York Legal Staff, International Labor Defense. "Outline: Study Group in the Law of Criminal Syndicalism." New York: International Labor Defense. [c. 1940.]

Nowak, Margaret Collingwood. *Two Who Were There: A Biography of Stanley Nowak.* Detroit: Wayne State University Press, 1989. . . . . 306–307, 316

"Our Lawless G-Men." *The Nation* (Mar. 2, 1940), p. 296.

‡Picasso, Pablo. "Why I Became a Communist." *New Masses* (Oct. 24, 1944). 410

Popper, Martin. "Report . . . to the War Convention [of the National Lawyers Guild]." *Lawyers Guild Rev.* III: 2, 4, 15 (1943). 388

"Proposal for a New Bill of Rights." *IJA Bull.* XI, 5, 49 (1942). 382

Quin, Mike. *The Big Strike.* Olema, CA: Olema Publishing Co., 1949. 164

Raineri, Vivian. *Red Angel: The Life and Times of Elaine Black Yoneda.* New York: International Publishers, 1991.

Roosevelt, Eleanor, to Franklin D. Roosevelt. June 9, 1942. Roosevelt Papers, Hyde Park. FDR MS, of 1750. 361

Roosevelt, Franklin D., to Eleanor Roosevelt. June 12, 1942. Roosevelt Papers, Hyde Park. FDR MS, of 1750 (xPP72). 361

Salisbury, Harrison E. "The Strange Correspondence of Morris Ernst & John Edgar Hoover 1939–1964." *The Nation* (Dec. 1, 1984).

Schneiderman, William. *Dissent on Trial.* Minneapolis: MEP Publications, 1983.

Schwartz, Stephen. "Intellectuals and Assassins — Annals of Stalin's Killerati." *NYT Book Review* (Jan. 24, 1988). 235, 289–291

Sen. Rep. No. 46, Pt. 3, 75th Cong., 2nd Sess. (1937) (La Follette Comm. on Industrial Espionage); "Amendments to the Wagner Act: I." *IJA Bull.* VII, 7, 73 (1939).

Sen. Rep. Investigating Wire Tapping, 76th Cong., 3rd Sess. (1940) (Comm. on Interstate Commerce by Sen. Wheeler re S. Res. 242).

Shirer, William L. *Berlin Diary: The Journal of a Foreign Correspondent 1934–1941.* New York: Grosset & Dunlap, 1943 reprint (1941 original).

"Sojourner Truth Homes." *IJA Bull.* X, 9, 93 (1942). 357

Stevenson, Janet. *The Undiminished Man: A Political Biography of Robert Walker Kenny.* Novato, Calif.: Chandler & Sharp, 1980.

Stone, I. F. "XXX and the FBI." *The Nation* (Sept. 25, 1943). 402

Theoharis, Athan. "The Hoover Menace: Who Created the Monster." *Rights.* (June–Aug. 1989), p. 4.

‡Trumbo, Dalton. *Harry Bridges: A discussion of the latest effort to deport Civil Liberties and the rights of American Labor.* Los Angeles: League of American Writers, 1941.

"W.R.A. [War Relocation Authority] v. Dies." *Lawyers Guild Rev.* III: 4, 61 (1943).

"Wartime Civil Liberties in Canada." *IJA Bull.* VIII, 12, 127 (1940).

"Wiretapping Congress & the Department of Justice." *IJA Bull.* IX, 9, 97 (1941).

XXX [a minor government official]. "Washington Gestapo." *The Nation* (July 17 and 24, 1943). 402

Yakovlev, Alexander. *The Events of 1939: Looking Back After Fifty Years.* Moscow: Novosti Press Agency, 1989.

Part IV

Cases

‡*ABDUL Uddin Ahmed, 00-99614/424; AR 1307647. 461

AMERICAN COMMITTEE FOR PROTECTION OF FOREIGN BORN v. Subversive Activities Control Board (organization registration requirement), United States Supreme Court, October term 1964 no. 44. ‡Brief for Petitioner on Writ of Certiorari (n.d.) pp. 6–14, 58–65. 433

AMERICAN COMMUNICATIONS ASSOCIATION v. Douds (Taft-Hartley non-Communist oath *upheld*), 339 U.S. 382 (1950). 500–501, 507

*U.S. ex rel. ALEXANDER BITTELMAN v. District Director (C.R.C. bail issue), 99 F. Supp. 306 (S.D. N.Y. 1951). 527

‡HARRY BRIDGES, et al. v. U.S. (criminal prosecution for conspiracy to defraud government re Bridges' naturalization petition), 86 F. Supp. 922, 931, and 87 F. Supp. 14 (N.D. Cal. 1949); (revoking Bridges' citizenship), 90 F. Supp. 973 (1950); (bail denied pending appeal), U.S. v. BRIDGES, 93 F. Supp. 989 (1950), *rev'd*, 184 F.2d 881 (9th Cir. 1950); (upholding convictions) 199 F.2d 811 (9th Cir. 1952); (upholding revocation of citizenship due to conviction) 199 F.2d 845 (9th Cir. 1952) and (*reh'g denied,*) 201 F.2d 254 (9th Cir. 1952); *conviction rev'd,* 346 U.S. 209 (1953); (citizenship not revoked) 133 F. Supp. 638 (N.D. Cal. 1955). ‡*The Law and Harry Bridges.* San Francisco: Bridges-Robertson-Schmidt Defense Committee (1952). 494, 503, 523, 527, 538–539

CANWELL COMMITTEE CASES (University of Washington "loyalty" firings); Sanders, Jane. *Cold War on the Campus: Academic Freedom at the University of Washington, 1946–64.* Seattle: University of Washington Press, 1979. 471–472

*FRANK CARLSON, et al. v. Landon (Terminal Island Four) (deportees release on bail *denied*), [94 F. Supp. 18 (S.D. Cal. 1950), *rev'd,* 186 F.2d 183, 190 (9th Cir. 1950); (bail *denied*), 187 F.2d 991 (9th Cir. 1951),] *aff'd,* 342 U.S. 524 (1952). 530, 538

Re MAURICE CHEVALIER (exclusion), *The Lamp* no. 67 (June–July 1951), p. 1. 520–521

*U.S. ex rel. KWONG HAI (HARRY) CHEW v. Colding (right of re-entry); The Sir John Franklin, [97 F. Supp. 592 (E.D. N.Y. 1951)]; (bail), 98 F. Supp. 717 (E.D. N.Y. 1951), 192 F.2d 1009 (2d Cir. 1951), [*rev'd,* 344 U.S. 590 (1953)]. 526, 530, 538

HAROLD CHRISTOFFEL v. U.S. (perjury before House Committee on Education and Labor), 171 F.2d 1004; *rev'd,* 338 U.S. 84 (1949); (perjury before Cong. Comm.) 200 F.2d 734 (D.C. Cir. 1952), (*cert. granted,* remanded for resentencing), 345 U.S. 947 (1953); 214 F.2d 265, (D.C. Cir. 1954); *cert. denied,* 348 U.S. 850 (1954). 524

‡*Clara DAINOFF (suspension of deportation of inactive IWO member), A 5-059-353 (Dec. 11, 1951). 520

EUGENE DENNIS (WILLIAM Z. FOSTER) v. U.S. (Foley Square CP Trial) (Smith Act constitutional), 183 F.2d 201 (2d Cir. 1950), *aff'd,* 341 U.S. 494, at 517 (Black, J., dissenting) (1951). 469, 471, 499, 522–523

*U.S. ex rel. CHARLES DOYLE, et al. v. District Director (deportee bail), 76 F. Supp. 739 (S.D. N.Y. 1948), 169 F.2d 753 (2d Cir. 1948); [DOYLE v. Shaughnessy (treatment of deportee during detention), 112 F. Supp. 143 (S.D. N.Y. 1953)]. 449, 497–498, 539

U.S. v. W.E.B. DU BOIS (failure to register as a foreign agent); *The Autobiography of W.E.B. Du Bois.* N.Y.: Int'l Publishers, 1968, pp. 361–95. 515

*GERHART EISLER, et al. v. Clark (Hunger strikers/APA injunction case), 77 F. Supp. 611 (D.D.C. 1948); POTASH v. Clark, *cert. denied,* 338 U.S. 879 (1949); [*rev'd,* McGrath v. POTASH and DOYLE, 199 F.2d 166 (D.C. Cir. 1952)]; ‡Affidavit of Carol King;

Lawyers Guild Rev. VIII: 6, 503 (1948). 448–457, 464–469, 472–473, 482–491, 493, 497, 505–506

*GERHART EISLER v. U.S. (making false statements on application for departure), 75 F. Supp. 634 (D.D.C. 1947), 75 F. Supp. 640 (D.D.C. 1948), [176 F.2d 21 (D.C. Cir. 1949)]; [extension of time to file cert. petition *denied,* 337 U.S. 912 (1949)], *cert. denied,* 337 U.S. 958 (1949). Eisler's petition to the United Nations, *The Lamp* no. 53 (May 1949), p. 1. . . . . 482–490, 493

*GERHART EISLER v. U.S. (contempt of Congress), 170 F.2d 273 (D.C. Cir. 1948); *cert. granted,* 335 U.S. 857 (1948); due to Petitioner's flight from United States after submission on merits, removed from docket, 338 U.S. 189 (1949). 482–490, 493

*U.S. ex rel. GERHART EISLER v. District Director (enemy alien case), release on bail *denied,* 71 F. Supp. 468 (S.D. N.Y. 1947), 162 F.2d 408 (2d Cir. 1947); (release on bail pending appeal), *denied,* 76 F. Supp. 737 (S.D. N.Y. 1948); *rev'd and remanded,* 167 F.2d 753 (2d Cir. 1948); after Pet's flight, *bail forfeited,* 87 F. Supp. 627 (S.D. N.Y. 1949). 482–490, 493

‡*Re HANNS EISLER (deportation), King, Carol. "Report." *The Lamp* no. 44 (Apr. 1948), p. 6. . . . . 445–448, 466

*Re HILDE EISLER (deportation), *The Lamp* no. 44 (Apr. 1948), p. 4; no. 54 (June–July 1949), p. 4. 493

*In re FRED W. ESTES (INS querying citizen re alien), [86 F. Supp. 769 (N.D. Tex. 1949),] 87 F. Supp. 461 *rev'd,* ESTES v. Potter, 183 F.2d 865 (5th Cir. 1950), [*cert. denied,* Potter v. ESTES, 340 U.S. 920 (1951)]. 507

U.S. v. ELIZABETH GURLEY FLYNN ("2d string" CP leaders trial under Smith Act), *aff'd,* 216 F.2d 354 (2d Cir. 1954), *cert. denied,* 348 U.S. 909 (1955). 525–526

*ABNER GREEN v. U.S. (contempt for not giving list of names), 193 F.2d 111 (2d Cir. 1951). 524–525, 530

U.S. v. Goering (Nazi war criminals), 6 F.R.D. 69 (Int'l Military Tribunal 1946). 431

VINCENT HALLINAN v. United States (income tax), *aff'd,* 182 F.2d 880 (1950), *cert. denied,* 341 U.S. 932 (1951). 523

Re LENA HALVERSON (denaturalization for IWO membership), *Lawyers Guild Rev.* VI: 1, 424, at 426 (1946). 433

*‡PETER HARISIADES v. Shaughnessy (deportation), A-5-300-756; 90 F. Supp. 397 and 431 (S.D. N.Y. 1950), 187 F.2d 137 (2d Cir. 1951), [w/ DORA COLEMAN and LUIGI MASCITTI, *aff'd,* 342 U.S. 580 (1952)]. 435–443, 479, 495–496, 505, 527, 530

*U.S. ex rel. KNUT HEIKKINEN v. Gordon (deportation), 190 F.2d 16 (8th Cir. 1951), [*cert. granted,* Gordon v. HEIKKINEN, 343 U.S. 903 (1952), *petition to vacate and remand denied,* 343 U.S. 945 (1952); *rev'd,* 355 U.S. 273 (1958)]. 513, 530, 540

U.S. v. ALGER HISS (perjury), 185 F.2d 822 2d Cir. (1950); *cert. denied,* 340 U.S. 948 (1951); *new trial motion denied,* 107 F. Supp 128 (S.D. N.Y. 1952); *aff'd,* 201 F2d 372 (2d Cir. 1953); *cert. denied,* 345 U.S. 942 (1953); *In Re ALGER HISS. Petition for a Writ of Error Coram Nobis.* Introduction by Thomas I. Emerson. Edited by Edith Tiger. New York: Hill and Wang, 1979. . . . . 481, 503–504

HUNGER STRIKERS, *see* Gerhart Eisler v. Clark.

INCORPORATION THEORY, *see* Adamson v. California.

INDONESIAN SEAMEN, *see* Soewapadji.

Application of Bohlinger (IWO licensing revoked), 106 N.Y.S. 2d 953 (1951); INTL. WORKERS ORDER v. New York by Bohlinger, 113 N.Y.S. 2d 755, 115 N.Y.S. 2d 824, 305 NY 258; *cert. denied*, 346 U.S. 857 (1953). Kahn, Albert E. *The People's Case: The Story of the IWO.* New York: The Hour Publishers, 1951. 520

‡*BEATRICE SISKIND JOHNSON (deportation): A-4-691-768, *NYT* (Sept. 9, 1949) 14:5. . . . .

JOINT ANTI-FASCIST REFUGEE COMMITTEE v. McGrath (International Workers Order v. McGrath, National Council of American-Soviet Friendship v. McGrath), (Attorney General's "subversive organizations" list unfairly compiled), 341 U.S. 123 (1951); Ginger, Ann Fagan. "Using Peace Law To Advance Human Rights." 46 *Nat'l. Lawyers Guild Practitioner* 33 (1989), pp. 36–37. . . . . 469, 520

‡*In the Matter of Application of JACOB KAMAIKO for writ (deportee held without bail) [(unrep.), (#29,832 N.D. Cal. June 22, 1950);] KAMAIKO v. Acheson, [(unrep.) (Civ. No. 1526-50 D.D.C. March 8, 1951) (McLaughlin, J.). 507

*U.S. ex rel. MYER KLIG (and sixteen others) v. Shaughnessy (bail for deportees), 94 F. Supp. 157 (S.D. N.Y. 1950). 511

*MYER KLIG v. Watkins, et al. (application for citizenship despite deportation warrant), *denied*, 84 F. Supp. 486 (S.D. N.Y. 1948). 511

JOHN HOWARD LAWSON v. U.S., Trumbo v. U.S. (HOLLYWOOD TEN) (contempt of Congress), 176 F.2d 49 (D. D.C. 1949), *cert. denied*, 339 U.S. 934 (1950). 470, 515

‡JOE LUKAS v. Ault (bail for deportee), (unrep.) (N.D. Ohio, E. Div. #27806) (Nov. 20, 1950). 504, 510, 514

*U.S. ex rel. GEORGE PIRINSKY v. Shaughnessy (bail pending appeal of bail question) *denied*, 70 S. Ct. 232 (1949), bail *granted*, 177 F.2d 708 (2d Cir. 1949); *The Lamp* no. 56 (Sept.–Oct. 1949), p. 5. 495–496

*IRVING POTASH v. Clark, *see* Eisler v. Clark.

*U.S. ex rel. IRVING POTASH v. District Director (bail for deportee), 169 F. 2d 747 (2d Cir. 1948). 502

JULIUS and ETHEL ROSENBERG v. U.S. (atomic espionage conspiracy charge), *aff'd*, 195 F.2d 583 (2d Cir. 1952); *cert. denied*, 344 U.S. 838, 889 (1952); 108 F. Supp. 798 (S.D. N.Y. 1952); *aff'd*, 200 F.2d 666 (2d Cir. 1952); *cert. denied*, 345 U.S. 965 (1953); 346 U.S. 271, 273 (1953); *reconsideration denied*, 346 U.S. 324 (1953). 508, 515, 519, 539

HARRY SACHER, et al. v. U.S. (attorneys convicted of contempt in *Dennis v. U.S.*), *aff'd*, 182 F.2d 416 (2d Cir. 1950), *cert. denied*, 341 U.S. 952 (1951). 499–500, 523, 530

‡*Matter of Application for Citizenship of BENNY SALTZMAN, (unrep.) (Cit. Pet. #2270–387387 S.D. N.Y. May 22, 1944) (Bright, J.). 477

*‡BENNY SALTZMAN v. Shaughnessy (deportee reporting requirement), (unrep.) (Civ. No. 51–43 S.D. N.Y. Aug. 8, 1949) (Kaufman, J.); *NY Post.* "Cruel & Inhumane" (Jan. 26, 1951). 475–479, 496, 520–521

*U.S. ex rel. JACK SCHNEIDER v. Esperdy (deportation), 108 F. Supp. 640 (S.D. N.Y. 1952); *The Lamp* no. 50 (Dec. 1948–Jan. 1949), p. 2. 433

*(CLAUDIA JONES) SCHOLNICK v. Clark (A.P.A. injunction.), 81 F. Supp. 298 (D.D.C. 1948), 94 F. Supp. 157 (S.D. N.Y. 1950). ‡Am. Comm. for Protection of Foreign Born, "Review of the Year 1948" (1948), p. 3. 462

‡*(CLAUDIA JONES) SCHOLNICK v. Shaughnessy (deportee reporting requirement) (unrep.) (Civ. No. 52-156 S.D. N.Y. Sept. 23, 1949) (Hulbert, J.). 462

Screws v. U.S. (Civil Rights Act violation), 325 U.S. 91 (1945). 502

*GEORGE SISKIND (deportee reporting requirement), 94 F. Supp. 157 (S.D. N.Y. 1950). 497

SOEWAPADJI, et al. v. Wixon (INDONESIAN SEAMEN), 9th Cir. #11375, 11391, *Lawyers Guild Rev.* VI: 3, 558 (1946). 427–428

*PHILIP STASIUKEVICH v. Nicolls (vacating order denying petition for naturalization), 168 F.2d 474 (1st Cir. 1948). 495

‡*ALEXANDER STEVENS (political deportation): A-3 404–243, *NYT* (Sept. 1–3, 1948); *The Lamp* no. 52 (Mar.–Apr. 1949), p. 3. 494

WONG YANG SUNG v. McGrath (INS subject to Administrative Procedure Act), 80 F. Supp. 235 (D.D.C. 1948), 174 F.2d 158 (D.C. Cir. 1949), 339 U.S. 33, *modified*, 339 U.S. 908 (1950). 469, 505–506, 510

‡*U.S. ex rel. MANUEL TARAZONA v. District Director (C.R.C. bail issue), (unrep.) (Civ. No. 69-19 S.D. N.Y. Aug. 16, 1951) (Weinfeld, J.). 527–528

TERMINAL ISLAND FOUR, *see* Carlson v. Landon.

U.S. v. DALTON TRUMBO, LARSON, et al., (HOLLYWOOD TEN) (contempt of Congress), *aff'd*, 176 F.2d 49 (D.C. Cir. 1949), *cert. denied*, 339 U.S. 934 (1950). 470, 515

*U.S. ex rel. JOHN WILLIAMSON v. District Director (deportee bail), *denied*, 76 F. Supp. 739 (S.D. N.Y. 1948). 448

NAT YANISH v. Phelan (political deportation), 86 F. Supp. 461 (N.D. Cal., S. Div. 1949). YANISH v. Barber (Douglas, J., granting deportee bail pending determination of appeal) 73 S. Ct. 1105 (1953). 449

* JOHN ZYDOK v. Butterfield (deportation), 94 F. Supp. 338 (E.D. Mich. 1950), *rev'd*, 187 F.2d 802 (6th Cir. 1951), *rev'd again*, Butterfield v. ZYDOK, 342 U.S. 524 (1952). 513–515, 530, 532–533, 537–538

Books, Articles, Pamphlets, Government Documents
‡In Carol Weiss King Collection at Meiklejohn Civil Liberties Institute

The Economic Crisis and the Cold War. Allen, James S., and Doxey A. Wilkerson, eds. New York: New Century Publishers, 1949.

‡American Committee for Protection of Foreign Born. "He Gave His Life . . . For What?" [re case of Benjamin Saltzman] 1951.

Churchill, Winston. "Alliance of English-Speaking People: A Shadow Has Fallen on Europe and Asia." [FULTON, MO. SPEECH]. *Vital Speeches of the Day.* vol. 12 (1946), p. 329. 424–425

Clark, Tom C. "Civil Rights: The Boundless Responsibility of Lawyers." 32 *ABA Journal* 453 (August 1946). 425–426

‡*The Communist Political Association: Some Things You May Want to Know About.* New York: New Century Publishers, Inc., c. 1945.

Donner, Frank. *The Un-Americans.* New York: Ballantine Books, 1961.

‡Eisler, Gerhart. *My Side of the Story: The Statement the Newspapers Refused to Print.* New York: Civil Rights Congress, March 1947.

‡Emerson, Thomas I. "Representing Communists: Experience in Conducting Case for Indicted Party Members Cited" (answer to Whitney North Seymour in *NYT*). *NY Guild Lawyer* (Feb. 1952), p. 3.

Ernst, Morris. "Why I No Longer Fear the F.B.I." *Reader's Digest* (Dec. 1950).

Field, Frederick Vanderbilt. *From Right to Left.* New York: Lawrence Hill, 1983. 525

‡Flynn, Elizabeth Gurley. "In Memory of Carol King." *Daily Worker.* (Feb. 14, 1952), p. 5. 536

Forer, Joseph. "Rein & Forer: Memories of the McCarthy Era and Before." 43 *Nat'l Lawyers Guild Practitioner* 94 (1986).

‡Fraenkel, Osmond. "Some Recollections of Youth and of the Law" Unpublished, pp. 80–81. . . . . 480, 499–500

Gellhorn, Walter. *Security, Loyalty and Science.* Ithaca: Cornell University, 1950.

Ginger, Ann Fagan. "Political Deportations: 1944–1954." 19 *Science & Society* 134 (1955).

Ginger, Ann Fagan, and David Christiano. *The Cold War Against Labor,* vols. 1, 2. Berkeley: Meiklejohn Civil Liberties Institute, 1987, pp. 258–260, 264–265, 306–313, 523–27. . . . . 501, 520

Green, Abner. "Two Views on Working with Movement Lawyers: United States 1951." 38 *National Lawyers Guild Practitioner* 45 (1981).

Horne, Gerald. *Communist Front? The Civil Rights Congress, 1946–1956.* Rutherford, NJ: Fairleigh Dickinson University Press, 1988.

H.R. Rep. No. 3123, 81st Cong., 2nd Sess. (1950) (House Comm. on Un-American Activities on National Lawyers Guild) (Sept. 25, 1950). 509

Kahn, Albert E. *High Treason.* With the assistance of Arthur Kahn. New York: Lear Publishers, 1950, pp. 240–59. 524

Kane, Francis Fisher. "More Serious Than 1920 Palmer Raids." *The Lamp* no. 64 (Dec. 1950–Jan. 1951), p. 2. 512

Katz, Richard N. *The Legal Struggle to Abolish the House Committee on Un-American Activities: The Papers of Jeremiah Gutman.* Berkeley: Meiklejohn Civil Liberties Institute, 1980.

King, Carol. "Aliens in the Post-War Period." *Lawyers Guild Rev.* V: 5, 329 (1945).

King, Carol. "Changes in Immigration Procedure." *Lawyers Guild Rev.* VI: 3, 555 (1946).

‡King, Carol. "Legal Aspects." *The Lamp,* no. 59 (Feb.–Mar. 1950), p. 4; no. 60 (Apr.–May 1950), p. 4; no. 62 (Aug.–Sept. 1950), p. 4. 507

‡King, Carol. "Persecution of Aliens Comes Home to Citizens." *Daily Worker* (June 12, 1949), p. M6. 1

King, Carol. "Treatment of Aliens in Two Wars." *Lawyers Guild Rev.* V: 3, 208 (1945).

King, Carol. Book review of *The Bending Cross* by Ray Ginger. *Lawyers Guild Rev.* X: 1, 218 (1950). 73

King, Carol, with Lee Epstein. Book review of *The Alien & the Asiatic in American Law* and *The Constitution and Civil Rights* by Milton R. Konvitz. *Lawyers Guild Rev.* VII: 4, 189 (1947).

[King, Carol]. "The End of the Bridges Case and After." *Lawyers Guild Rev.* VI: 1, 424 (1946).

[King, Carol]. "The Immigration Service and the Administrative Procedure Act." *Lawyers Guild Rev.* X: 1, 206 (1950).

[King, Carol]. "The Seaman Program." *Lawyers Guild Rev.* V: 2, 109 (1945).

King, Carol, and Ann Fagan Ginger. "The McCarran Act and the Immigration Laws." *Lawyers Guild Rev.* XI: 3, 128 (1951). 528, 530

Lowenthal, Max. Testimony before the House Committee on Un-American Activities, Sept. 15, 1950, pp. 2980–82 (re Carol King).

National Lawyers Guild. "Convention Resolutions and Statements of Policy. The Problem of Full Production and Employment in the Post-War Economy." *Lawyers Guild Rev.* VI, 2, 515 (1946). 429

National Lawyers Guild, Special Committee. "Report on Certain Alleged Practices of the FBI." *Lawyers Guild Rev.* X: 1: 185 (1950).

Navasky, Victor. *Naming Names.* New York: Viking Press, 1980.

Polier, Shad. "Law, Conscience and Society." *Lawyers Guild Rev.* IV, 2, 490 (1946). 428

Popper, Martin. "Report from San Francisco." *Lawyers Guild Rev.* V, 4, 213 (1945). 420

‡Pressman, Lee, O John Rogge, and other tributes to Carol King. *The Lamp* (Apr. 1948). 461

Report of the President's Commission on Immigration & Naturalization. *Whom We Shall Welcome: Report (1953).* New York: Da Capo Press, 1971.

‡Spivak, John L. *Pattern for American Fascism.* New York: New Century Publishers, 1947.

Thompson, Craig. "The Communist's Dearest Friend." *Saturday Evening Post* (Feb. 17, 1951). 458, 516–518

Sen. Comm. on Judiciary, 81st Cong., 1st Sess., (1949). *Report on Nomination of Tom C. Clark,* August 9–11, 1949, 359 pp. 502

Williamson, John. *Dangerous Scot: The Life and Work of an American "Undesirable."* New York: International Publishers, 1969, pp. 172–179. 453

Afterword

Cases

ADAMSON v. California (incorporation theory), 332 U.S. 46, at 74–75 (Black, J. dissenting) (1947); *see* Duncan v. Louisiana, 391 U.S. 145, 148 (1968). 541

COMMUNIST PARTY v. Subversive Activities Control Board (political registration), 223 F.2d 531 (D.C. Cir. 1954); *rev'd. and remanded,* 351 U.S. 115 (1956); *aff'd,* 367 U.S. 1 (1961). 541

ROBERT GALVAN v. Press (deportation), 347 U.S. 522 (1954). 539

‡WILLIAM HEIKKILA v. Barber (Douglas, J., granting bail pending deportation), 345 U.S. 229 (1953). 449, 539

DAVID HYUN v. Landon (deportation), *aff'd,* 219 F.2d 404 (9th Cir. 1955), *aff'd,* 350 U.S. 990 (1956). 539

ABRAHAM ISSERMAN v. U.S. (disbarment by U.S. Sup. Ct.), 345 U.S. 286 (1953), *rev'd,* 348 U.S. 1 (1954); N.Y. (fed'l.), *rev'd,* 271 F.2d 784 (2d. Cir. 1959); N.J. (state), *rev'd,* 172 A. 2d 425 (N.J. Sup. Ct. 1961); ‡"The Trials of Harry Sacher and Abraham Isserman," *New York Guild Lawyer* (Apr. 1952). 525

CYNTHIA KING v. U.S. Department of Justice (release of FBI files on Carol King), 586 F. Supp. 286 (D.D.C. 1983); *aff'd in part, rev'd in part,* 830 F.2d 210 (D.C. Cir. 1987). 540

CARLOS MARCELLO v. Bonds (upholding constitutionality of Act exempting Immigration Service from Administrative Procedure Act), 349 U.S. 302 (1955). 539

MICHAEL NUKK, et al. v. Shaughnessy (deportation), 350 U.S. 869 (1955). 539

U.S. v. MARTIN POPPER (contempt of Congress), *rev'd,* 306 F.2d 290 (D.C. Cir. 1962). 518

*‡CHARLES ROWOLDT v. Perfetto (deport-yourself act unconstitutional), 355 U.S. 115 (1957); United States Supreme Court No. 34, Oct term 1956. Ginger, Ann Fagan. Appendix to brief for petitioner. Study based on 307 political deportation cases. 512, 539–540

HARRY SACHER v. Association of Bar of City of New York (disbarment), 206 F.2d 358 (2d Cir. 1953), *rev'd,* 347 U.S. 388 (1954). 525

HARRY SACHER v. U.S. (contempt of Congress), *rev'd.* 356 U.S. 576 (1958); "The Trials of Harry Sacher and Abraham Isserman." ‡*New York Guild Lawyer* (April 1952). 518

PAUL SWEEZY v. New Hampshire (contempt of Atty. Genl's "Un-American investigation"), *rev'd,* 354 U.S. 234 (1957). 539

U.S. v ABRAHAM UNGER (contempt of Congress), *rev'd,* 236 F.2d 312 (2d Cir. 1956). 518

JOHN WATKINS v. U.S. (contempt of Congress), *rev'd,* 354 U.S. 178 (1957). 539

OLETA YATES (Schneiderman) v. U.S. (Smith Act prosecution of California Communist Party leaders), *rev'd,* 354 U.S. 298 (1957). 538, 539

Book, Articles
In Carol Weiss King Collection at Meiklejohn Civil Liberties Institute

"Brownell Reveals 22,000 Face Deportation as Reds." *Boston Daily Globe* (Mar. 15, 1953). 538

"Deportation Drive Now Focused on 38." *NYT* (Apr. 17, 1953). 538

Ginger, Ann Fagan. *Civil Liberties Docket* vols. 1–13. Berkeley: National Lawyers Guild, 1955–1968.

Index

Names in boldface contributed oral and/or written material to the book. For references to additional individuals contacted during writing of book, for descriptions of cases, and for citations to opinions, see General Sources/Specific References.

AAA (see also Agricultural Adjustment Administration), 215
ABA (see also American Bar Association): Committee on the Bill of Rights, 398; House of Delegates, 237; special committee on Communist tactics, strategy, and objectives, 515; special committee on the economic condition of the bar, 238
Abraham Lincoln Brigade, 312, 371
Abrams, 63
Abt, John, 123, 184–85, 216, 509, 511
Academic freedom, 139
ACA v. Douds (see also General Sources/Specific References), 500, 508, 523
Acheson, Dean, 355
ACLU (see also *Law and Freedom Bulletin*), 7, 26, 28, 31, 33, 35, 36, 72, 81, 85, 92, 109, 119–20, 125, 132, 142, 145, 159, 167, 173, 180, 187, 192, 195, 204, 217–19, 235, 236, 246, 310, 313, 361, 370, 374, 480, 499; amicus, 398; bail fund, 94–95 conference, 193; and FBI, 141, 351; leadership, Communists barred from, 195, 311–12; National Civil Liberties Union, 7
Acquittals, 16, 88, 189
Ades, Bernard, 167
Administrative Procedure Act (see also General Sources/Specific References), 455–56, 467–68, 471, 486, 503, 505–06, 509, 536, 539
Administrative Process, The, 259
Administrative remedies, 105
Advocating violent overthrow, 60, 343
Affiliation, definition of, 16, 417–18
AFL (American Federation of Labor), 26, 190, 194, 209, 220, 232, 253, 277, 306, 310, 348, 350, 354, 442, 500, 539
AFL Committee on Industrial Organization (see CIO)
AFL-Hod Carriers Union, 449
AFL-Painters Union, 456
Africa, 197
African-Americans (see also Blacks; Negroes), 85, 120, 171, 515
Afro-American, The, 121
Agents, undercover, 30

Agribusiness, 358
Agricultural Adjustment Act of 1933, 183, 213
Agricultural Adjustment Administration (AAA), 184, 210–11, 509
Agriculture, Secretary of, 324
Alabama: parole system, 323; state of, 97, 111–12, 170, 171, 173, 205, 230, 236; Supreme Court, 223
"Aldrich Family, The," 509
Alexander, Raymond Pace, 434
Alfano, Luigi, 86
Algonquin crowd, 58
Alien and Sedition Acts of 1798, 53, 443, 470
Alien and Sedition Acts of World War I, 16, 34, 55, 60
Alien-baiting, 323
Alien Enemy Act of 1789, 430
Alien Registration Act of 1940 (see Smith Act)
Aliens: burden of proof, 107 citizen children and wives of (see Children); due process rights of, 454; First Amendment rights of, 25, 353; little, 479; registration of, 206, 319; resident, 4, 92, 139, 510; rights of, 113, 419–20; statistics on (see also Immigration, statistics), 207, 310; undesirable, 62
Allen, Frederick, 277
Allen, James S., 111
Alliance of English-Speaking People, 424–25
ALP (see American Labor Party)
Amalgamated Clothing Workers Union, 6, 81
Amendments, U.S. Constitution (see First Amendment, etc.)
"America," 122, 141
American Association for Labor Legislation, 13–14, 114, 185
American Bar Association (ABA), 213, 221, 222, 249, 374, 420, 501, 515
American Civil Liberties Union (see ACLU)
American Committee Conference, 368
American Committee for Protection of Foreign Born, 1, 195–96, 208, 219, 230, 235, 306, 316, 328, 358–59, 393, 396, 401, 420, 433–34, 440, 442, 449, 451, 454, 458–59,

468, 474, 490–91, 493, 496, 502, 507, 512, 524, 528, 533
American Committee for the Defense of the Victims of German Fascism, 154
American Committee (see American Committee for Protection of Foreign Born)
American Council on Race Relations, 513
American Federation of Labor (see AFL)
American Federation of Teachers (AFT), 192
American Indians, rights of, 193
American Jewish Congress, 428
American Labor Party (ALP), 241, 364, 475, 498, 501–02, 508, 535
American Legion, 192, 330; California, 267, 282–83; Oregon Subversive Activities Committee of, 282
American Newspaper Association, 26
American Newspaper Guild, 219, 291
American Peace Mobilization, 344
American Protective Association, 54
American Psychoanalytic Association, 203
American Revolution, 47, 53, 493
American Slav Congress, 456
American Socialist Society, 16
American Steel & Wire, 224
American Student Union (ASU), 320
American Telephone & Telegraph (AT&T), 306
American Youth Congress, 328
Amici curiae briefs (friends of the court), 30, 203, 236, 250, 398, 500, 530
Amlie, Thomas R., 143
Amorroso, Nicholas, 80
Anarchism/Anarchists, 4, 11, 16, 32, 54, 63, 72, 107, 208, 233, 237
Anarchy, criminal, 32, 33, 62, 66–68
Anderson, Chief Judge, Ala. Supreme Court, 122
Anderson, George, 30, 33–34, 365
Anderson, Sherwood, 119
Andrews, John B., 14
Angel Island, Calif., 266, 271
Anti-alien legislation, 108, 206
Anti-Communist crusade, 203
Anti-Defamation League of B'nai B'rith, 13, 36
Anti-fascists, 80–90, 138, 189, 199, 505
Anti-lynching legislation, 193, 230
Anti-Nazi: demonstrations, 191; refugees, 208, 490
Anti-Negro, 120, 443
Anti-red hysteria, 34
Anti-Semitism, 13, 36, 167, 215
Anti-Soviet sentiment, 395
Anti-trust laws., 416
Anti-war meeting, 203
AP (Associated Press), 416
APA (see Administrative Procedure Act)
APA case (see *Sung v. McGrath*)
Apfel, Alfred, Dr., 117–18, 150
Appomattox, 65
Aragon, Louis, 410
Arkansas, 210
Armenian immigrants, 77
Armistice of 1918, 10, 16, 18, 64

Arnold, Thurman, 184
Arrests, 26, 30; false, 94; without warrants, 30
Arrest warrants, 206
Art galleries/dealers, 102, 122, 383
Asian immigrants, 54, 64, 358
Assassinations, 54
Associated Press (see AP)
Association of the Bar of the City of New York, 431–32, 498
Asylum, 538
Atomic: energy, 429; secrets, 519
Attorney, right to (see Right, to counsel)
Attorney General: abuse of discretion by, 472, 519; list of "subversive" organizations, 447–48, 468, 520, 527, 541; U.S. (see also name of Attorney General), 3, 16, 18, 19, 22, 23, 25, 30, 76, 357, 397, 416, 502;
Australia, 254, 427
Austria, 117, 194, 239, 466
Austrian immigrants, 91, 483
Auto workers (see also UAW-CIO), 219
Auto Workers Strike of 1937 (see also UAW-CIO), 222
Auto Workers Union (see UAW-CIO)
Avnet, Duke, 313
Axis, Nazi-Fascist (see also Fascism/fascists), 318, 324

Bail, 81, 94, 179, 364; administrative, 473; bondsmen, 130, 451; conditioned on reporting, 494, 497, 502; denial of, 40, 84, 98, 448–57, 472, 502, 511, 537; detention without, 26, 104, 352, 495; excessive, 159, 313, 495–96; forfeited, 490–91, 495; fund (ILD), 109; granted, 204, 242, 361, 456, 478, 484, 486, 514, 519, 528, 530, 538; revoked, 190, 508, 527; right of deportee to, 26, 491, 510; right to reasonable, 25, 31, 454, 466
Bakczy, Captain, 282
Bakers Union, New York Local 1, 463
Bakmatieff (Russian consul), 43
Baldwin, Roger, 187, 195, 351, 374, 519
Bales, Hay, 83, 93
Bante, Paul, 405
Bar Association of the City of New York, 189, 202, 535
Barbusse, Henri, 233
Bard, artist, 131(illus.)
Bard, Guy, Judge, 494
Barkley, Matthew, 49
Barkley, Matthew (Mrs.) (Mrs. B), 10, 48–49, 52, 69, 71–72, 75, 90, 96, 101, 102, 114, 173, 198, 245, 250, 260, 329, 410, 475, 489–90, 498, 536
Barnard Bulletin, 12
Barnard College, 12
Barnett, George, 309
Barron, Harriet, 434, 459
Bata Shoe Company, 304
Bates, Ruby, 170
Baxter, Charles, 478, 504
Bedacht, Max, 82
Belgium, 157, 318

Benson, Elmer A., 237
Berger, Harry (Mr. and Mrs.), 200
Berger, Victor L., 16
Berkman, Alexander, 4
Berle, A. A., 321, 405
Berlin, Germany, 89, 143
Bernays, Murray C., 63
Bernstein, Judge, 310
Bethlehem Steel, 31
BIA (see Board of Immigration Appeals)
Biddle, Francis, 236, 319, 342, 345, 356, 359–61, 394, 401–02, 417, 431, 502
Bifkins, Trashbasket and Brokenbasin, 202
Big business (see also Corporate, lawyers), 29, 184, 226, 387, 455
Bigelow, William, 449
Billings, Warren, 81, 386
Bill of attainder, 356, 388
Bill of particulars, 331
Bill of Rights, 1, 25, 32, 67, 419, 488, 495, 502, 526; economic, 382, 488; for workers (see Wagner National Labor Relations Act of 1935)
Binger, Carl, 504
Binswanger, Clara, 148, 229, 243, 245–47, 250, 260, 262, 266, 272–81, 283, 285–87, 329, 406, 414
Birth control, 12, 62, 192
Bittleman, Alexander (see also General Sources/Specific References), 527
Black, Hugo, 353, 428, 501, 508, 523, 533, 538, 541
Black Codes, 137, 175–76
Black Legion, 443
Blacklisting, 470
Blacks (see also African-Americans; Negroes), 18, 121, 231
Blackwell, Alice Stone, 82
Blackwell's Island, 8
Blichfeldt, Julius, 449
Bliven, Bruce, 205, 244
Bloch, Emmanuel, 435, 515
Bloor, Ella Reeve (Mother Bloor), 241
Blue Eagle Codes, 183
Board of Economic Warfare, 357
Board of Immigration Appeals (BIA), 350, 352, 356, 359, 478, 497, 519
Bohemians, 55, 75
Bolin, Jane M., 537
Bolsheviks, 19–20, 62
Bombs, 18, 35
Bond (see Bail)
Bondy, William, 242, 456–57, 472, 493, 537
Bone, Homer T., 220
Bonham, R. P., 268, 293, 301
Borah, William E., 31, 188, 314
Boss, The (see Hoover, J. Edgar)
Boston, Mass.: police, 99; raids by Justice Dept., 30, 33
Boudin, Leonard, 208
Boudin, Louis B., 208
Bourgeois, 169, 262; democratic principles, 493
Bourke-White, Margaret, 123
Boyd, John P., 442

Brandeis, Louis D., 25, 59, 60, 61, 67, 78, 121, 141, 214, 248
Brandeis briefs, 78
Brandt, Stefan (Mrs.), 235, 389–91
Brandt, Stefan (pseudonyms Ignacy Poretsky, Ignace Reiss), 234–35
Brazil, 200
Brecht, Bertold, 407
Bregman, Cynthia (see King, Cynthia Bregman)
Bridge of San Luis Rey, The, 395
Bridges, Harry (see also General Sources/Specific References), 206, 236, 251, 268, 278, 293
Bridges, Harry: as CIO Regional Director, 239, 259, 338, 348, 503; on the CP, 281, 340; Defense Committee, 260, 324, 329, 344, 347, 360, 372, 394, 405; deportation bill, 318–19, 345; as deportee, 467; and FBI, 256–364, 405–20, esp. 325, 329–30, 343, 408; and FDR, 240; as ILWU president, 239, 332, 338; and 1934 strike, 254–58, 281; on the offensive, 328; as witness, 267, 279–81, 301
Bridges, Nancy (Mrs. Harry), 285–86, 421
Bridges's, Harry: alleged CP affiliation, 256, 289, 301, 350, 359, 414, 417–18; alleged CP membership, 256, 267, 269, 289, 301, 350, 359, 416, 470; bail lifted, 527; case, rat file in, 269–70; character witnesses, 350; contempt case, 341, 347–48, 353, 414, 418; defense costs, 241, 299, 330; defense strategy, 240, 264–69, 271, 288–91, 350; defense tactics, 282; defense team, 263, 332–34; denaturalization, 539; isolationist stand, 1941, 347; luck, 273, 503; personality, 262, 267, 272–73, 277, 279, 281; philosophy, 254; relationships with women, 274, 285–86, 331; use of media, 302
Bridges's first hearing (Landis) (see also General Sources/Specific References), 256–303
Bridges's perjury in obtaining citizenship (see also General Sources/Specific References), 494, 503, 508, 523, 527, 538–39
Bridges's second hearing (Sears) (see also General Sources/Specific References), 325–62, 454
Bridgman, Mich., 81
Bright, John, 477
Brissenden, Paul F., 120, 205
British (see Englishmen)
Brodsky, Joseph R. (Joe), 10, 11, 20, 21, 32, 34, 36–38, 44, 62–63, 65, 68–69, 72–75, 84, 90, 100, 102, 109, 111–12, 114, 119–22, 129, 135, 136, 137, 154, 163, 170, 182, 195, 200, 208, 228, 231, 235, 236, 306, 309–10, 332, 430, 433, 441–42, 454, 459, 517–18, 520
Bronx Morning, A, 123, 125, 230
Brooklyn Navy Yard, 47
Broun, Heywood, 38, 45, 46, 219
Browder, Earl, election campaign (CP), 308, 312; expulsion from CP, 440
Browder, Raissa, 307, 322–23

Browder, Earl (see also General Sources/Specific References), 307–08, 311–12, 321, 372, 402, 406, 431
Brown, Harold Chapman, 290–91, 366
Brown, William Montgomery, 82
Brownell, Herbert, 538
Bryant, Louise, 5
Buck, Tim, 503
Building Service Employees Union, 440
Buitrago, Ann Marie, 403
Bulletin (see *IJA Bulletin*)
Bund (see German-American Bund)
Bureau of Investigation (later FBI), 4, 27
Burke-Wadsworth Conscription Bill, 322
Burns, William J., 65
Burton, Harold, 533, 538
Butterworth, Joe, 472

Caen, Herb, 260
Caesar, Julius, 94
California, 66; CIO, 259; Division of Immigration and Housing, 317; State Bureau of Criminal Identification, 268, 282
Callahan, Judge, 231
Calvary Baptist Church, 8, 47
Cammer, Harold, 525
Campos, Pedro Albizu, 208
Canada, 32, 120, 198, 320, 497
Canadians, 295
Cannalonga, Maurice J., 336–38, 340, 360
Cannery and Agricultural Workers Industrial Union (CAWIU), 167
Cannon, James P., 82
Canons of professional ethics, 518
Canwell Committee, Washington State legislature, 471–72
Capitalism, danger of overthrowing, 19
Capitalist system, 38, 123, 129, 132, 177, 185, 216, 302
Captial punishment (see Death penalty)
Capitol, U.S., 36
Capitol Hill, 143
Cardozo, Benjamin, 63, 64, 67, 121–122, 141, 167, 181
Carisi, Joseph, 80
Carnegie, Dale, 373
Carnegie-Illinois Steel, 224
Carr, Sam, 503
Carroll, Lewis, 487
Carusi, Ugo, 430
Cases on Labor Law, 259
Catholic-baiting, 443
Catholic Leader, 281
Catholics, Catholicism, 86, 199, 286, 315, 399
Caughlan, John, 171–73, 313, 471–72
CCNY (City College), 47, 167, 312
Central Conference of American Rabbis, 203
Centralia, Washington, lynching of 1919, 19, 81, 124
Certiorari, denial of, 121
Chafee, Zechariah, 27, 30, 188, 398, 405
Chain gang, 204
Chamber of Commerce (the Chamber), 212, 255

Chambers, Whittaker, 481, 504, 509
Chamlee, Attorney, 170
Chaplin, Ralph, 82
Chauvinism, white (see also Prejudice), 121
Cheatham, Elliott E., 390
Chen, Sylvia/Si-Lan (Mrs. Jay Leyda), 165
Chevalier, Maurice, 521
Chew, Harry/Kwong Hai (see also General Sources/Specific References), 538
Chiang Kai-shek, 234
Chicago, Illinois, 5, 19, 68, 99; race riots, strike of 1919, 18
Chicago Bar Association, 425
Chicago Star, 453
Chicago Tribune, 409
Chicherin, Soviet Foreign Minister, 43
Child labor, 62, 95, 214
Children, 9; citizens with alien parents, 235, 431, 435, 449, 453, 479, 498, 514, 538
Children's literature, 77
China, 54, 117, 138, 234, 373
China, Nationalist, 342
China, Red, 508
Chinese immigrants, 407
Christianity and Communism, 176
Christoffel, Harold (see also General Sources/Specific References), 524
Churchill, Winston, 424–28
Church League for Industrial Democracy, 192
Chutzpah, 73
CIO (Congress of Industrial Organizations), 232, 239, 243, 306, 309, 330, 350, 354, 365, 371, 447, 500, 508, 539; Bridges Defense Committee, 374; Chemical Workers, 497; Convention, 374; Council, 335; expulsion of unions, 500; general counsel, 461
CIO-Greater New York Council, 453
CIO-New York State Council, 453
CIO-Wayne County Council, 456
Citizens Committee, 346–347
Citizenship: applications, 235, 397, 449; granting to Asians, 407; native, 369; revocation of (see Denaturalization cases)
City College (see CCNY)
Civic Club, New York City, 38, 220
Civil Air Patrol, 528
Civilian Conservation Corps (CCC), 183
Civilian Works Administration (CWA), 189
Civil liberties, 15, 36, 117, 119; cases 66, 72
Civil rights, 113
Civil Rights Congress (CRC), 434, 458, 479, 493, 535; bail fund, 524–25, 527, 530
Civil service, 40–41, 355
Civil War, 24, 54, 65, 137, 213–14
Clark, Charles E., 495
Clark, Tom, 425–26, 428–29, 445, 451–52, 463, 468, 483, 488, 490, 493, 494, 502–03, 524; as Justice, 533
Clark, Judge (N.J.), 147
Class war prisoners (see also Political, prisoners), 82, 132
Clear and present danger doctrine test, 24, 221, 226, 433
Cleopatra, 94

Cleveland Art Museum, 429
Coal miners, 18, 112–13, 124–25, 136, 213; strike of 1919, 18
Coal Miners Union (see United Mine Workers)
Cocteau, Jean, 448
Coffee, John M., 316
Cohen, Aaron, 232
Cohen, Cole, Weiss & Wharton, 79, 111, 136
Cohen, Felix, 223
Cohen, Julius, 449
Cohn, Albert, Judge, 84–85, 87
Cohn, Roy, 87
Cohn, Sol H., 36–37, 44, 62, 72, 73, 75, 102, 119, 148, 158, 191, 229, 245, 309
Cold War, 87, 180, 351,424, 442, 447–48, 470, 481, 542
Coleman, William, 481
Collier's, 187–88
Collins, Charles, 456
Colman, Louis C., (Limey), 175, 197
Colorado Fuel and Iron Co., 8
Columbia Law Review, 78
Columbia Law School, 15, 39, 147, 158, 167, 179–80, 229, 390, 480
Columbia University, 290, 390
Commerce, Dept. of, 304
Commerce, Secretary of, 205–06, 442
Committee on Industrial Organization, 209–10
Communism: advocacy of international, 311; Communists, 72, 97, 104, 107, 121, 129, 142, 143, 147, 201, 233; theory of, 63
Communist: defendants, 66; lawyers, 129
Communist International (CI), 95, 97, 107, 142, 194
Communist Manifesto, 234, 332, 377–78
Communist Party (CP), 19, 21, 32, 36, 68, 109, 119, 133, 293, 306, 402, 447; advocacy of unlawful doctrines, 350, 399; advocacy of violent overthrow, 34, 471; affiliation with, as grounds for deportation, 352; assessment of situation in 1951, 523–24; candidates for office, 74, 122, 137, 360, 364; Central Committee, 95; club in FBI, 312; clubs, 492; constitution/platform, 379, 399; convention, 81; doctrine, legality of, 226, 288–91, 302, 379, 387, 399–401, 522–23, 541; doctrine, policies, 220, 225, 291, 358, 435, 493; during WWII, 37; expulsion from, 121, 308, 440; "foreign ideology," 307, 311; industrial clubs, 312; lawyers, 63, 177, 213, 216, 291, 365, 472, 500–01, 504, 509; lawyers' clubs, 501; lawyers for, 525–26, 528; leaders, 448, 452, 469–71, 522–27, 540; literature, newspapers, 4; meetings/conventions, 73, 208, 247; members, open, 217–19, 311; membership, 33–34, 367, 470, 477; members in U.S. Armed Forces, 377, 411; neighborhood clubs, 147, 216, 501; officials, secret meetings of, 269, 295; opposition to war preparation, 307, 343, 365; organizers, 175, 435; professors, 389; registration required,

510; underground, 216; "underground group," 481, 523–25
Communist Political Association, 402, 431
Communists, Black, 176, 192
Communist Workers Party, 19
Community Service System, 438
Concentration camps, 482
Conger, Edward A., 452
Congress, New Deal, 212–17, 224–25, 227, 253
Congress, Radical Republican, 214
Congress, U.S. (see also House and Senate Committees), 3, 6, 31, 37, 54, 59, 141, 182–84, 364
Congressional Record, 330
Congress of American Women, 453
Congress of Industrial Organizations (see CIO)
Connecticut, 26–27
Connecticut Bar Association, Character Committee, 167
Conscientious objectors, 7, 17, 193, 237, 519
Conscription bill, 320
Conspiracy: to advocate overthrow of government, 320, 401, 492, 522–24; against Bridges, 267, 283; charges, 66, 230; government-business, 266, 301; law, 522
Constitution, U.S., 3, 23, 25, 37, 42, 67, 97, 140, 174, 204, 225, 253, 356, 365, 366–67, 396, 398, 401, 418–19, 428, 454, 481, 491, 526
Constitutional: law, 28, 58, 179, 184; litigation, 35; rights (see also Civil liberties; Civil rights; Due process), 41, 132
Consumers Union, 168, 480
Contempt by publication, 537
Contempt of Congress, 472, 484, 488, 518
Contempt of court, 77–78, 84, 260, 414, 499, 523–24, 525–26
Contract, freedom of, 185, 214
Contract laborers, 430
Contract labor law, 304
Contradictions, 34, 37–38, 133; of the Left, 224
Coolidge, Calvin, 61, 64, 443
Cooper Union, 47
Corporal punishment, 199
Corporate: lawyers, 6, 14, 124, 135, 141, 248; power, 214
Corporations, rights of, 67
Correa, U.S. Attorney, 345
Costigan, Edward P., 142
Cotton, Eugene, 530
Cotton Textile Code, 184
Counsel, right to (see Right, to counsel)
Council for Social Action of the Congregational and Christian Churches of the U.S., 203
Cowley, Malcolm, 244
CP (see Communist Party)
CP-Bronx County, N.Y., 241
CP-Bulgaria, 150
CP-California, 539
CP-Detroit, 312
CP-France, 410, 431

CP-Georgia, 227
CP-Germany, 117, 149–50, 188–89, 192, 233, 389, 445, 466, 484
CP-Great Britain, 208, 247
CP-NY, 121
CP-Poland, 198–99
CP-USA, 75
CP-USSR, 115, 377
CP-Women's Commission, 462
CRC (see Civil Rights Congress)
Crimes, political, 89
Criminal: anarchy, 26, 62, 63; defense lawyers, 53; law/deportation law comparison, 42
Criminal syndicalism, 41, 62, 63, 66, 68, 113, 124, 221, 223, 387
Crockett, George, 493, 499
Cruel and unusual punishment, 25, 30, 428, 505
Crum, Bartley, 369, 374, 406, 459
Curfew order (see Japanese-Americans, curfew order)
Curtis, Charles, Vice President, 143
Custodial detention, 36; government's secret list for, 401–02
Custody, treatment in, 40
Customs, collector of, 146
Czechoslovakia, 304

Dahlberg, Edward, 143
Daily Compass, 536
Daily People's World, 449, 453
Daily Worker, 75, 85, 97, 98, 122, 141, 159, 176, 220, 233, 273, 312, 332, 372, 441, 453, 480, 536
Damon, Anna, 111, 136–37, 175, 197
DAR (Daughters of the American Revolution), 92
Darcy, Sam, 281, 334, 338
Darrow, Clarence, 26, 36, 50, 62–63, 80, 85–88, 135, 249, 260, 499
Davis, Benjamin J., Jr., 175–79, 227, 364, 441, 469, 492
Davis, John F., 533
Davis, John R., 277
Death penalty (see also Murder, charges), 27, 29, 111–12, 137, 140, 171, 175
Debs, Eugene V., 12, 34, 73, 82, 121, 499
Decker, Caroline (Mrs. Richard Gladstein), 241, 262, 264, 280–81
Declaration of Independence, 53, 133
Defense: mass, 517; NAACP, 176; radical, 35; strategy: CP, 517–18; tactics, 23
DeJonge (see also General Sources/Specific References), 223, 270, 290, 522
Del Guercio, Albert, 330–32, 334–40, 344, 347
De Lacy, Hugh, 420, 432
Delano, Frederick, 382
Delany, Hubert, 248
DeLappe, Pele, 265, 268, 272, 278
DeLeon, Daniel, 14
DeLeon, David C., 502
DeLeon, Solon, 13–14, 15, 48, 71, 157
Dell, Floyd, 120
Democrat, liberal, 259, 263

Democratic Party, 32, 182, 222, 379; lawyers, 215–16; platform, 137; Women's Division of, 45
Demonstrations/demonstrators, 104, 136, 147, 182
Denaturalization cases, 337, 365, 398–401, 507, 522, 539
Denmark, 318
Dennis, Eugene (see General Sources/Specific References)
Dennis (see Smith Act)
Dependent children, 31
Deportation (see also Communist Party): for affiliation with the CP/CI, 206, 352; for affiliation with an organization that advocates, 352; arrest for, 4, 19, 41, 186 (see also specific cases); for belief in violent overthrow, 194; canceled for nominal CP membership, 539; delirium, 42; evidence required for, 268; to Germany, Italy, 208, 242; grounds for, 31, 61, 104, 255–56, 522; hearings and due process, 31, 40–41, 54, 90, 108, 133, 264, 455, 506; history of, 21; to hostile nations, 42, 89; is/is not punishment, 41, 60; law, 16; mass, 430; for membership in the CP, 33; for membership in organization that advocates, 43, 107, 239, 256, 486; orders of, 18, 34, 107, 427; for past CP membership, 121, 238–39; for present CP membership, 138; statistics, 316, 512, 521; of strikers, 186, 189, 206; for trade union activity, 187, 208; to U.S., 187; warrants, 20, 34, 59, 61, 105, 236, 193; in WWII, 381
Deportees, political, 308
Deportees' spouses and children (see also Children, citizens with alien parents), 4, 539
Depression, 80, 95, 117, 120, 127–29, 143, 154, 163, 171, 179, 189, 196, 212–15, 225
Detroit, Mich., 4, 5, 99
Deutsch, Albert, 233
Deutsch, Babette, 12
Devaney, John P., 220, 237, 248
DeVoto, Bernard, 8, 48
Dewey, John, 322
Dewey, Tom, 408, 479
Dialectical materialism, 334
Dickerson, Earl, 386
Dickstein, Samuel, 432–33
Dictatorship of the proletariat, 67, 366, 399
Dies, Martin, 310, 404
Dies Committee on Un-American Activities (see HUAC)
Dies Deportation Bill of 1932 (House), 138
Dimitroff, Georgi (see also General Sources/Specific References), 150, 188–89, 386, 452, 517
Disbarment proceedings, 167, 525
Discovery, pre-trial, 269
Discretion: absolute, 452, 454, 510–11, 519; abuses of, 452
Discretionary relief for aliens, 532
Disorderly conduct, arrest for, 105
Dissell, Clayton, 411

Dix, Dorothy, 148
Dnieprostroy Dam, USSR, 114–17, 323
Dodd, William F., 388
Doho, 396
Donner, Frank, 434
Donovan, William, 124
Dorsey, Hugh, 203–04
Dos Passos, John, 233
Double jeopardy, 329, 414
Douglas, Melvyn, 260
Douglas, William O., 320, 378, 416–18, 463, 501, 508, 523, 533, 538
Dow-Jones average, 94
Downey, John J., 88
Doyle, Charles A. (see also General Sources/Specific References), 464, 467, 497–98, 539
Doyle, Larry Morton, 268, 282, 284, 294–96, 299–302, 343
Draft, opposition to (see also World War I, opposition to), 66
Dred Scott decision, 213
Dreiser, Theodore, 138
Dressmakers' strike of 1928, 92, 94
DuBois, W.E.B. (see also General Sources/Specific References), 515
Duclos, Jacques, 431
Due process: denial of, 33, 41, 84; in deportation hearings, 59, 60, 76, 259, 350; of law (see also Fifth Amendment), 1, 25, 31, 54, 65, 67, 113, 260, 367, 414, 492–93, 541; substantive, 185, 214
Dumbarton Oaks conference, 409
Dunaway, Lillian, 243, 375, 475
Dunaway, Philip, 243, 475
Dunham, Katherine, 434
Dunne's Insurance Report, 520

Eastern European immigrants, 64, 91
Economics of law practice, 7, 8, 42, 182–83, 202, 238, 458, 469
Edelstein, Michael, 312
Edgerton, Henry J., 488
Eggleston, Arthur D., 470
Eighth Amendment, 25
Einstein, Albert, 143
Eisenstein, Sergei, 127, 395
Eisler, Gerhart (see also General Sources/Specific References), 389, 464, 482–91, 493, 504, 518, 523
Eisler, Hilde (Brunhilde), 482, 493
Eisman, Julius, 485
Ellis Island, 4, 26, 36, 39–41, 43, 45, 133, 139, 186–87, 189, 190, 242, 482
Ellis Island Committee, 187, 190, 195, 455
Eluard, Paul, 410
Emergency Alien Bill, 352
Emergency Railroad Transportation Act, 183
Emerson, Bert (Paret), 354
Emerson, Ralph Waldo, 216
Emerson, Thomas I., 123–24, 167, 184, 224, 319, 344, 354–55, 528, 536, 544
Emory University, 176–77
Enemy alien, 483–84

Engels, Frederick, 37, 290, 332, 377
England, 33, 37, 47, 53, 75, 117, 151, 233, 307, 318, 424
Englander, Isidore, 454, 505
English classes, 3
English language/literacy, 23, 26, 33, 40, 60, 68, 86, 91, 107, 174
Englishmen (British), 55–56
Engstrom, government witness, 279
Ennis, Edward J., 347, 356, 361
Equal protection: of the law, 65, 97; for Negroes, 113
Equity, 73
Eriksson, Per, 449
Ernst, George, 190, 195
Ernst, Morris, 219, 220–21, 227, 248, 250, 311, 320, 355, 511
Ernst controversy, 248, 321
Espionage Act of 1917, 15, 16, 55
Esterwegen Concentration Camp, Germany, 242
Ethics, professional, 517
Everett, Wesley, 19
Evictions, 95, 128–29
Ex post facto laws, 61, 325, 414
Examiner (see *San Francisco Examiner*)
Exceptions, bill of, 174
Excess profits tax (World War II), 387
Exclusion: laws, 16, 39, 54, 65; order of, 482, 521
Exclusion Hearing Board, 396
Executive Order 8802, 387
Executive Order 9835, 470
Executive Order 9960, 357
Exhaustion of remedies, 105, 465, 469
Exit permit, 445, 484
Extradition, 88, 89

Fact, questions of, 84
Fagan, Ann, 391–92
Fagan, Peter, 399, 409
Fagan, Sarah, 391, 409
Fahy, Charles, 211, 344, 377–78, 413–14
Fair employment practices, 386, 407, 508
Fair Employment Practices Committee, 359
Fair Labor Standards Act, 386
Falangists, 233
Fallon, Bill, 62–63
False statements (see Perjury)
Fanelli, Joseph A.
Farm debtors and the New Deal, 185
Farmers, 183, 185, 192; relief to, 213
Farmers National Committee, 186
Fascism/fascists: 80, 161; rise of, 190, 194, 466, 492–93, 523
Fascist League of North America, Bronx Branch, 86
Fascist Party, U.S., 352
FBI (Federal Bureau of Investigation), 96, 305, 308, 337, 355, 368, 429, 430, 473, 482–83, 523; on anthropologists, 324; break-ins, 371; CP club in, 312; files, 74, 187, 235, 310; General Intelligence Division, 65; in *Harry Bridges* case, 256–364, 405–20

esp. 325, 329–30, 343, 408; illegal searches and seizures by, 312; illegal tactics of, 315; investigations of government employees, 324, 343, 351, 402–04; raids, 312; report on Bridges, 389–91; reports on Carol King, 75, 141–42, 161, 188, 201, 234, 326, 327–28, 333, 334, 377, 391, 393, 396, 446, 448–51, 467, 474, 476, 518, 529, 540; Sen. George Norris on, 314–15; tactics, 31, 315, 519; wiretapping, 343–48
FBI-Detroit, 312–15
FBI-Milwaukee, 312
Federal Bureau of Investigation (see FBI)
Federal Communications Act, 343
Federal Communications Commission (FCC), 222, 388, 455
Federal Emergency Relief Administration (FERA), 183
Federal employees, investigating, 324, 343, 351, 402–04
Federal government, 65, 174
Federalists, 53
Federal Security Agency, 388
Federal Surplus Relief Corporation, 184, 193
Federal Trade Commission (FTC), 259
Fellowship of Reconciliation, 192
Ferber, Edna, 45
Ferguson, Isaac, 294–95
Ferrin, S. P., 374–75
Feuchtwanger, Lion, 460
Field, Frederick V., 524–25
Field, Marshall, III, 202, 355, 513
Field, Noel, 389
Fierstein, Zusman (Fred Firestone) (see also General Sources/Specific References), 433, 467
Fifteenth Amendment, 65
Fifth Amendment, 25, 54, 60, 113, 253, 492
Fifth Amendment privilege, 30, 41, 76, 472
Fifth column activity, 358–59
Finland/Finnish, 32, 97, 121, 308; Red, 308; Right-wing, 313–14
Finnish Benevolent Society, 449
Finnish Workers Home, 121
First Amendment, 3, 16, 23–25, 28, 36, 55, 60, 63, 65, 90, 109, 113, 179, 227, 332, 353, 367, 414, 423, 470–71, 492, 500, 513, 522, 533, 541; absolute position on, 492; rights, 60, 70, 67, 133, 225, 229, 312
Fisher, Irving, 94
Fish Reduction Workers Union, 277
Fitzgerald, F. Scott, 48
Flag, right not to salute in public schools, 228–29
Flanagan, Hallie, 208
Flynn, Elizabeth Gurley (see also General Sources/Specific References), 17, 81, 311, 372, 434, 442, 473–74, 499, 525–26, 536
Food Workers Industrial Union (FWIU), 105–07, 186
Footnote Four (see also *U.S. v. Carolene Products Co.*, in General Sources/Specific References), 225–26, 418
Ford, Gerald, 481

Ford, Henry, 318
Ford, James, 137
Ford, T. F., 318
Ford Motor Co., 317
Forer, Joseph, 451, 467, 469, 506, 509
Forer and Rein, 467
Forsythe, Robert, 207, 209, 210
Fortas, Abe, 123–24, 184, 398
Foster, Henry, 171
Foster, William Z. (Bill), 18, 82, 95, 98–100, 133, 137, 189, 342, 379, 431, 441, 469
Fourteenth Amendment, 65, 67, 97, 214, 226, 541; incorporates First Amendment liberties, 353, 541
Fourth Amendment, 25
Fraenkel, Osmond K., 173, 218–19, 236, 309–11, 398, 480, 499–500
France, 58, 117, 198, 233, 307, 318, 424, 482
Franco, Francisco, 233, 313
Frank, Jerome, 120, 184, 215, 321
Frank & Weiss, 11
Frankensteen, Richard, 339
Frankfurter, Felix: as professor, 27, 30, 77, 123–24, 146, 184, 188, 378; as justice, 353, 400, 412, 533, 537–38
Franklin, Benjamin, 460
Fraternal organizations, 81
Fraud charges, 367
Frazier-Lemke Act of 1933, 213
Freedman, Blanch, 473–75, 511, 521, 531, 533
Freedman, David, 129, 219, 448, 473
Freedman, Michael, 473
Freedman & Unger, 473–75
Freedom: of advocacy, 371; of assembly, 221, 522; of association, 1, 367, 433; of the press; 1, 77, 133, 418; of religion, 228–29; of speech, 28, 55, 67, 113, 418, 433, 505, 522–23
Freedom of Information Act, 403, 542
Free speech: fights, 12, 125, 133; invasion of the right of, 33, 66–67, 139; rights of aliens, 347–48, 353
Freudians, 202
Freund, Ernst, 30
Frey, Alexander H., 223
Funduklian, Arto, 77, 101, 245
Furniture Workers Press, 453
Fur workers, 104, 146
Fur Workers International Union (FWIU) 194, 453

Gallacher, William, 208
Gallagher, Leo, 89, 150, 188–89, 313, 334
Gallagher, William J., 420
Garfield, John, 260, 395, 434
Garlin, Sender, 38, 85, 92, 372
Garner, John Nance, 143
Garrison, Lloyd K., 236, 237
Garrison, William Lloyd, 216
Gearhart, Bertram W., 420
Geer, John H., 175–76, 227
Gellhorn, Walter, 179–80, 200, 205, 227, 455, 541
General Assembly, 487

General Electric (GE), 424
General Motors (see GM)
Gentiles, 73, 203, 215
Georgia, 136, 176, 177, 204
German-American Bund, 352, 402, 448
German: attorneys, 119, 150; concentration camps, 242; gypsies, 233; homosexuals, 233; invasion of Poland, 296, 307; invasion of Soviet Union, 315; Jews, 233; judges, 188–89; refugees to U.S. in '30s, 191, 229, 242, 430, 483; sailors, 191, 235; trade unionists, 192, 233; troops, 241
Germany, 13, 82, 115, 117, 149, 150, 160, 187–89, 197, 318, 323, 390, 491
Gifford, James P., 205
Ginger, Ann Fagan, 391–92, 409–10, 499, 504, 510, 512, 520, 528–30
Ginger, Ray, 409–10, 499
Gitlow (see also General Sources/Specific References), 70, 76, 82, 85, 109, 122, 135, 140, 221, 223, 225, 226, 331–332, 353, 364
Gladstein, Nancy, 354
Gladstein, Richard (Richie), 240, 260, 263–66, 271–73, 276, 277, 280, 281–82, 287, 297, 299, 302, 313, 330–32, 334, 336–39, 341, 345–57, 361, 373–74, 406, 412, 420–21, 493, 499, 518
Glazer, Tom, 244, 322
GM, 222, 224, 306, 424
Goering, Hermann, 188, 431
Gold, Ben, 104, 146
Goldberg, Arthur, 313, 371
Goldblatt, Louis, 357–58, 393
Goldman, Emma (see also General Sources/Specific References), 262
Goldsborough, Thomas, 468, 486, 488, 495
Gollobin, Ira, 449, 454, 462–63, 469, 493, 498, 530
Goodelman, Leon, 346
Goodman, Ernest, 313, 314–15
Goodman, Leo, 305
Goodman, Louis E., 539
Gordon, David, 122, 141
Gorki, Maxim, 233
Graham, Frank P., 510
Great Britain (see England)
Great Depression (see Depression)
Great War (see also World War I)
Greco/Carillo (see also General Sources/Specific References), 135, 193, 227, 260, 499
Greco, Mrs., 87
Greece, Greek, 323, 505
Greek immigrants, 91, 441
Green, Abner, 434, 443, 451, 458–59, 464, 468, 510, 524–27, 530, 533–34, 536–37
Green, Gil, 523
Green, John Raeburn, 537
Green, William, 442
Greene, Nathan (Nuddy), 146, 148, 158, 169, 236, 246, 268, 317–18, 347, 368, 371, 380, 382, 386, 412–13, 420, 432, 495
Gregory, Attorney General, 18
Gropper, Bill, 106, 110, 132, 134, 209, 452

Grossman, Aubrey, 240, 260, 263–66, 269–73, 282–84, 286–89, 297, 302, 330, 334, 336, 341, 345, 346–47, 373, 394
Group Theatre, 109, 160
Guffey Coal Act of 1935, 213
Guild (see NLG)
Guild Lawyer, 536
Guild Quarterly (NLG), 249
Guilt, personal, 18, 32, 399
Guilt by association, 311, 432
Gutnecht, John, 249

Habeas corpus: aliens' petitions for, 42–43, 190, 316, 360–61, 484; citizens' petitions for, 246; petitions, 45, 76, 148, 452; petitions, hearings on, 30, 34, 427; petitions denied, 61, 88, 194, 242, 493, 527; petitions granted, 34, 105, 191, 478, 486, 496, 511
Hacker, Louis, 208
Hagen, Uta, 456
Hale, Nelles & **Shorr,** 6–8, 10, 11, 16, 20, 24, 25, 36, 44, 59, 62, 68–69, 86, 193
Hale, Ruth (Brown), 46
Hale, Swinburne, 7, 11, 21, 26, 27–28, 30, 36, 63, 68, 454, 459
Hall, Gus, 523
Halleck, Charles, 309
Hallinan, Vincent, 538
Halverson, Lena, 433
Hammett, Dashiell, 381, 456, 524
Hand, Learned, Judge, 16, 24, 27, 28, 62, 63, 89–90
Hanging, 13
Harap, Louis, 208
Harding, Warren G., 34, 108, 443
Harisiades, George, 479
Harisiades, Irene, 479
Harisiades, Peter (see also General Sources/Specific References), 104, 442–43, 467, 479, 496, 538
Harlan County, Ky., 113, 142, 162
Harper, Fowler, 388
Harris, George B., 508
Harrison, Earl G., 359, 388, 407, 429
Hart, Henry, 319
Hart, Pearl, 223, 461
Hartmann, Bertram, 48
Harvard Club, New York City, 38
Harvard College, 8, 47–48, 208, 290
Harvard Law Review, 123, 149
Harvard Law School, 15, 27, 32, 64, 115, 123–24, 146–47, 171, 175, 179, 184, 259
Hastie, William, 316
Hatton, Barry, 472
Hayden, Bits, 164, 257–58, 418
Hays, Alan, 500
Hays, Arthur Garfield, 85, 124–25, 227, 370, 499–500, 514
Hays, Lee, 329
Hays, Paul, 480
Haywood, William (Big Bill), 93, 130, 523
HB (see Bridges, Harry; Bridges's, Harry)
Healy, William, 408
Hearst International News Service, 360

Heikkila (see also General sources/Specific References), 449
Heikkinen, Knut, 513, 540
Heilbron, Seymour, 500
Hellerstein, Jerome, 148–49
Hendrickson, Jim, 165
Hepburn, Katherine, 316
Herndon, Angelo, 177, 234, 441, 479, 522
Herndon, Milton, 234
Herndon (see also General Sources/Specific References), 290
Herodotus, 77, 94
Herwitz, Leo, 165
Hewitt, Elsa, 142
Hewitt, George, 478, 502
Hillquit, Morris, 11
Hilton, Ned, 218
Hilty, John, 449
Hiroshima, Japan, 424
Hiss, Alger, 123, 184, 389, 420, 470, 481, 503–04, 509
History of the Communist Party of the U.S.S.R., The, 274
Hitler, Adolf, 97, 118, 144, 150, 233, 298, 304, 313, 370, 396
Hitler Germany (see Nazi Germany)
Hobbs, Samuel, 319
Hobbs Concentration Camp Bill, 468
Hoc, 144, 172
Hod Carriers Union-AFL, 449
Holland, 234, 318
Holly, William H., 220, 249, 388
Hollywood Ten (see also General Sources/Specific References), 515
Holmes, John Haynes, 195
Holmes, Oliver Wendell, Jr., 13, 23, 24, 28, 36, 59, 60, 63, 67, 90, 463
Holtzoff, Alexander, 469, 489
Homeless, 98
Home Relief Bureau, New York City, 147
Hoover, Herbert, 108, 128, 137, 139, 141–42, 186, 187, 212, 443
Hoover, J. Edgar (see also FBI), 4, 27, 31, 35, 65, 76, 248, 308, 312, 313–14, 324, 325, 328, 331, 344, 351, 355, 368, 371, 374, 404, 463, 483, 489, 510, 542
Hoovervilles, 182
Horace Mann School, 12
Horatio's Story, 94, 156
Horne, Lena, 456
Horse with the Union Label, The, 209
House Appropriations Committee, 256, 331, 343, 402
House Committee on Un-American Activities (see HUAC)
House of Representatives, 352
House Rules Committee, 26, 31
Housing Corporation, U.S., 47
Houston, Charles H., 168, 223, 227, 316, 459
Howard University Law School, 316
How to Keep Out of Trouble, 373
HUAC (House Committee on Un-American Activities), 220, 250, 270, 305, 309–10, 357,

405, 447, 466, 470, 472, 483–84, 489, 491, 509, 515, 539, 541
Hudson, Asst. Solicitor of Georgia, 175–76
Hughes, Charles Evans, 13, 32, 461; as Chief Justice, 122, 141, 221, 224
Hughes, Langston, 434
Hull, Cordell, 189
Hull House, 223
Human rights (see also specific right), 124, 226
Humphreys, Miles G., 365
Hungarian: immigrants, 64, 91; revolution, 64
Hungary, 197
Hungary, fascist, 82
Hunger marchers, 141–43, 159
Hunger strikers, 452–57, 464, 472, 497
Hunter College, 49
Hunton, Alpheus, 524
Husband/wife two-career relationships, 55–57
Hutcheson, Joseph C., 239
Hutchins, Grace, 92
Hutner, Daniel, 234
Hyman, Stanley Edgar, 244
Hynes, William F., 'Red,' 267, 334, 338, 365

Ickes, Harold, 358, 368
IJA-American Section, 119
IJA boys/IJAers, 148, 222, 243, 324, 344, 386, 420
IJA Bulletin, 121, 123–24, 136, 141, 145–49, 168, 184, 209, 260, 305, 388, 470, 518; articles, 171, 188, 206, 222, 224, 229, 243, 256, 259, 317, 344, 348, 354, 428, 455; Recent Items column, 386, 388; subscribers, circulation, 237, 243
IJA-Chicago Branch, 161
IJA-German Section, 117–18, 150, 233
IJA (International Juridical Association), 117, 119–21, 123–25, 139, 141, 150, 177, 189, 191, 207, 224, 227, 230, 234, 304–05; briefs, 319; Congressional investigation of, 304–06, 308–10; editors, 148, 243, 381–82, 387; finances, 158–59, 310; fund-raisers, 159, 317, 382; lawyers, 141, 157–58, 168–69, 178, 181, 184–85, 209, 210, 212–15, 219; Legal Research Committee, 149, 167, 185, 205, 210; victories, 386–87; wedding, 228
ILD (International Labor Defense, IRA–U.S.) (see also *Labor Defender*), 68, 81–84, 88–90, 111, 117, 119–21, 129–35, 138, 159, 170, 187, 192, 197, 200, 208, 310, 319, 349, 517; cases, 81, 89, 150, 167, 177–81, 217, 313; Conference of 1937, 230; fund-raising, 518; international delegation to Poland, 1935, 306; lawyers, legal staff, 129–32, 181, 217, 219, 234; members, 73, 192; of Poland (IRA), 197–200; sectarian errors of the, 132, 203
ILGWU (International Ladies Garment Workers Union), 13, 142, 185, 209
ILWU (International Longshoremen's and Warehousemen's Union), 239, 259, 263, 280, 306, 348, 357–58, 393, 479, 494, 503; con-

vention, 1941, 332; Ladies Auxiliary, 274, 280; officers, 421, 538–39; strikes, 253–58
Immigration, Commissioner of, 256
Immigration Act of 1906, 91
Immigration Act of 1924, 64
Immigration and Naturalization Service (see INS)
Immigration Appeals, Board of, 319
Immigration Border Patrols, 331
Immigration Bureau, Dept. of Labor, 3–4, 17, 31, 33, 39–40, 59, 60, 61, 62, 70, 104–05, 107, 108, 139, 186
Immigration: inspectors, 19; policy, evolution of, 28, 91–92, 108; quotas, 64, 65; racial barriers, 388; statistics, 91, 196
Immigration law: legislative reforms, 54; reforms, 108
Impeachment, 31, 167, 259
Imper, Thomas A., 352
Income tax, 377, 485
Incorporation theory, 65, 332, 353, 541
Index to Legal Periodicals, 243
Industrial Association of San Francisco, 254
Industrial Unions (see CIO)
Industrial Workers of the World (see IWW)
Injunctions: anti-labor, 139, 168; to prevent infringements of civil liberties, 125, 467–68, 486, 496
INS: alleged CP club in, 529; attorneys, 533; Board of Review, 316; Dept. of Justice (after 1940), 356, 430, 529; Dept. of Labor (1932–1940), 186, 189–90, 194, 206, 330; exempted from APA, 486; and FBI, 446, 529; policy, 235, 540; procedure, proposed reforms, 187, 316, 455; procedures, 239, 251, 335, 442, 451–52; rules/forms, 234; Seattle office, 259; strategy, 454; tactics, 239, 346–47, 436
Insurrection statute of Georgia, 136–37
Inter-American Bar Association, 407
Intercollegiate Socialist Society, 399
Internal Security Act (1950), 510, 528
International Delegation (see ILD)
International Fur and Leather Workers Union, 535
International Fur Workers Association–AFL, 190
International Harvester, 224
Internationalism/internationalists, 541
International Juridical Association (see IJA)
International Labor Defense (see ILD)
International Labour Organization (ILO), 19, 94, 304
International Ladies Garment Workers Union (see ILGWU)
International Longshoremen's and Warehousemen's Union (see ILWU)
International Longshoremen's Association-AFL (ILA), 253
International Military Tribunal, 431
International Red Aid (IRA), 82, 89, 117, 197, 517
International Seamen's Union–AFL, 254
International Unemployment Day, 97

International Woman's Day, 537
International Workers Order (see IWO), 109
Interstate Commerce Commission (ICC), 214
IRA-German (Rote Hilfe), 82
IRA-U.S. (see ILD)
IRA-USSR (MOPR), 82, 117
Irish: heritage, 150; immigrants, Irish-Americans, 54, 62, 133, 311, 532
Iron curtain, 425, 427–28
Irwin, Edward M., 143
Irwin, Frank, 171
Isserman, Abraham (Abe), 157–58, 168, 219, 223, 228–29, 395–96, 398, 434–35, 448, 488–89, 493, 499, 518
Isserman, Joan, 51
Issoki, George, 192
Italian: immigrants, Italian-American, 29, 68, 80–89, 91, 109, 120, 133, 236, 318, 323, 358; fascists, 80, 194, 241; nationalism, 80; seamen, 429
"Ivan the Terrible," 395
IWO-Finnish Benevolent Society, 449
IWO-Hellenic American Brotherhood, 479
IWO (International Workers Order), 119, 371, 430, 447, 495, 520, 527
IWW (Industrial Workers of the World), 12, 17, 18, 19, 32, 66, 124, 133; General Defense Committee, 113, 180
IWW News, 159
Izak, Ed V., 420

Jackson, Henry H., 420
Jackson, Robert H., 237, 313, 315, 321, 323, 325, 352, 377, 398, 400–01, 431, 502, 508, 533
Jackson, Shirley, 244
Japanese-American: curfew order, 401: relocation camps, 357–359, 368, 393, 430–31, 543; volunteers in WWII, 431
Japan/Japanese, 82, 197, 315, 323; attack on Pearl Harbor, 352; invasion of China, 138; scrap iron for, 306, 342; war with (see also World War II), 415
Jefferson, Thomas/Jeffersonian Tradition, 31, 53–54, 135, 161, 239, 379, 460
Jehovah's Witnesses, 228–29, 320, 396, 398
Jewish: intellectuals, 12, 64, 143, 147; lawyers, 6, 7, 11, 53, 60, 111, 178, 211, 231; quota, 15
Jewish People's Fraternal Order-IWO (JPFO), 430
Jewish Social Service Agency, 158–59
Jewish-sounding name/Jewish-looking, 273, 463
Jewish Workmen's Circle, 109
Jews, 48, 73, 133, 203, 220, 243, 260; defamation of, 161
Jim Crow segregation, 204
John, King of England, 42
Johns Hopkins University, 124
Johnson, Beatrice Siskind, 497, 540
Johnson, Crockett, 207
Johnson, Manning, 503

Joint Anti-Fascist Refugee Committee (see also General Sources/Specific References), 371, 469, 485–86
Joint Committee to Aid the Herndon Defense, 180
Joliot-Curie, Frederick, 410
Jones, Claudia (see also General Sources), 462, 479, 536, 540
Jones & Laughlin Steel Corp., 192, 317
Judicial notice, 289, 477
Judiciary Committee, House, 26
Julien Levy Gallery, N.Y., 123
Juries, 135, 145; exclusion of Negroes from, 120, 122, 171, 174, 178–79, 204–05, 232, 387; grand, 30, 32, 33, 81, 137, 170, 204, 492, 497, 524; instructions to, 177, 231;
Jury selection, 21, 84–85, 176; trial lawyers, 85; trials, 13, 29, 62, 66, 84–85, 88, 99, 120, 147, 170–71, 176–77, 229, 231, 293, 311, 323, 354, 503, 519
Justice, Dept. of: 18, 38, 96, 205–06, 215, 313, 329, 334, 344, 352, 356, 402, 429, 448–49, 468, 480, 502–03, 509–10, 538; Criminal Division, 313, 361; General Intelligence Division, 4; jurisdiction of, 27–35; raids by (see also Palmer Raids), 3, 7, 20

Kahn, Elinor, 413
Kahn, Peggy Stern, 49, 52, 58, 91, 122, 156, 229–30, 288, 384–85, 394, 437, 531
Kammet, Lawrence, 346
Kane, Francis Fisher, 25–26, 512
Kaufman, Irving, 519
Kaufman, Mary, 499, 524
Kaufman, Samuel H., 496
Keegan, John J., 267, 284, 301, 303, 343
Kelly, Edward J., 388
Kenny, Robert W., 320–21, 365, 407, 420, 428
Kent, Arthur, 240, 277
Kent, Rockwell, 442, 456
Kentucky, 113, 142, 162, 317
Kerensky regime, 42–43, 176
Kerr, anti-alien bill, 206
Kerr Committee, 388
Keynes, John Maynard/Keynesian economics, 184, 225, 232
Kilgore, Harley M., 510
King, Carol Weiss: and ACLU, 94–95; and *ACLU Law and Freedom Bulletin,* 65–66, 68, 76, 103, 119, 138; and ALP, 498; and American Association for Labor Legislation, 13–14; and American Committee, 328, 434, 491, 533; appearance of, 6, 12, 13, 38, 126, 149, 169, 180, 196, 200, 229–30, 241, 244–45, 260–64, 333, 375, 395, 410, 488–89, 516; arguing appeals, 406, 412; as art patron, 149, 394, 413, 429; and Association of Bar of City of New York, 431–32;as banker, 314; and Barnard College, 12–13; and brief on FBI investigation of suspected government employees, 402–05; and Brodsky, 10–11, 21, 37, 112–13, 120–21, 235, 272, 517–18; and Carl Stern, 15; and Carrie Stix (mother), 10; and clients, 74, 366, 372, 383–84, 415, 542; at college, 12–13; and CP and CPA, 472, 489–90, 492, 535; and CRC, 524–25, 527–28, 530; criticisms of, 321–22, 516–19; defeats, 50–53, 61–62, 89–90, 104–05, 235, 242, 448, 462, 466, 494, 497, 511, 520–21, 525, 527, 530; as defendant, 92–93; as editor, 148–49, 314, 528–30; and FBI, 312, 325, 374–75, 389–91, 402–05, 443–44, 446, 450, 462, 482–83, 518, 540; as friend, 122–23, 163, 166, 168, 229–30, 244–45, 287, 394–95, 437–38, 472, 475, 498–99; as great aunt, 406; housekeeping arrangements, 10, 49, 69, 71, 285; as human rights rapporteur, 159–60, 197–200; and hunger marchers, 141–43; and IJA, 117–25, 137, 139, 141, 149, 229, 246–47; and *IJA Bulletin,* 123–24, 129, 159, 179, 200, 232, 256, 260, 279, 303, 314, 323; and IJA "Recent Items," 159, 192, 208, 242, 245, 320, 388; and ILD, 130, 133; as innovator, 245–46, 344–49, 367, 541; as job seeker, 6, 155–56, 158, 161, 385; and juniors, 148, 167, 179, 271–72; as jury lawyer, 45, 50–53, 79, 84–85; at law school, 7, 10, 15, 16, 28, 34; and *Lawyers Guild Review,* 429; as legal administrator, 240, 363, 412, 436; as legal scholar, 78, 288, 509, 528; and legal stenographers/secretaries, 44, 274, 392; as legal strategist, 417, 440, 451–52, 454–56, 465–71; lifestyle, 6, 50, 58, 69, 161–66, 206; as lobbyist, 313, 319, 432–33, 519, 542; and Louis S. Weiss (see Weiss, Louis S.); and Lowenthal and Szold, 6, 20; as mentor, 179, 180, 243, 292, 344–47, 363, 391–92, 409–10, 461–62, 504, 528–30; as mother, 69, 71–72, 90, 156, 162, 163, 165, 240, 250, 280, 285, 299, 395, 462–63; and Mrs. Barkley, 10, 49, 69, 71, 173, 198, 245, 350, 489–90, 534, 536; and NLG, 429; and Nina Stern, 15, 475; and NLG Immigration Committee, 247, 432; obituaries, 535–37; and Peggy Stern Kahn, 52, 58, 91, 122–23, 156, 299–300, 384, 531; as plaintiff, 92, 94; and Pollak, Walter, 63, 76, 323; and *Report on Illegal Practices,* 31; and Samuel Weiss, 6, 11, 14; as secretary, 10; self-criticism, 298–99; self-description, 297, 406; as single parent, 101–02, 114, 118, 198, 497; small victories of, 42–43, 88–89, 90, 105–07, 191, 205–06, 223, 251, 288–91, 315, 386, 396, 433, 472, 495–96, 497–98, 502, 507, 511, 520, 527, 528, 530, 539, 541; as sole practitioner, 163, 228, 299–300; and son, Jonathan, 66, 69, 70–72, 76–77, 79, 90, 151, 153, 240, 285, 296, 328–29, 336, 396, 413–15; Stefan Brandt/Ignace Reiss, 234–35; testimonial dinner, 458–64; testimony before Congressional Committees, 308–10, 432–33, 502–03; and unions, 6, 13; as Weiss, 52, 135, 363; as widow, 100–03, 109, 127, 166, 245, 394–95; and William Weiss, 6, 15, 79, 111, 202, 373, 438;

and Willkie, 368–72, 375–80, 396–97, 401, 406, 408–10; as woman lawyer, 40, 45, 49, 50–53, 90, 145, 331, 366, 395, 438, 462, 532, 543
King, Cynthia Bregman, 408, 534, 540, 543
King, Earl, 279, 293–96, 352
King, Earl (Mrs.), 293
King, Edith, 118
King, Garfield, 293–94
King, Gordon, 8, 10, 15, 35, 46–49, 55–58, 59, 71–72, 76–77, 79, 92, 95–96, 100–03, 145, 156, 166, 287, 394–95; on women and men, 55–57; on writing, 8, 39, 46, 48, 55–58, 77, 79, 90, 94
King, Howard, 79, 118, 415–16
King, Jonathan (Johnny, JK), 71–72, 76–77, 79, 90, 92, 96, 100–03, 114, 118, 151, 153, 156, 162, 163, 165, 173, 198, 245, 260, 280, 285, 296, 299, 328–31, 336, 384, 396, 413, 415, 475, 534, 543; marriage, 408, 475, 534
King, Kittie Bruen, 47
King, Louis Cass, 47
King, views: on banquets, 464; on Biddle, 360–61; on birth control, 91–92; on Bridges, 240, 297; Bridges's co-counsel, 272–73, 283, 286–87, 300, 330, 344–47, 350, 353–54, 357, 361–62, 373–74, 394, 405–06, 421–22, 503; on child-rearing, 91, 274; on communism, 298; on contributions of aliens, 91–92; on CP, CP meetings, 73, 201, 296; on Darrow, 88; on deportation law abuses, 187, 303; on Eisler's bail jumping, 490–92; on fashion, 264, 375, 384; on fees, 473; on Hale, Nelles & Shorr, 7, 28, 44; on/to on her appearance, 49, 51, 241, 333, 384–85; on her family, 14, 262; on her first grandchild, 353, 534; on immigration history, 1, 53–55, 91, 429; on immigration law reform, 317; on inheritance, 391, 406–07; on intellectuals, 297; on Japanese-American detention camps, 357–58, 368, 393, 431; on Landis, 260; on life, 91, 292, 520; on little cases, 160, 299, 385, 421; on marriage, 153, 156–57, 161, 244, 280; on Marxism/political theory, 73, 288–90, 436–37, 492–93; on Poland, 197–200; on political prisoners, 200; on the press, 261–62, 273, 277–78, 281–82, 286, 297, 333, 445; on relaxation, 285, 287, 291–92, 416, 536; on reputation, 285, 373; on San Francisco, 292; on Sears, 350; on Shorr, Brodsky & King, 153–55; on significance of Bridges case, 296; on Soviet Union, 114–18; on victories in *Bridges, Schneiderman, Gitlow, APA* case, 317, 401, 506; on war, 298; on witnesses, 240; on women lawyers, 391

King & Freedman, 473–75, 498, 521, 533
King correspondence: to Clara Binswanger, 148, 245–47, 262, 266, 272–81, 283, 285–87, 291–92, 296–99, 405–07; to Jay Leyda, 148, 151–58, 161–66, 168, 177–78; to Roosevelt, 322; to Sylvia Chen, 166
King's: affair with Jay Leyda, 123–27, 145, 151–58, 161–66, 200, 395; "big aliens," 283; childhood, 11–12; courtship, 15, 48; family network/affairs, 202; FBI file, 75, 141–42, 188, 234, 325–27, 376, 390, 529; fees and finances, 8, 10, 44, 75, 79, 102, 153–55, 241, 299–300, 304–05, 347, 357, 366, 374, 383–84, 394, 473; Immigration Bureau file, 75; informal employment agency, 243–44; invisible contributions, 45, 63, 84–85, 121, 160, 217, 245, 368, 412, 348; legal apprenticeship, 6–8, 10, 20–23, 28, 34–35, 39–45, 50–53; legal mistakes, 302, 357–58, 393; legal network, 76, 135–36, 385, 427, 447, 510; "little aliens," 44, 52, 240, 460, 479; marriage, 38–39, 46, 48, 58, 76, 95–96, 100–03, 394–95; memory, 203–04; methods of work, 39–40, 44–45, 51–52, 63, 74–75, 78, 129, 135–36, 148–49, 167, 196, 246, 261–66, 271–87, 363–64, 496, 511; parents, 11–12; prestige at the bar, 495–96, 519, 532–33, 535–37; standard of living, 8, 163; trust fund, 10, 69, 79, 101–02, 391
King v. NYC Police Dept., 92–93, 145
Kirtein, Lincoln. 395
Klig v. Shaughnessy (see also General Sources), 511
Knowles, Harper, 267, 282–84, 301
Knox, John, 405, 537
Korean War, 508–09
Kovner, Joe, 124, 146, 168
Kramer, Charles, 509
Kramer, Jean, 307, 435
Krauthamar, Max, 233
Ku Klux Klan (KKK), 13, 54, 441, 443, 448
Kuntz, Ed, 129

Labor, Dept. of: 4, 17, 19, 34, 41, 65, 138, 186, 190, 206–07, 208, 269, 304–05, 470; Board of Review, 194, 316; jurisdiction of, 27–29
Labor, Secretary of, 17, 61, 108, 242
Labor Defender (ILD), 83–84, 88, 89, 93, 106, 110, 112, 122, 130, 138, 140, 144, 172, 197–98, 200, 201, 218, 227, 233
Labor Defense Council, 81–82
Labor Defense League, 159
Labor: law, 15, 28, 36, 66, 119, 541; lawyers, 53, 124, 210, 237, 249, 371, 434, 447, 451, 501; leaders, 470, 501; spies, 269–70, 405; unions (see Unions)
Labor's Non-Partisan League, 335
Lader, Lawrence, 241
Ladies Auxiliary (ILWU), 274, 280
La Follette, Bob, 64, 314, 448
La Follette, Philip F., 220, 237
La Follette, Robert M., Jr., 237

La Follette Civil Liberties Committee, 269–70, 283, 334
LaGuardia, Fiorello: as Mayor, 220, 228, 241, 372; as Rep., 138, 193
LaGuardia and Copeland bills for aliens, 196
Lamb, Edward, 313, 371
Lamont, Corliss, 311
Lamp, The, 490, 507, 530
Lampell, Millard, 329
Land, Yetta, 120
Landis, James M., 77, 259–60, 263–65, 267–71, 289, 291, 320, 329, 343, 365, 535
Landis: on Bridges, 301; on defense witnesses, 291, 294, 296; on government witnesses v. Bridges, 270–71, 275, 277, 279, 283–84
Landis's: children, 275; findings in *Bridges* case, 300–03, 417
Langer, William, 510
Langevin, Paul, 410
Lapham, Roger, 413
Larkin, Jim, 62
Laski, Harold J., 27, 247
Lattimore, Owen, 509
Law and Freedom Bulletin (ACLU), 33, 65–66, 68, 76, 103, 105, 113, 119, 138, 159, 519
Law: clerks, 21, 36, 68; commercial, 72, 74, 76, 79; development of, 77–78; domestic relations, 202; firms, integrated, 53; social functions of, 78
Lawrence, Thomas, 360
Lawyers, Supreme Court, 63, 179, 390
Lawyers: conservative, 179; criminal defense, 195; immigration, 195; left-wing, 53, 213, 226; liberal, 213; library (research), 119, 179; Negro, 130, 168, 175, 221, 386, 481; older women, 8; people's, 544; trial, 544; trial (pit), 179; women (see Women, lawyers)
Lawyers Guild (see NLG)
Lawyers Guild Review, 405, 410, 429
Lawyers' income/fees, 182–83, 202, 238, 458, 469
Lawyers Security League, 219, 234
Lazarus, Isidor, 249
Leafleting, arrests for, 21, 23, 74, 92, 94, 165
League for Industrial Democracy, 180, 192
League for the Rights of Man, 72
League of American Writers, 371
League of Nations, 19, 20, 189, 241, 304
League of Struggle for Negro Rights, 180
Leech, John, 271–72, 274–77
Lefkowitz, Louis I.
Lefkowitz, Louis J., 312
Left, U.S./Leftists, 84
Left ideology, 160, 216
Left-wing unions, 186, 263
Legal: clinic, neighborhood, 373; secretaries, 21, 44, 51, 196, 392; strategy, defense or offense, 59, 176; tactics, 23; theory, 34–35, 77–78; woodshed, 426–29
Legion (see American Legion)
Lehman & Greenman, 146
Lehman, Herbert, 146

Leibell, Vincent, 496, 505
Leibowitz, Samuel, 170, 173
Leipzig, Germany, 188
Lenin, V. I., 16, 42, 114, 176, 208, 399
Leonard, George B., 249–50
Leonard, Marjorie, 39, 229
Leonard, Norman, 39, 229, 299, 381
Leppold, John L., 277
Lerman, Shirley, 392
Letts, F. Dickinson, 467
Lewis, John L., 188, 222
Leyda, Jay, 123–27, 145, 149, 151–58, 161–66, 200, 395
Leyda, Si-Lan, 395
Li, Tao Hsuah, 138, 142
Liberal-Left Split, 1939, 308
Liberation theology, 399
Liberator, The, 176
Life and Struggles of the Negro Toilers, 176
Life magazine, 241
Lincoln, Abraham, 32, 413; second inaugural address, 135, 379
Lincoln Brigade (Spanish Civil War), 312; veterans, 371
Linder, Leo, 167, 227, 428
Literacy laws, 64, 91
Literature, seditious, 223
Little cases, 66, 78, 108, 159–60, 392, 479
"Little Italy," 80
Llewelyn, Karl N., 120, 200, 221, 247
Loeb and Leopold, 85
London police, 517
London Times, 425
Longshoremen's Strike of 1934, 163–64, 253–58
Lorac Lodge, Maine, 12, 163, 168
Los Angeles, 99; street railway strike, 365
Los Angeles Police Dept., subversive ("Red") squad, 150, 334
Los Angeles Times, 81, 353
Loucas, Loucas A., 104–05
Louisiana, 119
Lovett, Robert Morss, 82, 388, 460–61
Lowenthal, Max, 6, 20, 136, 155, 314
Lowenthal & Szold, 6, 20
Loyalists in Spain (see Spanish Loyalists)
Loyalty Board hearing, 480
"Loyalty/security," 470
Lucas, Charles P., 453
Ludlow, Colorado, strike of 1914, 8, 9 (illus.)
Lukas, Joe, 504, 510
Lundeberg, Harry, 338, 349, 393, 416
Luxembourg, 318
Lynching, 19, 36, 62, 124, 167, 173, 186, 204

MacArthur, Douglas, 509
McCabe, Louis, 313, 493
McCarran Internal Security Act (1950), 528, 536
McCarran, Pat, 324, 510–11
McCarran-Walter Immigration Act (1952), 519, 538
McCarthy, Joseph, 87, 510

McDonald, David J., 374
McGohey, John F.X., 524
McGrady, Edward, 190
McGrath, Comm. of Angel Island, 271
McGrath, J. Howard, 507, 512
Machado, Eduardo, 138
Machinists Union-AFL, 254
McKellar, Senator, 444
McKinley, William, 54
MacLean, Malcolm S., 359
MacLeish, Archibald, 316, 355
McNamara, J. B., 81
McReynolds, James, 219
McTernan, John, 532–33
McWilliams, Carey, 317
Madden, G. Warren, 211
Maddow, Doris, 13, 48, 101, 114–17, 123, 125, 154
Maine, 12, 100, 168
Malament, Edward, 210, 500
Malcolmson, Charles, 402
Male chauvinism, 285
Malone, Dudley Field, 124–25
Manchester Guardian, 77
Mann, Thomas, 460
Mann Act, 337
Mannerheim, Dictator of Finland, 121, 308
Manton, Martin T., 29
Mao Tse-tung, 234
Marcantonio, Vito (Marc), 68, 86, 193, 236, 241, 316, 319, 364, 420, 432, 441, 508, 512
Marcello v. Bonds (see also General Sources/Specific References), 539
Margolis, Benjamin (Ben), 240, 263, 287, 290, 299
Marine Cooks & Stewards Union, 352
Marine Firemen's Union, 293, 336
Marine Workers Industrial Union, 254, 257, 360
Maritime Workers Federation, 279, 284, 335
Market Street, San Francisco, 163–64
Marshall Plan, 447, 500
Martens, Ludwig C.A.K., 43
Martin, Charles H., 283
Marx, Karl, 184, 234, 290, 332, 377, 379
Marxist theory/Marxism/Marxists, 14, 34, 36–38, 104, 109, 132, 208, 288–90, 312, 366, 377, 384, 399–401, 434, 436, 493, 522; experts in, as witnesses, 290–91; lawyers, 11, 285; professors, 169
Maryland, 120, 124
Mascitti, Luigi, 533
Mason, Congressman, 433
Massachusetts, 3, 69
Mass defense, 176, 517
Masses, The, 9, 14, 16, 17, 24, 27, 28
Mass round-up of Mexican workers, 430
Massing, Hedda (see also Eisler, Gerhart) 234–35, 389, 504
Masters, Edgar Lee, 54, 364
Masters, Mates & Pilots-AFL, 254
Master/Servant, 16, 36
Matisse, Henri, 448

Matles, James, 104
Matthews, Judge, 406
Mauldin, Bill, 444
Maverick, Maury, 237
May Day, 124, 253, 490
Media, 264, 297, 370, 494
Medina, Harold R., 452, 499, 538
Melish, William Howard, 348
Melville, Herman, 395
Memorial Day Parade, 1927, 80, 87
Mentors, 8
Merriam, Frank, 255
Methodist Federation for Social Action, 192
Mexican migratory workers, 430
Mexicans, roundups in U.S. of, 139, 496
Mexico/Mexicans, 29, 482
Meyer, Howard N., 158, 180
Michael, Jerome, 179
Michigan Civil Rights Federation, 313–14
Middle class, 147, 163; backgrounds, 92
Military Intelligence Division of U.S. General Staff, 7, 26
Miller, Commissioner, 488
Milner, Lawrence A., 266, 269–70
Minor, Robert, 14, 372
Minton, Sherman, 533
Mission to Moscow, 395
Mooney, Tom (see also General Sources/Specific References), 81, 386
Morgan, J. Pierpont, 209
Morganthau, Henry, 355
Morrill, Clarence, 267
Moscow, U.S.S.R., 62, 95, 107, 114–15, 117, 132, 142, 151, 155, 516; gold, 517; treason trials, 322
Muezenberg, Willi, 192
Muir, Jean, 509
Mundt, Karl, 468
Munich nonaggression treaty, 321
Murder, 234, 390; charges, 29, 41, 80–81, 85, 113, 120, 167, 293
Murdock, John R., 309
Murphy, Frank, as Attorney General, 315; as Justice, 378, 398–401, 418–20, 428, 433, 471, 501–02, 523, 533; as Michigan governor, 222
Murray, James E., 358, 428
Murray, Philip, 374, 456, 501, 503
Murtha, Donald M., 470
Museum of Modern Art, 125–26, 395, 413
Mussolini, Benito, 80, 87, 94, 138, 194, 331
Mutiny charges, 205–06, 210, 541
Myers, Frederick, 456

NAACP (National Association for the Advancement of Colored People), 36, 109, 119–20, 132, 176, 192, 203, 316, 425, 453; Legal Defense Committee of, 513; legal strategy of, 176
Nagasaki, Japan, 424
Nation, The, 64, 143, 205, 328, 402, 453
National Association for the Advancement of Colored People (see NAACP)

National Association of Manufacturers (NAM), 212–13
National Bar Association, 168, 203
National Civil Liberties Bureau (see ACLU)
National Commission on Law Observance and Enforcement, 108
National Committee for the Defense of Political Prisoners, 159, 180
National Committee to Aid Striking Miners Fighting Starvation, 142
National Federation for Constitutional Liberties, 324, 434
National Guard, 222, 254
National health program, 307
National Industrial Recovery Act (NIRA, also NRA), 160, 184, 187, 193, 213, 253
National Institute of Immigrant Welfare, 316
National Labor Relations Act (NLRA), 309
National Labor Relations Board (see NLRB)
National Lawyers Guild (Lawyers Guild, Guild) (see NLG)
National Lawyers Guild Quarterly, 385–86
National Lawyers Guild Review, 388
National Longshoremen's Board, 255
National Maritime Union (NMU-CIO), 243, 448–49, 456, 500
National Popular Government League, 26, 30–31
National Recovery Administration (NRA), 183, 185, 211
National Resources Planning Board (NRPB), 382, 488
National Socialists (Nazis), 118
National Youth Administration (NYA), 193
National War Labor Board, 30
Naturalization: denial of, 54, 433; laws, 407; petition for, 238, 359, 388, 414, 420–21; revocation of (see also *Schneiderman*), 400, 494, 507
Nazi Germany, 189, 191–92, 244, 304, 315, 343, 388, 425
Nazi Party/Nazis/Nazism, 117, 119, 149–50, 188–89, 328, 424, 433, 490, 500; pro-Nazis, 405; in U.S., 352
Nazi-Soviet nonagression pact, 1939, 308, 315, 343, 365, 378
Nazi spies in Brooklyn, alleged, 351
Nearing, Scott, 16, 82
Needle Trades Workers Industrial Union (NTWIU), 189–90, 194
Negro-baiting, 177
Negro: Communists, 136, 137, 192; workers, 382; youths, 111
Negroes, 20, 113, 133; cases of, 111, 141; equal protection for, 237; FBI should hire, 429; rights of, 160, 193, 216, 357, 425, 448; voting rights of, 429
Negro Labor Victory Committee, 371
Nelles, Walter, 7, 8, 21, 26, 28–29, 33, 38, 60, 61, 62, 63, 65–67, 77–78, 159, 353, 393, 454, 459, 537
Nelson, Donald, 360
Neutrality Act, violations of, 313

New Deal: agencies, 147; civil liberties under, 192; constitutionality of, 212–15, 224, 227; era, 160, 185, 187, 227, 237, 307, 542; lawyers, 210, 365; legislation, 160, 184, 307, 488
New Jersey, 66, 109, 147, 158, 167, 186, 195, 223, 229
New Masses, The (CP), 208, 233, 375, 410
New Republic, The, 26, 82, 142, 244, 313
New School for Social Research, 481, 513
News Vendors Union Local, 75, 494
New York, 73, 220
New York, City College of (CCNY)
New York Board of Elections, 311
New York Call, 159
New York City, 3, 5, 21, 27, 28, 31, 114, 147; police, 3, 98, 186; police commissioner, 98, 107
New York City Council, 364, 492
New York County Lawyers Association, 238, 535
New York Daily News, 323
New Yorker, The, 58, 402, 487
New York Herald Tribune, 159, 371, 380, 402
New York Lusk Committee, 235
New York Post, 453, 521
New York Power Commission, 221
New York Star, 513
New York State: Assembly, 27, 32; Board of Law Examiners, 247; Labor Dept., 228, 243; Rapp-Coudert Committee, 343
New York Times, 4, 18, 19, 20, 24, 27, 57, 98, 101, 121, 139, 143, 146, 159, 202, 233, 234, 242, 255, 273, 296, 330, 332, 334, 370, 389, 490, 508, 523, 535–36
New York Times Book Review, 151
New York University Law School, 10, 11, 15, 16, 48, 51, 136
New York World, 98
Nicaragua, 122, 93
Niles, David K., 470
"Nine Old Men," 214, 216, 222
NIRA (see National Industrial Recovery Act)
Nixon, Richard, 468
NLG (National Lawyers Guild), 222–23, 230, 232, 234, 262, 291, 297, 313, 357, 365, 397, 407, 420, 425, 449, 461, 480, 501, 502, 525, 528, 530, 542; attempts to purge Leftists in, 248, 311, 320–21; Committee on American Citizenship, Immigration and Nationality, 247, 432; constitution, 222; conventions, 388; Founding Convention, 1937, 222–23; Fourth Convention 1941, 342; and HUAC, 509; Immigration Project, 542; lawyers in U.S. Armed Forces, 381, 386; National Executive Board (NLG–NEB), 237, 248, 250; NLG membership, 315; postwar Convention, 428–31; resignations from, 321; Second Convention, 1938, 237; Third Convention, 1939, 248
NLG-Detroit Chapter, 249
NLG-NYC Chapter, 247, 385, 480
NLRB (National Labor Relations Board, Labor Board), 211, 215, 249, 304–05, 309–10,

317, 348, 377, 441, 451, 500; congressional investigation of, 304–06, 308–10; field examiners/lawyers, 221
NMU (National Maritime Union-CIO), 210
Nonagression Munich treaty (see Munich nonaggression treaty)
Nonagression pact (see Soviet-Nazi pact)
Non-Communist oaths, 447, 480, 500–01, 507–08
Non-Partisan Labor Defense, 159, 180
Norene, R. J., 268
Norris, Clarence, 175, 439
Norris, George, 314–15
Norris, Kathleen, 151
Norris-LaGuardia Anti-Injunction Act, 124, 386
North American Aircraft strike, 1941, 338–40
North Korea, 508–09
Nowak, Margaret, 306–07
Nowak, Stanley, 306, 316, 396–97
Nuremberg, 424, 429, 431, 508

Oath: loyalty, 507–08; naturalization, 367; non-Communist, 447, 470, 500–01, 507–08
O'Brien, Pat, 249
Occupational health and safety, 13, 185
October magazine, 395
October Revolution (see Russian, Revolution of 1917)
Office of Civilian Defense, 354
Office of Price Administration (OPA), 381, 386, 388
Ohio, 5, 99, 123, 124
Oklahoma, 141, 185
Okolitenko, 42
Old age benefits/insurance (see Social Security)
Old Leftists, 542
Olson, Culbert, 352
O'Neil, James D., 335–36, 349–50, 352, 394, 408, 416, 418
One Third of a Nation, 208
"One World"/One-Worlders, 323–24, 368, 410, 424
Oppenheimer, Reuben, 108
Oregon, 124, 217
Oregon criminal syndicalist law, 217–19
Oregon State Dept. of Geology and Mineral Industries, 352
Oriental immigrants (see Asian immigrants)
Orsink, Melvin, 234
Overthrow: forcible, advocacy of, 16; personal belief in violent, 16, 198
Owens, Carl M., 370
Ozeran, Abe, 494

Pacific Coast maritime strike of 1934, 253–55
Padmore, George, 176
Padway, Joseph, 237
Palmer, A. Mitchell, 4, 18–19, 26–28, 30–35, 59
Palmer Raids, 6, 19–20, 21, 26–28, 30–35, 41–42, 62, 64, 81, 104, 108, 122, 313, 316, 430, 443, 463, 512; cases, 59; of 1950, 494, 510–15, 520–21, 528, 530

Pan-Americanism, 399–400
Paret, Bertha (Mrs. Thomas I. Emerson), 167
Parker, Dorothy, 45
Party Organizer, The (CP), 176
Passport: charges, 308, 311, 322; fraud, 308
Patterson, Haywood (see *Scottsboro*)
Patterson, William L. (Pat), 130–32, 363
Peace Information Center, 515
Pearl Harbor, Hawaii, 352, 355, 370
Pecora, Ferdinand, 237, 248–50
Pegler, Westbrook, 323
Pennsylvania, 4, 11, 25, 88–89, 99, 192
Pennsylvania Bar Association, 319
People's lawyers, 248
People's Radio Foundation, Inc., 430
Pepper, Claude, 316, 428, 432
Perjury, 29, 352, 478, 502, 524, 538
Perkins, Frances, 186–87, 195, 255–56, 259, 300, 302, 348, 353
Perlman, Philip P., 489
Peters, Jay, 516
Phelan, Arthur J., 442
Phi Beta Kappa, 13
Philadelphia Story, 316
Phillips, Wendell, 216
"Phony Imperialist War" (see World War II; Sitzkrieg)
Picasso, Pablo, 410, 448
Picketing: constitutionality of, 320; peaceful, 92, 139, 145, 320, 387
Picket lines/pickets/picketing, 21, 38, 104, 195, 453
Pins and Needles, 209
Pirinsky, George (see also General Sources/Specific References), 495–96
Pledge of Allegiance, 228–29
PM, 343, 355, 357, 416, 513
Poland, 60, 61, 117, 239, 296, 306–07, 490, 538
Poland, international delegation to, 197–200
Police, 39, 210; power, 66; shootings, 254; special, 8
Polier, Isadore (Shad), 123, 160, 168, 213, 219, 228, 428, 471
Polier, Justine Wise (Tulin), 158, 167–68, 203, 220, 228, 354–55, 481
Polish-Americans, 91, 109, 306, 396
Polish ILD (see ILD, of Poland)
Political parties, minority (see Third parties)
Political: persecution, 540; prisoners, 66, 82, 117, 198, 200, 230; questions, 73
Pollak, Louis H., 409, 488
Pollak, Marion, 49, 52, 64, 102, 323, 383, 409, 488
Pollak, Walter H., 63–65, 67, 76, 102, 122, 136, 140, 169, 173, 180, 184, 224, 323, 367, 383, 393, 409, 459
Pollitzer, Honi (see Weiss, Honi)
Popper, Martin, 220, 321, 407, 420, 518
Poretsky, Ignacy (pseud. Ignace Reiss) (see Brandt, Stefan)
Portland police, 268, 284
Portugal, 540
Post, Louis F., 27, 31–32, 34, 59, 65, 356

Postmaster General, 16, 170
Potash, Irving (see also General Sources), 146,
     453, 456, 461, 469
POUM, Trotskyist Marxist party, 389
Pound, Cuthbert, 63, 67
Pound, Roscoe, 27, 30, 78, 188
Powe, Ralph, 434–35
Powell, Adam Clayton, 434
Powell, Mary, 15
Powell, Thomas Reed, 123
Poyntz, Juliet Stuart, 13
Prejudice: anti-Negro, 85; disqualification for,
     489; sex, 45
Pressman, Lee, 123, 184, 210, 237, 239–40,
     412–13, 447, 461, 467, 508–09
Press (see Media)
Price, Victoria, 170, 231
Prison conditions, 100, 199, 230, 313
Private bill, 462
Progressive Party, 64, 448, 459, 461, 467, 479–
     80, 500, 524, 538
Propaganda, government, 30–31
Property rights, 124
Prussian Minister of Justice, 191
Psychiatric examinations, 352
Public Works of Art Project, 193
Puerto Rico, 120, 193, 230; independence
     movement of, 387; Nationalist Party of,
     208
Punishment, 26

Quakers, 53, 142
Quotas on immigration, racial, 519

Rabinowitz, Victor, 208, 500–01, 508
Racial discrimination, 387; in the armed forces,
     381, 387
Racism, 121
Radical literature, possessing, 29, 60
Radical Republican Congress, 213
Radin, Max, 374
Radin, Benjamin, 441
Radio Berlin, 360
Raids, 3–4, 7, 20, 69
Railroad workers and the New Deal, 213
Railroad workers' strike of 1919, 18
Rakosi, Mathias, 82
Ramsay, Ernest, 293–96, 352
Ramsay, Ernest (Mrs.), 294, 296
Rape, 141, 170
Rapp-Coudert Committee, 389
Raymond, Harry, 372
Rea, Gardner, 210
Real estate law, 95
Recent Items column (RIs), (see *IJA
     Bulletin*)
Recht, Charles, 63
Reconstruction Amendments, 113
Reconstruction Congress, 213
Red-baiting, 36, 186, 443; opposition to, 24
Red Cross, 130
Red Front Band, 143
Red International of Labor Unions, 107, 194
"Red Monday," 539

Red peril, 18, 97
Red scare of World War I, 37, 234
Reed, John (Jack), 5, 16, 18, 42, 62
Reed, Stanley F., 413, 428
Reedsville, W. Va. Homestead experiments, 193
Re-entry permit, 445, 497–98
Refugees: from Nazi Germany, 208, 229, 243,
     407; political, 193, 378
Reich (Third) (see Nazi Germany)
Reichstag: fire of 1933, 150, 188–89; fire trial
     (see also Dimitroff, Georgi), 517; German
     Parliament, 150, 192
Rein, David, 451, 467, 488–89, 533
Reiss, Ignace (pseud. Ignacy Poretsky) (see
     Brandt, Stefan)
Relief, public, 98, 129, 206
Relief funds, 95, 136
Religious freedom (see Freedom, of
     religion)
Relocation of Japanese-Americans (see Japa-
     nese-American, relocation camps)
Republican Party, 30, 108, 378, 379, 401, 408
Republicans: Black, 32, 175; Lincoln, 237,
     368; Red, 31, 241; Willkie, 470
Republic Steel, 230, 317
Res judicata, 414
Reuther, Walter, 447
Revolution: Hungarian, 64; right to, 133, 135
Revolutionary: ideas, 160; lawyer, 182
Reynolds, Robert, 360
Riemer, Mortimer, 220, 250
Right: of asylum, 208; to counsel (see also
     Sixth Amendment), 25, 27, 31, 41, 60,
     122, 245–47, 351, 497; to effective assis-
     tance of counsel, 140–41; to travel, 142; to
     trial (see Sixth Amendment)
Rights, economic, 382, 488
Rio de Janeiro, Brazil, 200
Riots, race, 16, 18, 36
Roberts, Owen J., 226, 379, 400, 418, 533
Robeson, Paul, 364, 441, 498
Rocco, Alexander, 86–87
Rochester, Anna, 92
Rockefeller, John D., 8–9
Roddy, Stephen, 111
Roemer, Ruth, 385
Rogge, O. John, 313, 463, 524
Rolph, James, 167
Romania, 98, 189–90, 323
Rome, Italy, 77, 94
Roosevelt, Eleanor, 45, 193, 250, 328, 354–55,
     361, 373, 383, 487
Roosevelt, Franklin D., (FDR), 237, 244, 254,
     304, 306–07, 313, 342, 414; aid to allies,
     351, 365; anti-alien actions, 186, 206–07,
     242, 319, 322, 353, 361; anti-communist
     actions, 1941, 372; anti-labor actions,
     1941, 351; brain trust, 212, 382; cabinet
     of, 250; court-packing plan, 222, 225, 227;
     Emergency Alien Bill, 352; as governor of
     N.Y., 88, 97–98, 187; greetings to Ameri-
     can Committee, 1942, 358, 468, to Na-
     tional Lawyers Guild, 407; New Deal
     strategy, 137, 212, 216, 225, 387; as Presi-

dent, 139, 182–84, 189, 207, 219; third term, 240, 259, 318, 323; veto, 320; as War President, 357, 360, 365, 382, 388, 455
Roosevelt, Theodore, 11
Roper, Daniel C., 205–06
Rosenberg, Beatrice, 530
Rosenberg, Ethel (see also General Sources/Specific References), 508, 515, 519, 539
Rosenberg, Julius (see also General Sources/Specific References), 508, 515, 519, 539
Rosenfeld, Herman, 210, 435, 500
Rosenfeld, Kurt, Dr., 191–92
Ross, Harold, 402
Rothschild, V. Henry, II, 206, 236
Rousseau, Jean Jacques, 47
Rowoldt, Charles (see also General Sources/Specific References), 539–40
Rubenstein, Barbara, 437–38
Ruling class, 37, 84, 136
Runaway shops, 223, 387
Russia (see Soviet Union)
Russian: czar, 3, 62; embassy, Washington, D.C., 42–43; ghettoes, 7; government, 42–43; immigrants, 91, 104; Jewish, 208; People's House, 3; Revolution of 1917, 19, 48, 114, 189, 217; War Relief, 371; white, 138
Rutledge, Wiley, 400, 414, 488–89, 501, 533
Ryan, Joseph, 254
Ryan, Sylvester, Judge, 525–26

Sabath, Adolph J., 456
Sacco-Vanzetti (see also General Sources/Specific References), 93, 120, 132, 197, 363, 443, 492
Sacher (attorney's contempt case) (see also General Sources/Specific References), 499
Sacher, Harry, 248–49, 493, 518, 525, 530
Sage, Sam, 456
Sailors, 104, 191, 219, 460
Sailors Union of the Pacific, 277, 338
St. Clair, Richard A., 360
St. John, "Teddy," 500
Salsedo, Andrea (Mrs.), 81
Saltzman, Benjamin (see also General Sources/Specific References), 477, 496, 520
Saltzman, Benjamin (Mrs.), 477–78
Saltzman, Bernard, 477
Saltzman, Isidore, 477
Sandburg, Carl, 413
San Francisco, Calif., 253, 286
San Francisco Examiner (Hearst), 261, 273, 277, 283, 296
San Francisco general strike of 1934, 253–55
San Francisco News, 302
San Francisco–New York comparison, 271–73, 285
San Quentin prison, 293–96
Saturday Evening Post (Satevepost), 38, 220, 458, 516
Savage, Charles R., 420
Sawyer, Hal, 331
S.B. & K. (see Shorr, Brodsky & King)
Scabs, 124

Schappes, Morris V., 343, 389
Schlesinger, Arthur M., 434
Schneider, Jack (see also General Sources/Specific References), 433
Schneiderman, Helen, 380
Schneiderman, Leah, 366, 380
Schneiderman, William (see also General Sources/Specific References), 104, 337, 341, 343, 344, 362, 364, 366, 371, 377, 413, 436, 438, 470, 501, 522, 538
Schofield, Lemuel B., 332–36, 340, 361
Schulman, John, 500
Schurz, Carl, 378
Schwab, Charles M., 31
Schwab, Irvin, 171
Schwartzbart, Elias (Eli), 112, 119, 154, 170, 173, 309
Schweinhaut, Henry, 315
Science and Society, 208, 219
Scott, Arthur, 284
Scottsboro (see also General Sources/Specific References), 140, 172, 439, 518
Scottsboro Boys, The (see General Sources/Specific References; specific defendants)
Scottsboro case, fund-raising, 171, 518
Scribner, David, 129, 434–35
Seabury Commission, 147
Seagartle, Fay, 10, 21, 44, 72, 102, 178
Seamen's strikes, 205–06, 293
Search and seizure, 25, 30, 60
Sears, Charles B., 329, 331–32, 335–41, 345, 347–48, 349–50, 360–61
Sears Roebuck, 306
Sectarian errors, 132, 203
Section 7A (see National Industrial Recovery Act)
Securities and Exchange Commission (SEC), 184, 222, 259, 260, 455, 511
Security clearances, 351, 354–55
Sedition Act of 1918, 16, 34, 55, 60
Sedition Act of 1940 (see Smith Act, sedition sections)
Sedition Bill of 1919, 26
Seeger, Pete, 329
Seeman Brothers, 11
Segregation, 36
Self-incrimination, 30, 41, 76, 472
Senate, U.S., 19
Senate Committee on Manufactures, 125
Senate Committee on RR securities, 314
Senate Judiciary Committee, 35, 502–03
Senate Subcommittee on Immigration Legislation, 319
Serio, Guido, 138
Service, the (see INS)
Seward, Ralph T., 316
Seymour, Whitney North, 180–81, 200, 205, 239, 278
Shanghai, China, 187
Shapiro, Henry, 115–17, 168, 373
Sherwood, Robert, 402
Shipley, Ruth Bielaski, 404–05
Shoemaker, Thomas B., 267, 269, 271–72, 291

Shorr, Brodsky & King (S.B. & K.), 70, 71–
76, 100, 107, 153–55, 158, 163, 200,
228, 249, 272; fees and finances, 75
Shorr, Isaac, 7, 11, 21, 26–28, 32, 37–38, 61,
62, 65, 68–69, 72–74, 80–85, 88–90, 95,
102, 104, 109, 153–55, 163, 182, 190,
194–95, 228, 235, 236, 272, 454, 459
Sicher, Dudley F., 537
Siegel, Mary Goldburt, 51
Silberstein, Robert J. (Bob), 219, 381
Silicosis, 387
Silverman, Samuel, 169, 201–02, 416
Silver Shirts, 161
Simon, Hans, 513
Simon & Schuster, 205
Simpson, Warren & Cardozo (see also Car-
dozo, Benjamin), 64
Sinclair, Upton, 82
Single parents, 497
Single tax, 27
Sing Sing Prison, 32, 389
Siskind, George (see also General Sources/Spe-
cific References), 497, 540
Sissman, Peter, 249
Sit-down strikes: 222, 236; legality of, 224
Sitzkrieg, 1939, 307, 318, 365
Sixth Amendment, 25, 247, 264
Slavery: chattel, 24, 65; Negro, 54, 214
Sloan, John, 9
Small Home Owners League, 185
Smith, Al, 70
Smith, Elmer S., 124
Smith, Ferdinand (see also General Sources/Spe-
cific References), 104, 445, 448, 452, 464,
540
Smith, Howard, 306, 318–19, 469
Smith, L.M.C., 368
Smith Act: cases (see also Dennis Yates in Gen-
eral Sources/Specific References), 476, 492,
499, 522–23, 525; sedition sections, 354,
405, 469, 471, 522, 536, 537, 539
Smith Alien Registration Act of 1940 (Smith
Act), 319–20, 325, 328–29, 334–35, 429,
436, 469
Smith Committee (House), 304, 308
Soapbox speeches, 21, 73
Sobell, Morton, 508, 519
Social Democrats, 117, 233
Socialism/Socialists, 8, 16, 17, 24, 32, 60, 66,
233
Socialist Labor Party, 14
Socialist Party, 11, 12, 19, 27, 38, 121, 159,
212, 249, 371–72, 377; Assemblymen of
NY, 32; candidates, 32; lawyers, 65; Left
Wing of, 18, 32, 62; revolution, fear of, 18–
19
Socialist Workers Party (SWP), 354, 470
Social legislation, 13
Social Security, 137, 167, 386, 508
Social Security Act, Administration, 215, 222,
227, 243, 387
Social Security plan, "womb to tomb," 383,
428

Society for the Aid of Revolutionary Fighters
(MOPR), 82, 117
Solitary confinement (see Prison
conditions)
Song of Russia, 395
South, the, 109, 111, 113, 124, 175, 204, 239,
541
Southern Tenant Farmers Union, 210
Southern Worker, 111
South Korea, 508, 540
Southwestern University Law School, 150
Soviet-Finnish War, 1939, 308, 314
Soviet-Nazi: Nonaggression pact, 306; Pact,
1939, 308, 315
Soviet: invasion of Poland, 306–08; Nazi inva-
sion, 349; resistance, 370; spy murder plot,
389–91
Soviet Russia, recognition of, 43, 95, 114, 154,
189
Soviet Union (USSR)(Soviet Russia), 3, 19, 20,
34, 36, 42–43, 60, 82, 97, 107, 114–17,
121, 127, 130, 132, 138, 140, 149, 152,
154, 157, 165, 194, 195, 216, 233, 342,
352, 355, 373, 424, 440; and Korean War,
508–09
Spain, Loyalist government of, 233, 241, 244,
308, 313, 342
Spanish Civil War, 233, 316; veterans, 445
Spanish Loyalists, 485–86
Special Committee on Communist Tactics,
Strategy and Objectives (ABA), 515
Stachel, Jack, 525
Stalin, Josef, 176, 189, 233, 235, 379, 389, 543
Stalingrad, USSR, 373, 375
Stalin's treason trials, 233, 390
Standard, William L., 210, 219, 449
Standard Oil, 11, 15, 122
Stander, Lionel, 260
Stanford University, 290
"Star-Spangled Banner," 40
Stasiukevich, Philip (see also General
Sources/Specific References), 495
State Dept., U.S.: 43, 65, 122, 143, 247, 470,
481, 485; Passport Division, 404, 445
State Police Officers Association (Calif.), 282
States' rights, 65, 213
Statue of Liberty, 4, 39
Statute of limitations, 308, 539
Stavis, Morton, 312
Steel Workers Organizing Committee (SWOC-
CIO), 210
Steelworkers strike of 1919, 18
Steffens, Lincoln, 86, 156, 233, 255
Steffens, Pete, 298–99
Steinbeck, John, 292
Steiner, Ralph, 123
Stenographers (see Legal, secretaries)
Stern, Anne, 94
Stern, Bernhard, 208
Stern, Carl, 64, 90, 136, 173, 372, 416, 475,
536, 538
Stern, Peggy (see Kahn, Peggy Stern)
Stevens, Alexander, 494, 516
Stevenson, Adlai, 184

Stewart, Donald Ogden, 298–99, 316, 459
Stewart, James, 316
Stix, Carrie (see Weiss, Carrie)
Stix, Margarite, 102
Stix, Thomas L., 482, 487
Stix family, 531
Stock Exchange, Senate investigation of, 237
Stockholm Peace Appeal, 508, 515, 521
Stock market crash, 95, 104
Stone, Harlan: as Attorney General, 61, 65; as
    Justice, 76, 180, 187, 215, 225–26, 400–
    01, 418
Stone, I. F. (Izzy), 128, 402–03, 536
Strakhov, A., 116
Strike, Pacific Coast maritime of 1934, 253–
    55, 418
Strikebreaking, 36
Strikes (see also specific name), 6, 8, 9, 14, 18–
    20, 41, 92, 94, 97, 105, 149, 163, 167,
    168, 200, 253, 348, 350; general, 254–55;
    nationwide, of 1919, 18–20; successful, 503
Striking miners, 18–20, 88
Strong, Anna Louise, 115
Struble, Sidney, 500
Subversive activities, 342–43, 402
Sugar, Maurice, 219, 222, 236, 313, 447
Sullivan & Cromwell, 64
Sung v. McGrath (see also General Sources/Spe-
    cific References), 469, 506, 510, 520
Supreme Court, appealing to, 22, 122, 173,
    185, 217, 239, 246, 344, 356, 361, 366,
    492
Supreme Court: arguments, 181, 219, 341,
    348, 373, 375, 380, 413–14; briefs, 173,
    180, 227, 370, 412; decisions on aliens, 21,
    41, 54, 60–61, 75–76, 96, 108–09, 398–
    401, 416–20, 505; decisions to hear, 49,
    120–21, 195, 203, 247, 367–68, 493, 530;
    Justices, liberal, 23, 243, 371; majority,
    221; on New Deal legislation, 185, 224,
    212–15, 317; new (1937 on), 227, 305; old
    (to 1937), 184, 212, 224; opinions on
    Bridges, 394, 416–20, 538–39; opinions on
    labor and civil rights, 23, 28, 36, 61–63,
    65–68, 139–41, 174–75, 221, 236, 317,
    320, 343–44, 353, 387, 388, 401, 470,
    507, 520, 522, 539; opinions on *Schneider-
    man*, 398–401, 539; opinions (see title of
    case in General Sources/Specific Refer-
    ences); prestige of, 225, 232; quiet revolu-
    tion in, 225–26; refusal to hear by (cert.
    denied), 194, 204, 229, 469, 527
Sutherland, W. A., 139, 227
Swedish Seamen's Union, 449
Sweet, Dr. Ossian, 85
Sweezy, Paul (see also General Sources/Specific
    References), 539
"Swing Mikado," 285
Switzerland, 234, 398
Syndicalism (see Criminal syndicalism)

Taft, William Howard, 61, 66, 167
Taft-Hartley Labor Relations Act, 441, 447–
    48, 470, 501, 507–08

Tarazonia, Manuel (Mr. and Mrs.), 527–28
Taub, Allan, 171
Tauber, Joe, 129
Tax, excess profits, 342
Taylor, Glen H., 420, 428
Teamsters Union, 354
Teapot Dome Scandal of 1923, 108
Tennessee, 111, 119, 125
Tennessee Coal and Iron, 224
Tennessee Valley Authority (TVA), 183, 386
"Terminal Island 4" (see also General
    Sources/Specific References), 514, 537
Terrorism, 464
Textile workers, 167
Thaelmann, Ernst, 192
Thin Man, The, 381, 456
Third degree, 3
Third parties (see also Progressive Party), 64,
    448
Thirteenth Amendment, 65
Thomas, Elbert D., 358
Thomas, J. Parnell, 484
Thompson, Craig, 458, 516–19
Thompson, John Oliver, 360
Thompson, Robert, 523
Thompson, Walter, 291, 366
Thurber, James M., 482, 487
Time magazine, 237
Times (see *New York Times*)
Tolan Committee (House), 357
Toland, Edmund M., 308
Torture, governmental, 150
Trade, 43
Trade unions (see Unions)
Trade Union Unity League (TUUL), 107, 189,
    194–95, 254
Transfer of trial (see Venue, change of)
Transportation, Secretary of, 481
Treasury Dept., 355
Tresca, Carlo, 81
Trotsky, Leon, 176, 322, 389–90
Truman, Harry, Pres., 423, 429, 442, 451, 470–
    71, 479–80, 500, 502, 509–10, 538; Sen.,
    314, 414
Trumbo, Dalton (see also General Sources/Spe-
    cific References), 515
Trust-busting, 11
Tucker, Ray, 187
Tulin, Justine Wise (see Polier, Justine Wise)
Tuttle, Elbert P., 246

UAW-CIO (United Auto Workers), 222, 313,
    447; Aviation Dept., 338–40
Ukrainian-Americans, 109
UN Charter, 383, 423
UN Conference on International Organization,
    420
Unemployed Councils of America, 138, 141,
    147, 185, 212, 232
Unemployment, 18–19, 59, 94, 97, 177, 182,
    186, 238, 305
Unemployment compensation/unemployment
    insurance, 13, 97–98, 100, 129, 137, 182,
    185, 212

Unger, Abraham, 129, 473–75, 492, 518
UN Human Rights Commission, 487
Union Now, 400
Union of Russian Workers, Federated (in U.S. and Canada), 4, 19, 32
Union of Soviet Socialist Republics (USSR), (see Soviet Union)
Union organizers, 237
Unions, 6, 21, 35, 54, 81, 97, 117, 147, 206, 306, 382; agitation in, 425, 523; legality of, 197, 387; right to organize, 36, 62, 187, 253
Union Theological Seminary, 124
United Auto Workers (see UAW-CIO)
United Chemical Workers, 449
United Electrical Workers (UE), 440, 453
United front against fascism, 189
United fronts, 321, 420
United Furniture Workers, 440
United Hospital Workers, 440
United Mine Workers (UMW), 113
United Nations, 358, 407, 409, 420, 424, 429, 430, 487, 508
United Organization of Unemployed and Relief Workers, 205
United Shoe Workers–CIO, 300, 304–05
Universal Declaration of Human Rights, 383, 487
University of California, Boalt Hall Law School, 374
University of Michigan (U of M), 222, 320, 399
University of Washington, 472
University of Wisconsin Law School, 236–37
Unlawful assembly, 139
Unprofessional conduct, 29
UN Security Counci., 508
Upper class, 163
U.S. Armed Forces, 3, 381, 386, 396, 424
U.S. Attorney, 25, 29, 43, 95, 468
U.S.-China treaty, 54
U.S. Dept. of Justice, illegal activities of, 3–4
U.S. Dept. of Labor (see Labor, Dept. of)
U.S. Embassy, Paris, 448
U.S. Expeditionary Force, 23
U.S. Intelligence Dept., 276
U.S. Marine Hospital, 457
U.S. Marines, 122
USSR (see Soviet Union)
U.S. Steel, 306
U.S. War Dept., 410
U.S. Woman Patriot Corporation, 143

V-Day, 429
Vajtauer (see also General Sources/Specific References), 408, 418, 515
van Druten, John, 48
Vanzetti, Bartolomeo (see also General Sources), 122
Venezuela, 47, 138
Venue, change of, 111, 170
Victorian era, 11
Victories, narrow, 190, 251
Vinson, Fred M., 508, 532, 539
Virginia State Corporation Commission, 430

Visas, applications for, 143
Voich, John, 449
Voir dire (see Jury selection)
Voltaire, 267
"Voluntary departure," 43, 89, 138, 194, 235, 242, 430, 466, 493, 494
Von Hindenburg, president of Germany, 150

Wages, hours, and working conditions, standards for, 19
Wagner, Robert, 97, 307
Wagner National Labor Relations Act of 1935 (Wagner Act), 224, 318, 386, 451
Waldman, Louis, 38–39, 220
Walker, Jimmy, 130
Wallace, Henry A., 184, 324, 357, 442, 448, 459, 500, 503, 509, 524
Wall Street, 123, 182; law firms/lawyers, 79, 136, 146, 184, 371, 432
Walsh, Frank P., 30, 188, 221
Walter-McCarran Immigration Act, 519, 538
War, opposition to, 36
Ward, Angela, 281, 285
Ward, Courtney, 456
Ward, Estolv, 260–61, 263–64, 281, 285, 372
Ward, Harry F., 311–12
War Labor Board, 381, 386
War Manpower Commission, 388, 407
Warner Brothers, 395
Warrants for arrest, 20, 25
Warren, Earl: as California D.A., 293, 295; as Chief Justice, 532–33
War Resources Board, 306–07
Warsaw, Poland, 198
Washington, bombings of 1919, 29
Washington, D.C., 31, 97, 125, 141–42; police, 99; race riots of 1919, 18
Washington Committee for Democratic Action, 344
Washington Post, 328
Washington State, 99, 124, 193, 220, 223
Washington Times-Herald, 405
Wasserman, Jack, 356, 533
Waterfront Employers' Association, 254, 282, 413
Watkins, John (see also General Sources/Specific References), 539
Watson, Goodwin, 388
Watt, Richard F., 533
Webster, Bethuel M., 227
Wechsler, Herbert, 167, 179, 200, 205, 227, 239, 278, 300, 321, 344, 371
Weinfeld, Edward, 527–28
Weiss, Carol (see King, Carol Weiss)
Weiss, Carrie, 10, 11, 12, 48, 262
Weiss, Honi (Mrs. Louis Weiss), 12, 203, 244
Weiss, Louis S., 6, 12, 38, 46, 53, 79, 136, 154, 202–03, 205, 244, 316, 344, 355, 364, 407, 416, 481, 503–04, 513
Weiss, Nina (Mrs. Carl Stern), 12, 90, 475
Weiss, Samuel, 11, 12, 13, 38, 135, 262
Weiss, William (Billy), 6, 12, 79, 111, 202, 373, 438
Weiss & Wharton (Louis's law firm), 38, 79

Weiss family, 11–12, 91, 100, 481
Weiss firm (see Cohen, Cole, Weiss & Wharton)
Weissking (see also King, Carol Weiss), 332
Welsh, Francis Ralston, 141–42
Welsh, Martin I., 393
Wendorf, Arthur P., 309
West Coast, 206, 239
West Germany, 500
West Virginia, 193
Western Worker (CP), 255, 281
Westinghouse, 424
Weyand, Ruth, 223
Whalen, Police Commr., 98
Wheeler, Burton K., 187, 314
White, Bouck, 8, 92
Whitehorn, Victor, 177–78
White House, 19
White primaries, 124
Whitman, Alden, 535
Whitman, Walt, 292
Wickersham Commission, 108, 186
Wiegel, Johannes, 235
Wilkins, Roy, 120
Williamson, John (see also Hunger strikers), 448, 452, 464, 540
Willkie, Wendell, 323–24, 358, 368–73, 391, 396–97, 401, 408–10, 413, 437, 459, 507, 526, 536; mother, 370
Wills, 74, 79
Wilmot, Robert P., 360
WILPF (see Women's International League for Peace and Freedom)
Wilson, Ellis, 394
Wilson, William B., 18, 34
Wilson, Woodrow, 15, 18, 23, 135, 263
Winston, Henry, 523
Winter, Ella, 298
Wiretapping, 343–49, 405, 419
Wiretapping by Justice Dept., 320, 344–48
Wise, Stephen S., 167
Witness against oneself (see Self-incrimination)
Witnesses, stool pigeon, 504
Witt, Nathan (Nat), 123–24, 211, 434–35, 461, 509, 518
Wobblies (see IWW)
Woman Question, The, 206
Women, 9; career of, 45; changing role of, 45; and children, 88, 95; lawyers, 6, 40, 44–45, 78, 145, 167, 223, 247, 370, 391, 438, 461, 499, 514, 530; as leaders, 45, 259; and men, 274; new kind of, 462, 487; Soviet, 116; working, 13, 40, 95, 382

Women's International League for Peace and Freedom (WILPF), 223
Women's suffrage, 12, 36, 45
Women's Trade Union League, 473
Wood, Charles Erskine Scott, 120
Wood, Howard C., 370
Woodshed speech, 425–29
Woolf, Virginia, 8, 101, 287
Woollcott, Alexander, 45
Woolsey, Judge, 105
Workers Alliance, 312
Workers' compensation, 13, 21, 95, 185
Workers Party of America, 365, 378
Workers' Republic of Russia, 23
Workers' Self-Defense in the Courts, 517
Workers' United Front Election Campaign Committee, 150
Working class, 37, 92, 102, 109, 128, 130; consciousness of, 128, 147; lawyers among, 130–32
Workmen's Circle, 11
World-Telegram, 323
World War I, 7, 15–16, 28, 30, 34, 48, 60, 64, 66, 80, 146, 209, 234, 429; opposition to, 7, 15–17, 31, 34, 46, 59, 60, 62
World War II, 296, 298, 304, 307, 320, 342, 357, 381, 408, 429
WPA Arts Project, 215
WPA Federal Theatre, 208
WPA (Works Progress Administration), 205, 219; lawyers, 205, 219, 220, 237; workers' strikes, 205
Wright, Roy (see also General Sources/Specific References; *Scottsboro*), 441
Wyatt, Judge, 177

Yale Law Journal, 160, 206
Yale Law School, 15, 68, 77, 124, 167, 355, 488, 528
Yale University, 11
Yannish, Nat (see also General Sources/Specific References), 449
Yates v. U.S. (also General Sources/Specific References), 538
"Yellow peril," 54, 358
Yiddish, 97
YMCA, Jane Street, NYC, 186
Young, Art, 17
Young Communist League (YCL), 122, 312

Zimmerman, Gilbert, 439, 440, 442, 479
Zorach, William, 48
Zydok, John (see also General Sources/Specific References), 513–15, 530, 532, 535, 537

GAYLORD
FG